Industrial Applications
of Technological Forecasting

Industrial Applications of Technological Forecasting

ITS UTILIZATION IN R&D MANAGEMENT

Marvin J. Cetron and Christine A. Ralph

WILEY-INTERSCIENCE, a Division of John Wiley & Sons, Inc.
New York · London · Sydney · Toronto

Dedication

This book, stressing the practical applications of technological forecasting in U.S. industry, is dedicated as a tribute to Ralph C. Lenz, Jr., whose contributions to technological forecasting have been its major guide posts. Lenz is deemed the Father of Technological Forecasting. His endowments to the subject are represented not only by his pathbreaking work, *Technological Forecasting*, but also by one of the technique's first large-scale applications in planning, described in a U.S. Air Force document entitled *Technology for Tomorrow* (known lovingly to practitioners in the field as "Tea for Two").

With the exception of substitution methodology, Ralph Lenz explained and illustrated in 1962 all technological forecasting techniques known today; since then, no other new exploratory techniques for forecasting have been devised or utilized which were not contained in that original work. Those of us who have enjoyed the privilege of close association with Lenz would be remiss if we did not also note the extent to which his innovativeness and brilliance are complemented by his personal helpfulness and capacity for friendship. It is Ralph Lenz, therefore, to whom this book is dedicated.

Foreword

Science and technology influence society and our national well-being in a very direct way, as even those not particularly interested in such problems have become acutely aware in recent years. The growing concern with the undesirable side effects of science and technology, our diminishing national resources, the need for environmental restoration, and our economic difficulties have made it mandatory to seek new methods which will permit the formulation of better, less speculative platforms for long-range planning and decision making, including, as early as possible, the projection of scientific trends, beneficial or undesirable, in order to distribute our resources more effectively and to have society gain to the greatest extent possible.

We need to understand more fully the outlines of future challenges brought about by currently recognizable trends in technology in time to develop the means to meet these challenges. The ostensibly obvious statements of need in the current era of recognized environmental, economic, social, and defense problems and opportunities are well documented in this book. We are in need of a better, more reliable, cross-correlated system of technological forecasting and planning—and the need is urgent.

During the last two years "technology assessment" (a term not even known five years ago) has become a household word, somewhat of a fad, exceeded in popularity only by "environment," "ecology," and "social indicators." These have seemingly replaced motherhood as things of which to be in favor, and air pollution and solid wastes have become things to be more against than sin. However, the term technological assessment is widely misunderstood. It is not the same as the protection and improvement of our environment; and if in overreaction to these problems we begin to allocate our resources predominantly for environmental or ecological restoration instead of in a more balanced and comprehensive program to improve the quality of life in general, we will suffer from imbalances and from secondary or tertiary side effects as well. This country cannot afford a reduction in its gross national product or a stagnation of technological innovation for the sake of an improved ecology. We will simply have to face the problem of priorities versus goals in an earnest attempt to reach an acceptable compromise, since we will not be able to solve simultaneously all of our problems, such as crime, inadequate transportation, insufficient power, environmental pollution, and solid waste.

During the last ten years technological forecasting has emerged as one technique which can aid us in the decision-making process for resources allocation and priority selection. It is broad enough to cover a range of items extending, for instance, from the planning of a research program to fight leukemia to the evaluation of technical alternatives for providing sufficient electrical power to the states along the eastern seaboard.

Unfortunately, technological forecasting as a quantitative input to technology assessment has developed some of the attributes of a specialized cult. The field contains groups of enthusiastic, evangelic advocates, who tend to use a special language that must be mastered before the uninitiated can converse with a practitioner. Articles and talks are often liberally sprinkled with catch words and phrases, of which QUEST, normative, PROFILE, Delphi, SOON, morphological analysis, scenario, BRAILLE, and relevance trees are only a few examples. Such a vocabulary, no doubt, allows a few experts to communicate rapidly with each other and at the same time lends an air of professionalism to an as-yet unproved field. However, the harassed manager who needs to decide when to undertake an exercise in technology assessment, how best to plan his programs, and what kind of forecasting to undertake is sometimes confused by the broad sweep of words, coupled with the dearth of data and specific, pertinent examples of plans, assessment, and forecasts upon which to lean. This volume helps to clarify some of the jargon and provide practical help in the application of forecasting.

Concurrently with the growing interest in this subject area, which has resulted more from dire necessity than clear conviction and belief in the techniques, has grown the need for good books to relate the specifics of the new planning tool to a broad and varied audience. Without exception, however, recent books have contained a preponderant amount of defense- or at least government-oriented methodologies and information that appeared to be nonapplicable to civilian-industrial purposes. This impression, although recognized by those working in the field as a misconception, certainly contributed, at least in the beginning, to the slow and reluctant diffusion of the new techniques. From several points of view, therefore, this new book by Cetron and Ralph is a most welcome addition to the literature. It gives a current overview of the activities in technological forecasting in various U.S. industries, as well as of the utilization of several of the more widely used methodologies. If not comprehensive, the chapters are at least representative of current activities, and show that technological forecasting is not the questionable art that some of its more conceptually oriented adversaries want to make it.

This book, it is hoped, will aid planners who need something more than just an initiation for their decision making.

BODO BARTOCHA
Deputy Executive Secretary
Executive Council
National Science Foundation

Preface

"*We judge ourselves by what we feel capable of doing, while others judge us by what we have already done.*"
Longfellow

In writing this book, it was our intention to look at various types of industry, and at companies of different size, in order to discover, if technological forecasting was being used, the methods being applied and the reasons for forecasting and for choosing particular techniques; or, if forecasting was not being used appreciably, the reason for its lack of popularity. The specific questions to which we wanted answers were the following:

1. What is the perceived importance of technological forecasting and the extent of its practice?
2. Is technological forecasting worth the cost, in terms of the resources that it takes away from "useful productive work"?
3. Can technological forecasting assist a corporation in identifying technological opportunities which will open up new markets for the corporation, or protect its current market by uncovering areas of technological vulnerability?
4. What is the role of technological forecasting in research and development planning and control?
5. What impacts are the results of forecasting having on planning and decision making in the firm?
6. Is technological forecasting being used to any significant extent in the allocation of resources?

7. Can any specific methodology be related to any type of corporation, by size, nature of industry, or degree of technological intensiveness?

8. What factors inhibit the effective implementation of technological forecasting?

Many theories have been developed for technological forecasting and for its use in a resource allocation system, and there is a great deal of literature on the subject. One point that seems to have been missed by many people, however, is that one does not need a "micrometer to measure a sewer pipe." Not only would this prove fruitless, but also, by assuming a greater degree of accuracy than is possible, needless errors are introduced into the system. Many of the sophisticated techniques developed for forecasting and resource allocation could not be used in practical situations because the necessary data were not available, too many errors were introduced, or the available data did not represent the real world. Another fact that few people have realized is that a forecasting and resource allocation system that works perfectly in, say, an electronics company cannot be used in the same manner for a pharmaceutical company. Also, when many of these techniques were developed, the means for relating their results to current operations were not mentioned. This is a great problem with the Delphi study, for example, unless one uses the information solely as an environmental forecast for writing scenarios. It is very interesting to know that a certain event will occur in 1989, give or take a year; but unless that event can be related and integrated into current programs or plans, it remains a useless piece of information.

Despite the problems involved in successful forecasting and resource allocation systems, many companies have on-going programs in these areas or are developing systems which incorporate both techniques. The reason seems to be that these companies realize that, no matter how experienced individuals or committees may be, they cannot make decisions at a corporate or division level merely on the basis of intuition. Technology is changing so rapidly that it is necessary to be aware of what is going on not only in a specific field of interest, but also in complementary and competitive fields, in the market place, and in the whole social-political-economic environment. Without some formalized method of sifting and weighing all this information, it cannot be used effectively. Additionally, if a decision has been made on an intuitive basis, the rationale or justification for it is lost and cannot be repeated or explained. A formalized method provides visibility (projects can be evaluated on the same basis), a dialog can be opened up between the decision makers and the engineers and scientists, and possibly, and more importantly, it can start people thinking about the future, not simply in terms of a bigger, better program of the same sort in which they are currently involved, but functionally in terms of what their work is for. In effect, the techniques provide the tools whereby the technical knowledge and judgment of the forecaster can be applied to logical, systematic thinking about the pattern of development of a particular technology.

Technological forecasting is not a panacea; it describes, not what the future *will* be, but only what the future *could* be. If money is not spent in a technological area, the predicted future will not come about; if money is spent, the event can occur, in most cases, in a time frame directly proportional to the level of funding. Frequently, an estimate of the likelihood of funding can be gained from a careful examination of the federal budget and, for the more distant future, from an assessment of the public's interest.

Why is it necessary to look at the more distant future? What makes this information so important to a planning system? Most companies already have long-range plans extending over the next 5 years. Why should they take the time and effort to look ahead any further? The main reasons for looking further into the future are long-term corporate growth and long-term investment. Since the first of these is obvious, let us consider long-term investment. The investment may be in terms of resources, such as personnel, equipment, and facilities, or in terms of research and development. It is just not cost-effective to build a plant, with a life of 30 years, to produce a particular product if a new technology may render the product obsolete in 5 years' time, or if needs may change, so that there will no longer be a market for it. Similarly, if the time taken for research is 5 to 8 years, and for development 3 to 5 years, the earliest possible production time is 8 years and the actual time could be as long as 13 years. It is therefore essential to know whether some other technology could offer severe competition, or whether needs might change, before resources are allocated to a research program.

When management realizes the need for technological forecasting, and recognizes its utility as an aid in the decision-making process, half of the battle of its being accepted has been won. Some top managements have willingly accepted such techniques, but others have shown great reluctance and some skepticism. Too often, one hears the argument, "Why should we change over to having a machine make our decisions? We've always had good planning, and we haven't lost any money yet, have we?" or "Joe's a good planner; he's been doing it for the last 10 years, and he always listens to the needs of each department." Frequently, such attitudes have prevented companies from making the best use of their resources. Many forecasts are performed only by the research and devel-

opment divisions of companies and are then not used to any great extent
except within these divisions. (Even then, they may have been subopti-
mizing for the corporation as a whole.) Frequently, terminology has had
to be changed, so that top management would not realize that the techniques used to develop a budget and long-range plan for a division were
in fact forecasting methods.

Our aim is to try to show that forecasting can be extremely useful in
providing *information* on which project selection and resource allocation
can be based. It does not take away any of management's decision-making power. It merely helps those who make decisions to assess the consequences more adequately.

We have tried to collect as much information as possible on the use
of these techniques in industry. We did not select only companies known
to have successful forecasts; rather, we have included also those that
have had all types of problems in performing them, and some that have
chosen not to use forecasting at all, along with their reasons. We, the
authors, have great hopes that in the future most of the decisions made in
business will be based on all the relevant information possible to collect.
We leave it to you, the readers, to judge for yourselves, from the evidence
before you, whether this is likely to come about.

The scene for the book is set in Chapter I, which describes the
philosophy of forecasting and planning. The next two chapters provide
an overview of the methods of technological forecasting and of its implementation in resource allocation systems, but the details of the methodologies have purposely been omitted from these chapters and are covered
later in Chapters XIII to XXIV.

The number and variety of techniques for forecasting technological
progress described in Chapters II and XIII to XIV of this book testify to
the importance of this field, but they also suggest that no one, fully
satisfactory, technique has been clearly identified. Some have face
validity, that is, they seem reasonable. Some have given correct answers
in certain cases. However, most arguments supporting one approach or
another must rely on historical data. It would take many years to compare today's long-range forecasts with actual results; moreover, the comparisons would not be fully valid if, because of the forecasts, resources
were concentrated in some areas at the expense of others. Progress is quite
sensitive to the availability and application of resources. Nevertheless,
it seems prudent to compare results with forecasts for a period of time
before leaning too heavily on any particular technique.

A careful manipulation of historical data could, conceivably, provide
some insight into the relative merits of the various techniques. On the
other hand, the data which we remember first are often biased in favor

of rapid progress. Once-promising developments which have not lived up to the expectations they evoked, such as dirigibles and public distribution of direct-current power, are easily forgotten. In contrast, who can forget transistors or lasers? Improper selection or use of data could lead to erroneous conclusions about which technique is best. In any event, it seems likely that technological forecasting will become less of an art and more of a science. The limits of its usefulness will surely be tested; it would be premature to define these limits now.

Too many brilliant decisions have come from the unfathomable subconsciousness of intelligent, experienced managers to discard mature judgment in favor of more mechanistic schemes. Perhaps these managers cannot always explain exactly how they reached their decisions, but the quality of the judgment is often more important than the mechanism by which it was made. It is hoped that those who seek the best forecasting technique will not arbitrarily rule out a role for the human mind, just because they do not understand how it operates. To do so might result in consistent, quantitative results but sacrifice originality and insight into the more subtle indicators of the future. And who can say that genius or intuition is not the product of some deep, logical processes? The flash of genius must, of course, be fueled by the prior accumulation and correlation of knowledge.

After we have determined the technology which probably will be needed at some point in time and the technology which could then actually be available, the next problem is to define the tasks required to bridge the difference. If future competitive threats, the new products needed to defeat these threats, the technology required to develop the defensive products, and the future availability of the requisite technology were all known precisely, the problem would not be especially difficult. Unfortunately, even when we make the effort to acquire this knowledge, we can have only estimates of these factors with associated levels of confidence. Furthermore, there is no assurance that all possibilities were covered in the process. Tasks should certainly be defined which address the most probable needs. However, it is not safe to ignore promising technological areas which do not obviously support any of the present or proposed products or services. Perhaps the safest prediction one can make in R&D is that more useful tasks can be defined than can be supported properly.

In Chapter III, we turn our attention to the relationship of the technological forecasting techniques discussed previously and resource allocation to the R&D planning process. We discuss the general applicability of technological forecasting to the planning of R&D in certain industries, and conclude by identifying specific applications of forecasting to the various elements of the planning process. Chapter IV presents our modus operandi, including the reasons for writing the book and the methods used for data collection, respectively. This concludes Section I.

In Chapters V to XI, we examine the actual applications of formal technological forecasting to research and development planning in various industries. In Chapter XII, "Some Conclusions," we discuss the advantages of technological forecasting. Also, we consider it appropriate—indeed, important—to discuss here, at the end of Section II, the pitfalls and limitations associated with the implementation of technological forecasting in industry.

In Chapter XIII, guest author Ralph Lenz gives us a preview of what is happening and what to expect from the basic technological forecasting extrapolation techniques. Most of his examples come from the military arena, which is only natural, since that is where technological forecasting was born and nurtured. Lenz also discusses the prerequisites for good forecasting and the effects of the competitive process on forecasting.

Murray Turoff, guest author of Chapter XIV, reports the results of an evaluation of an on-line (computer-automated) conference. He believes that merging the advantages of Delphi and of modern computer technology can have a synergistic effect. Turoff discusses this in detail in his chapter.

The Cross-impact and cross-support Matrix techniques are described and illustrated in Chapters XV and XVI by James Dalby and Christine Ralph, respectively. These matrix techniques are frequently thought to be the same, but this is not the case, despite some similarity. The cross-impact method assigns probabilities to all events in the matrix, and then proceeds to show the impact on other events of changes in the initial probabilities. Dalby explains why and how he made some refinements in the cross-impact technique, and then goes through a sample case to show how it can be used. Miss Ralph, on the other hand, by using the British fishing industry as an example, shows how cross-support can be an important decision-aiding technique, by measuring the magnitude of the relationships between parameters. She shows how complex problems can be broken down into smaller, better defined areas of study, so that only areas which are relevant are analyzed in detail. This is really an application of an old technique known as "management by exception."

Chapter XVII discusses the really new concept in technological forecasting—substitutability. Guest authors John Fisher and Robert Pry explain the methodology of this concept, and illustrate it with many good examples, in their chapter entitled, "A Simple Substitution Model of Technological Change." Substitutability is really not a technological forecasting methodology in the usual sense; it covers a much broader concept. It is really a macroforecast, or a combination of technological forecasts, economic forecasts, and sociopolitical forecasts that provides an environmental forecast, which says what the future *will* look like in a given technology, as opposed to what it *could* look like. The theory behind the substitution method is based on two major assumptions: (1) the old technology is completely substitutable by the new technology, and (2) once started (over 3%), complete substitution takes place.

Another example of the Delphi approach, this one in the area of social forecasting, is given in Chapter XVIII by Raul de Brigard and Olaf Helmer. This chapter describes the potential effects on society of technological development, and gives the estimated measure of these effects over the time period 1970 to 2000. This approach is rather different from the way in which Delphi has been used to forecast technological events.

Chapter XIX, by guest author Robert Prehoda, describes the detrimental effects that technology could have on society and its surroundings if it is not brought under sufficient control. He cites examples of many forms of pollution; among them are olfactory, water, thermal, data, and optical pollution. This chapter is the first one in Section III which leads away from the types of forecasting being used to the application of such forecasts—a theme which is then taken up by the succeeding guest authors.

Jay Mendell, in Chapter XX, points out the need for thinking about alternative futures at all levels of an organization. He believes that few people have a conceptual grasp of the forces molding their future environment, and that the majority do not realize there could be more than one possible future. In order to achieve realization of this concept, he feels that individuals should be encouraged to remove their blinders, cure their tunnel vision, and stretch their imaginations. In other words, Mendell's interesting article helps one to learn how to "blow his mind."

In Chapter XXI, Robert Ayres describes a new technique, which, with the aid of three classification schemes, can be used to define any process in any industry. Once the basic function of each process step has been identified, various analyses, such as sensitivity and deficiency analyses, can be performed in order to identify gaps in the technologies and key areas in which improvements would be of most benefit to a particular industry. This technique could provide a very useful tool for those interested in exploratory research and development.

The long-range planning activities in the U.S. aerospace industry are described by guest author Paul Polishuk in Chapter XXII. His study is based on an extensive survey questionnaire sent out to 260 companies in the aerospace business, and on some earlier work performed by David Cleland. Polishuk's findings cover a broad area of the companies' planning cycles, including such factors as company policy, internal factors (e.g., company growth, resources, and visibility), external factors (e.g., national focus, international focus, and competition), and methods for establishing a long-range planning effort.

One of the most widely known normative technological forecasting techniques—PATTERN—is discussed in Chapter XXIII. Guest authors Ross Alderson and William Sproull explain how Honeywell's PATTERN, which was originally developed for planning in the military area, has been modified and is being utilized in the industrial sector. Specifically, these authors show how this relevance tree technique has been successfully used to identify future needs and to aid in developing investment programs in hydrocarbon processing, building protection systems and housing, and identifying critical needs in the training of students in the public school system.

One of the more down-to-earth applications of technological forecasting is discussed in Chapter XXIV by Michael Cochran and Douglas Bender. It provides a description of a model which has been built to assist research and development management in its evaluation and selection of projects. The model is in two stages: project evaluation, which utilizes the concept of discounted cash flow, and project selection, which uses a linear programming algorithm. The technique does not make use of a technological forecast per se, but does incorporate the synthesized outputs from the forecasts described in Chapter VII, in terms of expected return on investment and probability of success.

In the last chapter, Marvin Cetron illustrates one method of tying all the pieces together in the macro-environment by relating technology to the nation's needs. He explains how each of the elements in the planning "package" (or "total system," to use the vernacular) could fit together to provide a system for allocating national resources to various technology areas, on the basis of national goals, and with the aid of technological forecasts.

A note of thanks is due to Captain Edmund B. Mahinske, USN, who served as special editor for us. With the able secretarial assistance of Mrs. Dorothy McGovern, he combined the chapters and improved the continuity of what we hope will be a book for a wide range of industrial managers.

Our gratitude is extended also to our business associates and colleagues for their help and cooperation in allowing us to interview them and for giving us the benefit of their time. A list of these individuals and their biographies are provided at the back of the book. To the guest authors of Chapters XIII to XXIV—Ralph Lenz, Murray Turoff, James Dalby, John Fisher, Robert Pry, Raul de Brigard, Olaf Helmer, Robert Prehoda, Jay Mendell, Robert Ayres, Paul Polishuk, Ross Alderson, William Sproull, Michael Cochran, and Douglas Bender—we owe a special word of thanks for giving us more than the state of the art of their techniques—a glimpse of the future.

We would also like to express our appreciation to our colleague, Bodo Bartocha, who gave his time and effort in the preparation of the foreword.

Appreciation is due to Theodore Taylor, Robert Ayres, and the staff of International Research and Technology Corporation for their counsel and assistance in the preparation of this book. Finally, we would like to acknowledge our gratitude to the National Science Foundation for its monetary support of Cetron's doctoral dissertation questionnaire, which provided us with a great deal of the background material for our study. The dissertation was written at American University under the guidance of his doctoral committee, chaired by Dr. Charles Bartfield, and composed of Dr. Bodo Bartocha, Dr. Lowell Hattery, Dr. Nick Perrone and Dr. Kenn Rogers. Since portions of Chapters 1 thru 12 and Appendix A have been adopted from the dissertation, the committee and Dr. Phorias, Head of the Doctoral Program, are also to be thanked.

Naturally, we accept full responsibility for any errors in the statistics and also in the interpretation of the various planning systems.

MARVIN J. CETRON
CHRISTINE A. RALPH

Fairfax, Virginia
Arlington, Virginia
February 1971

Contents

Industrial Applications
of Technological Forecasting

Section I

I. *Setting the Stage*

Small opportunities are often the beginning of great enterprises.   Demosthenes

INTRODUCTION

It is quite characteristic of our society to belabor to death the events of past history. Untold amounts of energy go into investigating why certain paths have led to disaster and how such disasters could have been avoided. We have, in this country, excellent 20/20 hindsight, as the saying goes. We are a race of voluble "Monday morning quarterbacks."

However, if attention is turned 180 degrees toward the future, the silence becomes equally unbearable and one suspects that he is surrounded by mutes. In this case, enormous amounts of energy must be consumed in prodding people to think of the future. Sometimes one despairs at the anomaly: the past is etched in the annals of history and no amount of energy can change it; yet the future, to which the expenditure of energy could be applied with greater effect and return, is not accorded a similar degree of voluntary concentration.

One of the God-given freedoms possessed by man is the ability to plan ahead for the future, to select among alternatives, and to reap the benefits or consequences of his choices. A basic underlying tenet of most religions demands that the individual look ahead; if he has not done so, it requires that he be penitent, rededicate himself, and subsequently mend his ways. No concept is more valid than the idea of a Day of Reckoning. Nothing is more obvious today than the fact

3

that many sad reckonings are at hand—all because of reluctance or inertia to *look ahead* and *plan* accordingly.

It takes us as long to get to work in the morning as to fly between cities, if not continents. We take pride in the supersonic speeds of our aircraft, but fail to face up to the ludicrous situation of ground transportation to the airports. We have befouled the environment, upset ecological balances, created urban monstrosities, and faltered in the face of burgeoning social problems. The rapid advance of technology, once heralded as a boon to mankind, is now viewed by many as a danger in disguise. This is not so. Theological concepts—if we may once more look to them—do not permit us to rationalize the blame away from where it belongs. We are at fault, not an inanimate entity of our own creation. We failed to plan ahead; we did not avail ourselves of the freedom of choice.

The point of all this is that all avenues of human experience give ample guidance and proof that the future must be planned for, and that actions or inactions have their consequences in the years ahead. In this book, we will discuss technological forecasting, a very necessary ingredient (indeed, the basis) of planning the future of technological endeavors. It is hoped that the general, prefactory remarks will be extended to this specific avenue and that the necessity for technological planning and its associated forecasting is logically and convincingly apparent.

TECHNOLOGICAL FORECASTS

Forecasting is not new. Early man doubtlessly recognized that he could live more comfortably and perhaps longer if he could predict changes in his environment. In the dawn of history, many "techniques" were employed to lessen perceived uncertainties about the future. Heavenly bodies proved useful in predicting seasons and floods, and the logical extension of astrology to the fate of peasants and empires created interesting anecdotes in history. Other once-popular predictive techniques now appear even less rational than charting celestial phenomena, but the reward for finding a method that evoked the awe and acceptance of those in power ensured a continuing search, even into the most improbable. Although science and practical observations thoroughly discredited astrology, palmistry, and other early practices, man's need to know more about tomorrow in order to prepare for it remained acute. The search continues to this day—and so does the idea that the solution lies in utterly simple mechanics.

The need for accurate forecasts can hardly be denied, but is there anything useful that a planner can do about it? Although some seem inclined to answer in the negative, others have pointed out quite accurately that all planning implies the use of forecasting:

A planner does not have the choice as to whether or not he will make a forecast. A forecast is implicit in planning. The only choice is whether the forecast will be made openly, rationally, and explicitly, so it can be subjected to the review and analysis of others, or whether the forecast will be made in the murky depths of the subconscious where no one else can ever know what the forecast is, let alone review or criticize it.[1]

In recent years, there has been an accelerating attempt to make forecasts more open, rational, explicit, and quantitative. Before the various techniques for accomplishing this are discussed, let us first examine exactly what technological forecasting is. There is a range of opinions on the matter. One recent survey disclosed roughly one hundred techniques related to technological forecasting.[2] For the purposes of this book, however, technological forecasting is defined as "the prediction, with a stated level of confidence, of the anticipated occurrence of a technological achievement within a given time frame with a specified level of support."[3] More specifically, it can be said:

A technological forecast is not a plan. It is a tool for planning and decision making. A forecast could become a plan if commitments were made to apply resources based on the forecast. It is emphasized that technological forecasting should consist of a systematic analysis which, when applied to specific technical data, will yield a consistent, quantitative technological conclusion, no matter which competent person performs the analysis.[4]

Even if technological forecasting is defined to exclude many of the less rational techniques, a rather unwieldy number of approaches remain. Some order can be achieved, however, by a systematic scheme of classification, such as the one in Chapter II.

[1] Joseph P. Martino et al., *Long-Range Forecasting and Planning, a Symposium Held at the U.S. Air Force Academy, Colorado,* Clearinghouse No. AD664108 (Springfield, Va.: U.S. Department of Commerce, 1966), p. 2.

[2] Arthur P. Lien, Paul Anton, and Joseph W. Duncan, *Technological Forecasting: Tools, Techniques, Applications,* AMA Management Bulletin No. 115 (New York: American Management Association, 1968), p. 5.

[3] Marvin J. Cetron, *Technological Forecasting: A Practical Approach* (New York: Gordon & Breach, 1969), p. 54.

[4] Marvin J. Cetron, "Forecasting Technology," *International Science and Technology,* September 1967, pp. 83–84.

GENERAL APPLICABILITY TO PLANNING

Technological forecasts, no matter how sophisticated the means used to derive them, no matter how adroitly they are carried out, no matter how accurate they prove to be, are useless unless they influence the actions of the planners, that is, are put to use. Technological forecasting is considered to have an important role as an input into the research and development planning process. It earns this role because it offers a methodical way to help identify and assess technological opportunities and threats.[5]

The Research Planner

The research planner can look to technological forecasts for help in identifying what appear to be the most fruitful areas for the investment of funds. He can rely on technological forecasts to provide a basis for decisions to initiate, increase, cut back, or terminate particular research projects.[6] He can use technological forecasts to discern where and when he will be in jeopardy if no action is mounted to effect a timely response to the hazards foreseen.

The Development Planner

Technological forecasts can provide guidance concerning the ability of the technological community to meet future system requirements, which are a principal concern of the development planner. The timing of future technology can be established by careful forecasting.[7]

Forecasts need not provide perfectly precise information about the future (which, in any case, would be impossible to achieve) in order to be useful. Research and development planning decisions can be improved by clearer delineation of future technological opportunities and threats than would otherwise be available without a formal forecast derived through a formal process.[8]

Among the lessons learned from Project Hindsight was that real needs

[5] James Brian Quinn, "Technological Forecasting," *Harvard Business Review*, Vol. 45, No. 2 (March–April 1967), p. 91.

[6] Joseph P. Martino, "The Use of Technological Forecasts for Planning Research," in *Technological Forecasting for Industry and Government*, ed. by James R. Bright (Englewood Cliffs, N.J.: Prentice-Hall, 1968), pp. 270–271.

[7] Marvin J. Cetron, "Using Technical Forecasts," *Science and Technology*, July 1968, p. 57.

[8] Quinn, *op. cit.*, p. 106.

resulted in accelerated technological growth.[9] Such a situation, in which technology has to be advanced to meet a specific requirement,[10] is classified as "demand pull" by J. P. Martino. Technological forecasting carried out in the normative sense can assist this process by identifying the specific technological barriers which must be overcome to meet the goal.

Martino's other classification of situations responsible for bringing about pioneering research or technological advancement is "science push," a complement to the "demand pull" concept. Exploratory technological forecasting can be applied in connection with the "science push" situation by identifying technological opportunities in closely allied or dependent scientific areas. An illustration of the two types can be seen in Figure 1.

Figure 1

TWO LEVELS OF PLANNING AT WHICH FORECASTS ARE VALUABLE

To summarize the general applicability of technological forecasts to the R&D planning process, it can be said that the importance of well-founded formal forecasts is reflected primarily at two levels in the planning process. One level involves assigning priorities to the overall R&D effort. The other level involves deciding which particular projects to undertake in connection with a specific system development program.[11]

[9] Raymond S. Isenson, "Technological Forecasting Lessons from Project Hindsight," in *Technological Forecasting for Industry and Government*, ed. by James R. Bright (Englewood Cliffs, N.J.: Prentice-Hall, 1968), p. 44.
[10] Martino, *op. cit.*, p. 273.
[11] Cetron, *op. cit.*, pp. 60, 61.

Examination of the various technological forecasting techniques also indicates that, in the context of the primary research question of this study, no useful purpose would be served by considering specific techniques for particular applications. Very probably any one of a large number of the various techniques might be equally applicable to any particular facet of the R&D planning process, depending on the nature and extent of the available data and the personal preference of the forecaster.

One of the major findings of our survey was that half of 1114 respondents to a questionnaire on technological forecasting, R&D planning, and project selection "always" or "frequently" used technological forecasting, and 42% used "normative" or quantitative methodologies for the allocation of resources. Two of the main reasons that others did not use technological forecasting were that its cost and applicability vary from company to company, and, as previously mentioned, its validity is uncertain. A forecast is useful only if it is integrated into a planning and resource allocation system. Unfortunately, people have tried to perform forecasts but then have discovered that they did not know how to apply the findings—that is to say, they could not translate a forecast into operational implications. This brings up another major point: there is no incentive to perform forecasts without an objective, formalized, and hopefully quantitative planning system.

II. *Historical Perspective of Technological Forecasting*

The most essential qualification for a politician is the ability to foretell what will happen tomorrow, next month, and next year, and to explain afterwards why it did not happen.   Winston Churchill

PRESENT STATUS OF TECHNOLOGICAL FORECASTING

One need only thumb through this chapter, checking the many references cited, to quickly surmise that a prodigious amount of energy has been expended in this new realm of technological forecasting. And yet, when the associated literature is examined, a constant observation runs through it: technological forecasting is in its "formative years." The reader is well advised to keep this in mind. What he sees of technological forecasting is what it is *now*, not what it can be if matured to full potential. It is well to remember the estimate of James R. Bright, to the effect that technological forecasting is about 50 years behind economic forecasting.[1] Edward B. Roberts is of the same mind.[2]

A little later herein, forecasting by means of growth curves will be presented as a technique. If you will, view technological forecasting

[1] James R. Bright, "Can We Forecast Technology?" *Management Thinking*, July 1968, p. 12.
[2] Edward B. Roberts, "Exploratory Normative Technological Forecasting: A Critical Appraisal," in *Technological Forecasting: A Practical Approach* by Marvin J. Cetron (New York: Gordon & Breach, 1969), p. 248.

itself as being in the lower portion of a growth curve. Do not precipitously demean its techniques as being oversimplifications. In large measure, the sustenance needed to mature technological forecasting into a science has been lacking. When new methods of managing science and technology arrive, the old die hard or, at least, are loathe to "move over." There must be an acceptance of the fact that technological forecasting *can* provide a powerful tool for planning that is, even in its infancy, several orders more logical than what now exist, and that it therefore warrants being put to the test on a serious scale. The refinements and sophistication *will then* come. The emotion and emphasis of our words are an indication that we are not at all happy with the acceptance—grudging at best—presently accorded to technological forecasting.

The literature searched during the research phase of this project injects a measure of confusion into the situation. Some semblance of standard terminology and definitions is just now emerging, but there is enough of what appears to be "jargon" to scare a novice off in a state of understandable confusion. Perhaps this is to be expected of something now characterized as an "art" but hopefully on its way to becoming a science. Nevertheless, the literature is profuse with "experts" saying exactly the same things, discussing the same or similar forecasting techniques, while simultaneously in apparent disagreement as to what the term technological forecasting means, what the usefulness of forecasting is, or what its relationship is to the long-range planning processes.

However, there was in the literature unanimous agreement—beyond the fact that technological forecasting is in an embryonic state, that it is an art trending toward a science—on one point: it is very difficult to accomplish.[3] Beyond this many differing views emerged. This apparent confusion or disagreement is probably due partly to semantic difficulties and partly to the individual preferences of the practitioners. Some definitions of technological forecasting appear forbiddingly broad, as that by Donald A. Schon, that is, the forecasting of technological change.[4] James Bright, on the other hand, provides an example of a definition that is too restrictive to be acceptable to a general survey effort of the type presented in this chapter:[5] true technological forecasting is

[3] Raymond S. Isenson, "Technological Forecasting in Perspective," *Management Science,* Vol. 13, No. 2 (October 1966), p. B-70.
[4] Donald A. Schou., et al., *The Role of the Federal Government in Technological Forecasting,* Interagency Task Groups on Technological Forecasting in Federal Government, January 1966.
[5] James R. Bright, *Research, Development, and Technological Innovation* (Homewood, Ill.: Richard D. Irwin, 1964), p. 757.

a process that yields a systematically reproducible result. This definition would seem to rule out so-called expert opinion and other techniques involving intuitive methods. Indeed, many of the techniques surveyed, in addition to the intuitive techniques, involve the application of subjective judgment to varying degrees. For this reason, the requirement for systematic reproducibility, in particular across different forecasters, may be unnecessarily stringent. Exact reproducibility is for machines, not people. If we had a situation where exact reproducibility were possible, we would not need the intelligent involvement of experts—in fact, we would not now be discussing forecasting.

The point is really this: it is not necessary that 100% agreement be achieved at "time zero" of a forecast—the opposite is expected. What some fail to realize is that technological forecasting is not a "one-shot" affair; it is a dynamic process as a function of time that tends toward smoothing out errors and differences of opinion. As a matter of fact, it provides the "forum" in which differing opinions "collide," interact, and are modified by the feedback of future events and the "give-and-take" between experts on different disciplines, such as planners and scientists or engineers. At least, this is what an ideal technological forecast process should do.

With this as background, let us proceed to see what pertinent literature has divulged as the various techniques espoused for technological forecasting.

TWO GENERAL APPROACHES

There are two general approaches to technological forecasting which are of interest to planners of research and development. One is "exploratory" technological forecasting, which seeks to project technological parameters and/or functional capabilities into the future by starting from a base of accumulated knowledge in relevant areas.

The other general approach is "normative" technological forecasting, in which future goals and missions are identified and assessed as to technological requirements. The process is then worked backward to the present, in order to identify the various technological "barriers" and deficiencies which must be overcome in order to achieve the goals.[6] Various elements and combinations of the specific technological forecasting techniques can be used in either or both the exploratory and norma-

[6] Erich Jantsch, *Technological Forecasting in Perspective* (Paris: Organization for Economic Cooperation and Development, 1967), pp. 29–38.

tive senses to explore and plan for the future. It can be said that:

In a general sense, the "purposes" of forecasting closely match the contrasting views of technological change. That is, one may ask (1) Where *is it possible* to go from here? Where are the dangers or opportunities? (thesis) or (2) Where do we *intend* (or desire) to go from here? What are the goals? (antithesis). Finally, (3) Where do we *expect* to go from here? What are the most probable paths? (synthesis). A forecast may be concerned with any one of these or with all of them.[7]

SPECIFIC TECHNIQUES

To best suit the purpose of this study, the technological forecasting techniques of interest have been grouped into the following categories:

Intuitive methods
Trend extrapolation
Trend correlation
Analogy
Dynamic predictive models

The ordering of the above categories might be regarded as reflecting a roughly ascending order of analytical sophistication. Employing any of the techniques is more of an art than a science, but with perhaps a few exceptions the ordering of the techniques in the above categories corresponds to increasingly firmer systematic analytical foundations and larger data banks.

INTUITIVE METHODS

The forecasting or prediction techniques in this category range from individual expert opinion and simple opinion polls to extensions of the Delphi technique developed at The Rand Corporation.[8] Expert opinion has been a fundamental prediction technique and is only now beginning to give way to trend extrapolation as the most widely employed method. The Interservice Technological Forecasting Methodology Study Group has identified four separate approaches under the "intuitive methods" category.[9]

[7] Robert U. Ayres, *Technological Forecasting and Long-Range Planning*, (New York: McGraw Hill Book Company, 1969).

[8] T. J. Gordon and Olaf Helmer, *Report on a Long-Range Forecasting Study* (Santa Monica, Calif.: The Rand Corporation, 1964), p. 5.

[9] Marvin J. Cetron et al., *A Proposal for a Navy Technological Forecast*, Part II, Headquarters, Naval Material Command, Washington, D.C. May 1, 1966 (A.D. 659-200), p. 16.

Individual Forecasting

It is quite possible that an individual who is expert in his special area and knowledgeable in related scientific technologies can produce meaningful forecasts. Not surprisingly, the quality of this type of forecast depends heavily on the particular expert doing the forecasting. A major shortcoming is that quite often there is a lack of explicit exposition regarding the logic involved and the underlying assumptions, so that critical evaluation of forecasts made by individual experts is often difficult if not impossible.[10]

Polls

Polls combine the judgment of a group of experts in the hope that some of the errors which might be present in individual predictions may be "integrated out" by others in the group. If the sample is poorly drawn, the forecast arrived at by polling a group of scientists or engineers will be very similar to an individual forecast.[11]

Panels

The panel approach to technological forecasting is the next logical step beyond polls. A desirable interaction among several experts can be achieved by bringing them into personal contact with one another. One disadvantage to this approach is that it provides the opportunity for the more forceful personalities present to generate the so-called band-wagon effect of a fallacious "majority" opinion.[12]

Delphi

The Delphi technique is an organized, systematic method to obtain a consensus of expert opinion and avoid many shortcomings of the panel and polling approaches. Some of the undesirable features of group or committee discussions are avoided by the use of questionnaires. The

[10] James R. Bright, "Can We Forecast Technology?" *op. cit.*, pp. 13–15.
[11] Marvin J. Cetron and Thomas I. Monahan, "An Evaluation and Appraisal of Various Approaches to Technological Forecasting," in *Technological Forecasting for Industry and Government*, ed. by James R. Bright (Englewood Cliffs, N.J.: Prentice-Hall, 1968), p. 146.
[12] Richard Simms, "Role of Technological Forecasting in Transportation R&D Planning," paper presented at the 1968 Transportation Engineering Conference, American Society of Mechanical Engineers, Washington, D.C., October 1968, p. 3.

technique is carried out in such a manner that many of the advantages of expert interaction are still achieved.[13]

In the Delphi approach to technological forecasting, direct debate is replaced by a carefully designed program of sequential interrogations, usually conducted by questionnaires, with controlled feedback. Individuals are first asked to predict the timing and implications of advances as a technology is developed toward its ultimate potential. Without allowing personal or face-to-face contact, the experts are provided with iterative controlled feedback to raise questions where divergent opinions exist and to identify areas of reasonable agreement.[14] However, again the opinions are only as good as the experts that have been selected.

TREND EXTRAPOLATION

Statistical extrapolation of existing trends, a common and popular technique of technological forecasting, is an old and familiar tool of engineers and applied scientists. It is generally agreed that the widespread application of the various trend extrapolation techniques is due primarily to their ease of use rather than to their accuracy.[15]

In the trend extrapolation method of technological forecasting, certain technological parameters, such as aircraft engine thrust-to-weight ratio, maximum aircraft speed, and operating energy of particle accelerators, are plotted over long periods as a function of time. It is then assumed that the nature of progress experienced in the past will continue in the future. That is to say, future inventions and advances will continue to occur at a rate which sustains the rate of growth shown. Most intuitive forecasts of progress are thought to be based on a subconscious model of this technique.

These extrapolations of time-series-related trends range from simple continuations of existing trends to more elaborate and elegant extrapolations using such techniques as linear and multiple regression and various curvilinear methods. A further extension of trend extrapolation forecasting involves judgment modification based on the consideration of exogenous factors.[16]

---

[13] Gordon and Helmer, op. cit., pp. 5–10.
[14] Arthur P. Lien, Paul Anton, and Joseph W. Duncan, Technological Forecasting: Tools, Techniques, Applications (New York: American Management Association, 1968), p. 22.
[15] Ralph C. Lenz Jr. Technological Forecasting, 2nd ed., Aeronautical Systems Division AFSC, ASD-TDR-62-414, Wright-Patterson Air Force Base, Ohio, June 1962 (AD408-085), p. 19.
[16] Cetron and Monahan, op. cit., p. 147.

Simple Extrapolation

The more simple mathematical-mechanical extrapolation techniques require that two basic assumptions be made. First, it is assumed that the factors which caused the prior pattern of progress will continue. Second, it is further assumed that the combined effect of these factors will perpetuate the previous pattern of progress rather than create a different one.[17]

It has been shown that these two assumptions are not as restrictive (within limits) as they might appear at first. Many technologies exhibit quantitative characteristics that approach very closely to an exponential growth over time, at least for quite significant periods.[18]

An example of this is seen when the energy-conversion efficiency of various means of illumination is plotted as a function of time. Over the span of a 100-year period, beginning with the paraffin candle and extending through the tungsten filament to the fluorescent lamp in about 1945, the efficiency, in lumens per watt, for each device falls very close to a straight line on a semilog plot. Measured trends appear to exhibit this kind of growth more often than not, at least during a significant period of the development life of a particular technology. However, problems arise (as might well be imagined) in trying to apply this technique to very young or very mature technologies. It is largely due to such difficulties that a modified approach has evolved, permitting the exercising of judgment as described in the following paragraphs.[19]

Substitution

The substitution forecast is a form of trend extrapolation, which is based, however, on an approach quite different from that used for single trend extrapolation, growth analogy, or correlation analysis, as defined above. In the substitution forecast, instead of measuring the increase in performance occurring in technology, the rate at which one technology is substituting for another in general usage is measured. For example, one may measure the rate of substitution, with time, of diesel engines versus steam for railroad locomotion. Of course, the relative increase

---

[17] Ralph C. Lenz, Jr., "Technological Forecasting," paper presented at the U.S. Air Force Symposium on Long-Range Forecasting and Planning, Colorado Springs, Colo., August 1966, pp. 155–157.

[18] Ralph C. Lenz, Jr., "Forecast of Exploding Technologies by Trend Extrapolation," in *Technological Forecasting for Industry and Government,* ed. by James R. Bright (Englewood Cliffs, N.J.: Prentice-Hall, 1968), pp. 65–69.

[19] General Electric Lamp Bulletin, January 1959.

in performance of the two technologies is the principal factor in the substitution process; however, the performance increments are not measured directly, but are only reflected in the rate of substitution.

The basic assumption in substitution forecasting is that substitition, once started, will proceed inexorably to conclusion, that is, that if the new technology can substitute completely for the old, it will. The substitution forecast proceeds at rates defined by the following formula:

$$f = \tfrac{1}{2}[1 + \tanh \alpha(t - t_0)]$$

where f = fraction of takeover by the new technology,
α = one-half of the initial annual exponential takeover rate,
t_0 = year in which $f = \tfrac{1}{2}$.

The forecast starts with the determination that a new technology is, in fact, starting to displace an older one. After selection of the measurement term which best defines the fraction of total usage of each technology, time-series data of the fraction of usage are gathered for both technologies. These data are used to establish the initial takeover rate and to predict the year in which takeover will reach 50%, on the basis of the formula. The formula is then used to forecast the dates at which various percentages of takeover will occur. The formula produces the characteristic S-curve in forecasting the rate of takeover. This subject has been treated in greater detail in Chapter XVII.

Modified Curve Fitting

As indicated above, technological progress, as reflected by functional capabilities or by technical parameters, often advances in an exponential manner similar to constant acceleration or to biological growth. At the outset, though, progress sometimes tends to be slow until the potential of a particular technical parameter is recognized and increased effort is directed toward its development. Its growth then accelerates. Eventually natural limitations are encountered, and the curve usually approaches a horizontal asymptote at some upper bound. We have identified five distinct types of trend curves.[20]

Linear with Flattening. This is a simple linear increase with a flattening effect as an upper limit is approached. This type is typified by curves of the efficiency of thermal power plants, for example.

Exponential with No Flattening. This second type exhibits an exponential increase with no flattening, or leveling off, in the time range under

[20] Cetron and Monahan, *op. cit.,* pp. 147–148.

consideration. The example mentioned above of energy-conversion efficiency in illumination technology is representative of this type of trend curve. Curves of the maximum speed of combat aircraft and the maximum speed of transport aircraft up to Mach 3.0 supersonic transport also are examples of this type.[21]

S-Shaped. The so-called S-shaped trend curve, characterized by a nearly exponential increase at the beginning, followed by a steeper slope in the midrange, and culminated by a flattening, or leveling off, is associated with many maturing technologies.

Double Exponential. The type of trend curve common to some functional capabilities in areas of concentrated research and development is classified as double-exponential with subsequent flattening. Curves of particle-accelerator operating energy plotted as a function of time are examples of this type, as are curves of the operating speed of commercial computers.[22]

Gradual-Rapid-Subsequent Flattening. The type of curve characterized by an initial gradual increase, followed by a very rapid increase and subsequent flattening, is descriptive of the maximum explosive power deliverable to a distant target. The very rapid increase corresponds to the advent of nuclear weapons. The subsequent flattening is due, not to technical limitations in this case, but rather to an effective utility limit at about 100 megatons.[23]

TREND CORRELATION

In the trend correlation technique, the forecaster assumes that one factor is the primary causal influence in the advancement of the technological parameter of interest. This technique is useful for applications in which the trend of a technical parameter is so complex and difficult to predict by itself that it might be more easily expressed as a result of a relationship between two or more related trends. Of course, this approach requires a knowledge not only of the primary trend or trends, but also of the probable relationships that the primary trends bear to the technological parameter of interest.

Trend correlation analysis is most useful for forecasting in situations

---

[21] Lenz, *Technological Forecasting, op. cit.* pp. 54, 55.

[22] Cetron et al., *op. cit.,* pp. 16–24.

[23] *Ibid.,* pp. 16–24.

where the development of a particular technological capability leads or lags in a predictable manner the development of a related capability. This is called forecasting by analysis of precursor events. It is predicated on correlation analysis of the progress trends between two developments, one of which is known or suspected to lead the other.[24] Jantsch mentions an example of this type of forecasting in which the prediction of the growth of future, fast nuclear reactor application is based on the projection of plutonium from the current generation of thermal reactors, on which the fast reactor applications are dependent.[25]

Another example has been developed by Ralph Lenz in forecasting the maximum speed of future commercial transport aircraft. The development of commercial aircraft is related to that of military combat aircraft in that the R&D effort which is originally applied to combat aircraft is eventually applied also to commercial aircraft.[26] There has been a fairly consistent sequential relationship in the correlation between maximum speed of combat aircraft and maximum speed of commercial transport planes. Transport speed has consistently lagged behind combat aircraft speed, with the lag increasing from about 6 years in the 1920s to approximately 11 years in the 1950s. Over the last 40 or 45 years the maximum speed of combat aircraft has doubled every 10 years and that of commercial transport planes has doubled every 12 years.[27] For more information in this regard, see Chapter XIII.

ANALOGY

Attempts to develop a theory that would explain why technological progress most often proceeds in an exponential manner are not new. Lenz cites what must be one of the earliest attempts, made in 1907, by Henry Adams.[28] Adams likened the advance of technology to a mass, initially in a state of equilibrium, which is acted upon by an external force and accelerates to a new equilibrium level. Since this early attempt, many other analogies have been drawn to theorize the rate of technological progress and to develop actual technological forecasts. Probably the most popular kinds of analogies are growth and historical analogies.[29]

---

[24] Cetron and Monahan, *op. cit.*, pp. 148–149.
[25] Jantsch, *op. cit.*, p. 159.
[26] Lenz, *Technological Forecasting, op. cit.*, pp. 54, 55.
[27] Jantsch, *op. cit.*, p. 160.
[28] Lenz, *Technological Forecasting, op. cit.*, p. 60.
[29] Cetron and Monahan, *op. cit.*, pp. 150–151.

Growth Analogy

Biological growth provides a useful analogy for many technologies. Growth equations similar to those for the rate of increase of fruit flies within a bottle, the rate of cell increase within a white rat, and the rate of growth of a beanstalk over time can be used to estimate the rate of growth and the time to a leveling off of progress in a maturing technology.[30]

Lenz has applied the biological growth analogy to a projection of military aircraft maximum speed trends. Application of the growth formula to a chosen upper limit of orbital velocity at an altitude of about 500,000 feet results in an extrapolation of maximum speed as a function of time which is asymptotic to the upper limit. According to Lenz's forecast by biological growth analogy, Mach 6 performance can be expected in 1979. Also, Mach 12 performance is predicted as being possible by 1995, which is 10 years later than the time predicted by the extrapolation of the present exponential trend.[31]

Historical Analogy

History has also been used to forecast the development of new technology. The General Electric Company has forecast the estimated proportion of electrical power that will be generated by nuclear fuels up to the year 2060. The estimate has been arrived at by employing the same type of development pattern as was observed for fossil fuels and hydroelectric power during the period from 1800 to 1960.[32]

DYNAMIC PREDICTIVE MODELS

An early application of dynamic forecasting was accomplished by Lenz, as an adaptation of a business simulation model developed by Professor Jay W. Forrester.[33] Forrester's model, which he termed "industrial dynamics," simulated complex business operations on a digital computer as a decision-making aid for industrial managers. Lenz utilized

[30] Lenz, *Technological Forecasting, op. cit.,* pp. 40–46.
[31] Ralph C. Lenz, Jr., "Forecasts of Exploding Technologies by Trend Extrapolation," in *Technological Forecasting for Industry and Government,* ed. by James R. Bright (Englewood Cliffs, N.J.: Prentice-Hall, 1968), pp. 66, 67.
[32] Cetron and Monahan, *op. cit.,* pp. 150–151.
[33] Jay W. Forrester, "Industrial Dynamics—A Major Breakthrough for Decision-Makers," *Harvard Business Review,* Vol. 36, No. 4 (July–August 1958), pp. 37–66.

Forrester's modeling structure and approach in order to model the important causal factors and relationships which govern the rate of advance of a functional technological capability.[34]

This method requires the forecaster to know a great deal about not only the technological area of interest, but also the factors that interact with each other to influence the growth of the technology in question. Equations must be developed using quantitative expressions of the effects of each important factor, their relationships to each other, and the feedback function. It is quite unusual, to say the least, to have such complete knowledge. Jantsch regards this technique as being "on the threshold of becoming useful for technological forecasting."[35]

There have been many serious attempts to employ this method because of its significant potential. Most technological forecasting methodology involves some kind of historical extrapolation. Dynamic predictive modeling provides the necessary tool or technique to investigate systematically how and to what extent future progress can be influenced by manipulating the factors over which control can be exercised.[36]

An early application of this technique, mentioned at the beginning of this section, involved a "knowledge-progress system."[37] In this model Lenz related thirty-seven variables and constants in nineteen different mathematical relationships to dynamically represent the development of a technology. Some of the factors reflected in the model were the number and the educational level of the people trained and employed to perform a particular R&D task, and the characteristics of the facilities provided. The output of the model was a description of technological progress, expressed as some "desired parameter of technical performance."[38]

A more recent example of the application of Forrester's "industrial dynamics" concept to technological forecasting is cited by Jantsch.[39] At the Xerox Corporation in Rochester, New York, a corporate-level forecasting staff utilizes an adaptation of the Xerox business model in connection with its technological forecasting function. The basic model is intended primarily for examining the effects of the introduction of

[34] Lenz, *Technological Forecasting, op. cit.*, pp. 63–72.

[35] Jantsch, *op. cit.*, p. 202.

[36] Marvin J. Cetron and Alan L. Weiser, "Technological Change, Technological Forecasting and Planning R&D—A View from the R&D Manager's Desk," *The George Washington Law Review—Technology Assessment and the Law*, Vol. 36, No. 5 (July 1968), pp. 1090, 1091.

[37] Lenz, *Technological Forecasting, op. cit.*, pp. 63–72.

[38] *Ibid.*

[39] Jantsch, *op. cit.*, pp. 203, 204.

a new product or a new development program. The greatest difficulty in using this model, or others like it, for technological forecasting is in obtaining reliable quantitative values for the 500 programmed variables and the many transfer functions which relate quantities of the input factors to quantities in which technological progress is expressed. However, even when considerable uncertainty is associated with many of the input variables, dynamic predictive models can be very useful in determining which factors are of overriding importance. Furthermore, many valuable insights into the problems involved are often gained in the process of attempting to construct a model of a real-world system or process.

MORPHOLOGICAL ANALYSIS

Dr. Fritz Zwicky describes "the method of the morphological box" as follows:[40]

First step: The problem which is to be solved must be exactly formulated.

Second step: All of the parameters which might enter into the solution of the given problem must be localized and characterized.

Third step: The morphological box, or multidimensional matrix, which contains all of the solutions of the given problem is constructed.

Fourth step: All of the solutions contained in the morphological box are closely analyzed and evaluated with respect to the purposes to be achieved.

Although the process outlined above related to problem solving, the author maintains that it is equally effective in forecasting. A fifth step concerns the selection and implementation of promising solutions and is deemed to lie outside the province of forecasting.

CROSS-IMPACT ANALYSIS

Cross-impact analysis was developed to overcome the lack of consideration of the relationships between events which is prevalent in the Delphi and other forecasting methodologies.[41] The major assumption on which

[40] Fritz Zwicky and A. G. Wilson, *New Methods of Thought and Procedure* (New York: Springer-Verlang New York, 1967), p. 285.
[41] T. J. Gordon and H. Hayward, "Initial Experiments with the Cross Impact Method of Forecasting," *Futures,* Vol. 1, 1968, p. 100.

the technique is based is that a probability of occurrence can be assigned to every event being considered. Cross-impact analysis then permits adjustment of the expected probability of each event in the set, on the basis of perceived interdependency among the events. Chapter XV describes some refinements to this method. Although both positive and negative (i.e., enhancing and inhibiting) relationships are taken into account, cause and effect relationships are not included.

CROSS-SUPPORT ANALYSIS

Cross-support analysis is a method of describing the cause and effect relationships between events, goals, technologies, and so on. It is based on the hypothesis that every event not only has the possibility of affecting every other event, but also can be affected by every other event, where the "effect" can be positive or negative. Thus, the total "value" or "contribution" of each event can be represented in terms of its causal and dependent relationships with the other events. The technique uses merely the magnitude of the relationships, not probabilistic estimates, nor does it require a high degree of quantification. Cross-support analysis is described in more detail in Chapter XVI.

RELATIONSHIP OF FORECASTING TO PLANNING

Among the important elements of research and development planning are corporate policy, goals, and objectives, the competitive environment, and the available resources. Technological forecasting is but one more element in the planning process. Although generally regarded as being an integral part of the R&D planning process, it is not a plan in itself.

Daniel Roman draws a meaningful, fundamental distinction between forecasting and planning.[42] He points out that a forecast does not develop or lay out a course of action to achieve stated goals or objectives. A good plan, of course, does exactly this. A technological forecast tries to predict what *could* be technologically, not what *will* be.

It should seem obvious that the forecast must precede the plan so that the nature of the R&D plan will be a consequence of the forecast and other factors. Monahan points out an improper use of exploratory technological forecasting in relation to planning, in which the plan pre-

[42] Daniel D. Roman, *Research and Development Management: The Economics and Administration of Technology* (New York: Appleton-Century-Crofts Division of Meredith Corporation, 1968), p. 340.

cedes the forecast.[43] In this case the forecast is used to "justify" or "validate" the plan and in reality is not a genuine forecast, but merely a rehash of the previously developed plan.

CHARACTERISTICS OF THE TECHNIQUES PRESENTED

The techniques of technological forecasting, if exercised properly, are based on careful analyses of past experience and require observation, measurement, and interpretation of the underlying data, trends, and interactions associated with the growth of a technology.[44] It was not our intention to offer any kind of critical assessment concerning the relative usefulness of the various techniques. Certainly, to have done so in this chapter would have been pointless. Although we will present a critique of each of the various techniques in Chapter XIII, it is maintained by at least some of our colleagues in the field (and we agree with them) that the success associated with any particular technological forecasting approach is more a matter of expertise in its use and development than of the intrinsic merit of the method selected. Jantsch states that he could find no discernible relationship between good forecasting and the use of specific techniques.[45] We believe that success really depends on the availability of a good data bank and on the seriousness and dedication with which the effort is undertaken.

[43] Thomas I. Monahan, "Current Approach to Forecasting Methodology," paper presented at the U.S. Air Force Symposium on Long-Range Forecasting and Planning, Colorado Springs, Colo., August 1966, p. 25.
[44] James Brian Quinn, "Technological Forecasting," *Harvard Business Review,* Vol. 45, No. 2 (March–April 1967), p. 91.
[45] Jantsch, *op. cit.,* p. 18.

III. *Historical Background of Technological Forecasting Used in Planning and Resource Allocation*

Life is a test, and this world a place of trial; always the problems—or it may be the same problem—will be presented to every generation in different forms.

Winston Churchill

THE NEED FOR RESOURCE ALLOCATION

As stated in the preceding chapters, there are never-enough resources to undertake all of the research projects that optimum planning would indicate. We are always in a pinch for funds, time, or competent personnel—a familiar story that holds true in all human endeavors, not just research. Any research program, if allowed, can develop an insatiable appetite for resources and will grow to fit the size of any pocketbook—and always with logical justification. But an enterprise cannot flourish and progress on one research program alone; it usually has many fields to explore, and its resources are finite and, most often, inadequate. Accordingly, one must "make the best of things" by doling out his resources among the various programs. Resource allocation answers the problem of how to make the best decisions under conditions of limited resources, imposed economics, and prescribed goals. It attempts to systematize these decisions in a fabric of logic.

The proponents of modern resource allocation techniques recognize that compromises must be made; however, they also recognize that among the myriad alternative compromises there are very few (often only one) that maximize a return on the investment. A principal aim of advocates of these techniques is to wean decision makers from top-of-the-head or arbitrary decisions with regard to allocating resources. The stakes involved are usually too high to place trust in methods that have little logical foundation. Again, as in the case of technological forecasting, logical resource allocation techniques do not represent a path of least resistance. They require an expenditure of effort and the indulgence of individuals who would prefer not to condescend to do the task. There is also a psychological stumbling block involved here, as will become apparent later.

Logical resource allocation methodologies start with the basic premise that relative values can be assessed for the importance of areas of endeavors and therefore values can be assigned to events or acquisitions occurring, or made to occur, in these areas. This is an everyday practice in the business world, where assessments of various alternatives include the attachment of values to intangibles and estimates of values for tangibles. The enlightened businessman will then process these values in a decision tree algorithm (perhaps computer-automated) to calculate the consequences of various alternatives. He then has his choices displayed before him for selection. Now, the businessman actually assessed the values; he probably devised the algorithm employed. He is not loathe to use the method or the results that it provides. It does not bother him that, perhaps, several million calculations were made in one hour of computer time without his lifting a finger. He will use the results without much compunction—he would not stay in business otherwise. He knows, of course, that he has not become a slave to the computer or a mechanistic process because these aids were of his own design. The tools were performing exactly as he would, had he had the time. How different the situation is in the world of research!

In research, the birthplace of the computer, the arena where mathematics, algorithms, and logic are commonplace, we find an anomaly. Research decision makers fear the use of these mechanized techniques. This might be all right if something as good existed in their place, but such is not the case. Some of the decision-making gyrations in this world make about as much sense as divination through the study of chicken entrails. Some glimmer of hope, however, is now appearing on the horizon. The idea of applying a precise rating system to research and development was, until fairly recently, highly suspect and somehow anti-intellectual; the old stereotype of the independent researcher following his private star dies hard. But the history of the last 25 years has sounded the death knell of this romantic approach. World War II, Sputnik, and Apollo lunar program—not to mention the new developments in electronics, medicine, and transportation—have all transformed science and technology into a big business of tremendous complexity. When the Department of Defense alone has an R&D budget of over $8 billion, there has to be a logical, rational way to select the tasks to be worked on and the resources to be expended on each of these efforts.

The fact is that research today is an input to an organization, whether government or private. Like production and sales, it must be subjected to examination and its usefulness to the organization's mission evaluated. This means that much of the aura of mysticism and infallibility usually attached to R&D must be discarded. Although most scientists and engineers are not romantics, they tend to resent the use of "relevance numbers," "figures of merit," and other techniques for evaluating their work. Procedures which they themselves have developed, like operations research, seem like Frankensteins when put to use in judging R&D itself.

But the job of allocating technical resources must be done. And as the scope of the effort becomes larger and the complexity increases, more and more factors must be considered in order to reach an effective decision. Soon the point is reached where even one small decision may affect the operation of all efforts, at least to some degree. When that happens, the human brain alone cannot do the job as well as is needed.

The situation is particularly hard to handle when many R&D projects must be considered for inclusion within a fixed government or corporation resource ceiling. Priorities must be set, or decisions made on which projects to back, or which to drop or delay. Numerous efforts are interrelated in time; therefore, choices must be made with regard to the total effect, including resources required, the purpose of each effort, and possible technological transfer between efforts. Every organization, whether a manufacturing firm, a service industry, a government agency, or a university laboratory, must seek the greatest payoff from its resource investments.

What alternative methods are available for helping to make allocations? How can they be evaluated? The basic point is that the resource allocation problem is usually too big to keep in one man's head. Data inputs come from areas completely outside of his control. Relevant inputs rapidly multiply to the hundreds or thousands when an allocation problem is subjected to really careful analysis.

SUMMARY OF GENERIC RESOURCE ALLOCATION METHODS

Level of Effort

History often plays a major role in resource allocation; that is, the resources provided to a given office or for a given task area tend to remain constant, or to change in proportion to the resources available to those responsible for the allocations. This approach can be represented by the following equation:

$$A(x)_{FY+1} = A(x)_{FY} \frac{R_{FY+1}}{R_{FY}}$$

where $A(x)_{FY}$ = allocation of the current year's resources for task area x,
$A(x)_{FY+1}$ = allocation of next year's resources for task area x,
R_{FY} = current year's resources available to office responsible for allocations,
R_{FY+1} = next year's resources available to office responsible for allocations.

Uses. This is the traditional approach to a large percentage of exploratory development allocations. Although it does not provide for new task areas, resources left over from completed task areas can sometimes be allocated for new work. If total resources are increasing, some of the increase can also be used for new work. However, the resources left over because of completed work seldom equal the needs for new work; and, as we are all aware, total resources have been decreasing, not increasing, in recent years.

Advantages
1. This approach simplifies the job of planning for future efforts. It is difficult to prepare meaningful plans for future work if the planner has little idea of the resources which will be available to him.
2. Men who are experienced in a particular type of work can usually continue work in their specialized areas. This prevents excessive retraining costs and can often increase productivity.
3. Many people will complain less and work harder if they believe that their projects are at least holding their own in the contest for funds and other resources.
4. Inefficient fluctuations of effort are usually avoided. Frequent and abrupt changes in a project can result in a great deal of activity with little net progress.

Disadvantages

1. Starting a new task area can be quite difficult, especially when total resources are being reduced.

2. Inertia can continue funding for a task area even though the primary goals have been achieved or the probability of achieving these goals has become small.

3. Some persons will complain that factors such as changing requirements, newly identified gaps in technology, and the expected results of the candidate task areas were not given proper consideration. Morale and productivity may be adversely affected.

4. The most serious disadvantage is that the potential values of the various task areas are not considered adequately.

Prestige of Supporters

Proposals are more likely to be accepted if they are advanced and supported by experts in the area concerned. An outstanding individual may well have his proposals accepted even if they do not fit the overall plan as neatly as desired. Highly respected administrators often find it easier to obtain funds than administrators who have not earned such confidence. Members of the latter group sometimes have to present their plans in greater detail and to support them with more compelling justification than their more favored colleagues.

Uses. Prestige is usually one of several factors which affect resource allocations. Although this is not always stated explicitly, few people ignore a man's reputation when evaluating his proposals. Prestige can play an especially crucial role in subjective evaluations, but it also influences the estimates used as data in more objective approaches.

Advantages

1. Prestige often reflects demonstrated ability. Those who have proved themselves in a given area usually have better than average ability to identify promising work in that area.

2. Most people are more likely to remain with an organization and to work harder if their proposals are accepted frequently. It is usually especially desirable to keep both the services and the enthusiasm of those with high prestige.

Disadvantages

1. Prestige is not always proportional to ability to select tasks with the highest expected utility.

2. A man's prestige may extend beyond his field of special competence.

Some men are careful to avoid questionable use of their prestige, but others are less scrupulous.

3. Competent men who do not have especially high prestige may react negatively.

Sunk Costs

Managers tend to continue support of task areas in which they have already invested substantial resources. It is psychologically uncomfortable to write off a mistake, especially an expensive mistake for which one is responsible. In addition, prestige and even job security may be lost when an error of judgment is admitted.

Uses. Although consideration of sunk costs is discouraged by decision-making theory, it plays a role in many resource allocation decisions in which continuing work is involved.

Advantages. There is little to be said in favor of permitting sunk costs to influence decisions concerning future expenditures. On the other hand, all of the possible future costs and gains should be considered. These include the possibility that some useful results can be obtained from a disappointing task area and the possibility that the work may have to be resumed at a later date and at greater expense. A manager may be tempted to cancel a shaky task area occasionally just to prove that he can do it. This temptation, of course, should be resisted. Although one should have the courage to admit a mistake, there is no virtue in prematurely writing off a decision just to prove a point.

Disadvantages
1. Task areas may be continued even though changes in requirements have reduced their usefulness or after problems have been identified which make successful completion very unlikely.
2. New task areas, which often respond to critical new requirements or exploit new technological breakthroughs, may be delayed because scarce resources are being diverted to work which should have been terminated.

Complaint Level

Under this alternative, funds would be allocated in some reasonable way, and the manager responsible would await the reaction. If nobody complained, or if everybody complained with equal fervor, he would consider the allocations satisfactory. If some reacted more strongly than others, he would make adjustments to equalize the noise level.

Uses. It seems unlikely that many managers decide consciously to use this approach, but things often work out in this way. A manager would seem unreasonable if he refused to listen to those immediately responsible for the task areas he sponsors, but he may find himself subjected to more high-volume emotion than reason. A manager being human, it should not be surprising if he sometimes responds to emotional appeals.

Advantages

1. Quite often, people who complain most loudly do so because they have the most about which to complain. To some extent, therefore, this approach can improve allocations.

2. The immediate noise level of the complaints may be minimized.

3. Those who complain will recognize that they are heard, that those above them are willing to listen to their problems and take appropriate action. This may improve their morale and productivity.

Disadvantages

1. The fervor of the complaints depends at least as much on the personality of the complainer as on his real needs. Such personality traits have little or no relevance to how resources should be allocated.

2. The morale and productivity of the less vocal worker can be affected adversely.

3. If the word gets around that a manager can be swayed by loudly expressed complaints, the noise can quickly approach an intolerable level.

Gains Matrix

Several decision-making techniques use a gains matrix similar to the one shown in Table 1.[1] A matrix such as this can sometimes be simplified, or even solved, if some of the alternatives available to the decision maker dominate others. (The dominant alternative will result in gains at least as large as those which would result from the dominated alternative, regardless of events beyond the control of the decision maker.)

This matrix, which is introduced for purpose of illustration, represents a hypothetical situation wherein a manager must determine which combination of three tasks he will support. One task would provide needed technology for a surface-to-surface missile (SSM), one would provide technology for countermeasures (CM) to enemy missiles, and the third would lead to improved counter-countermeasure (CCM) capability. A

[1] William T. Morris, *The Analysis of Management Decisions* (Homewood, Ill.: Richard D. Irwin, 1964), p. 383.

Table 1. Gains Matrix

U.S.	S_1 None	S_2 SSM	S_3 CM	S_4 CCM	S_5 SSM CM	S_6 SSM CCM	S_7 CM CCM	S_8 All
a_1 None	0	-3	1	1	-2	-2	2	-1
a_2 SSM	3	0	1	4	-2	-1	2	-1
a_3 CM	-1	-1	0	0	0	-2	1	-1
a_4 CCM	-1	-4	0	0	-3	-3	1	-1
a_5 SSM and CM	2	2	0	3	0	3	1	-1
a_6 SSM and CCM	2	1	2	3	-3	0	3	-2
a_7 CM and CCM	-2	-2	-1	-1	-1	-3	0	-4
a_8 All	1	1	1	2	1	2	4	0

possible enemy is faced with similar choices (S). Arbitrarily selected gains are assumed.

Table 1 contains several examples of dominance. No matter what choices an enemy makes, for example, a_1 is a better choice than a_4; a_2 is also a better choice than a_4 or a_7; a_5 is at least as good a choice as a_3, a_4, or a_7; and a_8 is at least as good a choice as a_1, a_3, a_4, or a_7. This makes it possible to reduce our choices from eight to four. The enemy would probably reduce his choices in the same way, or so it is sometimes assumed. The smaller matrix which results has new dominances, and these finally lead to a_8 and S_8 as the dominant strategies. Game theory, which can also be used to solve much more complex problems, gives an immediate solution to this problem.[2]

Several other techniques can be used if the S's represent possible states of the future rather than alternatives available to an opponent. If we can assign a meaningful probability to each possible state of the future, we can calculate expected gain. If the probability of one possible state of the future is especially large, it might be treated as if it were certain. If we have no basis for estimating probability, we can assume that each possible future is equally likely, and we can maximize our minimum possible gain (or minimize our maximum possible loss), or maximize

[2] Maurice Sasiene, Arthur Yaspan, and Lawrence Friedman, *Operations Research* (New York: John Wiley & Sons, 1959), p. 158.

our maximum gain. Several other techniques, including some which offer a compromise between optimism and pessimism, are also available.

Uses. Game theory, in the form of a gains matrix, can be useful for finding the best course of action when a limited number of options are open to each party in a two-sided contest and the gains or costs associated with each combination of options can be estimated. Expected gain can be determined when the probability of each possible state of the future can be estimated. Several techniques have been suggested for use when there is no basis for estimating probabilities.

Advantages

1. When there are only a few alternatives to consider in allocating resources, only a few possible contingencies to address, and adequate bases for estimating the gain or loss associated with each alternative-contingency combination, these techniques provide rational approaches for selecting a good alternative.

2. The process of preparing the matrix forces explicit consideration of alternatives, factors beyond the control of the decision maker, and the corresponding gains or losses. These factors are useful to decision making even if the matrix is never solved mathematically.

Disadvantages

1. The number of possible alternatives in most resource allocation problems is quite large. Possible enemies may pursue many courses of action, and many events are beyond the control of either opponent. A matrix which includes even the most interesting possibilities can become unwieldy.

2. A great deal of time and effort is necessary to prepare the matrix.

3. The theory of games approach postulates rational opponents. It has not been demonstrated convincingly, however, that the human mind is consistently rational, especially when entertaining thoughts of war.

Linear Programming

Suppose five candidate task areas have a linear relationship between resources allocated and gains expected. It is assumed that $1 million, 60 man-months of mechanical engineering time, and 84 man-months of electronic engineering time are available. It is also assumed that the following linear relationships apply:

$X_1 =$ units of task area 1 effort, where one unit requires $1000, 0.029 man-month of mechanical engineering time, and 0.100 man-month of electronic engineering time;

X_2 = units of task area 2 effort, where one unit requires $1000, 0.140 man-month of mechanical engineering time, and 0.160 man-month of electronic engineering time;

X_3 = units of task area 3 effort, where one unit requires $1000, 0.041 man-month of mechanical engineering time, and 0.053 man-month of electronic engineering time;

X_4 = units of task area 4 effort, where one unit requires $1000, 0.056 man-month of mechanical engineering time, and 0.038 man-month of electronic engineering time;

X_5 = units of task area 5 effort, where one unit requires $1000, 0.042 man-month of mechanical engineering time, and no electronic engineering time.

G_1 = gain from one unit of task area 1 = 9.8 when $X_1 \leq 510$,
= 0   when $X_1 > 510$;
G_2 = gain from one unit of task area 2 = 36.0 when $X_2 \leq 150$,
= 0   when $X_2 > 150$;
G_3 = gain from one unit of task area 3 = 4.7 when $X_3 \leq 510$,
= 0   when $X_3 > 510$;
G_4 = gain from one unit of task area 4 = 5.2 when $X_4 \leq 480$,
= 0   when $X_4 > 480$;
G_5 = gain from one unit of task area 5 = 2.8 when $X_5 \leq 360$,
= 0   when $X_5 > 360$.

The allocation of resources to maximize total gain may be calculated using the following set of equations and inequalities:

$$\text{Maximize } G_+ = G_1X_1 + G_2X_2 + G_3X_3 + G_4X_4 + G_5X_5$$
$$= 9.8X_1 + 36.0X_2 = 4.7X_3 + 5.2X_4 + 2.8X_5$$

where $X_1 \leq 510$, $X_2 \leq 150$, $X_3 \leq 510$, $X_4 \leq 480$, $X_5 \leq 360$.
Then

$$X_1 + X_2 + X_3 + X_4 + X_5 \leq 1000$$
$$29X_1 + 140X_2 + 41X_3 + 56X_4 + 42X_5 \leq 60000$$
$$100X_1 + 160X_2 + 53X_3 + 38X_4 \leq 72000$$

The linear programming technique can be used to solve this problem. Several variations of this technique are described by Gass.[3]

Uses. Linear programming is useful when relationships can be described by a set of equations and inequalities which are linear or can be converted to linear form. Unfortunately, the real world of resource allocation does not provide many problems which fit this very convenient solution. Relationships between resources and results tend to be non-

[3] Saul I. Gass, *Linear Programming: Methods and Applications* (New York: Mc-Graw-Hill Book Company, 1964).

linear. Employees often have varying degrees of competence in several types of work. Even if several factors are linear, at least one will usually fail to meet this test.

Advantages

1. If a linear problem does occur, this approach provides an excellent solution.

2. Proven techniques are also available for determining sensitivity to changes in the parameters. This is especially important in exploratory development because the values used are often estimated and are subject to change.

Disadvantages

1. Very few problems in exploratory development satisfy the linearity requirement.

2. Attempts to force a nonlinear problem into linear form can result in an explicit, numerical answer which has little relation to the real problem.

3. Even if a linear relationship exists between the inputs and outputs of candidate task areas, considerable effort would be required to determine what it is.

CURRENT INVESTIGATIONS

Although some of the techniques just described are in widespread use and others could be useful under certain conditions, improved methods are being sought. Much of this effort has been directed toward developing mathematical models which combine several criteria to provide a basis for resource allocations. Some of the results have been reported in the public literature, but much of the work is still in the formulative stage. Even if it were feasible to report all current information concerning progress in each of the armed services, this information would soon cease to be current. Therefore, only two current projects and projected trends in resource allocation will be discussed.

Torque

In 1968, Donald MacArthur, Deputy Director of Defense Research and Engineering (Research and Technology), pointed out that "no one has ever answered the question of how to allocate resources on a semi-quantitative basis."[4] However, TORQUE (<u>T</u>echnology <u>Or</u> <u>R</u>esearch <u>Q</u>uan-

---

[4] Walter Andrew, "AF to Try Systems Analysis on Exploratory Development," *Aerospace Technology*, April 8, 1968, p. 18.

titative Utility Evaluation) represents significant progress in providing the answer. TORQUE is "an analytical procedure for achieving balance in the allocation of exploratory development funds . . . formulated by an *ad hoc* tri-service committee, created by request of Dr. John S. Foster, Jr., Director of Defense Research and Engineering."[5] The *ad hoc* committee, which was under Marvin J. Cetron's chairmanship, included members from the army, navy, and air force and expert advisors from MacArthur's office, the Research Analysis Corporation, the Center for Naval Analysis, the University of North Carolina, The Rand Corporation, The Army's Behavioral Sciences Research Laboratory, and Stanford University.

In operation, TORQUE called for experts in operations, systems, and technology to estimate 10-year requirements, propose alternative approaches for the timely satisfaction of these requirements, identify technological needs and possibilities as a function of time and of the alternative approaches they support, and estimate costs involved. Although the estimates were quantitative, they reflected the judgment of the experts consulted, as well as any empirical data which might be both available and relevant. A mathematical model combined the various estimates and provided quantitative, time-phased values for each subdivision of exploratory development which was considered as a separate unit. These values were rank ordered, and the ranking provided useful information for managers who had to allocate exploratory development funds.

The military version of TORQUE has been reported, but not fully described,[6] in the public literature; and the air force has recently conducted an experiment to prove its feasibility. A closely related technique, designed for industrial use, has been described in some detail.[7]

Uses. This technique can be used by any or all of the armed services. If employed by all of them, approximately 12,000 Department of Defense (DOD) activities could be involved.[8]

---

[5] "TORQUE Presents System of Balancing R&D Program," *Army Research and Development* July–August 1967, p. 1.
[6] Ambrose Nutt, "Testing TORQUE—A Quantitative R&D Resource-Allocation System," *IEEE Transactions on Engineering Management,* Vol. EM-16, No. 4 (November 1969).
[7] Marvin J. Cetron and Harold F. Davidson, "MACRO R&D," *Industrial Management Review,* Spring 1969.
[8] "TORQUE Presents System of Balancing R&D Programs," *Army Research and Development,* July–August 1967, p. 1.

Advantages

1. This technique can provide a useful guide for those who must allocate exploratory development resources. Overall service needs, rather than the needs of the individual component parts of the service, would be emphasized.

2. It can also help in determining total exploratory development requirements.

3. It can be used to support requests for additional funds. Some men, both in the DOD and in Congress, are more impressed by explicit, mathematical techniques than by subjective judgment.

Disadvantages

1. A significant amount of time is required to make and review the many expert judgments.

2. Even though this techniuqe is planned as "a management tool, not a decision maker,"[9] it could lead to a situation where very few men would do the decision making. These would probably be highly competent men; nevertheless, they could hardly hope to understand each type of warfare addressed, systems concept considered, or technology involved as well as other competent men, each of whom has specialized in one of these areas for many years. Therefore, centralization of decision making could reduce the in depth knowledge of those who make the decisions.

A Probabilistic Risk Approach

One of the techniques being investigated by the Navy "addresses the problems of military utility. Military utility with respect to development atmosphere is a measure of R&D (research and development) work in terms of its usefulness in meeting U.S. Navy's General Operational Requirements (GOR)."[10] Although military utility includes value to naval warfare, responsiveness, and timeliness, the published version treats only value to naval warfare.

The technique depends on a series of appraisals. The first set provides relative values for satisfying the objectives of all Navy General Operational Requirements in each warfare category, such as Strike Warfare and Antisubmarine Warfare. Numerical values are assigned so that the total equals 100. Next, the value assigned to each category is divided

[9] *Ibid.*

[10] Marvin J. Cetron, *Prescription for the Military R&D Manager: Learn the Three R's,* Presentation to the NATO Defense Research Group, Teddington, England, November 12, 1968, p. 19.

among the Navy General Operational Requirements under that category. Each task area is then appraised to determine its possible impact on each General Operational Requirement. A number from 0 to 1 is assigned, with 0 indicating no impact and 1 indicating a radically important impact. This gives

$$\frac{VT_x}{S_x} = \frac{n}{\underset{g\,=\,1}{}} V_g 1(T_{xg})$$

where $V(T_x/S_x)$ = total value of Task Area X to naval warfare if task area objectives are achieved

n = number of General Operational Requirements considered

V_g = value assigned to General Operational Requirement G

$i(T_{xg})$ = impact of Task Area X on General Operational Requirement G if task area objectives are achieved

An appraisal is then made of the task areas to establish a probability of success. There may be several concurrent approaches to achieving the objectives of the task area, each with its own probability of success. If these probabilities are independent,

$$P(S_x) = 1 - \frac{m}{\underset{c\,=\,1}{}} [1 - P(S_c)]$$

where m = number of concurrent approaches

$P(S_x)$ = probability that Task Area objectives will be achieved

$P(S_c)$ = probability that concurrent approach C will prove successful

Thus

$$EV(T_x) = \frac{VT_x}{S_x} P(S_x)$$

$$= \text{expected value of Task Area X}$$

The optimum funding is estimated for each task area. The probability of achieving task area objectives will, of course, depend on the funding level selected. A desirability index can now be calculated.

$$D(T_x) = \frac{EV(T_x)}{C_x}$$

where $D(T_x)$ = desirability index for Task Area X

C_x = estimated optimum funding level for Task Area X

Task areas are then rank ordered on the basis of desirability index. If some task areas are assigned priorities, separate rankings can be provided for each priority level. Consideration may also be given to higher and lower funding level, and provision may be made for task areas that involve sequential operations as well as concurrent operations.

This technique is being developed and studied for possible use in the Navy. It would provide a basis for comparing all Navy task areas; but this technique, like the one tested by the Air Force, is intended to help the decision maker rather than replace him.

An industrial version of this technique is presented in much more detail under the name BRAILLE.[11]

Advantages and Disadvantages. This technique seems somewhat less complex than the one under investigation by the Air Force and the objectives appear somewhat less comprehensive. However, the advantages and disadvantages are similar.

The two illustrations just used came from the military; however, every businessman confronted with ranking or selecting the best candidates for allocating resources considers a few characteristics of each project: its development costs, the expected profit margin, the length of time needed to achieve a return on the investment, etc.—then looking at the complete list, he weighs each criterion in some manner and forms an index of worth (a desirability index) of each project. This manager has used a scoring model as an informal aid to his decision process.

Many types of scoring models have been derived, but the management scientists and operations researchers have put their main thrust into developing much more mathematically sophisticated models. These fall into two types: deterministic optimization models, such as the linear programming model previously described, and probabilistic risk models, which place emphasis on the structuring and weighing of subjective probabilities of success, distribution of costs and returns, and the like. (For a much more detailed treatment of the actual techniques, the optimization criteria, and factors to consider, the book *Technical Resource Management: Quantitative Methods* is recommended.)[12]

Each of these three classes of R&D ranking models—scoring, deterministic, and probabilistic—is in turn more complex in structure and requires larger numbers of data (most of the data are quantitative estimates, the reliability of which is not always high). (Techniques for quantifying subjective judgments will be discussed at some length in the next section of this chapter.)

---

[11] Marvin J. Cetron, *Technological Forecasting: A Practical Approach* (New York: Gordon and Breach, 1969), pp. 219–243.

[12] Marvin Cetron et al., *Technical Resource Management: Quantitative Methods,* (Cambridge, Mass.: The M.I.T. Press, 1970).

Moore and Baker question whether the costs entailed in the increase in complexity and data requirements are worthwhile.[13] They say their experiments show, in a mathematically simulated comparison, that the simple scoring models performed almost as well as the more complex ones. Our feeling is that, since the current models are based heavily on intuitive judgments, their best value may lie in forcing the user to think about the utilities (profits, market potentials, corporate goals, etc.), the probabilities of success (technological forecasts), and the costs (financial acceptability), as well as in the expressing of inconsistencies and possible consequences.

Techniques for Quantifying Subjective Judgments

The previous discussions have alluded to a number of techniques that can be useful for quantifying subjective judgments. At the core of most subjective analyses is some form of scaling; and although construction of the scale or scales may be accomplished by means of many response mechanisms (e.g., questionnaires, interviews, gaming, group dynamics), the output is almost always a numerical representation of an object or stimulus that somehow describes that object or stimulus as better than, equal to, or worse than others of the same or a different class. In subjective scaling, the number replaces semantics as a way of communicating one's judgments concerning vague or typically qualitative concepts.

There are four types of scales (nominal, ordinal, interval, and ratio), each with its own characteristics, and each with varying degrees of usefulness and of difficulty in deriving from subjective judgments. Table 2 summarizes the characteristics of each type.

In addition to the four types of scales, there are three major categories of scaling techniques.

1. Traditional Scaling Techniques. These emphasize the undimensionality of some latent attribute and rely on strong scaling assumptions. Some examples of traditional techniques are the following:

(a) *Thurstonian scaling,* which utilizes Thurston's law of comparative judgment. Interval (or sometimes ratio) scales are elicited by statistical analysis of a subject's degree of confusion about stimuli that are presented via a (large) number of paired comparisons.

[13] John R. Moore, Jr., and Norman R. Baker, "Computational Analysis of Scoring Models for R&D Project Selection," *Management Science,* December 1969.

Table 2.   Types of Scales[a]

Scale	Definition	Defining Relations	Examples
Nominal (or classifica-tory) scale	Weakest level of measurement, in which numbers or symbols are used simply to classify a characteristic.	Equivalence ($\equiv$)	(1) Baseball teams in the National League (2) Science vs. engineering objectives (3) Spacecraft vs. capsule objectives
Ordinal (or ranking) scale	Members of one class are in some kind of *relation* to members of another class (greater than, more preferred, stronger, etc.). If [A] > [B] for some but not all members of classes A and B, we have a *partially ordered scale;* if > holds for all pairs of classes, we have an *ordinal scale.*	(1) Equivalence (2) Greater than (>)	(1) Upper class > middle class > lower class (2) Sergeant > corporal > private (3) First priority > second priority > third priority (4) Primary > secondary > tertiary
Interval scale	Ordinal, plus the *distances* between any two numbers on the scale are of known size (there is no natural zero point, and the unit of measurement is arbitrary).	(1) Equivalence (2) Greater than (3) Known ratio of any two intervals	(1) Centigrade or Fahrenheit temperature scale
Ratio scale	Interval, plus the scale has a true zero point as its origin (the ratio of any two scale points is independent of the unit of measurement).	(1) Equivalence (2) Greater than (3) Known ratio of any two intervals (4) Known ratio of any two scale values	(1) Kelvin or absolute temperature scale (2) Mass or weight (3) Length

[a] Source: "A Methodological Study of Mission-Oriented, Basic Research Planning in the O.N.R.," ABT Associates report, December 1968.

(*b*) *Guttman scaling,* which produces ordinal scales of the attitudes of a group of subjects toward a stimulus. Guttman scaling is typified by a series of statements relating to the stimulus, with which the subject strongly agrees, is undecided, disagrees, or strongly disagrees.

(*c*) *Rating scales,* in which subjects rate their reaction stimuli on a series of equal-appearing intervals that represent degree of like or dislike for the stimuli. Interval scales of the stimuli are produced.

2. Nonmetric Scaling Techniques. These emphasize the multidimensionality of stimulus attributes, and produce a metric space of minimum dimensionality for describing the input data which, in turn, need only be rank ordered. Ratio scales of stimuli are produced. Two examples of nonmetric methods are the following:

(*a*) *Simple space programs,* in which rank-order similarity judgments on stimuli are used to produce a Euclidean type of minimum dimensionality. Interpoint distances (ratio scales) of stimuli "best" preserve the original rank orders.

(*b*) *Joint space programs,* in which rank-order similarity *and* preference judgments on stimuli produce not only the same results as simple space programs, but also an "ideal" point based on a subject's preferences for stimuli attributes. The distance (ratio scale) of each stimulus from the ideal point represents a "joint" space of similarity and preference.

3. Conjoint Measurement Techniques. These make it possible to combine weak (ordinal) scales of several (incommensurate) factors and to produce a strong (ratio or interval) scale representing all of the factors.

The application of any of the scaling techniques just described to a scientific subfield, research project area, or proposal evaluation depends largely on the outcome of the experiments described in the preceding section. Once certain techniques are determined to be appropriate, a procedure that utilizes the existing decision and review processes at the laboratory can be constructed. It would be quite appropriate, for instance, to inject scaling exercises into various research review meetings so that the judgment of the participants (as well as the meeting itself) could be structured and evaluated "on the spot."

Efforts are still being made to substitute mathematical models and computer programs for subjective judgment wherever feasible. Present trends suggest that these efforts will not decrease in the next few years. Although no way has been found to completely avoid subjective estimates when planning for an uncertain future, it is possible to exercise limited control over the kind of estimates which must be made.

LIMITATIONS AND PITFALLS

Most of this chapter has been concerned with the positive aspects of quantitative resource allocation and its application to R&D planning. It is necessary now, in the interest of attempting to achieve some degree of balance in this discussion, to mention some common pitfalls and limitations of quantitative resource allocation.

Limitations

Unpredictable Interactions. Technological advances in fields not suspected to be related to the area of interest can interact to cause totally unexpected consequences. For example, the miniaturization of many electronic devices, particularly computers, had far-reaching effects.[14]

Unprecedented Demands. It is extremely difficult, if not impossible, to anticipate completely all the uses to which a new technology will be put. Atomic energy, electronic computers, and dry-copying processes are examples of technological advances which have stimulated their own uses in applications not foreseen.[15]

Major Discoveries. The fact that major breakthroughs are very rarely foreseen is often used as a basis to discount attempts at technological forecasting and thus the probability of success input altogether. However, the frequency of discovery of wholly new technologies is regarded as sufficiently low to permit much useful forecasting.[16]

Inadequate Data. The supply of relevant, complete, credible, and timely data is often sparse. Schon cites an example of attempting to make a forecast in 1965 of conditions in 1975, based on 1958 data.[17]

Pitfalls

False Sense of Well-Being. A major pitfall, associated more with the application of technological forecasting than with making a forecast, is the euphoria sometimes attendant on the quantification of things diffi-

---

[14] Edwin Mansfield, *The Economics of Technological Change* (New York: W. W. Norton & Company, 1968), p. 39.
[15] James Brian Quinn, "Technological Forecasting," *Harvard Business Review,* Vol. 45, No. 2 (March–April 1967), p. 91.
[16] *Ibid.*
[17] Donald A. Schon, "Forecasting and Technological Forecasting," *Daedalus Journal of American Academy of Arts and Science,* Summer 1967, p. 765.

cult to quantitize. Edward B. Roberts discusses such a condition in one of his perceptive articles.[18] His example, discussed in the following subsection, is drawn from quantitative evaluation methods used in the allocation of funds for R&D projects.

Illusion of Rationality. Linstone[19] warns, "The illusion of sophistication and the aura of validity supplied by quantitative normative forecasts and resource allocation techniques are ideally suited to the bureaucratic style. The real danger is that methods such as those described may aggravate the tendency toward rigidity (and hence obsolescence) in the establishment which prepares and uses them."

As Roberts points out there are several evaluation methods which attempt to relate the importance of various military missions, the relevance of various research projects, and the likelihood of fruition of the research, all in quantitative terms.[20] Often, however, knowledge about the interrelationships between the factors is incomplete, and the numerical values assigned are sometimes only broad estimates.

The pitfall or danger, after these numbers have been manipulated to arrive at a ranking of the research projects, particularly if done by computer, is that the computer output is very precise, and often this precision is confused with accuracy.[21]

The Bold and Not-So-Bold. In Darracott's listing of pitfalls, he mentions both "lack of imagination" and "overcompensation." In essence, there is a very narrow middle ground between the two. There are numerous examples in the literature of both extremes.[22]

Narrow Point of View. Large errors of underestimation can result from concentration on specific configurations or on a small part of a scientific discipline rather than the broader technological area.[23]

---

[18] Edward B. Roberts, "The Myths of Research Management," *Science and Technology,* August 1968, pp. 41–42.

[19] Harold A. Linstone, "Book Review," *Technological Forecasting,* New York: American Elsevier Publisher, Vol. 1, No. 3 (March 1970), p. 330.

[20] For a comprehensive survey of a variety of methods see Marvin J. Cetron, Joseph Martino, and Lewis Roepcke, "The Selection of R&D Program Content— Survey of Quantitative Methods," *IEEE Transactions on Engineering Management,* Vol. EM-14, No. 1 (March 1967), pp. 4–13.

[21] Roberts, *op. cit.,* p. 41.

[22] For several famous examples see Mansfield, *loc. cit.*

[23] Halvor T. Darracott, Marvin J. Cetron, Howard Wells, et al., *Report on Technological Forecasting,* (Washington, D.C.: Interservice Technological Forecasting Methodology Study Group, June 1967), p. 7-5.

Intrinsic Uncertainties. Empirical methods of forecasting will be successful only to the extent that the forces causing the advancement of technology are understood and can be expressed in a useful form.[24] Experience has indicated that many advancements appear to depend on seemingly irrational actions or pure coincidence. Darracott refers to Ayres's belief that the creative process in human beings is probably the most significant force for technological advancement, but is presently too little understood.[25]

Inbreeding. There is some concern about the possibility of forecasts being self-fulfilling, particularly if they are made by people with official responsibilities for work leading to technological advancement in the area involved.[26] The uncertainty concerns whether the formally recorded forecast may prejudice the course of future events.[27]

WHY IS ONLY 42% OF INDUSTRY TESTING OR USING QUANTITATIVE RESOURCE METHODS?

Argyris[28] has written what we think is a classic on "Resistance to Rational Management Systems." Rather than try to paraphrase his thoughts (and lose something in the process), we will quote part of the article verbatim, with a recommendation that you read all of it.

Rationality is one of the highest order goals in civilization. To be sensible, to use the power of reason, to avoid emotionalism in making decisions—civilized people honor and value these characteristics and often strive to attain them. To be rational is to be good.

We have even created our organizations with rationality in mind: If every man behaves reasonably and sensibly, then bureaucratic structures (our dominant form of organization) can achieve their goals.

Of course, for organizational managers and executives to conduct their affairs rationally, they also need to know a lot of things. In American industry, for example, management requires a virtual torrent of information about its own

---

[24] James E. Hacke, Jr., "A Methodological Preface to Technological Forecasting," paper presented at the U.S. Air Force Symposium on Long-Range Forecasting and Planning, Colorado Springs, Colo., August 1966, p. 45.

[25] Darracott et al., *op. cit.,* p. 7–6.

[26] Marvin J. Cetron and Donald Dick, "Technological Forecasting—Practical Problems and Pitfalls," *European Business,* Paris, April 1969, p. 19.

[27] T. J. Gordon and Olaf Helmer, *Report on a Long Range Forecasting Study* (Santa Monica, Calif.: The Rand Corporation, 1964), p. 5.

[28] Chris Argyris, "Resistance to Rational Management Systems," *Innovation Magazine,* No. 10, 1970, p. 29.

operations, plus knowledge of its market environment, those hard-to-control forces operating beyond its doors.

If only we could cut the guesswork out of this decision. . . . If only we could shape up Department X. . . . If only we knew the consequences of this new policy. . . . Information, insight, foresight, in a word—rationality; with these we could do anything.

We all go through this "if only" fantasy in our work (and personal) lives. Because we all go through the fantasy, technicians constantly develop new methodologies and technologies in the pursuit of rationality—operations research, PPBS, and computer models are only recent examples.

Because we all experience the fantasy, then obviously new systems that provide more information, more accurate models of the world we live in—in short, more rational ways of choosing our next steps—are welcomed enthusiastically. People who can make such things happen are universally acclaimed, adopted as blood brothers, given succor, comfort, and honor.

So you might think. . . .

Unfortunately, the opposite usually happens. I've seen it over and over again. New developments for rational decision making often produce intense resentment in men who ordinarily view themselves as realistic, flexible, and definitely rational. Managers and executives who place a premium on rationality, and work hard to subdue emotionality, become resistant and combative in the back-alley ways of bureaucratic politics when such new technologies are introduced.

These reactions sound paradoxical. Yet they stem from ingrained, almost unconscious processes in American organizational life. Waves of fear, insecurity, and tenacious resistance arise unbidden from the bowels of the organization. Strange but true.

It's also understandable in human terms. It does not happen because men are stupid. It happens because of their long and successful education in organizational survival, where they learn deceit, manipulation, rivalry, and mistrust— qualities endemic to our present organizational structures.

When managers are asked why they do not use these techniques of forecasting, they express their opposition in terms of two specific issues: (1) they don't understand the new technology, and (2) they don't believe it's wise to use such technology before it has proved itself. These objections are reasonable, but they can be overcome. Probably the real reason for their objection is that they are uncertain how their past performances will appear in the light of these techniques, and that their prerogatives in the future may appear to be decreased, on the basis of their past performance and in the light of their new objectives.

IV.   *Our Modus Operandi*

It is difficult to know whether a man is a good administrator because he is so busy, or a bad one for the same reason.   Leo Rosten

THE PROCEDURE FOLLOWED

The foundation of this book is a two-part research program, designed to give a good coverage of the field. First, 40 case studies were conducted by personal interview, to provide a more intensive examination of the organizational context in which technological forecasting is, or is not, found. The companies were chosen from a fairly wide spectrum of industry, in terms of technological intensity and size. After the interviews, questionnaires for top management and for the user of, and the contributor to, the forecast were left for completion.

The second part of the program involved a questionnaire sent to 5900 individuals in American corporations, 1114 of whom responded. The purpose was to provide more representative evidence on the extent and nature of technological forecasting in industry.[1] A copy of the questionnaire follows as Figure 1 of this chapter. Chapters V–XI cover, by type of industry, the results of the case studies and the specific questionnaires. Chapter XII draws some conclusions.

[1] Work for this effort was supported, in part, by a grant from the National Science Foundation.

46

Objectives, Forecasting and Planning Information

How are your organization's objectives predominantly distributed for: (Circle one response in each line.)

	Written			
	Quantitative	Qualitative	Oral	No Objectives
The entire corporation	1	2	3	4
The R&D activities	1	2	3	4

How often are the objectives formally reviewed or revised for each of the following: (Circle one response in each line.)

	More Often Than Annually	Annually	1–3 Years	3–5 Years	5–9 Years	Over 10 Years	No Objectives
Entire corporation	1	2	3	4	5	6	7
R&D activities only	1	2	3	4	5	6	7

To what degree does your organization make any of the following forecasts: (Circle one response in each line.)

	Always	Often	Seldom	Never
Economic	1	2	3	4
Technological	1	2	3	4
Environmental	1	2	3	4
Market	1	2	3	4

When your organization makes technological forecasts, please indicate to what extent they are utilized for each of the following purposes: (Circle the response that applies in each line.)

	Always	Frequently	Occasionally	Never
As an aid in planning	1	2	3	4
As an aid in allocating resources	1	2	3	4
To help justify a previously made decision	1	2	3	4
To help in acquiring a government contract or subcontract	1	2	3	4
To satisfy a "fad" (considered to be fashionable)	1	2	3	4
Other (specify) _____	1	2	3	4

Figure 1   Questionnaire which served as one basis for this study.

If technological forecasts are used, who prepares them: (Circle one response.)

1   In-house staff   2   Outside consultants   3   Other (specify)———

For each staff group which prepares the technological forecasts, indicate what type of individuals are utilized: (Circle one response on each line.)

	Tech- nical Planners	Opera- tions Re- searchers	Scien- tists or Engi- neers	Combi- nation of the Fore- going	Forecasts Not Prepared by This Group
The corporate staff	1	2	3	4	5
The product (project) staff	1	2	3	4	5
The functional staff	1	2	3	4	5
The marketing staff	1	2	3	4	5
An *ad hoc* staff or joint committee	1	2	3	4	5

To what extent does your organization formulate specific long-range plans for its R&D effort: (Circle one response.)

Always	In Most Cases	Sometimes	Never	I Am Not Sure
1	2	3	4	5

To what degree are the technological forecasts used in preparing the long-range plans: (Circle one response.)

Great Extent	Most Times	Limited Extent	No Long-Range Plans
1	2	3	4

What is the approximate percent of each of the types of technological forecasts that make up your total technological forecasting program: (Circle one response in each line.)

	Less Than 5%	\% 5–10	11–20	21–30	31–40	40–50	Over 50%
Intuitive (consensus, "genius" type, Delphi, etc.)	1	2	3	4	5	6	7
Trend extrapolation (continu- ation of the past)	1	2	3	4	5	6	7
Trend correlation (follow the leader)	1	2	3	4	5	6	7
Growth analogy (S-shape curves)	1	2	3	4	5	6	7
Normative (goal-oriented)	1	2	3	4	5	6	7

Figure 1   (*Continued*).

What is *your* level of familiarity with each of the following exploratory forecasting techniques: (Circle one response in each line.)

	Never Heard of It	Heard of It	Con- sidered It	Used It	Plan to Use It	Cur- rently in Use
Intuitive (Delphi)	1	2	3	4	5	6
Trend extrapolation	1	2	3	4	5	6
Trend correlation	1	2	3	4	5	6
Growth analogy	1	2	3	4	5	6

How familiar are *you* with the following normative forecasting techniques: (Circle one item in each line.)

	No Famili- arity	Heard of It	Read about It	Con- sidered It	Plan to Use It	Tested It	Used It
Mottley Newton (scoring techniques)	1	2	3	4	5	6	7
Disman (discounted cash-flow optimization)	1	2	3	4	5	6	7
RDE (linear pro- gramming model)	1	2	3	4	5	6	7
BRAILLE (cost-effec- tive model based on technical feasibility)	1	2	3	4	5	6	7
PATTERN (heuristic relevance tree technique)	1	2	3	4	5	6	7
PROFILE (heuristic relevance tree technique)	1	2	3	4	5	6	7
QUEST (double- matrix technique)	1	2	3	4	5	6	7
TORQUE (marginal utility technique) (military)	1	2	3	4	5	6	7
MACRO (marginal utility technique) (civilian)	1	2	3	4	5	6	7
Other (specify)———	1	2	3	4	5	6	7

Are the organization's plans communicated (in writing) and used by the executive(s) in charge of allocating financial resources: (Circle one item.)

1   Yes   2   No   3   No corporate plans

Figure 1   (*Continued*).

Approximately how many years in the future do the organization's long-range plans extend: (Circle one response.)

Less than 1 Year	1 Year	1–5 Years	6–10 Years	11–15 Years	16–20 Years	Over 20 Years	No Long-Range Plans
1	2	3	4	5	6	7	8

How frequently are the long-range plans updated: (Circle one item.)

1 Monthly   2 Quarterly   3 Semiannually   4 Annually
5 Other (specify)_____   6 No long-range plans

Who is responsible for the formulation of the organization's long-range R&D plans: (Circle one response.)

1 Director of research   2 Single administrative officer of higher rank than the director of research

3 Committee of executive officers   4 No plans   5 Other (specify)
_____

To what degree do *you* personally believe meaningful objectives can be developed that can assist in the planning of applied research and development activities: (Circle one response.)

1 Can be developed and be extremely meaningful
2 Can be developed but not much help
3 Cannot be developed

What is *your* judgment as to the number of years into the future long-range R&D plans should be generated: (Circle one response for each line.)

	1 Year	2 Years	3 Years	4–5 Years	6–10 Years	11–20 Years
For applied research	1	2	3	4	5	6
For development	1	2	3	4	5	6

Project Selection

Do you consider the process used in your company to select R&D projects to be *primarily* subjective in nature, an objective process with assignment of weights or values to specific criteria, or a combination of the two, with the quantitative weighted data being used as an aid: (Circle one item.)

1 Subjective   2 Quantitative   3 Combination (quantitative as an aid)

Regardless of *your* previous answer, please give your opinion as to the *importance of* and the *accuracy* with which each of the following criteria can be estimated or quantified at the time the applied R&D proposal is being considered for *initial* funding: (Circle one importance factor and one accuracy rating in each line.)

Figure 1 (*Continued*).

Importance Factor					Accuracy Rating				
Criti- cal	Very Impor- tant	Impor- tant	Not Very Impor- tant	Criterion	Excel- lent	Good	Fair	Poor	Totally Unre- liable
1	2	3	4	1. Cost of the total research project	1	2	3	4	5
1	2	3	4	2. Cost of development if the research is successful	1	2	3	4	5
1	2	3	4	3. Probability of technical success	1	2	3	4	5
1	2	3	4	4. Time necessary to complete the research	1	2	3	4	5
1	2	3	4	5. Manpower requirements necessary to complete the research	1	2	3	4	5
1	2	3	4	6. Probability of market success	1	2	3	4	5
1	2	3	4	7. Time necessary to complete the development	1	2	3	4	5
1	2	3	4	8. Market life of the product if R&D efforts prove successful	1	2	3	4	5
1	2	3	4	9. Revenue from the sale of the product if R&D efforts are successful (potential value)	1	2	3	4	5
1	2	3	4	10. Cost reductions if R&D efforts are successful	1	2	3	4	5
1	2	3	4	11. Technological cross support (technology transfer to other products)	1	2	3	4	5
1	2	3	4	12. Good will or prestige to the firm	1	2	3	4	5
1	2	3	4	13. Management environment (top management support or not)	1	2	3	4	5
1	2	3	4	14. Competitors' position	1	2	3	4	5
1	2	3	4	15. Degree of ego involvement	1	2	3	4	5

What is *your* opinion as to the *importance of* and *accuracy* with which each of the following criteria can be estimated or quantified at the time an applied R&D task is being *reconsidered for continued* funding: (Circle one importance factor and one accuracy rating in each line)

Importance Factor					Accuracy Rating				
Criti- cal	Very Impor- tant	Impor- tant	Not Very Impor- tant	Criterion	Excel- lent	Good	Fair	Poor	Totally Unre- liable
1	2	3	4	1. Cost of the total research project	1	2	3	4	5
1	2	3	4	2. Cost of development if the research is successful	1	2	3	4	5
1	2	3	4	3. Probability of technical success	1	2	3	4	5
1	2	3	4	4. Time necessary to complete the research	1	2	3	4	5
1	2	3	4	5. Manpower requirements necessary to complete the research	1	2	3	4	5
1	2	3	4	6. Probability of market success	1	2	3	4	5

Figure 1   *(Continued).*

Importance Factor					Accuracy Rating				
Criti-cal	Very Impor-tant	Impor-tant	Not Very Impor-tant	Criterion	Excel-lent	Good	Fair	Poor	Totally Unre-liable
1	2	3	4	7. Time necessary to complete the development	1	2	3	4	5
1	2	3	4	8. Market life of the product if R&D efforts prove successful	1	2	3	4	5
1	2	3	4	9. Revenue from the sale of the product if R&D efforts are successful (potential value)	1	2	3	4	5
1	2	3	4	10. Cost reductions if R&D are successful	1	2	3	4	5
1	2	3	4	11. Technological cross support (technology transfer to other products)	1	2	3	4	5
1	2	3	4	12. Good will or prestige to the firm	1	2	3	4	5
1	2	3	4	13. Management environment (top management support or not)	1	2	3	4	5
1	2	3	4	14. Competitors' position	1	2	3	4	5
1	2	3	4	15. Degree of ego involvement	1	2	3	4	5
1	2	3	4	16. Resources spent to date (sunk cost)	1	2	3	4	5

Are there, in addition to the criteria mentioned in the questions above, qualitative criteria which cannot be expressed quantitatively but ought, you think, to be considered in the evaluation and selection of R&D projects: (Circle one response.)

1 Yes   2 No   If yes, please list_____

What is the average percentage of *new* R&D work started each year (by numbers of projects or dollars, whichever is easier to determine) by your organization: (Circle one item.)

	Less than 5%	%					More than 50%
		5–10	11–20	21–30	31–40	41–50	
$ or projects (cross out one)	1	2	3	4	5	6	7

Is a system for determining the balance between the selection of longer-term–payoff projects (research intensive) and shorter-term–payoff projects (development intensive) used in your organization: (Circle one response.)

1 Yes   2 No

If yes, is it: (Circle one.)

1 Subjective   2 Quantitative

Figure 1 *(Continued)*.

What is the average length of an R&D project in your organization: (Circle one response in each line.)

	Less than 1 Year	1–2 Years	3–5 Years	6–10 Years	Over 10 Years
Research	1	2	3	4	5
Development	1	2	3	4	5

Background Information

Does your organization operate more than one R&D Laboratory: (Circle one response.)

1   Yes   2   No

Did the answers to this questionnaire treat all your R&D activities as one unit: (Circle one response.)

1   Yes   2   No

Did your answers on this questionnaire refer to one laboratory only: (Circle one response.)

1   Yes   2   No

What is the official title of the person having prime management responsibility for R&D activities: (Circle one response.)

1   Vice president for R&D   3   Manager of R&D
2   Vice president for research   4   Director of R&D
5   Other (specify) _____

Approximately how many corporate officers have a rank equal to or greater than that of the individual responsible for the R&D activities: (Circle one response.)

None	One	Two	Three	Four	Five	More than Five
1	2	3	4	5	6	7

Are the company R&D activities performed in physically separate facilities (central or corporate): (Circle one response.)

1   Yes   2   No

Are R&D activities administered separately, with each under the immediate supervision of a different individual (decentralized or project management): (Circle one response.)

1   Yes   2   No

Figure 1   (*Continued*).

Indicate the number of persons involved in the R&D effort covered by your answers: (Circle one response.)

	1–25	26–100	101–400	400–750	Over 750
Technical and professional	1	2	3	4	5
Technicians, draftsmen, and support	1	2	3	4	5

Give the percentage of technical and professional personnel having the academic degree of: (Circle one response.)

				%				Over
	None	1–5	6–10	11–20	21–30	31–40	41–50	50%
Doctorate	1	2	3	4	5	6	7	8
Master's	1	2	3	4	5	6	7	8
Bachelor's	1	2	3	4	5	6	7	8
No degree	1	2	3	4	5	6	7	8

What proportion of your R&D effort (in terms of costs or manpower, whichever is easier to determine) is expended on: (Circle one response in each line.)

	Less Than 5%	5–10	% 10–20	20–30	30–40	Over 40%
Fundamental or pure research (knowledge for the sake of knowledge—not related to any product or process)	1	2	3	4	5	6
Applied research (need- or goal-oriented–directly related to a product(s) or process)	1	2	3	4	5	6
Development (application of scientific knowledge or new discoveries to the creation of specific products or processes)	1	2	3	4	5	6

Which classification best describes the primary organizational basis for your R&D activities: (Circle one response for each line.)

	Functional (e.g., circuit design) Basis	Discipline (e.g., electronics) Basis	Product or Project (e.g., TV sets) Basis	Other (specify)
Research labs	1	2	3	4
Development labs	1	2	3	4

Figure 1 (*Continued*).

What general industry group do you fall under: (Circle the one response most appropriate.)

1   Chemical and Pharmaceutical
2   Electronics
3   Plastics
4   Foods and feeds
5   Metallurgical and manufacturing of metals
6   Aerospace
7   R&D only firm, academic, or nonprofit
8   Government/military
9   Other (specify)_____

What age bracket do you fall under: (Circle one response.)

1   Under 20   4   31–35   7   46–50
2   21–25   5   36–40   8   51–60
3   26–30   6   41–45   9   Over 60

Are you, in your judgment, best described as: (Circle one response.)

1   A scientist
2   An engineer
3   An operations researcher
4   A manager
5   A planner or staff expert
6   A marketeer or salesman
7   Other (specify)_____

What is your role in the R&D planning and/or technological forecasting activities of your organization: (Circle one response.)

1   I am personally responsible for it
2   It is under my general jurisdiction
3   I participate in it in a staff capacity
4   I participate in it on an *ad hoc* basis
5   I have no direct role, although my organization does conduct such activities
6   No such activities can be identified explicitly in my organization

Figure 1   (*Continued*).

LIMITATIONS OF THE STUDY

It must be remembered, however, that, despite the number of interviews conducted and the number of responses to the questionnaires, the scope of the study was fairly limited. In our initial survey, when we were selecting companies to interview, we found that, if companies had thought at all about technological forecasting, they either had an on-going program on the subject or were not going to develop one. We found practically no companies that had considered forecasting and had decided to plan to use it later.

Another limitation, which was mentioned earlier, is that in many companies the techniques of forecasting have not been in operation long enough to constitute a real test. One final point that could also affect the results, particularly of the general questionnaire, is that different people in an organization frequently have different opinions as to how widely or how well a technique is being used. Although we sent the questionnaires to those who we believed were responsible for R&D planning, we have no guarantee that the responses came from these people themselves.

We feel, however, that the study provides an overview of the use and acceptance of technological forecasting in industry at the present time. In the future, a more detailed study of specific industries will be required in order to show exactly where the greatest potential of this tool lies.

In Section II we will proceed with an examination of several of these industries, commencing with electronics in Chapter V.

Section II

V. *Electronics*

What good is electricity, Madam? What good is a baby?   Michael Faraday

INTRODUCTION

The electronics industry today is in a position very similar to that of the aerospace industry. Its major R&D customer is the federal government, which means that not only is the industry's profit margin restricted, but its R&D operations are also limited. Except for the electronics companies dealing mainly in components and domestic electronic equipment, the business itself is of the low-volume, and supposedly high-margin, variety. This, in fact, is characteristic of highly technological and innovative industries, which are heavily R&D oriented, at least it would be so if the companies were competing to corner some commercial market.

When the customer is the government, however, the strategy must be different. In this case, the customer leads and the industry must follow. Thus, although the industry could and does make its own exploratory forecasts, its main forecasting effort is normative and lies in predicting what the government will need, or thinks it is going to need. This state of affairs frequently leads the company to have several on-going programs, of which only one is going to satisfy the customer's requirements—but this is one of the hazards of the game. The advantages lie in areas where the government requires research expertise and funds programs, because frequently a company would be unable to afford such large research efforts. The latest figures show that 59% of the money

59

spent on R&D in the electronics industry comes from the federal government.

Our sample of electronics companies was chosen to represent both the small $5-million-per-year companies and giants with several billion dollar sales and a number of divisions. Although 79% of these companies now have on-going programs in technological forecasting, these programs are still too new to be fully proved and tested. Communications between the people performing the forecasts and the managers, and in one case between the divisions and the corporate headquarters, seem to be rather inadequate or even nonexistent. In some instances, this is due to differing opinions as to what a forecast is, why forecasting should be done, and how the forecast should be utilized. In other cases, it is due to the "middle-management automation syndrome"—where overenthusiastic forecasters have claimed that such techniques can be used for decision making, and middle managers, rather than taking the initiative to encourage the introduction of forecasting in their domains as a source of information to supplement their own judgment, have panicked, feeling that they were in danger of being emasculated in their management role.

RESULTS OF QUESTIONNAIRE

The results from 234 responses to the questionnaires submitted to specific companies can be summarized as follows.

OBJECTIVES. Almost all the companies have corporate objectives, most of them (74%) written and quantitative. A large majority (77%) also have written quantitative R&D objectives. All of these objectives are updated at least annually.

FORECASTS. Technological and marketing forecasts are performed very often, whereas economic and environmental forecasts, although performed, are less frequent. The technological forecasts are used very frequently in planning and resource allocation, often to help in acquiring a government contract or subcontract, but hardly ever to justify a decision previously made or to satisfy a fad. On the whole, the forecasts are performed by in-house staff and, in some cases, by the corporate technical planners, together with a marketing planner and engineers and scientists, or else by the planners, operations-research staff and scientists or engineers of the R&D staff.

FORECASTING AND LONG-RANGE PLANNING. In almost every case, the companies always formulate specific long-range plans for their R&D

efforts. Some of these long-range R&D plans have incorporated techno-logical forecasting for a number of years, although only informally until recently. Technological forecasts are used quite extensively in the preparation of these long-range plans and objectives, the most popular method of forecasting being the intuitive, followed by trend extrapola-tion. Growth analogy and trend correlation are utilized to some extent, but the largest part of the forecasting effort is normative. In the prepara-tion of the long-range plans, the cost varies from a negligible amount to 5% of the total R&D budget; the cost for developing a forecast varies from a negligible amount to 3% of the R&D budget. The forecasts are updated at least annually, by a combination of individual inputs and group discussion. The long-range plans, extending about 5 years into the future, are also updated annually and are then communicated in document form to managers and program directors. In every case, the long-range plan forms a basis for resource allocation.

The responsibility for the development of the long-range R&D plans generally rests in one of two areas: mainly, vice president or director of R&D level; or, at the line management, manager of technological forecasting or manager of R&D level.

CONTRIBUTOR TO THE FORECAST. Although the most important tech-niques for forecasting have been mentioned in the previous section, the contributor uses several other approaches in the development of the forecasts. The committee approach is one of the most popular, followed by literature searches and then by genius or intuitive approaches. The number of contributors, in every case, was less than 20.

USERS OF THE FORECAST. The prime users of the forecasts are the planning staff, marketing staff, and programming and budgeting staff, although individual scientists and engineers, as well as study groups, occasionally utilize them. The frequency of use varies from monthly to yearly; the forecasts usually provide inputs to operational, rather than technical, planning and also serve as a source of general back-ground and intelligence information.

PROJECT SELECTION AND RESOURCE ALLOCATION. The current processes used for project selection are, on the whole, combinations of quantitative and subjective methods. The average amount of new R&D work under-taken each year is 20–30%, and subjective judgment is used for deter-mining the balance between longer-term–payoff projects (research inten-sive) and shorter-term–payoff projects (development intensive). Within almost all of the companies, research projects last an average of 5 years and development projects last about 4 years. The types of work performed by most companies include less than 5% of pure research, 35–45% of applied research, and 35–45% of development.

REMARKS. It was generally felt that there was a lack of continuity between the types of forecasts performed, their updating, and their implementation. In some companies, divisions were trying to reorganize so that their planning systems could take into account the results of the forecasts. In many cases, the forecasts did not satisfy the users' needs because of lack of detail or inability to relate future needs to current operations.

CASE STUDIES

The following case studies of electronics companies describe the planning operations performed in this type of industry.

General Dynamics—Electronics Division

CONTACT: GEORGE M. HAIR

The Electronics Division of General Dynamics comprises several smaller operations, each with particular areas of operation. It was considered desirable by top management that the planning for the entire division be as relevant and coordinated as possible. Therefore, as soon as various problems, such as the "middle-management automation syndrome" and the not-invented-here (NIH) factor had been overcome, the corporate headquarters laid down the ground rules for each division to perform a "relevance network" type of technological forecast. This is a forecast which relates the technology required for current programs to that required for future market needs; it assesses the competition in all areas, the risks involved, and the trade-offs between technology acquisition costs and potential market value.

In order to perform this forecast, the first step is to identify the area of technology involved. This is accomplished by dividing the product line into major segments, so that the current products, the market served, and the approximate sales value per year can be identified. Also the current "key technologies" (those capabilities in the product line which have no serious threat from competition) of the internal research and development (IR&D), as well as of customer-funded R&D, are identified.

An analysis is then performed of the capabilities of competitors, in terms of current programs, key technologies, and market penetration. As mentioned earlier, when the major customer is the federal government, an analysis is also needed to determine what the Department of Defense wants. This is performed by identifying the current emphasis of government-directed R&D and the technologies which are being supported, so that solutions to their current and future problems can be determined.

Market research is another vital part of a planning and research allocation system; in this case, it covers a detailed analysis of the budget activity of DOD and other relevant agencies in order to determine the time scale and potential value of future programs. All this information is then used to determine the potential future programs, technologies required, time scale, and market opportunities and threats. Once this information has been prepared, the engineers must evaluate the required technologies with respect to current capabilities and resources, and determine the level of effort needed (together with the associated costs) to achieve the technologies required for specific programs.

The forecast drawn up by the Electronics Division of General Dynamics included in flow-diagram and text form the various assessments mentioned above, which were then used by product-line management, operations management, and division management to select the optimum paths for achieving the long-term objectives of the division. The restrictions on the forecast were that work by DOD should not be duplicated, nor should the forecast be at odds with those developed by major customers, as the industry is essentially customer-oriented. The flow chart of the forecasting process in the entire Electronics Division is shown in Figure 1, and the actual forecasting process in Figure 2. For each major segment of product lines, the form shown in Figure 3 must be completed.

The final collated results of the technological forecast for the Electronics Division were presented in two volumes. The first contained the supporting information, in terms of an environmental forecast, product-line forecasts, support groups and facilities, and an overall analysis. The second volume contained PERT-type relevance networks for each major segment of the project lines, showing the interrelationships of current programs and key technologies to future programs and pacing technologies. Examples from the Communications/Avionics Sections of Volumes 1 and 2 are shown in Figures 4 and 5.

Each division of the corporation has to comply with the relevance network approach to market-technology forecasting; an example of one such relevance network for communications and avionics is shown in Figure 6.

After the forecasts have been prepared and the final documents drawn up, the technological forecast and the strategic plan can be integrated, as shown in Figure 7.

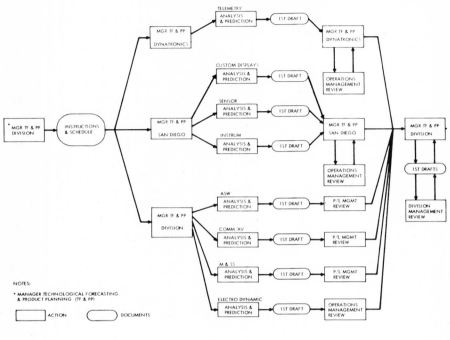

Figure 1   Flow chart of technological forecast process.

General Dynamics—Electronics Division, San Diego Operations

CONTACT: J. F. LANGSTON

The product lines of San Diego Operations lie mainly in the fields of instrumentation and sensors, where the technology base for such products is contained within a total systems capability. This capability has been developed over several years and is represented by a broad technology base; in order to continue along similar lines, it is necessary

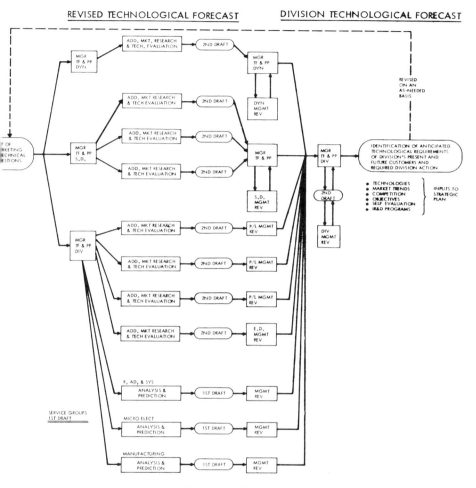

Figure 1   (*Continued*)

to support technology studies, as well as hardware concepts, both com-
pany- and customer-funded. Such systems programs, together with the
technology programs, lead to new programs and products, as well as
diversification into new fields. To take advantage of these potentialities,
a broader and more comprehensive evaluation of new business oppor-
the marketing has now been directed around specific areas. This provides
tunities and future needs in terms of both total systems and specific
technologies.

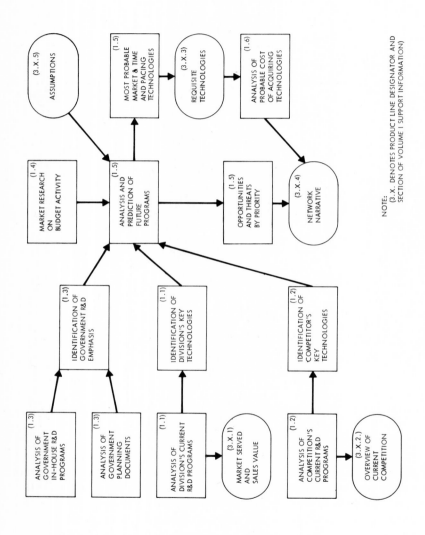

Figure 2   Analysis and prediction.

NOTE:
(3.X. DENOTES PRODUCT LINE DESIGNATOR AND SECTION OF VOLUME I SUPPORT INFORMATION)

MAJOR SEGMENT SUMMARY SHEET

	1970	1971	1972	1973	1974
TOTAL AWARDS POTENTIAL					
ON–CONTRACT SALES VALUE					
POTENTIAL SALES VALUE					
IR&D SUPPORT REQUIRED					
B&P SUPPORT REQUIRED					

PACING TECHNOLOGIES

LEVEL*	ON–HAND			REQUIRED														
	3	2	1	3	2	1	3	2	1	3	2	1	3	2	1			

* LEVEL 3   SUFFICIENT TO MANAGE R&D EFFORT
  LEVEL 2   SUFFICIENT TO PERFORM R&D EFFORT
  LEVEL 1   SUFFICIENT TO WRITE PROPOSALS

Figure 3   Major segment summary sheet.

67

Technological or Product Areas	Product	Leading Technology	Market Served	Sales Value per Year
HF Antennas	SC-883		GSA	18K
	SC-885		Army	
	SC-890	High-Power Hairpin	APOLLO	
	SC-891	Med.-Power Hairpin	Navy, CG	
	SC-892		ASA, International	
VHF Antennas	SC-882	Electrically Short	Air Force CG,	10K
	SC-893	Minimal Ground Effect	Army	
UHF Antennas	SC-884 Part of AN/URC-73		Air Force, International	5K
Coupler	SC-895		Army, AF International	25K
Communication Systems	AN/GRC-142/122	Radio Remote	U.S.A.	5M
	AN/GRC-108	Radio Relay	U.S. Air Force	
	AN/MRC-107	(FACTER)		
	FACTER	CFGI Antenna		
	Radio Remote			
HF/SSB	WRC-1	Freq. Stds.	Navy	6M
		Digital Synthesizers	Many Foreign	
		Broadband Amplifiers	Governments	

Figure 4   Radio—summary chart: Identification of area of technology

In accordance with the request by division headquarters for a relevance network approach to market-technology forecasting, San Diego Operations collated all the information determined in the manner above and assembled it in a document entitled "Technology Forecasts." However, either because of misinterpretation of division headquarters' request, or because of the difficulty of determining future programs, the required technology R&D programs were identified for only 2 years out, that is, until 1971. These programs were then used as inputs to the networks, which describe products or systems under completion in 1976.

Apart from the requisite relevance networks, San Diego Operations feels that any long-range planning must be based on some ideas of the future environment in which the company will exist. The first environmental forecast was based on already published forecast data and studies, together with the views of the author, the manager of long-range planning. The purpose of such a forecast was not to describe, with a great degree of accuracy, one possible future environment, but rather to stimulate thinking about the years to come. The future was described in broad terms of geopolitics, economics, sociology, technology and man-

VHF ANTENNAS

We currently offer two basic VHF Antennas: the SC-882 Center-fed Ground Independent Antenna (CFGI), which covers the high-band VHF, and the SC-893 low-silhouette 30-76 MHz tactical vehicle antenna. The SC-893 is a leading technology item. It has an extremely low-silhouette 30-76 MHz tactical vehicle antenna. The SC-893 is a leading technology item. It has an extremely low silhouette and may be obtained in manual, remote, and automatically tuned versions. The customer has a requirement for an antenna of this type and intends to evaluate four SC-893's.

UHF ANTENNA

We offer only the SC-884 CFGI. This item is a component of the AN/URC-73 UHF mobile radio set.

ANTENNA COUPLER

We offer the SC-895 HF automatically tuned antenna coupler. This is a 400 watt unit and ideally suited for use with the AN/GRC-106 Radio Set in any of its applications where a whip antenna is required.

Communications Systems Integration

AN/GRC-142/122

Developed to give the Army a Teletype Communication Central, cabability delivers 400 watts using AN/GRC-106—the Electronics Division developed equipment and won the follow-on competitive buy. In order to give the system a full duplex capability, the AN/GRC-122 was developed. Using the basic AN/GRC-142, the Army installs the additional hardware at the depot to convert to a full duplex system.

Figure 5

agement; and the narrower constraints were added, namely, the government, which was divided into defense environment, space environment, and the rest of the government environment. The last three sections contained material of direct relevance to the division, in terms of its market environment, technology environment, and management environment.

The next step, which is now underway, is a fully integrated planning

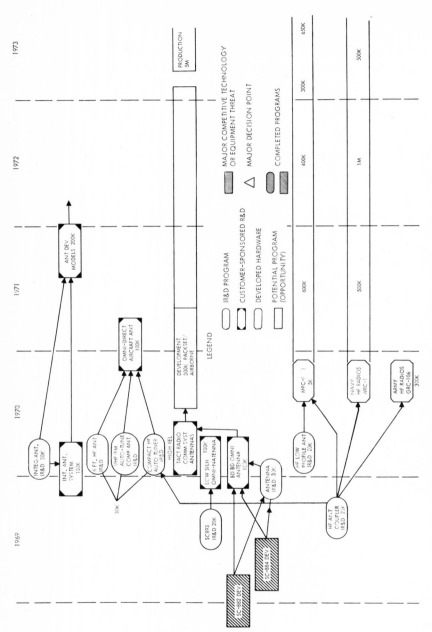

Figure 6 Communications and avionics product line; radio-antennas and couplers.

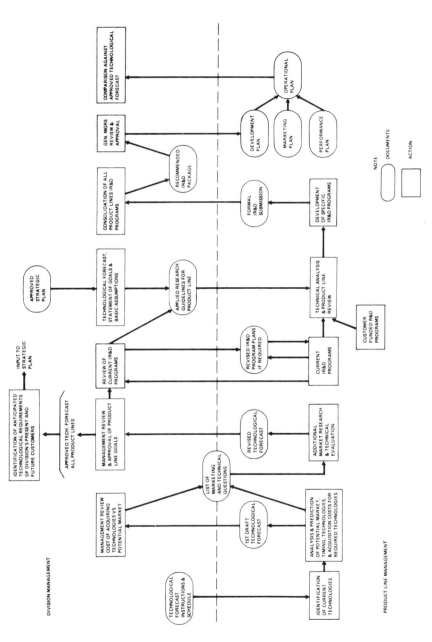

Figure 7 Technological forecasting, internal R&D planning and control, and division planning interface.

71

and forecasting system, using both the market-technology forecast and an updated environmental forecast.

General Dynamics—Electronics Division, Dynatronics Operation

CONTACT: WEBER IVY

Dynatronics Operation works very closely with the headquarters of the Electronics Division. Its forecasts, therefore, follow very closely the lines laid down for relevance networks. Rather than describing again the development and implementation of such networks, we felt that a market study, based on one specific area of Dynatronics' capabilities, would be more meaningful.

Over several years, Dynatronics has gained considerable experience and competence in applying advanced digital technologies to the telemetry requirements of DOD and NASA. These markets are fairly restricted, however, and it was felt that other ones could be found outside of these two agencies, possibly in the commercial world.

The study performed in this area took into account such factors as population growth, national goals and priorities, and their pressure to apply technology to the solution of social and ecological problems. Trends in federal spending, which are moving away from defense and space and toward social and domestic digital telemetry equipment, were also considered relevant.

The objectives of the study were threefold:

1. To investigate and analyze the U.S. markets, outside of DOD and NASA, applicable to specific digital acquisition and control systems of interest to Dynatronics.
2. To identify and evaluate specific areas within these markets that appear to hold the greatest new business and profit potential for Dynatronics.
3. To formulate and recommend a market strategy and plan for immediate and aggressive participation in these new markets.

The state of the art of each of the three major categories of digital systems was described in detail. Present applications of the systems were also described, and possible future applications as well. Because of a rapid increase in interest, and the availability of funds for industrial automated process control, water pollution control, air pollution control, and the monitor and control of ecological elements other than water and air, these areas appeared to be of great interest to the division. The outlook for U.S. spending was analyzed; then, on the basis of these

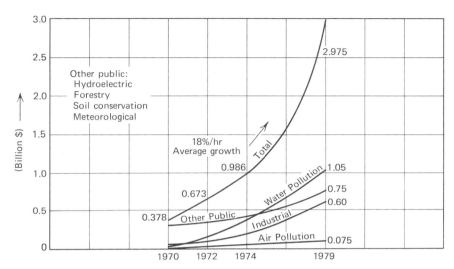

Figure 8 Total estimated market for electronic acquisition and control equipments in the United States, 1970–79. *Sources:* **SRI, FWPCA, FAPCA, others.**

funding estimates, the above areas of interest were analyzed in detail. Figure 8 shows an analysis in dollar terms of the total estimated market for electronic acquisition and control.

These estimated potential markets were then described in terms of their desirability to Dynatronics, and recommendations for future plans were made accordingly.

Radiation Systems Incorporated

CONTACT: ROBERT BAWER

Radiation Systems Incorporated (RSI), the youngest and smallest of all the companies considered in the case studies, serves as a good example to illustrate that forecasting can be extremely useful for any company which utilizes rapidly changing technologies.

The company was founded about 10 years ago and has grown quite rapidly into two major divisions, each with its own sales section. Various technological disciplines have been successfully combined to give RSI capabilities in various fields of communications. However, the size and age of the company, together with its particular capabilities, restricted its potential market almost wholly to the military and made it reliant on the customer for research opportunities.

A year ago, RSI felt that it had sufficient funds to begin an in-house research project with a view toward expanding its markets. The question was which direction to take. This small, young company could not hope to be a leader in the field of basic research in antennas, circuitry, or solid-state electronics. In these areas, it had to follow the leaders, and merely innovate or implement the results of others' research. There had to be other areas of research which would produce sufficient results for them to corner some potential market.

Before any of this could be accomplished, the company had to first draw up a formal list of quantified objectives. These were defined in financial terms which related to sales objectives, structured not in terms of products but in terms of known customers, their buying environment, and their present and future requirements. This method of definition was based on the belief that the personal goals of the people involved were going to be achieved, not by RSI maintaining an R&D image, but rather by its understanding and therefore contributing toward the underlying reasons for bidding on programs. These objectives and the rationale for the first formalized long-range plan were outlined in Volume 1 of the 5-year plan.

Once the objectives had been set, it was necessary to look at the

Technological Cross-Support

TECHNOLOGICAL AREAS

Microwave Components

Micro-miniature Components

Commercial Instruments

| | Microwave Components | Micro-Miniature Components | Commercial Instruments | . . . |

TECHNOLOGICAL AREAS

Figure 9 Technological cross-support.

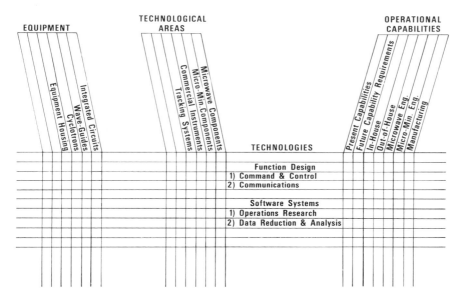

Figure 10   Planning matrix.

future in terms of the environment, the potential markets, and future customer needs. As an initial step, a consultant was called in to describe objectively the uses of such techniques as technological forecasting, and to explain how these techniques could be incorporated into a planning system. The system recommended made use of the four forms shown as Figures 9–12 for standardizing the project selection process.

One year later, the second volume of the 5-year plan, in which the marketing objectives were described in great detail, was published. It defined areas of interest, possible products, and potential markets, as well as determining the sales objectives even more quantitatively.

The first step was to identify RSI's capabilities in terms of technological disciplines, and experience in selecting materials, functional design, and economics. In addition to these broad categories of capability, there were also several areas of specialization.

Before further steps were taken, it was necessary to develop a marketing strategy which was consistent with the objectives. This led to the adoption of various specific criteria for the strategy.

With the aid of some environmental forecasts and expert knowledge

Value Sheet _____ Product _____

FIGURE OF MERIT	COLUMN 1	COLUMN 2				COLUMN 3
	CORPORATE OBJECTIVES	IMPACT OF PRODUCT CONTRIBUTION				
		0.8	0.5	0.2	0.1	
	1) Increase Volume of Sales					
	2) Increase Return on Sales					
	3) Increase Return on Investments					
	4) Increase Earnings Per Share					
	5) Increase Commercial Sales					
		TOTAL VALUE (V) TO CORPORATION				

Scale of definitions for "Impact of Product Contribution" (Column 2)

0.8 Critical line or service leading to proprietary production.

0.5 Extension of existing system/product lines.

0.2 Improvement of current system/product

0.1 Negligible (if any) affect on current system/product

Figure 11   Value sheet. From M. J. Cetron, *Technological Forecasting—A Practical Approach.*

of possible futures, together with the restrictions of consistency with the objectives, the divisions developed plans for future fields of interest, possible product lines, and potential markets. These were collated into the 5-year plan in terms of their financial benefits to the company, even to the inclusion of the desirability for acquisitions.

The next proposed step is to consider "sales tactics." It was made quite clear in the 5-year plan, however, that the plans and marketing objectives will be reviewed regularly, consolidated, and coordinated, to ensure that the company's assumptions, subject to both internal and external forces, are still valid.

Bell Telephone Laboratories

CONTACT: JACK MORTON

The Bell System comprises 4 major functions distributed among 24 companies. Most of the stock of these companies is held by AT&T, which also owns the Western Electric Company. Together with Western,

APPRAISAL SHEET   PRODUCT _____

Chance of meeting technical objectives with level of Confidence (c)

(   )   80 - 100%
(   )   60 - 80%
(   )   30 - 60%
(   )   0 - 30%

Number of different concurrent approaches (n) _____

Management environment

Board of Directors (   )
President   (   )
V. P. 1   (   )
V. P. 2   (   )

Appraisal Summary

Value (V) _____
Probability of success (Ps) _____
Expected Value (EV) _____
Funding required for 1 year (F1) _____
Funding required for 5 years (F5)_____
Desirability Index for 1 year (D1) _____
Desirability Index for 5 years (D5)_____

Figure 12 Appraisal sheet. From M. J. Cetron, *Technological Forecasting—A Practical Approach.*

AT&T owns the Bell Telephone Laboratories (BTL), where the research, development, and systems engineering relevant to the whole system is performed. The organization of these four groups is shown in Figure 13.

BTL operates under the "systems method," whereby, in the R&D part of the process, the necessary requirements are "people organized into a process structure, with a purpose." The prime requirement is capable, honest, professional scientists and engineers. This necessitates a careful selection process, followed by continuing education for such personnel. Each individual should find challenge and reward within his work, and for this reason the manager needs to understand and appreciate the roles which science and technology play in industrial innovation. This aspect will be discussed later.

The second requirement is purpose: the laboratory should know "what business it is in" and "what business it wants to be in." It has to have objectives, so that incentives and rewards can be related to the system

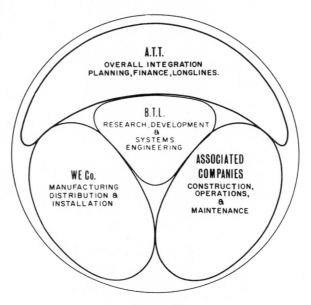

Figure 13

of achieving these objectives. Toward this end, the fields of specialization in the BTL are defined in terms of basic research, applied research, and development design. These functions are coupled to each other, and also to Western Electric's functions, as shown in Figure 14.

The basic research is limited to areas which are relevant to the field of communications, while the applied R&D programs are chosen in terms of their relevance and cost effectiveness in applying science to communications technology, which is part of the Bell System's goals. This can be illustrated as a laboratory goal, which is to generate, perceive, and

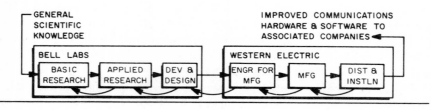

Figure 14

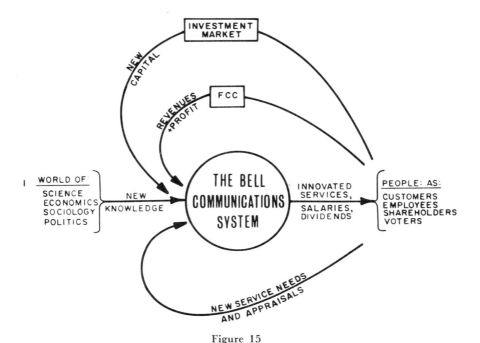

Figure 15

convert relevant basic research into a technology for a needed industrial purpose.

To achieve goals of this nature, the individual parts of each process involved must be coordinated to form a coherent whole. This requires the "creative, cooperative actions of people." The systems approach used by BTL takes into account the workers' need for self-motivation and for incentives: people are the laboratory's major concern. This can be seen in Figure 15, which illustrates the Bell Communications System's place in society.

Once the goals have been set, the functions of BTL can be described in greater detail. The basic research is not a haphazard operation from which breakthroughs occasionally appear. It is a searching for solutions to known problems and for responses to relevant opportunities. That is not to say that basic research enters the applied research field; rather, the close cooperation of the R&D people ensures that even the most basic research is performed in areas which appear to be of use in achieving BTL's goals. The interaction between the two groups also provides a feedback for needs from the development side and stimulus from the research side. In addition, it helps to reduce the time between invention and innovation, thus increasing the chances for successful innovation.

The function of applied research is to determine the most urgent needs in technology, as well as future opportunities, and to evaluate the technical feasibility of inventions in the fields of materials, machines, and systems which have a bearing on the overall Bell System. Such assessment includes a complete comprehension of both the potentialities and the limitations of the technology, so that its range of applicability can be made as wide as possible. Here again, the need for interaction between the basic researchers and the applied researchers and development engineers can be seen, as the development people must fully understand the results of basic research in order to apply them to their fullest advantage. The design engineers, in particular, have to deal much more quantitatively with the factors affecting performance, the specific requirements, the cost, the timing, and the tradeoffs among these.

Only when each of these groups has performed its part in close interaction with the others and the desired goal has been achieved, can the overall innovation process be considered successful. The process of innovation is performed under the total systems approach. Technological forecasting per se is not being performed in any formal manner, as systems engineering, under BTL, implicitly considers the future.

VI.   *Chemicals*

The age is running mad after innovation. All the business of the world is to be done in a new way. Men are to be hanged in a new way; Tyburn itself is not safe.   Samuel Johnson

INTRODUCTION

The category of "chemicals" covers a broad range of fields from synthetic fibers to paints, from petrochemicals to explosives, plastics, and agricultural products, and so on. It is extremely difficult to generalize about the chemical industry, for most chemical companies (or at least most divisions of chemical companies) tend to specialize in only one area, and in some cases in only one minute sector of an area, so that the problems involved in the R&D activities are different for each case. In some instances, the main problem is innovation: of what use is the invented substance—where can it be applied? In other cases, the problem is competition, or perhaps the lack of it: frequently, companies are unwilling to put an improved product on the market until a competitor does so. Another, fairly unusual problem is that until recently many companies have had almost unlimited funds and not enough ideas for projects, so that allocation of resources caused no difficulty. Perhaps exploratory forecasting could have been of assistance here. Some of the companies have DOD as a major customer; others do very little work for any governmental agency.

As long ago as the early fifties, some research people in the chemical industry were concerned because the flow of new technology into the industry was slowing. Firms from other fields—glass, petroleum, distilling, foods, etc.—were entering the industry and competing success-fully, with the aid of purchased technology. By the late fifties and early sixties, chemical marketers were discussing declining profitability because of commoditization of their principal products. Meanwhile, using in-dustries, such as television, were doing their own chemical development.

Although this kind of information was readily available, no one in-terpreted the significance of what was happening. Research managers continued to select projects and allocate resources by "seat of the pants" methods, depending on experience which was no longer applicable. Now corporate management is asking that research be planned, and research planners are reporting lack of ideas and difficulty in formulating objec-tives. Perhaps their real need is to formulate a new role for chemical research under pressure. At any rate, most of their problems could have been forecast, if only someone had bothered to investigate.

Specific case studies will provide a clearer picture of some of the area than any further generalizations can yield. The companies studied were chosen from as wide a range as possible. The size of these companies and divisions varies from 50 million to 16 billion dollars per year in gross sales. Planning personnel from a large petrochemicals company, an explosives company, a synthetic fibers division, a conglomerate with a bias toward chemicals, petrochemicals, and textiles, and a company with one very specific area of interest were interviewed. The case studies will be given in more detail later in the chapter.

RESULTS OF QUESTIONNAIRE

The results of the questionnaires submitted to these companies (98 in all) were as follows.

OBJECTIVES. Most of the companies have corporate objectives; most of these (80%) are written, but are a mixture of qualitative and quanti-tative goals. Most (80%) also have written R&D objectives, but these tend to be more qualitative than quantitative. The time frame for up-dating the corporate objectives varies from 1 to 5 years, whereas the R&D objectives are generally updated annually.

FORECASTS. Economic forecasts and marketing forecasts are performed almost always; technological and environmental forecasts, less often. The technological forecasts are used frequently as an aid in planning, occasionally as an aid in resource allocation or to justify a previously made decision, but only in rare cases to satisfy a fad or to help in acquiring a government contract or subcontract. The forecasts are always prepared by in-house staff, but there seems to be a complete division between the types of people involved. In about 50% of the cases, the forecasts are prepared by the planners, scientists, and engineers of the corporate staff, with some help from the marketing group; in the rest, by a joint committee of scientists and engineers from the product group and planners from the marketing staff.

FORECASTING AND LONG-RANGE PLANNING. On the whole, the companies nearly always formulate specific long-range plans for their R&D efforts. Where forecasting serves as an aid for this purpose, it has been underway for 2–4 years, although in one case for 8–10 years, but it is used to only a limited extent. Most of the forecasting effort (25–35%) is normative, with trend extrapolation being used about 30–40% of the time. Trend correlation and intuitive (25%) and growth analogy (10%) are also used some of the time by a few companies. The chemical industry as a whole spends very little of its R&D budget on planning (the answers to our question concerning amount ranged from "peanuts" to 1%), and even less is allotted to technological forecasting. The forecasts are updated at least annually, by a combination of individual input and group discussion. The long-range plans extend about 6–10 years (average, 7 years) into the future and are updated annually. They are then documented and circulated to managers and program directors, for use in their resource allocations. The responsibility for the formulation of the long-range plans is usually held by the vice president for research or for R&D.

CONTRIBUTORS TO THE FORECAST. The techniques used by the contributor have the same distribution as described in the previous paragraph. The size of groups generating inputs is usually around 2–5, but in some cases has reached 30. It is felt that participating in the forecast makes the personnel think more deeply about the business, and in some instances has precipitated a better definition of the company's goals.

USERS OF THE FORECAST. The prime users of the forecast are the planning staff, closely followed by study groups; marketing staff and individual scientists and engineers use it occasionally, and programming and budgeting staff even less. The frequency of use is at least once a year, usually as an input to short-range (0–3 years) technical and operational planning, as general information to provide a background for technical studies and concept generation, and for intelligence information.

PROJECT SELECTION AND RESOURCE ALLOCATION. The methods used for project selection are usually a combination of subjective and quantitative techniques, but with the emphasis on the subjective aspects. In only

50% of the companies questioned were forecasting methods used for determining the balance between long-term–payoff and short-term–payoff projects. The length of research projects is between 2 and 5 years (average, 4 years), and of development projects is 2–6 years (average, 5 years). The distribution of work performed by most companies breaks down as follows: less than 5% pure research, 35–45% applied research, and 35–45% development.

REMARKS. No one seemed to have any remarks which he considered pertinent to the study. However, it was noticeable that, of all the types of industries included, the chemical industry was by far the most reticent. In some cases, this was attributable to the fact that previous forecasting or decision-modeling efforts had failed miserably (usually because some important factors were excluded) and managements were unwilling to be bitten again. This was certainly not true, however, of many other companies that proved uncommunicative.

CASE STUDIES

Petrochemicals Research Company

Petrochemicals Research Company is organized as a "not-for-profit" institute. Its support comes from its operating affiliations with a parent company and one or two outside sources such as the government. The rights to the technologies used and to the forecasts belong to the parent organization and to the affiliates. The Research Company is divided into four quite independent sections:

1. Petroleum Processing and Product Group.
2. Chemical Group.
3. Engineering Group, which includes R&D, as well as design and project management.
4. Corporate Research Group, which deals with long-range research plans.

The planning Coordination Group monitors the long-range plans for each of the four sections.

The overall objectives of the Research Company have to do with its role as supplier of technical information for the parent company. However, these objectives are difficult to quantify in terms of the sub-objectives and technical objectives of the four groups.

The Planning Coordination Group has established a set of guidelines for each department, but there is much give-and-take in trying to specify what a good plan should be. Each group of Petrochemicals Research develops its own 5-year plan, which is updated annually. This is not a formal process, however, and it is left to the Planning Coordination Group to formalize these plans. There is considerable reluctance to devote time and effort to developing plans.

Basically, this planning group manages to assess a short-range plan fairly well. Potential market value is also looked at in some detail. The current programs are reassessed for technical output, but there is reluctance to expend effort in performing normative or exploratory forecasts.

As far as budgeting is concerned, until recently there has never been a limit to funds; rather, an insufficiency of research ideas has been the problem. This has had the effect of making budgeting extrapolative, and there has been a tendency to fill up the budget, which has resulted in a decrease in incentives for each research group.

Each of the four areas is identified with its own source of funds, so that there is no competition for one overall budget. Although the long-range corporate outlook is to 1975 and 1985, the plans do not encompass such long-term aspects. An annual "stewardship" report is prepared, in which the current objectives and performance are compared to their expected values from the previous year's report, and then the following year's goals are discussed. These meetings, which involve the entire top management of the company, are preceded by discussions on the long-range outlook, so that short-range plans can be "flavored" by the future possibilities. This has resulted in individual areas being asked to look realistically to 1985.

Last spring, the Vice President for the Petroleum Processing and Product Group realized the need for putting resources where the greatest effect could be felt. He went to the top management of the affiliates, and obtained their acceptance for a new planning development which was to focus on the Petroleum Group. Basically, his idea was a Delphi study on opportunities for the future. Then top management was asked to nominate individuals to perform the task of selecting participants with suitable backgrounds, and therefore credibility, but also with a talent for foresight. All the sections are now involved in this study, with most work falling on the Engineering Group.

The Delphi study itself involves 500 participants from the Research Company, regional and operating organizations, and affiliated research laboratories who have expertise in technical or business areas. The main purpose of this study is to produce more opportunities from which the research programs can be selected, and then to rank these opportunities to provide more information upon which the budget can be based. The approach being followed in the study consists of four phases, the first of which is currently underway:

1. Event generation.
2. Event cross-linking.
3. Evaluation.
4. Incorporation into research program.

Phase 1: Event Generation. The participants in this phase come from the three different groups mentioned above. The "internal" technology experts are individuals whose proficiency is in the fields of the parent company's activities; the "external" experts are those whose areas of technology lie outside the parent company's operations but are relevant to the overall technological environment; and the "business" experts are those who deal mainly in marketing, economics, government relations, and the like.

These experts forecast events which, if they occur, will represent significant changes in comparison to the current situation, or an extrapolation of current trends. Some of the sectors to be considered in the study are listed in Figure 1. The event then forecast by each group will be forwarded for sorting and assigning to the other two groups (as represented by the arrows in the figure) for cross-linking with other events.

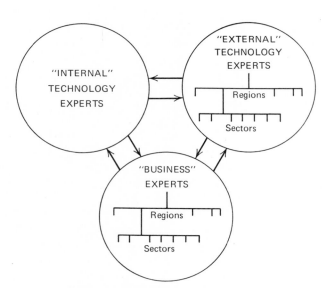

Figure 1   Phase 1: Event generation.

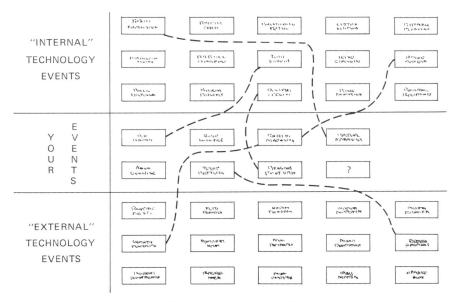

Figure 2   Phase 2: Event cross-linking.

Phase 2: Event Cross-Linking. Each expert will be asked to consider his own forecast in relation to the events forecast by other experts, in order to identify possible linkages which could produce a viable chain of events having some likelihood of future occurrence. He will also be asked to reconsider his own area, in the light of the other forecasts, to identify additional related events therein. Each participant will describe each chain of events in terms of the individual events involved, his idea of what might be involved in his area in order for the event to occur, and his rationale for the cross-linking. This phase is dia-grammed in Figure 2.

Phase 3: Evaluation. It is presently thought that this phase (Figure 3) will be performed on an individual basis by experts selected for their judgment in technical or business areas. Each chain of events will be sent to at least one expert in each area. The cost and probability of success of achieving the technical objective will be assessed by the tech-nical expert; the value of the objective and the probability of under-taking the venture, given a reasonable prospect of its technical success, will be left to the business expert.

It is expected that four outcomes will be possible, based on the business

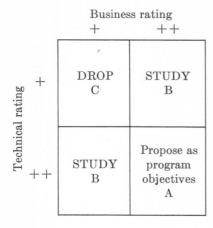

Figure 3   Phase 3: Evaluation.

and technical evaluations. These are shown in Figure 3, where category A items are those for which no further information is needed to reach a decision regarding their incorporation into the research program; category B items require further study in either technical or business areas before a decision can be made; and category C items will be deferred or dropped from further consideration.

Phase 4: Incorporation into Research Programs. Whenever the objectives in category A are consistent with the existing planning structure, they will be forwarded to the planning groups for consideration. Those which do not fall into the existing structure will be considered on a case-by-case basis by the relevant vice president and his staff. The items rejected will remain open for further analysis and reconsideration.

The B items will be assigned to *ad hoc* study groups, who will report back to the evaluators. After consideration, these persons will then reassign the objectives to category A or C.

Chemical Explosives Corporation

The Chemical Explosives Corporation comprises six separate departments which are semi-autonomous and have their own cost centers. Each operating group provides monthly, quarterly, annual, and 5-year forecasts, which are then consolidated by the Economics Research Division (ERD).

The preparation of the 5-year plan is vital to each operating group. There is no fixed format or type of presentation, nor must this planning be performed at any specific time of the year. The budget request is presented to the ERD one week before it is due to be presented to the Executive Committee. The ERD summarizes the information and makes a recommendation which then goes before the Executive Committee.

The 5-year plan essentially becomes a 5-year forecast in that the probabilities of achieving the stated quantity of sales, net sales value, profits, operating assets, and return on investment are assessed. The planners essentially think in terms of cash flow, as the most critical judgments for the company to make are the investment decisions.

Each operating group can make appropriation requests at any time of the year. Each request is considered on its own merits, as the company has virtually unlimited funds. Although the appropriation request is a formal document, there is no standard format for presenting the information. It contains detailed economic forecasts, a market analysis, and a threat analysis, in terms of both competitive companies and technologies, as well as estimated sales value, profit level expected, and other relevant data. The analyses are performed by the technical experts, market analysts, and finance people within each group, but the techniques used are not formalized.

The Operations Research Group does not perform a risk analysis in terms of rate of return on investment, which extends out for 10–15 years. The ERD would like to see a risk analysis incorporated into the appropriation requests, but more information would then be needed on the market and the costs involved.

The major problem encountered within the corporation is lack of ideas, particularly in the area of innovation. Until just recently, the main business of the corporation was war, and the chief customer was the federal government. Any research performed was mainly exploratory—there was little need-oriented research. The results of this research were quite often inventions for which no application could be found.

Now, despite the inertia and traditionalism of the top management, the validity of the research programs is being questioned. Although entrance into the commercial market is essential, the Chemical Explosives Corporation, recalling the experience of another company that spent 18 million dollars on an R&D program, only to find that within 6 months a competitive Japanese product was on the market, feels that it may be better to adopt the strategy of follow the leader. Alternatively, if it is possible to become a dominant factor in a market (30% or more), it can become a "me too" operation.

In 1967–1968 a new department was formed to provide additional investment potential by acquiring new companies. This was done because there were no R&D programs underway which would have paid off in the 1973–75 period. Now this department is looking for "need areas," such as housing, where the company can play a successful part.

On the whole, the company does not feel the need for much forecasting, other than extrapolation for specific appropriation requests. It requires, not distant trend extrapolations, but only breakthroughs or innovations and more product implications.

Man-Made Fibers Company

Reasons for Technological Forecasting. The management formally recognizes the continuing need for decisions in regard to:

- the allocation of research effort in the immediate future
- a 10-year plan for capital and expense outlays
- a reconsideration of the nature of the company's business

These decisions create a need for evaluation of just-emerging technologies that:

- compete for position or dominance
- require an estimate of success
- require an estimate of the delay before their impact on the market is significant

Profitability is usually only roughly known. Also, the technology is only just emerging, so little information can be derived from its history.

The basic problem is to forecast the development and commercialization of the technology, rather than its discovery. The company has tried several forecasting techniques, rather sporadically, over a period of 2 years, but has no specific formalized method. The following examples describe three of the exercises undertaken over a period of years in forecasts of various technologies. Features of the three exercises are shown in Exhibits I and II.

Exercise A. In 1963, conventional diagonal-ply tires and belted tires were being reinforced with rayon and nylon, but work was already underway on four other materials (steel wire, Fiberglas, modified nylon, and polyester). Those emerging technologies caused management to be faced with the following problems:

- whether to become a supplier of reinforcement material for tires
- what materials to choose as a primary target
- when to target for commercialization

Forecasting began with extensive open-ended discussions with both

Features of decision Problem	• Timing of commercial development critical for:
	  (a) immediate allocation of research effort
	  (b) reasonable 10-year planning
	• Evaluation of just-emerging technology
	• Only rough knowledge of potential profitability
	• Years of costly research before commercialization

Features of forecast problem	• Qualitative changes in technology to be forecast • Concern with material used, not value to user • Short time horizon (3–15 years)
Features of forecast approach	• "Ask-the-experts" • Development and commercialization of more interest than discovery of technology

Exhibit I   Common features of three exercises.

Feature	Exercise		
	A	B	C
Type of product	Reinforcement for tires	Textile material	Textured Yarn
Competition with our present products	None	Indirect	Direct
Marketing channel	Different	Different	Similar
Capital cost	High	High	Moderate
Major uncertainties	Cost effectiveness for user; consumer psychology	Relative production costs; esthetics	Timing of generic's commercial development; esthetics
Issue	What to commercialize next year	Direction and emphasis for research	Commercialization strategy; level of development effort
Decision alternatives	Well defined	Vague	Defined
Source for "experts"	External and some internal	Internal and selected external	Internal only

Exhibit II   Features distinguishing the decision problems.

internal and external experts. The resulting information was then incorporated into an analysis which identified the key factors, for each material's success, on which there was significant uncertainty. The major output of the forecast was a decision tree with four branches (i.e., four sets of assumptions for each market segment); an example is shown in Exhibit III.

For the assumptions used, the market share for each fiber was calculated. Then, with the assistance of the experts, the probability of each assumption being correct was estimated, giving a final result of the expected market share for each material.

Management accepted the parts of the forecast represented by the decision tree and by the market-share estimates, but expressed doubt about the probability estimates. However, these gave visibility to the different opinions and resulted in a structure which was acceptable and which aided in the final company decision.

The total time for this exercise was 3 months. It showed that the

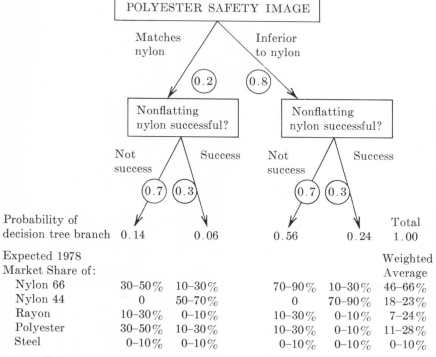

Probability of decision tree branch	0.14	0.06	0.56	0.24	Total 1.00

Expected 1978 Market Share of:					Weighted Average
Nylon 66	30–50%	10–30%	70–90%	10–30%	46–66%
Nylon 44	0	50–70%	0	70–90%	18–23%
Rayon	10–30%	0–10%	10–30%	0–10%	7–24%
Polyester	30–50%	10–30%	10–30%	0–10%	11–28%
Steel	0–10%	0–10%	0–10%	0–10%	0–10%

Exhibit III   **Decision tree for 1975 automobile replacement market.**

addition of technological forecasting to the more commonly used decision tree approach made possible a more logical analysis of alternatives.

Exercise B. As this exercise involved restricted development programs, the subject matter will not be discussed. The final product, however, was in indirect competition with some current products, as certain of the end-use areas overlapped. This had its advantages for forecasting, since those responsible had a reasonable overview of the area under consideration, but the range of specific alternatives was vague and broader than in Exercise A.

In this exercise, opinions were gathered from about 35 people by interviews inside and outside the company. After a literature and newspaper search, critical questions were defined for the interviews, but these were later revised in the light of the information obtained.

From the interviews the company obtained a good idea of the problems technology would have to solve, as well as first-hand information about the business-distribution methods, rates of growth, and basic economics. More important, however, was the better understanding of the overall problem, and the knowledge gained of the correct questions to ask in detail. In areas where the right questions were asked, timing estimates were obtained. Unfortunately, the company did not get a good feel for the overall range of possible answers.

Although the experts provided a clear consensus of the most likely events and their timing, the least and the most that could have been done within the time horizon were ill defined. The probable implications of the proposed actions were reasonably clear, but the reliability of the forecast was subjectively measured. The new information, although copious, was disorganized and required careful analysis.

The interviewing was carried out during a 5-month period, and in the following 2 months three major reports were prepared. The total cost, including support, up to the recommendations to management, was $30,000. The forecast itself cost about $15,000.

Exercise C. Again, the subject matter cannot be discussed here. However, the product involved in this exercise was one for which most of the right questions were known before the experts were consulted. For this reason, the Delphi approach seemed to be the most appropriate. Because of the nature of the problem, external experts could not be consulted, but 29 company people (covering a broad range of disciplines) took part in the panel. To ensure cooperation, the first questionnaire was hand-delivered and explained (Round 1). A typical questionnaire format for the first eight questions is shown in Exhibit IV (top).

Round 2 yielded small shifts in the third quartile for three questions, but no other changes. This round evoked many extensive "reason why" statements.

Three questions were also asked in a different way in the hope of extracting additional information regarding the individual's uncertainty. One of these was of the form: "What confidence do you have that event A will occur by the indicated year?" Each individual was given a scale on which to record his answer as a line (Exhibit V, top and middle). The bottom section of Exhibit V shows what the expert received in Round 2, where each black spot is the group's median answer for each cost level, and the shaded area is the inner quartile range. This appeared to offer a realistic picture of the experts' uncertainty, which

ROUND 1

QUESTIONNAIRE A

You are asked to supply four estimates for each question:
1. The earliest year the event is likely to happen (1 to 10 chance)
2. The year by which there is a 50-50 chance of occurrence
3. The latest year by which event is likely to occur (about 90% confidence that it will occur by this year)
4. Your estimate of your own qualifications for answering the question, using the scale:
   A. Competent to forecast
   B. Some competence to forecast
   C. Limited competence to forecast
   D. Marginal to my area of competence
   E. Outside my area of competence

Please use the back of the questionnaire for any additional comments or explanations you wish to make.

	(1) Earliest	(2) 50–50	(3) Latest	(4) Qualification
			Answer*	
4. By what year will the amount of *cotton* used in domestically produced and consumed textiles fall below 3.0 billion pounds (10% below the 3.3 billion lb used in 1968)?				

* Never is an acceptable answer.

ROUND 2

QUESTIONNAIRE A

Instructions: Record your new answer to each question. If your new answer is not in IQR or is "never," then state reason why.	Year by Which There Is a 50–50 Chance of Occurrence			Reason Why Your Answer is Not in IQR or Is "Never" (for more space use back of sheet)
	IQR	Your Old Answer	Your New Answer	
4. By what year will the amount of cotton used in domestically produced and consumed textiles fall below 3.0 billion pounds (10% below the 3.3 billion lb used in 1968)?	1972 to 1985			

Exhibit IV   Typical questionnaire format for first eight questions.

was extremely important from an analytical point of view. As the differences after Round 2 were relatively small, the experts decided that a third round was unnecessary. The results were summarized for top management and included in the information base as a start toward defining the research and marketing strategy in this product area.

Two rounds of questionnaires, including their design analysis and reporting, were completed in a period of 4 months, at a cost of about $5000.

Conclusions. In Exercise A, the interviews provided forecast information which was so diverse and entangled that it had little direct value. However, after the uncertainties in each market segment for which assumptions had to be made were analyzed and the results formed into a decision tree, the implications of the information were readily communicated to management, and they proved exceptionally useful.

Exercise B gave a good feel for the problems technology would have to solve. In addition, the information obtained was very useful, despite the subjectiveness of the reliability.

Exercise C provided quantifiable answers although, from the nature of the program, they were likely to have been inbred. One drawback

Confidence in event occurring
by indicated year

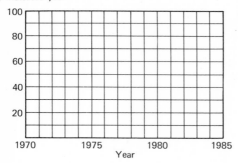

Round I Questionnaire

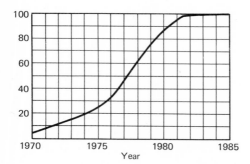

Typical Answer on Round I

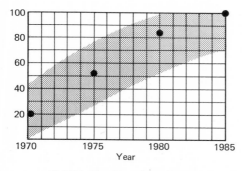

Round II Questionnaire

Exhibit V   Questionnaire and answers for Rounds 1 and 2.

96

to this technique is the need to frame the questions correctly, which can prove to be a major problem.

Generally, the chances of obtaining management action as a result of forecasting improved when the forecast was concise and well structured. Each of the three exercises, however, was valid and useful in its particular context.

Monsanto Corporation

CONTACT: J. KENNETH CRAVER

Monsanto has been conducting technological forecasts since early 1962. Initially these forecasts were used by the research staff of one of the major divisions of the company as guidelines for setting up new research programs. Key technical people within the research department were asked to identify and define long-term trends and critical events within their particular fields of expertise. These predictions were combined with events and trends gleaned from the scientific and technical literature, edited and reported annually. At first, no attempt was made to take into account sociopolitical or economic trends or events.

Currently, technological forecasting is a staff function with inputs into the Corporate Management Committee. Since it is realized that technical events *of themselves* can have little or no commercial impact, the technological forecasts are combined with economic and sociopolitical forecasts to create scenarios or "probable worlds of Monsanto," which are then used in planning and resource allocation at the corporate level. The forecasts are not intended to be all-encompassing. The subjects chosen for study must be pertinent to Monsanto and must have a reasonable probability of occurrence within a finite period of time (usually 10 years); also, their impact on Monsanto should be quantifiable and credible.

A variety of forecasting techniques is employed, no one of which is used to the exclusion of others. Delphi forecasts, trend extrapolations, and literature screens provide basic inputs into the technological forecasting sector. Economic models, such as the Battelle input-output matrix and the Wharton econometric model, are used, along with internally developed models, as inputs into the economic forecasts. The sociopolitical forecast is derived from a number of public and private sources.

An interesting tool for combining forecasts into one interacting scenario is the cross-impact matrix, originally described by T. G. Gordon and H. Hayward (*Futures*, Vol. 1, 1968, p. 100). An example of the technique is given in Figure 5. This is an actual matrix as used on a specific developmental product within Monsanto, but the events listed in Figure 4 are fictitious.

The participants, who are connected with the projects as managers or administrators, supply some of the events. Others are provided by the forecasting and analysis section. The items are chosen to include overall objectives, competitive and customer reactions, changes in technology and economics, and pertinent legal and social constraints. At the same time an estimate of the probability of any individual event is established, either intuitively or from other sources, such as Delphi

Event	P_{80}	P_{80}'
1. 700\overline{M}$ sales goal by 1980	75	95
2. Net return after taxes = $85\overline{M}$	75	95
3. License European distributors	80	99
4. European market = $100\overline{M}$ in 1980	80	99
5. $50\overline{M}$ investment by 1974	100	100
6. Company A captures cheese market	40	30
7. Company B introduces better product	20	26
8. Company D acquires Company E	70	85
9. 5B units to Company F in 1980	50	90
10. 2B units to Company G in 1980	65	91
11. 10B units to Company H in 1980	85	93
12. We develop an edible elastomer	90	90
13. Raw material costs = 9¢ in 1974	50	72
14. Raw material costs = 4¢ in 1980	65	99
15. Used containers remolded and reused	60	70
16. Vapor-phase deposition of coating	60	70
17. QEP used in textiles	90	85
18. Sunlight-degradable polymer developed	90	95
19. Fire-retardant QEP developed	80	95
20. German company J manufactures QEP in U.S.A.	90	96
21. Taste problem eliminated	90	94
22. Low-temperature brittleness solved	95	99
23. Pigmentation with approved colors	85	96
24. Nontoxic plasticizers available	60	78
25. Acceptance by food processors	80	98
26. Biodegradability demonstrated	90	91
27. QEP restricted to non-Kosher products	20	14
28. QEP films as synthetic paper	65	73
29. FDA approval for food uses	90	92
30. Regulations in force against nonreturn, noncombustible containers	60	70
31. Public rejects QEP on taste, appearance	15	10

Figure 4   List of events.

Figure 5 — data matrix (rotated on page). Columns are cross-impact items 1–30 plus Y_{10} and P_{80}; rows are Events 1–31. Diagonal cells are marked X. (Dense rotated numeric matrix; values read as accurately as possible, blank = empty cell.)

Event	P_{80}	Y_{10}	1	2	3	4	5	6	7	8	9	10	11	12	13	14	15	16	17	18	19	20	21	22	23	24	25	26	27	28	29	30
1	75	77	X	8	8	8	8	6	1	4	8	8	8	8	6	6	8	4	4	4	5	5	4	6	5	5	7	5	-6	6	1	6
2	75	77	8	X	8	8	8	4		4	4	4	4	4	6	6	6	3	4	6	6	6	3	6	5	4	3	2	-5	4	1	2
3	80	70	8	8	X	8								3	2		2	2	2				1	3								2
4	80	75	4	6	8	X		-2	2	4	2	3	2	-1	2	4	4	1	2	2	4	8	1	3	2	2	4	3	-2	2		2
5	100	70	8	8	8		X	-2	-2	-2	-2	-2	-2	-2		-2		-1				-2										
6	40	73	6	4		6		X	2	2	2	-6	2	6	2	4	2	3	4	4	2	6	3	3	4	1	5	3	-2	3		2
7	20	75	1		2	4	-2	-2	X	-2	-4	2	-2	2			2	2		3	2		3			4	6	4	-4		2	7
8	70	70	4	4	4	4	-2	-2	-2	X	8	2	2	6	4	4	4	3	5	4	4	7	4	4	4	4	6	4	-4	3		4
9	90	77	8	4	4	6	-2	-2	-2	8	X	4	6	6	8	5	4	2	4	4	4	6	4	4	4	4	6	3	-4	3		4
10	50	77	8	4	4	4	-2	-2	2	2	4	X	6	6	4	3	4	2	2	2	4	6	3	4	4	2	6	2	-3	6		4
11	65	72	8	4	3	3	-2	-2	-2	2	6	6	X	6	4	6	6	3	4	4	5	5	2	4	4	4	6	2	-2	6		4
12	85	75	8	4	3	1	-2	-2	2	6	6	3	6	X	5	3	4	3	4	4	4	4	2	5	2	4	6	2	-2	6		4
13	90	90	6	6	2	6		-2	2	4	8	3	4	8	X	6	6	3	4	2	4	4	3	5	4	4	6	3	-2	6		2
14	50	72	4	6	2	4	-2	-2	2	4	4	4	4	8	4	X	4	2	4	4	4	3	2	5	4	4	6	4	-3	4		2
15	65	72	8	8	4	8		-4	0	4	8	6	8	8	4	4	X	2	5	6	5	4	3	1	4	4	4	2	-6	6		2
16	60	77	6		2	6	-2	-4	-4	4	4	8	8	8	8	8	6	X	5	7	6	3	3	4	2	2	4		-8			2
17	60	71	8	8	4	8		-2	-4	4	8	2	2	2	4	2	3	2	X	3	1	2		5	4	4	6	2	-8		2	2
18	90	75	6	4	2	4		-2	-2	4	4	4	4	5	2	2	6	2	3	X	2	3	2	1	2	2	2	4	-4	2		4
19	80	71	2	6		2		-2	2	2	3	4	3	4	2	2	3	-1	2	3	X	3	3	4	4	2	4		-4		2	
20	90	73	2	8	7	2	3	-3	4	6	6	6	5	8	4	6	6		6	6	X	3		8		2	6		-2	2		2
21	90	70	6	5	3	3	2	-2		2	3	4	4	8		3	4	2	1	7	1	1	X	2	2	2	2			2	2	2
22	95	71	8	8	4	5	3	-2	1	3	6	6	6	4	4	8	3	2	2	6	2	4	2	X		4	4	6	-2			2
23	85	70	8	8	8	8	4	-2	3	3	6	4	6	4	4	4	3		1	7	X	1	8		X	4	6	6	-2	2	2	6
24	60	70	6	6	4	2	3	-3	2	4	6	6	6	5	1	8	6	2	5	2	3	2	2	8	2	X	X			2		6
25	80	70	6	8	4	8	3	-2	3	4	4	4	4	6	2	6	4	-2	2	2	2	4		1	4	3	X	X		X		
26	90	70	6	2	3	2	6	2	2	4	4	4	4	4	4	2	6	-2	1	6	2	1	6	6	2	X	-5	1	-1	3	X	6
27	20	77	-2	-2	-2	-2																2	2			X	X	X	X		X	
28	65	73	6	8	4	4	4	6	3	4	8	8	8	8	8	4	6	-6	2	2	2	44	8	8	4	4	5	6	-6	X	X	6
29	90	72	8	8	8	6	-8	4	2	4	4	4	4	4	4	2	4	-6	2	6	2	66	2	2	2	X	6	2	2	X	4	X
30	60	72	-2	-8	-8	-8	-8	4	0	4	6	6	6	6	2	6	8	-6	1	2	2	88	2	6	4	4	6	4	4	-2	-2	2
31	15	70	-8	-8	-8	-8	-8	4	8	4	8	8	8	8	4	8	4	-6	8	6	2	-3	6		2	4	8	-8	-8	-8	4	X

Figure 5 Matrix for "Product QEP."

study or trend extrapolation. This is shown in Figure 4 as P_n, where n = the year of maturity for the study (80 = 1980 in this case). The earliest date for which a probability of approximately 10% can be established is shown as Y_{10}. A matrix is then prepared, and the participants vote, as a group, on the probable impact of each event on every other event. They must first judge each impact as (a) favorable, (b) unfavorable, or (c) no effect, and then, in the case of (a) or (b), rate the intensity of the effect, using a scale of +8 to −8. The completed matrix is then processed using a computer program developed at the Institute for the Future. The computer output is a new set of probabilities, P_n'.

The shifts in probability $(\Delta P = P_n - P_n')$ are interpreted in light of the kind and the degree of impact shown in the matrix. The significance of any given event can be demonstrated by changing the event quantitatively or replacing it with another event and observing the change in ΔP.

Sherwin Williams Chemicals

CONTACT: ROBERT H. BALDWIN

In September 1969, Maumee Chemical Company, a subsidiary of Sherwin Williams was dissolved as such and was incorporated as part of a new division, Sherwin Williams Chemicals, comprising six plants and five laboratories.

The technological activity of the division takes place in two main areas: R&D and technical services. The technical services are for the manufacturing and sales groups, but if problems not soluble by existing knowledge arise within either of these groups, they are turned over to the R&D unit.

The prime purpose of this division is to support the established products and to develop new products in order to attract new markets, and to diversify. This means that most of the work performed, other than that for supporting on-going products, is of an exploratory nature, in both the research and the development stages; therefore, careful guidelines have had to be established, so that work is not prolonged on development which does not appear to have potential markets. For Sherwin Williams Chemicals, the dollar size of the potential market for a product should be in the range of $1–10 million. The cost of development would not justify a smaller market, and the division's resources would probably be insufficient for larger ventures.

The strategy used to approach the problems of exploratory development is that of "pioneering" development, which is explained in a set of guidelines. This strategy was developed from past experience in technology transfer and from published data relating to the Chemical Division's requirements. It provides a means of relating money-at-risk to successive stages of development over periods of time up to 20 years.

The outline of the pioneering development strategy is as follows:

1. Maintain strong flow of ideas.
   (a) Use suggestion system.
   (b) Carry out surveillance of patents and literature.
   (c) Stimulate outsiders with ads, seminars, etc.
2. Evaluate ideas and set priorities.
   (a) Aim at appropriate targets.
   (b) Integrate on established business.
   (c) Keep diversified.
   (d) Get extra mileage both ways—use and technology.
3. Limit commitment in early screening stages.
   (a) Invest only enough effort to get needed data.
   (b) Diversify total effort.
4. Increase commitment as risk falls and prospects rise.
   (a) As screening shows attractive utility.
   (b) As multiple uses enlarge.
   (c) As prospective markets grow.
   (d) As proprietary position is strengthened.
   (e) As technical and economic synergisms develop.
5. At development stage, be selective . . . and concentrate.
   (a) Undertake one major development at a time.
   (b) Use "task force" approach.

The first item of the strategy, "Maintain a strong Flow of Ideas," is based on the facts that in exploratory technology transfer there are no objectives to be achieved, and that for any given chemical the chance of reaching commercialization is about 1 in 3000 (as shown in Figure 6). This high mortality rate of ideas necessitates a strong suggestion system from both within and without the company.

The second item, "Evaluate ideas and set priorities," follows immediately from the first step, since there must be some standard means of determining which ideas get priority. The dollar size of the potential market provides one factor in determining priorities, as does the "functional chemical market" potential. A functional market is a general application area, served by a variety of chemicals. An example is shown in Figure 7, where the "plasticizers" market, totaling $215 million per year, is served by 35 chemicals selling for over $1 million per year. Other factors used in determining priority are company capability and

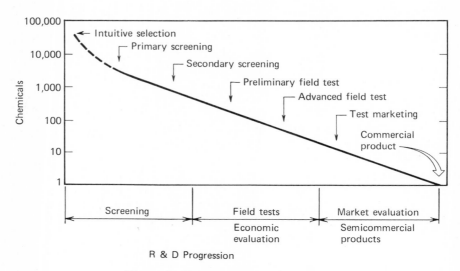

Figure 6 New product "decay" curve.

strengths, particularly utilization of proprietary techniques, and knowledge of markets already served by the company.

For more than 2 years, the remaining three steps were used in the qualitative form above; more recently, however, a quantitative form has been developed to supplement these steps. This guideline arose from a study of the problems involved in managing development programs, in terms of keeping the expenditures under control by increasing or decreasing efforts in proportion to payoff, or changing the emphasis or direction of a program. After observing the development of several programs over a number of years, the division became convinced that there was a basic pattern to pioneering developments. This pattern is illustrated in Figure 8, as "money-at-risk" versus time. The general characteristic of this curve is that the cumulative expenditure ("money-at-risk") increases gradually in the research stages and rises rapidly through the development stages, the start-up of a plant, and market introduction; then, as the production is successfully sold, the cash flow reverses.

The life cycle of an R&D program can range from 8 to 12 years or more; of this, the research can take from 1 to 10 years or longer, the development 5–7 years, and the plant construction, start-up, and

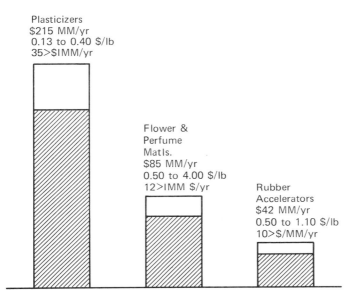

Figure 7   **Functional chemical markets. Crosshatching indicates portion of markets in products > $1 MM/year. Source of data: U.S. Department of Commerce.**

market introduction about 2–3 years. Thus the payoff can start to counterbalance the outflow of cash only after 10 years or longer, and the time taken to return the money-at-risk can be 13–19 or more years.

Because of the long time period during which substantial sums of money are at risk, the division required some means of assessing the program's development, in terms of out-flowing money. As a first step, the overall development section was broken down into five separate stages: conceptuality, activity, utility, marketability, and profitability. Those steps are shown in more detail in Figure 9.

"Conceptuality" takes place in the research stage—it is given in terms of the theory of chemical behaviors, or of analogy to other chemicals. Sometimes, when the research is radically different, the only conceptuality is curiosity.

The results of the research are then passed on for screening, before the activity stage. Because of the extra facilities and expertise sometimes required for this screening process, the division needs to augment its

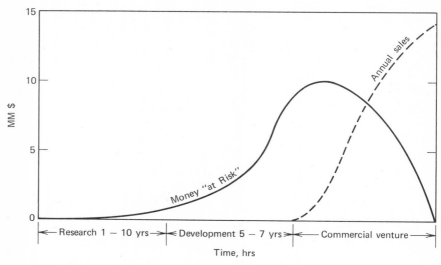

Figure 8   Time span versus cost for new product development.

own capabilities with those from outside, either through screening arrangements or by contract research, as shown in Figure 10.

"Activity" occurs between the research and the development stages; in fact, it is the state of the "activity" which determines whether a development program will be pursued, whether more research is required, or whether research will be dropped. If the "activity" looks good, then such questions as the following are considered: "Does the activity relate to a market of significant size?" "Is it likely to be profitable?" "Can it be integrated wih present business?" If the answers to these questions are favorable, then usually a development program is initiated.

The next step is determining the "utility." This is more than "activity," in that the program must avoid creating new problems, and the overall performance of the product under varying conditions must be demonstrated.

Once it has been determined that a compound has "utility," its "marketability" must be determined. Generally, a product must satisfy one of two criteria: it must do the same job, but at less cost than an existing product; or, for the same cost, it must do a better job. In other words, it must have a cost or a performance advantage over existing products. The next problem is to decide whether the new product will be able to penetrate the market for the existing products; or, if the product is radically new, whether it has good sale potential. In

Conceptuality	Activity	Utility	Marketability	Profitability
Initiating idea is that a particular chemical (or family) might be useful in one or more specifically visualized applications based on theory or analogy. Concept should include rough idea of size of market area.	Demonstration of activity in some useful application (kills weeds, bacteria, etc.; sweetens foods; inhibits corrosion; etc.) related to a market of size and significance.	Activity is coupled with other parameters in specific uses to show practical applications in actual use conditions. Competitive products, price ranges, and particular customers are now apparent.	Demonstration that the utility obtained is salable at a price that is not only competitive, but also attractive enough to penetrate the market in the face of established products and practices.	Demonstration that a plant can be built to make a profit selling products to specific customers for particular uses, in definite amounts, etc., and that the capital investment earns an attractive return.
SPECULATIVE OR EXPLORATORY RESEARCH	SCREENING AND EVALUATION	DEVELOPMENT FUNCTIONS APPLICATIONS RESEARCH PRODUCT DEVELOPMENT	MARKET DEVELOPMENT PROCESS DEVELOPMENT	CAPITAL PROJECT AUTHORIZATION AND PLANT DESIGN

⟶ Normal Development Progression ⟶

Figure 9 Stages or steps in the development of a new chemical product.

105

1. Screening arrangements (outside)
   Ag chemicals
   Pharmaceuticals
   Veterinary chemicals
   Biocides, fungicides, etc. (nonagricultural)
2. Contract research
   Polymers and polymer additives
   Electrolytic applications
3. "In-house" applied research
   Corrosion inhibiters
   Taste comparisons
   Ultraviolet absorbers

Figure 10   Applications research.

order to answer these questions, various economic studies are performed, including "value-in-use" both from a customer's viewpoint and in relation to the competition.

"Profitability" occurs when the program becomes a commercial venture in terms of a capital project with justifiable return on investment. The expected payoff is shown in terms of process developments, plant design, and estimates of construction and operating costs, as well as forecasts of sales and pricing schedules. At this stage, the decision is made to undertake the venture or to undertake more development—or in some cases even to abandon the project.

In order to profit from previous experience and to gain more effective control, the division made an attempt to quantify these five stages in terms of money-at-risk and time, which gave rise to the parameters on the curve shown in Figure 11. The first step was to find a maximum limit for the money-at-risk; this worked out to be less than or equal to the annual sales visualized at the "activity" stage in accordance with the tenet, "Aim at appropriate targets." The rationale for this was based on the characteristics of a typical profitable chemical, which generates a cash flow of 15–20% of the sales dollar. The generation of cash at such a rate results in a cash-flow break-even in 5–7 years (see point F on Figure 11).

Once the maximum money-at-risk (Point E, Figure 11) has been obtained, the other stages can be related to this limit. Previous case histories were used by the division to provide experience upon which to base quantitative assessments.

The "activity" and "profitability" stages were easily determined. Subjective judgment was required, however, in determining the "utility" and "marketability" periods, although past experience helped. The figures below show two specific cases (with fictitious product names), as well

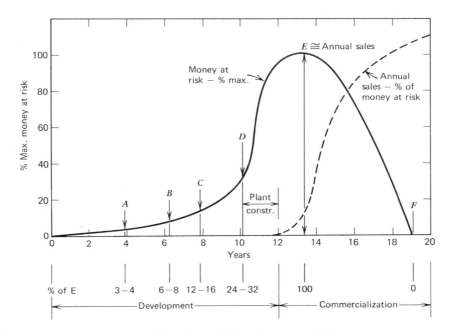

Figure 11 "Exploratory" development guideline.

as other miscellaneous cases; the last column lists the guidelines developed. The figures give the percentage of maximum money-at-risk at the point in question.

	"Parazines"	"Polyam"	Miscellaneous Cases	Guideline
Activity	2	3	2–4	3–4
Utility	10	6	8–10	6–8
Marketability	20	16	8–12	12–16
Profitability	33	25	30–40	24–32

The guideline values are shown in Figure 11. The guideline serves as an aid—as a means of checking, not as a rigid formula. Currently, it is being used to monitor three major programs. The conclusions arising from using the guideline retrospectively and currently are that market prospects need to be increased, and hence that new areas of "activity" must be sought. Also, some means of assessing the market more accurately is needed, so that the real requirements, the competition, and the whims of the customer are taken into consideration.

VII.　*Pharmaceuticals*

The highest reward for man's "work" is not what he gets for it but what he becomes by it.
                                                                    John Ruskin

INTRODUCTION

The pharmaceuticals industry is one which has greatly diversified in the last few years, and many companies now have interest in products quite removed from those found in bottles in a drug store or obtainable on prescription. From the field of drugs and other medicines, they have branched out into cosmetics and associated beauty preparations, biomedical electronics, ultrasonics, veterinary drugs, agricultural fertilizers and pesticides, and domestic chemical preparations. Within their R&D laboratories, they are developing equipment for recognizing and testing drugs and for reading labels on bottles, all of which have wide application in other areas.

Within the pharmaceuticals field itself, the problems involved in R&D are somewhat different from those encountered in other areas, as the industry relies more on invention and innovation than on the improvement of products, other than the reduction of side effects. Too, health and well-being are close to everyone's concern, and publicity, resulting in public or government pressure, often is responsible for the funding of programs which normally would not have been considered. All drugs and medicines have to undergo rigorous testing and must conform to FDA regulations. The pharmaceuticals industry makes much use of patenting and licensing procedures, another feature which sets it apart from other types of industry.

For this study three large pharmaceutical companies (with gross sales varying from $300 million to $600 million per year) were interviewed at length. All of them have on-going programs in forecasting, although two of these are environmental technological forecasts, rather than dealing with specific technologies. One of these companies has had included in its planning resource allocation, for many years, something which is rarely acknowledged outside of the military—a "sacred cow." Because of the brilliance and reputation of one particular scientist, it is deemed worthwhile to allow him a small portion of the funds for his own projects, in order to "keep him happy" and thereby enhance the prestige of the company. Unfortunately, the planning and forecasting systems used by another of the three companies contained too much proprietary information for publication.

RESULTS OF QUESTIONNAIRE

The results of the questionnaires submitted to approximately 40 specific companies, including some not mentioned above, yielded the following slightly different information.

OBJECTIVES. Most of the companies have written corporate objectives, which seem to be divided about equally between the qualitative and quantitative types. One company does not even consider its corporate objectives. All the companies have R&D objectives, but these are a mixture of oral goals and written qualitative objectives. In most cases, all the objectives are updated at least annually, but one company updates them every 1–3 years.

FORECASTS. Technological and marketing forecasts are performed most frequently, economic forecasts quite often, and environmental forecasts to a much lesser degree. The technological forecasts are almost always used as an aid in planning, often to assist in resource allocation, but only occasionally to help justify a previously made decision. Another two reasons for using the forecast are to increase cohesion and to give direction to research. The forecasts are always performed by in-house staff, but these persons come from two areas in the company: that of the product-program staff, who form a committee with scientists and engineers, and that of the corporate technical planners, sometimes with the aid of scientists and engineers, and marketing planners.

FORECASTING AND LONG-RANGE PLANNING. Almost all companies formulate specific long-range plans for their R&D efforts. Forecasting has been used in assisting long-range R&D efforts for as many as 15 years, but it is only recently (2–5 years) that such techniques have been formalized. Technological forecasts are employed quite extensively in the preparation of these long-range plans, the most popular methods being intuitive, followed by trend extrapolation; only about 5% use trend correlation. Normative types of forecasting are used about 20–30% of the time. The percentage of the R&D budget spent on planning varies from 1 to 2.3%, but the proportion of the budget spent on forecasting is negligible. The forecasts are updated at least annually, by a combination of individual input and group discussion. The long-range plans generally extend about 5–8 years into the future and are updated annually. These plans are then communicated in document form to managers and program directors. However, one company had research program plans extending up to 15 years into the future. The responsibility for the long-range R&D plans is generally held by the director for research, but in some cases it falls to a committee composed of executive officers and the planning department, or of the R&D operations staff.

CONTRIBUTIONS TO THE FORECAST. The techniques used by the contributors to the forecast are those described earlier. The size of groups generating inputs ranges from 4 to 30, but the usual size is 10. It was felt that participation in preparation of the forecast gave a better understanding of day-to-day operations, and of the planning involved, than the personnel had had previously, and also precipitated spin-off ideas for new projects.

USERS OF THE FORECAST. The major users of the forecast are the planning staff, followed by the laboratory management, although marketing staff and operations researchers and individual scientists and engineers also utilize them. The forecast is consulted on different occasions by different groups of people, but its main use is annual, immediately following the yearly revision. The forecast is used for technical and operational planning and as a source of intelligence information and general information to serve a background for studies and concept generation.

PROJECT SELECTION AND RESOURCE ALLOCATION. The processes used for project selection are usually a combination of subjective and quantitative methods, but the subjective aspects are emphasized. The amount of new R&D work taken on each year varies from 5% to 20%, but is generally in the region of 10%. Most companies have a subjective system for determining the balance between long-term–payoff projects and short-term ones. The length of research projects is about 5–8 years, the average being 7 years, but the development projects vary from 2–10 years, with an average of only 3 years. The type of work performed by the companies consists of 7–15% pure research, over 40% applied research, and 30–40% development.

REMARKS. It was felt that in the pharmaceuticals industry the contributor to the forecast is, in nearly all cases, also the user. Perhaps this situation results to some extent in the problems of in-breeding, but at least it gives more people an idea of what is going on.

CASE STUDIES

Smith Kline & French Laboratories

CONTACTS: A. DOUGLAS BENDER
MICHAEL L. COCHRAN

Three years ago the R&D Division of Smith Kline & French laboratories established a long-range planning function with the prime objective of helping management forecast and assess technological change in an effort to identify and highlight new research opportunities. Since that time the concept and practice of planning have been expanded, and presently an annual planning cycle integrates many activities, including technological forecasting, opportunity evaluation, establishment of goals and strategies, capability assessment, project and program evaluation and selection, resource allocation, project planning and control, and mission budgeting. The implementation of such a conceptual planning framework has achieved two major objectives. First, it has made possible the practical application of forecasting information (including Delphi data) to the generation of research options and opportunities and also to the evaluation and selection of various programs and projects. Second, it has emphasized the need for and the importance of strategic planning—an activity that is a direct responsibility of top research management. Furthermore, it has pointed out the obvious fact that planning and forecasting cannot take place in isolation and is not the sole responsibility of a planning staff. The success of this effort thus far has resulted from the fact that the planning staff is considered part of a continuing R&D process. Currently the planning staff responsibilities include technological forecasting, long-range planning, technical intelligence, project planning and resource allocation, budgeting, financial analysis, and operations research.

As noted, one of the major inputs to the planning cycle is a technological forecast. In addition to intraumural and extramural Delphi studies, normative forecasting studies have been conducted in an attempt to identify areas of significant and major medical need. Published forecast information has also been gathered, and this, together with the internally sponsored exploratory and normative forecast studies, has been used to construct scenarios of alternative futures. From this information bank potential opportunities are selected on the basis of commercial and technical considerations. These "areas of opportunity" are reviewed by research management, which selects from this list the ones which it wishes to have analyzed further in terms of their technical and commercial feasibility and the rewards that might be associated with various levels of investment.

A member of the research staff is then assigned to each one of these opportunity evaluations. Working with R&D and marketing research personnel, as well as outside consultants and experts in the field, he assesses the current technical state of the art, gathers information relevant to the commercial feasibility of the opportunity, and reduces all these data to investment recommendations highlighting both the cost and the potential benefits of the proposed management actions. These "opportunity evaluations" are incorporated into an "Annual Opportunity Forecast," which also includes a series of scenarios describing possible futures in areas highly relevant to the future of pharmaceuticals and is prefaced by an outline of the purpose, goals, and strategies of research and development. The R&D management reviews these recommendations and evaluates the potential of each in relationship to current commitments. A list of candidates for funding is then prepared. Each mission is further described in terms of its objective, feasibility, commercial potential, and the resources necessary to meet the objective, and a series of check points toward reaching the mission goal is drawn up.

A number of models have been constructed which permit management to relate economic potential and technical feasibility as an aid in its decision-making process, for both the selection of projects and the allocation of resources. Budgets are prepared which relate resource allocation (dollars) to selected missions. To assist project managers in planning their programs and exercising project control, network analysis (CPM and PERT) has been applied to all development projects and some research programs. Monthly reports highlighting significant deviations in project plans permit management to consider alternative courses of action.

As mentioned earlier, the Delphi technique has been employed for technological forecasting purposes. As with other forecast information, the application of these data to informed management action has been a source of concern. It has been found, however, that the data can be useful in identifying possible opportunities, but only when they are combined with other forecast information from normative studies and intuitive judgments of the research and administrative staff responsible for evaluating opportunities.

Two major Delphi studies have been completed. The remaining portion of this discussion describes the problems encountered, as well as some of the data derived from this work.

Intramural Delphi. Before the extramural Delphi study was conducted, two questionnaires were formulated and distributed to 196 members of the company's own R&D staff. In the first of these questionnaires the participants were asked to list the advances, breakthroughs, innovations, and trends which they considered to be importunate and feasible within the next 50 years in the areas of biomedical research and drug therapy. The second questionnaire asked the participants to designate, for each item, the time when they thought there would be a 50% probability that the event would be completed or widely accepted. The results of this study were most interesting and encouraging; however, the following problems were encountered:

1. *Ambiguity of questions or terms.* Many of the questions were worded ambiguously. Although this was unavoidable to a certain extent, greater care was taken in this regard in the later study.

2. *Duplications of responses.* On the first questionnaire, many of the participants' responses were similar or, in actuality, represented only minor variations on the same theme. On subsequent questionnaires, however, it was specified that only the clearest of similar suggestions should be proposed.

3. *Number of questions.* The second questionnaire consisted of 204 items. As the results illustrated, this was too great a concentration of questions in one area of inquiry. In subsequent studies, the number was kept to a minimum.

4. *Random order of presentation.* The items in the second questionnaire were presented in a random order which required the participants to constantly vary their frames of reference. Since this appeared to bother some of the respondents, the questionnaires are now formulated so that the questions are grouped according to subject matter.

Extramural Delphi. In formulating this Delphi, the study was divided into five sections, believed to be the most useful ones in long-range planning for a pharmaceutical company:

1. Biomedical research.
2. Diagnosis.
3. Medical therapy.
4. Health care.
5. Medical education.

Because of the close relationship among these topics, a single panel of experts was considered sufficient.

In the first questionnaire, each of the sections was briefly defined, and the participants were asked to list the breakthroughs, discoveries, and changes in method which they thought might occur in the next 50 years. The second questionnaire grouped the statements by subsections, as well as by the five main sections of inquiry.

In order to determine the level of expertise, each panelist was asked to rate his knowledge of the area by checking the appropriate answer: awareness, reading, or working. Members were also asked to rate the medical and social-ethical desirability of each event described.

Results of the Delphi. One hundred eleven individuals were contacted by mail and asked to participate in the study. The primary occupations of these individuals indicated that they possessed expertise in various sections of inquiry which would be applicable to a study of this type. From the 111 individuals initially contacted, a positive response was received from 78, and these people were then sent the first questionnaire to complete. Forty-two questionnaires were completed and returned for evaluation. From these 42 participants, a total of 867 statements or predictions was suggested for the five categories. Since many of these statements were very similar, they were combined in the formulation of the second questionnaire.

After the data from the first questionnaire had been compiled, a second one was sent out to all 78 individuals who had originally agreed to participate, regardless of whether or not they had completed the first questionnaire. Forty-one respondents returned the second questionnaire, but 1 was completed incorrectly and 5 arrived too late, leaving 35 questionnaires for final tabulation.

The following table compares the number of statements received in the first questionnaire with the number *used* in the second questionnaire.

Section	Number of Statements/ Predictions Received in Questionnaire 1	Number of Statements/ Predictions Used in Questionnaire 2
Biomedical research	238	71
Diagnosis	130	21
Medical therapy	219	75
Health care	142	29
Medical education	138	13
Totals	867	209

Figures 1 and 2 summarize the results of the questionnaires for the section on biomedical research; Figures 3 and 4, for the section on medical therapy.

BIOMEDICAL RESEARCH
MEDIAN AND QUARTILES

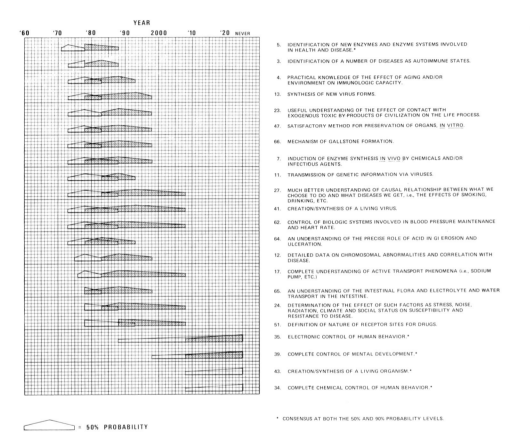

YEAR

'60   '70   '80   '90   2000   '10   '20 NEVER

5. IDENTIFICATION OF NEW ENZYMES AND ENZYME SYSTEMS INVOLVED IN HEALTH AND DISEASE.*

3. IDENTIFICATION OF A NUMBER OF DISEASES AS AUTOIMMUNE STATES.

4. PRACTICAL KNOWLEDGE OF THE EFFECT OF AGING AND/OR ENVIRONMENT ON IMMUNOLOGIC CAPACITY.

13. SYNTHESIS OF NEW VIRUS FORMS.

23. USEFUL UNDERSTANDING OF THE EFFECT OF CONTACT WITH EXOGENOUS TOXIC BY-PRODUCTS OF CIVILIZATION ON THE LIFE PROCESS.

47. SATISFACTORY METHOD FOR PRESERVATION OF ORGANS, IN VITRO.

66. MECHANISM OF GALLSTONE FORMATION.

7. INDUCTION OF ENZYME SYNTHESIS IN VIVO BY CHEMICALS AND/OR INFECTIOUS AGENTS.

11. TRANSMISSION OF GENETIC INFORMATION VIA VIRUSES.

27. MUCH BETTER UNDERSTANDING OF CAUSAL RELATIONSHIP BETWEEN WHAT WE CHOOSE TO DO AND WHAT DISEASES WE GET, i.e., THE EFFECTS OF SMOKING, DRINKING, ETC.

41. CREATION/SYNTHESIS OF A LIVING VIRUS.

62. CONTROL OF BIOLOGIC SYSTEMS INVOLVED IN BLOOD PRESSURE MAINTENANCE AND HEART RATE.

64. AN UNDERSTANDING OF THE PRECISE ROLE OF ACID IN GI EROSION AND ULCERATION.

12. DETAILED DATA ON CHROMOSOMAL ABNORMALITIES AND CORRELATION WITH DISEASE.

17. COMPLETE UNDERSTANDING OF ACTIVE TRANSPORT PHENOMENA (i.e., SODIUM PUMP, ETC.)

65. AN UNDERSTANDING OF THE INTESTINAL FLORA AND ELECTROLYTE AND WATER TRANSPORT IN THE INTESTINE.

24. DETERMINATION OF THE EFFECT OF SUCH FACTORS AS STRESS, NOISE, RADIATION, CLIMATE AND SOCIAL STATUS ON SUSCEPTIBILITY AND RESISTANCE TO DISEASE.

51. DEFINITION OF NATURE OF RECEPTOR SITES FOR DRUGS.

35. ELECTRONIC CONTROL OF HUMAN BEHAVIOR.*

39. COMPLETE CONTROL OF MENTAL DEVELOPMENT.*

43. CREATION/SYNTHESIS OF A LIVING ORGANISM.*

34. COMPLETE CHEMICAL CONTROL OF HUMAN BEHAVIOR.*

* CONSENSUS AT BOTH THE 50% AND 90% PROBABILITY LEVELS.

= 50% PROBABILITY

= 90% PROBABILITY

Figure 1   Future of biomedical research.

AREA / Knowledge of Area	BIOMEDICAL RESEARCH STATEMENT	MEDICAL NEED — Very Necessary	Necessary	Unnecessary	No. of Responses	SOCIAL-ETHICAL DESIRABILITY — Very Desirable	Desirable	Undesirable	Don't Care	No. of Responses	NUMBER OF YEARS IN WHICH EVENT COULD OCCUR — 50% Chance — Median	Inter-quartile Range	No. of Responses	90% Chance — Median	Inter-quartile Range	No. of Responses	Never
Immunology Working 7 Reading 16 Awareness 10	1. Complete understanding of mechanisms and factors involved in immunological response	79 %	21 %		33	76 %	18 %		6 %	33	15	10-25	24	30	20-40	25	3
	2. Chemical synthesis of specific antibodies	28 %	56 %	16 %	32	28 %	59 %		13 %	32	10	10-20	28	25	15-40	25	2
	3. Identification of a number of diseases as autoimmune states.	68 %	32 %		31	55 %	39 %		6 %	31	10	5-10	28	15	10-20	28	6
	4. Practical knowledge of the effect of aging and/or environment on immunologic capacity.	48 %	52 %		33	41 %	59 %			32	10	5-15	31	20	10-25	29	1
Enzymology 9 9 8	5. Identification of new enzymes and enzyme systems involved in health and disease.	67 %	33 %		33	56 %	37 %		7 %	32	5	3-10	27	10	10-20	27	1
	6. Complete knowledge of mechanism of action of enzymes.	50 %	43 %	7 %	32	47 %	43 %		10 %	30	20	10-25	25	30	25-40	20	
	7. Induction of enzyme synthesis *in vivo* by chemicals and/or infectious agents.	50 %	43 %	7 %	30	50 %	40 %		10 %	30	10	5-20	25	20	10-30	21	
	8. Partial or complete understanding of factors involved in biosynthesis of enzymes.	57 %	40 %	3 %	30	52 %	45 %		3 %	29	10	5-20	27	20	10-30	24	
Genetics 7 18 2	9. Acquisition of data necessary for establishment of human eugenic programs, either for prevention of disease or for transmission of superior and desirable human traits, i.e., genetic engineering.	45 %	49 %	6 %	31	42 %	48 %	10 %		31	15	10-20	27	30	25-40	21	3
	10. Understanding of the effect of the environment (radiation, pollution, noise, etc.) on genetic material.	74 %	26 %		31	72 %	28 %			32	10	5-20	28	25	10-40	25	3
	11. Transmission of genetic information via viruses.	52 %	41 %	7 %	29	50 %	40 %		7 %	30	10	5-20	27	20	15-25	22	1
	12. Detailed data on chromosomal abnormalities and correlation with disease.	69 %	28 %	3 %	32	62 %	34 %	3 %	4 %	32	10	7-15	28	20	15-30	24	

Figure 2 Future of medical therapy.

Molecular Biology

Knowledge of Area		
Awareness	Reading	Working
10	14	6

#	Item																
13.	Synthesis of new virus forms.	9%	63%	28%	32	3%	56%	6%	6%	35%	32	10	5–15	29	25	10–30	25	5
14.	Complete data on membrane structure and cellular organization.	67%	33%		33	46%	48%	6%		6%	33	20	10–30	26	40	25–40	22	3
15.	Understanding of factors which control function at the molecular level.	76%	24%		33	55%	39%	6%		6%	33	20	10–25	28	40	25–40	23	1
16.	Complete understanding of photosynthetic energy transduction.	36%	48%	16%	31	29%	61%	10%		10%	31	15	10–25	28	30	20–40	23	2
17.	Complete understanding of active transport phenomena (i.e., sodium pump).	79%	21%		33	55%	36%	9%		9%	33	10	8–15	29	20	15–40	26	2
18.	Detailed understanding of molecular changes involved in cell division, cell differentiation, and dedifferentiation.	70%	27%	3%	33	61%	30%	9%		9%	33	20	10–25	27	30	20–40	21	4
19.	Molecular mechanisms of brain function in health and disease.	84%	16%		32	75%	25%				32	20	15–30	26	40	30–40	21	4

Aging

Knowledge of Area		
Awareness	Reading	Working
11	16	4

#	Item																
20.	Discovery of fundamental mechanisms of aging.	71%	26%	3%	34	68%	26%	3%	3%		34	20	10–25	32	30	25–40	21	
21.	Ability to prevent, delay, or reverse the aging process.	44%	26%	30%	34	38%	28%	28%		6%	32	25	15–N	21	40	30–N	16	9
22.	Understanding of major role for nutrition, environment, and infectious diseases in the aging process.	56%	41%	3%	34	53%	44%	3%		3%	34	20	10–25	29	30	20–40	22	2

Environment

Knowledge of Area		
Awareness	Reading	Working
8	14	4

#	Item																
23.	Useful understanding of the effect of contact with exogenous toxic byproducts of civilization on the life process.	82%	18%		34	85%	15%			3%	34	10	5–15	31	20	15–30	26	1
24.	Determination of the effect of such factors as stress, noise, radiation, climate, and social status on susceptibility and resistance to disease.	68%	29%	3%	34	76%	21%	3%		3%	34	10	10–20	29	20	15–40	24	2
25.	Engineered control of environment (i.e., domed cities).	14%	43%	43%	33	18%	43%	24%	24%	15%	33	25	25–N	22	40	40–N	15	8
26.	Control of intrauterine and extrauterine environment of the child and an understanding of effects on development	38%	53%	9%	32	42%	52%	3%	3%		33	15	10–25	27	30	25–40	22	1
27.	Much better understanding of causal relationship between what we choose to do and what diseases we get, i.e., the effects of smoking, drinking, etc.	68%	32%		34	76%	24%			3%	33	10	5–20	30	25	15–40	25	2
28.	Meaningful data on transfer of disease by physical agents, i.e., cocarcinogens, etc.	76%	24%		34	82%	15%			3%	34	10	7–20	32	25	15–30	26	

117

AREA	BIOMEDICAL RESEARCH STATEMENT	MEDICAL NEED				SOCIAL-ETHICAL DESIRABILITY					NUMBER OF YEARS IN WHICH EVENT COULD OCCUR						
											50 % Chance			90 % Chance			
		Very Necessary	Necessary	Unnecessary	No. of Responses	Very Desirable	Desirable	Undesirable	Don't Care	No. of Responses	Median	Inter-quartile Range	No. of Responses	Median	Inter-quartile Range	No. of Responses	Never
Population Control Knowledge of Area (3, 17, 3)	29. Complete understanding of hormonal control of fertility.	62 %	35 %	3 %	34	68 %	32 %			34	10	7–20	31	25	15–40	24	2
	30. Control of sexual development, i.e., create males, females, and possibly neuters.	6 %	12 %	82 %	33	6 %	13 %	62 %	19 %	32	40	10–N	16	40	30–N	12	12
Nutrition (9, 14, 7)	31. Worldwide elimination of malnutrition and associated diseases.	82 %	18 %		33	88 %	12 %			33	40	20–N	16	N	40–N	12	16
	32. Understanding of role of nutrition in etiology of degenerative diseases.	71 %	29 %		34	71 %	26 %		3 %	34	20	10–25	32	30	20–40	25	1
	33. Development of new food sources (algae, plankton, etc.) for mass consumption, which are grown in an artificial environment.	59 %	32 %	9 %	34	74 %	20 %		6 %	34	10	10–25	31	25	20–30	25	
Learning, Memory, Intelligence, Thought Knowledge of Area Working 5 Reading 12 Awareness 11	34. Complete chemical control of human behavior.	15 %	18 %	67 %	33	16 %	12 %	69 %	3 %	32	N	40–N	7	N	N	5	21
	35. Electronic control of human behavior	3 %	16 %	81 %	32	6 %	13 %	71 %	10 %	31	N	20–N	10	N	40–N	9	17
	36. Full understanding of mechanisms involved in memory	60 %	30 %	10 %	33	52 %	45 %		3 %	31	25	20–N	20	40	40–N	14	10
	37. Control of biochemical factors involved in intelligence.	38 %	34 %	28 %	32	36 %	46 %	15 %	3 %	33	25	20–N	21	40	25–N	17	8
	38. Control of biochemical factors involved in mood.	39 %	49 %	12 %	33	33 %	55 %	9 %	3 %	33	10	10–25	24	25	20–40	22	5
	39. Complete control of mental development	40 %	10 %	50 %	30	27 %	21 %	46 %	6 %	33	N	30–N	8	N	40–N	8	19
	40. Chemical transfer of information via transplanted RNA.	23 %	42 %	35 %	31	26 %	39 %	19 %	16 %	31	30	20–N	19	40	40–N	15	9

No.	Item																
41.	Creation or synthesis of a living virus.	25%	41%	34%	32	25%	47%	3%	25%	32	10	5–20	24	25	10–40	17	2
42.	Creation or synthesis of a living cell.	23%	37%	40%	30	23%	52%	6%	19%	31	N	25–N	12	N	40–N	11	16
43.	Creation or synthesis of a living organism.	21%	24%	55%	29	25%	36%	18%	21%	28	N	40–N	9	N	N	5	21
44.	Development of methods for stimulation of regrowth of tissues or organs.	64%	33%	3%	30	63%	34%	3%		32	20	15–30	22	40	30–40	18	5
45.	Synthesis of artificial messenger RNA which will stimulate synthesis of proteins, cells, or organs.	48%	45%	6%	29	44%	53%	3%		32	20	10–30	21	30	20–40	18	
46.	Control of cellular reproduction to permit growth of organs from tissue or undifferentiated cells.	40%	43%	17%	30	44%	50%	6%		32	25	15–N	21	40	30–N	17	9
47.	Satisfactory method for preservation of organs *in vitro*.	61%	36%	3%	33	67%	27%	3%	3%	33	10	5–15	29	20	10–30	26	1

Life Creation | 12 | 11 | | 2 |

Organ Synthesis or Preservation | 11 | 16 | | 2 |

Figure 2   Future of medical therapy. (*Continued*)

119

MEDICAL THERAPY
MEDIAN AND QUARTILES

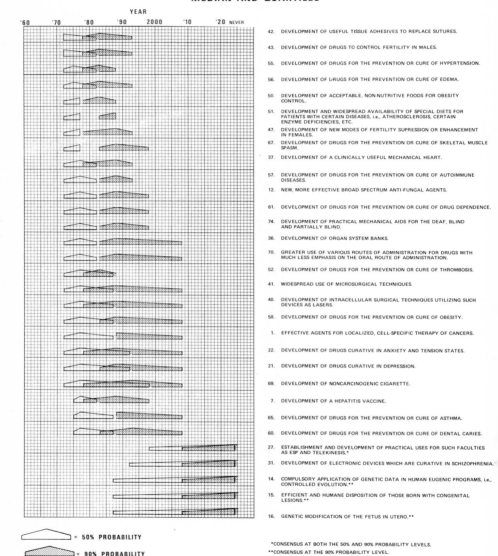

Figure 3

| AREA | MEDICAL THERAPY STATEMENT | MEDICAL NEED | | | | SOCIAL-ETHICAL DESIRABILITY | | | | | NUMBER OF YEARS IN WHICH EVENT COULD OCCUR | | | | | | |
| | | | | | | | | | | | 50% Chance | | | 90% Chance | | | |
		Very Necessary	Necessary	Unnecessary	No. of Responses	Very Desirable	Desirable	Undesirable	Don't Care	No. of Responses	Median	Inter-quartile Range	No. of Responses	Median	Inter-quartile Range	No. of Responses	Never
Cancer Knowledge of Area — Working 5, Reading 17, Awareness 7	1. Effective agents for localized, cell-specific therapy of cancers.	90 %	10 %		31	88 %	6 %		6 %	31	10	5–20	28	20	20–40	25	1
	2. Development of broad-spectrum anticancer agents.	74 %	23 %	3 %	31	84 %	10 %	3 %	3 %	31	20	10–30	24	40	25–40	23	
	3. Development of anticancer vaccines.	77 %	23 %		31	84 %	13 %		3 %	31	15	10–25	29	30	20–40	23	
	4. Development of physical methods (X-ray, lasers, irradiation) that are completely curative in cancer.	56 %	28 %	16 %	32	61 %	21 %	6 %	12 %	33	20	10–N	18	40	25–N	16	
Infectious Diseases — Working 6, Reading 13, Awareness 4	5. Development of effective "common cold" vaccines.	69 %	28 %	3 %	33	64 %	33 %		3 %	33	10	10–30	26	25	20–40	22	
	6. Development of effective broad-spectrum antiviral agents.	69 %	31 %		32	70 %	24 %		6 %	33	20	10–25	29	30	20–40	26	
	7. Development of a hepatitis vaccine.	74 %	26 %		31	63 %	34 %		3 %	32	10	8–15	30	20	10–30	25	
	8. Almost complete eradication of the common epidemic diseases via world-wide immunization programs.	61 %	39 %		33	68 %	32 %			34	25	20–N	22	40	30–N	17	11
	9. Widespread use of sterile areas in the treatment of patients with infectious diseases or for the quarantine of such patients.	29 %	26 %	45 %	31	37 %	40 %	16 %	7 %	30	11	5–40	22	25	10–N	16	6
	10. Effective treatment of most parasitic infestations.	71 %	29 %		34	71 %	23 %		6 %	34	15	10–25	29	30	20–40	23	1
	11. Use of synthetic antibodies to counteract infection.	38 %	47 %	15 %	32	37 %	48 %	9 %	6 %	33	20	15–40	23	40	20–N	17	7
	12. New, more effective broad-spectrum antifungal agents.	50 %	41 %	3 %	32	58 %	36 %	3 %	3 %	31	10	5–15	27	20	15–30	24	1

121

No.	Item															
13.	Development of drugs or mechanical devices for directly altering genetic material, thus controlling hereditary defects.	39%	39%	22%	31	37%	45%	18%		33	30	15–N	19	40	40–N	14	12
14.	Compulsory application of genetic data in human eugenic programs, i.e., controlled evolution.	13%	29%	58%	31	13%	28%	53%	6%	32	N	20–N	14	N	40–N	7	15
15.	Efficient and humane disposition of those born with congenital lesions	10%	45%	45%	31	12%	44%	44%		32	N	20–N	14	N	40–N	10	15
16.	Genetic modification of the fetus *in utero*.	21%	29%	50%	28	17%	37%	43%	3%	30	N	20–N	13	N	40–N	10	15
17.	Development of drugs that alter memory and learning processes.	37%	50%	13%	30	42%	52%	3%	3%	31	15	10–30	27	30	20–40	21	3
18.	Development of drugs that alter intellectual performance.	37%	40%	23%	30	39%	48%	3%	10%	31	10	10–30	24	25	20–40	18	5
19.	Development of drugs capable of controlling personality and behavior and their development and change.	41%	18%		29	40%	40%	17%	3%	30	15	10–30	24	40	20–40	20	6
20.	Development of drugs curative in schizophrenia.	77%	20%	3%	31	81%	16%	3%		32	25	10–40	24	40	20–N	18	7
21.	Development of drugs curative in depression.	82%	15%	3%	33	76%	21%	3%		33	10	5–25	25	20	15–40	21	6
22.	Development of drugs curative in anxiety and tension states.	70%	27%	3%	33	66%	28%		6%	32	10	5–25	25	20	10–40	21	5
23.	Widespread, accepted, and rational use of mind-expanding (psychedelic) drugs	13%	22%	65%	32	10%	27%	53%	10%	32	25	10–N	18	40	20–N	15	12
24.	Development of drugs that can cure or prevent mental retardation.	63%	31%	6%	32	63%	37%			32	40	15–N	17	N	30–N	12	14

Knowledge of Area		Genetics	The Mind
	Working	2	6
	Reading	15	12
	Awareness	8	8

Figure 4

Merck & Company, Inc.

CONTACT: JOSEPH M. FOX

The Merck Company comprises four main divisions and two subsidiaries. Each division operates with "decentralized" management, but the combined plans and finances are monitored by the corporate staff.

Most research takes place in the Research Laboratories, which constitutes one of the divisions. There is a great deal of interaction between the Research Laboratories and the other divisions, so that much of the research performed is need oriented or else has good market potential.

Development is regarded as a completely separate function from research. If a research project is deemed suitable for development, it goes before the Research and Development Committee, whose members, if they think it appropriate, request a development proposal. This contains a fairly detailed analysis of the program objectives, the methods for accomplishing them, and the manpower and funding necessary. Although it is now believed that a market analysis should also be included, this has not yet been accomplished. The development procedure is coordinated bimonthly to resolve differences and to monitor the programs.

The planning horizon for the divisions is 5 years, with annual updating. Each division has its own procedures for planning and for the annual presentation of its plans; however, if there are no changes in the plans from one year to the next, a division is not required to make a presentation. Although there are requirements for commitments, these are not mandatory.

Inputs from any departments within the divisions—in terms of new ideas, requests, and the like—are reviewed hierarchically.

The Research Division planning involves three distinct activities: research program plans, which deal with the scientific programs; long-range plans, which deal with important but nonscientific questions, such as facilities, personnel, and government relationships; and technological forecasts, which present assessments of the future environments but do not give implications or possible methods of achieving those environments. To emphasize that long-range planning starts in the present, it is usually referred to as "strategic programming."

The company realized that, in order to select programs for research and then development, it was necessary to consider such factors as the environment, both from a technological and from a marketing point of view. Approximately 2 years ago, therefore, the Research Task Force Groups were formed to look into these problems. Thirteen groups were set up, each with its own field of therapy, and one group to look into potential new research programs. The groups consider future technologies within the future environment. Their forecasts take the form of what will be, but their level of sophistication varies considerably, as some of the people involved suffer from "tunnel vision," whereas others have vivid imaginations. The groups meet on an *ad hoc* basis every 2 or 3 months, and marketing representatives are invited to at least one of these meetings during the year. Moreover, the marketeer associated with each particular area of the forecast sees the results, so that he can use them as he feels necessary.

These technological forecasts are circulated on a selected basis within the Research Division, as an input to its planning process. Although the task force is really a filter for ideas, at present it suffers from a lack of guidance, as far as forecasting is concerned.

Despite the quantitative aspects of the research program plans and the long-range plans, Research Division planning is essentially on a qualitative basis. Intuition and such factors as intrinsic value play a large part.

VIII. *Aerospace*

Minds are like parachutes; they only function when open.   Thomas Robert

INTRODUCTION

As mentioned earlier, the aerospace industry suffers from problems similar to those encountered in the electronics industry, but to an even greater degree. The field is narrower, the project or product tends to be of greater magnitude, and the competition is solely between the few large companies involved: there are no small companies in the aerospace business. The industry, which comprises, primarily, missiles and aircraft, has the federal government as its major customer; in fact, 81% of the dollars spent in R&D in this field come from the government. This has its advantages, but because of the peculiar characteristics of this type of business the scope of the R&D has become extremely limited.

In terms of the applied research, and even exploratory development performed by the industry, the companies are forced to "second-guess" the customer's needs. This often involves having several approaches to the same problem underway at the same time, so that, whichever way the Defense Department swings, at least one program is already aimed in the right direction. Not only does this prove extremely costly, but also the resources utilized could have been employed on in-house R&D projects. However, as the prime interest lies in developing systems applicable to the customer, most aerospace companies do not attempt to market detailed technology items, but try rather to apply state-of-the-art development to these needs. With a few exceptions, the method of devel-

125

opment follows a pattern of conceptual design approaches to the customer's needs, with identification of the leverage technology items which would provide the most advanced system. Often, a part of the organization is involved solely with keeping abreast of specialized technology developments throughout industry, and applying them to potential systems requirements. However, there are occasions, particularly if the marketing prospects look good, when large investments will be made in order to provide a technical breakthrough, or an order-of-magnitude change in a technology, for a specific application.

It is rather strange that, although several formal methods of technological forecasting have been proposed (and sometimes implemented in limited areas) at the R&D planning level, they have not been accepted at the corporate level. Top management appears to shy away from quantitative, formal techniques and to prefer a "committee" approach, where it, together with the contributor to and the user of the forecasts, integrates the technology available and the system requirements with the customer's needs. Usually, the user is the system manager, who will specify the technology areas he wishes to be forecast. The contributor then works with the user to identify alternative approaches which could serve the purpose. Their combined normative forecast is presented to top management.

The aerospace companies chosen for our study represent both parent companies, with over $2 billion per year sales, and also specific divisions, with $½ billion sales. Of these companies, 80% have programs for forecasting, although, as mentioned earlier, they are used to only a limited extent. In one case, an environmental forecast performed by a parent company was extremely well done and provided an excellent scenario, but more specific forecasts were restricted.

RESULTS OF QUESTIONNAIRE

The results obtained from the questionnaires sent out to 120 companies were as follows.

OBJECTIVES. Almost all the companies have corporate objectives (94%) most of which are written and quantitative. The R&D objectives, although written, are mostly qualitative. The corporate objectives are updated annually; the R&D objectives are generally updated a little more frequently.

FORECASTS. All the forecasts—technological, economic, marketing, and environmental—are almost always made, although to varying degrees, but they are not widely used. The divisions, which have more specific requirements, nearly always use the technological forecast as an aid in planning and the allocation of resources, whereas the parent companies use it much less frequently for these purposes. It is occasionally used to help in acquiring a government contract or subcontract, and sometimes to justify a previously made decision. The forecasts are always prepared by in-house staff, often comprising system specialists, together with operations researchers and technical planners. It was interesting to note that in several cases the marketing staff was not involved in preparing technological forecasts, and in one company the corporate staff was not involved.

FORECASTING AND LONG-RANGE PLANNING. The aerospace companies nearly always formulate specific long-range plans for their R&D efforts. However, in answer to the question, "for how long has forecasting been used in assisting long-range R&D efforts?" the answer was mainly, "For a very long time *informally* in the engineering or R&D departments, but only recently has it been formalized." From one company, the following was received: "The presumption is made that R&D planning is based on technological forecasting—this ignores budgets and customer needs, and the latter can dominate!" this is true, but a forecast can serve to estimate potential customer needs and also to provide the customer with extra information about what he can have. The degree to which technological forecasts are used in the preparation of the long-range plans varies from a limited to a great extent. The techniques preferred were again intuitive, closely followed by trend extrapolation, growth analogy, and trend correlation. Most of the companies have programs involving all four methods, but, surprisingly, the normative forecasts do not constitute as great a percentage as appeared from the interviews. The percentage of the total R&D budget used in the preparation of the long-range plans varies from less than 1% to 5%, but the amount spent on forecasting is negligible. The forecasts are updated annually by a combination of group discussion and individual input. The long-range plans, extending 6–10 years into the future, are updated annually and are then presented in document form to the persons involved in allocating resources. In some companies the responsibility for the formulation of the organization's long-range plans is held by the director of research; in others, by a committee of executive officers.

CONTRIBUTORS TO THE FORECAST. The techniques used by the contributor, in the preparation of his forecast, are the same as those mentioned earlier. It was felt that contributing to a forecast also helped in other aspects of the business, by promoting technology transfer and assisting in the formulation of new programs. Again, the size of the group generating the forecasts ranges from 5 to 20.

USER OF THE FORECAST. On the whole, the forecast is used by laboratory management, planning staff, and individual scientists and engineers; others who make use of the forecast, though not to such a great extent, are marketing staff, programming and budgeting staff, and study groups. Frequency of use varies; the most usual period is yearly, but it is consulted monthly in some cases. The forecasts seem to be used mainly as an input to mid-range (3–8 years) technical planning, as an input to and background for technical and operational studies, and as a means of justifying the budget.

PROJECT SELECTION AND RESOURCE ALLOCATION. The processes used in the aerospace industry for R&D project selection are usually a combination of subjective and quantitative techniques. Each year 20–30% of new R&D work is taken on, and subjective judgment is used to determine the balance between short- and long-term projects. In most companies, the time for development projects is 3–5 years (average, 4 years), whereas the research projects vary in length from 1 to 10 years (average, 7 years). The type of work performed by almost every company includes less than 5% pure research, 30–40% applied research, and over 40% development.

REMARKS. It was felt that some of the questions asked in the questionnaire were too detailed, and that the top management section was too long and complicated for most executives.

CASE STUDIES

The following case studies give examples of the planning and forecasting performed in different types and sizes of aerospace companies, including techniques which are used only in the R&D efforts of the divisions.

Lockheed Aircraft Corporation

CONTACT: HAROLD A. LINSTONE

Lockheed Aircraft Corporation comprises three large and six small divisions. Each division is required to prepare a 10-year plan annually. The plan includes the anticipated lines of business, as well as both profit and functional plans. The lines of business are categorized, with growth

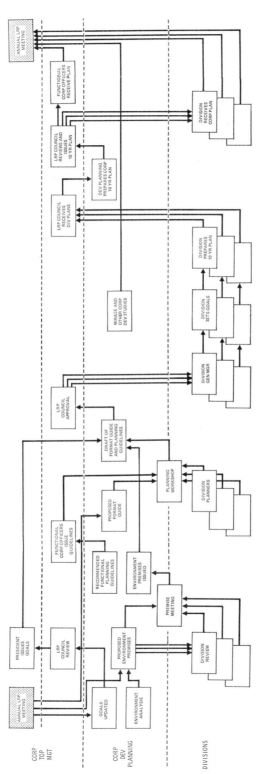

Figure 1 Corporate long-range planning cycle.

rates and sales goals shown for each one. The functional plans cover science and engineering activities, manufacturing and facility plans, marketing, financial operations, administration, and industrial relations. Wherever possible, the division planners are asked to estimate the probabilities associated with each of their programs, the degree of quantification being dependent on the planner's willingness to commit himself.

Figure 1 shows the planning cycle and indicates three levels of activity: corporate top management, Corporate Development Planning Department, and the divisions. Corporate top management includes the principal corporate decision makers individually, as well as the Corporate Long-Range Planning Council, an informal group consisting of half a dozen vice presidents under the chairmanship of an executive vice president. The Corporate Development Planning Department is a corporate analysis staff of about a dozen people. Their background spans business administration, economics, mathematics, operations research, physics, and engineering.

The focal point for the long-range planning activity is the annual long-range planning meeting, which brings together the top corporate and division executives for two full days. There are both formal and informal discussions, speeches, and panels. After the meeting, the Corporate Development Planning Department updates the statement of corporate goals for the forthcoming year. After review by the Corporate Long-Range Planning Council, the proposed goals are finalized by the president.

The Corporate Development Planning Department also develops environmental premises. It may specify alternative future worlds, implying alternative needs and markets. These are transmitted to the various divisions, and a premise meeting is then held jointly with the division planners. The environmental premises subsequently become part of the Planning Guidelines.

Functional planning guidelines are proposed by corporate specialists in the functional areas. At another joint session with the division planners, the proposed Format Guide and Planning Guidelines are reviewed and modified. Drafts of both documents are then submitted to the Corporate Long-Range Planning Council for review and approval. After approval, the Format Guide and Planning Guidelines are issued formally to the divisions, which then proceed to develop their own goals and 10-year plans. Figures 2–5 are excerpts from the Format Guide. The Corporate Development Planning Department may also undertake certain studies on its own, such as the MIRAGE needs analyses, discussed below.

Several months later, the division plans are transmitted to the Cor-

	1969	1970	1971	1972	1973	1974	1975	1976	1977	1978	10-Year Totals
INDEPENDENT EFFORT Bid & proposal											
MSD											
SSD											
R&D											
Total											
Independent development											
MSD											
SSD											
R&D											
General support											
Total											
Independent research											
Total B&P, ID, & IR											
Facilities											
Personnel (thousands) Direct Indirect											
Total											

Figure 2   Resource requirements (Dollars in Millions).

porate Long-Range Planning Council, and the task of integration, analysis, and synthesis by the Corporate Development Planning Department begins. This effort often raises questions whose resolution involves dialog with the divisions. The Council reviews the integrated 10-year plan, and upon approval this Lockheed Master Plan is transmitted to all divisions and corporate officers. The document provides the basis for the next annual long-range planning meeting. Corporate officers and division participants may use parts of this Master Plan as the starting point for their formal or informal discussions at the annual meeting.

Line of Business	1977						1978				
	Facil.	Sales $M		$K			Sales $M		$K		
		Pot.	Goal	B&P	ID	Facil.	Pot.	Goal	B&P	ID	Facil.
Construction Machinery	—	—		—	—	—	—		—	—	—
	—	—		—	—	—	—		—	—	—
	—	—		—	—	—	—		—	—	—
	—	—		—	—	—	—		—	—	—
	—	—		—	—	—	—		—	—	—
	—	—		—	—	—	—		—	—	—
	—	—		—	—	—	—		—	—	—
	—	—		—	—	—	—		—	—	—
	—	—		—	—	—	—		—	—	—
	—	700	310	425	—	—	810	315	475	—	—
Electrical Machinery											
———											
———											

Figure 3

Title	Description
Tractors	1. Pneumatic-tired, two-wheeled, diesel-powered tractors.
	2. Major competition from moving-track vehicles in certain areas; however, cannot replace product.
	3. Under this product are grouped various sizes of tractors which are all produced in same factory by lots.
Scrapers	1. Pneumatic-tired, two-wheeled scraper trailer.
	2. Major competition from dozers in some areas and special scraper vehicles; however, no major threats to market.
	3. No grouping.
Shovels	
Dozers	
Loaders	
Lub seals	Independent research program for high-temperature seal for bearings.
Hydra-control	Independent development program for hydraulic steering of tractors.
Tropical test	Special facility providing tropical environments for testing of tractors, scrapers, shovels, etc.
Auto-machine	Special facility for automatic machinery of standard parts used in tractors, scrapers, and dozers.

Figure 4   Programs—construction machinery.

Event Name	Organization	Description	Schedule	
			Start	Complete
Tractors #1	Marketing	Receive contract for 374 tractors from Army		
Plant Y-2	Manufacturing	Complete construction of Plant 7B, crawler tractor assembly plant—management approval required		
Test #74	Engineering test	Complete operational evaluation of new dozer, Model III, development laboratory		

Figure 5   Events 1968–69—construction machinery.

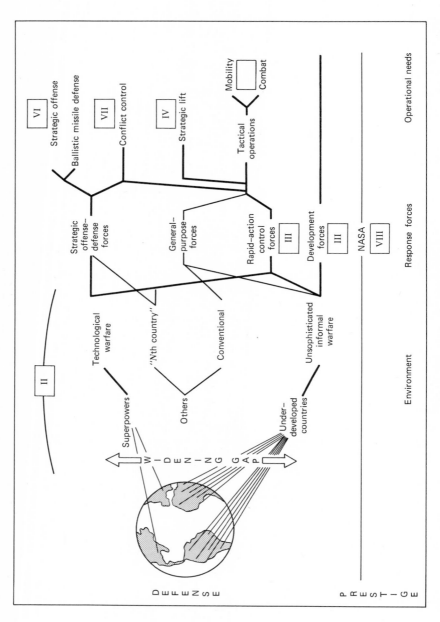

Figure 6 Report outline.

134

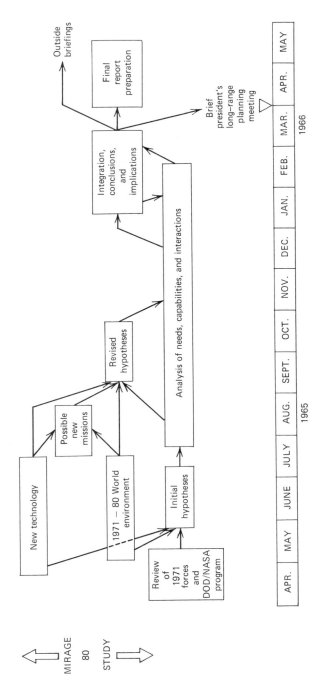

Figure 7 Work outline for MIRAGE 80 study.

135

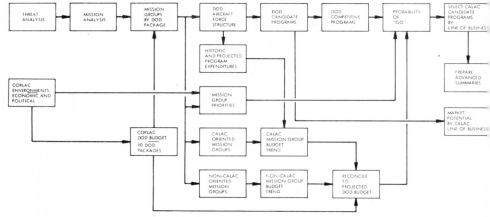

Figure 8   Candidate programs for funding.

The Lockheed Master Plan is *not* designed to be followed slavishly for 10 years. Its primary purposes are to encourage dynamic strategic planning and to provide insight for the improvement of current decision making at all levels.

One of the documents used for guidance of the divisions, as well as of corporate top management, is the MIRAGE study mentioned earlier. This is a long-range forecasting study covering the area which constitutes most of the corporation's business, namely, national security and space. The MIRAGE 80 study, for example, was carried out in 1965–66 and covers the period from 1970 to 1980. The most recent study, MIRAGE 85, extends to 1985.

The typical study includes discussions of the environment (international, socioeconomic, and technological), basic forces (new missions), strategic warfare (total war), strategic lift (air and sea), tactical operations (mobility and combat), conflict control (command and control), NASA, and conclusions. There is also a chapter on implications for the corporation. Figure 6 shows an outline of the nonproprietary portion of such a report.

The MIRAGE studies are undertaken in order to stimulate future thinking. It is believed that excessive reliance on the traditional sources of data in this area are likely to exacerbate the "more of the same but better" syndrome and to hinder creative thinking. The independent and unconstrained outlook possible in such studies is designed, therefore, to facilitate imaginative interaction between new needs and new technology and to identify "good risks" and "poor risks."

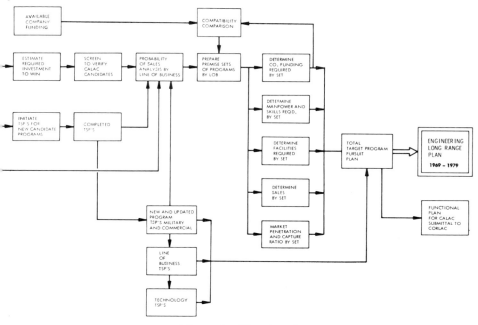

Figure 8   *(Continued)*

Figure 7 shows the work outline for the MIRAGE 80 study. An important aspect of this study was the development at an early stage of hypotheses. These took the form of potential conclusions generated by a committee on future need-technology interactions. Each hypothesis was then subjected to analysis to provide clues to its validity.

It should be emphasized that these studies do not rely on a single model or method of forecasting or analysis. A combination of trend extrapolations, systems analyses (e.g., tradeoff studies), Delphi, mission flow charts, and other tools is used in the analysis. It is also noted that the formats of the divisional 10-year plan and of forecasting studies such as the MIRAGE series vary with time. Rigidity of format leads to routinization, and conformity stifles creativity.

Lockheed-California Company

CONTACT: UGO A. COTY

Lockheed-California Company (Calac) is one of the major divisions of Lockheed Aircraft Corporation; its planning is based on the guidelines given by the corporate headquarters. The basic purpose of Calac's R&D

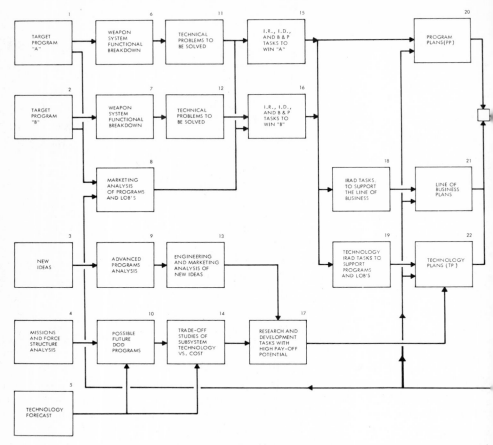

Figure 9   Methodology for research and development planning.

planning is to "determine the fundamental requirements of the missions to be performed, work on the basic technologies that best meet these requirements, and be in a good position to pursue whatever course evolves in the future."

Portions of the long-range R&D planning process are shown in Figures 8 and 9. The candidate programs which start the process in Figure 8 have been previously determined by analysis of the total force structure required to perform defense missions. By using mission priority and operational deficiencies, the future force structure is reconciled with defense budget, which is projected on the basis of a given world economic

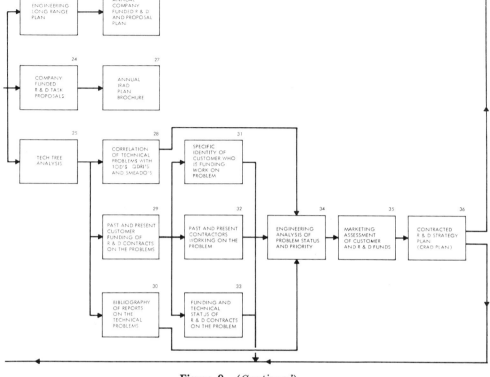

Figure 9   (*Continued*)

and political environment. Candidate programs are identified by mission(s) to be performed, total–life-cycle cost, timing, and probability that the program will be funded. The salient feature of the methodology shown in Figure 8 is that the R&D plan is based on projected company resources available. This precludes a plan which chases every program in sight. Figure 9 indicates the methodology by which possible contracted R&D programs which would supplement the company-funded R&D plan are identified.

Within Calac's planning system, one of the important programs concerns a means of determining the technology requirements for future fighter/attack aircraft. The objective of the program is to identify the technologies which would have the greatest beneficial effect on the future fighter/attack force mix.

Major Objectives	Missions	Mission Targets/Modes

"Control the air" (Air superiority, then air supremacy)	1. *Counterair*	A. *Offensive*
		 (1) Air-to-air (enemy fighters and/or interceptors)
		 (2) Air-to-ground
		   (a) Airfields (b) Parked aircraft
		   (c) Electronic facilities (d) Missile sites
		 B. Defensive
		 (1) Active
		   (a) Intercept
		   (b) Air escort of offensive aircraft
		 (2) Passive
		   All measures except active weapons

"Isolate battle area" (Prevent or hinder enemy use of an area or route)	2. *Interdiction*	A. Transportation and communications lines B. Supply, storage, repair, modification, and manufacturing facilities C. Staging areas and concentration points (includes armed reconnaissance for targets of opportunity)
"Support ground forces" (Neutralize or destroy enemy targets in close proximity to friendly ground forces)	3. *Close air support*	A. Strong points, fortifications B. Troop concentrations C. Armor, artillery, missile sites D. Escort airmobile columns, surface vehicle columns

Figure 10   The tactical air missions (exclusive of special air warfare).

140

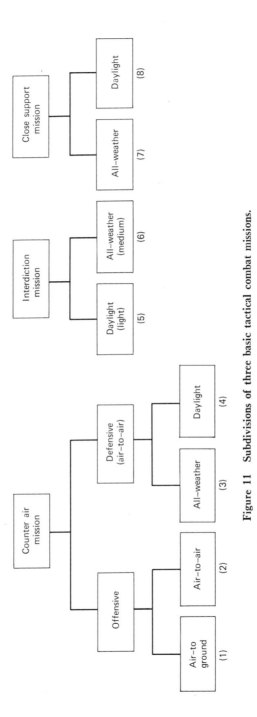

Figure 11 Subdivisions of three basic tactical combat missions.

141

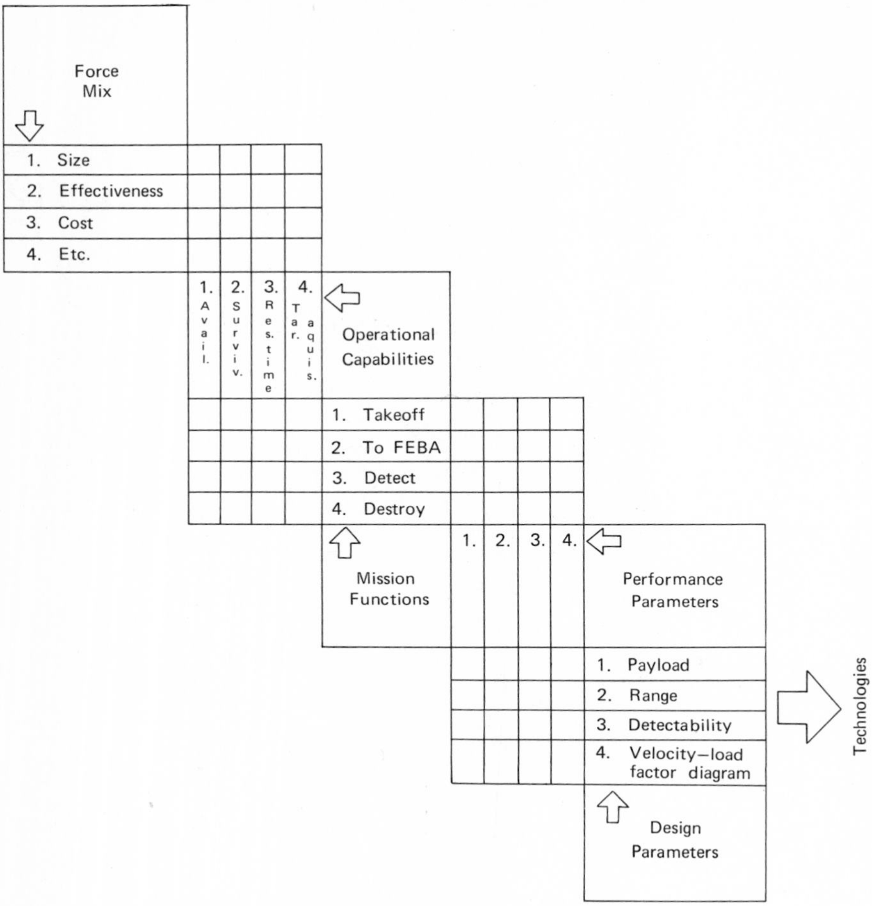

Figure 12   Impact matrix for technology tradeoffs.

The three basic missions which govern the fighter/attack force mix are shown in Figure 10. These can be subdivided into at least eight submissions, as indicated in Figure 11. Now, the approach to identifying a near-optimum force mix is to determine the degree of multimission capability each of the aircraft in the force mix should have. Operational people desire a single-purpose aircraft that can perform one mission better than anything else. Cost-oriented analysts, on the other hand, favor one aircraft that can perform all missions. The former approach is much too expensive; the latter will probably result in aircraft which

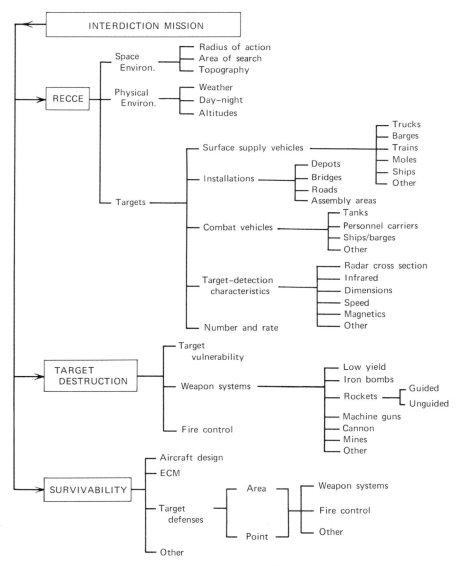

Figure 13 Mission analysis initial layout.

143

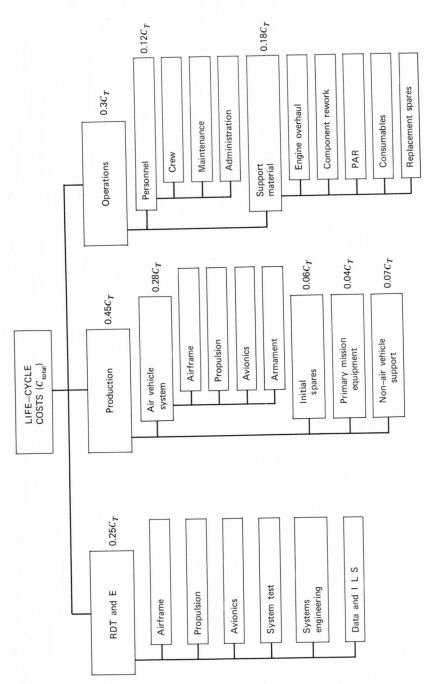

Figure 14 Life-cycle-cost program.

cannot perform any mission well. The best solution generally lies some-where between the two extremes.

The approach being used by Calac is to start with a single-purpose design for each of the submissions of Figure 11. To simplify the initial analysis, assumptions can be made which reduce the number of single-purpose designs. For example, if it is assumed that (a) all-weather close support is not technically feasible during the period of interest, (b) all-weather interceptors can come from the strategic defense interceptors, and (c) one aircraft can be used for daylight air-to-air missions in both offense and defense, only five single-purpose designs remain.

The first step is mission analysis (Figure 12 illustrates the start of one), which provides a means of relating design parameters to mission capabilities. Next, the impact-matrix program (Figure 13) determines the force level required for a given scenario of missions, based on the levels of knowledge which are assumed to be available in the applicable technologies. These assumed levels are varied to measure the sensitivity of force level to technology levels. The life-cycle–cost program (Figure 14), taking into account the assumed levels of technology being applied, calculates the total cost of any force mix.

With these tools available, the cost of the first force mix, consisting of single-purpose designs, can be calculated. The next step is to add an increment of multimission capability to one or more of the single-purpose designs and to note the effects on force mix and total costs. Two constraints must be observed each time that this is done. First, the original mission performance of the aircraft cannot be reduced when the increment of multimission capability is added. This will usually result in an increase in cost for that aircraft. The second constraint is that the force-mix capability must always meet the mission performance requirements of the scenario.

As the process is repeated, the need for some of the original single-purpose aircraft may be completely eliminated. Eventually, force mixes will evolve which indicate that certain combinations of aircraft with particular multimission capabilities result in the lowest total costs. These are the force mixes and the fighter/attack aircraft designs of greatest interest because they are closest to optimum cost effectiveness.

At this point, sensitivity analyses will identify the technologies which have the greatest payoffs in terms of total costs. Allocation of R&D funding can then be determined by three basic criteria:

1. The sensitivity of the system-life-cycle cost to increases in the levels of particular technologies.

2. The estimate of the funding required to achieve a given level of capability and knowledge in each technology.

3. The estimate of the probability of technical success in a given time frame.

Although the entire model is not yet complete, portions have been tested successfully. The indications are that the method is feasible and constitutes a powerful R&D planning tool.

ABC Aerospace Company

Technological forecasting is used, in this aerospace company, to improve planning and budgeting procedures so that the effectiveness of research programs can be increased. To accomplish this purpose, it is first necessary to establish a strategic plan for achieving long- and short-range objectives, and, consistent with this, to set up a long-range corporate development plan and a short-range operations plan.

Before this can be done, it is necessary to have organizational goals which must be communicated to all levels of the organization. Typical of these goals are the following:

- the businesses the company wants to be in
- the general size of the company
- the desired rate of company growth (relative to some base, usually the whole economy)
- the desired direction of growth (by product groupings)
- the percentage of market to be held
- the method of growth intended (acquisition, internal, merger, etc.)
- the degree of diversification sought
- the degree of flexibility desired
- the profit/volume ratio desired (i.e., whether to be a high-volume/low-margin company, or conversely)
- the degree of market stability wanted
- the geographical markets to be attacked
- the company image to be sought
- the allowable degree of dependence on outside suppliers and specific raw materials
- the degree of organization decentralization intended
- the minimum and desired rate of return on capital
- the quality-price market to be competed in
- the kind of ownership desired (broad-base, family-held, public, etc.)
- the degree of government control to be tolerated

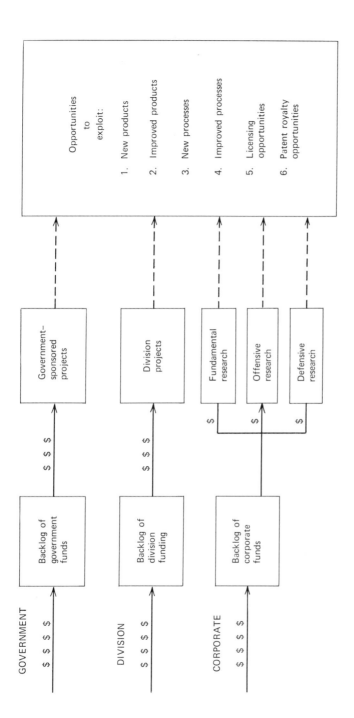

Figure 15 Funding and information flows in a typical industrial research laboratory.

147

	Division 1		Division 2, etc.		$\cdots$
Future Technology Requirement	WO_1	WD_1	WO_2	WD_2	$\sum_{n=1}^{n} WO_n + WD_n = 1.0$
T_1	RO_{11}	RD_{11}	RO_{12}	RD_{12}	
T_2	RO_{21}	RD_{21}	RO_{22}	RD_{22}	
$\cdot$	$\cdot$	$\cdot$	$\cdot$		
$\cdot$	$\cdot$	$\cdot$	$\cdot$		
$\cdot$	$\cdot$	$\cdot$	$\cdot$		

$$\sum_{i=1}^{n} RO_{ij} = 1.0 \quad \sum_{i=1}^{n} RD_{ij} = 1.0$$

Figure 16   Technology relevance assessment.

Long-Range Corporate Development Plan. Once these objectives have been specified, the long-range technology requirements can be established. These, however, are also dependent to a great extent on the funding allocated and on the source of the funding. Figure 15 shows the funding of a typical central research laboratory of a multidivisional firm. With these funding constraints, it is then possible to rank-order the future requirements for fundamental research (see Figure 16) through the assignment of technology relevance numbers. There are, however, offensive and defensive research programs, which require a different type of planning; these will be mentioned later.

The first column of Figure 16 is a compilation of corporate technology requirements—these are considered for a 10-year planning period, which was suggested because the lag between the initiation of a fundamental research project and the implementation of the results is of this order. The technology listing should be related to long-term corporate goals. A relevance number is then assigned to reflect the offensive and defensive technology requirements of each corporate division. For example, in Figure 16 the number RO_{11} represents the percentage of the total projected offensive technology requirements of Division 1 which is related to technology area T_1. The relevance numbers in each of the offensive and defensive columns should sum to 1. A ranking of the criticality of a technology area to the corporate requirements can be formulated by the following equation:

$$H_1 = WO_1RO_{11} + WD_1RD_{11} + WO_2RO_{12} + WD_2RD_{12} + \cdots \quad (1)$$

where H = criticality index of a technology,

   WO = weighting factor reflecting the criticality of a division's need for offensive technology in relation to the needs of other divisions,

   WD = weighting factor reflecting the criticality of a division's need for defensive technology in relation to the needs of other divisions,

   RO = relevance number of offensive technology,

   RD = relevance number of defensive technology.

The weighting factors can be related to the corporation's 10-year sales forecasts as illustrated in Figure 17. For each division using data from the existing corporate 10-year sales forecasts, projections would be made of the total sales and of the distribution of sales from the currently existing product mix and from new products to be added. The offensive and defensive technology weighting factors for a division would be determined as:

$$WO_n = \frac{\text{forecast of } n\text{th division's offensive sales 10 years from current year}}{\text{forecast of total corporate sales 10 years from current year}} \qquad (2)$$

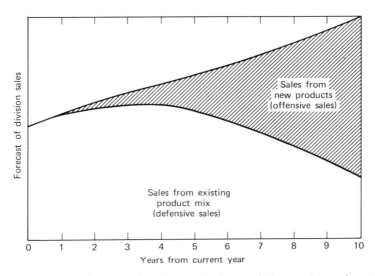

Figure 17   Ten-year forecast of division sales from existing product mix and new products.

$$WD_n = \frac{\begin{array}{c}\text{forecast of } n\text{th division's defensive sales}\\ \text{10 years from current year}\end{array}}{\begin{array}{c}\text{forecast of total corporate sales}\\ \text{10 years from current year}\end{array}} \qquad (3)$$

It can be seen that the summation of the weighting factors for all the corporate divisions equals 1. Solving Eq. 1 for each of the technologies makes possible a rank ordering of the technologies according to their expected criticalities.

It is also necessary to relate technology requirements to scientific disciplines, so that the relevancy of the discipline to the technological area of interest can be determined. This can be accomplished in a manner similar to that above. Figure 18 shows the procedure used. Each relevance number represents the percentage of the technology requirement in a particular area which is contributed by a given discipline (e.g., $20\% \equiv 0.20$). A critically ranking of the disciplines can then be established by multiplying the relevance numbers by the criticality of the technology area, H, and summing for each column. The disciplines having the highest sums are the most critical, and the various disciplines can be arranged in a hierarchy of criticality. On the basis of this information, decisions can be made in regard to the disciplines to be supported, and, if necessary, additional personnel can be hired.

Once these steps have been completed, it remains only to establish

Technology	Thermodynamics	Quantum theory of solids	Electrochemistry	Organic chemistry	Defect solid state	Mathematical analysis	Electromagnetism	Kinetic theory	Continuum mechanics	X-ray crystallography	Superconductivity	Nuclear structure	Stochastics	Zoology	Spectroscopy	Chemistry and physics of surfaces
Propulsion	x			x		x		x	x						x	
Nuclear power	x	x		x	x			x	x	x	x	x			x	
Chemicals		x	x	x						x		x			x	x
Aircraft				x	x			x	x							
Oceanography	x			x			x							x	x	
Computers		x			x	x	x			x	x		x			
Ceramics					x					x						x
Structural metals		x			x			x	x							x

Figure 18   Selection procedure for relevant scientific disciplines (x = relevancy number; see text)

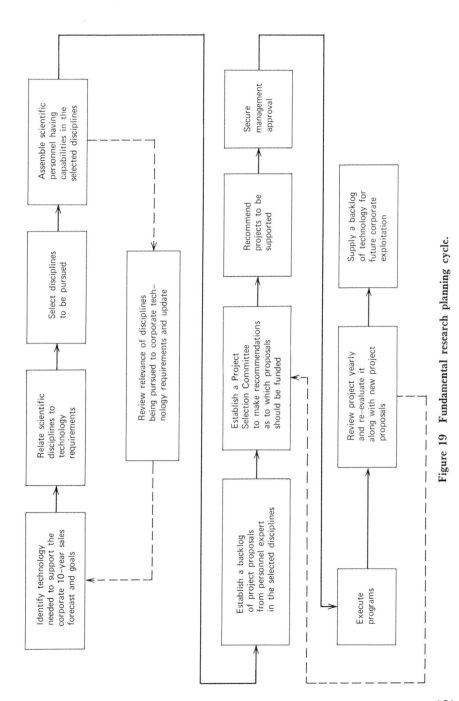

Figure 19 Fundamental research planning cycle.

151

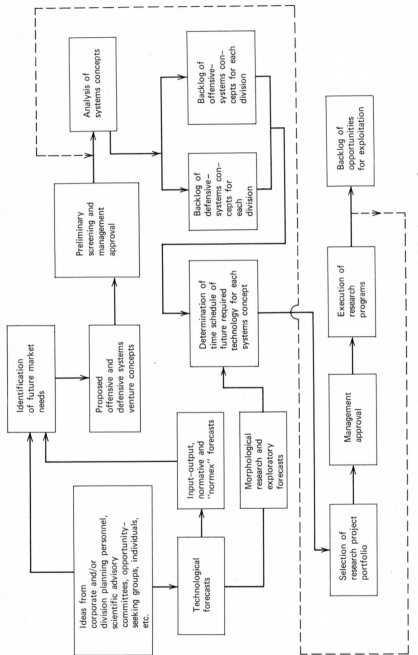

Figure 20 Planning cycle for offensive and defensive research.

152

the methodology for selecting the research projects to be pursued, within the various disciplines.

In the case of fundamental research, project selection is achieved through the use of a Project Selection Committee, made up of a small group who possess scientific expertise and are sensitive to the corporation's objectives and long-term technology requirements. A backlog of project proposals is established by the scientists who are specialists in the various disciplines. Those proposals clearly define the objectives of the various projects and indicate how these objectives are related to corporate technology requirements. They include the overall cost estimated to achieve the objectives, as well as a schedule of required yearly expenditures over the life of the project. The proposals are ranked by the Project Selection Committee, and recommendations made to management. Bayesian statistical concepts can be used as an aid in this project selection process. The planning cycle for fundamental research is shown in Figure 19.

The research planning for offensive and defensive research, as mentioned earlier, is rather different, as it is more applied in nature and is oriented to a greater extent toward new products and existing products. Because the results produced by this form of research are more direct and product related than those from fundamental research, evaluation and planning lend themselves to a more quantified, less intuitive approach. The planning cycle for offensive and defensive research is shown in Figure 20. The first step is to identify needs not currently satisfied, and those which are expected to develop as a result of the changing social-political-economic and technological environments. Technological forecasts are useful in identifying the capabilities of technology to respond to these needs.

A method found to be useful for this purpose is the "normex" technique, which is a combination of exploratory and normative forecasting methods.[1] The point of departure for the application of normex forecasting is an analysis of the salient characteristics of as large a segment of the total market as possible; ideally, it should be based on annual world sales. This analysis should include a determination of the time variation of product market shares and a delineation of the pertinent technological characteristics of the products making up the market.

The next problem which must be faced in applying the normex procedure is that of finding a mathematical function which will provide an adequate approximation to the frequency distribution of sales (or mar-

[1] A. Wade Blackman, "Application of the Normex Forecasting Technique to the Commercial Jet Aircraft Engine Market," *Technological Forecasting,* Vol. 2, No. 2.

ket shares) as functions of pertinent technological performance parameters selected on the basis on their influence on sales.

Histograms used to relate the specific system parameters to market shares in a given year revealed a general skewness in the distributions, with the long tail extending to the right. In this study, it appeared that a normal distribution would not be likely to provide an adequate approximation but that a log-normal distribution might provide the desired characteristics. It would not be implausible to assume that market shares in a given period of time might be determined by the product, rather than the sum, of performance factors, as would be the case with a log-normal distribution. The logarithm of the performance parameter would be the sum of independent random factors; and as the number of these random factors increased, the distribution of the logarithm of the performance parameter would approach the normal distribution according to the central limit theorem.

The characteristics of the log-normal distribution are very appealing; it is a distribution which can be made sufficiently symmetric or asymmetric to yield a good fit to a wide variety of distributions and can be estimated easily in practical applications. Also, the parameters of the distribution can be readily estimated, using either graphic or nongraphic procedures. The graphic procedure may be applied by measuring, on a cumulative frequency plot on log-normal probability paper, the points at which the fitted straight line crosses the 0.5 line and the 0.84

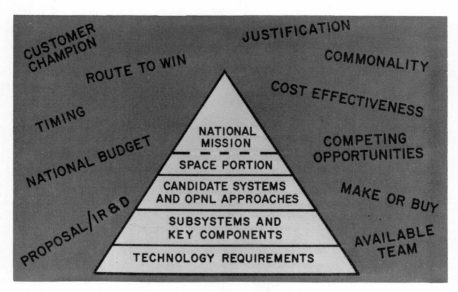

Figure 21   Schematic pyramid.

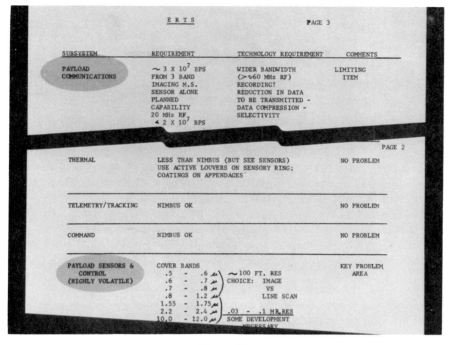

Figure 22

line on the probability scale, and the shape parameters of the underlying normal distribution can be estimated from the following relationships:

$$\mu = \ln X_{0.5} \tag{4}$$

and

$$\sigma = \ln \frac{X_{0.84}}{X_{0.5}} \tag{5}$$

where μ = mean of underlying normal distribution,
σ = standard deviation of underlying normal distribution,
X = variable.

When the shape parameters (μ and σ) are known, a log-normal frequency curve may be fitted to histograms (e.g., constructed by plotting market shares on the ordinate and selected engine performance parameters on the abscissa), utilizing the following equation:

$$Y = \frac{0.398\, Ni}{X\sigma} \exp \frac{-(\ln X - \mu)^2}{2\sigma^2} \tag{6}$$

where Y = value of ordinate,

X = value of abscissa,

N = number of items in sample (e.g., total units sold in a given year),

i = class interval,

μ = mean of underlying normal distribution,

σ = standard deviation of underlying normal distribution.

The analytical procedures utilized in this study may be summarized as follows:

• Historical data were assembled on annual world sales and on the technological performance characteristics of the products which contributed to these annual sales.

• For selected years, histograms were constructed of the frequency distributions of sales as functions of engine performance parameters.

• For each of these histograms, cumulative frequency plots were con-

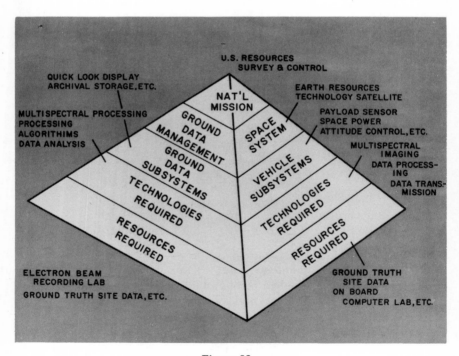

Figure 23

structed on log-normal probability paper, and the mean and standard deviation of the underlying normal distribution were estimated graphically.

- Values of the mean and standard deviation of the underlying normal distributions, as determined for the selected years, were plotted versus time and extrapolated into the future. Similar plots were constructed of annual unit sales and were also extrapolated into the future.
- By use of the extrapolated values obtained in the previous step, frequency distributions of sales as a function of technological performance parameters were calculated, utilizing Eq. 6 for future years of interest.

Conclusions. The results of the forecast gave an indication of the technical requirements for future product designs, and served to assist in the formulation of goals and priorities for future research programs.

The forecast indicated market-oriented tradeoffs between technological performance parameters and indicated the desired interface between technological capability and market demand. It also gave an evaluation

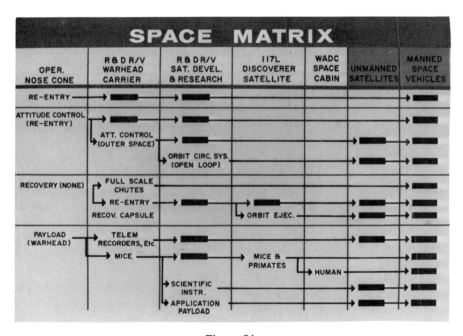

Figure 24

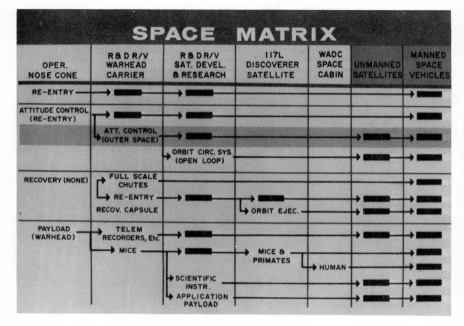

Figure 25

of the mean and variance of the technological parameter forecasts, providing a clear indication of the uncertainty associated with future forecasts.

Thus it can be seen that a forecasting technique such as the one used by the ABC Aerospace Company can provide useful information about the future, upon which planning decisions can be based.

PQR Electric Company—Space Division

Like most large, technically oriented corporations, the PQR Electric Company has found that, unless an organization is structured in a manner which will allow, and even enforce, "technical interaction," a confrontation gap will result. To alleviate this problem, a system of technological cross-support has been established. At the top level of this system is the Corporate Development Council, which is focused on a spectrum of technologies. It is composed of a number of subcouncils, which are staffed by senior technical leaders from each of the technologies involved. One such subcouncil is the Space Division.

The Space Division, like the rest of PQR Electric, has combined its systems planning and research and its technology planning operations into one organization called Mission Requirements and Advanced Programs. As a result, all of the elements, such as requirements, advanced systems engineering, technology planning, and advanced programs, necessary for efficient long-range planning are "under one roof." Also included in this group, and of paramount importance, are resources and resource management. This assures the Space Division of a certain amount of "dollar reality."

To ensure technical interaction or technological cross-support, a Technology Council is in operation. The main function of this council is to see that sufficient resources are directed toward meeting future program requirements. However, this is not its only function. The council also investigates the technical content of programs, both present and proposed, as well as insuring that the advanced technology efforts of the Space Division fulfill the requirements of future missions.

After the Technology Council has determined which missions are of significant importance and interest, a presentation is made to the Space Division. After this is completed, the Council then embarks on the task of formulating a schematic pyramid for each mission, with the national

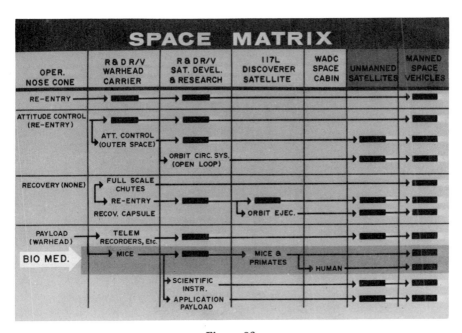

Figure 26

mission itself occupying the apex of this pyramid (Figure 21). The national mission is followed by (a) the candidate systems and operational approaches, (b) the subsystems and key components, and (c) the technology requirements, which form the base of the pyramid. When the requirements thus shown are compared against the state of the art, any discontinuity in the technology becomes obvious. An example constructed for the Earth Resources Technology Satellite is shown in Figure 22.

By comparing or cross-correlating two such pyramids, the Space Division can see whether there is any technology or subsystem commonality. After this is determined, it is possible to establish, on a broader knowledge base, the need for effort in a particular technology or system. This was clearly shown in the common need for a light-weight roll-out solar array power subsystem for eight prospective mission areas (Figure 23).

Since the "pyramid approach" is basically a static one, another method which brings in the dynamics is also used. In this method, called the "road map approach," the "map" shows the flow as well as the development of skills and other relevant factors. The best way is to illustrate it by the use of diagrams from a Space Division case study; these are shown in Figures 24–26.

One of the most important things that this approach enabled the division to do was to face the emergence of a new technology. Although many new technological areas do not survive because of lack of applications, a "critical" technology is pursued even if there is only one apparent use for it.

IX.　*Conglomerates*

It's easier to do a job right than to explain why you didn't.　Martin Van Buren

INTRODUCTION

The very name of this particular industrial category seems pregnant with meaning. Conglomerates are assemblies (sometimes apparently haphazard) of various types of industry, which provide corporate planners with no simple task when it comes to the problem of long-range planning. In fact, these corporations, perhaps more than any other, need to consider a large number of factors which have some effect on the future. Usually, however, conglomerates have an emphasis on some particular industry, and for our case studies we chose one with a bias toward aerospace and one with a bias toward electronics and aerospace.

As is true of most aerospace and electronics companies, there is really only one customer, namely, the federal government—and with it, go all the same problems. On the positive side, one of the advantages of being a conglomerate is the ability to diversify, to look for new areas of interest.

Both of the people contacted for information on their planning systems have been in the planning and forecasting business for a number of years. None of their techniques, however, had such wide acceptance as they had hoped.

RESULTS OF QUESTIONNAIRE

The results of the questionnaires given to the corporations are as follows.

OBJECTIVES. Both companies have written corporate objectives; in one case they are entirely quantitative, and in the other, a combination of quantitative and qualitative. The R&D objectives for both corporations are written and qualitative. All the objectives are updated annually.

FORECASTS. The two companies make technological forecasts and economic, marketing, and environmental forecasts to the same degree within the organization—one makes them all "often"; the other maintains them. The technological forecasts are frequently used as an aid in planning and resource allocation, as well as, in one case, occasionally to help in justifying a previously made decision, and in the other case, occasionally to assist in acquiring a government contract or subcontract. The forecasts are prepared by in-house staff, in conjunction with outside consultants. The in-house staff usually consists of corporate planners, operations research staff, and scientists and engineers, together with project scientists and engineers and marketing staff.

FORECASTING AND LONG-RANGE PLANNING. In both organizations, long-range plans are formulated for R&D efforts in most cases. Although forecasting has been used informally for several years, only in the last 4 years has it been used formally in assisting long-range R&D efforts. In one of the conglomerates, technological forecasting is used to a great extent in preparing long-range plans; in the other, its application is slightly less frequent. The percentage of the R&D budget spent on planning is 5% in one corporation and none in the other; neither organization spends any of its R&D budget on technological forecasting. The two techniques currently in use in both corporations are the intuitive approach (11–20% in one, and 30–40% in the other) and trend correlation (20–30% and 10–20%); trend correlation and growth analogy have either been used previously or considered for use. Only one of the companies produces 20–30% goal-oriented forecasts. In one case, the forecast is updated annually; in the other, it is updated continually by a combination of individual inputs and group discussions. The long-range plans, extending 6–10 years into the future, are updated annually and are communicated in document form to the personnel in charge of resource allocation. The responsibility for developing long-range R&D plans is held by a committee of executive officers.

CONTRIBUTORS TO THE FORECAST. To the techniques mentioned earlier, the contributor adds literature searches as a means for providing inputs to the forecast. In one corporation, the size of the group used to generate these inputs was 76 persons; in the other, 14 panels, each having 17 members, served as contributors. In both cases, as the participants were, in fact, the users of the forecasts, they became stimulated to look ahead and to cross-correlate ideas. Also, in one company, participation by management was felt to increase its confidence in the data.

USERS OF THE FORECAST. The major users of the forecast are the planning staff and the marketing staff. The other users differ in that, in one organization, the programming and budgeting staff often consult the forecast, whereas in the other it is used more by laboratory management, scientists and engineers, operations research staff, and study groups.

PROJECT SELECTION AND RESOURCE ALLOCATION. The current processes used for the selection of R&D projects are combinations of subjective and quantitative techniques. The amount of new R&D work taken on each year is 5–10% in one corporation and 11–20% in the other. The company with the larger amount of new work uses a system for obtaining a balance between long-term payoff and short-term payoff projects. In one company, research projects last 3–5 years, and development projects 6–10 years. In the other, the relative lengths of time are reversed: research projects last 6–10 years, and development projects 1–2 years. The type of work performed by both companies breaks down into less than 5% pure research, 20–30% applied research, and over 40% development.

REMARKS. One of the largest problems encountered is that of finding a workable method of enabling managers to make more effective use of the data in order to foresee the long-term impacts of technical decisions and, in turn, to relate these to business operations.

CASE STUDIES

Thompson Ramo Wooldridge, Inc.

CONTACT: DONALD L. PYKE

Thompson Ramo Wooldridge (TRW) is structured basically in six groups, each of which functions as a separate corporation. Within each group are divisions which have their own cost centers; some are more autonomous than others, and some are in the form of separate corporations or subsidiaries. Each division is responsible for its own 5-year plan. The 5-year plans of the various divisions are collated to form group 5-year plans, which are in turn collated by the corporate staff to form TRW's corporate 5-year plan. There is no standard format for the 5-year plan, but the head of planning at the group level directs the divisions in this work.

As a corporation committed to "growth through technology," TRW realized, in the middle sixties, that to grow (in fact, even to survive) a technology-oriented company must anticipate and prepare for the environment in which it will operate in the future. Trend extrapolation did not provide sufficient information to prepare for breakthroughs; and after studying the results achieved by Helmer and Gordon in their Delphi study, TRW decided to adopt this technique as the most likely one to provide the additional information needed.

In 1965, the first TRW Delphi study was conducted. Later, several modifications were made on the original Delphi study. The events to be forecast were limited in time up to 1985, except for those which might occur at a later date but would have an effect on TRW's current operations.

Group executives nominated 27 of TRW's most talented and creative people to the panel. In Round 1, each panelist was asked to list the technical events which he believed might have a significant impact on TRW's near-term planning. He was then asked to indicate, for each event, a date by which he felt there was a 50% probability that the event would have occurred. He was invited to consult freely with anyone throughout the company, but his list was to contain only the events which *he* thought would occur.

By that time, TRW realized that the socioeconomic environment of the future would have a major impact on the directions which technology would take. As no real picture of that environment was available, each panelist was given copies of a McGraw-Hill economic forecast, the results of the Helmer and Gordon study, a *Time* essay of the future, and a *U.S. News and World Report* article entitled, "Blueprinting the Future U.S." Apart from these, each member was asked to make his own assumptions in regard to the future, excluding only all-out nuclear war.

After approximately 1 month, the lists of events were edited, combined, and grouped according to technologies. The first draft was then returned to each panelist with the request that he edit freely in areas of his own expertise. At the end of this second round, the results were incorporated into a 50-page booklet (Probe I) listing 401 events grouped within 14 technical categories. In addition, the results of this study were presented at the annual conference of TRW's top management.

Despite the fact that the forecast had been performed under the auspices of Dr. Ramo, the assistant chairman of the Board, and despite the external publicity and internal interest, a follow-up 6 months later led to the disappointing revelation that little or no direct use was being made of Probe I in the preparation of specific long-range plans. Although it was being used as a check list, it had not become a base for the planning of R&D programs.

The reason was that, although Probe I had provided the planners with specific events that appeared likely in the future, it had not shown them the means for achieving these events, or the connections between them. In other words, the implications to TRW of these events were not shown.

This realization led to the development of logic networks and SOON charts, to provide information concerning alternative routes to "interesting events." Although they appeared to provide the necessary "missing link," their preparation required a substantial amount of time and effort. By that time, it was realized that the modified Delphi method could be improved, and the planners were reluctant to expend the effort to prepare SOON charts based on data in which they lacked sufficient confidence. However, in July 1967, a SOON chart concerned with developments prerequisite to the widespread availability of electric automobiles was presented to top management. The discussion generated by this presentation paved the way for Probe II, in which some of the shortcomings of Probe I were corrected.

For Probe II, the Delphi method was expanded substantially to include the following:

1. An index of desirability was developed, as considered from the viewpoint of those who might be affected by the occurrence of a forecast event—that is, if a product or service, by those who might purchase it; if a process, by those who might use it.

2. An index of feasibility was drawn up, reflecting both the technical and the economic difficulties likely to be encountered by those engaged in efforts to make an "event" happen.

3. In an attempt to eliminate the confusion typically encountered in soliciting estimates of probable dates of occurrence, two separate judgments were sought:

   (a) An estimate of the probability that the event would ever occur.
   (b) An estimate (assuming the probability of occurrence to be 1.0) of the date by which the probability would be 0.5 that the event would have happened, and the degree of uncertainty associated with that estimate; that is, the date by which there would be a reasonable chance ($P = 0.1$) that the event might have occurred, and the date by which it would be almost certain ($P = 0.9$) to have occurred.

4. In view of the breadth of the categories selected for investigation, each panelist was also asked (in Round 2) to record his familiarity with one or more technologies relevant to an event, rating himself as "excellent" if he were a specialist; "good" if he had a working knowledge; and "fair" if he had a layman's knowledge. It was suggested that panelists "skip" events about which they knew little or nothing.

Probe II was launched in the fall of 1967 with the support of TRW's senior executives. It was realized that in any planning activity the support and participation of key managers is essential to success. The general managers of each of the six groups nominated senior technical executives to serve as group captains. The responsibilities of those individuals were (a) to function as a committee for the selection of categories of critical importance to TRW, for inclusion in the list of those to be "probed," (b) to ensure that each TRW division which might be affected by the occurrence of an event in a specific category was represented on the panel chosen to probe that category, and (c) to perform such management functions as might be required for successful completion of the exercise.

Figure 1 shows an example of the list of categories selected, and the way in which 140 panelists, including a chairman for each panel, were selected from more than 7000 members of TRW's technical staff. Those selected attended one of two briefings, at which general instructions and background material were issued, and questions were answered. This was the only time that the panelists met as a group.

Each panelist was assigned a number to preserve anonymity. In Round 1, panelists were asked to develop a list of technical events which they considered likely to occur in the anticipated environment. Although they were asked to concern themselves primarily with events significant to their own category, contributions to other categories were not discouraged. An example of such a list is shown in Figure 2. This was prepared by Panelist 102—the event numbers were selected so that they could be referenced to the original source document. The numbers written above the text indicate a preliminary decision to expose a particular event to panels on different categories. Although not essential, indications of desirability and feasibility were requested as a guide to the elimination of trivia.

By the cutoff date, 128 of the 140 panelists who responded to this round had provided 2500 events. These were screened four times, to ensure that the events were discrete, to eliminate duplication, to delete trivia, to ensure technical relevance, and, finally, to ensure that the Round 2 questionnaires were meaningful and were organized under logi-

Probe II Categories	Systems						Equipment							Electronics						Automotive							
	Instruments	SL	SEID	SVD	PSD	ESD	Staff	Mark 46	Magna	Metals	J & O	Accessories	Equip. labs	Globe IND.	Electro. insul.	UTC	Capacitors	Semiconductors	El. components	Ramsey	Staff	TP. LTD.	Replacement	Valve	Ross gear	NRC	Michigan
Technologies																											
Electronics and electro-optics	X	X		X	X	X		X	X	X	X	X	X	X	X	X	X	X	X	X	X			X		X	X
Materials (incl. coatings, fuels, and lubricants)	X	X			X				X			X	X	X		X	X	X	X	X	X	X	X	X	X	X	
Mechanics and hydraulics		X		X	X			X				X	X	X			X	X	X	X	X				X	X	
Power sources, conversion and conditioning	X			X		X						X	X			X			X		X						
Information processing	X	X	X	X	X	X	X	X	X	X	X	X	X	X	X	X	X	X	X	X	X	X	X	X	X	X	X
Instrumentation and control	X	X	X	X	X			X	X		X	X	X					X			X					X	
Manufacturing processes		X	X			X	X											X			X						
Systems and subsystems																											
Plant automation-production and business		X	X	X	X	X	X					X	X	X		X	X	X	X	X	X	X	X	X	X	X	X
Transportation		X	X	X	X	X	X					X	X					X	X	X	X	X	X	X	X	X	X
Defense and weapons (exclude missiles)		X	X		X	X	X			X	X	X	X	X	X	X	X	X	X		X				X	X	
Aerospace (include missiles)		X	X			X	X	X	X		X			X		X		X	X		X					X	
Oceans		X	X			X	X											X	X								
Personal and medical	X	X	X	X		X	X							X		X		X									
Urban and international	X	X			X	X	X											X			X					X	X
Environmental control	X	X				X							X	X				X									

Figure 1   List of categories and selection of panelists.

167

1. List below *all* anticipated *technical* events (indicating source, if external source) which will have a *significant* effect on TRW in the above category.
2. Evaluate each predicted event with respect to the three factors at the right in view of the anticipated environment.

	Customer Desirability			Producer Feasibility			Probable Timing		
	Needed Desperately	Desirable	Undesirable but Possible	Highly Feasible	Likely	Unlikely but Possible	Year by Which the Probability is x That the Event Will Have Occurred		
							$x = 0.20$	$x = 0.50$	$x = 0.90$
10) 50% of all financial transactions will be made by electronic signals.		x		x			1980	1985	1990
11) TV will be available to 90% of world's population.		x		x			1977	1980	1983
12) Composite integrated circuits to produce 1 kW CW power at 400 MHz will be available.		x		x			1970	1972	1974
13) An average of 20 or more integrated circuits will be used in each new automobile for non-radio or TV applications.		x		x			1973	1977	1980
14) LSI (Large-Scale Integration) will provide computer gate functions at one cent each or less.		x		x			1970	1972	1974

Received from Panelist 102

Figure 2 TRW'S probe of the future—Round 1 questionnaire.

cal subcategories. At the completion of the editing, the number of events was reduced to 1438. An example of a Round 2 questionnaire and the responses to it is shown in Figure 3.

At the cutoff date, responses had been received from 91% of the 135 panelists, and this particular set of evaluations became one of 22,355 individual records which were subjected to computer analysis. An example of one of five outputs in this analysis which were related to event No. 108010 is shown in Figure 4. This one was prepared for the chairman of Panel 6, allowing him to compare responses by his panelists with each other, with the summary for his panel, with the summary for other panels, and, finally, with the summary of all panels. Similar outputs were given to the chairman of the other four panels which considered this event.

Round 3 was limited to a resurvey by "experts" who might have been aware of information not generally available to all panelists but possibly having a significant bearing on the event. The 75 "experts" contacted were those who rated their familiarity as excellent, and whose judgment concerning any parameter lay outside arbitrarily established limits. An example of the Round 3 questionnaire, given to Panelist 508, is shown in Figure 5. Printouts similar to the one in Figure 3 were attached to the questionnaire for each of the four events "challenged" (the average was six challenges per panelist). These printouts allowed the panelist to make the same comparisons that were available to the panel chairman.

The responses to this round fell into three categories. In view of the evidence presented, some panelists revised their judgments, moving toward the corporate consensus. Others maintained their own positions but offered no supporting logic. The third group maintained their positions and gave reasons to support their judgments. A response of this nature from Panelist 508 is shown in Figure 6.

It was determined that Round 3 should be the last, as the benefits previously gained from a further round were marginal. The information in the data bank was adjusted accordingly, and the final entry was made in Figure 7. This contained a statement of the event, indices of its desirability and feasibility, and the probability of its occurrence. The dot represents the median (.5) data, and the ends of the line indicate the median .1 and .9 probability dates.

Probe II covered 14 areas, 7 technologies, and 7 applications. Although these are fairly broad areas, they are being mapped with respect to a three-level concept: the critical environmental forces, the responses of technology to these forces, and the applications of technological developments. The map is a "collage" of SOON charts, which relate the

Probe Category 6 INSTITUTION AND COMPANY　　　　Panel Member 508

Event Number / Event Description	Panels Evaluating	Familiarity	Desirability	Feasibility	Probable Event	Probability Dates
309021 Prototype tested	01 06	1 Fair 2 Good 3 Excellent	1 Needed 2 Desirable 3 Undesirable	1 Simple 2 Possible 3 Unlikely		.1 Date .5 Date .9 Date
309022 Production design completed	01 06	1 Fair 2 Good 3 Excellent	1 Needed 2 Desirable 3 Undesirable	1 Simple 2 Possible 3 Unlikely		.1 Date .5 Date .9 Date
309023 Available commercially	01 06	1 Fair 2 Good 3 Excellent	1 Needed 2 Desirable 3 Undesirable	1 Simple 2 Possible 3 Unlikely		.1 Date .5 Date .9 Date
108010 Large scale integrated (LSI) circuit costs will drop to 1% gate function permitting special digital operations in machines such as small process controls, machine tools, and others	01 05 06 07 08	① Fair 2 Good 3 Excellent	① Needed 2 Desirable 3 Undesirable	1 Simple ② Possible 3 Unlikely		.1 Date 1970 .5 Date 1971 .9 Date 1972
211330 Automatic electronic gauging and machine compensation will be in general use for mass produced item operations	01 06 08	1 Fair 2 Good 3 Excellent	1 Needed 2 Desirable 3 Undesirable	1 Simple 2 Possible 3 Unlikely		.1 Date .5 Date .9 Date
209060 Fluidics will replace electronic control on 20% of the applications in production equipment	01 03 06 07 08	① Fair 2 Good 3 Excellent	1 Needed ② Desirable 3 Undesirable	1 Simple ② Possible 3 Unlikely		.1 Date 1975 .5 Date 1980 .9 Date 1985

Figure 3　A Round 2 questionnaire and responses to it.

TRW PROBE 11

EVALUATION OF EVENT 108010
LSI (LARGE SCALE INTEGRATED) CIRCUIT COSTS WILL DROP TO ONE CENT
PER GATE FUNCTION PERMITTING SPECIAL DIGITAL OPERATIONS IN MACHINES
SUCH AS SMALL PROCESS CONTROLS, MACHINE TOOLS, ETC.   0105060708

JUDGE	FAMIL- IARITY	DESIRA- BILITY	FEASI- BILITY	PROB of EVENT	A
					L11 1 1 1 1 1 2 2 2 2 BEYOND
					R99 9 9 9 9 9 0 0 0 0 2020
					D67 7 8 8 9 9 0 0 0 0 ·1·5·9 NEVER
					Y9012345678901234567890123456789012345678901234567890123456789
PANEL 01					
PANEL SUMMARY	·25	⁻·25	·50	*-M-*	
PANEL 05					
PANEL SUMMARY	·86	·29	·78	*--M--*	
PANEL 06					
305	G	0	0	·80	1 5 9
508	E	1	0		159
310	G	1	0	·99	5 9
PANEL 06					
PANEL SUMMARY	·67	0 ·00	·89	*---M-*	
PANEL 07					
PANEL SUMMARY	·50	0 ·00	·67	*-----M---*	
PANEL 08					
PANEL SUMMARY	·33	- ·33	·80	*----M--*	
TRW SUMMARY	·57	0 ·00	·72	*--M----*	
VALUE - 1 STD. DEVIATION			·24		

Figure 4 Example of computer analysis of evaluations.

sequence of developments of technologies to their environmental precursors and to their applications. In the mapping process, technologies have been reclassified into categories compatible with those used by National Science Foundation and Engineering Joint Council and applications have been reclassified into categories compatible with SIC codes and those used in U.S. Department of Commerce I/O tables.

Although the maps are not yet available, the results of TRW's Probe II have been applied in five or six significant instances, including use by one of the six major groups of the corporation as a basis for its long-range planning, and as a basis for a thorough review of metal-processing techniques.

Ling-Temco-Vought Inc.

CONTACT: WILLIAM G. MCLOUGHLIN,
DIRECTOR OF TECHNOLOGICAL PLANNING

The purpose of performing a technological forecast was to assist Ling-Temco-Vought (LTV) and its nine subsidiaries in providing an annual analysis of the technologies applicable to their products and product

To panelist no. 508   Page 1 of 1

   Round 2 of TRW's Probe II has been completed and the resulting data have been
analyzed by the chairman of your panel who prepared this form. Round 3 is being
restricted to contact with specialists whose evaluations on specific events are sufficiently outside the TRW "consensus" to indicate that they may have based their
judgement on information not available to other panel members. Accordingly, you
are being contacted with respect to the event(s) listed below. Enclosed are copies of
the data printout for each of these events. These will enable you to compare your
responses with (a) those of other members of your panel, (b) the summary for your
panel, (c) the summary for other panels evaluating the event, and (d) the summary
for all TRW panels.

   The set of printouts constitutes your Round 3 "questionnaire" and you are asked
to enter your response for each event directly thereon in one of two ways: (1) if you
wish to reconsider your evaluation in the light of other responses, please make appropriate changes in the line which reports your judgements; or (2) if you still disagree
strongly with the TRW consensus in any respect, please indicate which respect and
state your reasons for your differing opinion.

   As one of TRW's experts in this area, your complete and candid comments are
solicited in this third round of Probe II—responses to which may enable the company to gain a significant lead in some areas and to avoid wasteful pursuit of elusive
goals in others. To encourage complete candor and objectivity, the continuing preservation of your anonymity is assured. Be assured also that your efforts in Round III
will be appreciated by TRW management even though anonymity precludes personal
acknowledgment.

   In order to complete the exercise before this date it is necessary that your questionnaire be returned to Mr. Donald L. Pyke, TRW Systems, One Space Park, El/5017,
Redondo Beach, Calif. 90278 no later than July 1 and hopefully much earlier.

Event No.   Question
  411400   Why so pessimistic when panel member No. 411 believes 90% probabil-
                ity will occur in 1972?
  525040   Why so optimistic when panel member No. 432 lists the 90% probabil-
                ity date of the event as 1990?
  108010   Based on recent LSI problem at (company name deleted), are you still
                optimistic?
  525090   Is there evidence that there are data to support a 10% probability in
                the near future?

Figure 5   Example of a Round 3 questionnaire.

lines. This analysis provides a base for each subsidiary's 5-year business
plan. In order to further assist the subsidiaries, the LTV Corporate
Plans Office each year issues a World Outlook Report, which provides
analyses of the predictable social, political, economic, and technological
environments. These take the form of chapters on:

   U.S. Economic Trends.
   U.S. Political and Social Trends.

TRW PROBE 11

EVALUATION OF EVENT 108010
LSI (LARGE SCALE INTEGRATED) CIRCUIT COSTS WILL DROP TO ONE CENT
PER GATE FUNCTION PERMITTING SPECIAL DIGITAL OPERATIONS IN MACHINES
SUCH AS SMALL PROCESS CONTROLS, MACHINE TOOLS, ETC.   0105060708

JUDGE	FAMIL-IARITY	DESIRA-BILITY	FEASI-BILITY	PROB of EVENT	A L11 R99 D67	1 9 7	1 9 8	1 9 8	1 9 9	1 9 9	2 0 0	2 0 0	2 0 1	2 0 1	BEYOND 2020 ·1·5·9 NEVER

Y90123456789012345678901234567890123456789

PANEL   01

	PANEL SUMMARY	·25	⁻·25	·50	*-M-*

PANEL   05

	PANEL SUMMARY	·86	·29	·78	*--M--*

PANEL   06

305	G	0	0	·80	1 5 9
508	E	1	0		159
310	G	1	0	·99	5 9

PANEL   06

	PANEL SUMMARY	·67	0 ·00	·89	*---M-*

PANEL   07

	PANEL SUMMARY	·50	0 ·00	·67	*-----M---*

PANEL   08

	PANEL SUMMARY	·33	⁻·33	·80	*----M--*

TRW SUMMARY   ·57   0 ·00   ·72   *--M----*

VALUE - 1 STD. DEVIATION   ·24

I am not familiar with (company name deleted) problems with LSI but (company name deleted) is building LSI's for a Japanese desk calculator where over 1 300 gate functions are contained in five LSI's. The total cost of the calculator is less than $500. Subtracting the cost of indicators, the cost per gate function less than ⅓ cent. This is already here. Obviously this cost is for a large volume so the manufacturer would need to design a somewhat 'general purpose' machine to keep costs down.

Figure 6   Example of a response to the Round 3 questionnaire.

The U.S. Government Customer.
International Outlook.
Technological Scenarios.

In late 1967, the Corporate Plans Office decided to extend and increasingly formalize the subsidiaries' technological analyses, by providing a broader-based technological forecast. The initial forecast was begun early in 1968 for inclusion in the World Outlook Report for the same year.

Realizing that a technological forecast is a dynamic interpretation of future events, since it is a prediction, made at a single point in time,

Event Description	Desir-ability $\bar{d}$	Feas-ibility $\bar{f}$	Prob-ability $\bar{p}$	1970	1975	1980	1980	1985	1990	1990	1995	1999	2000 and Beyond .1	.5	.9
LSI (Large Scale Integrated) circuit costs will drop to one cent per gate function, permitting special digital operations in machines such as small process controls and machine tools.*	+ .57	− .09	.72												

* Indicates existence of minority opinion(s) (see Appendix).

Figure 7 TRW'S probe II: sample of final output.

of events which have no certainty of occurrence, LTV performed the forecast with the knowledge that it could be altered at any time as the result of changes in the environment. Another major problem was recognized: that of convincing top management of the benefits of such long-range forecasting. The responsibility for forecasting belongs to top management, and if it is to be successful, then these executives must give the direction essential to its conduct. In addition to the need to convince top management, the participation of other personnel at the intermediate and control levels had to be obtained.

Initially, the vice president of corporate plans sent a letter to the presidents of the then eight key subsidiaries of LTV, in which he explained the objectives of the study and the means for their accomplishment. Each president was asked to designate a responsible coordinator within any division or subsidiary of his particular key subsidiary. These coordinators were then contacted directly, and the first stages of the forecasting procedure were initiated. Each coordinator was asked to select participants, and he himself was encouraged to take part. One of the largest problems encountered was that of convincing prospective participants that there would be absolute anonymity regarding specific predictions made by panelists.

Altogether, there were 50 participants: 12 vice presidents from engineering, planning, marketing, and general management; and 38 other persons, of at least project-manager level from the R&D personnel, long-range planners, marketeers, and financial personnel—giving a good cross-section of management skills. This formal participation by management prevented the forecasting activity from becoming informal and separated from the realities of the company.

Although the Delphi technique was believed to offer the best possibility for corporate-wide participation, there were several problems to be solved:

1. The Delphi technique is supposed to eliminate the bandwagon effect, but can any method which restricts the scope of the answer provide the objectivity necessary to prevent some degree of bandwagon effect?

2. Since the future state of the art of technology is interdependent with developments and changes in the economic, sociological, and geopolitical environment, can a purely scientific and technical panel make objective predictions?

3. A date on which a future event may occur is meaningless if there is no measure of the prediction reliability of the actual occurrence of the event, and no measure of such reliability is possible with a Delphi methodology.

4. The standard Delphi results provide no means of relating a forecast to the long-range planning of a company.

As a test, 14 students took part in a Delphi study, in which 17 event statements were listed. None of the students had a technical background, but all were well read and interested. The test Delphi was conducted in the standard manner, with four iterations. When the student median dates were compared to those of the original scientific panelists, there was surprising correspondence on all dates before 1985.

The bandwagon effect was noticeable; however, this was subsequently reduced by performing a nonstandard Delphi, in which NEVER was an acceptable date for an event. More importantly, the percentage of NEVER replies to a statement, expressed in terms of the total number of replies, was stated in the second and subsequent questionnaires.

In the spring of 1968, the modified Delphi technique was initiated for the LTV Technological Forecast 1968. A number of statements of future technologies and events affecting the current and future business of LTV and its subsidiaries were assembled from sources within and without the company. Each panelist was asked to assign an expected occurrence date to each event, as well as to any other events which he added to the questionnaire. In the instructions, it was emphasized that NEVER was an acceptable answer.

When the second questionnaire was prepared, all the original statements were reworded with a median date, a range of middle-quartile years, the date extremes, and the percentage of NEVER replies to each statement. The additional event statements supplied by the panelists were also included, but only the panelists' occurrence dates were given for these items. The median dates and quartile ranges were determined only by the positive date answers—the NEVER answers were excluded.

Arguments offered by panelists on any of the questionnaires were included with the appropriate statement in the subsequent round (see Figure 8). The study went through three iterations. As the process proceeded, some statements had an increasing percentage of NEVER answers, whereas others had a decreasing percentage. In every case, the range of the middle-quartile years narrowed substantially. The range was less than 5 years for 39 of the 84 event statements, and was equal to 5 years for 34 of the rest.

The next step was to assess the confidence of probability of the occurrence of an event. Expressed as a confidence factor, the probability of NEVER answers was subtracted from 100%. As no event is ever a certainty, it was thought prudent to reduce all 100% confidence factors by 1 percentage point.

Statement: A majority of new home construction will include internal power (i.e., fuel cells, solar cells, etc.) by the year _____.

Arguments Previously Offered: (Never) Power supplied from nuclear plants will be too economical. (Never) It will not be economically feasible to produce a unit of this type and compete with a central power plant. (Never) The only possibility is a safe, reliable, compact, cheap nuclear power plant. It may be safe, reliable, and compact, but it will not be cheap. (2010) Community power sources will be more economical and cheaper to the user until a meaningful breakthrough is made. (2006) I agree that the only possibility is a reliable nuclear power unit in the home. This cannot occur before the year 2000. Also consider the efficiency and economy of centrally generated and distributed power that is being used now. (2000) It is assumed that this question refers only to the United States. (2000) It is possible if internal power assumes no distribution lines of any kind. (1990) Experiments have been made on the concept of this project for over 7 years. Most of the gross concept has been worked out; only the details remain for solution. (1990) I think the nonthinkers who say "never" are ridiculous, for it is just a matter of time and money. Drawing power from long distance with lines running everywhere is *not* in the future with our rapidly growing power needs. (1975) The American Gas Association has conducted successful experiments with natural gas fuel cells and contends that they will be competitive with conventionally generated and distributed electricity by 1970 or 1971. See *Science-News*, November 1968.

Median: 1998   *Inner quartile:* 1995–2000   *Extremes:* 1975 and 2010

% Nevers: 9.1   Your new estimate:

Your arguments:

Figure 8

Finally, it was necessary to determine the value of the derived data for long-range planning. Not all the event statements could be regarded as of equal importance. However, given a confidence factor and a median date for any event statement, it was thought possible to place that event in a priority spectrum. In the determination of priority, LTV used the following criteria for measuring each forecasted event:

Priority I: Any event statement requiring industrial entry within the next 5 years for which there is a confidence factor of 95% or greater.
Priority II: Any event statement requiring industrial entry within the next 5 years for which there is a confidence factor of 85–94.9%; or any event statement requiring industrial entry within the next 10 years for which there is a confidence factor of 95% or greater.

Priority III: Any event statement requiring industrial entry within the next 5 years for which there is a confidence factor of 75–84.9%; or any event statement requiring industrial entry within the next 10 years for which there is a confidence factor of 85–94.9%.

Priority IV: All other event statements.

In order to make these priorities meaningful to the company, it was necessary to consider product life cycles. The form of life cycle used is shown in Figure 9.[1] The ratio of values and the span of time in each phase differed according to product, but the form remained essentially the same.

As an example of the interaction of the life cycle and the priority as derived from the LTV methodology, consider a prediction such as the following: "Integrated microcircuitry will constitute the major sales volume in the hi-fi home entertainment field by the year 1973." If a firm waits until 1973 to begin its competition with integrated microcircuitry, that firm should expect to find itself in the "maturity" phase of the cycle, and this phase is characterized by declining profit margins. In such a situation, the firm has lost its best opportunity to compete with a product using integrated microcircuitry.

On the basis of a long history of electronic products introduction, it is known that the product introduction and market growth phases of the life cycle probably take between 5 and 8 years. Thus a firm in the high-fidelity home entertainment field should take the Delphi forecast date of 1973 and subtract 8 to establish the year in which it should begin planning for the introduction of microcircuitry into its product line. Also, the firm should have made its technical plans for the introduction of microcircuitry not later than 1966. Subtracting 5 years from the 1973 date would have established a product introduction date of 1968. Before 1969, the firm should have completed its initial product designs, made experimental models, conducted testing, made engineering refinements, planned the production phase, including whatever plant conversion is necessary, mapped out the marketing program, and, most importantly, planned the financial program.

These results of the LTV Delphi were evaluated in cooperation with a panel of faculty members from the engineering schools of Oklahoma State University (OSU), who participated in a Delphi with identical event statements. Out of 57 statements, 30 had comparative confidence factors 5 percentage points apart; only 5 confidence factors had a spread between 10 and 15 percentage points, 6 had between 15 and 20 percentage

[1] William G. McLoughlin, *Fundamentals of Research Management* (New York: American Management Association, 1970).

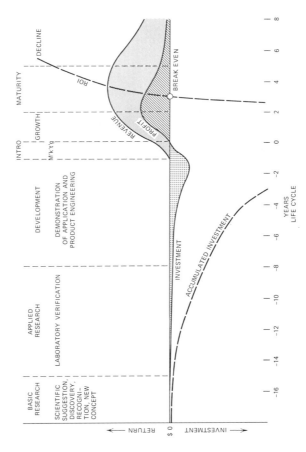

Figure 9 Example of product life cycle.

Forecast Scenario—1975

Techniques for utilizing high-power, pulsed lasers in commercial applications of holography for (a) recording dynamic objects and/or transient environment, (b) microscopy with infinite depths of focus (resolution to the order of a wavelength of light), and (c) differential interferometry for 3-D recording of asymmetrical fluid flow, will be commercially available and widely used in both manufacturing and research. Other high-power, high-efficiency, continuously emitting lasers, using direct conversion of chemical energy or other means, will be used for precision-controlled machining of materials. Sonic and ultrasonic drivers with resonant vibrators also will be in common use for cutting.

Forecast Scenario—1975

In the office, a majority of intra- and intercompany business will be conducted on a checkless, cashless computer exchange basis. Direct-voice-transcription-to-draft-letter-form dictation machines will be a reality, greatly simplifying the secretarial load problem. Scramble telephone service for both business and home use will be in general use. An internal facsimile transcription service paralleling the video-phone will replace the majority of inter- and intracompany business letters, memoranda, and orders. In terms of "mail," the Post Office will offer same-day, carrier-delivered, facsimile-transmitted letters as a substitute for air mail service.

Figure 10   Prediction scenarios for business methods and industrial processes.

Forecast Scenario—1975

Within the United States, there will be no shortage of instructors and teachers for the primary and secondary (precollege) grade levels. Hence, within these grade levels, the teaching machine will be widely used only in the teaching of the disadvantaged and the handicapped. The teaching machine market for primary and secondary school levels will be largest overseas and will be especially strong in the underdeveloped countries, where teachers will still be in extremely short supply. In the United States, the teaching machine will have won a major, though limited, market in routine college instruction such as language and engineering fundamentals.

Forecast Scenario—1980

A major impact on the teaching load will have occurred with the adoption of the metric system by the United States. Another potential impact will be the initial trial experiments with comprehension stimulation and acceleration drugs, as well as electrical conditioning methods. All educational objectives will be based on building as much knowledge within each individual as that individual can absorb; and these objectives will be aimed at accomplishing this within the minimum period of time. As a result, all education will be more meaningful and effective.

Figure 11   Prediction scenarios for education and educational systems.

Forecast Scenario—1975

The forerunner of synthetic foods will be very much in evidence. Meat substitute products such as vegetable-based frankfurters and hamburgers will be widely accepted and less expensive than true meat. Over 5000 tons of petroleum-derived foodstuffs will be fed to cattle and poultry, while the introduction of petroleum-based foods for human consumption will have already occurred. Similarly, both natural and artificial protein concentrates in liquid, solid, and flour form will constitute a major international sales product from the United States.

Forecast Scenario—1980

Synthesis of food will have been carried to the point where 5000 pounds of high-protein and vitamin-enriched powder can be produced from the fermentation of only 1000 pounds of bacteria, certain yeasts, water, crude oil stock, nitrogen, and phosphate. Through the addition of essences, the resultant product will be made to look and taste like meat or fish at a fraction of the cost of the real item. Such petrochemical-derived food will be moving toward a significant percentage of the total world food market.

Figure 12   Prediction scenarios for food.

Forecast Scenario—1975

Prosthetic and orthotic medical technology will have advanced significantly. Spurs to this development will be integrated microelectronics and such power developments as radioisotope batteries in microminiature size for human implants, as well as 200 watt-hour/pound dry batteries for driving substitute electromechanical muscles. Prosthetic limbs will be commonly fitted to a patient at the time of amputation. Bioelectronic arms, hands, and feet will be activated by muscle nerve impulses, with the user only subconsciously thinking of the movement required to affect the desired physical response.

Forecast Scenario—1980

Most cancers will be curable or preventable. Secondary radiation from laser and electron beams will be in common use for the selective treatment of cancers, while vaccines will be available to prevent or cure limited cancers in their early stages. A greater understanding of and tolerance for cancer will remove cancer from the hideous or dread disease category. Studies of cancer will have led, either directly or indirectly, to the synthesis of live matter. This breakthrough will have opened an enormous new era in biology. Similarly, development of a fetus which has been removed completely from the mother and transferred to an artificial placenta will have been demonstrated.

Figure 13   Prediction scenarios for health.

points, and 4 had more than 20 percentage points. Because of ambiguity in the statements, which led to misinterpretation, 2 had to be disregarded. Among the remaining 55 statements, the standard deviation between the LTV and OSU median dates was 3.68 years. For events predicted for 1990 or earlier, the standard deviation was 3.54 years; for 1985 or earlier, 2.64 years.

This shows that 68% of the comparative answers are included within the span of 1 standard deviation, and 85% within the span of 2 standard deviations. The only point for concern in this study was the large differences in the confidence factors.

To assist the planners and managers of LTV and its subsidiary companies, the data from the Technological Forecast 1968 were made avail-

Forecast Scenario—1975

On the job site, major contractors will be using a vast array of labor-saving devices and equipment. Heavy-duty staple guns and powered drivers for fasteners will have completely replaced the hammer. Virtually all lumber and other materials will be precut to size and delivered to the site for erection without further cutting or specialized fitting. Unitized wiring and plumbing systems will fit into place with a minimum of labor. Painting will be minimized by the use of prepainted exterior panels and/or siding; inside, the spray gun will have completely replaced the brush or roller. Flooring will be available in panels with carpeting preapplied. Similarly, roofs will be erected with interlocking panels which provide greater strength, durability, and safety than the best roofs of 1968.

Forecast Scenario—1980

The last half of the decade will see the completion of the major changes in the construction industry. Giant corporations will have entered the industry to mass-produce relatively low-cost, completely engineered, advanced housing completely based on the modular concept. A buyer will be able to visit a showroom where sample modules and a catalog of options are available to select the specific style and form of a house. Each module will be completed in the "factory" on an assembly line. All built-ins will be in place, carpets of the proper color will be on the floor, and electric, plumbing, and air-conditioning features will be ready for plugging into one of the standard service modules, nominally sized to meet the needs of varying sizes of families. The completely assembled home will be better air-conditioned, be more fireproof inside and out, and substantially easier to maintain than the best construction of a decade earlier. To make this change possible, the government will have raised its annual subsidies for housing to above $3 billion annually.

Figure 14   Prediction scenarios for housing and construction.

able as event statements with median dates and interquartile ranges, as well as being incorporated into a series of prediction scenarios for the years 1975 and 1980 (see Figures 10–14). These scenarios were drawn from both LTV's Delphi data and other Delphi data provided in a mutual exchange with other companies.

In order to use all this Delphi data effectively, cross-correlation cards provide single event statements and Delphi exercises resulting in related dates. Twenty-one key business areas are identified by the numbers on the upper right of the cards, and the affected subsidiaries by the letter code at the lower right. Key words converted to an alphanumeric code are given at the bottom. Ultimately, it will be possible to use key words to identify all related event statements, and key business area codes to identify all events within selected areas or all events which will have an impact on various LTV subsidiaries.

X. *Metallurgy and Machinery*

Experience is the cheapest thing you can buy, if you're smart enough to get it second hand.

Anonymous

INTRODUCTION

The problems encountered in the metals business are of a completely different nature from those found elsewhere. The companies are, at present, in the position of not having quite the supply of raw materials to meet the demand. However, this currently certain market does not prevent them from looking into the future for new markets and new uses for metals, because there may well come a day when many requirements currently satisfied by metals will be met even more fully or more cheaply by plastics and ceramics.

There are three aspects to the metals business, and a large company usually includes at least two of these stages in its field of operation. The first is that of mining and refining the metal and adding alloys as required; the second consists of shaping and treating the metal (e.g., forming it into tubing, rods, sheets, etc.); and the third is concerned with making consumer products. In terms of forecasting potential markets, a mining company has to forecast each customer's customers' needs, and then must relate the results to what the customer feels are its customers' needs. Also, until fairly recently, there were very few improvements in mining and refining processes; and, as the mines were too far away for personnel at headquarters to visit them very often, it was difficult to keep track of funds and resources.

184

For case studies the following were chosen: one metal and mining company, to represent the first stage; a division of a metal mining company to represent the second stage; and one machine company to represent the third. It should be pointed out that these companies were exceptions in their respective industries, in that their planning and forecasting were done on a formal basis, unlike the majority of firms in this area. If classified under one broad category, as the title of the chapter suggests, the size of the companies varied from $300,000 to $1 billion gross sales per year.

RESULTS OF QUESTIONNAIRE

The results of the questionnaire submitted to 80 specific companies were as follows.

OBJECTIVES. Most of the companies (96%) have corporate objectives, but they are equally divided among oral, written, qualitative, and written quantitative objectives. The R&D objectives tend to be divided between written qualitative and written quantitative ones. All the objectives are revised at least annually.

FORECASTS. The majority of the machine companies often perform technological, economic, and marketing forecasts, and slightly less often environmental ones. The metal companies, on the other hand, always perform economic and marketing forecasts and occasionally environmental forecasts; but some companies always perform technological forecasting, whereas others seldom use it. The technological forecasts frequently serve as an aid in planning, but rarely for anything else, except in one machine company which occasionally uses them for resource allocation and for justifying a previously made decision. In every case, the forecasts are made by in-house staff, usually by corporate planners, operations research staff, and scientists and engineers; in one company, the product and marketing staff are also included.

FORECASTING AND LONG-RANGE PLANNING. In almost every case, the companies always formulate specific long-range plans for their R&D efforts. Formal technological forecasts have been used by at least one machine company for as long as 10 or 12 years in the formulation of its long-range plans, and by the metal companies for 2–3 years. The degree to which the technological forecast is used in preparing the long-range plans is, in the machine companies very great, but in the metal companies is limited. The popular techniques being used for forecasting are the intuitive approach (15%) and trend extrapolation (27%). The forecast is updated at intervals varying from 6 months to 2 years by individual input and group discussion. The long-range plans, extending, in the case of the machine companies, 1–5 years into the future, are then communicated in writing and used by those in charge of resource allocation. The long-range plans of the metals companies extend 6–10 years into the future but are not communicated to the allocator of resources.

CONTRIBUTOR TO THE FORECAST. The techniques used by the contributor are the same as those mentioned earlier. The number of contributors varies. It was felt that their participation helped in the development of new projects, because of improved understanding of company objectives.

USER OF THE FORECAST. The major users of the forecast are the planning staff and laboratory management, followed by the marketing groups and individual scientists and engineers. The forecast serves mainly as an input to the operational plans and for general and intelligence information, as well as providing a background for studies.

PROJECT SELECTION AND RESOURCE ALLOCATION. The processes used for project selection are, on the whole, combinations of quantitative and subjective methods, but in one company only quantitative techniques are used. The average amount of new R&D work undertaken in each year is 15–25%; in two cases, quantitative methods are used for obtaining a balance between long-term–payoff projects and short-term ones. There appeared to be no correlation between the lengths of research and the development projects undertaken—probably because our category was rather broad, and, in terms of the type of work performed, the only agreement was on 40% or more development. However, for whatever use the information may be, the average length of time for research and development projects seems to be 4 years in each case.

REMARKS. It was the general opinion that forecasting could help in improving the processes currently used in the machinery and metals industries, and could also assist in identifying potentially marketable areas of business. Such forecasts could be especially valuable for companies that use the metals in their fabrication processes.

CASE STUDIES

Large Copper Corporation

The purpose of technological forecasting here is to help in the development of a corporate applied research laboratory and the formulation of its objectives and activities. The laboratory was already doing applied research in the fields of solidification and liquid metal processing, but despite reductions in fabrication costs it was evident that a high cost was associated with converting the intermediate cast form of the metal into its final fabricated shape. Thus it appeared that casting technology would represent the next wave of progress.

This was, in a sense, a technological forecast, although no sophisticated

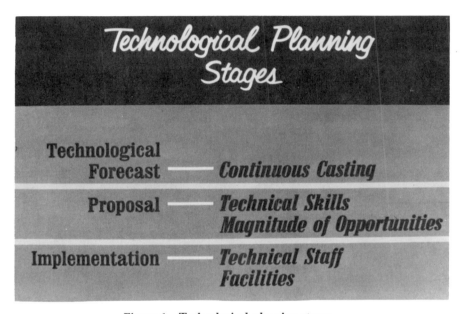

Figure 1   Technological planning stages.

techniques were used; and it provided a basis on which future technological activities were planned. It was the first stage of the technological planning process and led to the second stage: the development of a proposal to capture the technology.

In 1965, a proposal was prepared for a casting-oriented research activity, which served as a basis for creating a commitment to establish a moderate-sized development effort. In 1966, a second proposal was prepared. This called for an expanded effort, with specific emphasis on applied research in the areas outlined in the first proposal. Both proposals focused on two areas: the potential economic implications of casting improvements for the corporation, and the technical activities that would be required to achieve these benefits.

The final proposal provided a preliminary, broad-brush evaluation of the economic benefits of casting longer and closer to the final shape for several product-process combinations in the corporation. It established the order of magnitude of the opportunities and in addition specified the requirements of each. This broad-brush analysis served as the

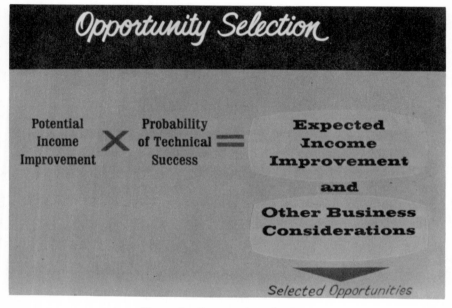

Figure 2   Opportunity selection.

basis for identifying the specific research skills, disciplines, and facilities necessary to achieve the technologies required to capture the potential economic benefits, and for proposing that they be acquired.

The proposal phase provided a more detailed description of the concept. The opportunity for cost reductions was quantified (in a preliminary way) and specified for several product-process combinations. Included in the assessment that continuous casting could provide the technology were the technical disciplines and facilities necessary for the development of the process.

The proposal was accepted and implemented. Highly qualified technical people were acquired, and facilities constructed. The implementation of the proposal provided the ability to advance the technological planning one more step. Proposals were prepared, in five technical disciplines, for specific research activities directed at gaining an understanding of solidification and liquid metal processing as related to continuous casting. In addition, a proposal was made for activities which could assist in the identification, evaluation, and selection of research opportunities.

Technical Objective

LOWER OVERALL COST AND IMPROVE PRODUCT QUALITY BY ECONOMICALLY:

☐ CASTING CLOSER TO FINAL SHAPE
SOLIDIFICATION PROCESSING

☐ USING UPGRADED SCRAP
LIQUID METAL PROCESSING

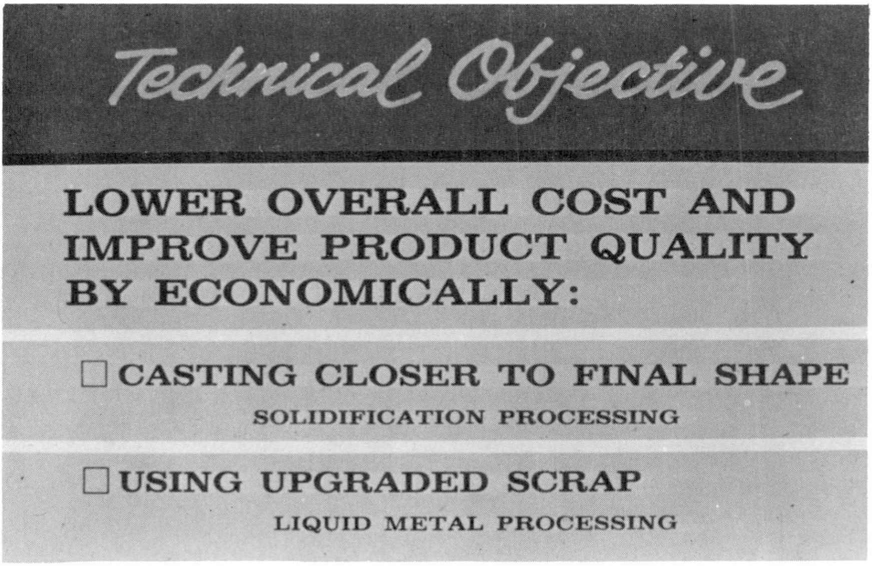

Figure 3   Other objectives to be considered.

The implementation provided an even finer focusing of technological efforts, as the proposals were translated into specific research goals and programs to support continuous casting research. Re-evaluation of research opportunities provided information which was used to evaluate more adequately the economic benefits of the proposed research.

When the first three stages of the planning process—namely, forecasting the technology, formulating proposals to capture the technology, and implementing the proposals (see Figure 1)—had been accomplished, there was a sound basis on which to build the applied research effort, as well as a foundation and stimulus for future planning. The planning process then began to diverge, in order to organize efforts to capture specific continuous casting opportunities. The first step in this process was to focus technical activities on a particular opportunity. It was necessary to ensure that the corporate requirements and technical activity interacted. Each opportunity had associated with it an estimated potential improvement in operating income, resulting from the successful development of a continuous casting process.

Figure 4   Relevance matrix.

First, the opportunities were listed, each with its appropriate potential improvement in operating income. Next, this potential improvement was adjusted by the probability of technical success in order to reflect an expected improvement in operating income (see Figure 2).

A group of corporate executives were then asked to examine the ranking of the opportunities by expected value, and to superimpose their own judgments of what the ranking should be, taking into account other business considerations which are not easily quantified, such as the objectives shown in Figure 3. On the basis of these two evaluations, specific research opportunities were selected.

Once the research opportunities had been chosen, it was necessary to examine the technical disciplines needed to accomplish them. Since much interaction between disciplines was required, it was necessary to evaluate the amount which the various disciplines contributed, not only

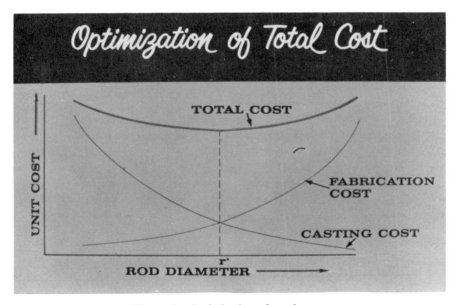

Figure 5   Optimization of total cost.

to their own technical objectives, but also to the research programs of the disciplines.

To accomplish this, a relevance matrix technique was used. The rows of the matrix were formed by listing the research programs, and the columns by the technical objectives of the five disciplines, as shown in Figure 4. On the basis of the research proposals prepared for the specific continuous casting opportunity, each technical manager was asked to evaluate the relevance or importance that each research program had to his technical objective, and to quantify that relevance according to a defined scale. These numerical assessments were entered in the matrix elements.

This technique allowed each technical manager to express his opinions concerning where and to what degree he expected interaction to take place, in relation to specific research programs. Disagreement between managers regarding the value assigned to a specific element stimulated interest and exchange of information that might not otherwise have occurred. Also, the matrix could then be updated—something which

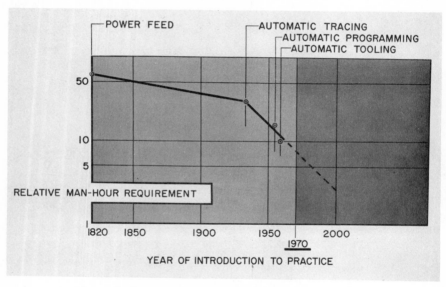

Figure 6   Improvement of automation of metal removal.

should, in any case, be done periodically. Furthermore, the director could see and evaluate the viewpoints expressed by his managers. Finally, the relevance matrix could also be used to establish research program priorities.

In order to assess more adequately the research contribution to corporate requirements, additional economic and systems analyses were also performed. These included optimization of total cost, as shown in Figure 5.

Technological forecasting offers considerable promise of assisting industry and government in utilizing more fully their technical and economic resources. For this copper corporation, each phase of the technical planning process led to the finer focusing of research activities and provided visibility, so that communications and exchange of information could take place more freely.

International Nickel Company Incorporated

CONTACTS: MARCEL A. CORDOVI AND WILLIAM S. MOUNCE,
Market Development Department

The International Nickel Company Incorporated (INCO) is one of the principal subsidiaries of the International Nickel Company of Canada, Limited. Although competition is increasing, INCO mines and refines more than half the total amount of nickel which is consumed today, as well as copper, cobalt, iron, and the other metals found in the same ore. Since the demand for nickel is still greater than the supply, INCO has not had to search for new markets. However, this has not prevented

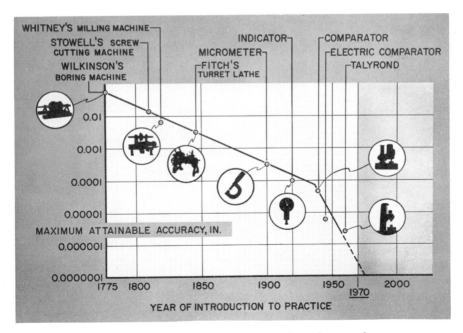

Figure 7   Improvement of accuracy of metal removal.

the company from performing research and development to discover new uses for nickel; in particular, the Market Development Department has a large Application Engineering Group, with 13 separate divisions which study the end uses of nickel from the points of view of the chemical industry, electrical and electronics industry, aerospace and power industry, aerospace and power industry, automotive industry, etc.

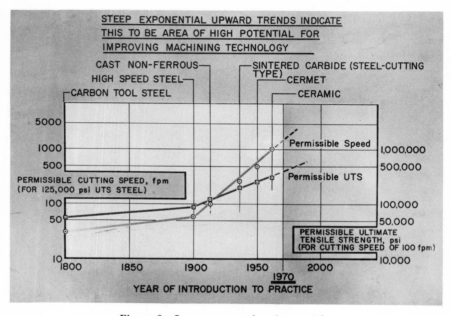

Figure 8   Improvement of tool materials.

The major objective of the Market Development Department is to increase the total market for nickel, by increasing present markets and by creating completely new ones. In order to do this, rather than going to the companies which purchase nickel directly from INCO, the Market Development Department approaches companies which use nickel as an end product, such as Pratt & Whitney and Edison. When approaching such companies, the purpose is not to probe, but rather to help by determining what requirements made them choose nickel-containing materials: did such materials provide longer service, increase productivity, reduce maintenance costs, or permit more appealing design? Once these technical and economic requirements have been defined, it is necessary to determine the quantity of nickel in the material purchased by the end user, as well as the amount of the material that he buys.

Any forecasting performed by INCO, in terms of the quantity of nickel which will be consumed, is, of necessity, dependent on the forecasts made by the end user. For example, if the power industry forecasts

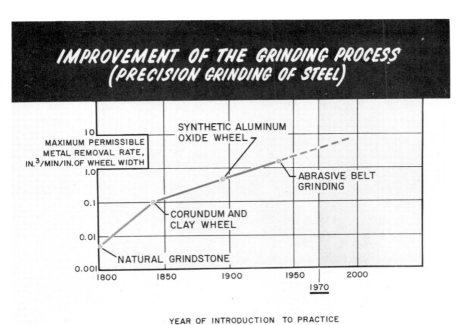

IMPROVEMENT OF THE GRINDING PROCESS
(PRECISION GRINDING OF STEEL)

YEAR OF INTRODUCTION TO PRACTICE

Figure 9   Improvement of the grinding process (precision grinding of steel).

a need for X new power plants, which will use condensers requiring Y pounds of copper-nickel alloy, INCO can establish which group of customers will be buying nickel and, often, when and where the demand is likely to increase or decrease.

Once the customer specifies his requirements for material with specific capabilities, the R&D Division performs normative forecasts in the efforts to achieve these requirements. On the exploratory side, the group tries to find new uses and new characteristics for materials containing nickel.

At present, INCO's knowledge of requirements by the end user is dependent on individual application engineers. To reduce the loss of knowledge if one leaves, the Marketing Development Department is building an input/output model to take into account all the factors determining the quantity of nickel used at every stage in the end-users' processes, and the factors (technical, economic, social, political, etc.) which can affect each step, so that the impact of any changes in these factors can be measured in terms of the effects on INCO.

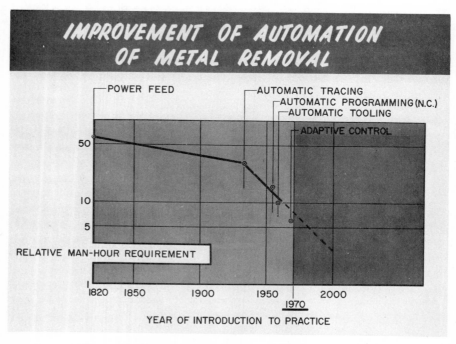

Figure 10   Improvement of automation of metal removal.

Once the criteria have been identified, opportunities can be identified, and action defined, through the marketing plan. Several different kinds of opportunities may be selected for the marketing plan; many may even deal with applications which are still quite small but appear to have good growth potential, either in specific areas or by adaptation for more general use.

The marketing plan describes how the various tools available within INCO should be used to achieve these goals. Frequently the R&D Division provides essential technical data, and then the Marketing Development Department works with these to enlist the interest and support of the customer. To gain added approval, INCO maintains close contact with the specification and code bodies that can endorse the materials and applications, and also with trade associations, which use some of the ideas in promoting their programs.

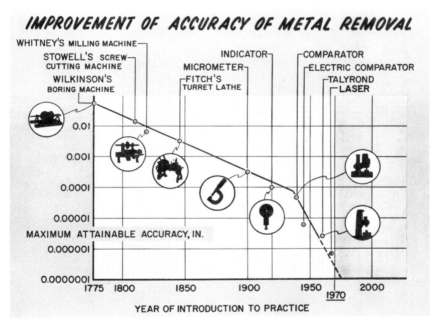

Figure 11   Improvement of accuracy of metal removal.

Once a development appears to be increasing in potential value, its worth should have been demonstrated sufficiently so that the direct suppliers and producers will continue its exploitation. At this point the Marketing Development Department can look for new opportunities.

XYZ Milling Machine Company

About 10 years ago, XYZ Milling came to the realization that, because of the rapid increase of technological change in industry, a more efficient and effective means of forecasting the future was needed. Before this early forecasting was performed, a purely intuitive method of determining technological change was used in long-range planning.

Since the intuitive method was felt to be inadequate for the investigation of future areas of improvement and innovation in manufacturing engineering, the company decided to make a simple future projection

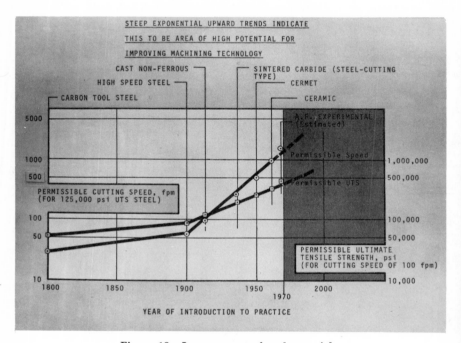

Figure 12   Improvement of tool materials.

of previously observed changes or trends. In doing this, it assumed that the rate of change and direction observed in the past would continue in the future. This approach was later known as trend extrapolation.

The major results of these extrapolations can be seen in Figures 6–9. These results have recently been updated as shown in Figures 10–13. By comparing the points plotted in the last four figures to those in the first four, one will find that they are on the same trend line, or are relatively close to the earlier extrapolated line.

Although this method of extrapolation proved to be very useful in forecasting, the company felt a need for more "qualitative" information about the years to come. This was obtained by face-to-face interviews with experts to determine what the nature of new developments in the future might be.

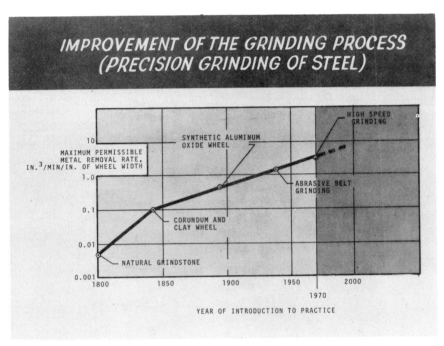

Figure 13   Improvement of the grinding process (precision grinding of steel).

The combination of trend extrapolation and expert opinion was extremely successful and resulted in the further application of these methods in later studies. One such study attempted to define some of the long-range trends and needs of manufacturing. Five of the major results of this study were as follows:

1. There is a growing need for more economical production of small lots, resulting from the diversification of various types and numbers of manufactured products.

2. There is a need for more economical means of working to higher accuracies.

3. There is a growing need for more economical means to work less conventional and higher-strength materials.

4. There is an increasing need for manufacturing processes to be less wasteful of material.

5. There is a rapidly growing need for improved communication and feedback between the manufacturing process and the design process.

Although the face-to-face interviews with experts were successful, they also had some obvious drawbacks, such as the influence of other panel members on an individual's opinion. Since the Delphi method was becoming well known and apparently had an acceptable accuracy rate, as indicated by the studies of Helmer and Gordon, it was adopted and is now being used by the technical and managerial staffs in their technological forecasting.

XI.   *Foods and Feeds*

Only the supremely wise and the abysmally ignorant do not change.   Confucius

INTRODUCTION

The foods and feeds business can generally be classified as "technologically static," that is, it is characterized by an R&D investment of about 2–3% of profits. It is only very recently that processes for manufacturing all types of foods quickly and cheaply have come into being; even now, there has not been very much invention or innovation in these areas. The only exception found to this general rule was the company chosen for the case study. Out of the 1170 companies that returned the more general questionnaire, only 30 were from the foods and feeds area.

RESULTS OF QUESTIONNAIRE

The results of the questionnaire left with the specific company, which, as stated above, may well be an exceptional firm, are as follows.

OBJECTIVES. The company has written quantitative corporate objectives and written qualitative R&D objectives, all of which are updated annually.

FORECASTS. The company always makes technological, economic, environmental, and marketing forecasts. The technological forecast is always used as an aid in planning and resource allocation, and occasionally for help in acquiring a government contract or subcontract. The forecasts are performed in-house by corporate planners, operations research staff, and scientists and engineers, together with the marketing staff.

FORECASTING AND LONG-RANGE PLANNING. In most cases, the company formulates specific long-range plans for its R&D effort. Forecasting has been used in assisting long-range planning efforts for 7 years and is ordinarily utilized in preparing the long-range plans. The major technique employed is intuitive, followed by trend extrapolation. The cost of preparing the long-range plans is 10% of the annual R&D budget; another 10% of the R&D budget is spent on technological forecasting in the first year, and 5% each additional year. Revisions to the forecast are made every 6 months by group discussion. The long-range plans extend 1–5 years into the future, are updated annually, and are then communicated in writing to the persons in charge of allocating resources, who use them. The responsibility for the formulation of the organization's long-range plans is held by the director of research.

CONTRIBUTOR TO THE FORECAST. Although the most important techniques used are those mentioned previously, the contributor also uses trend correlation to provide inputs to the forecast. The size of the groups generating these inputs is about 2 persons.

USER OF THE FORECAST. The major users of the forecast are the planning staff, marketing staff, manufacturing staff, and programming and budgeting staff. The forecast is used monthly as an input to short-range operational plans, operational concept generation, justification of budget, and intelligence information.

PROJECT SELECTION AND RESOURCE ALLOCATION. The current process used for the selection of R&D projects is subjective. The amount of new R&D work taken on each year is 21–30%, and a subjective system is used for obtaining a balance between long-term–payoff projects and short-term ones. Both the research and the development projects last about 1–2 years. The type of work performed by the company consists of 10–20% pure research, over 40% applied research, and 5–10% development.

REMARKS. The results from the questionnaires from the other 29 foods and feeds companies are as follows: average time for research is 4 years; for development, 2 years. Although most of the firms have objectives and formulate long-range plans, very little forecasting is performed.

Food Products Company

The Food Products Company is the corporate headquarters of 4 main divisions and 12 manufacturing plants in the United States. The divisions are broadly classed as follows: Product Line Division; Marketing Division, whose main interest is in chocolate, coffee, and tea; Commercial Products Division, specializing in restaurant service, chocolate coatings, etc.; and Government Division. Within each of these are several subsidiaries.

The marketing functions for each division are decentralized, but the other staff services are centralized. Each division creates its own short- and long-term profit plans. The short-term plan, covering 1 year, is updated every 6 months; the long-term 5 year plan, annually. The divisions' plans are collated by the corporate staff into one overall plan, which is then approved by the Swiss parent company. The overall plan encompasses an economic forecast, proposed development of new products, new ideas, projected building of new facilities, research and development plans, and promotion and sales plans. Before preparing the plans, each division must perform some market research and, once ideas have been formed, must examine consumers' requirements (taste-profile) and the marketability of proposed products. On the whole, the estimated profitability establishes the priority of proposed projects; however, if product interaction is required (e.g., building up a market for freeze-dried coffee while regular instant coffee is still available), the initial profitability is not taken into account. In other words, the aggregate profitability picture is evaluated on an aggregate basis.

Basically, the techniques used for short- and long-term planning are intuitive, although a computer model has been built for warehouse distribution, and a model known as COMPASS is used for selecting and optimum mix of advertising media. Some of the market research utilizes sensing devices to detect consumer attitudes to product areas and various products, by measuring consumers' perceptions in terms of taste, convenience, economy, social acceptability, etc. Also, exploratory studies are conducted on samples of the population, in order to quantify consumers' criteria for product selection. The results of these studies are analyzed by means of perceptual mapping and are then fed back to the R&D groups. This type of study opens up avenues for product development and, by improving market segmentation, can provide added strategies for the marketing and production people to use in their plans. The plans are directed toward the profit goals of the divisions, which are established by the parent company with the agreement of the divisions.

The foreign parent company keeps tight control over all its divisions, not only by approving their goals and monitoring their planning systems, but also by reviewing all proposed projects. If the laboratory facilities or expertise in the United States proves insufficient for some R&D projects, the foreign capabilities can be used, on payment of royalties. Similarly, if the foreign laboratories discover a new product believed to have market potential in the United States, the divisions here can manufacture and market it, on payment of royalties to the parent.

Essentially, although the Food Products Company is engaged in work of a highly technological nature in the food area, this is not as high a technological area, as, for instance, is the Aerospace Industry. Forecasts in terms of customer needs, market demands, and new processes can greatly assist in the development of the company's long-range plans.

XII.   *Some Conclusions*

It is not what you know about the present or the future, but what you do with what you know that really counts.   Bodo Bartocha

The information in this chapter originated in eight sectors: chemical and pharmaceutical, electronics, aerospace, plastics, metallurgical and metal, foods and feeds, R&D firms and academic, and government and military. Besides the specific case studies carried out, 1114 executives, most of them at the level of vice president for R&D or director of research, responded to our questionnaire.

SUMMARY OF LONG-RANGE PLANNING ACTIVITIES

Here are the main points emerging from the survey of long-range planning activities in the reporting companies.

1. Formal long-range planning activities of some form are reported by the overwhelming majority (95%) of the companies. Among the very few (5%) who report no long-range planning are extremely small organizations and those whose preoccupation with short-term survival preclude, in their eyes, planning much further ahead than 1 month.

2. Increases or decreases of company size in concert with the economic environment are included in the long-range plans of over half the companies (60%).

3. Concurrent approaches and alternative actions are provided for

in the long-range plans of many companies, as protection against changes in the social-political-economic environment.

4. A specific time for review of their long-range plans is scheduled by most companies (85%), although the planning process itself goes on continuously.

5. Most long-range planning activities were begun after 1945. The use of planning has increased steadily since 1960, and the tendency toward planning continues.

6. At the lower levels of the corporation, support for planning is usually obtained by persuasion or the formulation of suitable policy instruments, whereas at higher levels it is obtained by education of executives.

7. Internal factors responsible for increased adoption of long-range planning include company growth, diversification, decentralization, and increased efficiency.

8. Relevant external factors are competition, loss of patent protection, technological change, diverging markets, government spending, diminishing product lifetime, and lengthening market lead-time.

9. The length of time ahead for which companies plan (the planning period) is usually dependent on product development time, market development time, and the availability of accurate information.

10. Many companies report a fixed planning period. Some are considering extending their planning farther into the future.

11. The main tendency is to concentrate long-range planning in a formal group reporting directly to the president or vice-president, whereas planning formerly was an extra task for an already overburdened executive.

12. Particularly in marketing, technology, and management, the long-range planning staff is the basis for the creative, dynamic aspect of the organization.

13. If planning is to succeed, all levels of a company must participate in the long-range effort.

14. Customer requirements loom large in development of a company's long-range plans.

15. Critical areas of long-range planning include product research and development, marketing, budgeting, facilities, product engineering, and competition.

16. Input information to long-range plans includes sales forecasts, technological forecasts, appraisals of state of the art, market forecasts, and financial data.

17. Some companies employ *ad hoc* or standing planning committees to coordinate long-range planning. Most respondents, however, say that they employ normal interstaff coordination.

18. Such aids as classical methods (sales, budgets, return on invest-ment), operations research, modeling, and information science are used in current planning systems.

19. Such techniques as game theory, simulations, and improved man-agement information systems could be employed in future planning sys-tems, our respondents report.

20. Long-range plans are usually communicated to the operating levels responsible for their implementation by integrating them in a master plan which is distributed to line managers, or by intracompany briefings.

21. Major difficulties and limitations in long-range planning are due to preoccupation of higher management with other matters and operating pressures, lack of adequate information, and inadequate forecasts.

22. Major results of long-range planning reported by our respondents include organizational changes, product changes, diversification, new facilities, and new equipment.

23. Adequate methods for evaluating the effectiveness of long-range planning have not yet been developed, our respondents feel.

SUMMARY OF FORECASTING ACTIVITIES

Here are the main points emerging from the survey of forecasting in the reporting companies.[1]

1. Written corporate objectives were reported by 77% of the respon-dents—43% reporting written *quantitative* objectives; 34%, written *qualitative* objectives. Written R&D objectives are reported by 78% of the respondents—36% having written *quantitative* objectives; 42%, written *qualitative* objectives. Over half of the written R&D objectives are updated annually or more frequently.

2. The types of forecasts used in the reporting organizations, and their percentage frequencies of use, are shown in Table 1.

3. Among the organizations that use them, technological forecasts serve the purposes shown in Table 2.

4. A large majority (83%) of respondents report that forecasts are performed in-house. A small minority (7%) report that forecasts are performed externally. The remaining 10% report that some forecasts are done by in-house staff and some by contractors.

5. When a corporation prepares technological forecasts in-house, the work is done most commonly by the product staff. The second and third

[1] The work for this effort was supported, in part, by a grant from the National Science Foundation.

Table 1

Type of Forecast	Percentage Frequency of Use				
	Always	Often	*Always + Often*	Seldom	Never
Marketing	39	34	*73*	14	13
Technological	32	37	*69*	25	5
Economic	35	30	*65*	21	14
Environmental	19	25	*44*	34	22

most common sources of technological forecasts are the corporate staff and the marketing staff.

When the forecast is prepared by the product staff, the personnel involved are mainly engineers and scientists. When the corporate staff is responsible, a combination of technical planners and operations researchers collaborate in the research, and technical planners prepare the forecast. When the forecast is prepared by the marketing staff, it is done by technical planners assisted by technical personnel from the R&D division.

Table 2

Purpose	Percentage Frequency of Use				
	Always	Frequently	*Always + Frequently*	Occasionally	Never
As an aid in planning	40	33	*73*	21	5
As an aid in allocating resources	28	33	*61*	27	11
To justify previously made decisions	4	21	*25*	48	28
To help acquire a government contract	5	19	*24*	24	53
To satisfy a "fad"	1	7	*8*	36	56
Other—to gain insight into competition, etc.	17	13	*30*	10	60

6. The types of technological forecasts most used (in percentage decreasing order of use by firms) are listed in Table 3.

7. Normative forecasting techniques or quantitative resource allocation methods are used (or were tested) by 54% of the 1114 respondents. Another 3% plan to use them. The remaining 43% neither use them nor plan to use them.

8. Table 4 shows a breakdown of normative forecasting techniques and their utilization, listed in decreasing order of use.

9. A large majority (90%) of the respondents believe that appropriate models can be developed and made extremely meaningful in planning R&D activities. The remaining 10% say that they can be developed but will not be of much help. No one thinks that the models cannot be developed.

Table 3

Type of Forecast	Less than 5%	5–10%	11–20%	21–30%	31–40%	41–50%	Over 50%
	Types of Technological Forecasts Used by Percentage						
Trend extrapolation	13	11	17	19	16	11	13
Intuitive, including Delphi	22	16	15	13	9	10	14
Trend correlation	34	18	21	13	7	4	3
Growth analogy	48	18	15	10	4	3	3

10. The process used in their companies is a combination of quantitative and qualitative techniques, say a preponderance of our respondents (61%). Quantitative techniques alone are reported by more respondents (30%) than report qualitative techniques alone (9%).

11. The number of years that a long-range plan for *applied research* should extend into the future is estimated in the various industries as shown in Table 5.

12. The number of years that a long-range plan for *development* should extend into the future is estimated in the various industries as shown in Table 6.

In the following sections (13–16) respondents were asked to evaluate the *importance* and *accuracy* of the tabulated items. The scale for *im-

Table 4

Forecasting Technique	Number of Firms That Have:		
	Tested or Used the Technique	Plan to Use the Technique	Have No "Familiarity" with the Technique, or Have "Considered" the Technique
RDE (linear programming model)	20	3	77
Disman (discounted cash-flow optimization)	19	2	79
BRAILLE (cost-effective model based on technical feasibility)	15	2	83
PROFILE (heuristic relevance tree technique)	11	4	85
PATTERN (heuristic relevance tree technique)	12	1	87
QUEST (double-matrix technique)	9	3	88
Mottley Newton (scoring technique)	6	0	94
TORQUE (marginal utility technique—military)	5	1	94
MACRO (marginal utility technique—civilian)	4	2	94
Other quantitative methods (miscellaneous)	11	2	87

Table 5

Industry	Average Number of Years
Chemical and pharmaceutical	7
Aerospace	6
Government/or military	6
Electronics	5
Plastics	4
Foods and feeds	4
Metallurgical and metals	4
R&D (firm only) or academic	4

portance is as follows:

1: critical
2: very important
3: important
4: not very important

The scale for *accuracy* (how accurately the criteria can be quantified for evaluation purposes) is as follows:

1: excellent
2: good
3: fair
4: poor
5: totally unreliable

The numbers assigned to the criteria in Tables 7–10 are mean values of the responses.

Table 6

Industry	Average Number of Years
Government/military	7
Plastics	5
Electronics	4
R&D (firm only) or academic	4
Metallurgical and metals	4
Aerospace	4
Chemical and pharmaceutical	3
Foods and feeds	2

13. The criteria considered important for project selection on the basis of *initial funding* are listed, in decreasing order of *importance,* in Table 7.

14. The criteria considered important for project selection on the basis of *continued funding* are listed, in decreasing order of *importance,* in Table 8.

15. The criteria considered important for project selection on the basis of *initial funding* are listed, in decreasing order of *accuracy,* in Table 9. The figures in *italics,* which check closely with our own, are from Robert E. Seiler's *Improving the Effectiveness of Research and Development,* McGraw-Hill Book Company, New York, 1965.

16. The criteria considered important for project selection on the basis

of *continued funding* are listed in Table 10 in the order of how accurately they can be quantified for evaluation purposes.

A more detailed analysis of the results, broken down by industry, occupation, role, size, and age, is presented in the Appendix at the end of the book. The size and the makeup of the sample are included there.

Table 7

Criterion	Mean Value of Responses
Probability of market success	1.84
Management environment (top management support or not)	1.89
Revenue from the sale of the product if R&D efforts are successful (potential value)	1.96
Probability of technical success	2.03
Cost of development if the research is successful	2.29
Competitors' position	2.34
Cost of the total research project	2.36
Time necessary to complete the development	2.41
Market life of the product if R&D efforts prove successful	2.44
Time necessary to complete the research	2.55
Manpower requirements necessary to complete the research	2.61
Cost reductions if R&D efforts are successful	2.65
Degree of ego involvement	2.91
Technological cross support (technology transfer) to the firm	3.08
Good will or prestige to the firm	3.10

REASONS FOR NOT USING FORECASTING

Since we believe that normative technological forecasting can be very useful, especially in technological companies, we must now account for the fact that only 54% of the companies questioned report using it. What factors are inhibiting the application of technological forecasting?

The single most obvious finding is that, if a firm has no meaningful planning system, it is not likely to find technological forecasting very useful. Four factors are prerequisites for the implementation of a technological forecast:

1. A planning system which is the basis for decisions.
2. A planning system which is used in the programming of resources.
3. Integration of the forecast into the planning process.
4. Support by management at all levels of the organization.

In short, unless forecasts have an impact on decision making or resource allocation, they are useless. This necessity is illustrated by Figure 1 from Donald Pyke, showing the role of forecasting in the planning process.[2]

Table 8

Criterion	Mean Value of Responses
Probability of market success	1.77
Management environment (top management support or not)	1.76
Probability of technical success	1.77
Revenue from the sale of the product if R&D efforts are successful (potential value)	1.88
Cost of development if the research is successful	2.11
Cost of the total research project	2.11
Competitors' position	2.17
Time necessary to complete the development	2.20
Time necessary to complete the research	2.28
Market life of the product if R&D efforts are successful	2.32
Manpower requirements necessary to complete the research	2.42
Cost reductions if R&D efforts are successful	2.56
Degree of ego involvement	2.79
Technological cross support (technology transfer to other products	2.96
Good will or prestige to the firm	3.06
Resources spent to date (sunk cost)	3.40

One of our respondents from an aerospace company that does not use forecasting expressed the same idea in this way:

The value of technological forecasting as a planning technique will depend to a large measure on the extent to which it is integrated and applied within the framework of a comprehensive long-range planning program directed toward the selection of research projects and the allocation of resources consistent with overall corporate objectives. The results of technological forecasts by themselves will be interesting but of limited planning value.

[2] Donald Pyke, "Technological Forecasting: A Framework for Consideration," *Futures,* December 1970, p. 327.

Table 9

Criterion	Accuracy Rating					Ordinal Rank by Reliability Based on Responses of "Poor" or "Totally Unreliable"
	1 (Excellent)	2 (Good)	3 (Fair)	4 (Poor)	5 (Totally Unreliable)	
Management environment (top management support)	18	48	24	7	2	1
	—	—	—	—	—	—
Probability of technical success	8	39	39	13	1	2
	3.5	*51.3*	*39.9*	*6.3*	*0.0*	*1*
Competitors' position	7	41	37	13	3	3
	—	—	—	—	—	—
Manpower requirements to complete the research	4	37	42	14	2	4
	2.6	*34.2*	*53.5*	*7.0*	*2.7*	*2*
Cost reductions if R&D efforts are successful	8	36	37	15	5	5
	10.7	*57.1*	*14.3*	*14.3*	*3.6*	*5*
Cost of development if the research is successful	5	31	38	23	3	8
	2.6	*38.8*	*46.6*	*9.5*	*2.5*	*3*
Time necessary to complete the development	3	28	45	21	3	6
	1.8	*34.5*	*41.8*	*17.3*	*4.6*	*6*
Degree of ego involvement	9	32	31	15	13	10
	—	—	—	—	—	—
Revenue from sale of the product if R&D efforts prove successful (potential value)	7	29	37	22	4	9
	5.3	*36.0*	*28.9*	*27.2*	*2.6*	*8*
Cost of the total research project	3	23	51	21	3	7
	3.5	*27.8*	*52.2*	*14.8*	*1.7*	*4*
Probability of market success	4	28	40	25	4	11
	3.6	*33.6*	*38.2*	*14.5*	*10.1*	*7*
Good will or prestige to the firm	8	30	31	19	12	13
	—	—	—	—	—	—
Market life of the product	5	28	39	21	8	12
	4.6	*28.0*	*29.0*	*23.4*	*15.0*	*10*
Time to complete research	2	20	47	28	3	14
	0.9	*18.6*	*50.4*	*24.8*	*5.3*	*9*
Technological cross support	5	24	33	28	10	15
	—	—	—	—	—	—

214

Another contributor from the aerospace industry justified technological forecasting in these words:

Our forecasts had a direct impact on planning and the subsequent allocation of funds, because the man who initiated the planning effort was the director of technology planning and he had "the ear of corporate management."

Table 10

Criterion	Mean Value of Rating
Resources spent to date (sunk cost)	1.84
Management environment (top management support or not)	2.08
Probability of technical success	2.19
Manpower requirements necessary to complete the research	2.30
Cost of the total research project	2.33
Cost of development if the research is successful	2.39
Competitors' position	2.41
Time necessary to complete the research	2.50
Time necessary to complete the development	2.51
Cost reductions if R&D efforts are successful	2.55
Degree of ego involvement	2.59
Probability of market success	2.65
Revenue from the sale of the product if R&D efforts are successful (potential value)	2.66
Technological cross support (technology transfer to other products)	2.78
Market life of the product if R&D efforts prove successful	2.81
Good will or prestige to the firm	2.82

Perhaps this quotation from the vice-president of a medium-sized electronics company serves as the best summary:

Decisions are based on the personal interests of the researchers, the pet projects of key administrators, and a variety of other criteria which may well be at odds with the strategic interests of the firm. Major decisions are determined by "internal power dynamics" which permit a substantial amount of "hobby-work" or pet projects. Even though I realize that individual project allocations might provide a better basis for control, putting it bluntly, without the need for objective cost justification of research projects there is little incentive among R&D decision makers for either planning or forecasting technology. With this new squeeze on resources, however, the picture may well change.

THE ROLE OF FORECASTING IN THE PLANNING PROCESS

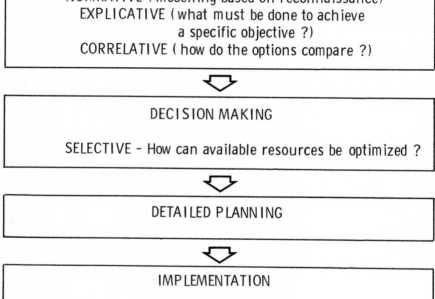

Figure 1   The role of forecasting in the planning process.

Two other factors seem to be necessary (but not sufficient) for the implementation of a planning program. The first is the presence of a catalyst or key man. In every successful application of technological forecasting one or two key men played a decisive role. In all but two cases, technological forecasting programs were sold from the bottom up. Even in the two exceptions in which forecasting was initiated at the top, the right man—one with initiative and a broad background—had to be available. This is clearly shown in Figure 2, a caricature from *Innovation Magazine*, Vol. 12, 1970.

The second necessity for planning program implementation is the willingness of top management to accept change. We are all familiar with the "resistance-to-change" syndrome. This must be overcome if a company is to take advantage of new technological opportunities or to stop work in progress that has little potential.

"The payoff from technological forecasting is a long time coming," wrote the R&D vice president of a large chemical company, "and the big corporation has no memory for a long-term investment." As the responsible official for a profit center, this man had to make short-term decisions the results of which would show up as soon as possible on his profit-and-loss statement. Thus he identified the last impediment

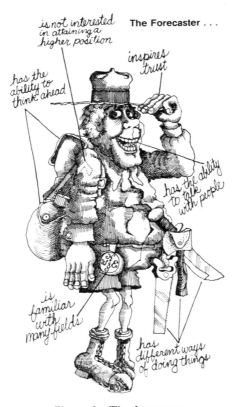

Figure 2   The forecaster.

to the successful application of technological forecasting—*the time value of information.*

THE SELECTION OF A FORECASTING TECHNIQUE

We are often asked by executives who expect to embark on a technological forecasting venture, "What forecasting technique is best?" Actually there is no "best" technique. In this connection Tables 11 and 12, adapted from data by the National Research Council-National Materials Advisory Board, are of interest. The first column represents the amount of time involved in preparing a forecast, where 1 is a brief time and 10 a long one. The second column represents the amount of data required; the third column, the degree of reproducibility in three different time frames—1–3 years, 3–10 years, and 10 or more years. The fourth column refers to the objectivity or visibility of the method to the potential user. The fifth column is a measure of confidence in the accuracy of the method or technique, again detailed in three time frames. The sixth column lists assumptions implicit in each technique, and the seventh column contains special remarks.

Although no one technique is optimum for every purpose, there are three major requisites of a good technological forecast:

1. A reliable data base, which normally consists of the knowledge bases of scientific specialists in the subject, as well as any supporting data.

2. Astute judgment and common sense on the part of the forecaster.

3. An understanding of applicable forecasting techniques, and of how and why to apply them.

In regard to the selection of a technique, we suggest that the most satisfactory choice will depend on the circumstances under which the forecaster is working; his needs; the reliability, completeness, and quantitative precision of the data base; the purpose of the forecast; the length of the forecast period; and the time and effort that can be invested in preparing the forecast.

A few examples will illustrate the usefulness of Tables 11 and 12. Let's assume that management has asked us to prepare a forecast in the field of praetersonics. We want the pacing physical parameters, let's say. This science is too new for us to know the natural limits or the likely areas of utility. Consequently, few or no data exist. Theoretically, we might take several steps to build up our data base. We might analyze in great detail whatever data exist. We might examine laboratory experi-

Table 11 Exploratory Techniques

Technique (All Extrapolative)	Time Involved	Data Required	Reproducibility (years) 1–3	3–10	10 or More	Objectivity	Confidence in Accuracy of the Method (0 when no data available) 1–3	3–10	10 or Higher	Assumptions	Remarks
1. Single trend extrapolation	Medium / 5	High / 4–5	Excel. / 10	Excel. / 9	Excel. / 8	High / 8	Very good / 7	Good / 6	Poor to mod. / 0–4	Future—an extrapolation on past continuity	Work high if data obscure—low available. Confidence depends on adequate data over sufficient time. Only possible if data are available.
2. Growth analogy	Medium / 6	High / 6	Excel. / 10	Excel. / 9	Excel. / 8	High / 8	Very good / 7	Very good / 7	Poor to mod. / 0–5	Above and natural limits	Same as (1) above—treatment of natural limits is improvement.
3. Correlation analysis	High / 8–10	High to very high / 8–10	Excel. / 9	Very good / 8	Mod. / 6	High to moderate / 7	Very good / 7	Very good / 8–9	Poor to mod. / 1–6	Above plus tradeoffs	As in (1) and (2) above. Long-range forecast confidence depends on abundant and detailed data.
4. Substitution	Medium / 6	High / 6	Very good / 9	Very good / 9	Very good / 9	High / 8	Very good / 7	Very good / 7	Poor to mod. / 0–5	Once started, substitutions inevitable	Long-term analysis better for item substituted; valuable for process trend analysis. (Fatalistic—not as useful to control the future.)

Table 12 Intuitive and Normative Techniques

Technique (5–8 Intuitive; 9 Normative)	Time Involved	Data Required	Reproducibility (years)			Objectivity	Confidence in Accuracy of the Method (0 when no data available)			Assumptions	Remarks
			1–3	3–10	10 or More		1–3	3–10	10 or Higher		
5. Personal judgment	Very small 1	No 0	Good 5	Mod. to poor 3	Worthless 0	Low 2	Good 6	Poor 1	Poor 0	Hidden	Highly dependent on the individual.
6. Genius (means knowledgeable person)	Very small 2	No 1	Good 6	Mod. 4	Poor 0	Low 0	Very good 7	Mod. 4	Poor 1	Hidden	Identification of individual difficult. Reputation protection leads to conservatism.
7. Consensus	Small 4	No 1	Very good 8	Mod. to good 5	Poor+ 2	Moderate 4	Very good 8	Mod. 4	Poor to mod. 2–4	Partially visible	Initial choice and balance very important—social pressures to conform may be high.
8. Delphi	Small to large 3–7	Some 2	Very good 8	Good 6	Mod. 4	High 5	Very good 8	Mod. 5	Mod. 2–4	Partially visible	Comparatively good long-term where data base is poor or nonexistent. Depends heavily on question formulation and programming. (Trend analysis can be helpful.)
9. Normative	Large 8–10	High to very high 8–10	Very good 8	Good 6	Mod. 4	High 6	Very good 7	Good 6	Poor to Mod. 2–4	Specific desirable future exists	Total range of assumptions rarely specified (social, economic, and political). Tends to limit exploratory solutions.

ments in progress, with an eye to the technical barriers to which praeter-sonics is the possible solution. But unless we can afford to invest our resources in this sort of analysis, which does, after all, require extremely sophisticated methods, we might be better off using an intuitive forecast.

For a quick, inexpensive, moderately reliable, short-term forecast, we would do well to solicit the opinion of an expert in the technological field. Perhaps this will satisfy our needs. For better credibility and a longer time span—and providing we are ready to pay for the extra effort—we might employ a committee of experts or use a Delphi exercise, the additional experts giving an increment of objectivity to the forecast. If our resources of time and effort are even more substantial, we might undertake a correlation analysis using all available data, which can then be employed as the basis of a Delphi exercise; and the Delphi panel itself may serve as the starting point for a consensus panel, to provide the additional intuitive insight inspired by vigorous open discussion.

Now suppose instead that we have been asked to prepare a 3–10 year forecast in a stable but expanding field like jet engine R&D or process steel making. We can be sure that copious data exist. Therefore, on the assumption that data would be available easily in suitable form, we would incline toward the use of trend analysis, which provides great objectivity, reproducibility, and confidence. Even sophisticated trend techniques require little time, once the necessary data are at hand. The trouble is that, for reasons of secrecy traceable to security or proprietary considerations, the assumption that data are readily available in the fields we mentioned is not justified. Since data collection for trend analysis is often harder work than the analysis itself, we would do better to save ourselves some time by turning to intuitive methods. (As a matter of fact, even if we conducted a trend analysis, we would be well advised to conduct a back-up intuitive forecast as insurance against gaps in technology and the effects of competing technology.)

Of course, if we are willing to settle for the cheapest, most subjective, nonreproducible forecast—one that requires no data but provides almost no confidence—we can always guess the future ourselves.

THE PRESENT STATUS OF FORECASTING

Good forecasting tools *are* available for the 8–10 year period, providing the necessary data are at hand. The principal shortcoming in technological forecasting today is the unavailability of an adequate data base in useful form.

The significance of technological forecasting is dependent to a great extent on the technological dynamism of a company and on its strategies for innovation. Most companies employ a mix of normative and exploratory forecasting techniques, but the more innovative companies stress the former type.

Many companies find technological forecasting useful for cataloging and quantifying subjective judgments and for dealing in a systematic manner with a large number of uncertain factors. Unfortunately, however, doubts concerning the validity and acceptability of forecasting, and reservations about the cost of implementation, remain in the minds of even those who now use these techniques. Indeed, we have encountered cases in which forecasting might better have never been undertaken, since it was not part of a long-range planning system and thus was invalid from the beginning, having no real purpose.

A most important breakthrough in technological forecasting will occur when a major company proves decisively and incontrovertibly that it is a valuable tool of industry. When such a company can demonstrate to others that forecasting has increased its effectiveness in attaining its corporate objectives, we will be able to say truthfully that technological forecasting *can be* and *must be* an integral part of long-range planning.

Section III

XIII. *Technological Forecasting Methodology*

RALPH C. LENZ, JR.

That piece of equipment is so ingenious; looks so beautiful; and works so well; it almost makes one forget how utterly useless it is. Commander, Royal Navy

INTRODUCTION

All uses of extrapolation are suspect to some degree, and most of us, as scientists, engineers, or technicians, much prefer interpolative methodology for analysis and design. *Unfortunately, interpolation is not available to us for predicting future technological advance, since any forecast of the future is inherently extrapolative.* This necessity for extrapolation is the root problem in much of the resistance still prevalent to the subject and practice of technological forecasting. To those who are irrevocably opposed to extrapolation, speculation about the future is completely foreclosed. For those who wish to guide their destiny by some rational expectation of future events, extrapolation becomes a lesser evil.

With this preamble, some of the possible techniques for prediction of the trends of technological progress may be presented. *A first condition for any form of extrapolation is, of course, the necessity for some kind of regularity in empirical data, which regularity may be expressed in a form suitable for extension beyond the observed data.* A second condition is that the form chosen for extension should conform to natural laws, insofar as these are expected to have effect in the region of the

225

extrapolation. A third condition, not always met, is the existence or development of a theory which adequately accounts for the observed data, and which will permit extrapolation on the basis of known facts.

All of the methods of technological trend prediction offered here meet the first condition of regularity of data presented in a form suitable for extrapolation. Some of the methods meet the second condition by providing accommodation for the physical limits of natural law. Since technological forecasting has only been accepted as a topic for serious study in this decade, however, the third condition, calling for theory supporting the extrapolations, is seldom met. However, two recent articles, one written by the Secretary of the Air Force, Dr. Robert C. Seamans, Jr., and one by Alan Fusfeld, offer new opportunities for the development of a theoretical explantation for some observed phenomena of technological progression.

Six extrapolative methods will be presented in this chapter:

1. Extension of technological performance at a constant percentage rate of improvement.

2. Prediction of technological performance in accordance with growth analogies.

3. Projection of technological performance by correlation with precursor trends.

4. Synthesis of future technological capabilities by projection of interrelated performance trends, constrained by those relationships.

5. Projection of technological performance as a result of competitive processes.

6. Extrapolation of technological progress on the basis of cumulative production quantities.

Before each of these methods is described, certain comments should be made concerning previous use and misuse of extrapolative techniques.

Projection of improvement in technological performance at the same rate which has prevailed in the past has served as the basis of most forecasts that have been made. The forecaster's personal view of the past rate of improvement was often more significant than the actual rate. If the forecaster was unaware of past improvements, his forecasts were like a stab in the dark. If he viewed progress as a random occurrence, his forecasts were similarly random. If he felt that advances were made only very slowly and at great cost, he projected a similar conservatism or stagnation in his forecasts. If he truly believed that necessity is the mother of invention, his forecasts were projected solutions to current problems. On the contrary, if he believed that invention is the father of necessity, the forecaster predicted rates of improvement based on schedules for the completion of development projects. Finally, the true genius intuitively analyzed remembered data and extrapolated actual rates of past improvement to obtain his forecasts. The objective of the methods presented herein is to rationalize the process of intuition used by the genius to produce his forecasts.

CONSTANT PERCENTAGE RATE OF IMPROVEMENT

The rationale for the first method, that is, improvement of technological performance at a constant percentage rate, begins with the intuitive belief that prior rates of improvement are indeed significant to future expectations. In fact, it has even been suggested that one cannot reasonably extrapolate from a single point of data. On the assumption that this intuitive view is correct, the next step in developing the rationale is the identification of patterns of behavior in technological progress. The majority of researchers on this subject, starting with Henry Adams at the turn of the century, have concluded that technological performance improves exponentially in most cases. Thus the empirical evidence strongly favors forecasting of continued constant percentage rates of improvement in cases where the data indicate the existence of such rates up to the time when the forecast is made.

In brief, the rationale is that progress in most technical areas will proceed exponentially, that is, at constant percentage rates of improvement, because this is the pattern evident in our technologically oriented societies.

The logical method of developing a forecast of technological performance which increases exponentially is, of course, to plot data for past performance on semilogarithmic graphs, with time as the abscissa. Constant percentage rates of increase may then be plotted as straight lines fitted to the data for past performance. The forecast is simply an extension of the established trend at the same percentage rate of increase. Typically, such a forecast may be presented in the form shown in Figure 1.

Some examples of performance trends which at least appear to follow the pattern of constant exponential increase are shown in Figures 2 and 3. Figure 2 shows that the horsepower of the average U.S. automobile has increased at an average rate of 3.7% per year since 1900. The projection of this trend indicates a further increase from the present average of 200 horsepower to 600 horsepower by the year 2000. Whether or not such a projection is valid, it remains the most logical choice unless

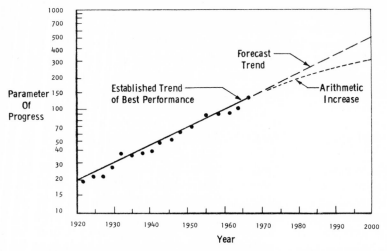

Figure 1 Elements of exponential trend forecasting of technological progress.

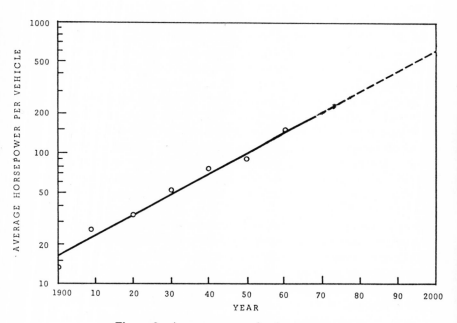

Figure 2 Average automotive horsepower.

228

and until additional evidence is introduced. Figure 3, presenting 1958 and 1967 forecasts of combat aircraft speed trends, shows the change which may occur in a forecast as a result of later information. In this case the earlier forecast proved optimistic by only 12% after a period of 9 years.

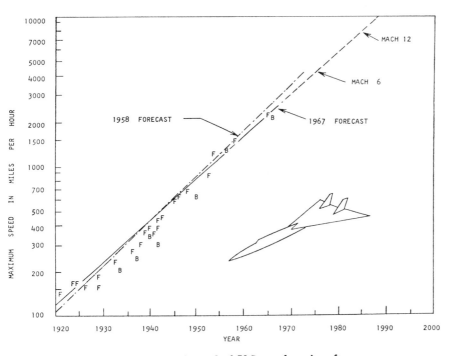

Figure 3   Speed trend of U.S. combat aircraft.

GROWTH ANALOGIES

Many processes proceed initially at an exponential rate which gradually slows as some ultimate limit is approached. These processes, including autocatalytic chemical reaction and biological growth patterns, have been used frequently as analogs for technological progress. As indicated in the preceding section, early investigators of technological progress discovered that performance most often increased exponentially. However, some of these investigators also presented cases in which the initial rate of progress decreased gradually to the point that further advance was imperceptible. Such empirical data may be neatly reduced to fit the formula of any of the several analog processes. The rationale for these analogs is simply that mathematical formulas which match the empirical observations are provided for use in extrapolation. Beyond empiricism, some qualitative descriptions of the analog relationships provide a hint that logical models for this pattern of technological development can ultimately be developed. However, the quantitative relationships necessary for acceptance of any of the analog models as a satisfactory explanation for the process of technological improvement have yet to be developed.

Nevertheless, the rationale of empiricism can be accepted for the use of this method in forecasting, since the analogies make possible the development of trend curves which provide a better fit to existing performance data. In addition, the analog formulas often provide reasonable consideration of the effects of factors which inhibit or limit progress in a given technical field.

Development of a forecast using any one of the analogies which describe processes expanding to an upper limit naturally starts with selection of the desired analogy. In the absence of any better reason, the selection may be based on the forecaster's familiarity with the analog process or his belief that qualitative logic supports a comparison between the model and the parameter of progress to be forecast. Data for the past performance of the parameter to be forecast are then introduced into a proper transform of the existing formula for the analog model. Units of time are ordinarily exponents in such models, so that the forecast is made by calculation of results using increasing exponential values.

Graphic presentation of the forecast, on a semilog plot with time as the abscissa, ordinarily results in an initially straight line representing exponential increase, followed by a gradual curve approaching an asymptotic limit. Figure 4, showing a prediction of combat aircraft speeds, is based on an analogy of population growth originally developed by L. G. Pearl. The upper limit of progress is assumed to be the point at which orbital velocity is reached, at which point the vehicle ceases to depend on aerodynamic forces to sustain it. Thus, although higher speeds may be (in fact, already have been) attained with ballistic and space vehicles, the orbital condition represents a practical limit for vehicles intended to operate entirely within the atmosphere. Comparison of Figure 4 with the straight exponential forecast of the same parameter shown in Figure 3 indicates typical differences between these two forecasting techniques.

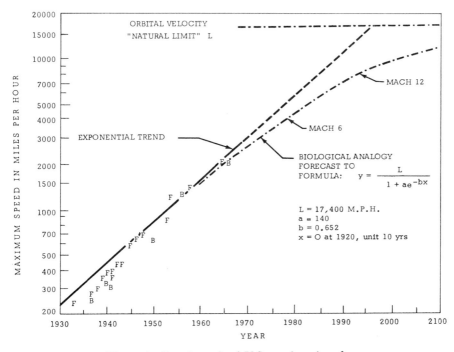

Figure 4   Speed trends of U.S. combat aircraft.

CORRELATION WITH PRECURSOR TRENDS

Any situation in which the attainment of particular values by a given quantity have regularly and consistently preceded the attainment of the same values by a related quantity offers the possibility of forecasting future values of the dependent quantity on the basis of presently attained values of the initial quantity. This method thus provides a forecast into the future equal to the lead time of the initial quantity over the dependent quantity. In cases where the dependent quantity has a cause-and-effect relationship with the initial quantity, the validity of this method of forecasting is scarcely questionable. Often, forecasts based on such relationships provide ample lead time for planning purposes. In some cases, even though the cause-and-effect relationship may be obscure or questionable, the regularity apparent in the relationship may provide a rational basis for forecasting.

Preparation of a precursor trend forecast requires finding a quantity whose variations have regularly preceded similar variations in the quantity to be forecast. If the nature, or the unit of measurement, of the two quantities is the same (such as velocity or size), the relationship between the two may be simply described. In any case the relationship may be developed mathematically or graphically to establish the basis for a forecast. For graphical presentation, a plot of the two quantities, with time as the common abscissa, and with appropriate ordinate scales, will depict the relationship. (Ordinarily, such plots of technological

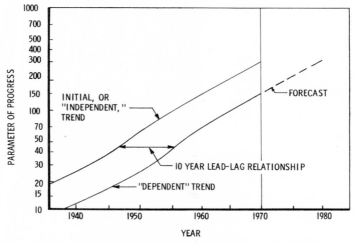

Figure 5   Precursor trend forecast of technological progress.

progress are best accomplished on semilog graphs, since they follow the same principles indicated in the examples mentioned earlier.) The forecast is then made by extending the dependent variable as far into the future as it ordinarily lags the independent variable. If a forecast has been made separately for the independent variable, a further extension of the dependent variable may be made. Confidence in this extension will be limited, however, to the confidence placed on the forecast of the independent variable.

The general nature of a forecast based on precursor trends is indicated in Figure 5. An example of such a forecast is shown in Figure 6, which depicts the relationship between combat aircraft speeds and the speeds of commercial transport aircraft. In this case, commercial transport speeds have lagged combat aircraft speeds by a regularly increasing

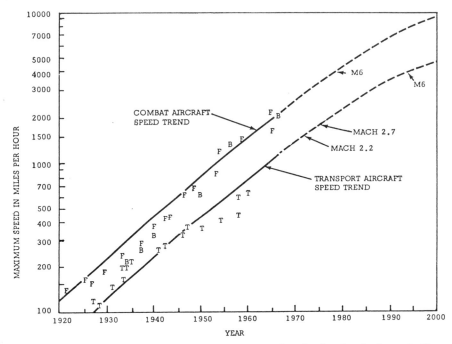

Figure 6   Speed trends of combat versus transport aircraft, showing lead trend effect.

period of time. Therefore, the demonstrated speed performance of combat aircraft has been used as a precursor to predict the date of attainment of similar speeds by commercial aircraft.

One form of precursor trend forecasting is based on comparison of the rate of development of two similar technologies. For example, the historical rates of development in radio technology may be used in predicting the rates of development in television technology at a later period. The validity of such predictions is highly dependent both on the degree of identity between the two technologies, and on the similarity of environmental conditions at the two different periods of time.

SYNTHESIS FROM INTERRELATED TRENDS

A common and valid criticism of forecasts made by extrapolation of single trends is that such forecasts often produce absurd results at some point of extension. For example, if the gross national product is increasing at a constant average rate of 7% per year, while R&D expenditures are increasing at an annual rate of 10%, the two trends will intersect at some point in the future, with obvious indication that R&D expenditures will consume the entire GNP at the point of intersection. Critics would like to assume that absurdities of this type invalidate trend extrapolation as a useful forecasting technique. One answer to this criticism is that trends should not be extended beyond the point at which the existence of such conflict first requires a modification of the trends. Another answer is that such situations often indicate the existence of an upper limit on the extension of the trend, in which case one of the growth analogies may be used to extend the trend asymptotically to the upper limit, thus avoiding the conflict. Occasionally a precursor trend may exist which will indicate the probability of a change in the trend being extended, so as to avoid the apparent conflict.

By far the best answer to absurdities created by unlimited trend extrapolation, however, is to use the apparent trends in an iterative synthesis which takes proper account of known relationships between the factors being forecast. The physical relationships between various parameters which represent technological progress in a given field are well known to design engineers and may be used effectively in conjunction with trend analysis to forecast future progress.

For example, aircraft speed, altitude, wing area, and lift coefficient are physically related in a known manner. Trend projections of the separate quantities may be examined collectively to see whether the known physical relationships are satisfied by the values forecast at various points of time. If not, one or more of the trends may be modified so that the necessary physical conditions are met. The choice of the trends to be modified depends heavily on the judgment of the forecaster, and his knowledge of the dominant and subordinate factors involved. In the case just cited, if extension of the altitude trend projected beyond the sensible atmosphere, then no combination of speed, wing area, and lift coefficient would be sufficient to sustain flight. Therefore the altitude trend would logically be subject to downward revision.

Figure 7 provides an example of forecasting by using interrelated trends. In this example, the total passenger-miles per year for U.S. trunk airlines, the total plane-miles, the average seating capacity per plane, and the average load factor are the factors being forecast. The trend of total passenger-miles is a function of market demand, which, within reasonable limits, is independent of the other three variables. Average seating capacity per plane is the technological trend of interest to the aircraft designer and operator, while total plane-miles is a demand trend

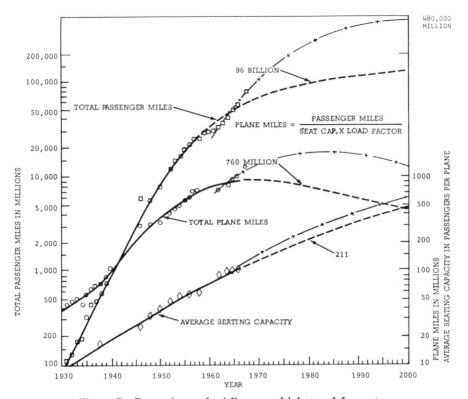

Figure 7   Domestic trunk airlines—multiple-trend forecast.

for air route and airport control services. Load factor trends are of primary significance for economic analyses. As shown by the chart, if the average seating capacity per plane, that is, aircraft size, increases at a greater rate than total passenger-miles, either total plane-miles or average load factor must decline. Although Figure 7 represents an actual forecast based on real data, it is shown principally to demonstrate the method of analyzing and synthesizing forecasts from a number of related trends.

ANALYSIS OF COMPETITIVE PROCESSES

A recent addition to the literature of exploratory forecasting was Air Force Secretary Robert Seamans' article on "Action and Reaction," published in *Technological Forecasting*, June 1969. One portion of this article outlined the rates of technological advance which would be expected under various assumptions for competitive action and reaction. The most interesting of the assumed cases, shown in Figure 8, starts when Competitor A initiates a new product. When this product is disclosed, Competitor B initiates action to develop a better product (assumed here to be 20% better), while A concentrates on production of the initial product. When B discloses his product, this stimulates A to attempt a 20% improvement over B's product. This "leap-frogging" continues as long as competition is maintained.

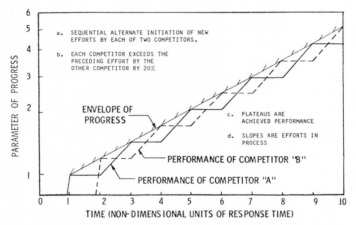

Figure 8   Technological progress as a function of competitive processes.

Secretary Seamans' development of this new concept is highly significant, since it represents one of the very few attempts to explain why technological progress proceeds exponentially. Although stylized in its presentation, this model nevertheless depicts real-world processes which are familiar to everyone.

Even more significant is the possibility that this model can be developed to provide a new technique for exploratory forecasting. With this concept progress is a function of (a) number of competitors, (b) length of time for development of new models, (c) timing of responses, (d) percentage of advance attempted, and (e) probability of success (which should be included as a stochastic function). Historical values of these quantities can be ascertained for various technical areas, with the aid of regression analyses. These values can then be combined in equations, or used in models, to forecast future rates of progress or to permit the examination of alternative possibilities. For example, the effect of competition on progress could be quantified from past experience, and then projected for various levels of competition in the future.

CORRELATION WITH CUMULATIVE PRODUCTION QUANTITIES

Alan Fusfeld, in a paper on "The Technological Progress Function," delivered at the annual meeting of The Industrial Management Society in Atlanta, October 1969, introduced another new technique for exploratory forecasting. The essence of Mr. Fusfeld's approach is that technological progress is correlated to cumulative production quantities of technological artifacts. The underlying premises of this approach are consistent with those of the Seamans model. The models differ in many significant respects, however, since the Seamans model is inherently dependent on competition between producers, whereas the Fusfeld concept is simply linked to production quantities without specific consideration of competition, which may or may not be present.

The rationale for the Fusfeld model is that technological progress is analogous to the "learning curve" function. Fusfeld equates improvement through repetition (in the learning process) with improvement (progress) in technology through repetitive production. This rationale may be challenged by the contention that continuous production of identical articles does not indicate progress. However, in modern technological societies most production articles do change (even the Volkswagen) and are replaced by later models.

Fusfeld's thesis is supported by several factors inherent to industrial societies. One is that the margin of return on industrial production permits investment in research and development of new products. Thus increases in production quantities should support greater R&D investment, leading to higher rates of technological advance. Also, technological progress is supported by large numbers of highly skilled engineering, management, and production personnel, who develop such skills primarily by employment related to production. Therefore, higher production quantities provide a larger base for sustained technological advance. In addition, production quantities are related to demand, from which it may be inferred that increases in production quantities indicate greater demand for higher performance as well as larger quantity.

Fusfeld has completed a number of studies in support of his thesis,

one of which is shown in Figure 9. This example presents a correlation
of improvement in two turbojet-engine performance parameters with
the cumulative production of such engines in the United States. The
other examples developed by Fusfeld generally show similar correlations.
However, anomalies appear in some of the cases studied, in that lower
rates of increase in production quantities have coincided with higher
rates of technological progress.

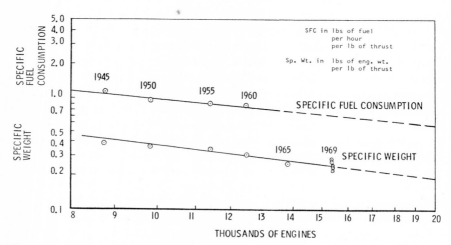

**Figure 9   Correlation of turbojet engine performance with cumulative production
quantities.**

This technique provides a useful new tool for forecasting when applied
in conjunction with other methods. Once a correlation between production
quantities and technological progress has been established for a given
parameter, a projection of future rates of production must follow, if
a prediction with respect to time is desired. If production quantity forecasts are reasonably straightforward and generally accepted, a good basis
is provided for the more difficult technological projection. Similarly, if
significant changes are projected in production quantities, the correlation
may point to probable changes in technological trends. The correlation
between production quantities and progress may also provide a quantitative explanation of historical lags and spurts in progress, which previously were attributed only qualitatively to depressions, wars, and similar
occurrences.

Further work on this concept will increase its utility. The alternative of a correlation between the cumulative number of new models of a given product, and the rate of technological progress, should certainly be explored. Such a correlation might provide data to verify and quantify the Seamans model.

EXPLORATORY AND (OR VERSUS) NORMATIVE FORECASTING

The term technological forecasting was first applied to methods of forecasting which were fundamentally extrapolative. Subsequently, Erich Jantsch collected, under the name "technological forecasting,"[1] both a group of extrapolative techniques of forecasting, and a group of techniques for determining the future through methods of resource allocation and goal setting. Jantsch defined the group of extrapolative techniques as "exploratory forecasting," and the second group as "normative forecasting." Since all the methods discussed in this chapter have been of the extrapolative or "exploratory" type, a brief comment concerning the relationships between these two groups is appropriate.

Of prime importance is that these two forecasting groups are not competitive, but are complementary. Therefore neither is "best;" and if the question is asked, "Which group of forecasting techniques should be used?" the answer is "both."

Extrapolative forecasts may be made for any technological parameter for which a data base of past performance exists. However, the forecaster usually has at least an intuitive feel that worthwhile goals exist for the future development of the technology he is forecasting. Additionally, he may modify the trend on the basis of knowledge concerning the value of the predicted progress. Thus "normative" or goal-oriented factors are an inherent part of exploratory forecasting.

Conversely, it is difficult to imagine the establishment of a "normative" goal for progress in any technological area which is not based on an intuitive recognition of previous rates of progress in that area. If the goal is significantly greater than can be met by the continuance of these previous rates, the "normative" forecaster almost always includes an appeal for increased effort in the area, thereby reflecting some knowledge of the rates of progress in the past.

Knowledge and use of both exploratory and normative methods are essential for effective technological forecasting. Visibility and discipline

[1] Erich Jantsch, *Technological Forecasting in Perspective* (Paris: Organization for Economic Cooperation and Development, 1967).

can be gained through the use of exploratory forecasting to define what may be possible. Vision and inspiration can be gained through the use of normative forecasting to define what is useful and desirable.

AN EXAMPLE OF THE APPLICATION OF FORECASTING IN R&D PLANNING

Obviously all valid methods for the exploratory forecasting of technology may be applied in R&D planning, since any indications of probable future developments in a given technology are useful in establishing objectives and determining areas of emphasis. Even an outline of such applications is beyond the scope of this chapter. One specific application, as actually prepared and used for guidance in R&D planning, may serve as an example of potential uses, for the benefit of those who wish to explore additional possibilities. This example, in the field of subsonic transport design, was developed by the Aeronautical Systems Division, Wright-Patterson Air Force Base, Ohio, by R. R. Swab, J. P. Kuhns, and J. L. Wilkins, under the guidance of S. M. Nehez and R. C. Lenz.[2]

The first step was to determine the historical trends of 40 parameters considered significant in the design and development of large subsonic transport aircraft. On the basis of these trends, the future trend of each parameter was forecast. When contradictions became apparent in the projected trends of interrelated parameters, adjustments were made in the forecast to minimize these contradictions. The historical forecast trends were reported under the title, "Technology Trends for Subsonic Transports," to serve as the basis for R&D planning directed toward the ultimate achievement of air transport capabilities exceeding current aircraft by a large margin.

The application of this forecast to planning is following two major paths. The first path is the use of the projected trend characteristics in design studies of new transports. The projected 1985 value of each characteristic is being used in various design layouts, both to test the reasonableness of the projections and to identify significant changes in configuration. Figure 10 represents one such design layout and shows some of the major characteristics of the design.

The second path in the application to planning is the use of the projected values to determine the technological gains in component perfor-

[2] Robert R. Swab, John P. Kuhns, John L. Wilkins are all in the Directorate of Airlift Systems Plans, Stephen M. Nehez is Director of Airlift Systems Plans and Deputy for Development Planning. Ralph C. Lenz, Jr., is Assistant Deputy for Development Planning.

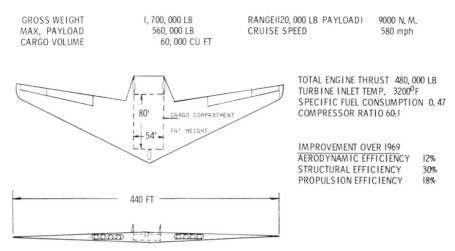

GROSS WEIGHT   1, 700, 000 LB   RANGE(120, 000 LB PAYLOAD)   9000 N. M.
MAX. PAYLOAD   560, 000 LB   CRUISE SPEED   580 mph
CARGO VOLUME   60, 000 CU FT

80'
CARGO COMPARTMENT
54'   14' HEIGHT

440 FT

TOTAL ENGINE THRUST   480, 000 LB
TURBINE INLET TEMP.   3200°F
SPECIFIC FUEL CONSUMPTION 0. 47
COMPRESSOR RATIO 60:1

IMPROVEMENT OVER 1969
AERODYNAMIC EFFICIENCY   12%
STRUCTURAL EFFICIENCY   30%
PROPULSION EFFICIENCY   18%

Figure 10   Possible design considerations drawn from technology trends for subsonic transports—1985.

mance which will be required in order to achieve the overall capabilities projected. Necessary gains in engine performance, aircraft structures, and aerodynamic characteristics have been quantified. These gains are being used in establishing objectives for R&D programs, so that the technology in each component area will have advanced to the necessary level by the time that a decision to initiate the next new large transport becomes appropriate.

PROBLEMS AND PITFALLS IN FORECASTING

Problems in technological forecasting fall into two major categories, those having to do with utilization of the forecast, and those involved in making the forecast. Utilization of the forecast commences with a consideration of the environment of the organization. Frequently this environment is hostile. In order to establish a sound basis for forecasting, the key individuals in the organization must have an introspective understanding of the appropriate ultimate objectives for the organization, and this situation does not always prevail. If the environment is favorable to the creation of a forecast, the next problem is the development of a plan based on the forecast. Comments are often made that forecasts are self-fulfilling. This is true only if the organization makes plans to participate in the fulfillment; otherwise the competition will fulfill the forecast.

Next in the list of problems is making the forecast (and the plan) have an impact on current decisions and actions. All too often the forecast and the long-range plan are assumed to be relevant only to some future course. Like *mañana*, the time for "future action" never comes. If it is forecast that new supplies of wood will be needed in 20 years, now is the time to buy the land to plant the seedlings. The last problem in utilizing the forecast is failure to update it regularly. Almost imperceptible drifts and small perturbations may snowball over a period of time into large divergences from the original forecast. Resetting the course of action is much easier if the forecast is updated regularly.

The problems of making the forecast are difficult in spite of the number of methods available. The first problem is the lack of adequate data on product performance in many technical fields. Many do not agree with this statement until they attempt their first forecast, at which point they abandon further efforts. A second problem in the compilation of forecasts is the tendency to substitute hyperbolic narrative for performance data. Thick documents, full of pictures and words (and devoid of performance data and specific dates of achievement), prepared under executive pressures to get on the technological forecasting bandwagon, are impressive but useless.

A third problem is the distortion of forecasts by strong "desirements." Unreasonable increases in rates of progress may be predicted, particularly if the forecast is extrapolated from the single point of present capability without regard to the rate of past progress. Lack of rigor in the application of forecasting methodology, and failure to analyze and iterate the forecasts, lead to unsatisfactory forecasts and disillusionment. The blame for creating this pitfall lies with the forecaster himself, who ultimately becomes the victim.

A final problem is that engendered by failure to document the forecast. Documentation is not an end in itself, but it is a vital step in communicating the forecast to those who must use it, to those who may constructively criticize it, and to the forecaster himself, who must review and revise it periodically. The danger that a well-documented forecast will later prove that the forecaster erred is a small price to pay for the visibility it provides into alternative futures.

Although most individuals and organizations do poorly in their first attempts at forecasting, persistence and continued search for improvement eventually result in forecasts which provide a sound basis for planning.

XIV. *Delphi + Computers + Communications = ?*

MURRAY TUROFF

You pays your money and takes your choice: Two heads are better than one, or too many cooks spoil the broth.
Anonymous

BACKGROUND

This chapter represents a summary of my views on the results of an on-line (computer-automated) conference[1] conducted in the spring of 1970 out of the Systems Evaluation Division of the Office of Emergency Preparedness in the Executive Office of the President.

The conference involved 20 individuals spread across the country and about equally divided, in regard to affiliations, among government, industry, nonprofit organizations, and universities. The group was also professionally mixed, being composed of persons in the areas of Delphi design, corporate planning, computer science, information systems, management systems, and operations research. About one-quarter of the indi-

---

[1] A comprehensive bibliography and further explanation of the Delphi techniques may be found in "The Design of a Policy Delphi," by Murray Turoff, *Technological Forecasting,* Vol. 2, No. 2, 1970.

viduals had no previous experience with computers or terminals.[2]

The purpose of the conference was to evaluate the potential utilization of computer-communication systems of this type, as well as my design of the delphi-type communication formats being used. During the first five weeks no conferee had any knowledge of the identity of the other 19 participants. For this reason the exercise could be considered a "Delphi conference."

A more complete and detailed report on the exercise is given in "Delphi Conferencing," technical memorandum of the Systems Evaluation Division in the Office of Emergency Preparedness.

INTRODUCTION

Significant advances often result today from the merger of techniques employed by separate disciplines. It is my belief that the use of Delphi techniques in modern computer-communication systems will result in a major advance in the ability of a group of individuals to apply a collective intelligence capability to complex issues and problems. To put this premise into some perspective, a brief review of each of these two areas is in order.

COMPUTERS

Computers have held the promise of bringing about a revolution which compares in scope with the Industrial Revolution. This is largely due to the analogy between the earlier use of the steam engine to bring

[2] I should like to acknowledge the indirect but significant contribution made to this chapter by the individuals who participated in the Delphi conference described herein (in some cases two individuals acted as one respondent). *Government:* Mr. J. Coates, National Science Foundation; Lt. Col. J. Martino, United States Air Force; Mr. T. Pyke and Dr. H. Grosch, National Bureau of Standards; Mr. R. See and Dr. R. Davis, National Institute of Health; Dr. H. Wiedemann, State Department; Mr. R. Wilcox, Office of Emergency Preparedness. *Industry:* Dr. A. Bender and Mr. M. Cochran, Smith Kline & French; Mr. J. Craver, Monsanto; Mr. J. Goodman, Lockheed; Mr. D. Pyke, TRW. *Nonprofit Organizations:* Mr. C. Darling III, National Industrial Conference Board; Mr. D. Delguidice and Dr. J. Strange, National Academy of Public Administration; Mr. S. Enzer and Dr. O. Helmer, Institute for the Future; Dr. M. Kay and Dr. W. Graham, the Rand Corporation; Dr. S. Rosen, Hudson Institute. *Universities:* Professor J. Bright and Dr. H. Johnson, University of Texas; Professor A. Jones and Dr. R. Piccirelli, Wayne State University; Prof. A. Oettinger, Harvard University; Dr. A. Sheldon, Harvard Medical School; Dr. J. Williamson, John Hopkins University.

about a sizable extension of man's physical powers, and the current application of the computer to effect a sizable extension of at least a portion of man's mental power—namely, his memory and his ability to process information logically. To only a limited extent, however, has the promise of the computer been realized.

Computers have reached the level of being tools for individuals or organizations; they remember data and they do calculations on these data as requested. In this capacity they have at least offered society a mechanism for coping with an increasingly complex civilization and the growing number of information-handling problems generated by that complexity. It is unlikely, however, that anyone can infer from current applications of computers that they have in themselves produced a revolution or significantly altered man's mental horizons.

In part, this is due to the fact that the average computer today does not communicate well with the average man. We have not as yet produced the computer equivalent of the Model-T. A computer of medium to large size still represents a massive capital investment, particularly when all associated costs are included. For this reason most applications, aside from the research area, have involved areas where the payoff can be quantified in an accounting sense. This same cost pressure has also produced computer system designs, particularly in software, where the actual users of the system must first pass their problems and applications to individuals trained to obtain the most efficient possible performance from the computer. In a sense, this impedes the actual user in his attempts to apply the computer as a direct extension of his mentality. The current generation of immediate-access or time-sharing systems has not really broken this barrier. These systems usually only provide the user with a restricted subset of the computer's power, limited to well-defined, separate classes of applications—numerical calculations and retrieval on previously prepared data bases.

This emphasis on efficiency in the use of computers has also meant that the design of computer software has been influenced for the most part by mathematicians, logisticians, and linguistic specialists. As a result, the user has found it difficult to apply the computer to any problem which is not reducible to a set of logical expressions. There has been comparatively little impact on computer systems from the social sciences or other disciplines dealing with problems which do not always lend themselves to this logical deduction process. The R&D effort in the area of computer systems has perhaps overemphasized attempts at utilizing the computer to simulate intelligence, as opposed to efforts to reduce the interface difficulty involved in allowing human beings to supply the intelligence.

We appear to be entering a decade of significant change in this situation. The rapidly declining cost of computer power, coupled with a greater recognition of the full meaning of the "information" problem facing society, seems to be breaking down the barriers between users and computers. An important cornerstone in this effort is the rather new Delphi discipline.

THE DELPHI DISCIPLINE

The Delphi technique, as it is now known, is more than 10 years old (perhaps older if one considers the analogy with the jury system); however, only in recent years has it come into wide use. As a result, it is only in the infancy stage of becoming a recognized discipline. Its increasing use is accompanied by a growing realization that most serious problems facing organizations within our society, and facing society itself, cut across the established compartmentalization of disciplines and organizations. The Delphi technique appears to make its maximum contribution when it allows individuals in separate endeavors to establish meaningful, constructive communication. The problem which poses the greatest challenge for the professional Delphi designer is perhaps best expressed by Gibran:

> It takes two of us to create a truth,
> One to utter it and one to understand it.

It may very well be that the profession of Delphi design will contribute more to society in the area of defining usable communication structures among individuals than through any particular result of the current emphasis on using Delphi exercises to produce technological forecasts. The practiced Delphi designer has come to realize that the biggest problem he faces is the definition of a communication structure which allows a group of individuals in separate endeavors both to comprehend, as a group, highly specialized concepts, and to contribute their individual intellects meaningfully to a group analysis of the issues involved in the particular subject under consideration. Most Delphi designers devote a great deal of effort to such problems as the different shadings that words take on to individuals of differing backgrounds.

Today Delphi techniques are being applied to complex and meaningful problems in the society. The studies are being staffed with the individuals who deal with these subjects. When psychologists have attempted to investigate group communication structures, they have been severely hampered by the lack of opportunity to conduct meaningful exercises on meaningful groups. Although Delphi designers may be accused of jumping ahead of scientific rigor in applying new design techniques without adequate experimentation, they are meeting a real demand for improving group communication structures. It is evident to those who have looked carefully at the current scope of Delphi designs that a number of useful techniques for handling the communication and presentation of various types of complex issues have already been produced.

THE DELPHI CONFERENCE

It should be obvious that any set of procedures which can establish a communication structure among a group of individuals through the mechanisms of paper, pencil, and the mails in principle can be automated on a time-shared computer-communication system. This allows, of course, for the limitation on pictorial or graphic presentations if the terminal is of a typewriter type. What may be less obvious is my contention that the result of this automation is no longer a "Delphi exercise" but rather a new entity, with significantly different properties, which I shall refer to as a "Delphi conference."

The computer in a system of this sort operates as a real-time accounting system. This is a well-established capability for modern computer systems and does not represent an attempt to push the state of the art in the computer sciences. The computer performs an accounting function in storing the discussion items entered by members of the group and in accumulating votes on these items, as opposed to the usual accounting functions involving sales, stock, and shipping records. Since the computer maintains the status of the conference in real time, the individual getting on the terminal to interact, or just to view, has available to him whatever has occurred up to that point. Moreover, if he utilizes a terminal with print capability, he has immediate hard copy on the results as they stand at that time.

Perhaps more important is the fact that the individual is free to determine when and how often he will interact. The paper-and-pencil Delphi may force him to wait weeks between interactions, so that he must often rethink the whole set of issues involved. The conference call ties him to a set time which can sometimes be very inconvenient, especially when the participants are spread over a number of time zones. A committee or panel meeting also creates a time constraint, and any travel involved may add the further inconvenience of lost time.

Another advantage of the Delphi conference is the feasibility of providing a capability for interaction with a much larger group than is possible in verbal or face-to-face exchange. A conference call, for example, limits the exchange of information to 5–10 individuals.

The location of the individual is unimportant, as long as he has access to a telephone line and a terminal. The decreasing cost of terminals, together with their increasing availability and portability, will soon eliminate any current inconvenience.

Comparison of the Delphi Conference with Other Groups Communications Techniques

Table 1 provides a qualitative comparison among group communication techniques and thereby places the Delphi conference in the context of a communication process, either as a supplement or an alternative to the other group processes. From this perspective it is no longer necessary to attempt to justify the use of the Delphi on the basis of producing a correct result. It is necessary only to determine whether the Delphi will allow a greater ease of communication among the participants with respect to the application under consideration.

Considerations in the Design of a Delphi Conference

The design for a Delphi conference must emphasize the goal of allowing the participants as much freedom as possible in expressing their views and judgments. The individuals must supply the intelligence, not the computer system or the monitor. The sample specifications for a Delphi conference system which follow are based on three premises:

1. The terminals used are typewriter, teletype, or alphanumeric display types (no graphic capabilities are assumed).

2. Hard-copy summaries of the proceedings are made available every few weeks.

3. The conference group either utilizes the system on a continuous basis or has an opportunity to practice with the system before the real conference begins.

A single application of a Delphi conference to a group which has not had experience with such systems may have to utilize a design somewhat more constrained than the one described in the following pages. Also the design as given represents a considerable improvement over the initial system and results in part from the suggestions made by the conference group evaluating the original design. From my viewpoint the potential utility of such systems for the collective evaluation of a topic was demonstrated in the first conference by the production of a number of obviously beneficial suggestions which had not occurred to me in my original design effort. This process, it must be admitted, is not always rewarding to a designer's ego.

Table 1 Comparison of Group Communication Techniques

Criterion	Conference Telephone Call	Committee Meeting	Formal Conference or Seminar	Delphi Exercise	Delphi Conference
Effective group size	Small	Small to medium	Small to large	Small to large	Small to large
Occurrence of interaction by individual	Coincident with group	Coincident with group	Coincident with group	Random	Random
Length of interaction	Short	Medium to long	Long	Short to medium	Short
Number of interactions	Multiple, as required by group	Multiple, necessary time delays between	Single	Multiple, necessary time delays between	Multiple, as required by individual
Normal mode range	Equality to chairman control (flexible)	Equality to chairman control (flexible)	Presentation (directed)	Equality to monitor control (structured)	Equality to monitor control or group control and no monitor (structured)
Principal costs	Communications	(1) Travel (2) Individuals' time	(1) Travel (2) Individuals' time (3) Fees	(1) Monitor time (2) Clerical (3) Secretarial	(1) Communications (2) Computer usage
Other characteristics	(1) Time-urgent considerations (2) Equal flow of information to and from all (3) Can maximize psychological effects	(1) Equal flow of information to and from all (2) Can maximize psychological effects (3) Forced delays	(1) Efficient flow of information from few to many	(1) Equal flow of information to and from all (2) Can minimize psychological effects (3) Written record	(1) Time-urgent considerations (2) Equal flow of information to and from all (3) Can minimize psychological effects (4) Written record

When a conference member gets on the terminal, he may exercise any or all of the following options:

1. View an activity summary of the conference proceedings.
2. View the text of any particular discussion items in the conference proceedings at that time.
3. Express a judgment or vote on any discussion items he has not previously judged or change earlier votes and judgments if he so desires.
4. Add one or more discussion items to the proceedings for consideration by the whole group.
5. Add to the system a message which is a comment that is not to be evaluated by the group and may only have a limited lifetime in the on-line proceedings.
6. Obtain a summary of his vote for all the items.

The discussion items are of three types:

Comments, which are evaluated on a primary scale of importance as related to the general subject of the conference. A typical importance scale is:

VERY IMPORTANT
IMPORTANT
SLIGHTLY IMPORTANT
UNIMPORTANT
REJECT
NO JUDGMENT

Proposals, which are evaluated on a primary scale of desirability, such as the following:

VERY DESIRABLE
DESIRABLE
UNDESIRABLE
VERY UNDESIRABLE
NO JUDGMENT

Estimates, which request the supplying of a numeric estimate from the conference members and a vote on a primary scale of importance (see above) with respect to the estimate being actually obtained.

The REJECT choice allows a respondent to express the judgment that a particular item should not be included in the proceedings because it is not related to the basic subject of the conference. A sufficiently high REJECT vote should cause the computer to automatically purge the item.

When the conferee enters an item, he designates which of the three types—comment, proposal, or estimate—it is. He also chooses a secondary scale to be applied to his item for evaluation by the group. Such secondary scales may be:

Agreement
STRONGLY AGREE
AGREE
NEUTRAL
DISAGREE
STRONGLY DISAGREE
NO JUDGMENT

Confidence
CERTAIN
RELIABLE
NOT DETERMINABLE
RISKY
UNRELIABLE
NO JUDGMENT

Probability
VERY PROBABLE
PROBABLE
EITHER WAY
IMPROBABLE
VERY IMPROBABLE
NO JUDGMENT

Feasibility
DEFINITELY FEASIBLE
POSSIBLY FEASIBLE
NOT DETERMINABLE
POSSIBLY INFEASIBLE
DEFINITELY INFEASIBLE
NO JUDGMENT

A comment may have a secondary scale, for example, of *agreement* with the comment or *confidence* in its validity. A proposal will usually have a secondary scale of *feasibility*. An estimate may have a secondary scale of *confidence* in the estimate, or *probability* of occurrence if it is an event-type estimate. Also, in a cost estimate the *feasibility* of obtaining funds might be an appropriate secondary scale. The important consideration here is to allow the author of the item his choice in choosing the secondary scale or the freedom to adapt or tailor the system to his requirements.

When the item is first entered, it is placed in a PENDING classification. When 80% or more of the possible votes (not including NO JUDGMENT votes) have been entered for an item, it may fall into any of the following classifications:

ACCEPTED

If the average vote is high on both the primary and the secondary scale (e.g., average vote of IMPORTANT or better and AGREE or better for a comment).

SIGNIFICANT

If the average vote is high on the primary scale but not on the secondary scale.

INSIGNIFICANT
   If the average vote is low on the primary scale (e.g., SLIGHTLY
   IMPORTANT or less).
REJECTED
   If the average vote is low on both scales or a majority (better than
   50% of the whole group) has chosen the REJECT vote. This classifica-
   tion causes the item to be purged from the proceedings and to be
   no longer available to the group for consideration.

Items may move from a higher to a lower class, or vice versa, as
votes are changed. The only classification which is permanent is RE-
JECTED. If the discussion item does not fit into any of the above
classes, it remains PENDING.

The individual who entered an item may also choose, if he wishes,
to associate his item with 1–5 earlier items. However, the first association
specified is considered primary, and the others secondary. As each item
is entered, it is given a number which signifies the order in which it
occurred and which is used to retrieve the item, to view the item, to
vote on the item, and to express associations among the items.

As long as the item is in the PENDING class, its author can reword
it, but this capability should be used only to improve the wording, not
to change the content or intent of the item. The author cannot change
the item type or associations. When an item is modified, a date of modification is entered in the activity summary. The activity summary prints
out one line per item, containing the item number, its current classification, its associations, its type, the number of votes that have been entered, the date entered or modified, and the number of vote changes
that have occurred for the item.

A conferee may also enter a message, which similarly receives a number. Only a finite number of messages are allowed (say 100); when
this limit has been reached, the first message is purged to make room
for an addition at the end of the list. Messages are usually associated
with a particular item and may be of the type: "Item 10 would be
more acceptable if the wording were changed to . . . ."

When a conferee goes to the terminal to view or vote on the discussion
items, he should have a number of options regarding the order of presentation of the items, so that he may act in whatever manner suits him.
Such options are as follows:

By Numeric Order
   Where he specifies a start and a stop item number, and all items
   between are presented.

By Associations Order

Where he specifies an item number, and all primary and then secondary associations (if he desires) are presented.

By Item Number

Where one item at a time is retrieved by specifying the item number.

By No Vote

Where the items which the conferee has not voted on are retrieved.

By a Particular Class

For example, ACCEPTED, SIGNIFICANT, PENDING, INSIG-
NIFICANT.

The conferee cannot see the vote distribution on an item until after
he and more than 60% of the conference group have voted on it. The
NO JUDGMENT votes are included in this percentage calculation for
exposing the vote to viewing.

Each conferee has a personal code word which he must supply at
the beginning and which allows him to vote and to add items or messages.
In addition, there may be a set of code words for individuals viewing
the proceedings but not participating. It is also possible to set up restrictions whereby some individuals are allowed to add items but not vote,
and vise versa.

DESIGN FACTORS FACILITATING INTERACTION
BETWEEN MAN AND MACHINE

Basically, a complete description of a Delphi conference system has
now been given. However, a number of crucial items are related to the
interface of a human being with a terminal and computer system. It
is critical that this system can be used by individuals with no more
than a half hour of terminal instruction and no previous experience
with computers. This category includes secretaries in particular, who
may be doing the actual leg work for their bosses.

Except when the user is entering a security code, an item, or a message,
he should never have to type more than a numeric code to indicate
a choice for proceeding through his interaction. Also, there must be two
versions of the interaction program: one that offers a complete explanation of each choice available and, figuratively, leads the user by the
hand, and another that is extremely abbreviated in its explanation for
use by an experienced person. Here is an example of what may be typed

out in each of the two versions:

Long Form	Short Form
DO YOU WISH TO:	MODE CHOICE: ?
VIEW ACTIVITY SUMMARY	(1)
VIEW ITEMS	(2)
VIEW VOTE	(3)
VIEW ITEM AND VOTE	(4)
VIEW MESSAGES	(5)
VOTE	(6)
ADD AN ITEM	(7)
ADD A MESSAGE	(8)
WAIT MODE	(9)
MODE CHOICE: ?	

The user then enters a numeric digit (1–9 in this case) after the "?" to indicate his choice. In the short form it is assumed the conferee knows from previous interactions that there are eight mode choices and what they are by number. It is almost impossible to satisfy the experienced user and the beginner with the same interaction program. Also, a number of individuals in any group always prefer the long form even though it lengthens their interaction time on the terminal.

When entering an item or message, the conferee should see it printed back by the computer and be given a chance to confirm its accuracy before it is logged into the system. In this connection, the system must always be forgiving in that, if the wrong key is typed or a wrong choice is made, the conferee can recover and return easily to a point in the interaction which allows him to correct the mistake or proceed as he desires.

If the system is to be used in an emergency mode, or in a mode where an individual is asked to enter the conference within hours, a complete explanation regarding the use of the system should be available as an option from the terminal. In this instance only the log-in procedure need be given over the phone.

Ideally the monitor should have nothing to do; however, he should have the ability to edit, correct, or purge items or messages should the need arise. If the conference is being held to provide information for a user who is not directly participating, the monitor may also have to add items to ensure that certain subtopics are covered.

A system such as the one described here is fairly flexible, even within the limits imposed by a typewriter-type terminal. It may be a little too sophisticated, however, for use on a single-shot application if the conference group has not had a chance to practice with it before starting the "real" application. Where a series of single-shot applications is to take place, it becomes important to create the system in a user-oriented computer language such as BASIC or JOSS, so that it can be quickly tailored by the designers to each application. The original conference system mentioned at the beginning of the chapter was written in an extended form of the BASIC language (X BASIC)[3] which had the following critical features for creating a conferencing system:

Executive-Level Control by a BASIC Program[4]

The ability to execute executive-level commands within a BASIC language program so that a common file on the conference proceedings can be exclusively assigned to a member of the conference just long enough to include in it his additions (items and/or votes) and then the file can be freed for use by any other member who happens to be simultaneously on a terminal interacting with the system.

String-Variable Storage and Manipulation[5]

The ability to store the items entered by the conference members. The ability to manipulate a string is needed only to be able to catch errors due to incorrect typing of a numerical choice (hitting an alphabetical key) or to prevent noise on the communication line being read as spurious symbols.

Format or Form Control

The ability to generate neat, easily readable output for vote summaries and activity summaries.

Many individuals in the computer industry feel very strongly that one user system (i.e., BASIC) should not be used to build another user system (i.e., an on-line conferencing system) because of the resulting "inefficient use" of the computer hardware. When the system is written in an assembly-level language, inefficiencies also exist in the process of the designers translating their requirements to programmers and in the delays inherent in either developing or modifying a system to meet changing requirements. Any organization considering such a system must examine this recurring tradeoff between the machine and human inefficiencies. In any case, it is desirable to do the initial development in a user-oriented computer language, since the first few applications to any real user group will probably result in required changes. The un-

---

[3] Developed by Language and Systems Development, Inc., Silver Springs, Md.
[4] The executive-level software of a computer is the package that controls the operation of the computer and schedules the sharing of the machine among different simultaneous users in an on-line operation. It has available all the flexibility of the machine, whereas most user languages (BASIC) do not.
[5] A string variable is a set of alphanumeric characters which can be labeled by a symbol in the same manner as a numeric variable.

awareness of this fact of life has proved the undoing of many computer-ized management information system efforts.

Additional comments that I have made on the utilization of on-line computer systems in user environments may be found in the following articles:

"Immediate Access and the User Revisited," *DATAMATION Magazine,* May 1969.
"Immediate Access and the User," *DATAMATION Magazine,* August 1966.

Incidentally, the group which participated in the on-line conference mentioned at the beginning of the chapter included approximately five individuals who previously had not had any direct contact (terminal experience or programming) with a computer. Also, before the conference was over, at least six secretaries were utilizing the terminal to obtain recent items or to supply items or votes as directed by their bosses.

Potential Applications of the Delphi Conference

In the Delphi conference mentioned at the beginning of this chapter, a number of potential applications were presented and evaluated by the conference group. Some of these are listed here to illustrate the potential utility of Delphi conferences:

This system could be used by a committee or panel before its meeting to ensure that all issues were on the table and that all concerned had had an opportunity to consider their views on these issues.

This system could be used by a committee or panel between meetings to keep the group abreast of developments and to maintain a dialog or continuous conference, especially when meetings were weeks or months apart.

This system could be used after a committee or panel process as a means of summarizing the results.

This system could be used by a peer group (management team, group of scientists, or any group engaged in a common endeavor) to maintain continuous contact for the exchange and group evaluation of information and ideas.

This system could be used to convene in a day a conference on a time-urgent issue.

This system could be used to completely replace committees formed for certain purposes.

This system could be used by a management peer group to reach agreement on a decision or to agree to pass the issue to a higher-level group.

This system could be used by a group of Congressmen, seeking a common objective or piece of legislation, to maintain a continuous caucus.

This system could allow a three-way anonymous exchange and evaluation among the editor of a professional journal, the panel of specialist referees, and the author of a paper submitted for publication.

Systems of this type could be used in labor-management or citizen-government relations, with labor or citizens supplying items and management or public officials supplying votes to indicate the level of formal consideration each item will receive.

Systems of this type could be used as a real-time scenario simulation or exercise by incorporating a wait mode to cause new discussion items, as generated at one terminal, to appear on all others.

Although all these applications are potentially possible, their desirability and feasibility depend on the particular circumstances of the individual application. It is interesting that in some of these areas of application there are notable variations in the actual mechanism of exercising the system. For example, in some cases (professional peer group) it is desirable that the individuals participating be known to each other; in others (refereeing), it is not. In one instance the voting group differs from the group adding the items. In some cases it may be necessary to give more weight to votes by certain individuals in the group, or a person may choose the option of signing his name to a comment if he represents a particular expertise not possessed by the other participants.

On the other hand, the ability to provide anonymity for the author of an item or for the originator of a particular vote is crucial to the utilization of such systems by individuals with significant reputations. Since a well-known person does not have to take a public position on an issue, he is more likely to consider modifying his judgment during this type of exchange, as opposed to the committee meeting. The actual Delphi conference described here at vote changes in excess of 20% of the total vote.

THE OUTLOOK FOR IMPLEMENTATION
OF DELPHI CONFERENCE SYSTEMS

The actual speed with which systems of this sort will come into play depends critically on a number of factors. For organizations unable to afford a computer operation of sufficient size to provide a Delphi conference capability, the still-unresolved issue of whether or not this type of on-line computer system is a communication system in the regulatory sense may inhibit the availability of such a system as a time-sharing service to be bought on a use basis, as are other accounting services. Also, these systems are ideal for improving lateral communication within an organization or across organizations. It is not likely, however, that the many organizations still promoting hierarchic communication and discouraging lateral communication will find these systems attractive. Finally, the issue of professional peer groups cuts across the organizations themselves, so that persons in these groups may have an even longer wait until these systems are readily available to them as a professional service.

XV. Practical Refinements to the Cross-Impact Matrix Technique of Technological Forecasting

JAMES F. DALBY

A committee is made up of the unready—appointed by the unwilling—to do the unnecessary.
Anonymous

BACKGROUND

In his 1967 book *Technological Forecasting in Perspective*, Erich Jantsch makes the observation, "The thought process of an individual who is seeking to arrive at a decision concerning a development program . . . is often described as the intuitive development of separate 'scenarios' with subsequent iteration through synopsis." The idea was used as far back as 1963 by Ronald Brech for the set of forecasts used in his book *Britain 1984*. Basically, he described developments in different disciplines and then modified the descriptions through an iterative process in which each was made compatible with the others.

More recently, in 1968, the idea was systematized and put on a quantitative basis by T. Gordon and H. Haywood in their article, "Initial Experiments with the Cross-Impact Matrix Method of Forecasting," *Futures*, December 1968. A careful analysis of the technique used by

Gordon and Haywood has revealed four areas, to date, where improvements could readily be made. The purpose of this chapter is to explain these improvements. This is most logically done by developing the theory, following Gordon and Haywood, and pointing out the improvements as the opportunities present themselves in the development and in illustrative examples.

THE CROSS-IMPACT MATRIX THEORY

What is meant by a cross-impact effect is the change in the probability of individual future events with the occurrence or nonoccurrence of related events. Suppose that a set of developments is forecast as likely to occur on individual future dates with specified levels of probability. If these developments are designated D_i $(i = 1, 2, \ldots, n)$, with associated probabilities P_i, then the question can be posed, "If $P_m = 1$ (i.e., if D_m occurs), how do the other P_i change?" By way of illustration, if the following developments and probabilities were forecast for a given year:

Development, D_i	Probability, P_i
1. SALT talks fail	0.4
2. MIRV becomes operational	0.9
3. Surface-ship ICBM-launch system developed	0.5
4. Laser anti-ICBM developed	0.2

then these might be arranged in matrix form as follows:

If this development were to occur:	then the probability of			
	D_1	D_2	D_3	D_4
D_1	—	↑	↑	↑
D_2	↑	—	↓	↓
D_3	↑	↓	—	↓
D_4	↓	—	—	—

where the upward arrows indicate an increase in probability. This kind of array is called a cross-impact matrix.

Note that a cross-impact matrix based on the nonoccurrence of events may also be constructed and used in the same way as the occurrence matrix. Thus, if the SALT talks indeed fail, it is likely that the probabilities of development of a surface-ship ICBM-launch system and operational MIRV's will increase, as indicated by the upward arrows.

The interconnections between items are much more complex, in general, than can be indicated by a simple arrow. In addition to the direction of the likely change, one must consider the intensity of the influence and the time available for diffusion of the effects of the predecessor event; that is, one must consider mode (the plus or minus linkage effect), strength of linkage, and the length of interval required before another item is influenced.

The mode of the linkages between events may be enhancing, inhibiting, or neutral. For example, tight federal controls over air pollution would enhance entry of an electric car into the market. A severely curtailed NASA budget would inhibit development of the space shuttle system. With respect to strength of linkage, in the limit, the lower the strength of the linkage, the more closely the relationship approaches are uncon- nected mode.

The time effect is important since, even if two events are strongly linked in the enhancing mode, there is little chance that the probability of a dependent event will increase significantly immediately after the occurrence of a first event. Depending on the nature of the events, the time required to realize the higher probability will range from hours to years, even decades. (A Department of Defense study, Project Hind- sight, indicates a time delay of the order of 10 years from scientific discovery to utilization in weapon systems.)

With these concepts understood, it can now be asked how the prob- ability of D_i might change if D_m occurs. If P_i' is the probability of D_i some time after the occurrence of D_m, then

$$P_i' = f(P_i, M, S, t_m, t)$$

where P_i is the probability of D_i before the occurrence of D_m,
$\qquad M$ is a function of the connection mode,
$\qquad S$ is a measure of the strength of connection,
$\qquad t_m$ is the time of the occurrence of D_m,
$\qquad t$ is the time in the future for which the probabilities are being estimated.

From probability theory, it is known that both P_i and P_i' must lie between 0 and 1; furthermore $P_i' = 0$ for $P_i = 0$, and when $P_i = 1$, P_i' must equal 1. This holds true regardless of whether the mode is enhancing or inhibiting, as can be seen in Figure 1.

When $t_m = t$, no time is allowed for the adjustment of probability of P_i to P_i', so P_i must equal P_i'.

In Figure 2, the area above the diagonal contains the enhancing mode, and the area below contains the inhibiting mode, since above the line $P_i' > P_i$ and below it $P_i' < P_i$.

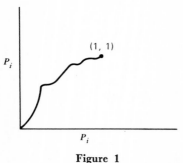

Figure 1   Figure 2

It seems reasonable to assume, with Gordon and Haywood, that within these regions the value of P_i' will vary monotonically with time available and linkage strength, that is, the stronger the connection and the greater the time, the greater will be the ratio P_i'/P_i for enhancing or inhibiting modes.

If the relationship is assumed to be quadratic in P_i, then

$$P_i' = aP_i^2 + bP_i + c$$

Substituting in the known conditions gives

$$P_i' = 1 \quad \text{when } P_i = 1, \quad \text{and} \quad P_i' = 0 \quad \text{when } P_i = 0$$

so that we obtain $b = 1 - a$, $c = 0$, and

$$P_i' = aP_i^2 + (1 - a)P_i$$

For the inhibiting case, $\quad 0 < a < 1$

and for the enhancing case, $\quad -1 < a < 0$

In general, P_i' does not approach 0 or 1 asymptotically except in very special cases. This may be seen as follows:

$$P_i' = aP_i^2 + (1 - a)P_i$$

$$\frac{\partial P_i'}{\partial P_i} = 2aP_i + (1 - a) = a(2P_i - 1) + 1$$

To establish the a required for a zero-slope approach to a P_i' of 0 or 1, we set

$$\frac{\partial P_i'}{\partial P_i} = 0 = a(2P_i - 1) + 1 \quad \text{or} \quad P_i = \frac{a - 1}{2a}$$

For $P_i = 1$: $a - 1 = 2a$ and $a = -1$
For $P_i = 0$: $a - 1 = 0$ and $a = +1$

Therefore, if $\lim_{P_i \to 1} P_i' \to 1$,   then $\lim_{P_i \to 1} a \to -1$

and if $\lim_{P_i \to 0} P_i' \to 0$,   then $\lim_{P_i \to 0} a \to +1$

But, in general, a is not equal to ± 1; it varies in the range $-1 < a < +1$. Therefore, in general,

$$\frac{\partial P_i'}{\partial P_i} \neq 0 \quad \text{as } P_i \to 1 \quad \text{or as} \quad P_i \to 0$$

This implies that, in using the technique, care must be taken to prevent rapid convergence to 1 or 0, as there is a built-in proclivity for the P_i' to advance steadily (monotonically) toward one or the other of these limits each iteration. At the same time, means must be provided to reflect pronounced upward or downward adjustments when judgment so dictates. These two features have been built into the iterative technique for updating event probabilities to be described later.

The question remains as to how t_m, t, and S affect the parameter a. It is reasonable to assume that the relationship is linear in both S and in time, that is,

$$a = kS \left(\frac{t - t_m}{t} \right)$$

where k is $+1$ or -1 as determined by the mode,
    S is a number which varies between 0 and τ,
    t_m is the time of occurrence of event D_m,
    t is the time in the future for which the probabilities are being estimated,

and $$\tau = \left(\frac{t_{\max} - t_m}{t_{\max}} \right)^{-1}$$

where $t_{\max}$ is the maximum time for which probabilities are being estimated.

The effect of allowing S to vary over this range is to permit the parameter a to cover the entire spectrum of its possible value in a given application. This is vital for permitting rapid upward (or downward) P_i' adjustments when the situation calls for them:

$$P_i' = kS \left(\frac{t - t_m}{t} \right) P_i^2 + \left[1 - kS \left(\frac{t - t_m}{t} \right) \right] P_i$$

USE OF THE TECHNIQUE

The initial task in getting the technique going is the assembly of a list of events which have bearing on the decision(s) one is trying to make. If the decision involves where to seek business in a new field and when to do it, experts in the area are consulted in the preparation of the list. The size of the list depends on the computing capacity available, as the storage requirements rise proportionally as the square of the number of events. It should be noted that the list need not be "scrubbed" at the outset for self-consistency, as the technique is designed to handle seeming inconsistencies (mutually exclusive events) in stride. In fact, that is the whole point of the technique—to make a probabilistic picture of the future (in a given area) internally consistent. Each of the items on the list is assigned years of occurrence associated with the probability levels 0.1, 0.5, and 0.9. This is a departure from the technique used in published examples illustrating the technique, but is necessary if important results are not to be disregarded.

Once the list is prepared, the occurrence and nonoccurrence cross-impact matrices, described earlier, are formed. This process involves recording judgment decision on both mode and strength in every element of both matrices. Elements are, of course, left blank if the occurrence or nonoccurrence of an event has no discernible effect on a given event (i.e., if the events are totally independent). It often makes sense to judge whether one event must necessarily precede another, and this judgment may also be recorded in the element.

After both matrices are formed, the main business of determining truer, more consistent values of probabilities of event occurrence can be started. This is done by first considering the predecessor events at the 0.1 probability level. In general, these will be associated with different years of occurrence. By means of a random number generator, it is found whether or not the first event occurred at the 0.1 probability level. If it did, then the probabilities of all other affected events are updated. Since the years associated with initial probabilities of 0.1, 0.5, and 0.9 have been identified, if these years are all later than the year of occurrence of the first event, then probabilities are updated at each of the years stipulated. This prevents any data from being lost, for if there was a 0.5 initial probability that an event would occur in the same year that the first event did occur, the updating formula would show no change in the probability of the second event occurrence for that year even if the linkage is strong. Although this is correct, the probability should be updated at a later year, that is, the 0.9 probability should be updated. This consideration does not appear to have been recognized in the examples published heretofore. In the event of nonoccurrence of the development, the same procedure is followed. The nonoccurrence matrix, however, is used instead.

It is then decided whether the second event occurred at the 0.1 probability level, and probabilities for all later occurring events are calculated as described above, continuing until the last item is decided. This completes the first "round." Notice that, during the round, event probabilities are updated on a continuous basis, that is, the $\Delta P_i'$ are not computed and algebraically combined before modifying the initial P_i for that round. The latter approach implies denial of events which have been assumed to have occurred.

At the end of a round, the values of P_i' are stored for later use. The next round begins with the initial values of the P_i, because a new future is being decided and no connection with the results of the last round should be made.

At the end of R rounds (1000 rounds are commonly made), the P_i' are averaged for each event at each of 3 years—the years associated with the initial probabilities of 0.1, 0.5, and 0.9. This provides a conservative factor to the analysis by invoking Tchebycheff's theorem; the danger of artificial convergence of probabilities to 0 or 1 is virtually ruled out.

SUMMARY OF GUIDELINES FOR IMPROVEMENT OF THE TECHNIQUE

The four guidelines for improvements to the cross-impact matrix technique for technological forecasting brought out in this paper may be summarized as follows:

1. The effects of nonoccurrence of events should be taken into consideration by the formation and use of a nonoccurrence cross-impact matrix.

2. Probabilities should be updated at the years corresponding to initial 0.1, 0.5, and 0.9 probabilities to avoid loss of meaningful data.

3. The strength parameter should be calculated to permit the quadratic parameter a to assume its full possible range of values.

4. The probabilities should be calculated in a cumulative mode during rounds, followed by an averaging over the sum of the rounds.

EXAMPLE OF THE TECHNIQUE

In this section, an example of event forecasting with the cross-impact matrix technique will be described. The so-called cross-impact approach is a mathematical methodology for technological forecasting which, as stated previously, draws its strength from the recognition of mutual effects between events and developments. The modes of linkage between events and developments can be grouped into several categories, namely, strength, timing, and direction of change, each with its own properties. This generalization permits at least a primitive analysis of the potential interactions between the events and developments considered. In the case examined here, this analysis led to some insight about the future which was not available by inspection of the items alone; it came when the interactions between these items were explored.

In setting up a cross-impact matrix (described later), for use in a computer program, questions of the following type were asked: "If development X happens, how is the probability of development Y likely to be affected?" In asking such questions over and over again, attention was forced onto issue of causality. If the fields being dealt with had been exact sciences, precise answers could have been produced. However, there is no theory of causality in the fields considered, and in these inexact areas there is no substitute for judgment. The answers, recorded in numerical form in the matrix, therefore took the form "From experience and intuition it appears that the probability of development Y might be enhanced (or inhibited) if development X were to occur." Certainly some of these judgments were in error; however, the orderliness of the matrix forces one to be explicit about the relationships that he believes to be functioning.

The cross-impact matrix used in this case took the following form:

If this development occurred:	then the probabilities of these developments are affected as follows:		
	D_1	D_2 $\cdot$ $\cdot$ $\cdot$	D_{15}
D_1	—	4↑	6↑
D_2	2↓		4↑
$\cdot$			
$\cdot$			
$\cdot$			
D_{15}		7↓ $\cdot$ $\cdot$ $\cdot$	

An upward-arrow in a matrix element signifies enhancement, and the number (on a 0–9 scale) indicates the strength of the linkage.

The list of developments and the actual matrix used in the Ballistic Missile Division (BMD) case considered are given below. (An upward

	EVENTS	YEAR AT PROB. LEVEL		
		0.1	0.5	0.9
1	SAFEGUARD CONCEPT CHANGE	1972	1975	1976
2	SALT TALKS RESULT IN INS.S.	1973	1973	1975
3	NEW BMD SERVICE	1975	1977	1980
4	RED CHINA IN UN	1972	1972	1976
5	SABMIS REALITY	1974	1978	1982
6	ULMS REALITY	1974	1975	1977
7	ARPA - NEW ABM IDEA	1975	1974	1980
8	FOBS REALITY	1971	1970	1970
9	MINOR SAFEGUARD CHANGE	1974	1972	1973
10	AMSA REALITY	1972	1974	1976
11	MANNED ARMS CONTROL SATELLITE	1976	1977	1978
12	SHIFT IN R&D POLICY	1971	1972	1972
13	TEST SATELLITE REALITY	1973	1975	1976
14	LASER ABM CAPABILITY	1975	1978	1982
15	USSR MANNED SPACE BASE	1970	1972	1973

If this development occurred:

Then the probabilities of these developments are affected as follows:

	1	2	3	4	5	6	7	8	9	10	11	12	13	14	15
1	0	-4	-2	-2	-9	0	0	0	0	-7	0	8	-9	-7	0
2	5	0	-1	-1	9	9	0	5	0	7	-9	-9	2	1	0
3	0	1	0	0	-8	-4	-2	01	1	-1	-1	-2	-8	-8	0
4	1	-3	0	0	1	1	0	1	0	1	-3	-1	1	1	0
5	-9	-5	-9	-1	0	0	2	-6	0	4	0	-4	-8	-2	0
6	6	-5	-7	-1	1	0	0	-5	0	7	-1	-1	0	0	0
7	-9	0	-2	-1	6	3	0	3	5	6	0	-3	-3	0	0
8	-4	-4	-8	-2	-6	-4	-1	0	0	-5	-6	8	-3	-4	1
9	-9	0	-1	0	-7	-2	-5	-1	0	-2	0	-1	-4	-2	0
10	2	-1	2	-1	1	1	5	0	-3	0	0	-2	1	0	0
11	-1	-7	0	-4	-1	-1	0	-1	0	-1	0	-4	-1	0	-6
12	8	-5	2	0	2	4	-7	1	0	-4	-5	0	0	2	-1
13	-6	-2	-1	0	-2	0	-2	0	-7	0	0	0	0	0	0
14	-9	0	0	0	-1	0	0	3	0	0	0	0	-6	0	0
15	0	0	0	0	0	0	-1	0	0	0	-4	-1	1	-1	0

arrow is represented by a minus sign for convenience in the mathematics.)

The way in which the technique works will now be described. Input data are received via questionnaires from a number of individuals, familiar in varying degrees with the developments postulated. In this case, nine questionnaires were received from personnel in various operating groups. The questionnaires elicited estimates of the years in which each event is likely to occur at the 0.1, 0.5, and 0.9 probability levels; an example of a completed questionnaire follows:

Sample Questionnaire

BMD
Postulated Future Events for a Forecast Exercise

"IN WHAT YEARS IS IT PROBABLE (.1, .5, .9) THAT—"	PROBABILITY		
	.1	.5	.9
	YEARS		
1. Before deployment of the ABM defense systems for hard sites (Safeguard) and regions is complete, the current concepts and commitments yield to substantially different ABM commitments? (This provides latitude on Safeguard schedule firmness as well as the durability and workability of the concepts, the stability of the threat definition, the economic affluence of the U.S.A., etc.)	72	77	80
2. SALT (Strategic Arms Limitations Talks) or other discussion leads to some measure of mutual arms limitations that by their nature will give ascendency to satellite surveillance—inspection—control systems? (Perhaps at the expense of the importance of ABM defense)	74	77	85
3. The BMD function gains sufficient focus that the strategic satellite surveillance functions of the Air Force, and the ABM functions of the Army and Navy, are brought together in a unified BMD service? (Perhaps as a fourth armed service)	75	78	82
4. Communist China becomes a member of the UN?	71	72	74
5. The SABMIS (Seaborne, ABM, Intercept System) becomes a reality? (Perhaps thought of as an official commitment to deploy)	80	83	85
6. The ULMS (Undersea Long-Range Missile System) becomes a reality of sufficient capability to carry a significant part of the present ICBMs? (And perhaps have a deterrent effect that inhibits the prospect of being attacked)	72	74	76

Sample Questionnaire (*Continued*)

BMD

"IN WHAT YEARS IS IT PROBABLE (.1, .5, .9) THAT—"	PROBABILITY		
	.1	.5	.9
	YEARS		
7. ARPA specifies the system or makes the invention that enables serious pursuit of a significantly more cost-effective approach to BMD than the ABM-hard site, regional-urban defense now conceived and committed?	72	75	80
8. The FOBS (Fractional Orbit Bombardment System) deployment decision is made by U.S.S.R.?	70	71	75
9. The much-contended information system soft-ware problem of Safeguard (incl. hard site and regional defense) proves to be intractable to the point that major or minor alterations to Safeguard becomes necessary? (Perhaps including compromises in performance)	76	73	71
10. The AMSA (Advanced Manned Strategic Aircraft) becomes a reality (is deployed)? (And as a strike capability has some deterrent value which in the defensive sense inhibits being attacked)	72	74	76
11. A manned arms—control—inspection—monitor satellite becomes a workable, effective reality to the point that initial flights are committed?	76	78	80
12. Internal sociopolitical pressures mount, forcing a national policy of "intensified R&D—prototype" approach to preparedness at the expense of existing practices and policies of deployment of weapon systems? (Can take form of fewer deployments, partial deployments, stretch-outs, etc., of defensive and offensive weapon systems)	70	71	72
13. Test and evaluation of our BMD system will be done with a satellite system especially designed for the purpose and capable of ejecting re-entry expendables, emitting signals simulating missile threats, or other threats.	72	75	80
14. A high-power laser capability is realized of power density "at the target" sufficient to neutralize attacking missiles? (Demonstrated in an aerospace mission environment?)	75	78	80
15. The U.S.S.R. puts a manned space station in orbit capable of supporting work crews for periods exceeding a minimum period of roughly thirty days?	70	71	72

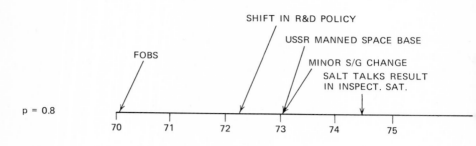

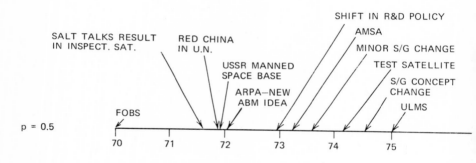

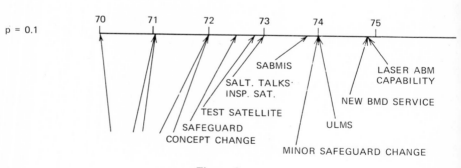

Figure 3

270

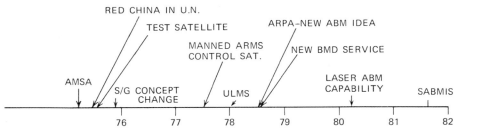

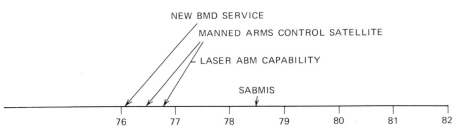

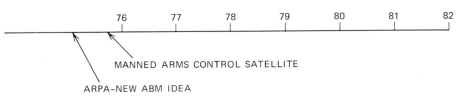

Figure 4

EVENT TITLE	MAX UPDATED PROBABILITY	.1 PROB. YEAR	UPDATED PROB.	.5 PROB. YEAR	UPDATED PROB.	.9 PROB. YEAR	UPDATED PROB.
STEVE—REALITY	0.999	1973	0.147	1975	0.799	1976	0.999
LASER ABM CAPABILITY	0.999	1975	0.136	1978	0.771	1982	0.999
NEW BMD SERVICE	0.999	1975	0.171	1977	0.807	1980	0.999
PANNED ARMS CONTROL SATELLITE	0.997	1976	0.257	1977	0.840	1978	0.997
ARPA—NEW ABM IDEA	0.995	1975	0.192	1974	0.625	1980	0.995
AMSA—REALITY	0.991	1972	0.124	1974	0.753	1976	0.991
SALT TALKS RESULTS IN INS.S.	0.990	1973	0.194	1973	0.694	1975	0.990
RED CHINA IN UN	0.964	1972	0.109	1972	0.524	1976	0.964
SAFEGUARD CONCEPT CHANGE	0.963	1972	0.117	1975	0.594	1976	0.963
SABMIS—REALITY	0.942	1974	0.112	1978	0.463	1982	0.942
USSR MANNED SPACE BASE	0.925	1970	0.100	1972	0.519	1973	0.925
FOBS—REALITY	0.900	1971	0.117	1970	0.500	1970	0.900
MINOR SAFEGUARD CHANGE	0.880	1974	0.063	1972	0.500	1973	0.880
SHIFT IN R AND D POLICY	0.816	1971	0.059	1972	0.294	1972	0.816
ULMS REALITY	0.779	1974	0.106	1975	0.506	1977	0.779

Figure 5 Cross-impact matrix analysis updated probabilities table (ranked by decreasing maximum updated probability).

The results of the questionnaires are merged, and the median year is found at each probability level and used as the consensus input. A Monte Carlo computer program then calculates the mean effect of 1000 completely different "futures." In other words, the program decides mathematically whether or not each event occurred at the specified probability levels and, if it did, updates the probabilities of all affected events accordingly, using the stored cross-input matrix and the formula:

$$P_i' = ks \left(\frac{t - t_m}{t}\right) P_i{}^2 + \left\{ 1 - \left[ks \left(\frac{t - t_m}{t}\right) \right] \right\} P_i$$

where P_i' = updated event probability,
$\quad P_i$ = initial event probability,
$\quad k$ = -1 or $+1$, depending on whether the mode of change is enhancing or inhibiting,
$\quad s$ = strength of linkage,
$\quad t$ = year of event under consideration,
$\quad t_m$ = year of event determined to have occurred.

The printout results are then graphed, as in Figures 3 and 4, in order to determine the new years corresponding to the 0.1, 0.5, and 0.9 probability levels. These results permit the construction of a maximum likelihood chronology of events probability level. These chronologies for the BMD case are shown in Figure 5. Figure 5 is a sample of the printout and shows, at each initial probability level, the corresponding year and the updated (maximum likelihood) probability for that same year. Note that the events are ranked in order of probability resulting from updates to the 0.9 level.

XVI.   *The Beginnings of Cross-Support Analysis (DIANA) As Applied to the Fishing Industry*[1]

CHRISTINE A. RALPH

Men occasionally stumble over the truth, but most of them pick themselves up and hurry off as if nothing had happened.   Winston Churchill

INTRODUCTION

The technique known as decision impact analysis (DIANA) has been evolved to aid in technological forecasting by the study and operational analysis of the effect of making and implementing complex decisions which affect and are affected by a large number of factors. A complex or ill-defined problem can be broken down into smaller, better-defined areas of study by a systematic approach of this nature, so that only the areas shown to be most relevant to the field of study need be analyzed in detail. The power of the technique lies in its recursive nature, as the results of analyses can alter the initially chosen subjects, assump-

[1] This chapter is adapted from "Decision Impact Analysis Applied to the U.K. Fishing Industry" by Christine A. Ralph, published as a report by Plessey Radar Ltd., 1968.

tions, and constraints, so that no initial or subsequent error can prevent the emergence of the most relevant information. Any effects of decisions or assumptions made at any stage in the analysis, on any other stages, past or yet to come, are considered.

The rigor of the analysis is determined by the quantity and availability of data and the other constraints imposed on the study. These factors, together with a nonrigorous definition and the multidimensionality of the variables, prevent there being a unique solution to the problem. The recursive and adaptive nature of the technique, however, ensures that the best balanced and considered information is derived from the study.

APPLICATION OF DECISION IMPACT ANALYSIS TO THE FISHING INDUSTRY

In accordance with the complexity of the operational structure of the system under study, the technique can be applied to the whole system or to each operational area. For example, in the fishing industry the system can be resolved into three main areas, namely, marine operations, wholesale operations, and retail operations (see Figure 1a). The relationships between the operational and the suboperational areas can also be determined by use of the cross-support technique to be described later; in fact, in highly technical industries, this method is more useful for relating technologies to other technologies through their contributions to operational functions. For illustrative purposes, however, the fishing industry is considered to be less complex than it is in reality, and the example treats the system as a whole.

The realization of the "global" systems concept is begun with a statement of the "systems envelope" (see Figure 1b). This is a statement of the field of study and an initial statement of all the variables which may affect the field of study or be affected by it, as well as the scales upon which these variables act. This initial statement, however, contains no data.

The problem is to examine the relationship between the field of study and the scaled variables, so that the effects of changes in one may be seen in the other. The variables themselves are not independent, and therefore their dependence relationships must be determined. This can be accomplished by means of the cross-support technique, which relates one factor to all the rest in terms of its positive or negative contribution.

In the next step, the systems envelope is rewritten as a "statement

276

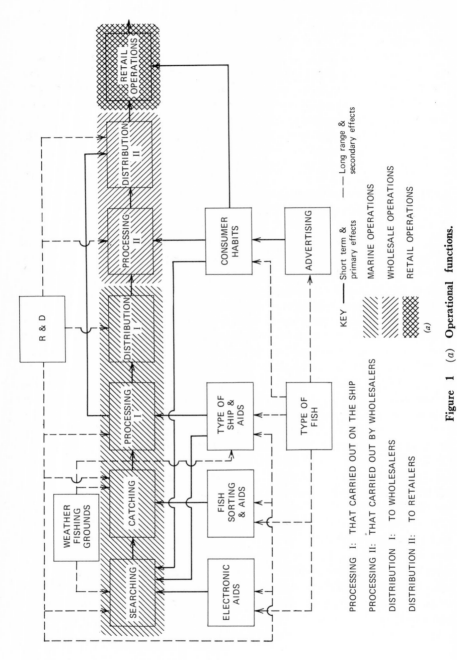

PROCESSING I: THAT CARRIED OUT ON THE SHIP
PROCESSING II: THAT CARRIED OUT BY WHOLESALERS

DISTRIBUTION I: TO WHOLESALERS
DISTRIBUTION II: TO RETAILERS

KEY ——— Short term & primary effects
——— Long range & secondary effects

MARINE OPERATIONS

WHOLESALE OPERATIONS

RETAIL OPERATIONS

(a)

Figure 1 (a) **Operational functions.**

Field of study
  Fish population
  Fishing systems
  Processing and distribution of fish
  Fish marketing opportunity
Causal/Dependent Variables
  Fishing technique development
  Development in processing
  Fish farming
  Ship and communications design and development
  GNP
  Cost of systems and processing
  Present and future organizational structure
  Consumer demand for fish and products (quantity)
  Consumer requirements (quality, etc.)
  Quality/cost to consumer
  Human protein demand
  Supply of personnel
  Safety and health on board
  Zone restrictions
  Fishing areas and detection of shoals
  Position and capability of fishing ports
  Links from ports (transportation)
  International competition
  Present capability (catching and processing)
  Advertising
  Weather
  Population (human) health
Scale
  Intra United Kingdom operational areas
  Extra United Kingdom operational areas

Figure 1 (*b*) **The U.K. fishing industry—systems envelope.**

matrix" in which the columns represent the cause and the effect of the field of study, and the rows represent the scaled causal/dependent variables (see Figure 2). It is processed by entering, in each element of the matrix, an estimate of the correlation between that particular section of the field of study and the variable. The correlation need only be rated as coarse, high, medium, low, or zero, represented by H, M, and L, respectively. In a similar manner, the "cross-support matrix" is drawn up to determine the relationships between the variables themselves (see Figure 3). In this case, the variables are not scaled; they are considered at all scales, and the greatest value is entered.

FIELD OF STUDY

CAUSAL/ DEPENDENT VARIABLES

SCALE (OPERATIONAL AREAS)	FISH POPULATION AFFECTED BY		DECISION TO CHANGE FISH POPULATION AFFECTS		FISHING SYSTEMS AFFECTED BY		CHANGE IN FISHING SYSTEMS AFFECTS		PROCESSING AND DISTRIBUTION AFFECTED BY		DECISION TO CHANGE PROCESSING AND DISTRIBUTION AFFECTS		MARKETING OPPORTUNITY FOR FISH AFFECTED BY		CHANGE IN MARKETING METHODS FOR FISH AFFECTS	
	INT U.K	EXT U.K	INT U.K	EXT U.K	INT U.K	EXT U.K	INT U.K	EXT U.K	INT U.K	EXT U.K	INT U.K	EXT U.K	INT U.K	EXT U.K	INT U.K	EXT U.K
DEVELOPMENT IN FISHING TECHNIQUES	M	M			H	H	H	M	M	M	M	L	M	M	M	L
DEVELOPMENT IN PROCESSING OF FISH							H	M	H	H	H	H	H	H	M	
FISH FARMING	H	H			M	L	L		M				M		M	
SHIP AND COMMUNICATIONS DESIGN AND DEVELOPMENT			H		H	H	H	H	H	H	M				M	
G.N.P.			L		H		L		L		H		L		H	
COST OF SYSTEMS AND PROCESSING			L		H	H	H	H	H	H	H	H	M		M	
PRESENT AND FUTURE ORGANIZATIONAL STRUCTURE					H				H				H		M	
CONSUMER DEMAND FOR FISH & FISH PRODUCTS (QUANTITY)	M	M			M	M			H	H			H	H	H	L
CONSUMER REQUIREMENTS (QUALITY...ETC.)	L	L			M	M			M	M			H	H		
QUALITY/COST TO CONSUMER			L	L	L	L	M	M			H	H	H	M		
HUMAN PROTEIN DEMAND	L	L	L	L					M	M			M	M		
SUPPLY OF PERSONNEL			L		H		H		M		H		M			
SAFETY AND HEALTH (ON BOARD)			M		H		H		L		L					
ZONE RESTRICTIONS					L											
FISHING AREAS AND SHOAL DETECTION	L	L	M		M	M	L	L								
POSITION & CAPABILITY OF FISHING PORTS					L		M		H		M		L		L	
LINKS FROM PORTS (TRANSPORTATION)			L		L				L		M		M		L	
INTERNATIONAL COMPETITION	L	L			L	L	L	M	M		L		M	M	M	M
PRESENT CAPABILITY (CATCHING & PROCESSING	L	L			H				H				M			
ADVERTISING													H	L	M	
WEATHER	L	L			H				M							
POPULATION (HUMAN) HEALTH					L	L			M	M	M	M				

Figure 2   Statement matrix.

278

Figure 3 Cross-support matrix.

DEPENDENT VARIABLES	DEVELOPMENT IN FISHING TECHNIQUES	DEVELOPMENT IN PROCESSING	FISH FARMING	SHIP & COMMUNICATIONS DESIGN & DEVELOPMENT	G. N. P.	COST OF SYSTEMS & PROCESSING	PRESENT & FUTURE ORGANIZATIONAL STRUCTURE	CONSUMER DEMAND FOR FISH & FISH PRODUCTS	CONSUMER REQUIREMENTS (QLTY, ETC)	QUALITY/COST TO CONSUMER	HUMAN PROTEIN DEMAND	SUPPLY OF PERSONNEL	SAFETY & HEALTH ON BOARD	ZONE RESTRICTIONS	FISHING AREAS & SHOAL DETECTION	POSITION & CAPABILITY OF FISHING PORTS	LINKS FROM PORTS (TRANSPORTATION)	INTERNATIONAL COMPETITION	PRESENT CAPABILITY (CATCHING & PROCESSING)	ADVERTISING	WEATHER	POPULATION (HUMAN) HEALTH
DEVELOPMENT IN FISHING TECHNIQUES		M	M	H	H	H	H	M	M	L		L	M		H			L				
DEVELOPMENT IN PROCESSING OF FISH	H			H	H	H	L	H	H	H	M	L				L		L				
FISH FARMING	L	L		M		L	M	H	H	M	H	L	H									
SHIP & COMMUNICATIONS DESIGN & DEVELOPMENT	M	M	L		H	M	H					M	H			L	M		L			
G. N. P.	L	L	L	L		M				L		L				L	L		L	L	L	
COST OF SYSTEMS & PROCESSING	H	H		L			L	M	M	M	L	L				L	L	L	L			
PRESENT & FUTURE ORGANIZATIONAL STRUCTURE	M	M	L	M	M						L		L						L			
CONSUMER DEMAND FOR FISH & FISH PRODUCTS (QNTY)	H	L		L	L				H	H	H										H	
CONSUMER REQUIREMENTS (QUALITY...ETC.)	H	L		L						H											H	
QUALITY COST TO CONSUMER	H	H	H	M	L	H	L	H	H		L				L	L	M	M	H	H	M	M
HUMAN PROTEIN DEMAND																						
SUPPLY OF PERSONNEL	H	H	H	L			M	M					H			L	M					L
SAFETY & HEALTH ON BOARD	H	H	H	H	L																H	
ZONE RESTRICTIONS																		M				
FISHING AREAS AND SHOAL DETECTION	H		H			M				L				H							M	
POSITION & CAPABILITY OF FISHING PORTS				M	H	L	H		L				H	M		M		H			H	
LINKS FROM PORTS (TRANSPORTATION)				H																		
INTERNATIONAL COMPETITION	H	H	H	M									H	M	M					M		
PRESENT CAPABILITY (CATCHING & PROCESSING)		H					H	H				H	M	L	L	H	L				H	
ADVERTISING							L		L													
WEATHER	L																					
POPULATION (HUMAN) HEALTH		M	L		M					M	H								L			

279

Each element of the two matrices represents a coarse first-order correlation, which is estimated by applying (*a*) relevant constraints, (*b*) professionally based assumptions, and (*c*) trend forecasting techniques.

The Qualitative Selection Process

In order to determine which variables should be analyzed in more detail, it is necessary to assess not only their relevance, which is esti-

	SCALE	
	INTRA UK	EXTRA UK
DEVELOPMENT IN FISHING TECHNIQUES	4	2
DEVELOPMENT IN PROCESSING OF FISH	4	2
FISH FARMING	4	1
SHIP DESIGN & DEVELOPMENT	4	2
G. N. P.	4	1
COST OF SYSTEMS & PROCESSING	2	1
PRESENT & FUTURE ORGANIZATIONAL STRUCTURE	8	1
CONSUMER DEMAND FOR FISH & PRODUCTS (QUANTITY	8	4
CONSUMER REQUIREMENTS (QUALITY, ETC.)	4	2
QUALITY/COST TO CONSUMER	8	2
PROTEIN DEMAND	8	8
SUPPLY OF PERSONNEL	8	1
SAFETY	8	8
ZONE RESTRICTIONS	2	2
FISHING AREAS & SHOAL DETECTION	2	1
POSITION & CAPABILITY OF FISHING PORTS	4	1
LINKS FROM PORTS (TRANSPORTATION)	4	1
INTERNATIONAL COMPETITION	4	2
PRESENT CAPABILITY (CATCHING & PROCESSING)	1	1
ADVERTISING	2	1
WEATHER	2	1
POPULATION (HUMAN) HEALTH	8	8

(left margin vertical labels: CAUSAL DEPENDENT VARIABLE)

Figure 4 Weight matrix.

mated from the correlation, but also their importance to the field of study. This can be expressed in the form of a "weight matrix" whose elements are the scaled variables (see Figure 4). Each element represents the importance which the decision-making body, acting in its frame of reference, attaches to each variable. The importance need only be rated as coarse, 8, 4, 2, or 1, the four numbers representing high, medium, low, and zero, respectively.[2]

The elements of the statement matrix are then multiplied by the weights of the appropriate scaled variables, and each row is summed to form a bar chart (see Figure 5). The elements of the bar chart are summed (high = 4, medium = 2, low = 1) to form "weighted sums" of correlation units which can be ordered. A threshold, depending on the constraints of time, money, and personnel available for the study, is now set, and the variables whose sums exceed this threshold are the ones which should be analyzed in greater detail.

It is at this stage that the qualitative selection process comes to an end. The areas of most importance have been determined; and now, if required, more detailed quantitative methods can be used on each of these areas. One such method is described in the following paragraphs.

Application of Quantitative Method

Each variable of this subset of most important variables is now expanded into its component subvariables (covering its multidimensionality), and new matrices ("expanded statements") are formed between the field of study and the subvariables. The cross-support matrix is consulted for variables which are highly dependent on, or causal to, those which have been expanded, and these are included in the expanded statement. It is then processed in the same manner as the statement matrix (see Figures 6–10). The areas of high correlation in each expanded matrix define the fields for intensive analysis, which typically takes the form of data collection and collation, followed by multiple regressional analysis and trend forecasting.

An overall review is then made of the results of the detailed studies, and the factors which were used in their derivation. If any of the initial assumptions or constraints appear to have been invalid, or if some additional variable should have been included, amendments are made

---

[2] These numbers were chosen because it has been shown that people think logarithmically.

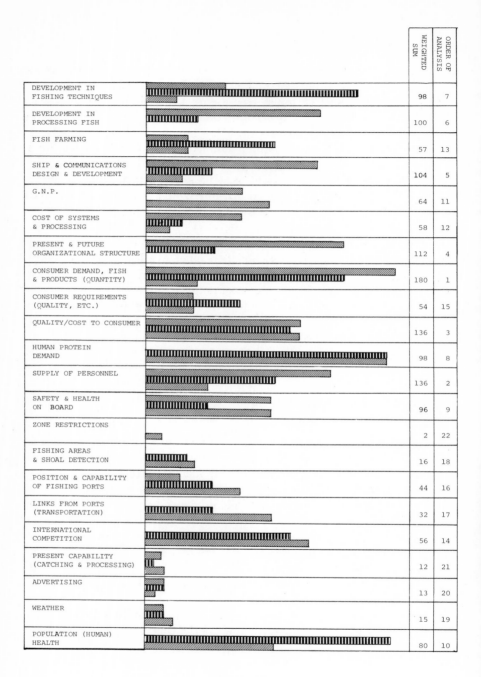

	WEIGHTED SUM	ORDER OF ANALYSIS
DEVELOPMENT IN FISHING TECHNIQUES	98	7
DEVELOPMENT IN PROCESSING FISH	100	6
FISH FARMING	57	13
SHIP & COMMUNICATIONS DESIGN & DEVELOPMENT	104	5
G.N.P.	64	11
COST OF SYSTEMS & PROCESSING	58	12
PRESENT & FUTURE ORGANIZATIONAL STRUCTURE	112	4
CONSUMER DEMAND, FISH & PRODUCTS (QUANTITY)	180	1
CONSUMER REQUIREMENTS (QUALITY, ETC.)	54	15
QUALITY/COST TO CONSUMER	136	3
HUMAN PROTEIN DEMAND	98	8
SUPPLY OF PERSONNEL	136	2
SAFETY & HEALTH ON BOARD	96	9
ZONE RESTRICTIONS	2	22
FISHING AREAS & SHOAL DETECTION	16	18
POSITION & CAPABILITY OF FISHING PORTS	44	16
LINKS FROM PORTS (TRANSPORTATION)	32	17
INTERNATIONAL COMPETITION	56	14
PRESENT CAPABILITY (CATCHING & PROCESSING)	12	21
ADVERTISING	13	20
WEATHER	15	19
POPULATION (HUMAN) HEALTH	80	10

KEY   HIGH
      MED
      LOW

Figure 5   Weight correlation bar chart.

Figure 6 — Expanded statement matrix for consumer demand for fish and fish product.

CAUSAL/DEPENDENT VARIABLES

FIELD OF STUDY

SCALE (OPERATIONAL AREAS)	FISH POPULATION AFFECTED BY — INT U.K	FISH POPULATION AFFECTED BY — EXT U.K	DECISION TO CHANGE FISH POPULATION AFFECTS — INT U.K	DECISION TO CHANGE FISH POPULATION AFFECTS — EXT U.K	FISHING SYSTEMS AFFECTED BY — INT U.K	FISHING SYSTEMS AFFECTED BY — EXT U.K	CHANGE IN FISHING SYSTEMS AFFECTS — INT U.K	CHANGE IN FISHING SYSTEMS AFFECTS — EXT U.K	PROCESSING AND DISTRIBUTION AFFECTED BY — INT U.K	PROCESSING AND DISTRIBUTION AFFECTED BY — EXT U.K	DECISION TO CHANGE PROCESSING AND DISTRIBUTION AFFECTS — INT U.K	DECISION TO CHANGE PROCESSING AND DISTRIBUTION AFFECTS — EXT U.K	MARKETING OPPORTUNITY FOR FISH AFFECTED BY — INT U.K	MARKETING OPPORTUNITY FOR FISH AFFECTED BY — EXT U.K	CHANGE IN MARKETING METHODS FOR FISH AFFECTS — INT U.K	CHANGE IN MARKETING METHODS FOR FISH AFFECTS — EXT U.K	DEVELOPMENT IN PROCESSING — ANY	FISH FARMING — ANY	CONSUMER REQUIREMENT — ANY	QUALITY/COST TO CONSUMER — ANY	PROTEIN DEMAND — ANY	ADVERTISING — ANY
DEMAND FOR FRESH FISH	H	L			M				H		H		H		M		H	H	H	H		M
DEMAND FOR WHITE FISH					L				M		M		H		H				H	H		M
DEMAND FOR RED FISH					L				M		M		H		H				H	H		H
DEMAND FOR SHELL FISH									M		M		H		H		M	H	H	H		H
DEMAND FOR FISH MEAL	L	L			L				M				H						H			
DEMAND FOR FISH OIL	L	L			L				M				H						H		M	
DEMAND FOR DRIED/SMOKED FISH									L				H	H			M		H			
DEMAND FOR TINNED FISH									M				H	H	M				H	L		
DEMAND FOR PREPARED 'READY' TO COOK FISH (FROZEN, FILLETED, BREADCRUMBED ETC.)									H		H		H	H	H		H		H	H		H
DEMAND FOR FISH AS A SOURCE OF PROTEIN	H	H							M				H	H							H	

EXPANSION OF VARIABLE

Figure 7 — Expanded statement matrix for supply of personnel.

FIELD OF STUDY / CAUSAL/DEPENDENT VARIABLES

Row labels (down the left) are grouped under the heading **EXPANSION OF VARIABLES**.

SCALE (OPERATIONAL AREAS)	FISH POPULATION AFFECTED BY	DECISION TO CHANGE FISH POPULATION AFFECTS	FISHINGS SYSTEMS AFFECTED BY	CHANGE IN FISHING SYSTEMS AFFECTS	PROCESSING AND DISTRIBUTION AFFECTED BY	DECISION TO CHANGE PROCESSING AND DISTRIBUTION AFFECTS	MARKETING OPPORTUNITY FOR FISH AFFECTED BY	CHANGE IN MARKETING METHODS FOR FISH AFFECTS	DEVELOPMENT IN FISHING TECHNIQUES	DEVELOPMENT IN PROCESSING	FISH FARMING	SHIP DESIGN AND DEVELOPMENT	PRESENT AND FUTURE ORGANIZATIONAL STRUCTURE	SAFETY	POSITION AND CAPABILITY OF PORTS	PRESENT CAPABILITY (CATCHING & PROCESSING)
	INT	EXT	INT	EXT	INT	EXT	INT	EXT	ANY	ANY	ANY	ANY	ANY	ANY	ANY	ANY
	U.K	U.K	U.K	U.K	U.K	U.K	U.K	U.K	ANY	ANY	ANY	ANY	ANY	ANY	ANY	ANY
TYPES OF PERSONNEL REQUIRED		M		H		H		M	H	H	H	H			M	H
WAGES								M	M	M			H			
BENEFITS													H			
QUALITY OF EMPLOYER													H			
CONDITIONS AND AMENITIES				M		M			H			H	H			
"IMAGE"				M					H							
COMPETING LOCAL EMPLOYMENT			H		H										H	H
PRESENT STATE OF THE INDUSTRY	L		H	M	H	M				L						H
WILLINGNESS TO WORK IN FISHING INDUSTRY				M					H			H	H	H	M	H

Figure 8 Expanded statement matrix for quality and cost to consumer.

SCALE (OPERATIONAL AREAS)	FISH POPULATION AFFECTED BY INT U.K	FISH POPULATION AFFECTED BY EXT U.K	DECISION TO CHANGE FISH POPULATION AFFECTS INT U.K	DECISION TO CHANGE FISH POPULATION AFFECTS EXT U.K	FISHING SYSTEMS AFFECTED BY INT U.K	FISHING SYSTEMS AFFECTED BY EXT U.K	CHANGE IN FISHING SYSTEMS AFFECTS INT U.K	CHANGE IN FISHING SYSTEMS AFFECTS EXT U.K	PROCESSING AND DISTRIBUTION AFFECTED BY INT U.K	PROCESSING AND DISTRIBUTION AFFECTED BY EXT U.K	DECISION TO CHANGE PROCESSING AND DISTRIBUTION AFFECTS INT U.K	DECISION TO CHANGE PROCESSING AND DISTRIBUTION AFFECTS EXT U.K	MARKETING OPPORTUNITY FOR FISH AFFECTED BY INT U.K	MARKETING OPPORTUNITY FOR FISH AFFECTED BY EXT U.K	CHANGE IN MARKETING METHODS FOR FISH AFFECTS INT U.K	CHANGE IN MARKETING METHODS FOR FISH AFFECTS EXT U.K	DEVELOPMENT IN FISHING TECHNIQUES ANY	DEVELOPMENT IN PROCESSING ANY	FISH FARMING ANY	COST OF SYSTEMS AND PROCESSING ANY	CONSUMER DEMAND AND FISH PRODUCTS ANY	CONSUMER REQUIREMENT ANY	INTERNATIONAL COMPETITION ANY	PRESENT CAPABILITY (CATCHING & PROCESSI) ANY
COST OF FRESHNESS							H	M			H		H		H		H	H	M			H		H
COST OF ATTRACTIVENESS							H	M			H		M		H		H	H	M			H		L
COST OF FRESH FISH		L					M	M			H		H		H			H	H	H	H			H
COST OF FROZEN FISH		L					M	M			H		M		M			H	L	H	H			
COST OF CANNED FISH		L					M	M			L		L		L			M	L	M	H			
COMPARISON OF COSTS OF FRESH, FROZEN, CANNED FISH											M		H		H			L				M	H	
COMPARISON OF COSTS TO OTHER PROTEIN SOURCES													H		H			M			H	H	M	
COST OF FISH MEAL AND FISH OIL							H				L		H		H			L	M	M	H		M	
NEW AVAILABILITY AND SERVICES													H		H	M	M	M	L	L	H	M		

FIELD OF STUDY

CAUSAL/DEPENDENT VARIABLES

EXPANSION OF VARIABLE

Figure 9 (a) Expanded statement matrix for present and future organizational structure.

EXPANSION

SCALE (OPERATIONAL AREAS)	FISH POPULATION AFFECTED BY		DECISION TO CHANGE FISH POPULATION AFFECTS		FISHING SYSTEMS AFFECTED BY		CHANGE IN FISHING SYSTEMS AFFECTS		PROCESSING AND DISTRIBUTION AFFECTED BY		DECISION TO CHANGE PROCESSING AND DISTRIBUTION AFFECTS		MARKETING OPPORTUNITY FOR FISH AFFECTED BY		CHANGE IN MARKETING METHODS FOR FISH AFFECTS		DEVELOPMENT IN FISHING TECHNIQUES	SHIP DESIGN & DEVELOPMENT	SUPPLY OF PERSONNEL	POSITION & CAPABILITY OF PORTS	PRESENT CAPABILITY (CATCHING & PROCESSING)
	INT U.K	EXT U.K	INT U.K	EXT U.K	INT U.K	EXT U.K	INT U.K	EXT U.K	INT U.K	EXT U.K	INT U.K	EXT U.K	INT U.K	EXT U.K	INT U.K	EXT U.K	ANY	ANY	ANY	ANY ANY	ANY ANY
SMALL OWNERS TAKING/ PLOUGHING BACK PROFITS					H		H		H		H		H		H		H	H	H	H	H
LARGE COMPANIES TAKING/PLOUGHING BACK PROFITS					H		M		H		M		H		M		H	H	H	H	H
INTERESTS IN OTHER BRANCHES OF FISHING INDUSTRY (E.G. TRAWLING AND MARKETING)					L				H		M		H		H		M	M	M	H	
WILLINGNESS TO OUTLAY CAPITAL					H		M		H								M	M	H	H	M

286

A matrix (Figure 9(b)) cross-tabulating FIELD OF STUDY variables (rows) against CAUSAL/DEPENDENT VARIABLES (columns), with cells marked H (high), M (medium), or L (low).

Row labels (FIELD OF STUDY variables):

FIELD OF STUDY												
NATIONALISATION	H					M			H		M	M
COMPANY MONOPOLY	H		H		M		H	M	H	H	H	M
INTEGRATION OF INDUSTRY (I.E., FISHING, PACKING, DISTRIBUTION, ETC.)	H		H		H	H	H	H	H	H	H	H
USE OF O.R. TECHNIQUES	M		M		M		M	M	H	M	H	H
NATIONAL PLANNING	M		M		L		M	L	M	M	H	
DIRECT MARKETING (VESTED INTEREST IN WHOLESALES)	H		H	H	H	H	H	H	H		H	H
INTERNATIONAL COMPETITION AT SEA	H	M			M		H	M			H	
CORRUPTION	H		H		H		H	H	H		H	
BONUS INCENTIVES AND EFFECT	H		H		H		H				H	
INTERNATIONAL COLLABORATION			L	L	L		H	L	L	L		

FIELD OF STUDY   CAUSAL/DEPENDENT VARIABLES

Figure 9 (*b*)

287

Figure 10 (matrix chart). The chart cross-tabulates operational areas (rows, under the stub "SCALE (OPERATIONAL AREAS)", the "FIELD OF STUDY" axis) against the "CAUSAL/DEPENDENT VARIABLES" (columns). Cell values are H (high), M (medium), or L (low).

Variable (scope)	Side Trawlers & Development	Stern Trawlers & Development	Large Freezer/Storer/Packer Ships with Small Satellite Ships & Development	Small Freezer Ships & Development	Methods of Converting Old Ships	New Ships Incorporating New Techniques	Submarine Fishing Vessels Development	Stern Chute for Landing Catch	Export Possibilities for New Ships & Systems	Development in Communications
SHOAL DETECTION (ANY)						H				H
SAFETY (ANY)	H	H	H	H	H	H	H	H	M	
SUPPLY OF PERSONNEL (ANY)	M	M	H	L	L	H	H	L		
ORGANIZATIONAL STRUCTURE PRESENT & FUTURE (ANY)	M	M	M	M	H	M	M			
G.N.P. (ANY)	H	H	H	H	M	H	H	M	H	
DEVELOPMENT IN FISHING TECHNIQUES (ANY)	L	L	H	H	H	H	H	H		
CHANGE IN MARKETING METHODS FOR FISH AFFECTS (INT EXT U.K)									M	
CHANGE IN MARKETING (INT U.K)			M		M					
MARKETING OPPORTUNITY FOR FISH AFFECTED BY (INT EXT U.K)			M		L					
DECISION TO CHANGE PROCESSING & DISTRIBUTION AFFECTS (INT EXT U.K)			M		L		M			
PROCESSING & DISTRIBUTION AFFECTED BY (INT EXT U.K)	L	L	H		H	H	L			L
CHANGE IN FISHING SYSTEMS AFFECTS (INT EXT U.K)	L	M	L	L		L	L	L	H	
CHANGE IN FISHING SYSTEMS AFFECTS (INT EXT U.K)	M	H	H	H	L	H	H	M		
FISHING SYSTEMS AFFECTED BY (INT EXT U.K)	H	H	H	H		H	H	H		H
FISHING SYSTEMS AFFECTED BY (INT EXT U.K)	H	H	H	M	M	H	H	H		H
DECISION TO CHANGE FISH POPULATION AFFECTS (INT EXT U.K)										
FISH POPULATION AFFECTED BY (INT EXT U.K)										

CAUSAL/DEPENDENT VARIABLES

FIELD OF STUDY

EXPANSION OF VARIABLE

Figure 10 Expanded statement matrix for ship and communication design and development

288

and the whole process is repeated, until all unwanted "noise" is smoothed out of the system.

RESULTS

The results take the form, typically, of predictions of several possible futures and of the ways in which they may be attained. These alternatives take into account all the relevant technologies but not, of course, any unforeseen technological breakthrough which may occur.

XVII. *A Simple Substitution Model of Technological Change*

JOHN C. FISHER AND ROBERT H. PRY

What we see depends mainly on what we look for.　　　　　John Lubbock

INTRODUCTION

For people who attempt to forecast the future, there is a continuing need for simple models that describe the course of unfolding events. Each such model should be based on easily understood assumptions that are not available for unconscious or invisible tampering by the forecaster in his efforts to make the future what he wants it to be. The model should be readily applicable to a wide variety of circumstances and should be easy to interpret. It is our purpose to describe such a model and, by way of example, to apply it to a few illustrative forecasts.

If one admits that man has relatively few broad basic needs to be satisfied—food, clothing, shelter, transportation, communication, education, and the like—then it follows that technological evolution consists mainly of substituting a new form of satisfaction for the old one. Thus, as technology advances, we may successively substitute coal for wood, hydrocarbons for coal, and nuclear fuel for fossil fuel in the production of energy. In war we may substitute guns for bows and arrows, or tanks for horses. Even in a much more narrow and confined framework, substitutions are constantly encountered. For example, we substitute water-based paints for oil-based paints, detergents for soap, and plastic floors for wood floors in houses.

The view of advancing technology as a set of substitution processes may seem evolutionary or revolutionary, depending on the time scale of the substitution. Regardless of the pace of the change, however, the end result to the user is almost always to allow him to perform an existing function or satisfy an ongoing need differently from before. The function or need rarely undergoes radical change. Whenever exceptions to this view are found, the notion of competitive substitution as a model for technological change does not apply.

THE MODEL

The model is based on three assumptions:

1. Many technological advances can be considered as competitive substitutions of one method of satisfying a need for another.
2. If a substitution has progressed as far as a few per cent of the total consumption, it will proceed to completion.
3. The fractional rate of fractional substitution of new for old is proportional to the remaining amount of the old left to be substituted.

When a new method is first introduced, it is less well developed than the older method with which it is competing. Therefore it is likely to have greater potential for improvement and for reduction in cost. Our second assumption is based on the idea that any substitution that has gained a few per cent of the available market has shown economic viability, even without the improvement and cost reduction that will come with increased volume, and hence that the substitution will proceed to 100%.

Experience shows that substitutions tend to proceed exponentially (i.e., with a constant percentage of annual growth increment) in the early years, and to follow an S-shaped curve. The simplest such curve is characterized by two constants: the early growth rate and the time at which the substitution is half complete. The corresponding fraction substituted is given by the relationship

$$f = \tfrac{1}{2}[1 + \tanh \alpha(t - t_0)] \tag{1}$$

where α is half the annual fractional growth in the early years, and t_0 is the time at which $f = \frac{1}{2}$. This equation can be derived from our third assumption, which in mathematical form is

$$\left(\frac{1}{f}\right)\left(\frac{df}{dt}\right) = 2\alpha(1 - f) \tag{2}$$

Before proceeding with some examples of the application of the model, a few useful characteristics of the S-shaped expression given as Eq. 1 will be developed. First, recall that $f = \frac{1}{2}$ when $t = t_0$. Thus t_0 signifies the point in time when the substitution is half complete. It will be convenient, in addition, to characterize a substitution by its "takeover time," defined as the time required to go from $f = 0.1$ to $f = 0.9$. This time is inversely proportional to α:

$$t = t_{0.9} - t_{0.1} = \frac{2.2}{\alpha} \tag{3}$$

A more convenient form of the substitution expression given as Eq. 1 is

$$\frac{f}{1 - f} = \exp 2\alpha(t - t_0) \tag{4}$$

This expression allows one to plot the substitution data in the form of $f/(1 - f)$ as a function of time on semilog paper and to fit a straight line through the resulting points, as illustrated in Figure 1. The slope of the line is 2, the time t_0 is found at $f/(1 - f) = 1$, and the takeover time is easily measured as the time between $f/(1 - f) = 0.11$ and $f/(1 - f) = 9$. The resulting curve can then be replotted on linear graph paper for display.

It will be readily recognized that the model contains at least one obvious flaw: in reality, all substitutions start at a specific point in time, whereas the model predicts that all substitutions began in the infinite past. In practical circumstances, however, this is of little consequence, since the model, by our first assumption, is not to be applied to substitutions prior to their achieving a magnitude of a few per cent, at which time a definite growth pattern is established and the very early history has little effect on the trend extrapolation.

APPLICATIONS OF THE MODEL

Synthetic versus Natural Fibers

Table 1 shows the history of the U.S. consumption of natural and man-made or synthetic fibers since 1930. Wool, silk, and flax have been

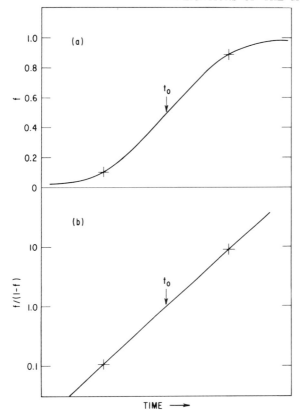

Figure 1   General form of the substitution model function.

lumped together under Other Natural. The fraction, f, of synthetic to
total fibers is listed in this table. The function $f/(1-f)$ versus time
has been plotted in Figure 2. This indicates a half-substitution date
of 1969 and a takeover time of 58 years, from an $f = 0.1$ in 1940 to
0.9 in 1998.

If one wishes to use this projection to forecast the total use of synthetics or natural fibers, two additional pieces of information are required: projections of population growth and of per capita fiber consumption in the United States. Per capita consumption is listed in Table 1
and is shown in Figure 3, including a linear trend projection into the
future. By combining these curves with the U.S. Bureau of the Census
population projection,[1] assuming 1962–66 fertility levels, a forecast of

[1] U.S. Department of Commerce, *Statistical Abstracts of the United States,* 1969.

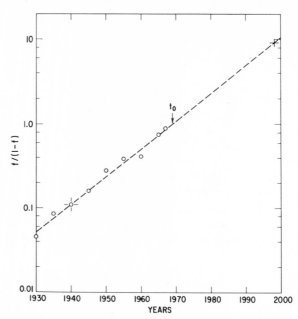

Figure 2 Synthetic for natural fiber substitution versus years—substitution model fit to data.

Table 1   Mill Consumption of Natural and Synthetic Fibers

Year	Synthetics $\times 10^9$ lb	Synthetics lb per capita	Cotton $\times 10^9$ lb	Cotton lb per capita	Other Natural $\times 10^9$ lb	Other Natural lb per capita	Total per Capita	Fraction Synthetic
1930	0.12	1.0	2.62	21.3	0.36	2.88	22.66	0.044
1935	0.27	2.2	2.76	21.7	0.50	3.97	27.87	0.079
1940	0.50	3.7	3.96	30.0	0.47	3.55	37.25	0.10
1945	0.85	6.1	4.52	32.3	0.65	4.66	43.06	0.14
1950	1.82	10.1	4.68	30.0	0.66	4.34	45.34	0.22
1955	1.90	11.5	4.38	26.5	0.433	2.62	40.62	0.28
1960	1.89	10.4	4.19	23.2	0.423	2.37	35.97	0.29
1965	3.62	18.6	4.47	23.0	0.40	2.07	43.67	0.43
1967	4.24	21.3	4.42	22.2	0.32	1.65	45.15	0.47

294

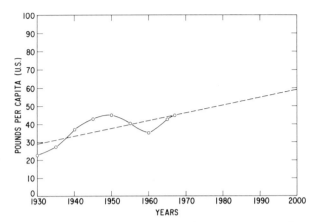

Figure 3   Total per capita U.S. fiber consumption versus years—data and straight-line projection.

U.S. consumption of synthetic and all natural fibers through the year 2000 is obtained. This forecast, shown in Figure 4, suggests a substantial increase in the consumption of synthetics and a decline in the consumption of natural fibers. The degree of concern that this should cause the producers of natural fibers depends on one's confidence in the forecast.

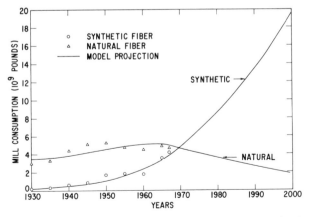

Figure 4   U.S. fiber consumption versus years—data and projection using the substitution model.

Plastic versus Leather

A similar example is the substitution of plastic for leather. Everyday experience suggests that plastic materials have been substituting for leather in the United States. The per capita consumption of leather has undergone a steady decline since about 1930, but we were not able to find data on the consumption of plastic substitutes for leather. How-

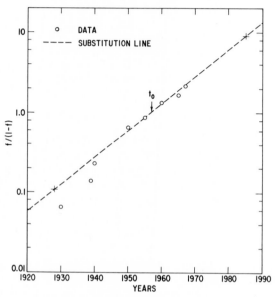

Figure 5 Synthetic for natural leather substitution versus years—substitution model fit to data.

ever, assuming a constant per capita consumption of the combined materials over the past few decades, it is possible to deduce the fraction of plastic for any given year. Figure 5 shows the substitution curve generated in this way.

If the curve in Figure 5 is projected ahead, assuming a constant per capita consumption of combined leather and plastic substitutes, and using the same population projection as in the fiber example, one obtains the curve of Figure 6. This shows the forecast total of tanned animal hides to be sold in the United States as a function of time. Again, if one believes the model, a rapid and continuing reduction in the sale of leather products will take place. As these two examples illustrate, the proposed substitution analysis model can be used not only to forecast expanding opportunities but also to identify areas where additional attention may be needed to adjust to potential adverse changes.

Two of the principal advantages of this substitution analysis can now be seen. First, the analysis is simple to perform and is not open to much subjective judgment by the forecaster. Second, the various elements of the forecast—that is, the fractional substitution competition, the per capita consumption, and the projected population growth—are separated.

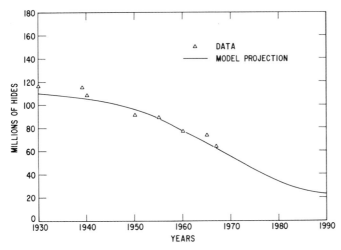

Figure 6   U.S. consumption of tanned animal hides versus years—data and substitution model projection.

This not only allows but also demands that independent projections be made for each element. The substitution model is fatalistic in the sense that it projects a specific and undeviating future based on past events. This is not to imply that a particular future is inevitable, but rather to suggest that, in a normal competitive environment in which no large forces are discontinuously brought into play, the future is predictable from past events. A demonstrable exception is the following case.

Synthetic versus Natural Rubber

In the 1930s synthetic rubber was slowly being substituted for natural rubber, which was largely imported from offshore plantations. Synthetic rubber was, at that stage, inferior in some ways to the natural product. Very early in World War II, however, offshore sources of natural rubber were largely cut off, while at the same time the demand for rubber as an essential material for the conduct of the war increased considerably. At this time, a large national effort was undertaken to substitute synthetic for natural rubber. During these years progress was made in

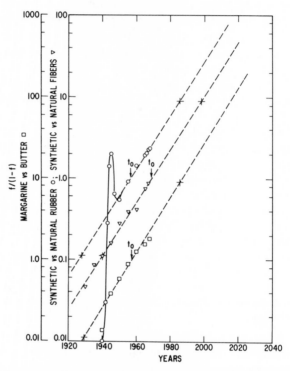

Figure 7 U.S. consumption versus years and fit to substitution model for three agriculture-based products.

improving both the properties and the production cost of the synthetic product. After the war ended, the offshore sources of natural rubber again became available, and, since purely synthetic rubber had not yet passed natural rubber in properties and cost, the relative use of the two products readjusted itself to a new substitute fraction. Then, in subsequent years, the substitution proceeded ahead at an orderly pace.

Figure 7 shows the substitution competition of synthetic for natural rubber, along with two other agricultural product substitutions. It is interesting to note that the rate of substitution of synthetic for natural rubber after 1946 is nearly the same as the rates of oleomargarine for butter and of synthetic for natural fibers, two other broad agricultural substitutions.

CHOICE OF UNIT FOR COMPARISON

In order to examine the breadth of applicability of the substitution model, seventeen different cases of competitive substitutions have been considered, including those already described. Included are the substitutions of plastic for metal in cars, of open-hearth steel for Bessemer steel, of detergents for soap, and of plastic floors for hardwood floors in houses.

In considering such a wide range of substitutions, a question arises as to the appropriate units to be used in each instance. Since the substitution of synthetic for natural fibers is reasonably direct, fiber weight was used as a basis for comparison. Weight will generally suffice also when considering competing processes for manufacturing essentially the same end-product, such as open-hearth versus Bessemer steel and sulfate versus tree-tapped turpentine. But what about substitutions like plastic floors for wood floors, or the use of plastic for metal in cars, or of Fiberglas for other materials in pleasure boats? A weight comparison may be inappropriate in these cases. A comparison based on dollars of sales is equally inappropriate when, as in the case of processes, cost saving may be the motivation for the substitution.

One must examine each case individually to determine the best equivalent units, and then hope that data are at hand or attainable in these units. For example, in the case of plastic substituting for hardwood in floors, data were available for the number of pounds of plastic, as well as for the number of board-feet of hardwood flooring, used in new homes. Clearly the equivalent unit needed is the number of square feet used in homes. By converting the number of pounds of plastic into the equivalent number of pounds of filled plastic, and dividing by the filled density and by the average thickness of a plastic floor covering, the pounds of plastic could be converted to square feet of plastic floor covering. Since the sum of this number plus the number of square feet of hardwood floor covering in new residential construction came within about 10% of the total floor area of new housing starts for a number of years, confidence was increased in the validity of the data to be used in the substitution analysis.

In the case of substitution in the materials for pleasure boats, numbers of boats of each type were used. In the substitution of plastics for leather, the surface area expressed in numbers of equivalent hides served as an appropriate unit.

SOME FURTHER EXAMPLES OF SUBSTITUTION DATA

Data are given in Table 2 for a number of such substitutions. The takeover time, Δt, the midpoint time, t_0, and the units are given for

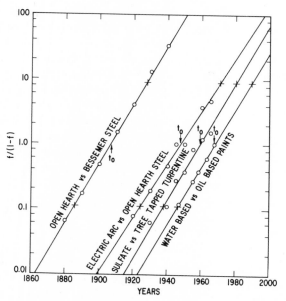

Figure 8 (*a*) **Substitution data and fit to model for a number of products and processes. All data U.S. except in the case of detergents for soap as noted.**

each case. Special problems exist for items with an asterisk in the unit column. Because the electric arc furnace is used primarily for the production of specialty steels, it was assumed to substitute for only 11% of steel production tonnage. The density of plastic is approximately one-eighth that of metal, but the strength and stiffness are much less; hence it was assumed that 1 pound of plastic would replace 3 pounds of metal in cars. In the case of detergents substituting for soap, approximately 15% of total washing products are not considered available for replacement. These are mostly facial soaps and similar products. Since this is as true in Japan as in the United States, this amount was subtracted from the total in arriving at the fraction substituted in each of these cases. Figures 8a–d display the data and the fit to the model for the cases of Table 2, using the function $f/(1-f)$ versus time.

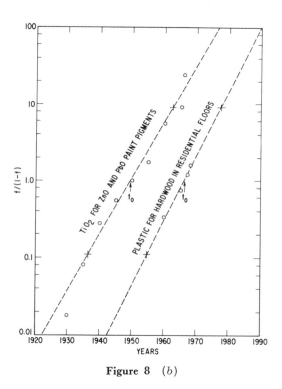

Figure 8 (b)

A further test of the degree to which the form of the model proposed fits the actual history of many competitive substitutions taking place over the last nearly 100 years is shown in Figures 9a and b. The ordinates used in these figures are $f/(1-f)$ and f, respectively. The abcissa used in both figures is the dimensionless parameter $2(t-t_0)/\Delta t$, which normalizes all of the data to a single mathematical form. All of the data points for the seventeen cases considered are plotted together in these figures. The solid curves shown are the theoretical curves for the substitution model, that is,

$$f = \tfrac{1}{2}\left[1 + \tanh 1.1\,\frac{2(t - t_0)}{\Delta t} \right]$$

$$\frac{f}{1 - f} = 2.2\,\frac{2(t - t_0)}{\Delta t}$$

(5)

The fit of the data to the mathematical form of the model is remarkably good over this wide range of examples.

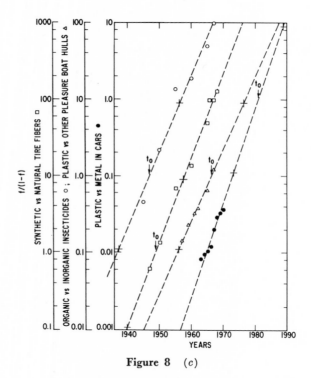

Figure 8   (c)

Although these data increase the confidence in the model for forecasting, the data as displayed in this form raise many questions from the standpoint of understanding technological change. For example, is there an underlying reason for the great similarity in takeover time of the first four substitutions of Table 2 (particularly considering the major perturbation that occurred in synthetic rubber production during World

War II)? Is their relationship to agriculture important? The takeover time of synthetic tire fibers for natural tire fibers is substantially shorter than that of all natural fibers; how is this time related to the diversity of product of the industry involved? How much of the very short time required for BOF takeover from the open-hearth process, compared to open-hearth takeover from Bessemer, is related to the fact that the BOF process was imported, fully developed, from Germany and Austria?

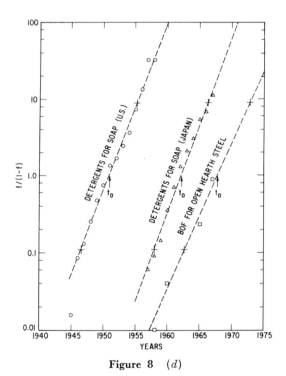

Figure 8 (*d*)

How much of this difference is related to the timing of equipment replacement and to investment policy? Does the striking similarity between the detergent-from-soap takeover times in the United States and Japan, even with a midtime lag of a decade, have any particular significance? It is not within the scope of this paper to attempt answers to these questions. Rather, the questions are raised to indicate the diversity of broad topics which may be addressed with the aid of this simple model.

Table 2   Takeover Times (ΔT) and Substitution Midpoints (T_0) for a Number of Substitution Cases

Substitution	Units	ΔT, years	T_0, year	Reference Source[a]
Synthetic/natural rubber	Pounds	58	1956	1
Synthetic/natural fibers	Pounds	58	1969	1
Plastics/natural leather	Equiv. hides	57	1957	1
Margarine/butter	Pounds	56	1957	1
Electric arc/open-hearth specialty steels	Tons*[b]	47	1947	2
Water-based/oil-based house paint	Gallons	43	1967	3
Open-hearth/Bessemer steel	Tons	42	1907	2
Sulfate/tree-tapped turpentine	Pounds	42	1959	3
TiO_2/PbO-ZnO paint pigments	Pounds	26	1949	3
Plastic/hardwood residence floors	Square feet	25	1966	1
Plastic/other materials for pleasure boat hulls	Hulls	20	1966	4
Organic/inorganic insecticides	Pounds	19	1946	3
Synthetic/natural tire fibers	Pounds	17.5	1948	1
Plastics/metal for cars	Pounds*	16	1981	4
BOF/open-hearth steels	Tons	10.5	1968	2
Detergent/natural soaps (U.S.)	Pounds*	8.75	1951	5
Detergent/natural soaps (Japan)	Pounds*	8.25	1962	5

[a] References:

1. U.S. Department of Commerce, *Statistical Abstracts of the United States*, 1969.
2. Illinois Institute of Technology Research Institute, Ceramics Bulletin No. 24, November–December 1969.
3. *Chemical Economics Handbook*, Stanford Research Institute.
4. D. V. Rosato, W. K. Fallon, and D. V. Rosato, *Markets for Plastics*, New York: Van Nostrand-Reinhold Co., 1969.
5. *Chemical Week*, September 26, 1969, p. 69.

[b] See text for qualifying comments about items with asterisks.

Although it is well to exercise some caution in drawing conclusions from a set of examples whose sole criterion for choice was the availability of data with which to perform the analysis, a few general remarks will be made. If one characterizes these examples by the date at which the substitution was 10% complete, the set can be said to cover a span of time of about 90 years. In spite of the large variation in takeover

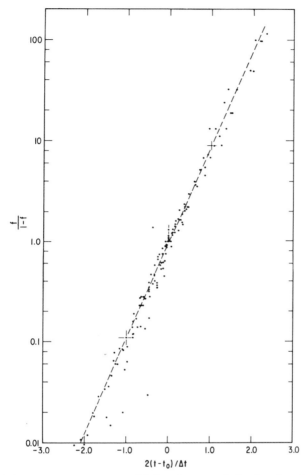

Figure 9 (a) **Fit of substitution model function to substitution data for all 17 cases versus normalized units of time.**

times between examples in the set, there seems to be little correlation between the takeover time and the date at which the substitution started. On the other hand, it is commonly believed that the pace of technical change has increased dramatically in this century. The apparent discrepancy in these statements might be resolved by recognizing that the pace of change in a society is probably measured less by the speed with which a single isolated substitution occurs than by the number and magnitude of such substitutions taking place simultaneously. It might be enlightening to examine this question in a given country as a function of time or between countries to determine the correlation between the number of such substitutions and the abundance of technical, economic, educational, and other resources available.

The speed with which a substitution takes place is not a simple measure of the pace of technical advance, or of manufacturing, marketing, distribution, or any other individual substitution element. It is rather a measure of the unbalance in these factors between the competitive elements of the substitution. When a substitution begins, the new prod-

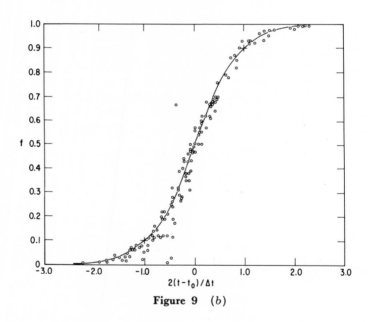

Figure 9 (*b*)

uct, process, or service struggles hard to improve and to demonstrate its advantages over the dominant product, process, or service. However, as the new substitution element becomes recognized by commanding a few per cent of the total market, the threatened element redoubles its own efforts to maintain or improve its position. Thus the pace of technical innovative effort—indeed, the competitive pace of all aspects of the substitution—may increase markedly during the course of the substitution struggle.

A major conclusion that we draw from the successful application of the substitution model is that, all of these considerations notwithstanding, the rate constant of a substitution, once begun, does not change throughout its history. The rate at which a given substitution proceeds seems to be determined by the complex interplay of economic forces responding to the inherent superiority of a new method.

SUMMARY

A substitution model of technological change based on a simple set of assumptions has been advanced. The mathematical form of the model is shown to fit existing data in a wide variety of substitutions remarkably well.

It is suggested that the model can prove useful to a number of types of investigations, such as forecasting technological opportunities, recognizing the onset of technologically-based catastrophies, investigating the similarities and differences in innovative change in various economic sectors, studying the rate of technical change in different countries and different cultures, and investigating the features limiting technological change.

XVIII. *Some Societal Consequences of Technological and Scientific Developments*[1]

RAUL DE BRIGARD AND OLAF HELMER

Success is the ability to get along with some people and ahead of others.

G. R. Wasserman

INTRODUCTION

The material in this chapter represents an overview of various aspects of the future of our society, according to expectations held either jointly or individually by a group of persons well informed in numerous disciplines. It is intended to serve, not so much as a detailed description of what the future may hold, but rather as a preview for more detailed investigations that should be undertaken in order to relate the consequences of developments and policies in one sector of society to those in others and to the future expectations and needs of society as a whole.

Obtaining a preliminary overview of this kind was considered of particular importance for the primary sponsor of this work, the Educational

[1] This chapter contains excerpts from Report R-7, "Some Potential Societal Developments," by Raul de Brigard and Olaf Helmer (Middleton, Conn.: Institute for the Future, April 1970).

Policy Research Center at Syracuse (EPRC). In order to assess the long-term consequences of alternative courses for the total educating system, it is desirable to have at hand a reasonable set of assumptions on what the future of society may be like. The construction of a reliable set of assumptions of this kind is clearly a long-range task requiring the use of a variety of sources and techniques, and the effort presented here may be viewed as one of the initial steps toward obtaining such a set.

Even the preliminary construction of a relatively comprehensive view of society, especially a future society, is subject to severe limitations. No formal theoretical framework within which to derive such a picture is available, and it is necessary to rely on relatively informal methods of surveying and reconciling the judgments, insights, and expectations of persons who are likely to have at their disposal relevant information on many facets of society.

Thus the following sections assemble a set of such expectations obtained from a group of individuals knowledgeable in different areas and use the combined insight of this group to assess each of these expectations. Although the results are not the outcome of a formal investigation of any of the factors influencing the development of our society, they do reveal some of the expectations regarding society as perceived by professionals in various disciplines.

The Method Used

The Delphi method was the procedure used to assemble a combined set of expectations which describe possible future directions of our society. This technique consists of an iterative process which allows for the anonymous presentation, feedback, and re-evaluation of a set of judgments supplied by a group of informed individuals. It serves here as a method (*a*) to elicit relatively brief statements regarding the course of expected major developments in a variety of fields, (*b*) to present these points of view to other members of the group and elicit their opinions on the subject matter, and thereby (*c*) to establish an overall set of expectations without entailing a great deal of argumentation. In sum, the method allows for an ordered process which produces a cumulative assessment of the group's expectations without requiring elaborate investigation of each area under consideration. However, when applied to such a complex subject as the future of our society, this approach has certain drawbacks, which should be taken into account in the interpretation of the results.

Shortcomings of the Method and Other Problems

These shortcomings can perhaps best be understood by comparison with a parallel Delphi study of expected developments in the areas of physical and biomedical technology. Although the procedures in that technological forecasting study and in the present societal forecasting study were similar, substantial differences in the quality of the output had to be anticipated. These were traceable not only to inexperience in applying the method to a new and highly complex subject matter, but also (and, we believe, even primarily) to the difficulty in matching, in the social sciences, the crispness associated with statements in the physical sciences.

For instance, whereas the question of when electric power plants driven by thermonuclear fusion will come into existence is reasonably unambiguous, the same cannot be said of the question of when the alienation and impersonality of urban life will reach its maximum. There are two differences here. First, societal terminology is not as precise as physical terminology, so that in general the circumstances under which a statement would be considered true are not as clearly determined. In addition, there is a certain inevitability about many physical developments, the only question being one of the precise time at which they will come to fruition; whereas for most societal developments their occurrence or nonoccurrence depends greatly on the presence and the form of human intervention. Thus the future of society, factually as well as semantically, is less determinate than the future of technological progress.

A closely related problem in this study resulted from the need to deal with certain situations in which quantitative statistics convey an exaggerated impression of precision, whereas the interpretation of such data is extremely delicate. If, for example, we are dealing with the non-white percentage of central city population, not only is it difficult to obtain really precise figures but also such statistics, to the extent that they are available, are often quite controversial. This controversy is further enhanced by the fact that even small discrepancies or changes in the numbers may have very considerable implications for society. Thus the respondents in this study, aside from expressing their expectations regarding the future, were required both to interpret the statistics themselves and to account for their own perceptions as to the long-run significance of phenomena implied by the statistical trends. These perceptions, even if they were judged to be accurate, in the end involve a subjective assessment of the meaning of particular indicators and are based very significantly on personal values. It is therefore important to remember that the results stated in this report represent only general expectations regarding the future direction of our society, and that these expectations cannot be divorced from the value judgments made by the panel.

Finally, it may be important to note that during the course of this study a number of developments were suggested, such as the advent of nuclear war or of a very strong authoritarian government, that could be classified, at least in terms of our present values, as "extreme possibilities." It is one thing to speculate on how such developments could come about; it is another to expect a group of individuals to concur unequivocally that we are likely to move increasingly toward such eventualities without considering some change in priorities. In some cases, we may well come to accept what at present would seem an extremely precarious situation; in other cases, strenuous attempts may be made to alter the chain of predicted events. It is here that the question of tradeoffs among goals and consequent resetting of priorities must be introduced, and it is in this regard that the following sections are quite revealing.

Most of the extreme possibilities are clearly discernible, in that they not only were considered very important but also generated the most controversy as to their outcomes. This study, to some extent, begins to present these extreme possibilities in context with one another. It does so also with a number of less crucial developments which commonly have been mentioned in such discussions about the future. For example, the concept of a so-called leisure society does not stand isolated but is seen in the light of a continuing cause for social ferment, growth in the service sector of our economy, technological advancement and its implications on our way of life, and substantial efforts to readjust our institutions to allow for different forms of personal involvement. Viewing such events in relation to each other is both enlightening and stimulating for further inquiry.

Forms Used to Present Results

Because the investigators considered it particularly important that the results convey a multifaceted view of society, the study not only encompasses a variety of areas but also attempts to approach the subject matter from several starting points. The results therefore appear in several forms. The principal output of this work consists of a set of descriptions in paragraph form which enumerate for each of ten sectors of society some potential future developments which the panel considered likely. An evaluation of each particular development is then given separately.

Two other sections are appended to this set of paragraphs. One of these presents expectations regarding specific trends. The purpose of this part of the presentation is not so much to make definitive statements as to the future course of each of the trends as to identify those which, in the opinion of the panel, might shift considerably from their present direction. It also was considered important to identify the trends which appeared most controversial or uncertain. The other section is devoted to delineating some possible consequences of a set of foreseeable technological innovations. This work is at best preliminary. It does, however, reveal the major thrust of the panel's expectations, particularly its members' concern over the side effects that many of these developments might have on both international and domestic social conflict. A general summary at the end of this report reviews the total scope of the work as seen by the authors of the study.

In February 1970, a two-day seminar, attended by senior staff members of the Institute for the Future and the full staff of EPRC, was held at Syracuse University to review the output of this investigation. Many of the considerations previously mentioned were clarified during the course of this discussion. In addition, a consensus emerged among the participants of this seminar that the nature of the study required this report to incorporate some examples of the type of questions raised by its conclusions.

Types of Questions Raised by the Study

One of the primary values of this study may be seen in the fact that it raises two sets of questions in the reader's mind. The first is of this kind: if one or another of these trends or social developments were to materialize, what might be its consequences for me, for the institutions and organizations with which I am affiliated, and for the society of which I am a member? (Indeed, it is by attempting to explicate such consequences that one begins to get a feeling for the policy issues which arise when serious thought is given to weighing alternative possibilities for dealing with the future.)

The second set of questions, which is more directly policy-oriented, asks whether these trends and developments should be encouraged or inhibited. Policy is, by nature, an intervention in the development of perceived trends. What, then, are the policy questions one might want to raise, given the forecasts described in this report? This study may assist us, as individuals and as citizens, in examining our values, culture, and institutions, as well as the directions in which science and technology appear to be taking us.

During the two-day seminar at Syracuse University, a number of each kind of questions emerged. Examples of some of these have been included in this report. Far from intended to be exhaustive, these examples are presented to spur the reader to ask the questions which are relevant and important to him. This returns us to the original intent of the study: to produce not so much a forecast of the future as an overview of expectations held by individuals knowledgeable in various fields—an overview which, in turn, may provide an additional frame of reference for those who must consider specific policy options likely to have major impact on different aspects of society.

DESCRIPTION OF THE STUDY

The objective of this study was to assess the future of our society as seen by a small group of informed individuals with expertise in a wide variety of fields. It was hoped that such an overview would highlight the trends which are of greatest significance to more than one sector of society, and provide some further insight into determining the most critical areas of uncertainty.

The enormous scope of the subject matter—it was, after all, intended to exclude no major aspect of society—suggested a division into the following twelve areas:

Urban problems
Family structure
The economy
Education
Food and population
International relations
Law and order

Leisure
Government and political
  structure
Divisions in American
  society
Values and mores
Science and technology

Each participant was required to respond to questions within only some of these areas. Some were assigned to him according to his specialty; he elected others according to his interests. In the first two rounds, each aspect treated by the Delphi study was examined by approximately ten different individuals. In the last round the subject matter was significantly compressed, so that the initial estimates could be exposed to more individuals.

RESULTS OF THE DELPHI STUDY

The Delphi study was divided into four parts, presented in this section under the following subheads: Current Trends, Future Developments, Implications of Technology, and Societal Indicators.

The section on *current trends* is intended primarily as an indication of how the panel views the present social environment in both a present and a future context. Because this study is based on the viewpoints of a rather disparate panel, it was considered necessary to gain some understanding of how this group might interpret present phenomena before attempting to identify specific future developments which might have an impact on the course of social events. The developments listed in this section are for the most part quite apparent already.

The section on *future developments* comprises the primary output of this study. It is organized under ten headings, each of which presents, and invites the evaluation of, the future expectations of the Delphi panel within a given area. The developments presented are primarily future-oriented, even though they no doubt reflect some of our present social concerns.

The section on *implications of technology* singles out eighteen potential breakthroughs in physical and biomedical technology, attempting to derive an initial understanding of their possible effects on society at large.

The final section, on *societal indicators,* seeks to relate the expectations of the panel to changes in specific statistical indices of social trends. Because the extensions of the various curves into the future represent the subjective assessment of a group, they should not be confused with the results of a more mechanical or studied form of extrapolation. They are intended to represent instead the actual expectations of the group with regard to each trend, thus forming a backdrop for the expectations presented in each of the other areas.

Current Trends

The respondents were asked in the first round to formulate statements descriptive of what they considered current trends of important aspects of each of the twelve societal areas. Each such trend description submitted by a participant was subsequently rated by the other panelists in terms of the present as well as the future importance of the trend.

Below is a selection of the current trends in six areas considered by a majority to be of high importance now or of increasing importance in the future:

Urban problems
   The benefits of technology to cities, which used to be high and then declined, are beginning to rise again.
   Political jurisdictional lines are becoming more visibly obsolete.
   There is an unresolved conflict in urban policy between programs requiring centralization (transportation and land-use planning), decentralization (health and welfare services), and some of each (education).

Family structure
   There is a greater acceptance of change and flexibility as normal.
   There is a much greater emphasis on the psychological rewards of life; there

are high expectations of, and a greater demand for, sexual expression and satisfaction.

Abortion is becoming acceptable, and limitations on it are rapidly disappearing.

The economy

There is a manpower revolution, in the sense that high economic returns on the uses of labor are required, with manpower for marginal economic activities becoming unavailable. There is a concomitant rapid elevation of the educational level of those entering the labor market.

The thesis that economic development will take care of poverty via the filtering down of benefits is being disproved.

Concentrated investment schemes associated with pension systems are gaining acceptance.

The income aspirations of the below-average economic class are growing ever faster and more demandingly; it is from this segment that the main thrust of future expansion will come. National policy has promised an end to poverty, and the poor are expecting the promise to be kept.

Research and development activities are on the increase.

There is an increased understanding of the role of innovation.

More attention is being paid to social goals, for which economic stability is but a means.

Education

There is a rising need of professional persons for retraining.

There is a growing disillusion with the idea of the school as the agent of total socialization, or at least with present programs in civics, government, history, and so on.

The number of young people continuing education beyond high school is increasing.

Student challenges to authority, although sometimes excessive, may be a vehicle through which major changes into the education process are introduced.

Much quiet progress is occurring at many major universities in response to examples such as Columbia and San Francisco State University.

Food and population

We are on the verge of a great breakthrough in applied agricultural technology, as well as in pure-food and protein research.

Some new adaptive agricultural research efforts have begun to pay off, particularly in fertilizers and new seed hybrids.

International relations

Atomic armament by such states as Israel and Egypt is in the offing.

The expectation gap in underdeveloped countries is further threatening any prospect for international stability.

The rise of China and France as nuclear powers is upsetting "reciprocal nuclear deterrence."

The United States is gradually withdrawing from its role of universal champion of democracy and universal dispenser of economic assistance.

Future Developments

The material presented in this section is the result of an attempt to elicit from the panel a description of possible future societal developments which might occur during the next decades and which would represent major changes from current patterns. In the first round of questionnaires each panelist was asked to suggest future developments in four of the twelve societal areas under consideration. The responses, in the form of suggested developments, were given back to the panel for evaluation of strength and importance in several time periods. In a final round, the panel was asked to reconsider the developments which had generated the greatest disagreement. Some of the statements were rewritten in this round to remove possible ambiguities.

In evaluating each development, two nominative scales were used: one for rating its "importance" (A, B, C, D), and another for indicating the "strength of trend" (+3 to —3). Five time periods were considered: early seventies, late seventies, eighties, nineties, after 2000. The statement used to describe each trend corresponded almost exactly to that used by the respondent who submitted it. In some cases this generated confusion, since the expression "strength of trend" could refer either to cumulative or to incremental change over time. The effect of this ambiguity was to widen the amount of disagreement over events, especially when timing became crucial. In this regard it should be noted that three types of ambiguities are involved in the evaluation of each statement: (1) ambiguity in the statement itself (what does it mean?); (2) ambiguity in the scale (when does a trend become "strongly noticeable"?); and (3) ambiguity in the scale over time (how long does a trend remain "strongly noticeable" and from whose point of view?). A more precise application of the technique within each area would be necessary in order to identify specific differences in interpretation.

The results of this process were presented in the following form. The trends were organized under ten headings:

Urbanization
The Family
Leisure and the Economy
Education
Food and Population
International Relations

Conflict in Society; Law
   Enforcement
National Political Structure
Values
Impact of Technology on
   Government and Society

In this chapter, the output of the panel in regard to the last of these categories will be used as illustrative of all of them.

Under each heading the trends are first combined into a narrative summary, and then presented as they were actually predicted. A certain amount of reorganization was necessary in order to present the results in a coherent manner. The original twelve societal areas were reduced to ten and given titles which reflect more accurately the scope of the forecasts. In addition there were many cases in which the trends studied under various societal areas dealt with closely related phenomena. In such cases the trends themselves were regrouped and sometimes even repeated, so as to ensure that in every instance the reader would have a more complete view of the material produced by this investigation.

A supportive tabulation follows the narrative. It presents each individual development as contributed and evaluated by the Delphi panel. The graph next to each statement displays the opinions of the panel regarding the anticipated strength of the development over several time periods. The quartile spread is shown in dotted lines, whereas the median is indicated with a continuous line. Importance ratings are also shown. In addition, two types of trends are highlighted for each section. The symbol "●" indicates a trend which was considered to be both strong and very important for the context in which it is presented. The symbol "○" singles out trends of admitted major importance if they materialized, but exhibiting considerable dissensus as to whether they were in fact to be expected or even as to what direction they would take. The latter trends might be particularly important in that they represent the panel's most significant areas of uncertainty.

A third paragraph follows the tabulation within each section. It presents some of the potential policy issues which might arise from the preceding expectations. These were derived, as explained previously, from a seminar conducted with the primary sponsor of this investigation, the Educational Policy Research Institute at Syracuse University. Staff members were asked to consider the expectations of the Delphi panel and to identify the issues which they would regard as most critical to social policy making. This material was subsequently reorganized into a brief statement covering each area of consideration. Each paragraph is only exemplary of the types of issues which could be raised in light of the future presented. It does not attempt to reproduce the viewpoints of a wide spectrum of society.

These three presentations—the narrative, the supportive tabulation, and the paragraph on policy issues—follow for the category "Impact of Technology on Government and Society."

Summary of the Panel's Expectations

Starting in the early 1970s and becoming very noticeable after 1980, there will be, in the panel's opinion, an increasing search for a new symbiosis between power and knowledge, be it in the form of policy-oriented research, so-called think-tank organizations, or new types of professional policy advisers. The respondents foresaw that, especially toward the end of the century, progress in social technology will specifically call attention to the need for monitoring and predictive devices to relate technical change to social impact. Most of them expected at least a moderately increasing rate of investment by the federal government in social science research, as well as greater involvement of higher education in urban problems through the development of new, problem-oriented societal laboratories in the real world. Economic policy making is expected to be integrated with social policy making as new tools, including governmental controls, are evolved, and policy planning to concern itself more with such specific areas as income redistribution, education, and recreation than with GNP or stability generally. The panel, however, had strong doubts as to whether or not there would be a major redirection of resources from military and space programs to urban programs, especially in the near future.

Most respondents did not foresee the development of a technocratic elite in the near future, though for the far future a few respondents considered this a possibility. The emergence of today's youth from the student years was expected to lead, to a moderate extent, to new political institutions or to other developments allowing for greater individual or community participation in government, industry, education, and the church. The panel agreed that these experiments with new political forms would bring about their own social catastrophes.

The respondents foresaw that, in an effort to dispel frustration and alienation and to regain citizen support, city governments might be reorganized to improve civic services and devise better feedback mechanisms for the discovery of citizen attitudes. Instant referenda and polls can be expected to play a somewhat larger role in shaping the direction of public policy, though many respondents had serious doubts that such things as "instant polls" would allow for direct public participation in major policy decisions. Similarly, in spite of the general belief that increasing speed in obtaining feedback would allow for faster change of community values, there was strong disagreement on whether or not attempts by the state to direct and channel community values would become increasingly effective. A substantial minority felt that the opposite would be the case. A moderately noticeable trend was seen toward a social revolution leading to humanistic laws and social order. Though the respondents anticipated only a moderate tendency toward a multivalued society with various subgroups and disagreed strongly on whether or not any major upsurge in antiscientific ideologies will occur to repudiate so-called rationally based economic and political activities, they did express some hope that technological cooperation on the international level will take place with respect to the conquest of space and the peaceful organization of the world.

Supportive Tabulation

Each statement below originated with an individual panelist. It was submitted to a group of approximately ten other panelists for evaluation as to direction, strength and importance. The graph to the right shows the group's response: the solid line is the median; dashed lines are the upper and lower quartiles.

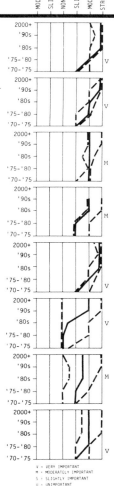

There will be an increasing search for new forms of symbiosis between power and knowledge, be it in the form of policy-oriented research, "think-tank" organizations, or new forms of professional government policy advisors.

Progress in social technology will specifically call for the establishment of monitoring and predictive devices for relating technical change to social impact.

There will be increasing investment in social science research by the federal government, but the payoff will not be felt until about the year 2000.

The development of a new, problem-oriented social science with laboratories in the real world will cause higher education to be involved with urban problems in a relevant and effective manner. (See also Section 4.)

Economic policy-making will be integrated with social policy-making, with new goals and tools, including novel governmental controls; there will be more emphasis on specific areas (income redistribution, education, recreation, and so on) rather than on GNP or stability.

There will be a major redirection of resources from military and space programs to urban programs.(See also Sections 1, 6.)

Increased political action by technocrats will become highly contested, but as a result technocrats will gain in power.

The revolt against institutions that deny individual participation may, as today's youth emerge from the student years, lead to new political institutions or to new possibilities of "community participation" in government, industry, education, professions, the church, and so on. (See also Sections 1, 7, 9.)

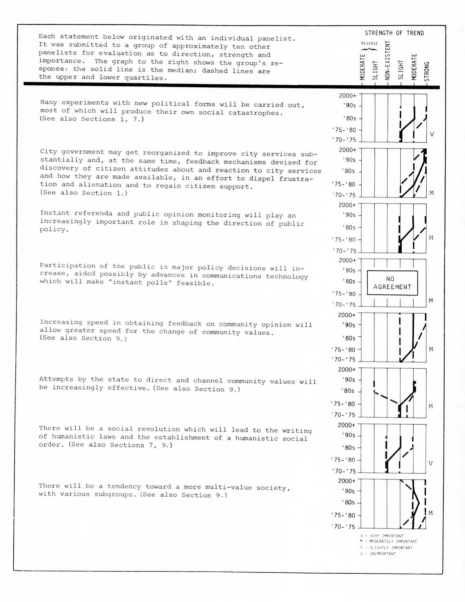

Each statement below originated with an individual panelist. It was submitted to a group of approximately ten other panelists for evaluation as to direction, strength and importance. The graph to the right shows the group's response: the solid line is the median; dashed lines are the upper and lower quartiles.

STRENGTH OF TREND

REVERSE
MODERATE | SLIGHT | NON-EXISTENT | SLIGHT | MODERATE | STRONG

Many experiments with new political forms will be carried out, most of which will produce their own social catastrophes. (See also Sections 1, 7.)

City government may get reorganized to improve city services substantially and, at the same time, feedback mechanisms devised for discovery of citizen attitudes about and reaction to city services and how they are made available, in an effort to dispel frustration and alienation and to regain citizen support. (See also Section 1.)

Instant referenda and public opinion monitoring will play an increasingly important role in shaping the direction of public policy.

Participation of the public in major policy decisions will increase, aided possibly by advances in communications technology which will make "instant polls" feasible.

Increasing speed in obtaining feedback on community opinion will allow greater speed for the change of community values. (See also Section 9.)

Attempts by the state to direct and channel community values will be increasingly effective. (See also Section 9.)

There will be a social revolution which will lead to the writing of humanistic laws and the establishment of a humanistic social order. (See also Sections 7, 9.)

There will be a tendency toward a more multi-value society, with various subgroups. (See also Section 9.)

V = VERY IMPORTANT
M = MODERATELY IMPORTANT
S = SLIGHTLY IMPORTANT
U = UNIMPORTANT

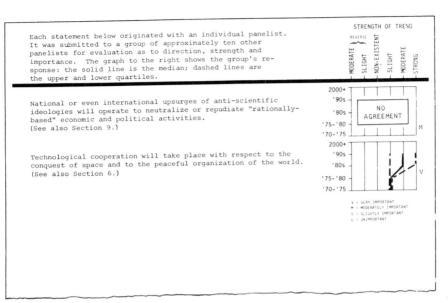

Some Policy Issues Raised by the Preceding Expectations

There are many questions to be raised here. In another part of this report, the study attempts to deal more specifically with some societal consequences of technological breakthroughs. But an examination of the material on the impact of technology on government and society contained in this section raises the enormously powerful issue of the role of a technocratic elite. What are the conditions under which it is likely to emerge? Have these conditions already been met? It is important to note that, while the panel disagreed on the likelihood of such an elite gaining a formal power base in society, there was a good deal of agreement about an extremely strong trend toward a symbiosis of knowledge and power. The manner in which society functionally relates these two sets of variables may indeed be the ball game for traditional notions of participatory democracy and representative government. What will be the demands on the body politic to manage this symbiosis? What human capacities are needed—knowledge, skills, attitudes—and how broadly held are they likely to become? To put it another way, who will control the technocrats?

Or, just as important perhaps, has not technology also overwhelmingly enhanced the effective power of the man in the street? Do we not also need control here? Will it be the technocrat or the grass-roots leader who will be more effective in protecting society from constant exposure to violence or threats of violence? What does a symbiosis of power and knowledge mean in this context?

A second broad and extremely significant range of questions concerns the forecasting, monitoring, and especially the control of technological developments.

Do we need new institutions to control technological research? Should means be devised for halting research which appears to have clearly negative or disastrous social consequences? How can the innovative process be controlled? What value structure could be used to discriminate between socially useful and socially harmful consequences?

Implications of Technology

This section of the report deals with forecasts of possible societal developments in the light of foreseeable technological breakthroughs. It parallels a similar effort in Report R-6 of the Institute for the Future,[2] except that in this case the panel evaluating the effect of technologies on society is composed of experts in the social rather than the physical sciences.

A list of twenty possible physical and biological breakthroughs was presented to the panel in the first round. Each respondent was asked to select a number of these and to indicate what possible consequences these breakthroughs might have on our society. This material was then arranged into a list of possible societal implications that might result from given technological breakthroughs. The respondents were asked in the second-round questionnaire to indicate whether they regarded each consequence as favorable or unfavorable, and how likely they considered its occurrence to be within a period of 10 years after the breakthrough. In the third round the panel re-estimated the breakthroughs that generated greatest controversy. For this round the investigators rewrote many of the statements, eliminating a number of ambiguities.

The results are presented in the charts which follow. An approximate date has been given for each technological breakthrough, based on the forecasts described in IFF Report R-6. The likelihood of each implication is then shown in terms of medians and quartiles, using the following notation:

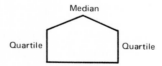

For the importance rating, a ■ was used to display the opinion of the respondents. A □ □ shows polarity of opinion, while ■-■ indicates

[2] Theodore J. Gordon and Robert H. Ament, Report R-6, "Forecasts of Some Technological and Scientific Developments and Their Societal Consequences" (Middletown, Conn.: Institute for the Future, September 1969).

BREAKTHROUGHS IN PHYSICAL TECHNOLOGIES

IF THESE DEVELOPMENTS WERE TO OCCUR,	THEY MIGHT RESULT IN:	HOW LIKELY IS IT THAT THE RESULT WILL BE A CONSEQUENCE OF THE DEVELOPMENT?				WHAT WILL THE EFFECT OF THE CONSEQUENCE BE?				
		VIRTUALLY CERTAIN	PROBABLE	POSSIBLE	ALMOST IMPOSSIBLE	VERY FAVORABLE	FAVORABLE	LITTLE OR NO IMPORTANCE	DETRIMENTAL	VERY DETRIMENTAL
1. Demonstration of large-scale desalination plants capable of producing useful water economically for agricultural purposes. (1980)	A. The food supply would be raised throughout the world.	▱				■				
	B. The development of industrialized agriculture would be accelerated by opening up presently sparsely populated areas for development of large tracts.	◻					■			
	C. Desirable, warm, low-rainfall areas, which are now deserted, would be settled on a wider scale.	◹					■			
	D. Disputes over fresh-water sources and tensions among nations fighting for water rights would be reduced.		◿				■			
	E. Productivity of Near Eastern countries would increase, making them less dependent on foreign aid.		◺			■				
	F. This development will be of considerable help to those nations most affected by the threat of famine.	⌂					■			
	G. Coastline populations will be able to suburbanize more easily.	⌂					■			
	H. To establish such plants will become a major form of aid from rich to poor countries.		◹				■			
	I. This breakthrough will contribute substantially to the settlement and development of major areas in this country, such as the Southwest.	◺					■			

323

BREAKTHROUGHS IN PHYSICAL TECHNOLOGIES		HOW LIKELY IS IT THAT THE RESULT WILL BE A CONSEQUENCE OF THE DEVELOPMENT?				WHAT WILL THE EFFECT OF THE CONSEQUENCE BE?				
IF THESE DEVELOPMENTS WERE TO OCCUR,	THEY MIGHT RESULT IN:	VIRTUALLY CERTAIN	PROBABLE	POSSIBLE	ALMOST IMPOSSIBLE	VERY FAVORABLE	FAVORABLE	LITTLE OR NO IMPORTANCE	DETRIMENTAL	VERY DETRIMENTAL
6. Establishment of a central data storage facility (or several regional or disciplinary facilities' with wide public access (perhaps in the home) for general or specialized information retrieval primarily in the areas of library, medical, and legal data. (1980)	A. The development of powerful data reduction and retrieval systems would be necessary.	◻				■				
	B. Such banks would be used heavily by professionals and would restructure the operations of the professions.	◻					■			
	C. Important improvements in law and medicine would result.		◻			■				
	D. Grave privacy problems would be created.	◻							■	
	E. Many societal functions would be decentralized.				◻	■				
	F. Data would become available to all instead of just to the elite in our society.				◻	■				
13. Development of sophisticated teaching machines utilizing adaptive programs which respond not only to the students' answers but also to certain physiological responses of the students such as extreme tension. (1980)	A. A substantial number of educators will have to leave the system in order to stay in the system.	◻							■	■
	B. Human contact will still remain as an essential part of teaching, especially in cases of difficult physiological or psychological responses in students.	◻					■			
	C. Reliance on person-to-person interaction would be reduced.	◻							■	
	D. Children will be enrolled in school as soon as they are able to verbalize.			◻			■		■	
	E. Within a decade, the use of this development will be sufficiently wide-spread to cause a noticeable acceleration in scientific, technological, and cultural rates of productivity.			◻		■				

324

BREAKTHROUGHS IN PHYSICAL TECHNOLOGIES		HOW LIKELY IS IT THAT THE RESULT WILL BE A CONSEQUENCE OF THE DEVELOPMENT?				WHAT WILL THE EFFECT OF THE CONSEQUENCE BE?				
IF THESE DEVELOPMENTS WERE TO OCCUR,	THEY MIGHT RESULT IN:	VIRTUALLY CERTAIN	PROBABLE	POSSIBLE	ALMOST IMPOSSIBLE	VERY FAVORABLE	FAVORABLE	LITTLE OR NO IMPORTANCE	DETRIMENTAL	VERY DETRIMENTAL
13. Development of sophisticated teaching machines utilizing adaptive programs which respond not only to the students' answers but also to certain physiological responses of the students such as extreme tension. (1980) (continued)	F. Ignorance and illiteracy throughout the world will be noticeably reduced because of this system.			△			■			
	G. Education would become more effective.			△			■			
	H. Internationalism would be enhanced because people would be better educated and thus could be expected to achieve more effective trans-national contacts.			△			■			
	I. This development is not likely to be accepted or to have any effect in the next few decades.			△						■
21. Wide-spread availability of new types of automobiles which have acceptable performance, are economically competitive with other forms of transportation, and permit operation without harmful exhaust. (1980)	A. We will see more developments aimed at relieving traffic congestion.		△			■				
	B. The prospects for car tunnels and underground parking facilities will be enhanced.		△			■				
	C. The trend toward the multi-car family will continue its present course in the United States.		△				□		□	
	D. The effect on health would be beneficial.	△				■				
	E. Decentralization of urban and suburban areas will be reinforced.		△				■—■			
	F. A serious constraint on the growth of the megalopolis would be temporarily relieved, temporarily only because of other forms of pollution generated by the automobile, namely noise, dirt, and congestion.	△						□		□

BREAKTHROUGHS IN PHYSICAL TECHNOLOGIES		HOW LIKELY IS IT THAT THE RESULT WILL BE A CONSEQUENCE OF THE DEVELOPMENT?				WHAT WILL THE EFFECT OF THE CONSEQUENCE BE?				
IF THESE DEVELOPMENTS WERE TO OCCUR,	THEY MIGHT RESULT IN:	VIRTUALLY CERTAIN	PROBABLE	POSSIBLE	ALMOST IMPOSSIBLE	VERY FAVORABLE	FAVORABLE	LITTLE OR NO IMPORTANCE	DETRIMENTAL	VERY DETRIMENTAL
21. Wide-spread availability of new types of automobiles which have acceptable performance, are economically competitive with other forms of transportation, and permit operation without harmful exhaust. (1980) (continued)	G. Radical changes would be forestalled that would otherwise be necessitated by the acutely polluted atmosphere.	△				■				
	H. The introduction of auxiliary transportation from parking complexes to employment, home, or shopping would become necessary.	⌂					□		□	
	I. The early introduction of innovations such as audio signals to drivers to supplement video signals automatic traffic interval regulating devices, and (later) automated highways would be necessitated.		⌂					■		
5. Availability of cheap electric power from thermo-nuclear (fusion) power plants. (Laboratory demonstration of continuously controlled thermonuclear power.) (1985)	A. Living standards will increase generally, due to a rise in the use of consumer durables powered by electricity.	△				■				
	B. Problems of thermal water pollution would be created because of the vast amounts of coolant needed for nuclear piles.	△								■
	C. Less developed countries would undergo more rapid industrialization.	△				■				
	D. Electric heating on a broader scale would be facilitated.	△					■			
	E. This development will lead to greater dispersal of urban areas.	⌂					■			
	F. Political and economic factors will tend to delay the introduction of these plants into relatively small and poor nations.		□							■

BREAKTHROUGHS IN PHYSICAL TECHNOLOGIES		HOW LIKELY IS IT THAT THE RESULT WILL BE A CONSEQUENCE OF THE DEVELOPMENT?				WHAT WILL THE EFFECT OF THE CONSEQUENCE BE?				
IF THESE DEVELOPMENTS WERE TO OCCUR,	THEY MIGHT RESULT IN:	VIRTUALLY CERTAIN	PROBABLE	POSSIBLE	ALMOST IMPOSSIBLE	VERY FAVORABLE	FAVORABLE	LITTLE OR NO IMPORTANCE	DETRIMENTAL	VERY DETRIMENTAL
5. Availability of cheap electric power from thermo-nuclear (fusion) power plants. (Laboratory demonstration of continuously controlled thermonuclear power.) (1985) (continued)	G. Food shortages will be overcome.	□				■				
	H. The gap between rich and poor nations would be narrowed.	△				■				
	I. The birth rate would decline as TV and electric light become wide-spread.	△					■			
19. Individual portable telephones, carried by most Americans. (1990)	A. Persons would be subjected to intrusion at all times, thereby interfering with their capacity for reflection.	△								■
	B. Interpersonal relationships and communication and intimacy beyond the family would be facilitated.	△					■			
	C. Traffic control would be aided.	△					■			
	D. Many more mobile forms of work will come into existence with many individuals "in the field" rather than in offices.	△					■			
	E. The need for travel would be reduced by allowing quick consultation without it.		△				■			
	F. Families will spend more time apart.		△							
	G. Difficulties caused by separations that still persist would be reduced.	△					■			
	H. Families will spend more time together.			△						

327

that most respondents felt that the implication had both favorable and unfavorable aspects. Shaded boxes indicate implications considered by the panel to be both detrimental and fairly probable.

Societal Indicators

In order to obtain insight into the panel's view of the future, the investigation included an attempt to forecast specific parameters describing particular characteristics of our society.

Forty-six statistical indicators were selected for this purpose, describing some of the major trends in each of the twelve societal areas. These were presented graphically, most curves covering at least 15 years. In the first round the panel was asked to extend the graphs to the year 2000. The second round fed this information back to the panelists (as medians and quartiles) asking them to reconsider their estimate in light of the range of the group and to state any reasons they might have to substantiate their point of view. The panelists were also given the choice of indicating that their estimate was a pure guess, or that it was intuitive. The third round concentrated on a smaller set of indicators, asking for a final estimate in view of the reasons presented as well as for some indication of the certainty each panel member associated with the central range of group opinions.

The results cannot be interpreted as very accurate forecasts, if for no other reason than that the panelists were given only a very limited time. They represent, at best, an intuitive assessment of the direction a trend might take over the coming decades. The purpose of this exercise was primarily to highlight (1) factors that might cause a reversal of past trends, (2) suitability of a particular indicator in describing foreseeable future developments, and (3) natural "ceilings" of certain trends based on anticipated social priorities.

Even from this point of view, however, the results cannot always be considered equally satisfactory. In some cases the panelists expressed considerable concern over foreseeable changes in definition which would make any forecast of trends difficult to interpret or evaluate. Words such as "educational system," "married," "nonwhite," "metropolitan," and even "gross national product" might refer to different concepts in the future. In other cases, this was further complicated by the awkward relationship between the indicator and the issue in question.

For some graphs, these difficulties tended to become less crucial once the first estimate had been made. For other graphs the problems became more pronounced, as the inquiry progressed. In order to give some indi-

Estimates	Reasons
Purchasing power of the consumer dollar (1957–1959 = 1.00) 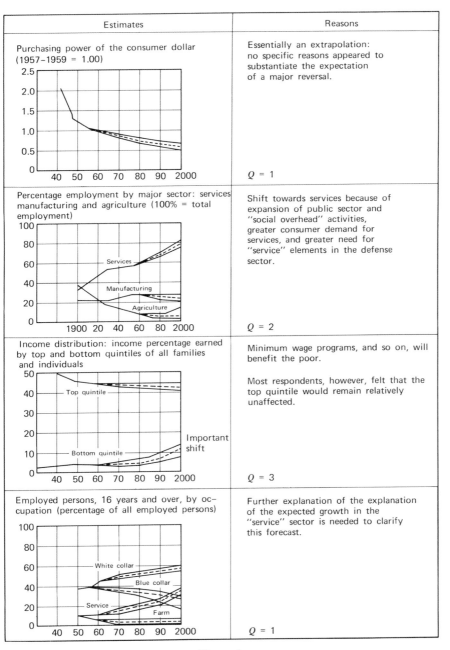	Essentially an extrapolation: no specific reasons appeared to substantiate the expectation of a major reversal. Q = 1
Percentage employment by major sector: services manufacturing and agriculture (100% = total employment)	Shift towards services because of expansion of public sector and "social overhead" activities, greater consumer demand for services, and greater need for "service" elements in the defense sector. Q = 2
Income distribution: income percentage earned by top and bottom quintiles of all families and individuals	Minimum wage programs, and so on, will benefit the poor. Most respondents, however, felt that the top quintile would remain relatively unaffected. Q = 3
Employed persons, 16 years and over, by occupation (percentage of all employed persons)	Further explanation of the explanation of the expected growth in the "service" sector is needed to clarify this forecast. Q = 1

Figure 1

329

cation of the impact of these problems, each graph has been rated as follows:

Q = 3 means above average consistency of response
Q = 2 means average consistency of response
Q = 1 means below average consistency of response

For those graphs rated $Q = 3$, note the following:

- The panel make-up was ample and consistent from round to round.
- Additions or substitutions to the panel did not markedly shift the group estimate from round to round.
- The reasons provided by the respondents were consonant with the nature of the difference of opinion.
- There was relatively little difference between the group reply of those who felt they had substantive reasons for their guess and those who indicated they were primarily making a more "intuitive" assessment.

Graphs rated $Q = 1$ were quite deficient in one or more of these respects.

The graph of each curve shows the group forecast in terms of its median (dotted central line) and its quartiles (solid lines on either side of median) (see Figure 1). The median and quartile convention is a considerable simplification of a multiple set of replies. Thus two additional notations have been added to ensure proper interpretation.

1. Complete Disagreement. The actual responses deviated widely from the median, rather than clustering around the median.

2. Important Shift. Regardless of the disposition of the responses, the large majority of the panel expected an eventual shift in the curve.

XIX. Technological Forecasting and Terra's Ecological Crisis

ROBERT W. PREHODA

The greatest of faults, I should say, is to be conscious of none.   Thomas Carlyle

INTRODUCTION

Ecology—the word is derived from the Greek *oikos* (house) and *-logia* (the science or study of)—is likely to be the most important discipline in the remaining years of this century. The reasons are painfully obvious to anyone who attempts to live, breathe, or simply concentrate in one of our major cities, for ecology is the framework science of the living environment or "life-support system" of a badly polluted spacecraft called Terra. As with the Apollo 13 spacecraft, Aquarius, things are starting to break down throughout Terra, which is racing through the heavens toward an unknown goal—a destination which lies in the hands of Divine Providence. The final mission objectives of Terra are "top secret," and unfortunately we crew members do not have the requisite security clearance or "need to know." The purpose of this chapter is to define new ways of "maintaining" and "repairing" Terra so that its crew of several billion human beings and trillions of other *vital* living shipmates can continue the mission after the year 2000.

THE PROBLEM

The Terranian astronauts have been worshiping at the altars of several false gods including (a) technology for the sake of technology, (b) unrestrained growth of crew population and GNP, and (c) a complete disregard of the effects of various agents such as chlorinated pesticides on Terra's infinitely complex life-support system. Leading ecologists are now in agreement that Terra's crew faces its most severe crisis since written mission records were started more than five millenia ago.

Terra's life-support contaminants include atmospheric, olfactory, radioactivity, water, thermal, solid- and liquid-waste, pesticide, acoustical, optical, data, esthetic and demographic categories of general pollution. It is clear that we must rethink, redesign, and then rebuild almost everything in our society in order to achieve the requisite ecological balance that will allow Terra's crew to survive.

THE USE OF TECHNOLOGY FORECASTING IN PLANNING

The process of "rethinking" and "redesign" has been enhanced in the past few years by a new long-range planning tool called technological forecasting (T/F). I have defined T/F as "the description or prediction of a foreseeable invention, specific technological refinement, or likely scientific discovery promising to serve some useful function, including better health and longer life."[1] Technological forecasting is a relatively new discipline that has been refined during the past 12 years primarily to meet military system and space requirements. We now find that T/F is a sword that can be "beaten into a most useful plowshare" to meet a host of nonmilitary requirements, foremost of which will be the salvaging of Terra's life-support system.

This chapter is a scenario for further refinement, using T/F as a means to provide *practical* answers to Terra's ecological crisis. An interdisciplinarian team will use the *synthesis forecasting* methodology approach, which I have been refining during the past 12 years. It attempts to combine the best features of other predictive methodologies. Synthesis T/F can start with an initial forecast (such as this chapter) which may be arrived at by using trend curves and morphological networks, along with interviews and correspondence with experts. This can follow

---

[1] Robert W. Prehoda, *Designing the Future: The Role of Technological Forecasting* (Philadelphia: Chilton Books, 1967), p. 2.

the basic Delphi technique. A combination of methodologies is used to prepare a preliminary forecast for the T/F refinement team.

The smallest T/F refinement group consists of 1 team moderator (an experienced forecaster) and 4 specialists in the one or more areas being reviewed. The upper limit, or point of diminishing returns, appears to be about 11 members including the moderator. The optimum is 7–9 members.

If the group is kept relatively small, objections to forecasting through committee discussion are almost totally eliminated. Experience shows that the greatest problem is the undue influence of a prestigious member or participant with an overriding personality. Such influence can be reduced by the tactful influence of the moderator, who can shift discussion to other subjects or direct specific questions to less vocal specialists. Some brilliant scientists tend to be introverts and exhibit reluctance to express their views—a problem that seems to exist in direct proportion to the size of the T/F team. If the group remains small, the problem is significantly reduced or even eliminated.

The "bandwagon" effect of majority opinion can also be a serious problem in large forecasting teams. This is not significant, however, when the group is small and the moderator is able to exercise tactful control over discussion. A stimulating preliminary forecast is presented to the team a week or two before its first formal meeting, providing time for serious thought and, in some cases, an opportunity to look up specific references in journals or to refresh memory in other ways. Also, it is necessary to distribute a preliminary agenda to members before the initial meeting.

The moderator prepares a refined forecast based on the first working session, which is then passed on to members to review before the next meeting. The second meeting is usually more interesting because members are far better prepared, and a certain element of gamesmanship is evident. New information has been secured, sometimes from obscure sources previously overlooked. After the second meeting, the moderator prepares a second refined forecast, which is again sent to the members. At the third meeting the team offers final comments and sums up an evaluation of the field(s) under study.

The final forecast session usually reflects consensus among diverse experts. The moderator then prepares a final forecast draft, which is sent to the team. Members can suggest changes or modifications, which the moderator may incorporate into the final T/F document projecting trends in specific areas or related fields.

The T/F discovery stage is often called the *Hahn-Strassmann point* (named for Otto Hahn and Fritz Strassmann, who discovered uranium-235 fission in December 1938). Publication of the Hahn-Strassmann experiments permitted an accurate forecast of contemporary nuclear technology which would not have been possible before the breakthrough announcement. It is extremely important to recognize a new Hahn-Strassmann point. This is comparatively easy when it results from a dramatic research breakthrough, but harder when it is a synergistic result of evolutionary progress.

The final T/F document is an integrated forecast containing:

1. Long-term state-of-the-art projections.
2. Possible Hahn-Strassmann point discoveries.
3. Key applied research objectives.
4. Economic and funding projections at alternative R&D levels.
5. Possible synergistic relationships between technologies.

In addition, the final T/F document serves the following purposes:

1. It brings to light relatively unknown physical and biological phenomena that may offer basic research promise of Hahn-Strassmann point discoveries.
2. It defines basic research areas where increased support may result in Hahn-Strassmann point discoveries.
3. It attempts to clarify supposed "natural barriers" to determine whether they are really fundamental limitations.

TYPES OF CRISES AND POSSIBLE SOLUTIONS

The following sections describe possible developments in regard to various types of pollution afflicting the spaceship Terra.

Atmospheric Pollution

Caused primarily by the use of coal, gas, and other hydrocarbons in power production, and the continued use of the internal-combustion engine in ground transportation, atmospheric pollution has reached the critical stage. Millions of tons of toxic gaseous substances are injected into our atmosphere from factories, vehicles, ships, and homes.

Fission power plants can replace fossil fuel plants in the next 30 years if a practical breeder reactor can be developed to supply the requisite quantity of fissionable fuel. In nuclear fission, a uranium or plutonium nucleus splits, releasing neutrons and energy and creating lighter elements (fission products) toward the middle of the periodic table. Most of these new elements are radioactive, but the majority are solids that can easily be extracted in fuel processing, where they are safely sealed in cement or used for some practical purpose. However, two fission products, xenon-135 and krypton-85, present severe containment problems. These noble gases tend to escape into the atmosphere from conventional reactors and nuclear fuel reprocessing plants. Xenon-135 is particularly soluble in human blood plasma, and krypton-85 can also be a biological hazard.

The Atomic Energy Commission is developing an entirely new type of breeder reactor in which fluoride salts of lithium-7, beryllium, uranium, and thorium are circulated through a liquid reactor core (moderated by solid graphite) to produce power and additional fissionable fuel. Nuclear physicists are confident that future versions of this molten-salt reactor can generate electricity with a thermal efficiency of 44%, somewhat higher than most modern power plants. Since the fuel is in a liquid state, it can be passed through a system which will continuously remove the radioactive xenon and krypton. Xenon will form stable compounds with fluorine, allowing it to be safely stored. Although krypton forms only unstable fluorine compounds, it can be stored in cryogenic liquid form. In the 1990s radioactive xenon and krypton, along with other radioactive wastes, may be economically transferred into low orbit by a one-stage "Escher" space shuttle. There, it could be ejected into deep space to be carried away by the solar wind. Accelerated development of the molten-salt breeder reactor would allow all nuclear power plants constructed after 1980 to employ this basic design, which could eliminate atmospheric radioactive pollution from fission reactors.

Controlled thermonuclear fusion research on tritium, deuterium, and helium-3 promises a pollution-free power source from fuels that will not be exhausted for millions of years. In 1969, Soviet scientists achieved a breakthrough in the field with a toroidal (doughnut-shaped) magnetic containment device called *Tokamak Three*. A tritium-deuterium plasma of 50,000 billion particles per cubic centimeter was held at 10 million degrees Kelvin for 0.05 second—ten times longer than any previous experiment. Soviet, British, and American plasma physicists are now convinced that a large Tokamak-type fusion power plant could be demonstrated within 10 years—providing that an Apollo-scale effort is instituted within the next 2 years.

Thermonuclear power plants would be exceptionally large, producing power at less than half of today's cost. Neutrons produced in the fusion process could be used to "breed" tritium fuel from lithium-6, or fissionable fuel from uranium-238 and thorium-233. The fusion reactor would eliminate the need for complex nuclear breeder reactors, and small fission power systems (molten-salt type to contain radioactive noble gases) could be used in situations where small power plants are indicated—for example, isolated communities or ships.

The internal-combustion engine is actually a high-pressure chemical reactor producing two forms of deadly pollution: smog and acoustical (noise) damage. Elimination of the noise would require an impractical soundproofing system. Detroit's current efforts to salvage the internal-combustion engine, motivated by an $8 billion investment in production facilities, are ludicrous, pathetic, and doomed to failure. The latest approach is to use nonleaded gasoline with the exhaust being passed through two different catalytic systems in succession, reducing the contaminants to water vapor, carbon dioxide, and nitrogen. Lead poisons the catalysts. Such a power plant system would be extremely expensive, and catalyst-bed replacement might cost $500–$1000 a year.

External-combustion engines such as the Stirling or the steam engine would significantly reduce atmospheric pollution. Fluorocarbons similar to Freon, which do not decompose, offer many advantages over steam in a Rankine-cycle engine. Simple catalytic systems could reduce the atmospheric contaminants of external-cycle engines of less than 1% of internal-combustion engine levels.

Although the electric car offers the ideal solution, conventional lead-acid batteries store only about 10 watt-hours of electricity per pound. A sodium-sulfur battery storing 100–150 watt-hours per pound is being developed. Liquid sodium and liquid sulfur are separated by a unique crystalline ceramic electrolyte, which can selectively pass sodium atoms while containing all other liquids. Each sodium atom gives up an electron as it passes through the ceramic and combines with the sulfur electrode. The electrons flow through an external circuit to the sulfur electrode, providing the electric current. The operating temperature of 250–300°C would require effective insulation and a resistance heating start-up system when the battery is cold. The low cost of sodium and sulfur make this battery particularly attractive. In addition, room-temperature, non-aqueous systems using lithium may eventually provide practical batteries in the 150 watt-hour per pound range.

Large amounts of energy can be stored in superconducting solenoids, and inductive energy-storage devices may be practicable in buses and trucks if hydrogen can be used as the cryogenic refrigerant. The development of superconductors with transition temperatures 5–10° higher than 21°K could play a vital role in the development of many areas of pollution-free technology.

Hybrid vehicles using a combination of batteries (or other power-storage devices) and a small external-combustion engine driving a generator may be the best near-term compromise. Battery power alone could be used for short trips.

Ultrahigh-strength carbon and boron filaments may be the key to a superflywheel-powered car in which the flywheel container is mounted in gimbals. A recent study concludes that a superflywheel could propel a vehicle for 2 hours at 55 miles per hour if the flywheel accounted for 25% of the total system weight. The superflywheel would be supported by magnetic suspension in a vacuum chamber.

Systems combining the advantages of the car and mass transportation are feasible. An electric car could turn off a road into an underground tube, where contact would be made with two rails and power picked up from a third rail under the car. The inside of the rubber wheels would be integrated with a smaller metal wheel that would contact the rails. Travel in the tube would be under complete computer control, allowing optimized speed and vehicle spacing. The driver would resume manual control after exiting to normal streets. Any type of electric or hybrid vehicle could use this system if it had uniformly spaced wheels.

Perfect "pollution-free" combustion of hydrocarbons still produces one contaminant—carbon dioxide. There is mounting concern that an increase of atmospheric CO_2 levels will produce the "greenhouse" effect, causing a temperature increase in Terra's atmosphere. The solution is simply to convert all hydrocarbon fuels to hydrogen, which can be used as a liquid cryogenic fuel. The pure carbon would be a valuable by-product to be used in filtering systems and in many other useful products. It should also be mentioned that coal burning (a major CO_2 source) must be stopped as quickly as possible. Coal could still be used in the chemical industry, however, as a raw material for plastics, dyes, and synthetic food.

Cryogenic hydrogen fuel in turbofan transports and other aircraft would eliminate the serious problem of airport pollution and would double the range of aircraft for a comparable hydrocarbon fuel weight. Superinsulation would permit it to be used also in trucks, buses, and all seacraft too small for nuclear power. The liquid hydrogen could be used in external-combustion engines, turbines, and fuel cells for many power requirements.

Methane and other hydrocarbons could be converted to gaseous hydrogen and transported via pipeline to residence, office building, or factory. There it would serve to provide heat or run an air conditioner, or it could be converted into fuel cell electricity. In Century 21, Terra's scarce hydrocarbons will become too valuable in petrochemical processing to be used as fuels. Hydrogen will then be obtained through water electrolysis.

Reusable "Escher"-class Terra-to-orbit spacecraft will use nonpollutant hydrogen-oxygen propellants. Nuclear rocket engines will be started only in orbit, where there is no atmospheric contamination problem.

Factory and other industrial pollutants can be eliminated through a variety of recycling approaches, catalytic conversion, and redesign of production processes. Frequently the reclaimed wastes will have sufficient value to pay for the reclaiming system.

The availability of pollution-free electric power is essential to all of Terra's future technology. *Thermonuclear power plants will play the most important role in maintaining our atmosphere in Century 21 and the years beyond.*

Radioactivity Pollution

This type of pollution is found in many surprising places. A coal-fueled power plant releases more than twice as much radioactive contaminants into the atmosphere as a contemporary nuclear fission power plant because there are small quantities of uranium and thorium in the coal. The final answer is controlled fusion to eliminate coal burning and reduce fission power systems to the relatively small sizes needed to power ships and spacecraft (at a sufficiently high orbit-start to preclude atmospheric contamination). Thick plates of lead glass or novel solid-state flat projector designs can eliminate the X-rays produced by contemporary television picture tubes. New means of viewing the interior of the body using harmless acoustical waves can replace many medical X-rays. In addition, ultrasensitive film can significantly reduce the X-ray dosage needed to provide sufficient resolution for diagnostic purposes. Every device that employs radioactive isotopes or emits any kind of ionizing radiation must be carefully redesigned to ensure that the isotopes are properly contained, and that radiation emission controls are fail-safe under all reasonable conditions.

Water Pollution

In many ways, water pollution poses an even more serious threat to Terra's ecology than atmospheric contamination. The answer is complete recycling, a process being refined for use on smaller, more sophisticated spacecraft than Terra. Every system that uses large quantities of water must become a closed loop so that no wastes are dumped into our streams, rivers, lakes, or oceans. With proper design, most of these systems will pay for themselves.

All processed human sewage will be sterilized by heat or radiation, homogenized, and then pumped into a sealed, pathogen-free, hydroponic factory, where these human wastes—a slurry containing every chemical necessary for the growth of all of man's food plants—will be converted into vegetable products suitable for human beings and domestic animals. Fresh water will be extracted from one end of the hydroponic system so that it can be returned to the urban closed-cycle environment. Laws will forbid the sale of products that would poison the hydroponic system.

The automated hydroponic factories for the supply of food will allow much farmland to be converted into parks and attractive grazing areas for a variety of domestic animals. The use of artificial fertilizers on conventional farms will be severely restricted, so that the drainoff into rivers and lakes will not upset the ecology and add harmful compounds to city drinking water. In time, all of Terra's vegetables will be produced through hydroponics and organic agriculture.

All utensils used in the preparation and consumption of food will be cleaned in an ultrasonic dishwasher which may use dilute hydrogen peroxide or safe enzymes in an open cycle. Existing methods of producing pure hydrogen peroxide as a low-cost rocket propellant will make it possible to use diluted solutions for all household and industrial drain-pipe cleaning. Soap and body detergents will be largely replaced by the scrubbing brush, steam bath, and hot bubble massage bath. Hair can be shampooed in a small closed-cycle shower system. The electric razor has already eliminated the need for shaving lather.

Every mineral extraction and manufacturing process can be converted to a closed-cycle water system. In some cases extracted byproducts will pay for the added cost, but more frequently it will be passed on, step by step, until the final consumer pays a higher retail price. The ingenuity of countless inventors, however, will result in many clever refinements in industrial closed water systems, reducing their expense to a negligible percentage of total manufacturing cost.

Thermal Pollution

The excess heat produced by power plants which frequently use ocean or river water for cooling is the primary source of thermal pollution. Heat from countless buildings, air conditioning systems, and factories in large cities can raise the environmental temperature by several degrees. The term thermal enrichment has been used by offending power companies, and indeed there is a possibility that the name is justified. Thermal enrichment, however, is likely to be expensive and restricted to coastal regions. The best solution is to build most of our large power plants on artificial islands 5–10 miles out on the continental shelf. These would contain huge breeder reactors in the 1975–90 time period and fusion reactors thereafter. Fusion reactors would emit less than half the waste heat produced by fossil fuel and fission power plants. Some of the waste heat could be used for saline water conversion, with the brine pumped past the continental shelf. The hot sea water used for cooling would be pumped many miles to the edge of the continental shelf, where it could be released on the sea floor at a depth of 2000 feet or lower. The stream of warm water would create an artificial sea floor current which would cause phosphates and other minerals to rise to the surface, increasing the potential harvest of many oceanic life forms used for human nutrition.

Some of the electricity produced on the artificial islands would be used directly in adjacent facilities for power-intensive mineral processing and manufacturing. These operations would be automated, so that only a small maintenance and control crew would be required. The artificial island would grow rapidly to an optimum size as industrial operations that now clutter Terra's increasingly valuable shoreline were moved out to the artificial islands. Power would be transmitted to the continent in underwater, super-conducting cryogenic lines cooled with liquid hydrogen, and transmission to cities a thousand miles or more inland without significant loss would be feasible.

Interior communities in which the coastal superconductive power grid would not prove economic could have small fission plants which could use water towers for cooling. If humidity became a problem, large fans could direct air against a circular array of cooling pipes with the cooling water in a closed circuit.

The collective thermal rise in large cities can best be solved by better insulation in office, factory, and residential buildings. Several orders of magnitude of improvement in insulation effectiveness is theoretically possible, and economic insulation design would pay for itself in lower heating and cooling costs. Interior air would be filtered with electrostatic and other systems which would reduce cleaning requirements, and the microbe count in the interior air would also be much lower.

Solid- and Liquid-Waste Pollution

As many carelessly discard things that are no longer useful, these types of pollution are painfully evident. Liquid wastes are primarily industrial chemicals which can be converted into useful products by adding more cycles to the manufacturing process. The solid-waste problem, however, will require the adoption of entirely new design and financing philosophies. Recycling and reuse will offer many economic solutions.

Containers should be made sufficiently durable that they can be returned for a small refund and reused countless times. The *unbreakable beer bottle* can serve as an example. Beer containers could be made of a strong glass or ceramic that would not break under normal usage—say, even if, they were dropped on a cement floor. These bottles would have a hinged-swing plastic top (similar to some used in Germany), allowing the bottle to be resealed if only part of the beer was consumed. Not even the top would be thrown away. The consumer might pay 30 cents more for a six-pack, but this deposit would be returned to him when he brought the bottles back to any food or beverage store. All other liquid food products could be sold in similar containers, which would eventually result in appreciable savings for the public.

All used cans should be collected separately from the solid wastes and then reprocessed into aluminum and steel. Hard or slick paper could be collected separately to be reconverted into fresh white paper. Newspapers and other forms of soft paper have already been converted by microorganisms into economic cattle feed; today's gloomy news is thereby transformed into steaks for the Saturday barbecue. Old clothes can be made into high-quality paper and other products. Plastic containers can be made of collagen compounds that will dissolve or provide direct nutrition for cattle. Application of a similar reuse or alternate-use philosophy would eliminate the bulk of our present solid wastes.

Sophisticated means of reclaiming solid wastes will emerge from the alchemy of research. By the year 2000, a *plasma torch* diverted from a thermonuclear power reactor may be used to ionize all solid wastes, and the individual elements will then be separated through electromagnetic methods. Of course, careful use must be made of the thermal energy (perhaps saline water conversion) to avoid serious thermal pollution. The plasma torch may provide the final solid-waste solution in Century 21.

Meanwhile, Terra's crew must change its basic manufacturing and financing philosophy. The automobile is typical of our present planned-obsolescence approach. Cars are designed and manufactured so that they will operate effectively for 3–5 years. After that time constant repair costs frustrate the consumer so that he buys a new vehicle. Most cars are now financed on a 3-year amortization schedule. Precise aerospace fail-safe design combined with "Rolls Royce"-quality manufacturing standards could easily provide cars that would be trouble-free for 10 years and could be used for twice that length of time without excessive repairs. They would be amortized over a 10–20 year period at a cost outlay comparable to what we pay each year for our contemporary vehicles. The same basic approach could be applied to products throughout industry, and junkyards full of rusty cars and discarded appliances would then disappear.

Similarly, we terrarians tend to discard many smaller items as soon as they need repair and to buy new replacements. The approach inherent in shoe or watch repair should be extended to all of our possessions.

Pesticide Pollution

This may be defined as "pollution stemming from the deliberate introduction of known toxins into the environment." Outside of agents used in warfare, the most serious problem is the widespread use of cholorinated hydrocarbons such as DDT and all other pesticides used to control insects that damage crops or domestic animals. The use of chemical pesticides is analogous to a situation in which a particular workman is known to be causing sabotage in a large factory. One can set off a bomb in the vicinity of the saboteur and hope that not many loyal workers will be killed and that useful machinery will not be severely damaged. An alternative approach would be to have a skilled marksman eliminate the saboteur with a single bullet without causing any other harm. What we need are "bullets" that will kill specific insect pests without damaging beneficial insects or other living creatures essential to Terra's life-support system. The determination of which of our shipmate species are "pests" and which are useful should be the subject of careful investigation. We will probably find that wolves, eagles, and tigers all occupy essential ecological niches.

The term biological control refers to any means of selectively eliminating offending pests. This has been accomplished, for example, by introducing large numbers of sterilized males into a geographic area in which the females of the species breed only once. Introducing predators that relish the offending pests is a particularly suitable form of biological control. Compounds that sterilize urban rats are in the experimental stage.

The real breakthrough in replacing all chemical pesticides will come from the investigation of bacteria and viruses that are highly specific in causing fatal diseases in certain species of insects. The deplorable R&D in germ warfare conducted in advanced countries during the past 30 years has refined laboratory techniques by which a specific germ or virus can be mutated until a passive disease becomes fatal, or the microbe becomes more infectious. Some very promising experiments are underway to refine the use of viruses that kill only crop-damaging insects and have no effect on human beings or other beneficial life forms. An aerosol is sprayed on the crops, using techniques similar to those required for chemical pesticides.

At first, biological control will be more expensive than contemporary techniques, but it can sometimes result in the total elimination of an offending species in one season. The rabbit menace in Australia was quickly reduced to manageable levels through the introduction of a specific virus. In addition to breeding selective microbes, scientists are investigating the possibility of mass-producing specific insect hormones that will halt growth or reproduction in only the offending species. The alchemy of DNA research may uncover a cornucopia of selective bullets for biological control on Terra.

Acoustical Pollution

This type of pollution, which includes sound and vibration, is becoming a serious health hazard. There is strong evidence that excessive noise, now directly linked to cardiovascular disease, can actually shorten the lifespan, since deaf people live, on the average, longer than the normal lifetime. The noise in Terra's large cities makes people nervous and irritable, lowers productivity, and may even add to the tensions that explode in urban riots.

Insulation technology can solve half of the problem. All buildings should employ soundproof construction, which also provides better insulation. Double panes of sealed glass will eliminate most noise in transparent structures.

Sound and vibration must also be eliminated or reduced at their source. External-combustion engines and electric cars will run quietly, and a blinking red strobe light will replace the auto horn. A blinking light in each room could replace the telephone ring. In the late 1980s perfect hollow ball bearings, constructed in orbital space factories, will reduce the noise and raise the efficiency of all forms of rotating machinery. Sound-absorbing material will be placed around all noise emitters, and machinery will rest on an elastic base. Ear-protecting helmets will be worn by workers in factories which have a dangerously high acoustic environment. Legislation will outlaw amplified musical instruments.

Powerboats will have quiet internal waterjet propulsion, reducing their noise level to that of sailboats. Electric motorcycles will sound like bicycles. A "quiet airplane" developed for military purposes, using a very-large-diameter, slow-moving propeller mated to a glider fuselage and wing design has already flown. An alternative approach is to employ slow-moving propellers with five or six blades. Quiet helicopters based on the same fundamental approach are under design, and quiet submarines are being developed for the navy. Although quieter jet engines have been demonstrated, there are fundamental limitations that cannot be easily overcome. The SST will be restricted to overseas routes, and optimized airport location will minimize noise from subsonic jet aircraft.

Optical Pollution

Design solutions for optical pollution, better known as "glare" or the reflection of sufficient light to cause visual discomfort, are quite simple. Aluminum surfaces can be painted with new long-lasting paint that reduces the reflection to a pleasant shade. Special Polaroid filters can be placed over headlights and windshields so that the driver will see only a fraction of on-coming headlights, but retain the full forward illumination from the lights of his own vehicle. Illumination in the home and workplace can be of the "indirect lighting" design, and Polaroid filters over reading lamps can eliminate the glare from reading white or glossy pages, which are the principal cause of eye fatigue. A simple redesign of every reflective surface and illumination source, using existing technology, can eliminate optical pollution.

Data Pollution

This type of pollution stems from the proliferation of journals, books, and other scholarly publications. Terra's total volume of printed material—not necessarily its new knowledge—doubles every 7 years. Scientists often write 10–20 separate papers and articles on a single experiment or hypothesis over a period of years. They frequently reinterpret the results of their old experiment in the light of new knowledge, or simply write another paper because a new society (with its journal) has been formed.

The solution may well be a sophisticated, computerized, abstracting technique centered entirely around the individual experiment, hypothesis, or theory. A complete description of the experiment would be stored on electronic tape or some other medium. If two scientists, unknown to each other, conducted the same experiment, their names and efforts would be cross-referenced. The computerized abstract would actually contain all essential data relative to the experiment, and the human semanticist would ensure that the text employed terms that would be understood by scholars in the disciplines most likely to profit from knowledge of the experiment. Reinterpretation of the experiment in the light of new knowledge would usually require only a simple abstract addition (with reference) to the basic description of the experiment.

In some cases, however, new information might require that the stored data be completely rewritten or restructured.

This approach to vital scholarly data would allow the specialist to gather quickly all the essential facts relevant to a new project, while permitting everyone else to continue the proliferation of papers and articles in our "publish or perish" academic environment. Journals and other publications would be simply bypassed by anyone engaged in a scientific data search. Hard copy for the investigator might be reproduced (from a distant source) though an electrostatic printout system adjacent to his desk, or it could be mailed to him at a lower cost.

Esthetic Pollution

Such unsightly man-made objects as billboards, overhead power and telephone lines, surface urban highways, and buildings of unimaginative design constitute esthetic pollution. Some solutions are simple. Billboards in areas of natural beauty can be eliminated by legislation. Telephone lines can be easily placed underground with little cost penalty. The further refinement of superconductors with transition temperatures in the liquid hydrogen range will permit the development of cryogenic underground power lines that offer the added advantage of negligible power loss over long distances. The electric car and other pollution-free vehicles will make it possible to build most of our urban highways underground, with the surface area covered with beautiful parks, fountains, and pleasant walk-ways.

Terra's current crew contains a large number of talented architects and city planners. An esthetically pleasing building—perhaps based on organic design—does not cost much more than the unattractive "boxes" that have been proliferating throughout our cities in recent years. Toward the end of the century, many will prefer underground homes with economic temperature, humidity, and air filtering systems. The illusion of being in the desert, the mountains, or ancient Rome, at the seashore, or even on the surface of Mars will be provided by three-dimensional holographic wall projections that can be changed automatically to fit the mood or the occasion.

People Pollution

Finally, some solution must be found to people pollution, Terra's most serious ecological hazard. Demographic pressures seriously intensify all other forms of environmental insult. Every cause is doomed to failure unless the population problem is solved. Moreover, increases in the human lifespan, perhaps to as much as 200 years, will intensify the problem in Century 21.

Experts agree that Terra's crew should be in the 1–2 billion range, a number which would require a reduction in the world's present population. This can be achieved only if a large percentage of the crew can be persuaded to limit reproduction to *one child per family* until the optimum population is reached after three or more generations.

Parents could be sterilized after the birth of one child. As biological insurance against the premature death of offspring, ova and sperm could be collected from the parents before sterilization and stored at cryogenic temperatures. In addition, there are many promising research options in contraception, abortion, and sterilization.

The question of pursuasion or enforcement of population control is the greatest dilemma in Terra's ecological crisis. Adoption of the one-child family rule for several generations would be easier to enforce in a totalitarian state, but it is to be hoped that advanced educational and propaganda techniques will bring acceptance of the program without excessive erosion of personal liberties. Unless population is brought into proper balance with nature, every society on Terra will evolve into a totalitarian state.

SUMMARY

This brief scenario shows that T/F can point the way to a permanent solution to Terra's life-support system crisis. Some of the requisite technologies can be developed in the near future; others will require generously funded R&D before the practical stage is reached. Advanced forecasting techniques will permit a permanent monitoring of all new technological possibilities stemming from basic research, allowing priorities to be constantly reassessed.

Solutions will be expensive and may often be contradictory to established custom or religious belief. Nevertheless, compliance must extend throughout Terra's crew if our spacecraft is to continue to maintain a high-quality human environment.

XX. *Futuristics—An Approach to Thinking about the Future*

JAY S. MENDELL

I am interested in the future because that's where I intend to live.   Anonymous

INTRODUCTION

When Peter Drucker, the philosopher of management, wrote a book on the future of business, he called it *The Age of Discontinuity*, to underscore the revolutionary nature of the social, technological, economic, and political forces[1] which comprise the environment of business. Tomorrow's business will be molded by revolutions in the social, technological, economic, and political spheres. The technology-based corporation will feel these forces because it is a purveyor of technology and because it is an institution—which, like all institutions, will adopt new goals, attitudes, concepts, practices, and organizational forms in response to new threats and opportunities.

"Invention and discovery, social change, and economic growth are seen as overshadowing anything we have seen in the past. The industrial world will face dramatic alterations as entire new industries based on technological advances, services, and human needs become realities," Carl Madden of the U.S. Chamber of Commerce has stated.

"Technology can be directed creatively so as to bring human society

[1] Henceforth I will refer to the STEP system, which is my acronym for the Social-Technological-Economic-Political environment.

347

into close harmony with its natural environment. It can be made to create wealth. . . . It can be made to create beauty. . . . It can be made to bring man both greater security and more individual freedom. What it does, however, will be accomplished only when we stop blaming it for our shortcomings, reassert our mastery over it, and agree what we want to do with it," wrote Glenn Seaborg, expressing his hopes for better management of technology.

Many corporations have indicated an interest in adapting to future conditions. This is simply good business. But will they be able to adapt? Adaptation to the environment will certainly demand a *sensitivity* to the environment and a willingness to think about it *speculatively* and *creatively,* and these attributes are all too clearly held in low esteem by technologists accustomed to working under the extreme pressure of day-to-day crises.

Can the corporation tear its attention away from today long enough to think about tomorrow?

SOMETHING IS MISSING—A CONCEPTUAL GRASP OF THE FUTURE

Unfortunately, when our marketers and managers look to the future, they see a blur, a fog, or a kaleidoscope. Ideally they should be able to draw pictures of what they think is almost certain to happen; what cannot be eliminated as a possibility; what might be made to happen or not happen if specified steps are taken; and how the corporation must be transformed if these steps are to be taken. But because they have no conceptual grasp of the future, they cannot carry out their jobs effectively. Not only are they unable to predict or plan, but also they are unable to understand the processes of "discontinuity" well enough to describe and discuss the business environment. They lack a conceptual grasp of the forces molding their future environment.

It is difficult to overstate the importance of conceptual thinking. Conceptual thinking lets us relate the different parts of a problem, gain new insights, and communicate our ideas. It helps us to gather information by letting us decide what to look for. It stimulates creativity. It allows us to see the structural similarity between systems. It assists us in thinking on very large or small scales when these scales are beyond our range of experience. Conceptual thinking helps us to think far into the future or about unfamiliar parts of the STEP system.

A student of psychology will point out that new concepts not only give us fresh views of what we already know, but also help us to absorb large quantities of new information. Without concepts to help us sort out the bits of information and relate them one to another, our sensory input would be a jumble. The better equipped we are with concepts, the more we can learn and the more effectively we can organize for action.

Most of us stumble through life with the same old concepts we learned in our youth. Consequently, because their employees are devoid of new concepts, corporations blunder along, avoiding opportunities that require new thinking and colliding with dangers that might have been avoided.

The most urgent need would appear to be for a better understanding of how human behavior governs the rate and direction of technological change and how technology exerts an impact on the human condition. This requires bringing an understanding of sociology and political science into the corporation and demands that we recognize economics, business administration, and technological innovation as dependent on human considerations. In the last few years, scholars have built a behavioral science that is more pertinent to technological planning: our problem is to get the new concepts into the corporation and to put them to use. *The only way to get the new concepts into the collective corporate intelligence is first to get them into the minds of individual employees—* not only managers but also all the technologists and executives who create the pervading atmosphere in which the corporation is managed.

WHAT IS FUTURISTICS?

Futuristic thinking (futuristics, for short) is a catch-all term for various ideas, attitudes, bits of knowledge, and methods that help us to think about and discuss the future. Technological forecasting is certainly part of futuristics. The scholarly content of futuristics consists of studies in management, social and political analysis, economics, the history and philosophy of science, technological innovation, creativity, and other fields that attempt to explain how human beings and the systems they create will behave in various circumstances.

There are three practical problems of futuristics:

1. How to infuse massive quantities of new concepts into all levels of a corporation; or, more to the point, how to stimulate an insatiable appetite for new concepts among all the employees.
2. How to increase employees' confidence in their own creativity and persuade them to become aggressively creative.
3. How to wean employees away from their obsession with day-to-day

operations and short-range problems so they may devote time to speculative and creative discussion of threats and opportunities in their environment.

A TECHNOLOGICAL HORROR STORY

Government and public pressures are forcing a certain corporation to curtail the smoke and noise output of its product. I talked with the engineer in charge of nuisance abatement. After a late start and many recriminations, he was succeeding in a crash program to roll back smoke and noise, though at great expense in time, men, and dollars.

"Air and water pollution, solid wastes, waste heat, noise, and radionuclides have all been branded ecologically harmful," I remarked. "No one understands better than you the importance of acting early to eliminate the pollution incidental to product use. If you had started a few years earlier, wouldn't your clean-up job have been much easier?

"You deserve great credit for what you have accomplished in a short time," I continued. "But tell me: how long do you think you will be able to rest on your oars? Don't you suppose that the environmentalists will be back in a few years, demanding an even cleaner product? When they come, what will they want? Still lower levels of noise and smoke? Lower levels of the invisible pollutants? Which pollutants? And how strong will the environmentalists be politically? Will their demands be backed by legislative standards?"

I asked whether the corporation was monitoring the activities of the environmentalists. "Who are their allies in Congress and in the federal departments? When do you expect your next headache, and what are you doing to avoid the need of another crash program?"

The engineer thought for a few moments before answering. "Yes," he said; he realized there would be more stringent requirements someday. But he hadn't given much thought to when they would occur or what they would demand. His job, I had to understand, was power plant engineering. As an engineer, he was concerned with well-defined problems, certainly not *speculation*.

"Who *is* concerned with speculation?" I asked. To his knowledge, no one.

Here is the exact opposite of the futuristic attitude. This engineer couldn't be bothered with speculation; he wanted *a well-defined* problem. He wanted to stay with his narrowly defined technological job, to live with his old and reliable concepts.

What made his attitude appalling was the fact that this man had actually experienced the agonies of a crash program caused by *insufficient* speculative attention to environmental considerations. He had bled because he (and everyone else) had been asleep at the switch, but he would sooner bleed again than make it his business to monitor the environmental movement and predict its future demands.

MANY TECHNOLOGISTS WANT TO UNDERSTAND THE FUTURE

At this point we have to ask, "Are technologists natural-born Philistines, or can they be persuaded to broaden their outlook?" For several years, I have felt that most graduates are motivated by a desire to understand the world around them, and I have believed that, given encouragement, many would attempt to form a concept of the future.

My suspicions were confirmed recently when a group of sixteen engineering graduates enrolled for my Seminar in Technological Forecasting in the evening program of the Graduate School of Business, University of Connecticut in Hartford. (My "students" emphatically preferred to think of themselves as businessmen-engineers who happened to be going to school at night. They were either candidates for the M.B.A. degree or recent M.B.A. graduates.) Early in the semester, I decided their interests lay not in the methodologies of technological forecasting, but rather in the conceptual framework of futuristic thinking. They were less interested in decision making based on forecasting, more interested in developing an understanding of change.

On the second evening of the semester, I showed them that classic example of technological growth, the timewise exponential increase of nuclear accelerator energies (Figure 1). "Can the curve be expected to grow to higher and higher energies?" I asked.

One student asked whether any law of physics would prevent an atomic or nuclear particle being accelerated to energies of 100,000 MeV or higher. I assured him that, as an ex-physicist, I could see no physical limit at that level.

Immediately another student asked whether bigger accelerators are cost-effective. If not, he implied, society would choose not to buy them. "Very good," I said. "What constitutes effectiveness in an accelerator? What are they good for? What do they give society in return for lavish outlays of tax dollars?"

Now the students were stumped. No one seemed to be sure exactly what the big machines give us. Vaguely they understood that accelerators are used in experimental nuclear and particle physics, and that these

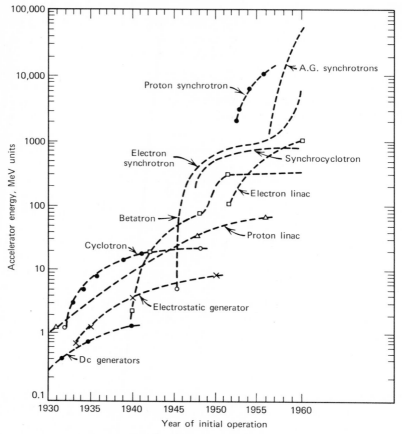

Figure 1 **Typical envelope curve—rate of increase of operating energy in particle accelerators.**

fields are at the very cutting edge of physical research; but the utility of physics research was an enigma. Who needs it?

I tried to explain. I launched myself into a passionate speech on the value of basic research. Particle accelerators, I asserted, were partly responsible for the revolution in physics that occurred during the first half of the century. And the New Physics, in turn, revolutionized man's view of matter, energy, and the universe. With the possible exception of Freud's psychiatry, no other scientific developments so profoundly influenced twentieth-century man.

My businessmen-engineers thought about my explanation. After a while, one of them remarked that there might be better ways to spend money. "I think most of us assumed, when you posed the question, that accelerators have some concrete, utilitarian function which we didn't happen to understand," he said. "Because we didn't understand the objective of pure science, we couldn't understand what scientists accomplished with accelerators." (Engineers sometimes understand the contents of science, but they seldom understand the purpose of "pure" science.)

My student continued: "Naturally, if the object of physics is to increase our understanding of the universe, it must be in competition with other branches of science that also provide understanding. Speaking for myself, I would rather put money into biology, since I am interested in understanding the nature of life. Maybe the guy sitting next to me is interested in understanding how his mind works, in which case I'm sure he would opt for spending money on psychology. So instead of looking at the trend curve of accelerator energies, why don't we discuss what sort of understanding science can offer us and try to decide what value society will place on this understanding?"

You will agree, I am sure, that this is a perceptive statement. It shows that this man quickly saw we were dealing with a social question (one of value systems) rather than a scientific one. As a matter of fact, my experience throughout the course was that students wanted to discuss technological issues in the context of their full social, economic, and political implications.

TECHNOLOGISTS CAN ADAPT TO FUTURISTIC THINKING

One evening after class a student showed me an article that Paul R. Ehrlich had written for the magazine *Ramparts*. The article was called "Eco-Catastrophe!", and it took the form of a scenario. (Incidentally, "Eco-Catastrophe!" has been reprinted in *The Environmental Handbook*, a paperback available in every college bookstore.)

A scenario is a narrative description of one version of the future. It purports to show how a certain train of events will lead to a desirable or (more usually) undesirable result. The scenario has been popularized by Herman Kahn in such books as *On Thermonuclear War* and *On Escalation*, but the pre-eminent exponent of ecological scenarios is Dr. Ehrlich, a biology professor at Stanford University.

In "Eco-Catastrophe!" Ehrlich argues that worldwide catastrophe is only a few years away unless man can learn to manage his natural resources. Against a background of steadily deteriorating international relations, Ehrlich depicts the collapse of agriculture in the underdeveloped countries (UDCs), followed by the ruination of the ocean as a source of food and finally by the outbreak of strategic war among the nations.

The story starts in the early 1970s, when, as part of an attempt to regain lost prestige among the UDCs (and to build a market abroad for American agricultural products), the United States launched a vigorous foreign aid program aimed at an agricultural "Green Revolution." The UDCs were furnished seeds of "miracle," high-yield grains. Owing to economic and ecological circumstances (which Ehrlich describes in detail), the Green Revolution failed. As a reaction to the frustration of great expectations, the UDCs became increasingly hostile to the United States.

Expecting to capitalize on this resentment, the Soviet Union launched its own attack on worldwide famine by supplying the UDCs with facilities for the manufacture of Thanodrin, a "miracle" pesticide. In 1975 the Soviet economic-political penetration of the UDCs was spear-headed by the appearance of Thanodrin factories throughout the under-developed world. At first the results were dramatic. But because the Thanodrin Revolution, too, was built on unsound ecological premises, it also ultimately foundered, as nature evolved superpests resistant to the super-pesticide. To counter the appearance of the pests, the Soviets counseled more liberal application of Thanodrin, resulting in an upward spiral of Thanodrin resistance and Thanodrin application (which, Ehrlich pointedly remarks, is exactly what should have been expected). As Thanodrin poured into the ecosystem, its effect on the human population proved to be lethal. Throughout the world, angry mobs attacked Thanodrin plants, destroyed them, and poured tons of the chemical into rivers and oceans.

By January 1979, the ecology of the oceans themselves had been knocked into a downspin by massive infusions of Thanodrin. "By September," Ehrlich writes, ". . . all important animal life in the sea was extinct. . . . Japan and China were faced with almost instant starvation from a total loss of the seafood on which they were so dependent. Both blamed Russia for their situation and demanded immediate mass shipment of food. Russia had none to send. On October 13, Chinese armies attacked Russia on a broad front. . . ."

I asked the student who brought me *Ramparts* how he felt about "Eco-Catastrophe!" Did he think, for instance, that Ehrlich was deliberately exaggerating the dangers of resource mismanagement? And how was he (the student) influenced by the scenario?

His reply was satisfyingly perceptive. "Well, Ehrlich has a valid viewpoint to present. While it is true that he chose an improbable train of events, all occurring one after another in the worst possible sequence, as nearly as I can determine Ehrlich has not actually premised his scenario on anything known to be false. He constructed his scenario by always picking the worst possible outcome of the unknowns. No one can call him a liar: we can only wonder if he is an alarmist."

"The scenario was an excellent introduction to ecology," he continued. "I'd never understood the fragility of the ecosystem or taken an interest in it before I read Ehrlich's article. The scenario form is an attention-grabber."

How did he feel about "Eco-Catastrophe!" as a forecast? "Well, I don't think of it as a forecast. Ehrlich's intention may have been to show how little we know about managing our resources. I think he underscored the unknowns by deliberately exaggerating them. As I see it, the scenario was not supposed to be taken as a prediction so much as a warning. His article was educational. Ehrlich *wants* to be proved wrong."

This student understood that statements about the future should not always be taken as forecasts: their purpose may be educational.

FUTURISTICS IN THE LIBRARY

Have I given the impression that futuristic thinking is a scarce resource? It isn't. The libraries are full of it: our problem is to bring it into the corporation.

A nonprofit organization, The World Future Society (P.O. Box 19285, Twentieth Street Station, Washington, D.C., 20036) publishes a bimonthly journal of forecasts, trends, and ideas about the future, *The Futurist.* Here are the contents of a typical issue of this journal:

- An article on mankind's search for long-range goals, written by Gerald Feinberg, author of a book on that subject.
- A review of a recent copy of *Nation's Business* (a publication of the U.S. Chamber of Commerce) which surveyed the future of 34 industries (aerospace, aluminum, airlines, automobiles, banking, etc.).
- An article on the future of mental health ("During the 1960s, psychiatry developed the concepts of community psychiatry into an operating nucleus for a nationwide program of comprehensive mental health services. The central concern of the mental health professions in the 1970s will be to expand this program to provide human services appropriate to the needs of all groups within the population. . . .").

- An article on plans to build a 30,000-inhabitant city in the ocean.
- A description of how a subsidiary of a natural gas company is trying to diversify into a vendor of educational programs.
- An article from a communications specialist in The Rand Corporation which appraises the societal impact of cheap, long-distance communications.
- A précise of progress toward the facsimile transmission of newspapers.
- "Reflections of a 21st Century Manager," a scenario by George Kozmetsky, the Dean of Business at the University of Texas ("Back in the early 1970s . . . managers began to recognize new kinds of organizations. For convenience, these developing organizations were known as *non-routine industries*. . . . The education industry was a leading non-routine industry.").
- Articles on technological and economic forecasting.
- A review of a home-study course in creativity.
- News of local chapters of The World Future Society. (One chapter discussed the possibility that the general public wants a slowdown in regard to science and technology.)

Most readers agree that exposure to futuristic material is broadening and stimulating. Reading *The Futurist*, I realized that corporations have done a rather effective job of isolating themselves from such broadening and stimulating experiences. One of the very few established mechanisms that can act as a stimulus is the corporate library, and that institution is too often regarded as a reference department rather than a pipeline of rejuvenating ideas. Libraries are full of futuristic concepts which cannot break into the corporate consciousness *because the library is disastrously underutilized by employees.* (In addition to the corporate library, employees have access to the local public library and often to the facilities of a nearby university. But if they don't know how to use one library, they won't know how to use the others.)

Half the problem is that engineers and executives do not spend much time in the library. In fact, the more influential executives claim to operate under such intense day-to-day pressure that they can never find time to go there.

The second half of the problem is that, when they appear at the library, they don't carry out the one pattern of behavior guaranteed to expose them to new materials: they don't browse. Quite simply, browsing consists of reading briefly from a variety of books, journals, and newspapers to determine whether anything therein might be useful in the near or distant future. One advantage of browsing is that you develop an interest in, and then an understanding of, dozens of subjects which otherwise would not have entered your life. But the real payoff comes when, after years of browsing, you begin to see the long-range relevance of practically everything to your business. Practiced on a massive scale (I use seven libraries and seven bookstores), browsing is bound to turn anyone into a futuristic thinker.

At the end of this chapter is the reading list that I gave my students of technological forecasting. I call it a "browser's list" because it is the result of years of prowling among the stacks of bookstores and libraries. There is no other way in the world that I could have developed an interest in such diverse, insightful, and relevant subjects as creativity, the history of science and technology, and technological forecasting except by surrendering to my natural curiosity. And if I hadn't developed the habit of regularly reading such journals as *Science, Science News, The Futurist,* and *The Harvard Business Review,* I would be intellectually crippled in my attempts to monitor the environment in which my corporation must operate.

To sum up, there exists within easy reach of everyone a vast body of literature which can help him to understand the present and future environment of his corporation. Every effort must be made to induce people to use this resource.

STIMULATING INSIGHTFUL PERCEPTION

The key to innovation and adaptability is the capacity for fresh perception. Futuristic thinking requires us to search for unusual properties and new uses in what we take for granted.

In my evening course at the University of Connecticut I included training in creative perception. One evening I asked a student to imagine that he was the owner of a coal mine. After he had reflected on the state of the coal industry and the predicament of a mine owner, he was supposed to explain the nature of his business *as he perceived it.* He identified his business quite simply as coal mining: "I dig it up and ship it out." Couldn't he see his business in a broader context, I asked, by relating, for example, to other basic industries? No, he couldn't.

A second student suggested that coal was actually part of the *energy business,* which opened the possibility that the mine owner might prefer to manufacture electricity and "ship it out" by high-voltage transmission line. A third student also saw coal as part of the fuel business. Why not manufacture synthetic fuel gas or gasoline at the mouth of the mine and transmit it to the customer by pipeline?

I immediately pointed out that by shifting our attention away from the commonplace perception of coal (a mineral to be dug up and then transmitted great distances to its ultimate place of consumption) we had been able to enumerate two possibilities for reforming the coal business. I paused for additional ideas. When none were forthcoming, I resorted to a technique that I knew would stimulate the insight-generating process: I invited the students to write down the attributes of coal—every description that in any way seemed to fit coal. The resulting list included *hard, soft, black, brown, carbon, carbonaceous, hydrogen, hydrocarbon, fuel, heat, combustible mineral, dense, raw material, railroad,* and many other words that, in the students' minds, denoted or connoted coal.

Again we took up the discussion of coal mining. One student remembered reading that coal is the starting point for the synthesis of industrial chemicals. He vaguely remembered that several clothing fabrics are derived from coal. I asked why coal is so useful as a raw material, and, after a good deal of thought, the student decided that the rich variety of organic chemical linkages makes coal the starting point for organic chemicals which would be difficult to build up from the base elements. Also, he guessed, the latent energy of coal serves to drive the chemical reactions.

At this point we were seeing coal as a complicated, chemically rich, energy-rich substance. No longer was it a mineral to be ripped out of the ground and carelessly burned.

Here the dialog took an insightful turn. A student remarked, "From coal we can obtain heat, which is equivalent in my mind to shelter, and fabrics, which I equate with clothing. So here we have two very basic human needs. But can we satisfy an even more fundamental need? Can we eat coal?"

Because the students were now seeing coal as an energy-rich organic substance, they willingly visualized coal as having the essential attributes of a food. I pointed out that in fact experiments were under way to develop bacteria which would consume protein, an edible residue. Then why not food from coal?

And so we had identified shelter, clothing, and food as needs to be served by the coal industry. Could we hope to find anything else?

After several minutes of silence, someone remarked, "All the while we have been focusing on what comes out of the hole—the coal. But why can't we use the hole itself? In a few years our cities will be burying themselves under a mountain of solid waste products—bottles, cans, and other trash. Why can't some of this waste be loaded into the empty railroad cars headed back to the coal mines for disposal in abandoned mines?" This last comment was perhaps the most insightful of all, in that it represented a shift of attention from the mineral to the hole it leaves behind.

The point of my exercise was that, with a little effort, many new facets can be found in a rather ordinary operation.

In the reading list at the end of this article are several books on creativity that explain how the insight-generating process may be brought out. I am convinced that perception training can play an important role in helping a corporation to perceive new opportunities.

FORECASTERS NEED FUTURISTICS

For several years James Bright collected technological forecasts, including some that turned out well and others that turned out poorly. Analyzing their fabric of assumptions, logic, and input information, he was able to spotlight several sources of error. Two are worth mentioning here.

1. A forecaster often pays insufficient attention to easily available information on events and trends outside his own company and industry. Furthermore, forecasters often overlook work unfolding in the early stages of R&D because they cannot imaginatively perceive its long-range consequences.

2. Attempting to predict happenings in the technological system, forecasters forget that this is merely a part of the social-technological-economic-political system. They ignore, for example, needs generated by the economic and political system and the climate of social opinion.

In other words, forecasters tend to fail when they are too narrow. Perhaps they are too snugly wrapped up in their methodologies. Whatever the reason, they are clearly prime candidates for training in the broader futuristic viewpoint. Though futuristics is important everywhere in the corporation, one man needs it more than anyone else. He is the technological forecaster.

READINGS

Two Articles on the Aims and Limitations of Technological Forecasting

David M. Kiefer, "The Future's Business," *Chemical and Engineering News*, August 11, 1969.

James Brian Quinn, "Technological Forecasting," *Harvard Business Review,* March–April 1967.

Three Reports Available from the Commerce Department Clearinghouse ($3.00 each)

Joseph P. Martino et al., "Long-Range Forecasting and Planning, a Symposium Held at the U.S. Air Force Academy, 16–17 August 1966," AD 664 108.

"Report on Technological Forecasting, Prepared by the Interservice Technological Forecasting Methodology Study Group" June 30, 1967, AD 664 165.

Joseph P. Martino and Thomas Overbeck, "Long-Range Forecasting Methodology, a Symposium Held at Alomogordo, New Mexico, 11–12 October 1967," AD 679 176.

Four Comprehensive Texts on Technological Forecasting

Robert U. Ayres, *Technological Forecasting and Long-Range Planning.* New York: McGraw-Hill, 1969.

James R. Bright, *Technological Forecasting for Industry and Government.* Englewood Cliffs, N.J.: Prentice-Hall, 1968.

Marvin J. Cetron, *Technological Forecasting: a Practical Approach.* New York: Gordon and Breach, 1969.

Erich Jantsch, *Technological Forecasting in Perspective.* Organization for Economic Cooperation and Development, 1967.

Four Books on the Role of Technology in World-Wide Future Conditions

Arthur C. Clarke, *Profiles of the Future.* New York: Harper and Row.

Harrison Brown, *The Challenge of Man's Future.* New York: Viking.

Harrison Brown et al., *The Next Hundred Years.* New York: Viking.

Richard P. Shuster, Ed., *The Next Ninety Years,* (sequel to the *Next Hundred Years*). California: California Institute of Technology Press, 1967.

Periodicals on Forecasting Planning

The Futurist
World Future Society Bulletin
Futures
Technological Forecasting
Long-Range Forecasting/Planning Reports of the Stanford Research Institute

Three Books of Unusual Interest

Stafford Beer, *Management Science: The Business Use of Operations Research,* New York: Doubleday, 1968.

James R. Bright, *Research, Development, and Technological Innovation,* New York: Irwin, 1964.

Arthur D. Hall, *A Methodology for Systems Engineering.* New York: Van Nostrand, 1962.

Also Helpful

William F. Butler and Robert A. Kavesh, Eds., *How Business Economists Forecast.* New York: Prentice-Hall, 1966.

K. A. Yeomans, *Statistics for the Social Scientist (Introducing Statistics,* Vol. 1; *Applied Statistics,* Vol. 2). New York: Penguin, 1968.

On the History and Philosophy of Science

David Killefer, *How Did You Think of That?—An Introduction to the Scientific Method.* New York: Doubleday, 1969.

Thomas Kuhn, *The Structure of Scientific Revolutions.* Chicago, Ill.: U. of Chicago Press, 1962.

Jay S. Mendell, "Will the 21st Century Repeal the Laws of Nature?" *The Futurist,* August 1968.

Stephen Toulmin, *The Philosophy of Science.* New York: Harper and Row.

Stephen Toulmin, *Foresight and Understanding.* New York: Harper and Row.

Stephen Toulmin and June Goodfield, *The Architecture of Matter.* New York: Harper and Row.

Stephen Toulmin and June Goodfield, *The Fabric of the Heavens.* New York: Harper and Row.

Stephen Toulmin and June Goodfield, *The Discovery of Time.* New York: Harper and Row.

Charles H. Townes, "Quantum Electronics and Surprise in Development of Technology—The Problem of Research Planning," *Science,* February 16, 1968.

Marshall Walker, *The Nature of Scientific Thought.* Englewood Cliffs, N.J.: Prentice-Hall, 1963.

Derek J. deSolla Price, "A Calculus of Science," *International Science and Technology,* March 1963.

Nancy T. Gammara, "Erroneous Predictions and Negative Comments Concerning Exploration, Territorial Expansion, Scientific and Technological Development," The Library of Congress Legislative Reference Service, April 10, 1969.

From The Harvard Business Review

H. Igor Ansoff and John M. Stewart, "Strategies for a Technology-Based Business," November–December 1967.

Laurence D. McLaughlin, "Long-Range Technical Planning," July–August 1968.

John K. Baker and Robert H. Shaffer, "Making Staff Consulting More Effective," January–February 1969.

Paul R. Lawrence, "How to Deal with Resistance to Change," January–February 1969.

Robert H. Hayes, "Qualitative Insight from Quantitative Methods," July–August 1969.

Maxwell W. Hunter, II, "Are Technological Upheavals Inevitable?" September–October 1969.

James Brian Quinn, "Long-Range Planning of Industrial Research," the HRB R-and-D Series, Part I.

James Brian Quinn and Robert M. Cavanaugh, "Fundamental research can be planned."

Important Journals

American Scientist
Endeavour
Innovation
New Scientist
Science
Science Journal (especially October 1967 issue on "The Future")
Science News
Scientific American
Scientific Research
Science and Technology (formerly *International Science and Technology*)
Science Year (*The World Book Science Annual*)
Psychology Today
Trans-Action

On Creativity

Edward deBono, *The Five-Day Course in Thinking*. New York: Signet, 1967.
William J. J. Gordon, *Synectics*. New York: Collier, 1961.
Alex F. Osborn, *Applied Imagination*. New York: Scribners, 1963.

Sidney J. Parnes, *Creative Behavior Guidebook* and *Creative Behavior Workbook*. New York: Scribners, 1967.

Darold Powers, *The Idea Machine*, Cider Press, 1963.

Persuasion and Communication

Henry M. Boettinger, "The Art and Craft of Moving Executive Mountains," *Business Management*, July, August, September 1969.

Dale Carnegie, *How to Win Friends and Influence People*. New York: Cardinal, 1967.

Rudolf Flesh, *How to Write, Speak and Think More Effectively*. New York: Signet, 1960.

Roy Garn, *The Magic Power of Emotional Appeal*. New York: Ace, 1960.

Haim G. Ginnot, *Between Parent and Child*. New York: MacMillan, 1965.

Gerard I. Nierenberg, *The Art of Negotiating*. New York: Hawthorn, 1968.

Odds and Ends

Fritz Zwicky, *The Morphology of Propulsive Power*. California: California Institute of Technology Press.

Various books by Herman Kahn, Isaac Asimov, and Nigel Calder.

XXI.   *A Model for Resource Allocation in Materials Processing for Research and Development*

ROBERT U. AYRES

When you can measure what you are speaking about, and express it in numbers, you know something about it.   Lord Kelvin

BACKGROUND—THE PROBLEM

Most R&D expenditures at any given time—whether government- or corporation-sponsored—are "mission-oriented;" that is, they are directed at solving a problem in terms more or less defined by the client or the would-be user. The problem of resource allocation for government or industrial research laboratories operating within this framework boils down to evaluating the relative contribution a given research project will make toward the specified goal, in relation to the cost of the effort. There exists a rather large literature on this topic, which need not be recapitulated here and to which we are not called upon to add at this stage.[1]

In contrast to the above, however, there exists another type of R&D effort, which has traditionally been carried on in a rather unstructured fashion by individual inventors, product developers, or even basic researchers. Certain organizations, notably The Battelle Development Corporation, as well as various venture capital firms and independent product development firms, make a profitable business of inventing—or supporting the further development of inventions. Here the focus is on recognizing and assessing opportunities or, in a sense, matching potential problems with existing solutions. Resource allocation in this framework has never been reduced to a formalized "model," primarily because of the obvious difficulty of characterizing potential markets for inventions whose costs and functional capabilities cannot be described in detail—precisely because the necessary R&D has not yet been carried out.

On the other hand, it is clear from the historical performance of some of the more successful invention investment programs that intelligence and experience can be applied systematically and successfully to the resource allocation problem. The question which has been posed, then, is whether it is possible to improve on this decision-making methodology by providing a "model," that is, a data bank and some logical analysis reduced to a set of repetitive algorithms suitable for programming on a computer. Rather than discussing the question in abstract terms, the approach of the International Research and Technology Corporation has been to attempt to devise a model to improve resource allocation for the development of inventions, and to discuss the more general issue in the light of the specific problems of model implementation and data acquisition, as well as underlying questions of validity and relevance.

The field of materials processing is particularly appropriate for initial exploratory studies because it is fundamental to so many industries, and because there exists a large quantity of fairly good data. However, what we propose hereafter, in general terms at least, could probably be applied as well (if it can be applied at all) to any other functionally defined area of technology, such as energy conversion, energy transmis-

---

[1] Some general references include:

M. J. Cetron, J. Martino, and L. Roepcke, "The Selection of R&D Program Content—Survey of Quantitative Methods," *IEEE Transcript on Engineering Management, EM-14,* No. 1, March 1967.

James R. Bright, ed., *Technological Forecasting for Industry and Government* (Englewood Cliffs, N.J.: Prentice-Hall, 1968).

M. J. Cetron, R. Isenson, J. N. Johnson, A. B. Nutt, and H. A. Wells, *Technical Resource Management: Quantitative Methods* (Cambridge, Mass.: The M.I.T. Press, 1969).

sion, information processing, information transmission, or information display.

In summary, the model approach proposed and discussed hereafter involves the following three steps:

• **Morphological analysis** (for a given industry) of all possible sequences of material transformations, leading from specified raw materials to specified "final" (i.e., processed) materials.[2] Each transformation sequence (or *macroprocess*) is broken down into individual process steps (or *microprocesses*). The number of possible transformation sequences can be limited in various ways, for example, to the extent that either initial or final "states" are prescribed. For instance, one may focus attention on a specific raw material, such as iron ore, or on a specific final material, such as plate glass or nylon fiber. Any definite choice, such as these, tends to eliminate the vast majority of possible combination and permutation of processing steps. Moreover, the number of possible macroprocesses is greatly limited by the fact that most microprocesses are applicable only to specific *forms* of material (i.e., solid, powder, fiber, gel, liquid, etc.), and only process sequences applicable to the same forms are allowed unless the microprocess itself causes an appropriate change in form. Other microprocesses are applicable only to certain physical or chemical substances, for example, ferrous metals, superconductors, semiconductors, insulators, or polymers. Finally, it can be shown that microprocesses occur in certain characteristic subsequences, which in turn occur only in certain logical orderings. Further details of a morphological analysis of materials processing are described later. Once the rules governing allowable sequences are articulated, possible process sequences can be programmed for a computer.

• **Economic analysis** (again, for a given industry), consisting of an identification of microprocess technologies actually in use, or used in the past, to determine fixed (capital) and variable (labor and energy) costs, and other measures of transformation efficiency (e.g., materials wasted or lost as materials), specified as to form or composition. On the basis of these data, *total* costs, energy consumption, losses, etc., can be estimated for arbitrary microprocess sequences and optimum sequences can be chosen in a manner analogous to the "critical path method" commonly used for project scheduling.

---

[2] The term morphological analysis was first applied in this context in connection with studies of hypothetical rocket engines; see F. Zwicky, *Morphology of Propulsive Power* (Pasadena, Calif.: Society for Morphological Research, 1962). A more up-to-date (and accessible) discussion can be found in Chapter 5 of R. U. Ayres, *Technological Forecasting and Long-Range Planning* (New York: McGraw-Hill Book Company, 1969).

• **Technological sensitivity analysis** (again, for a given industry), involving the determination, by means analogous to the calculus of variations, where in the macroprocess a technological improvement would have the greatest potential for upgrading overall cost effectiveness. One essential component of the sensitivity analysis is to assess the potential payoff from research on particular microprocesses, measured in percentage improvement likely to be achieveable per dollar of expenditure. A preliminary schematic approach is described later; in a slightly different context the proposed method has already been applied successfully on a fairly large scale by the U.S. Navy Material Command as part of its technological forecasting activities.[3]

The second major component of technological sensitivity analysis involves varying the performance of individual microprocesses to determine the overall multiplier effect of hypothetical changes. By "performance" is meant either *quantity* of output per unit of energy or material input, *cost* per unit output, or any pertinent measure of output *quality* (depending on the process). A computerized model is essential at this stage because multiplier effects may be very large indeed and calculation is nontrivial, since individual microprocess changes may affect not only the capital and labor costs of a particular step, but also the material *flow* requirements, which in turn affect, in principle, the capital and labor costs of every other microprocess. Moreover, it must be noted that, since large multiplier effects are indeed possible, the *optimum sequence*, that is, *the optimum macroprocess, may change as a result of a fairly small change in a single microprocess.* Although this sort of "trigger" effect may be relatively uncommon in technological practice, its potential economic importance if and when it occurs is such that a considerable expense is justified in identifying opportunities of this kind to guide the allocation of R&D resources.

The third and final major element of the sensitivity analysis involves systematically testing (on the computer) alternative permutations of microprocesses and synthesizing new hypothetical macroprocesses. The degree to which this third stage, in particular, can be carried out effectively in practice remains highly uncertain at present.

MORPHOLOGICAL ANALYSIS OF POSSIBLE MATERIAL TRANSFORMATIONS

As noted previously, the morphological analysis involves breaking down all existing processes into individual process steps or *micropro-*

---

[3] *U.S. Navy Technological Projections,* Headquarters, Naval Material Command, Washington, D.C., to be published in 1971.

Table 1 Classification of Materials by Form

Form	Example
Simple Forms	Example
S: Solid	Wood, stone, glass, metal castings
G: Granular or powder	Sand, sawdust, metal powder, cells
F: Filamentary	Hair, feathers, vegetable fiber, muscle, synthetic fiber, wire
M: Mesh (equivalent to F-F)	Paper, woven textiles, wire, screens
L: Liquid or fluid	Water, fats and oils
V: Vapor or gas	Air
Selected Composite Forms	Example
S-S: Solid-solid (laminated) structure)	Plywood
S-G: Solid-granule	Frozen soil, concrete
S-F: Solid-filament	Fiberglas, fiberboard
S-M: Solid-mesh	Epoxy-impregnated fabric
S-L: Liquid in solid matrix	Wet sponge
S-V: Vapor in solid matrix	Foam rubber, pumice, coke
G-G: Granule-granule	Mixture of granulated or powdered materials
G-F: Granule-filament	Plant or animal tissue
G-L: Granule-liquid (slurry, solution)[a]	Mud, paint, syrup, brine
G-V: Granule-vapor	Dust cloud
F-L: Filament-liquid (gel)	Gelatin, silica gel
F-V: Filament-vapor	Cotton fluff
M-L: Mesh-liquid	Wet cloth or paper
L-L: Liquid-liquid (emulsion)	Cream, gravy
L-V: Liquid droplet in vapor (aerosol)	Aerosol spray (water, paint, etc.)
V-L: Vapor in liquid (foam)	Soap suds

(Other composites are conceivable and will be considered as appropriate in the model.)

[a] By convention, a solution of polar or nonpolar solid material in a liquid is classed as a granule-liquid (G-L) composite (rather than a solid-liquid or filament-liquid, etc.).

Table 2   Electrochemical Classification of Basic Material Forms

Type		S: Solid	G: Granular	F: Filamentary	M: Mesh	L: Liquid	V: Vapor
				Examples			
M_1	Metals only (conductors)	Metals or alloys	Metal powder or filings	Metal whiskers or wire	Wire screen	Molten metal	N.A.
M_2	Polar electrolytes, soluble in H_2O	Metal chlorides, nitrates, sulfates, hydroxides, some phosphates, some carbonates	Powdered salts			Fused salts: H_2SO_4, HNO_3, H_2CO_3, NH_4OH	HCL
M_3	Polar nonelectrolytes, soluble in H_2O	Sugars, amino acids, soap	Powdered sugar, powdered soap, powdered amino acids	Spun sugar		Alcohols, H_2O, ethers, organic acids, phenols	SO_2, SO_3, NO, NO_2, NH_3, O_2
M_4	Nonpolar compounds, soluble in nonpolar HC (benzene, etc.)	Resins, plastics, waxes, fats	Tetraethyl lead, iodine	Many synthetic polymers, e.g., rayon	Rayon cloth	Hydrocarbons, saturates, olefins, aromatics bromine	Chlorine
M_5	Insoluble, organic (insulators)	Rubber, Teflon, lignin, coal, some proteins, cellulose	Powdered coal, etc.	Hair and wool, silk, muscle fiber, cotton, jute, wood pulp (cellulose)	Wool, silk, cotton, linen, sponge	Latex, fluorocarbons	Freons, refrigerants
M_6	Insoluble, inorganic (insulators)	Metal oxides, silicates, phosphates, carbonates, igneous rocks, glass	Powdered oxides, powdered glass, sand, clay, soil, gravel, sulfur	Asbestos, glass fiber	Asbestos or glass cloth	Fused rock, molten glass, liquid nitrogen	Helium, nitrogen, carbon dioxide, carbon monoxide, hydrogen, fluorine

369

cesses, from which (presumably) all possible macroprocesses can be logically synthesized. Microprocesses tend to be very material-specific; hence a good starting point is a taxonomic classification of materials as such. The following is offered as a tentative classification scheme, based on work that I have done previously.[4] Table 1 lists twenty-two distinct material forms, with examples of each. This classification scheme will serve as the basis for most of the following analysis. Table 2 shows a further breakdown into six types according to basic electrical and

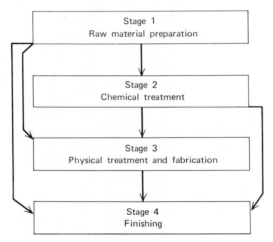

Figure 1   Generalized sequence of macroprocesses.

chemical properties. This breakdown applies separately to each component element of any composite material. It must be recalled that, although most microprocesses are applicable to only a small number of materials (as classified by either Table 1 or Table 2), a good many processes result in *changing* materials from one form or classification to another. For instance, the form of a material may be changed by heating, cooling, cutting, grinding, weaving, or dissolving.[5] Similarly, the

[4] R. U. Ayres, "A Materials-Process-Product Model," IRT-P-15/4 for the Resources for the Future Conference on Environmental Quality and the Social Sciences: Theoretical and Methodological Studies, June 16–18, 1970; to be published in book form by Johns Hopkins University Press, Spring 1971.

[5] *Ibid.*

electrochemical composition of a material—hence its electrochemical properties—may be altered by a variety of microprocesses involving for example, oxidation, electrolysis, decomposition, fermentation, or cooking.

The next step is to identify the various microprocesses and their allowable interrelationships. Figure 1 displays a generalized group of macroprocesses and indicates alternative sequences. Table 3 shows a fairly comprehensive taxonomy of elementary microprocesses which minimizes, although perhaps does not entirely eliminate, ambiguities and omissions. Experimental applications of this taxonomy to several industries (paper pulp, sugar beet refining, and wool reprocessing) have confirmed that actual macroprocesses can successfully be characterized as sequences of microprocesses from Table 3. A preliminary application to the iron and steel industry is presented in Figures 8–14 at the end of this chapter.

The next step is to articulate the permissible (or impermissible) sequences of microprocesses. This information can best be conveyed in two separate sets of relationships, those resulting from simple material forms, and those from composites. In the case of composite materials, in which each of the component elements may be transformed separately, a much larger number of hypothetical combinations is possible than for simple materials. Thus it appears to be convenient to focus initially on the six "simple" forms, treating the fourteen composite forms essentially as associations of two (or more) basic materials insofar as possible.

To determine which microprocesses can operate upon the various materials (specified by electrochemical classification and simple form) a matrix of materials versus microprocesses is drawn up, as in Table 4. Each checked element represents a material form upon which the specific microprocess can probably operate. For example, the matrix element represented by the row reading "M, Metal or alloy, M" (for mesh) and the column $P_{4.4}$ signifies that a metal mesh can be operated upon by processes involving mechanical joining, whereas the element defined by the same column ($P_{4.4}$) and the row "M, Metal or alloy, L" (for liquid) signifies that it is not possible to weave molten metal. However, some of the microprocesses from Table 3 can operate, not upon simple materials, but only upon composite ones.

Table 5 illustrates a matrix of possible composite materials which can be formed from the six basic electrochemical categories of materials, shown in Table 2, multiplied by the six basic material forms, shown in Table 1. For example, the matrix element represented by the column heading "Filament (M_5)" and the row reading "Granule (M_6)" represents a composite of filamentary insoluble organics and insoluble inor-

Table 3 Elementary Microprocesses

P_1 Transportation (solids or fluids)

    $P_{1.1}$ Vehicle, self–propelled (truck) (Solid or containerized fluid)
    $P_{1.2}$ Vehicle, passive (pallet; cable car, pneumatic tube, etc.) ''
    $P_{1.3}$ Conveyor belt ''
    $P_{1.4}$ Gravity flow (channel or pipe) (Fluid)
    $P_{1.5}$ Pressure flow (pump or pipe ''
    $P_{1.6}$ Convective flow ''
    $P_{1.7}$ Capillary flow ''

P_2 Change of Energy State (solid or fluid)

    $P_{2.1}$ Irradiation
    $P_{2.2}$ Electrification or magnetization
    $P_{2.3}$ Heating
        2.3.1 No change of phase
        2.3.2 Change of phase
    $P_{2.4}$ Refrigeration
        2.4.1 No change of phase
        2.4.2 Change of phase

P_3 Change in Physical Form (mainly solids)

    $P_{3.1}$ Pressure forming (or compression, for fluids)
    $P_{3.2}$ Extension or expansion (or evacuation, for gases)
    $P_{3.3}$ Torsion (twist)
    $P_{3.4}$ Shear (bend)
    $P_{3.5}$ Alignment of fibers or filaments (carding, comb)
    $P_{3.6}$ Winding of fibers or filaments (cone, quill, spool)
    $P_{3.7}$ Randomization of fibers or filaments (felting)

P_4 Physical Integration (solids or mesh)

    $P_{4.1}$ Fusion or sintering
    $P_{4.2}$ Adhesion
    $P_{4.3}$ Weaving of filaments (spinning, braiding, roving, etc.)
    $P_{4.4}$ Mechanical joining (sew, rivet, screw, bolt, nail, etc.)
    $P_{4.5}$ Implantation in a surrounding medium

Table 3 Elementary Microprocesses (*Continued*)

P$_5$ Physical Disintegration (solids or mesh)   ———————→O— — — — →

  P$_{5.1}$ Shock
      5.1.1   Mechanical impact (chopping, splitting, etc.)
      5.1.2   Explosive impact (blasting)
      5.1.3   Acoustic
  P$_{5.2}$ Tooth cutting (sawing, slicing, drilling, milling, etc.)
  P$_{5.3}$ Crushing
  P$_{5.4}$ Tearing or picking

P$_6$ Physical Association

  P$_{6.1}$ Mechanical stirring or blending
  P$_{6.2}$ Mixing by acoustic agitation
  P$_{6.3}$ Entrainment and suspension by moving fluid stream
  P$_{6.4}$ Solution
  P$_{6.5}$ Absorption
  P$_{6.6}$ Adsorption
  P$_{6.7}$ Electrostatic deposition
  P$_{6.8}$ Diffusion

P$_7$ Physical Dissociation or Separation

  P$_{7.1}$ Mechanical dismantling
  P$_{7.2}$ Sifting and sorting
  P$_{7.3}$ Filtration
  P$_{7.4}$ Centrifugal separation
  P$_{7.5}$ Flocculation/precipitation
  P$_{7.6}$ Settle/drain
  P$_{7.7}$ Crystallization
  P$_{7.8}$ Evaporation, melting or sublimation (see P$_{2.3.2}$ or P$_{3.2}$)
  P$_{7.9}$ Condensation or freezing (see P$_{2.4.3}$ of P$_{3.1}$)

P$_8$ Surface Treatment or Finishing (solids)

  P$_{8.1}$ Surface Removal
      P$_{8.1.1}$ Abrasion (grinding, polishing, sanding, napping, etc.)
      P$_{8.1.3.}$ Etching
      P$_{8.1.2.}$ Coating removal (pickling, sealing, bleaching, stripping)

Table 3 Elementary Microprocesses (*Continued*)

$P_{8.2}$ Surface non–additive treatment

   $P_{8.2.1.}$ Work hardening
   $P_{8.2.2}$ Heat treatment
   $P_{8.2.3.}$ Pressing

$P_{8.3}$ Surface additive treatment

   $P_{8.3.1.}$ Lubrication
   $P_{8.3.2.}$ Wetting or fulling (detergent, surfactant)
   $P_{8.3.3}$ Coating (paint, dye, was, shellac, oil polish, etc.)
   $P_{8.3.4.}$ Metal plating
   $P_{8.3.5.}$ Reactant coating (anodizing, passivating, nitriding, carbonizing, etc.)

P_9 Chemical Dissociation or Decomposition

   $P_{9.1}$ Thermal activation (e.g., thermal cracking, dehydration, etc.)
   $P_{9.2}$ Electrolytic (e.g., anode reactions)
   $P_{9.3}$ Catalytic intermediary (e.g., catalytic cracking)
   $P_{9.4}$ Hydrolysis (e.g., ions in solution)
   $P_{9.5}$ Photolysis
   $P_{9.6}$ Biological digestion (e.g., proteins → amino acids)

P_{10} Chemical association or snythesis

   $P_{10.1}$ Thermal activation (e.g., combustion)
   $P_{10.2}$ Electrolytic (e.g., cathode reactions)
   $P_{10.3}$ Catalytic intermediary (e.g., polymerization)
   $P_{10.4}$ Hydration
   $P_{10.5}$ Photochemical reaction (e.g., smog)
   $P_{10.6}$ Biological synthesis (e.g., amino acids → proteins)

P_{11} Isomerization

Table 4 Processes Applicable to Simple Material Forms

		P₂						P₃							P₄					P₅				P₈										P₉				P
		.1	.2	.3.1	.3.2	.4.1	.4.2	.1	.2	.3	.4	.5	.6	.7	.1	.2	.3	.4	.5	.1	.2	.3	.4	.1.1	.1.2	.2.1	.2.2	.2.3	.3.1	.3.2	.3.3	.3.4	.3.5	.1	.3	.5	.6	.1
M₁ Metal or alloy (conductor)	S	X	X	X	X	X		X	X	X	X				X	X		X	X	X	X						X		X	X	X	X	X					
	G	X	X	X	X	X		X	X	X	X	X	X	X	X	X		X	X	X	X						X		X	X	X	X	X					
	F	X	X	X	X	X		X	X	X	X				X	X		X	X	X	X						X		X									
	M	X	X	X	X	X	X			X	X	X	X	X	X	X	X	X	X	X	X	X	X															
	L	X					X				X	X	X	X	X	X		X	X			X	X															
M₂ Polar electrolytes soluble in H₂O	S	X	X	X	X	X									X	X	X	X	?	X		X	X											X	X	?		
	G	X	X	X	X	X									X	X	X	X	?	X		X	X											X	X	?		
	L	X		X	X	X	X			X										X		X	X															
	V		X	X	X	X	X													X		X	X															
M₃ Polar nonelectro-lytes soluble in H₂O	S	X	X	X	X	X		X	X	X	X	X	X	X	X	X		X	?	X	X	X	X											X	X	?	X	X
	G	X	X	X	X	X				X	X	X	X	X	X	X		X	?	X		X	X											X	X	?		
	L	X		X	X	X	X	X	X	X	X	X	X	X						X	X	X	X															
	V		X	X	X	X	X													X	X	X	X															
M₄ nonpolar compounds soluble in nonpolar	S	X	X	X	X	X		X	X	X	X	X	X	X	X	X		X	X	X	X	X	X			?	X	X	X	X	X	X	X	X	X		X	X
	G	X	X	X	X	X		X		X	X	X	X	X	X	X		X	X	X	X	X	X				X	X	X	X	X	X	X	X	X		X	X
	F	X	X	X	X	X				X	X	X	X	X	X	X		X	X	X	X	X	X				X	X	X	X	X	X	X					
	M	X	X	X	X	X	X	X	X	X	X	X	X	X	X	X	X	X	X	X	X	X	X				X	X	X	X	X	X	X					
	L	X		X	X	X	X			X	X	X	X	X	X	X		X	X	X	X	X	X											X	X		X	X
	V		X	X	X	X	X			X	X	X	X	X	X	X		X	X	X	X	X	X											X	X		X	X
M₅ insoluble organic	S	X	X	X	X	X		X	X	X	X	X	X	X	X	X		X	X	X	X	X	X			?	X	X	X	X	X	X	X	X	X		X	X
	G	X	X	X	X	X		X		X	X	X	X	X	X	X		X	X	X	X	X	X				X	X	X	X	X	X	X	X	X		X	X
	F	X	X	X	X	X				X	X	X	X	X	X	X		X	X	X	X	X	X				X	X	X	X	X	X	X					
	M	X	X	X	X	X	X	X	X	X	X	X	X	X	X	X	X	X	X	X	X	X	X				X	X	X	X	X	X	X					
	L	X		X	X	X	X			X	X	X	X	X	X	X		X	X	X	X	X	X											X	X		X	X
M₆ insoluble inor-ganic compounds	S	X	X	X	X	X		X	X	X	X	X	X	X	X	X		X	X	X	X	X	X			?	X	X	X	X	X	X	X	X	X		X	X (12)
	G	X	X	?	X	X		X		X	X	X	X	X	X	X		X	X	X	X	X	X				X	X	X	X	X	X	X	X	X		X	
	F	X	X	X	X	X				X	X	X	X	X	X	X		X	X	X	X	X	X				X	X	X	X	X	X	X					
	M	X	X	X	X	X	X	X	X	X	X	X	X	X	X	X	X	X	X	X	X	X	X				X	X	X	X	X	X	X					
	L	X		X	X	X	X			X	X	X	X	X	X	X		X	X	X	X	X	X											X	X		X	X
	V		X	X	X	X	X			X	X	X	X	X	X	X		X	X	X	X	X	X											X	X		X	X

375

Table 5 Possible Composite Materials

Solid						Granule						Filament				Mesh				Liquid						Vapor						
M_1	M_2	M_3	M_4	M_5	M_6	M_1	M_2	M_3	M_4	M_5	M_6	M_1	M_4	M_5	M_6	M_1	M_4	M_5	M_6	M_1	M_2	M_3	M_4	M_5	M_6	M_2	M_3	M_4	M_5	M_6		
			X	X	X											X											X			X	Solid	M_1
	X						X	X			X																				Solid	M_2
		X					X	X																							Solid	M_3
X			X	X	X	X			X	X	X	X	X	X	X	X	X	X	X		X	X		X	X		X		X	X	Solid	M_4
X			X	X	X	X			X	X	X	X	X	X	X	X	X	X	X		X	X	X	X	X		X	X	X	X	Solid	M_5
X			X	X	X	X					X	X			X	X	X		X		X	X	X	X	X		X	X	X	X	Solid	M_6
						X	X	X	X	X	X	X	X	X	X						X	X	X	X	X	?	X	X	X	X	Granule	M_1
						X	X	X	X	X	X	X	X	X	X						X	X	X	X	X			X	X	X	Granule	M_2
						X	X	X	X	X	X	X	X	X	X						X	X	X	X	X			X	X	X	Granule	M_3
						X	X	X	X	X	X	X	X	X	X						X	X		X	X	X	X		X	X	Granule	M_4
						X	X	X	X	X	X	X	X	X	X						X	X	X	X	X	X	X	X	X	X	Granule	M_5
						X	X	X	X	X	X	X	X	X	X					X	X	X	X	X	X	X	X	X	X	X	Granule	M_6
						X	X	X	X	X	X	X	X	X	X														X		Filament	M_1
						X	X	X	X	X	X	X	X	X	X																Filament	M_4
						X	X	X	X	X	X	X	X	X	X								X								Filament	M_5
						X	X	X	X	X	X	X	X	X	X																Filament	M_6
						X			X	X	X										X	X	X	X	X		X	X	X	X	Mesh	M_1
						X			X	X	X										X	X		X	X	X	X		X	X	Mesh	M_4
						X			X	X	X										X	X	X	X	X	X	X	X	X	X	Mesh	M_5
						X			X	X	X										X	X	X	X	X	X	X	X	X	X	Mesh	M_6
											X				X					X					X					X	Liquid	M_1
						X			X	X	X	X	X	X	X						X	X	X	X		X	X	X	X	X	Liquid	M_2
						X			X	X	X	X	X	X	X						X	X	X	X		X	X	X	X	X	Liquid	M_3
						X	X	X		X	X	X		X	X						X	X	X	X		X	X	X	X	X	Liquid	M_4
						X	X	X	X	X	X	X	X	X	X						X	X	X	X		X	X	X	X	X	Liquid	M_5
						X	X	X	X	X	X	X		X	X					X					X	X	X	X	X	X	Liquid	M_6
						?		?	X	X	X		X	X	X						X	X	X	X	X	X	X	X	X	X	Vapor	M_2
						X			X	X	X	X	X	X	X						X	X	X	X	X	X	X	X	X	X	Vapor	M_3
						X	X	X		X	X	X		X	X						X	X	X	X	X	X	X	X			Vapor	M_4
						X	X	X	X	X	X	X	X	X	X						X	X	X	X	X	X	X	X	X	X	Vapor	M_5
						X	X	X	X	X	X	X	X	X	X						X	X	X	X	X	X	X	X	X	X	Vapor	M_6

Table 6 Processes Affecting Composite Materials

	P6								P7									P8	P9		P10					
	.1	.2	.3	.4	.5	.6	.7	.8	.1	.2	.3	.4	.5	.6	.7	.8	.9	.1.3	.2	.4	.1	.2	.3	.4	.5	.6
S-S									X									X								
G-S							X									X					X					
F-S																X					X					
M-S									X							X					X					
L-S					X	X	X							X		X			X		X	X	X	X		
V-S					X	X	X									X	X		X		X	X	X	X		
G-G	X	X								X		X				X					X					
F-G = G-F	X	X								X		?				X					X					
L-G		X			X	X	X							X		X			X		X	X	X	X		
V-G		X			X	X	X									X			X		X	X	X	X		
F-F	X	X								X		X				X					X					
G-M												X				X			X		X		X	X		
L-M						X						X		X		X			X		X	X	X	X		
V-M						X										X	X		X		X	X	X			
G-L*	X	X	X	X				X		X	X	X	X	X	X*	X			X	X	X	X	X	X	X	X
F-L	X	X	X	X						X	X	X	X	X		X			X		X	X	X	X	X	X
L-L	X	X	X	X				X				X		X		X					X					
V-L		X	X	X										X			X				X			?	X	
G-V		X	X					X			X	X		X			X		X		X	X		X	X	
F-V		X	X								X	X		X			X		X		X	X	X	X	X	
L-V		X										X		X			X				X		X	X	X	
V-V								X									X				X			X	X	

* (Includes solutions.) By convention, a solution of polar or nonpolar solid material in a liquid is classed as a granule-liquid (G-L) composite (rather than a solid-liquid or filament-liquid, etc.).

377

ganic granules, such as dirty raw sheep's wool. A possible combination of this type is denoted by X, where the row and columns are interchangeable. As another example, the matrix element represented by the column "Vapor (M_6)" and the row "Liquid (M_5)" represents a composite of insoluble inorganic vapor and insoluble organic liquid. In this case, it is taken to be a vapor-in-liquid (V-L) composite or foam (e.g., beaten egg white). Here, however, the row and the column are not interchange-

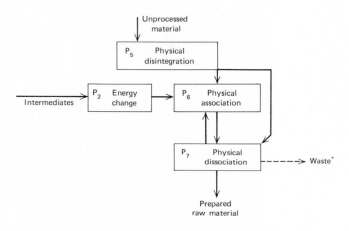

* Waste streams are generally associated with P_7 (physical dissociation) processes simply because the waste must be separated from the usable materials by such a process. Losses can occur, of course, at any point in the system.

Figure 2   Stage 1 flow diagram: raw material preparation.

able; the L-V composite evidently describes an aerosol rather than a foam.

The possible composites can then be listed in columns in a matrix of composites versus processes. This can be completed, as in Table 6, by identifying the microprocesses which can operate upon these composite materials.

The second set of determinative relationships defines characteristic *subsequences* of microprocesses. In Figure 1 four basic macroprocesses in a generalized industry are illustrated:

Stage 1: Raw material preparation
          (mining, harvesting and crude physical separation)

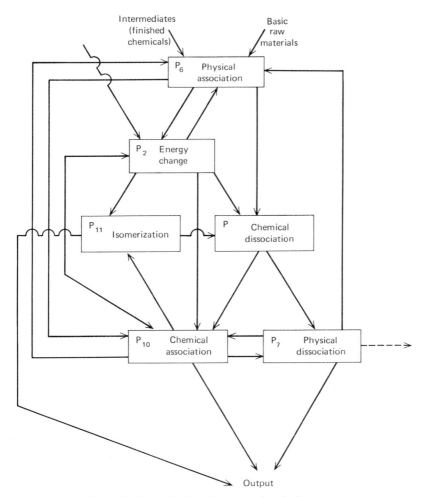

Figure 3   Stage 2 flow diagram: chemical treatment.

Stage 2: Chemical treatment
Stage 3: Physical treatment and fabrication
Stage 4: Finishing

Of course, either stage 2 or stage 3 (or both) may be omitted in some cases, as indicated by the generalized flow diagram.

Each of these stages may be analyzed separately to elucidate the various possible paths. We note that transportation processes (P_1) may (and do) occur at virtually any point in a sequence. These processes can put constraints on the processes which follow because of the nature of the transportation medium. The cost of the process is also dependent

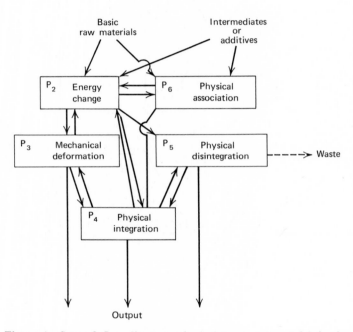

Figure 4   Stage 3 flow diagram: physical treatment and fabrication.

on the transportation medium, because of possible losses of material, speed of transportation and possible need for cleaning the materials: these costs will be taken into account in the sensitivity analysis to be performed on the matrices. Four basic processes can occur in Stage 1:

P_2 Energy input
P_5 Physical disintegration
P_6 Physical association
P_7 Physical dissociation

Of course P_6 may involve the use of intermediate materials (other than the raw material in question), such as water, explosives, detergents, or chemicals. Prior processing, such as purification, deionization, or heating, is often necessary; however (with the exception of energy inputs), such treatment is characterized as chemical treatment or "finishing" for the chemical intermediate in question. Thus Stage 1 can be analyzed

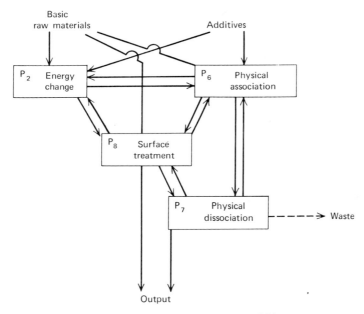

Figure 5   Stage 4 flow diagram: finishing.

in terms of the flow diagram shown in Figure 2. The P_6 step can be skipped; alternatively, the P_6–P_7 loop can be cycled several times with the same, or different, chemical intermediates. Examples of this sort of loop would be successive washings of wool or coal. Figures 3–5 show the basic flows in the other stages of processing. All of these relationships can be expressed in matrix form, as indicated in Table 7.

Examples of the flows of macroprocesses in the iron and steel industry are given in Figures 8–14 at the end of the chapter. Many different combinations of the processes, as well as different configurations of the pro-

Table 7   Relationships Between Basic Flows Through the Processes

						Output					
Input	P_1	P_2	P_3	P_4	P_5	P_6	P_7	P_8	P_9	P_{10}	P_{11}
P_1		③④			①	② ③④		④			
P_2			③	③	① ③	③④		④	②	②	②
P_3	③	③	③								
P_4	③	③	③		③						
P_5	③			③		①	①				
P_6		② ③④		③			① ④	④	②	②	
P_7	①② ④					①② ④		④		②	
P_8	④	④				④	④				
P_9		②				②					
P_{10}		②				②	②				②
P_{11}		②							②		

cesses themselves, have been shown, but an attempt has been made, for purposes of the example, to keep the processes as basic as possible. In some cases, information of the nature required was not available; the greatest level of detail is shown for the iron-making blast furnace process. It is hoped that such information may be obtained also for the subsequent processes.

In Table 7 the symbol ① in the i–jth matrix element signifies that the sequence $P_i \rightarrow P_j$ is likely to occur in Stage 1. This possible sequence

Table 8 Costs Involved in Woolen Industry

| Process | Form of Matter | Fixed Cost per Unit Capacity | | Variable Cost per Unit Capacity | | Energy Cost per Unit Output | | Material Loss in Process, % |
		Total Cost $/lb dww	Cost of Hot Water $/lb dww	Total Cost $/lb dww	Cost of Hot Water $/lb dww	Btu, $/lb dww	kWh, $/lb dww	
Fulling	M,L	0.004 (a)		0.041 (a)			0.0016 (a)	1 (a)
		0.007 (c)		0.041 (c)			0.0016 (c)	1 (c)
Scouring	M,L	0.002 (a)	0.001 (a)	0.048 (a)	0.0140 (a)		0.0006 (a)	Neg. (a)
			0.0006 (b)		0.0083 (b)	0.0089 (b)		
		0.005 (c)	0.0022 (c)	0.048 (c)	0.0135 (c)	0.0155 (c)	0.0006 (c)	Neg. (c)
			0.0014 (d)		0.0083 (d)	0.0097 (d)		
Stripping	M,L	0.003 (a)	0.0004 (a)	0.029 (a)	0.0060 (a)		0.0003 (a)	Neg. (a)
			0.00013 (b)		0.0023 (b)	0.0024 (b)		
		0.008 (c)	0.0008 (c)	0.027 (c)	0.0064 (c)	0.0072 (c)	0.0003 (c)	Neg. (c)
			0.0006 (d)		0.0023 (d)	0.0029 (d)		
Dyeing	M,L	0.004 (a)	0.0002 (a)	0.107 (a)	0.0030 (a)		0.0003 (a)	Neg. (a)
			0.0001 (b)		0.0017 (b)	0.0018 (b)		
		0.007 (c)	0.0004 (c)	0.107 (c)	0.0027 (c)	0.003 (c)	0.0003 (c)	Neg. (c)
			0.0003 (d)		0.0017 (d)	0.0020 (d)		

Note. Flow through processes in plants is based on pounds of dry wool weight (dww), where:
(a) Plant is as it exists currently (equipment totally depreciated) with existing liquid flow rate.
(b) Plant as above, with liquid flow rate half of present level.
(c) Plant with equipment replaced at current prices, existing flow rate.
(d) Plant as above, half of present flow rate.

is represented by an arrow between P_i and P_j on the flow chart for Stage 1 (Figure 2). Actually, Figures 2–5 should specify processes at the two or three-digit level of disaggregation shown in Table 3, and Table 7 should be similarly expanded to accommodate the finer grain.

ECONOMIC ANALYSIS

This phase of the analysis comprises identifying and characterizing actual microprocesses (applicable to a particular industry) to determine relevant fixed and variable costs and efficiencies as functions of material throughput. Ultimately, the microprocesses are listed, together with pertinent data, as shown in Table 8, which describes the cost of processes involved in the woolen industry.[6] Note that these costs and performance indices correspond to current, existing technology. For each macroprocess, that is, each allowable sequence of microprocesses, the overall costs,

[6] *Ibid.*

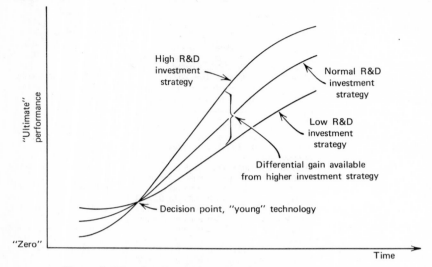

Figure 6 Development versus time for a "young" technology.

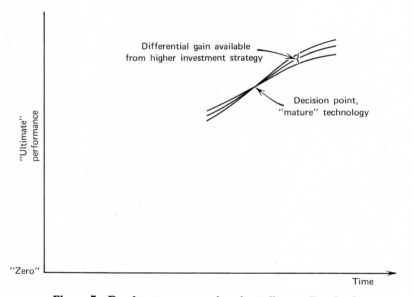

Figure 7 Development versus time for a "mature" technology.

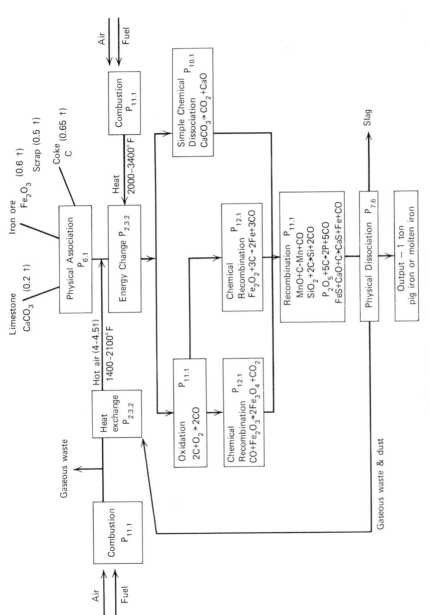

Figure 8 Iron making—blast furnace.

385

materials inputs and outputs, and residuals can all be calculated, also by computer, and the best alternative selected according to any pertinent criteria, for example, to minimize direct (internal) cost or some combination of internal and external costs.

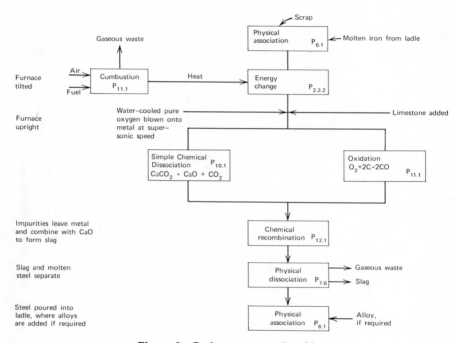

Figure 9   Basic oxygen steel making.

In principle every industry (at least, every firm) should have carried out some such optimization as this in designing its production facilities. In practice, very few firms have actually done so—partly because of lack of sophistication regarding the intricacies of computer simulation. It would not be surprising, therefore, to discover that existing macroprocesses can be improved upon considerably, even, in some cases, *without* the introduction of new technology.

TECHNOLOGICAL SENSITIVITY ANALYSIS

As noted earlier, there are two components of this analysis. The first is an assessment of the cost effectiveness of research as related to the improvement of specific microprocesses. There is no direct way of evaluating the probable effectiveness of a research effort. However, a phenomenological model is available to describe the capabilities of any well-defined technology as a function of time. On the assumption that

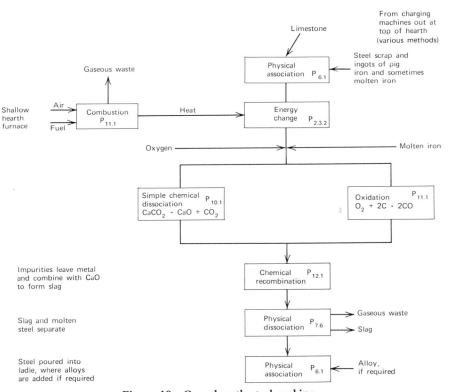

Figure 10   Open-hearth steel making.

there exists an initial point, which can be equated to zero on some scale, and an ultimate point corresponding to the achievement of whatever natural limit is applicable to the technology in question, development versus time generally resembles the so-called S-shaped or logistic curve illustrated in Figure 6.

Note that the development process can be speeded up or slowed down relative to the normal rate of progress, but the initial and ultimate points remain the same and the *shape* of the curve also is generally unchanged. Given that this phenomenological model is reasonably valid, the crucial questions are (*a*) *where* on the curve are we now, and (*b*) *which* curve are we on? If the existing technology is somewhere in the lower half of the chart, the upward trend of the technology growth curve is accelerating, and the gap between low-investment and high-investment curves in increasing. Thus any incremental investment in

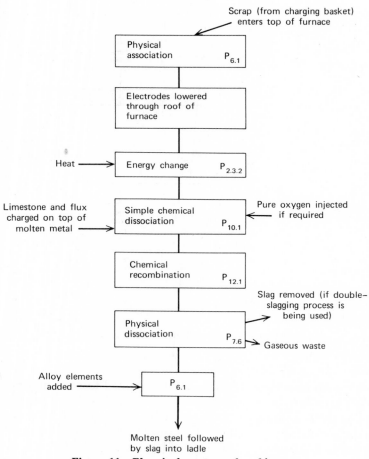

Figure 11   Electric furnace steel making.

research at this stage has a relatively high potential payoff, since it moves the technology toward the steepest part of its growth curve. By contrast, when the technology begins to mature, that is, to approach its ultimate limiting capability, the differential gains available from a higher level of investment in R&D are considerably reduced, as Figure 7 shows.

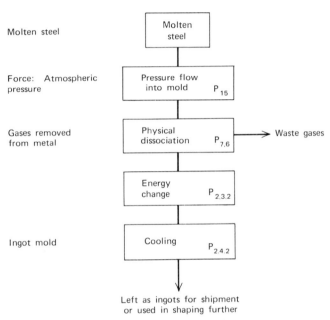

Figure 12   Vacuum degassing.

The development of a set of growth curves for each microprocess technology would be a major undertaking. It appears to be feasible, however, and much work of this type has already been done, particularly by the U.S. Naval Material Command.[7] I believe that a family of twenty to thirty curves of this type, corresponding to each of the major microprocesses in, say, the iron and steel industry could be assembled with

[7] Marvin Cetron et al., "Proposal for a Navy Technological Forecast," Parts I and II, May 1966 (AD 659-199 and AD 659-200).

reasonable effort from information now (or shortly to become) available from a variety of sources. Equating the differential gain in performance for a higher investment level (Figures 6 and 7) with the desired cost-effectiveness index completes the data base needed to carry out the final step in the sensitivity analysis.

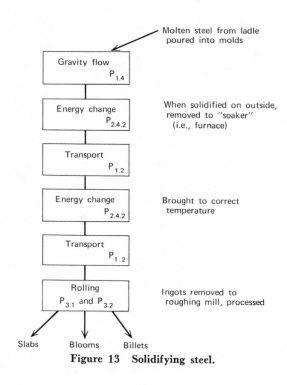

Figure 13   Solidifying steel.

The completed analytical tool is a generalized LP-type materials-flow simulation model of the industry in question. As already noted, such models now exist for some processing activities—if not whole industries—inasmuch as they are useful for other purposes. A computer model designed for the task of determining the altered materials-flow patterns required by various microprocess innovations, to permit the computation of macroprocess cost and efficiency, should ultimately be built. In the shorter term, however, *ad hoc* methods should be sufficient to provide evidence of the utility of the overall analysis described here for the

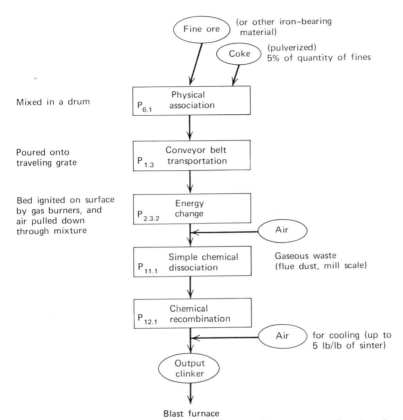

Figure 14 Sintering, the process used to convert fine ores or other iron-bearing materials into "lump" form for use in a blast furnace.

purpose of upgrading R&D resource allocation in an opportunity-oriented environment.

PRELIMINARY APPLICATION OF MODEL

Figures 8-14 illustrate the preliminary application of the model to the iron and steel industry.

XXII.   *A Potpourri of Planning*[1]

PAUL POLISHUK

A good idea that is not shared with others will gradually fade away and bear no fruit, but when it is shared it lives forever because it is passed on from one person to another and grows as it goes.   Lowell Fillmore

INTRODUCTION

Contemporary thought concerning long-range planning (LRP) manifests itself in the literature of the period and in the practices and policies of business organizations. The thinking of various organizations on long-range planning is reflected in how they are organized for it, how they were motivated in effecting it, and what approaches have been taken in establishing and operating a LRP endeavor. This chapter examines the results of a survey made on LRP in the U.S. aerospace industry. Responses to the questionnaire are analyzed so as to develop the evolving framework of the philosophy within contemporary times. The questionnaire, as developed by David Cleland,[2] sought to identify certain factors, forces, and effects which have been influential in the contemporary philosophy of LRP in the aerospace industry. The data presented herein

---

[1] This chapter is taken from U.S. Air Force Report FDP-MM-70-6, entitled "Long Range Planning in the Aerospace Industry," by Paul Polishuk, Air Force Flight Dynamics Laboratory, first published in December 1969 and revised in May 1970.
[2] David I. Cleland, "Long-Range Planning in the Aerospace Industry," Ph.D. thesis at Ohio State University.

have been organized around the framework originally developed by Cleland:

1. Factors motivating and influencing the development of long-range planning.
2. The determination of how far ahead to plan.
3. Organizational and procedural arrangements for long-range planning.
4. The accomplishment of long-range planning.

NATURE AND SCOPE OF THE SURVEY

Since the subject of LRP in the U.S. aerospace industry is relatively new and is not well reported in existing literature, an extensive survey questionnaire was used to obtain data from a representative number of companies in the aerospace business. Table 1 summarizes the number and type of organizations contacted in this study, together with the studies of Cleland and the *National Industrial Conference Board* (NICB) *Business Record.* In all, approximately 260 questionnaires were sent to various segments of the aerospace industry. Of the 117 replies received, 11 produced no information. Only 6 of these respondents said that they did no formal LRP; the reasons given were as follows:

1. Current plans are limited to product planning and relatively short-term programs.

Table 1   Comparison of Results of Three Studies on Long-Range Planning

Type of Company	No. of Questionnaires Distributed	No. of Responses to Questionnaires	Doing LRP? Yes	No	No. of Companies Responding but Not Contributing	Percentage of Respondents Doing LRP
Industrials	150	61	55	3	3	90
Merchandising	15	8	6		2	75
Utilities	15	7	7			100
Commercial banks	15	6	5	1		83
Life insurance companies	15	5	2	3		40
Transportation (Cleland)	15	4	4			100
	225	91	79	7	5	Av. 86.4%
Manufacturing (Conference Board Record Study)		165				90
Aerospace (This study)	250	122	106	5	11	95

2. No formal techniques exist.
3. Long-range planning is handled by the top management on a very informal basis.
4. There is preoccupation with day-to-day problems of the business; no time is available to commit plans to writing.
5. It is easier to hire outside consultants.

The other 5 respondents in this category indicated that they were doing LRP but declined to submit completed questionnaires for the following reasons:

1. Company procedures do not allow the release of information regarding the specific techniques used.
2. The business is mostly commercial, and the type of planning is not applicable to the technological planning of the aerospace industry.
3. A long-range planning function was only recently established.
4. The process is too complicated to represent properly by a questionnaire, no matter how comprehensive.

It should be pointed out from the outset that no claim is made for statistical exactness of the data. In some cases, companies failed to respond, or multiple responses by one company to a specific question created a pattern of answers more or less than the total number of companies doing LRP. Statistical analysis of these data has not been done in this chapter but is planned in subsequent reports. In spite of the lack of statistical data analysis, however, it has been possible to obtain an indication of the general trend of LRP in the companies surveyed.

As can be seen from Table 1, this study indicates that approximately 95% of the aerospace firms surveyed did some form of formal LRP. This is to be compared with an average of 86.4% from Cleland's study of industrial, merchandising, utilities, commercial banking, life insurance, and transportation companies and the NICB's results of greater than 90%. Although such comparisons may not be valid since Cleland's data were published in 1962 and those of the NICB in 1966, they serve to indicate the general acceptance of the need for LRP in American Industry. Both this study and that of Cleland indicate that the number of firms doing LRP varies with the industry.

In this survey, responding companies were asked to submit unclassified copies of company regulations, standard operating procedures, literature, organizational charts, policy instruments, and any such related publications that were used directly in their LRP activities. Although a large

number replied that this type of company documentation was proprietary, several firms submitted material. No attempt was made in this
study to review these documents in detail. One interesting reply pointed
out the following:

> The corporate objectives of growth and financial performance were set forty
> years ago by the chief executive officer. These objectives have remained constant
> and are well communicated to the entire organization through annual reviews
> of each decision by the corporate officer body (management committee).

EXTENT OF LONG-RANGE PLANNING
IN THE AEROSPACE INDUSTRY

Table 2 is a comparison of the results of this survey and those of
Cleland's study in regard to growth and contraction plans. In this table
and the following ones, P = Polishuk (this survey), C = Cleland. Table
2 shows that in both studies a significant majority of the companies
engaged in LRP report the development of contraction as well as growth
plans.

In effecting LRP, a business corporation has several alternatives concerning the development of specific plans or just one best long-range
plan for the corporation. Table 3 indicates the results from the aerospace
industry in regard to the creation of alternative plans versus one best
long-range plan. As can be seen from this table, the majority of the
businesses create alternative long-range plans as opposed to the formula-

Table 2   Analysis of Companies Reporting
Growth and Contraction Plans

Type of Company	Growth and Contraction Plans		Growth Plans Only	
	C	P	C	P
Industrials	47 (85%)		8	17
Utilities	4		3	
Merchandising	2		4	
Commercial banks	4		1	
Transportation	4		0	
Life insurance	2		0	
Totals	63	88 (84%)	16	17

tion of just one best plan. However, a significant number endeavor to establish just one best long-range plan. A number reported that they sometimes submit supplementary plans, consider alternative plans before adopting a final plan, or have back-up plans and planning options to the base-line plan.

Table 3   Companies Reporting Creation of Alternative versus One Best Long-Range Plan

Type of Company	Alternative Plans		One Best LRP	
	C	P	C	P
Industrials	37	64 (67%)	18	32
Utilities	5		2	
Merchandising	3		3	
Commercial banks	3		2	
Transportation	3		1	
Life insurance	2		0	
Totals	53	64 (67%)	26	32

Table 4   Companies Reporting on Continuous or Intermittent Frequency of Long-Range Planning

Type of Company	Continuous		Intermittent	
	C	P	C	P
Industrial	42		15	25
Utilities	5		3	
Merchandising	2		4	
Commercial banks	2		3	
Transportation	3		1	
Life insurance	2		0	
Totals	56	80 (76%)	26	25

Long-range planning is a continuous effort in the majority of the companies responding. Table 4 reflects whether the respondents effect LRP on a continuous or an intermittent basis. As a continuous effort the activity is presumably performed by a full-time staff specifically appointed for the LRP corporate effort. Long-range planning, in its infancy, was probably performed on an intermittent basis, as executives had other immediate tasks, such as planning, organizing, and controlling the day-to-day operational activities. As more time was given to future factors, however, special staffs were appointed and LRP as a formal activity came to be conducted on a continual basis.

DERIVATION OF LONG-RANGE PLANNING NEED

In the questionnaire, the respondents were requested to indicate why they had initiated long-range planning efforts. These answers have been categorized as to *internal* and *external factors*. Where possible, similar answers have been grouped together in an attempt to quantify the data.

Internal Factors

Internal company conditions necessitating the development of a LRP activity are varied and complex. No attempt was made to group these replies. The following are frequent internal causes:

Resource allocation
Need for company growth
Need for diversification of product or customer line
Profit improvement
Coordination of diverse operation
Increased business complexity
Rapid growth of company
Good management practice
Business survival
Decentralization of operations
High technology content, long product life-cycles
Need to promote management development
Future visibility
Financial requirements
Internal integration
Facilities and manpower requirements

External Factors

External factors and forces of a national, international, and competitive nature which motivated the development of LRP are many and varied. The major external factor seems to be, by far, increased competitive activity. Other factors of lesser importance include:

Large systems business
Long-range planning activity needed to compete

Fluctuations of customer budget or requirements
Change of growth of market
Short lifetime of product due to rapid technological advances
Long lead nature of market

It is interesting to note the realization that, in order to compete, LRP is a necessity.

Changes in policy on the part of the research establishment have required defense contractors to assume a greater responsibility for financing their own working capital and their long-range capital investments in research facilities and company-initiated R&D activities. These external factors have pointed up the need for a more systematic study of long-term trends in the defense business and for better tools for selecting among long-term investment opportunities.

From the small number of replies (6) indicating that companies were not doing formal LRP, it is difficult to draw any conclusions with regard to the reasons. Those that reported no formal LRP effort were either preoccupied with operational or short-term problems, were small in size, or did their planning on an *ad hoc* basis. There are many external reasons why it might be rational not to do formal LRP in the aerospace industry (e.g., volatility of the market, uncertainty of future business trends, and influence of significant and unpredictable national and international events); however, none of these was reported. Moreover, although the literature is replete with articles on LRP, few contain case histories of successes or failures, especially in the aerospace industry.

A classic example of apparently unproductive LRP can be found in the airline industry. A number of years ago, several international airlines placed orders for jet transports, based on an anticipated number of future air passengers determined through LRP decisions. Today, many of the new aircraft are flying with passenger loads well under capacity. On the other hand, although these companies sustained losses because of the failure of their long-range plans to materialize as envisioned, the losses might have been relatively greater if no LRP had been effected. This case points up the difficulty in measuring the productivity of LRP.

ESTABLISHMENT OF THE LONG-RANGE PLANNING EFFORT

Time of Initiation

The answers to the question regarding the year in which "somewhat *formal* LRP" was initiated are tabulated in Table 5. The data indicate that LRP is a relatively new formal management function, with the

Table 5   Year in Which Somewhat Formal LRP Activities Was Initiated

1900	1	1953	1	1961	10
1940	1	1954	1	1962	11
1951	1	1955	4	1963	4
1945	1	1956	2	1964	7
1948	1	1957	2	1965	6
1950	4	1958	5	1966	8
1951	3	1959	1	1967	3
1952	3	1960	8	1968	4

largest number of respondents initiating it within the last 10 years. These results agree with those of Cleland, which indicate that the majority of respondents started LRP between 1950 and 1961, supporting the claim in management literature that LRP is a post-World War II phenomenon.

Methods Used to Establish Initial Effort

The establishment of LRP effort is approached in a variety of ways. Table 6 lists the methods reported in this survey and that of Cleland. Many of the organizations reported one, two, or three of the methods listed. As may be noted, major dependence was placed on the creative ability of company personnel. The study of methods used by other companies and research in the current periodical and book literature also play significant parts in establishing the initial effort.

Methods Used in Gaining Support for Long-Range Planning

Concurrently with the task of setting up the LRP effort, businesses have concerned themselves with changing the attitude of middle and

Table 6   Method Used to Establish Initial LRP Effort

Method	P	C
Depended on creative ability of company demand	92	73
Studied other companies' methods	62	49
Studied current periodical and book literature	67	49
Sought help from management consultants	29	22
Sought help from universities and colleges	10	14
Sought help from government agencies	8	6

Table 7   Methods Used by Companies to Gain
Middle and Lower Management Support for
Long-Range Planning

Method	P	C
Used executive persuasion	59	48
Published suitable policy instruments	67	33
Conducted seminars in LRP	37	25
Provided formal instruction in LRP for executive personnel	39	9

lower management to appreciate and support the evolving philosophy of LRP. The methods used are listed in Table 7.

Although planning is considered an integral part of management, the support of middle and lower management must be gained by the planning organization either by persuasion or through a more formal method, such as the publication of suitable policy instruments. A formal method of enlisting executive support is required, as shown by both surveys. This study indicated a greater reliance on suitable published policy instruments than did Cleland's. Although formal instruction was rated as the method least used for gaining acceptance for LRP in Cleland's study, a finding which he attributed to the newness of the concept and the lack of qualified people to provide the necessary instruction, this study indicated a strong application of this method.

Experience indicates that successful LRP requires support and participation at all levels. Without this support, the implementation of any LRP effort is extremely difficult, if not impossible, and those who must supply many of the input data for the plan will be uncooperative unless properly conditioned. All this emphasizes the need, as indicated in the surveys, for participation, from classroom attendance to actual engagement, in the LRP activities, either in a seminar or through executive contact.

TIME ELEMENTS OF LONG-RANGE PLANNING

Long- and short-range planning, although somewhat similar in technique, differ in application and time dimensions. Short-range planning usually involves planning within a year's time frame a definite program for implementation. Ordinarily the resources are fixed and well defined, and the program is laid out. Long-range planning, on the other hand, involves a prognostication into the future, based on past performance and on projections or other indications of the future. It is usually performed for time periods greater than one year and may extend as far as 50 years, depending on the industry. The further one looks into the future, of course, the more uncertain things become. In some organizations short- and long-range plans are considered together in one overall plan, with the first year of the plan constituting the short-range plan.

Determining How Far Ahead to Plan

The determination of how far into the future to plan is a complex function of the industry, market demand, availability of resources, lead time involved in product life cycle, product obsolescence, and specific objectives of the company. Whenever one talks of "how far corporations plan ahead," it is necessary to clarify whether overall corporate long-range plans, functional long-range plans, or financial, facility, raw materials, etc., plans are being discussed.

The length of the future period for which plans should be made is one of the most important factors of long-range planning. A company should plan ahead as far as is useful, but only as far as it is possible to proceed with reasonable accuracy. Table 8 indicates the periods of overall corporate long-range planning reported.

Most of the contemporary literature cites 5 years as the common overall long-range planning period. The results of this survey bear this out, with the majority reporting over 5 years, and small but significant numbers over 3 and 10 years.

Table 8   Overall Corporate LRP Period

Period, years	P	C
Over 1	3	7
Over 3	18	14
Over 5	78	45
Over 10	14	21
Over 20	5	3
Over 30	1	0
Over 50	0	2

Table 9   Factors Determining Length of Period for Which Corporations Plan Ahead

Factor	P	C
Market development time	67	58
Product development time	83	43
Facilities constructions time	32	37
Availability of accurate data	48	31
Payoff time for capital investment	37	27
Capital acquisition time	19	21
Raw materials availability	6	12
Research and development	66	...

Factors Determining the Length of the Long-Range Planning Period

The factors determining the length of the LRP period are shown in Table 9. In many of the replies several of the factors listed in the table were checked, accounting for the large number of responses. In comparison to Cleland's survey, product development time was more important in this survey than market development time. In both studies, availability of raw materials and capital acquisition cost played relatively minor roles. As might be expected in the aerospace industry, R&D is of major significance.

Extension or Contraction of Planning Period

Most of the companies reported that either the present planning period was adequate or an extension was contemplated; the results are tabulated in Table 10. The reasons for these responses are many and varied and have been listed in other sections of this study. In general, they include long development cycles for new products, as well as increasingly heavy company commitments in capital and in research undertakings. Longer

Table 10   Suitability of Planning Period

	P	C
Present period suitable	73	59
Will extend	27	15
Will contract	1	0

planning periods will result from better market intelligence, improved forecasting techniques, and the development of other long-range planning techniques.

Planning Area Period Determinants

The planning periods reported for the various functional and other areas of LRP reflect the fact that significantly different time periods are used for planning in the same functional areas within the same industry. Table 11 reflects the planning period for each functional area. In general, long-range planning in functional and other areas is carried out mostly for periods of 5 and 10 years, although considerable numbers report planning for 2 and 3 years. Relatively few companies indicated planning periods of 4, 6, 7, 8, or 9 years. These results corroborate the results of Cleland's survey with respect to industrial firms.

ORGANIZATIONAL AND PROCEDURAL ARRANGEMENTS FOR LONG-RANGE PLANNING

As planning gains greater and greater importance as a management tool, the organizational structure is changed to reflect the new function. This section is devoted to reporting how the present aerospace companies have been structured to perform the planning function.

Initial Organizational Structure for Long-Range Planning

Most of the reporting companies established a specific organizational function for LRP after World War II, particularly during the period between 1950 and the present. Table 5 listed the years in which participating companies established specific organizational entities for LRP. The fact that most companies consider LRP as a top-level management function is indicated by an analysis of the organizational levels to which the individuals in charge of LRP are assigned, as shown in Table 12. The high-level organizational status of LRP is further substantiated by a listing of the titles of respondents to this study.

Before a formal long-range planning function was established, the function was performed by various individuals and groups. *Ad hoc* groups, executive committees, coordinating committees, and product planning offices are a few of the alternatives mentioned. Table 13 reflects

Table 11   Planning Periods by Functional Areas

Area	Period of Planning, Years										
	1	2	3	4	5	6	7	10	15	20	25
Product research and development	5	8	7	1	38	...	2	16	2	1	...
Product costing	18	9	10	...	21	...	...	6	1	1	...
Facilities	6	6	10	1	44	...	1	8	1	...	...
Manufacturing/production	15	10	12	...	29	...	...	7	1	...	...
Finance	6	5	12	...	41	1	1	6	1	1	...
Credit	11	7	10	...	17	...	...	2	...	1	...
Marketing	6	8	8	...	45	1	...	9	2	1	...
Organizational structure	18	9	9	...	24	...	...	3	...	...	...
Executive development	7	10	9	...	24	...	...	4	1	...	...
Industrial relations	10	7	14	...	16	...	...	4	1	...	...
Personnel	15	7	9	...	21	...	1	7	2	...	...
Policy formulation	11	5	5	...	28	...	...	2	...	...	...
Public relations	12	10	8	...	15	...	...	2	1	...	...
Sources of raw materials	17	5	3	...	16	...	−5	5	...	...	...
Sources of supplies	18	6	5	...	9	...	...	5	...	...	...
Subcontracting	17	10	4	...	18	...	...	4	...	...	...
Product distribution	10	4	6	...	25	...	...	4	2	...	...
	1	2	...	...	5	...	...	...	...	1	...
Product engineering	9	8	10	...	32	...	...	7	2	...	...
Real estate	6	6	5	...	27	...	1	9	...	1	1
Manufacturing methods and processes	9	8	12	...	24	...	...	5	1	...	...
Product competition	5	8	9	...	37	...	...	8	1	...	...
	1	1	1	...	3	...	...	...	...	1	...
"Size Planning," that is, developing long-term objectives as to how large the business should be	3	1	1	...	44	...	...	15	1	2	...

these findings. The majority of the responses indicate that the president, vice president, other top officers, or marketing sales manager performed the LRP, perhaps with the help of the functional departments. The results of this study differ from Cleland's in that here the marketing sales manager played an important role in LRP before a formal organization was set up. Both studies show that, contrary to the contemporary literature, the financial officer has not engaged in LRP to a significantly greater extent than other executive personnel. In summary, before a formal organization was set up, LRP was still a high-level function.

Table 12 Organizational Assignment Level of Individual in Charge of Long-Range Planning

Organizational Level	P	C
Vice president	29	37
Controller		8
Staff assistant to president		5
President	2	5
Chairman of the board	2	4
Department head		4
General manager	9	3
Treasurer		3
Reports to president	13	2
Assistant general manager		2
Staff assistant to vice president	6	
Top management staff	16	

Table 13 Organizational Element Performing Long-Range Planning before Appointment of Specific Entity for This Purpose

Element	P	C
President or executive vice president	52	47
Other top officer personnel	39	31
Board of directors	13	15
Financial officer	19	15
Marketing sales manager	38	13
Additional duty of key officer	8	11
Other	17	

Present Organizational Structure for Long-Range Planning

With the increasing trend to LRP, separate organizational entities have been set up to carry out this function. As was pointed out in the previous section, such an entity is usually at a high level of the organization. Table 14 gives the results of the question concerning the present organizational structure used to accomplish LRP.

Table 14   Present Organizational Structure
Used to Accomplish Long-Range Planning

Structure	P	C
Assigned as specific responsibility to a major functional area of effort	39	30
Long-range planning office per se	47	17
Long-range planning committee	25	21
"Assistant to" used for long-range planning	13	2

The results of this survey seem to indicate a tendency to move from using a committee toward allotting LRP responsibility to the functional manager or to a planning office. Committee planning activities can play an important role, however, in gaining participation in the LRP effort.

Size of Staffs for Long-Range Planning

The number of personnel assigned full time for the LRP function is, as shown in Table 15, relatively small, according to the data. This number is easy to obtain, but it is very difficult to determine the total number of personnel who spend part of their time in planning or who provide inputs to the plan. Hence the total manpower resources that are actually going into LRP are not evident from these data. A number of responders indicated that they had no full-time planners; one claimed

Table 15   Number of
Personnel Assigned Full Time
to the LRP Function

No. of People	P	C
1– 3	43	21
3– 6	19	14
6– 12	9	9
12– 18	10	3
18– 36	2	5
36– 72	2	2
200–250	1	

that planning was everyone's job; others pointed out that, while the staff at the corporate level was small, a large number were used in either a part-time or a full-time capacity at the division level; another reported that the planning was separated, that is, R&D, financial pricing, etc., planning activities were carried out.

Composition of Long-Range Planning Staffs

The composition of LRP staffs by professional area is given in Table 16. Marketing, technical, management, and finance appear to be the predominant disciplines represented on LRP staffs. These results are not in disagreement with those of Cleland, except in regard to economics.

Table 16   Professional Areas of Effort Represented on LRP Staff

Area	P	C
Marketing	61	45
Technical	65	42
Economics	38	41
Management	57	41
Statistics	31	33
Finance (including accounting)	42	31
Production	25	21
Legal	8	10
Personnel	6	8
Real estate	5	4
Medical	5	1

Organizational Participation in Long-Range Planning

Participation in the formulation of LRP at all levels of management is necessary for the accomplishment of long-term objectives. Table 17 lists the results of this survey in regard to the depth of the participation in planning in the organization. When these results are compared with Cleland's, there are indications here of greater involvement all the way down through the section level. This may be explained by the fact that in a highly technological business like the aerospace industry the techno-

Table 17   Depth of Long-Range Planning
by Organizational Hierarchy

Depth of Participation	P	C
Through: Executive vice president	14	16
Vice president for functional area of effort	22	29
General manager	35	32
Superintendent	18	12
Department chiefs	38	20
Section chiefs	31	13

logical forecasts that go into the plan must come from the working level.

ORGANIZATIONAL LEVEL OF INDIVIDUAL
IN CHARGE OF LRP

As was pointed out earlier, LRP responsibility is located near the top of the organizational structure. The persons to whom the heads of the LRP function report are listed in Table 18. A number of other

Table 18   Organizational Level of Planning

Person Ultimately Responsible for LRP	P	C
Chairman of the board	3	4
President	12	5
Vice president	29	37
Comptroller	. . .	8
Staff assistant to president or vice president	6	2
Department head	2	4
General manager	8	4
Treasurer	. . .	3
Assistant general manager		2
Corporate director	2	
Director of marketing	3	
Staff	10	

answers by respondents include director of research (2), executive committee (2), and various other individuals at the group or corporate level.
The list of different positions named is quite diverse. It is interesting
to note the absence of anyone reporting a person in finance, the comp-
troller or treasurer, as being the one to whom the LRP head reported,
as compared to Cleland's results. This may be indicative of the fact
that the financial aspects of an organization are on the same level as
the LRP group or that LRP may be on the same plane as finances,
R&D, and similar functions.

THE USE OF OUTSIDE AGENCIES
IN LONG-RANGE PLANNING

Consultants

In our planning operations survey, it was found that from time to
time external assistance was obtained for a number of reasons, such
as (a) obtaining economic data, market trends, or technological forecasts,
(b) making a critical review of the planning operation, or (c) gaining
assistance in setting up a new planning function. One of the common
methods is to hire outside consultants.

Table 19   Questions on the Use of Consultants

	Yes		No	
	P	C	P	C
1. Have you ever used consultants in LRP?	29	29	77	48
2. Do you presently use consultants to do your LRP?	10	13	95	66
3. Do you use management consultants to furnish specific LRP information?	49	42	53	36

Table 19 lists the responses to two questions on this subject. In both
cases, it does not appear that the use of consultants is very widespread.
Although a significant number of companies reported using consultants,
this was done mainly to provide specific data or capability.
Some of the reasons for using outside consultants may include:

1. Lack of qualified company personnel.
2. Need for an "outside" evaluation.

3. A company workload that precludes internal accomplishment of LRP.
4. A policy of using consultants only for *ad hoc* LRP projects.

The principal objections reported to using consultants include:

1. The belief that planning must be done by the individual responsible for the results.
2. Availability of internal capability.
3. The feeling that consultants are too far removed from the pulse of the business.
4. The unfamiliarity of consultants with the business.
5. The high cost of using consultants.
6. Classified nature of the business data available.
7. Consultants' lack of adequate hard-core knowledge.
8. The view that LRP is a significant and inseparable function of management.
9. The belief that LRP is a full-time job.
10. Lack of acceptance by working elements, hence usually a disregard, of any plan prepared by an outsider.
11. Nature of business and corporate policy.
12. Highly specialized product and customer.
13. Impossibility of effecting better integration of plans.
14. Lack of confidence in outsider.

Others may include:

1. Time required by consultant.
2. Lack of realism.
3. A belief that use of a consultant does not improve company skills.
4. A loss of the "Byproducts" of planning if outside agencies do LRP.

Companies that used consultants reported that they did so for the following reasons:

1. Systems development.
2. Augmentation of expertise.
3. Assistance in specific areas where company not as well informed.
4. Executive ties.
5. Planning methods.
6. Objective overview of marketing strategies.
7. Aids in the planning process.
8. Some markets and/or products.
9. Occasional specialist efforts, which, however, are not economic to maintain.

Four respondents expressed no objections to the use of consultants. From question 3 in Table 19, it is clear that almost half of the respondents use consultants to provide some LRP data.

In instances where assistance or information is required, the types sought are as shown in Table 20. No one type of information appears

Table 20   Type of Assistance or Information Sought from Consultant

Type of Assistance or Information	P	C
Economic indicators	35	41
Economic predictors	29	44
Gross national product statistics	29	33
Census of business data	23	20
Statistical summonses	14	17
Census of manufacturers' data	28	16
Legislative and technological evaluations	29	34
Other	15	

to be sought above the others in either survey, although in Cleland's study there seemed to be more interest in economic indicators, as one might expect in a civilian economy. The last item in Table 20 covers other sources of data, which were reported as:

1. Department of Defense at all levels.
2. Market intelligence.
3. Market surveys.
4. Government planning.
5. Market forcasts, that is, Stanford Research Institute, A. D. Little, ICE (Phoenix), Frost and Sullivan, etc.
6. Instruction in planning methodology.

Method for Obtaining Economic Data

The methods used in obtaining economic data for LRP are shown in Table 21. Major reliance is placed on subscribing to outside economic

Table 21   Sources of Economic Data for
Long-Range Planning

Method	P	C
Subscribing to outside advisory services	43	38
Perusal by company executives of trade publications, periodicals, newspapers, etc.	58	35
Use of trade associations	35	26
Attendance at professional meetings	37	24
Part-time duty of specific company executive	21	19
Retaining professional economist	6	10
Hiring economist on *ad hoc* basis	6	9
University contracts	5	7
No specific effort made to follow current economic conditions	2	2

advisory resources, as well as on company executives' perusal of the literature, attendance at professional meetings, and assistance from trade associations. Several companies reported that they received economic data from corporate staffs or from financial institutions and government.

Table 22   Assistance from
Trade Associations

Yes		No	
P	C	P	C
48	48	57	26

Table 22 lists responses regarding assistance from trade associations. The responses to this study are essentially split on this question, whereas in Cleland's survey a significant number indicated that trade associations were used in LRP activities.

Other techniques reported as being used in establishing LRP included seminars; existing corporate policy especially in the case of acquired companies; the hiring of a set of outstanding planners, from either a nonprofit organization or the government; the process of evaluation; formal courses; and, finally, the hiring of people with experience.

Table 23   Planning Tools Employed by
Corporations in Effecting Long-Range
Planning

Tool	P	C
Statistical analysis and inference	69	66
Correlational and trend analysis	68	59
Game theory	9	9
Operations research	32	24
Linear programming	22	21
Break-even charts	56	37
Budgets	92	69
Financial statement	83	65
Mathematical models	31	20
Operation models	19	1
Ecological models	5	1
Input-output theory	19	10

TOOLS OF LONG-RANGE PLANNING

The tools of LRP are the methods and techniques used by planners
to assist in the identification and interpretation of significant data relative
to this function. Some of these tools may be considered "classical" in
that they have been used in business areas for long periods of time,
such as budgets and financial statements, while others are more recent
innovations and a third group is still in the development stage. Table
23 lists some of the tools used by present businesses in their LRP
activities.

Although the classical techniques of budgets, financial statements, statistical analysis, and correlational a d trend analysis are reported as
being in most frequent use, the mathematical techniques employed in
operations research, such as game theory, linear programming, and input-output theory, are being utilized to a greater extent. Increased application of mathematical techniques can be expected in the future. A number of newer techniques, such as the Delphi method, the systems analysis
approach, the matrix method, Honeywell's PATTERN, Lockheed's
Mirage, and technical tree analysis have recently become popular in
aerospace industry planning. Similar system, such as QUEST, RDE,
TORQUE, and PPBS, have been developed within the government.[3]

[3] Others include PROFILE, MACRO, NEDEEP, and BRAILLE.

Perhaps the greatest area of development is the field of technological forecasting. Recent literature has contained a number of articles on this subject. In such a rapidly changing technological environment as the aerospace industry, it is only reasonable to expect that technological forecasting will become a more important aspect of LRP.

The use of these tools does not negate, in any sense of the word, the requirement for the exercise of executive judgment in the LRP process. Reflective thinking and the mental balancing of the pros and cons of a long-term decision still must be accomplished by the executive, regardless of the degree of refinement of his planning tools.

ACCOMPLISHMENT OF LONG-RANGE PLANNING

Once the organizational and procedural managements for LRP are established, the company must develop the long-range plan. Objectives must be established, planning by functional area identified, limitations and difficulties considered, plans coordinated and integrated, and the mechanics of review, pretesting, and measurement of results developed. The next few sections examine how present business organizations accomplish LRP with respect to the above areas.

Establishment of Objectives

The setting of LRP objectives and goals for the organization is a fundamental task of management. Objectives should be realistic, attainable, and compatible with the organizational capabilities. A basic question arises as to whether long-range goals or objectives are set before the LRP process is initiated, or whether they grow out of such a plan.

Table 24 represents the results of the survey on this question. It is

Table 24   Policy for Establishing LRP Objectives

Policy	P	C
Objectives are established before entering into long-range planning	59	29
Objectives grow out of preliminary long-range planning activities	58	57
Board of directors select long-term objectives upon which to predicate long-range planning	7	6
Long-term objectives can be established notwithstanding absence of long-range planning activities	4	3

clear that approximately equal numbers established objectives before entering into LRP and had objectives grow out of preliminary LRP. These results are in disagreement with the claim that the objectives always grow out of planning. As pointed out by Cleland, the far-out objectives cannot be established without some sort of LRP.

Pretesting of Long-Range Plans

After a planning process has been developed, there must be some method to convince management that the plan will operate and produce results as envisioned by the planners. Several techniques are available for testing the plan; one of these is the use of the plan on a trial basis, and another is the actual implementation of the plan under the assumption that several iterations will be required to work the bugs out of the plan, gain its acceptance, and measure its results. If management can gain its acceptance, the latter approach is perhaps the one used most often.

The actual survey results are shown in Table 25. From these results, it is evident that a great deal of executive judgment and discussion, rather than exotic techniques, enters into the pretesting of a long-range plan. This would also indicate that techniques for evaluating or pretesting plans have not been developed. Some of the techniques reported in the questionnaire included:

1. Profit assurance plan.
2. Iterative process through reviews.
3. Market and development plans tested by customer survey.
4. Operations research, mathematical markets, executive seminars, and executive judgment.
5. Review prior efforts.

As was pointed out earlier, contemporary literature is almost devoid of material on the pretesting of long-range plans except for an article by William J. Platt and N. Robert Maines.[4]

Functional Areas of Long-Range Planning

In general there are few functions which are not subject to planning on a long-term basis. Not every field of activity is planned in every company, and there are differences in the period for which LRP is formulated. (See discussions of the period of planning by functional area of

[4] "Pretest Your Long-Range Plans," *Harvard Business Review*, January–February 1959, pp. 119–127.

effort.) Table 26 indicates the functions reported and those considered as the most important.

Difficulties and Limitations of Long-Range Planning

Although over 90% of the companies surveyed reported that they were actively engaged in LRP, such planning is not without difficulties or limitations, and Table 27 lists these as reported. The two primary major limitations reported were lack of accurate data and management's preoccupation with immediate operating problems. Secondary major limitations involved personnel, organizations, and forecasting.

Many of the difficulties are within the jurisdiction of the management and can be reduced by improvements in internal organization, policies, and procedures.

Table 25   Methods Used by Corporations to Pretest Long-Range Planning

Method	P	C
Operations research	11	18
Mathematical models	15	15
Executive seminars	45	17
Computer techniques	14	16
"Business games"	11	2
Operational models	14	10
Ecological models	1	1
Coordination with management consultant agencies	2	11
No attempt to pretest	9	3
Executive judgment	88	63

The main difficulty reported in Cleland's survey involved the establishing of LRP policies, procedures, and techniques. This was of minor consequence, however, in this study.

Overcoming Difficulties and Limitations in Implementing

The difficulties and limitations experienced in implementing LRP are those which are normally associated with the development and introduction of any new concept. The previous section attempted to define the most important of these factors. In the study, cooperating organizations

Table 26   Functional and Other Areas of Effort Where Long-Range Planning Is Reported by Cooperating Companies

Area of Effort	Frequency Reported		Frequency Reported as One of Five Most Critical Areas	
	P	C	P	C
Product research and development	11	48	66	44
Product costing	20	25	11	10
Facilities	24	50	26	38
Manufacturing/Production	25	36	20	24
Finances	15	50	34	36
Credit	12	15	2	2
Marketing	16	57	51	52
Organizational Structure	31	32	5	9
Executive Development	32	23	10	9
Industrial Relations	17	17	2	6
Personnel	22	31	14	17
Policy formulation	16	24	5	9
Public relations	14	15	1	1
Sources of raw materials	17	21		11
Sources of supplies	20	17		2
Subcontracting	20	14		1
Product distribution	17	26	7	6
Product engineering	17	25	25	13
Real estate	20	17	1	7
Manufacturing methods and processes	21	26	9	14
Product competition	21	38	25	21
"Size planning," i.e., developing long-term objectives as to how large the business should be	18	28	19	16

were asked to comment on how they attempted to overcome the difficulties and limitations of planning. The techniques which appear to be used to the greatest extent include better data and forecasting techniques, increased internal communications, and executive persuasion.

Extraorganizational Factors Affecting Long-Range Planning

Business is affected by a great many factors which are beyond its control, such as the economy of the country, access to foreign markets, tariff protection against imports, general availability of money for capi-

Table 27 Reported Limitations of Long-Range Planning Corporations

Limitation	Criticality of Limitation Based on Actual Number of Response										Percentage	
	(1)	(2)	(3)	(4)	(5)	(6)	(7)	(8)	(9)	(10)	P	C
Lack of accurate data	15	15	8	9	2	1	...	...	...	...	65	45
Gaining wholehearted top management support	6	1	2	1	2	...	1	...	...	...	19	14
Personnel limitations	8	3	5	5	1	...	...	...	...	...	29	28
Preoccupation of management with immediate operating problems	21	15	8	3	...	2	...	...	...	...	69	45
Establishing long-range objectives	1	2	7	2	3	1	1	...	...	...	25	35
Establishing long-range planning policies, procedures, and techniques	1	4	3	1	...	2	...	...	...	...	16	72
Having suitable organizational structure to effect long-range planning	2	10	7	8	3	...	...	...	...	...	35	24
Effecting intracompany coordination of long-range planning activities	1	4	6	3	...	...	...	...	...	...	22	29
Business cycle influences	4	3	2	3	...	...	...	...	...	...	15	14
Government controls	1	1	1	2	4	1	1	1	...	...	17	22
Reviewing, revising, and updating long-range plan	...	2	1	8	...	...	...	...	...	1	20	15
Industry peculiarities (Please explain)	4	2	1	...	...	...	...	...	1	...	15	15
No difficulties or limitations	...	...	...	...	...	...	...	...	...	...	2	2

Table 28   External Factors Considered in LRP Activities

Extraorganizational Factor	P	C
Legislative actions	64	51
Gross National Product Changes	54	47
Government expenditures	94	44
Technological progress	91	63
Business cycles	47	49
Industry trends	89	69
Competitors' actions	95	67
International matters	64	43
Social mores	17	10
Political environment	47	36
Employment	36	23
Government fiscal policy	72	43
Government controls	58	46

tal, government controls, and other factors which must be identified and evaluated as part of the LRP effort. External factors are not just related to the general economy and the individual company's position in the market; they also necessitate a careful appraisal of what the competition is doing with product lines, prices, distribution methods, and long-range planning.

Table 28 lists the external factors that were reported by the respondent companies. As may be noted, government expenditures, technological progress, competitors' actions, and industry trends are cited as the most important. Government expenditures are of unique significance to the aerospace industry because of the heavy reliance on this customer. Other factors reported included market trends, life cycle of products, public concern (i.e., in regard to noise, pollution), universe and related phemomena, aircraft development, and national security policy.

Key Industry Influences

Particular external factors include the industry in which a company is located. Table 29 lists the key influences of the aerospace industry. It appears that all those listed are important except LRP techniques. Perhaps this is due to the fact that it is difficult to obtain information on long-range internal company plans. In this study, for example, ques-

Table 29   Key Influences or Factors in Company Industry, Evaluated by Select Corporations

Factor	P	C
Competitive position	95	73
Growth or decline trends	83	74
Industry demands	76	63
Individual firm's position	83	66
Long-range planning techniques	31	35
Other (Please specify)	11	

tion 53 requested copies of plans or procedures; a large number of firms claimed its method and techniques were proprietary information.

Although a specific question was not included in this study on the evaluation of LRP by competitors, Cleland's survey collected data on this subject and found that the following techniques were used:

1. Thorough examination of key decisions of competitors versus apparent direction and payoff of these decisions.
2. Judgment of planners, based on informal visits and discussions.
3. Trade association contacts.
4. Statistical studies.
5. Published reports of competitors.
6. Thorough use of published government data.
7. Company executive seminars.

Identification and Integration of Customer Viewpoint

Probably one of the most important factors in any industry is the identification of customers viewpoint and data and its integration into LRP deliberations. This question was the one which received the greatest number of written responses. There is a clear indication that close communication with the customer in regard to his needs is maintained through constant contacts and that these play a very important part in the formulation of long-range plans.

Use of Published Source Data for Long-Range Planning

An important source of economic and market data for LRP is published material. Table 30 reflects the frequency of use of published source data for LRP purposes. The data presented in the table suggest that an integral part of the LRP organization should be an information collection agency organized along the lines of an intelligence office or of a military staff. Such an organization could be provided to collect raw intelligence information, interpret it, and disseminate it for the use and guidance of other parts of the company engaged in planning. Personal discussions which I held with members of planning functions in various companies in the aerospace industry indicate that extensive intelligence networks are in operation.

Table 30   Frequency of Use of Published Source Material for Long-Range Planning

Source Material	P	C
Government statistics	82	75
Commerce Department reports	53	61
Trade association data	82	60
Books	54	48
Government technology needs	78	
AMA special reports	38	44
University business research reports	43	43
Periodicals	74	58

Forecasting in Long-Range Planning

Drucker defines long-range planning by what it is not rather than by what it is: ". . . it is not forecasting. It is not masterminding the future, . . . long-range planning is necessary precisely because we cannot forecast." Forecasting attempts to find the most probable course of events or at least a range of probabilities by assessing the past, present, and future impact of such environments on the organization and the impact of the organization on the environments. Planning occurs at a later date when the company evaluates the forecast information and converts it into objectives, plans, policies, programs, and procedures which will guide the corporate action.

Table 31 lists the internal company data used for forecasting and LRP as reported. The main types are sales forecasts, present sales data, financial data, defense requirements, and technological forecasts. The

Table 31 Internal Company Data Used in Long-Range Planning

Type of Data	P	C
Sales forecasts	116	76
Present sales data	101	71
Plant and equipment maturity data	44	47
Credit data	20	15
Financial data	91	66
Cost data	78	62
Personnel data	66	50
Personnel capabilities	69	46
Organization posture	63	35
Manufacturing techniques	76	50
Labor availability	56	29
Product data	74	55
Technological forecasts	94	

last of these has recently received a great deal of attention, and some sophisticated techniques for this type of forecasting have been developed and are reported in other chapters.

External data and specific forecasts effected in relation to LRP are listed in Table 32 as reported. From the number of replies to the question about forecasting, there seems to be a considerable amount of management attention to this activity. The broad range of functional and other areas of LRP which has been facilitated by forecasting indicates that this will continue to be an important activity. Complex factors and forces affecting the company dictate that a firm engaged in LRP should try to develop comprehensive and accurate forecasting techniques.

Results of Long-Range Planning

The results of LRP may manifest themselves in both direct and indirect ways. This study attempts only to identify the direct results; these are listed in Table 33.

In accord with a frequently echoed saying, "Planning means change," this table indicates that LRP resulted in changes of some sort. Very few respondents reported no changes, with the majority reporting major changes in product lines, acquisitions, reorganizations, product diversification, facilities, and new capabilities.

**Table 32   External Factors and Forecasts
Effected Relative to Long-Range Planning**

Type of Forecast	P	C
Sales	105	74
Technological progress	93	51
Political environment	55	29
International conditions	62	36
Legislative	31	24
Technical intelligence	72	51
Gross national product changes	42	48
Government expenditures	86	45
Prices	67	53
Costs	72	55
Total customer potential	88	63
Standard of living progression	19	24
Capital availability	46	44
Profit	91	67
Marketing	90	36
Share of market	84	66
Product life	75	44
Product diversification	76	52
Employment requirements	52	38
Social mores	12	10
Industry trends	81	68
New construction	36	36
Raw material prices	28	30

Another result of the LRP process is the creation of "planning documents" to implement the long-range plans. These are summarized in Table 34. In addition to those listed, other plans reported were profit plans, facilities plans, new product plans, strategic (master) plan, development plan (5 years), and functional plans (1 year).

The Communication of Long-Range Planning
After Development and Acceptance

After a long-range planning procedure has been developed and accepted, the problem arises of how to communicate it to those responsible for implementing it. Table 35 lists the ways in which the participating companies reported that they carried out this communication. In general,

Table 33 Direct Results of Long-Range Planning

Changes Reported	P	C
New product lines	61	39
Organizational decentralization	26	18
Company mergers	20	16
Company acquisitions	46	36
Executive development program	25	26
Company reorganizations	44	26
Product diversification	64	38
No changes	8	13
New facilities	66	
New capabilities	67	

Table 34 Planning Documents Created as the Result of Long-Range Planning

Planning Document	P	C
"Master" plan for future	70	39
Functional area long-range plans	67	57
Long-range plan for specific segments of the company	56	45
Economic predictions	37	36
Technical forecasts	50	

two main techniques were used to communicate long-range plans: (1) integration into the master plan and distribution to line managers, and (2) use of intracompany briefings. These results do not agree with those of Cleland's survey, which indicate no particular preference outside of using intracompany briefings.

Coordination and Review of Long-Range Plan

Coordination of the LRP includes both vertical and horizontal activities. It involves the synchronization of related activities with respect to time and performance. Coordination of LRP may be accomplished by either formal or informal techniques. The most frequently used method is that performed by individual executives in developing their input to the LRP.

Table 36 reflects the internal policies and procedures used for coordinating the LRP activities of the responding companies. Normal staff coordination predominates as the method usually employed for coordinating LRP, with the use of a standing planning committee and *ad hoc* "coordination" also receiving significant responses.

Review and Revalidation of the Long-Range Plan

Review and revalidation of the LRP are closely related to coordination. The review process is an essential keynote to the entire planning

Table 35   Method of Communicating Long-Range Planning After It Has Been Developed and Accepted

Method Reported	P	C
Integrate into "master plan" and distribute to line managers	49	12
Use company seminars	22	14
Use intracompany briefings	44	23
Distribute functional area long-range plans only; no attempt made to distribute "master plan"	12	13
Integrate into "master plan" and distribute to all echelons responsible for implementing a portion of "master plan"	17	12
Limited distribution of "master plan"	17	15
No distribution effected; line managers responsible for implementing own long-range plans and for company coordination	15	4

Table 36   Internal Policies and Procedures Used for Coordinating LRP Activities

Method of Obtaining Coordination	P	C
Standing planning committee	38	25
Departmental seminar	18	13
Intracompany routing of master plan	28	14
Normal intrastaff coordination	63	49
Ad hoc "coordination"	39	28
Board of directors	12	15

operation; from it assumptions, premises, and changed economic conditions for the past period can be used to test the existing applicability of the plan. A review period may be determined by the actions of customers or competitors; the development of a new product by a competitor, for example, may motivate the review of existing LRP in order to meet this challenge. In the aerospace industry, the review period may be based on the government budget cycle.

Table 37 indicates the frequency with which corporations reporting reviewed their long-range plans. The majority of respondents answered that they carried out such reviews either semiannually or annually. A significant number reviewed the long-range plan continuously. It could be that some part of the plan is always being reviewed.

Table 37   Frequency of Review of Long-Range Planning

Period	P	C
Quarterly	11	8
Semiannually	24	10
Annually	58	36
Every 2 years		3
Continuously	25	30

The method used to determine the period for review varies and is dependent on many factors. Some of the replies to this question include:

1. Rate of technical change.
2. An arbitrary decision.
3. Parent company directives.
4. Corporate policy.
5. New data that make a review desirable.
6. Executive judgment.
7. Budget allocation from the corporate.
8. Trial and error.
9. Arbitrary determination of 1 year.
10. Fiscal period.
11. Determination in accord with the need for flexibility.
12. Need to make key decisions or to meet market situation changes.

13. Dependence on detailed plan.
14. Executive availability.

It should be recognized that much review of the long-range plan is done on a continuous basis as new developments in the planning process are identified. Formal review, however, is usually carried out at recurring periods, at which time the top management group reviews the overall corporate plan, adjusts corporate goals as required, and directs the establishment of new objectives.

This formal review is considered apart from the normal review that the functional area manager conducts in relation to his area of responsibility. The period for this review varies and depends on the following factors:

1. Functional area involved and length of time for which the plan has been devised.
2. Dynamics of the competitive environment of the company.
3. Actions of competitors, customers, and government agencies.
4. Internal factors which influence the long-range plan, such as mergers, consolidations, or corporate reorganizations.
5. General fluctuations of extraordinary action in the economy which significantly and rapidly render obsolete existing long-range plans.

Future Innovations in Long-Range Planning

The existing state of the art of LRP planning is so new as a concept and philosophy that many innovations and techniques will be developed and implemented in order to improve and refine present planning. In reply to a question in the survey, however, 35 of the 117 respondents replied that no future refinements were planned. Of those answering that future refinements were planned, a large number indicated the following general trends:

1. Improved collection, evaluation, and dissemination of market intelligence.
2. Improved techniques for advanced identification of product competition.
3. Greater use of computer techniques.
4. More formalized LRP effort.
5. Better quantitative methods and molding techniques.
6. Better technological forecasting.
7. Greater management commitment to LRP.
8. Continual refinement of LRP process.
9. Use of the data obtained in this survey.

XXIII.   *Requirement Analysis, Need Forecasting, and Technology Planning, Using the Honeywell PATTERN Technique*

ROSS C. ALDERSON AND WILLIAM C. SPROULL

Churchill has said, "We shape our buildings and afterwards our buildings shape us." The same holds true in our contemplation of a subject—we organize our thoughts and afterwards the structure of our organization shapes future thinking.

Donald Pyke

INTRODUCTION

Over the last few years, Honeywell has developed and implemented a methodology for forecasting, and assigning priorities to, future technology needs that has proved useful in selecting long-range R&D investment programs. A great many techniques are currently being employed to forecast technological change, ranging from intuitive thinking (brainstorming) to sophisticated systems analysis techniques using dynamic mathematical models. Honeywell needed something in between these two extremes, however, that would adequately structure the problem, yet be simple enough for a small planning staff to use on a continuing basis.

To meet this need, Honeywell developed a normative forecasting technique employing a relevance tree. The technique was selected for three reasons. First, Honeywell operates over a broad technology base which lends itself well to need-oriented analysis. Second, the approach permits structuring the problem in such a way as to break down the many complex interrelated variables affecting development decisions into small manageable elements for evaluation. Third, the approach helps to assure the consideration of all types of alternatives.

As a result of the accelerated pace of technology, there are generally many more feasible technical alternatives available to solve a particular problem than can be economically supported by either the government or industry. As a result alternative solutions must be weighed very carefully in terms of how well a particular solution supports overall objectives. This is particularly true in the early stages of development, since expenditures on a particular program generally accelerate with time. In view of this complex and costly development environment, some auxiliary aids are needed to help assess the impacts of these many alternatives and to assist industry in deciding where to place its R&D dollars in order to continue its growth.

To meet this increasing need for requirements analysis, Honeywell's Military and Space Sciences Department developed a technique called PATTERN (Planning Assistance Through Technical Evaluation of Relevance Numbers), which uses a relevance tree to aid corporate planners in identifying critical needs and in presenting carefully evaluated alternatives in corporate decision matters. Although PATTERN was originally developed and used most extensively for planning in the military area, the methodology has proved flexible and is currently being applied in several areas in which decisions must be made under conditions of uncertainty. For example, the PATTERN technique has been used effectively to forecast future technology requirements in the biomedical field. More recently, the PATTERN methodology has served to identify future needs and to aid in mapping out investment programs in hydrocarbon processing, in building protection systems and housing, and in identifying critical needs in the training of students in the public school system.

PATTERN finds a decentralized usage within the Honeywell organization. Although originating within the technical planning staff of the Aerospace and Defense Group, the technique has been further refined through extensive use by Honeywell's Systems Analysis Department within its corporate research activity. Operating from this position, planning and analytical support has provided assistance to many parts of the corporate structure.

In producing any meaningful technology forecast, Honeywell has learned through experience that a number of problems must be dealt with. The first, and probably most difficult problem, is to develop and maintain communications between the organizational levels responsible for corporate objectives and the levels charged with identification of the technology needs which support these objectives. This communication problem exists among people throughout the various levels of the corporate structure and affects their understanding of the interrelationship between technology and corporate objectives. This is essentially a structuring problem involving both scope and definitions. The government, recognizing the problem, decided in 1965 to implement the Planning Programming Budgeting System (PPBS) in an attempt to improve communications among and within the various departments by stressing mission-oriented programming and budgeting.

Another difficult problem is putting a forecast into the correct time frame. Information on the status of the various technologies and their projected rate of growth must be used to determine the time and capability required to meet the future technical needs that have been identified.

A third major problem is the selection of the criteria by which the relative importance of various alternatives at a given level in the structure can be assessed. The criteria selected must be appropriate to the level at which the decision is being made. The criteria at the various levels of analysis should be mutually exclusive, and above all they must be understood by the decision makers.

It has been said that normative technology forecasting is an attempt to invent the future. Perhaps this is correct. However, when a company with limited resources is considering making R&D investments in just a few of the many technical areas open to it, the management would like first to establish the future need for a particular technology and the priority of that need. Assuming that rational men will attempt to fulfill these needs on a basis consistent with their priorities and with available resources, one is next faced with the problem of which alternative solution best meets a particular need on a cost-effective basis. How then do we make a knowledgeable decision faced with x number of alternatives?

Evaluations of the capability of the human mind to interrelate and correlate a large number of variables has shown that there is a very sharp knee in the curve in the region of about 20 alternatives. As the number of alternatives to be considered increases much beyond 20, the probability of making a knowledgeable decision is greatly reduced. Therefore, it would seem advisable to reduce the number of variables being considered at any given time in a decision process to something under 20, and preferably under 10, to assure that the mind can assimilate all of the relevant factors associated with the decision being made.

Experience has also shown that it is necessary to express the relative importance of the various items in quantitative terms. These not only are more exact than qualitative expressions, but also can be used in a computer program whereby considerable time and effort can be saved in analyzing and updating the decision data.

PATTERN METHODOLOGY

There are seven components of the PATTERN methodology:

1. Relevance tree structure.
2. Criteria.
3. Data entry.
4. Assumptions or reference data.
5. Relevance number determination.
6. Output data.
7. Data processing.

Relevance Tree Structure

The relevance tree structure provides a means of organizing the study material to permit the determination of releative priorities among large numbers of independent variables. The basic approach to structuring is to determine and define the area to be investigated and then to subdivide it as necessary in a tree structure to permit accurate assignment of priorities. There are four basic guidelines governing the relevance tree structure:

- *Understandability:* The structure must be understandable to those entering data, and to those analyzing the study results.
- *Applicability:* The structure must be capable of being used to develop data which will enable accomplishment of the study objective. Normally, the relevance structure is functional rather than hardware-oriented.
- *Completeness:* The area of interest must be completely contained in the division. Any areas omitted in the structure will not appear in the output.
- *Independence:* The structure elements must not contain each other.

An example of a tree structure is given in Figure 1 in a partial depiction of the automobile on a functional basis. For the purpose of simplified

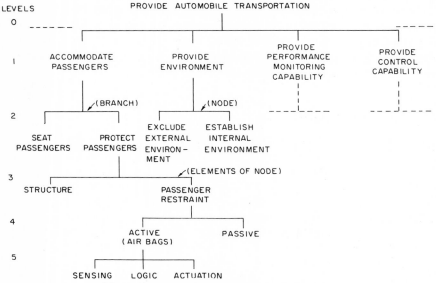

Figure 1   Example of relevance tree structure.

explanation, however, the partial depiction will be considered complete. Let us assume a primary (Level 0) function of "Provide automobile transportation." Some subfunctions of the primary function might be "Accommodate passengers," "Provide environment," "Provide control capability," and "Provide performance-monitoring capability." (Obviously additional subfunctions are contained in the area of interest, but, as previously indicated, a partial structure has been developed for simplicity).

In the figure the structuring of the relevance tree starts with the broad objective of "Providing automobile transportation" and continues to be divided into progressively more detailed levels of objectives. The detailing should continue to the point where specific objective and needs can be identified which have a direct relationship to the capability or potential capability of the organization.

Figure 1 also depicts several structural elements which are indicated in parentheses ( ). It will be observed that the structure is organized by levels, with the lower levels being effectively contained in and comprising the upper levels with which they are associated. For example, "Seat passengers" and "Protect passengers" (Level 2) are contained in "Accommodate passengers" (Level 1). Note that the requirement for independence of structural elements applies at specific levels, that is, Level 1 items cannot contain other Level 1 items or parts thereof; and between levels, that is, Level 2 items cannot contain Level 1 items or parts thereof or other Level 2 items or parts thereof, etc. Multiple appearances of items or parts thereof will result in multiple weightings and will distort the results of analysis.

Criteria

Criteria are used in the study methodology to enable the persons entering data to make meaningful judgments about the relative priorities among the variables as they relate to each other. Criteria may be considered as priority objectives, bases of judgment, and/or reasons for change or upgrading. The guidelines for criteria are similar to those stated previously for the structure.

- *Understandability:* The criteria must be understandable to those entering data, and to those analyzing the data entered.
- *Applicability:* The criteria must allow the making of judgments required to meet the study objectives.
- *Independence:* The criteria must not contain each other.
- *Completeness:* The criteria must constitute all factors of judgment. Omissions will result in nonobservable shortcomings in the study end product.

The development and application of criteria can be illustrated by returning to the example of providing transportation. Assume that it is desired to determine the priority (e.g., upgrading needed) of subfunctions to meet transportation needs at a selected time in the future. This is provided by first defining objectives which will enable an evaluation of relative functional upgrading needs. With the guidelines for criteria in mind, the following list of objectives could be developed:

1. To reduce costs of automobile transportation.
2. To increase passenger safety.
3. To increase efficiency of automobile transportation.
4. To increase passenger comfort.

It is important to note that the judgmental process is incremental because of the structural division of the area of interest. Accordingly, different criteria sets may be used to formulate judgments at different levels of the structure while meeting the completeness requirement.

PROVIDE AUTOMOBILE TRANSPORTATION

CRITERIA 1 UPGRADING NEED TO REDUCE COSTS OF AUTOMOBILE TRANSPORTATION
          2 UPGRADING NEED TO INCREASE PASSENGER SAFETY
          3 UPGRADING NEED TO INCREASE EFFICIENCY OF AUTOMOBILE TRANSPORTATION
          4 UPGRADING NEED TO INCREASE PASSENGER COMFORT

Criteria ID	01	02	03	04
Criteria Weight	.20	.50	.20	.10
1 Accommodate passengers	.05	.25	.40	.35
2 Provide environment	.30	.05	.15	.50
3 Provide performance-monitoring capability	.60	.10	.40	.05
4 Provide control capability	.05	.60	.05	.10

Figure 2 Data entry form ("ballot").

Data Entry

As previously stated, the relevance tree structure involves the division of the area of interest into "pieces" which can be meaningfully evaluated. The criteria are the bases for evaluation of these pieces. The structure and criteria are combined into data entry forms called "ballots" to permit the balloters to enter their judgments. Two forms of ballots are used (Figures 2 and 3). These ballots are functionally identical, and the choice between them may be made by the study developer.

NAME_____ ORG _____

TO PROVIDE AUTOMOBILE TRANSPORTATION

MKT
TECH   (CIRCLE ONE)
Balloter Expertise Self Rating:
None   Low   Medium   High   (Circle One)

What is the relative importance of each of the following in determining the Upgrading Need in Providing Automobile Transportation?

1.	Reduce Costs of Automobile Transporation	20
2.	Increase Passenger Safety	50
3.	Increase Efficiency of Automobile Transporation	20
4.	Increase Passenger Comfort	10
		100

1. To reduce, Costs of Automobile Transportation, what is the relative Upgrading Need among the following?

1.	Accommodate Passengers	05
2.	Provide Environment	30
3.	Provide Performance Monitoring Capability	60
4.	Provide Control Capability	05
		100

2. To Increase Passenger Safety, what is the relative Upgrading Need among the following?

1.	Accommodate Passengers	25
2.	Provide Environment	05
3.	Provide Performance Monitoring Capability	10
4.	Provide Control Capability	60
		100

3. To Increase Efficiency of Automobile Transporation, what is the relative Upgrading Need among the following?

1.	Accommodate Passengers	40
2.	Provide Environment	15
3.	Provide Performance Monitoring Capability	40
4.	Provide Control Capability	05
		100

4. To Increase Passenger Comfort, what is the relative Upgrading Need among the following?

1.	Accommodate Passengers	35
2.	Provide Environment	50
3.	Provide Performance Monitoring Capability	05
4.	Provide Control Capability	10
		100

Figure 3   Alternative data entry form.

The data to be entered in the ballots are the quantitative representations of each balloter's judgments (weighting assessments) regarding the priorities of the criteria or structural elements in question. In each case, the weighting assignments are made on an allocation basis, with the total summing to 100 points (or 1.0 at the balloter's choice) among each criteria group. This constraint is imposed by the logic of the structure and emphasizes the fact that each group of weighting assignments constitutes a complete judgment based on the questions asked and the available data. Allocations which by mistake do not sum to 100 (or 1.0) are normalized in processing the data; hence their relationship is preserved and the results are not affected.

In examining the ballots onto which data have been entered, as a continuation of the transportation example, observe that:

- Values have been assigned to the criteria in relation to their importance in determining the upgrading needed in "Providing transportation." (The relative influences of the criteria have been entered by relative weighting.)
- Values have been assigned to the functions on the basis of their relative need for upgrading as that need is defined by evaluation against the criterion under consideration. (The relative priority among variables as dictated by a specific criterion has been entered by relative weighting.)
- The sum of individual weighting allocations across criteria sets and structure branches is 1. (In our example, the "point" total is 100, which, of course, may be normalized to 1.)
- Although the ballot formats shown in Figures 2 and 3 are different, they both permit the entering of equivalent technical data.

Assumptions or Reference Data

The study data may have their origin in either implicit or explicit assumptions. *Implicit* assumptions rest on the background and experience of those supplying the data and generally are operative as a projection of "normal trends" through the time period of interest. *Explicit* assumptions must rest on a scenario specifically defining future events on a basis chosen by the developer. It might, for example, define economic, political, and social environments. The scenario must also define conditions relevant to the study that results from the future assumptions. A scenario making explicit assumptions about future conditions obviously need not conform to present real-world conditions. The scenario assumes that the data supplier has knowledge of the present status of study-related developments.

Relevance Number Determination

Local relevance numbers are developed across each level of the structure. They are the sums of partial relevance numbers for variables of interest. The partial relevance is the product of the weighting of the criterion of interest and the weighting of the variable when evaluated against that criterion:

$$R_p = c_i v_j$$

where R_p = partial relevance, c = criterion weighting, and v = variable weighting; and the local relevance number is accordingly:

$$R_L = \sum_{\substack{i=1 \\ j=n}}^{\substack{i=n}} c_i v_j$$

where R_L = local relevance.

As an example, partial relevances will be developed for the weightings previously given. You will note that in Figures 2 and 3, Criterion 1 ("To reduce costs of automobile transportation") was given a weighting of 20 when compared to the other criteria. The partial relevance numbers for the functions listed as determined by Criterion 1 would accordingly be:

Accommodate passengers	$0.05 \times 0.20 = 0.01$
Provide environment	$0.30 \times 0.20 = 0.06$
Provide performance-monitoring capability	$0.60 \times 0.20 = 0.12$
Provide control capability	$0.05 \times 0.20 = 0.01$

(Note that the scale of the weighting figures has been shifted, because of normalization, to 1.)

The local relevance for each of the variables listed is the sum of its ratings across all criteria. Computations for the rest of the local relevance figures will be found in the appendix on methodology at the end of the chapter.

Total direct relevance numbers represent the judgment of the rater as reflected through the levels of the tree. The total direct relevance number, R, of any variable in the relevance structure is developed as a product:

$$R = r_v \prod_{n=1}^{N} r_n$$

where r_v represents the local relevance value of the variable of interest (this may be a single value for a single ballot or an average value for multiple-ballot inputs),

N represents the local relevance structure level of interest (the level of the node containing the variable of interest),

r_n represents the local relevance values of related branch nodes (nodes connected by branches below Level 1) from $n \ldots N$ (single value or average value),

II is the multiplication operator which instructs that all values of r_n be multiplied.

Computations for total direct relevance numbers for the variables of the example will be found in the appendix at the end of the chapter.

Output Data

There are a number of output options with different functions:

- Total direct relevance listings of all input data (R_B), organized by level and sequenced both by relevance ranking and ID (title identification) number. This relevance ranking displays relative priority among the variables. A sample printout is shown in Figure 4.
- Total direct relevance listings of all input data with the relevance of selected variables summed (R_N). This summation is usually on the basis of similarity of functions or combinations of functions which are supplied by a hardware system. These listings display relative priorities among the variables, with groupings of selected variables which are considered as a whole. Horizontal summation may be effected at any selected tree level. The summed items are indicated in the ID-sequenced printout.
- Total direct relevance listings based on input data (ballots) as selected. These listings permit display of the data by selected organizations or classifications of individual inputs.
- Total direct relevance listings with selected criteria set to zero (R_{cn}). These listings permit display of the sensitivity of variable priorities to selected objectives or bases of judgment.
- Intersection listings, which define cross containment of separate listings. These listings permit display of the highest ranked variables in two separate lists.
- Equal-expectation value output listings for the relevance structure (R_U). These listings permit display of the total direct relevance values which would occur if weightings were uniform across all criteria and all variables at each node.
- Ratios of selected listings. These listings permit display of the relationship between selected relevance rankings.

The data dispersion is approximated by root sum square (RSS) listings. The RSS listing is computed from the square root of the sums of the squared standard deviations of the variable of interest and each related node above it in the structure, expressed as a percentage of the average relevance of the variable:

$$\text{RSS of } R_n = (\sigma R_N{}^2 + \sigma R_{N1}{}^2 + \sigma R_{N2}{}^2 + \cdots + \sigma R_{Nn}{}^2)^{\frac{1}{2}} \left(\frac{100}{R_N}\right)$$

where R_N = variable of interest, and $R_{N1\ldots n}$ = nodes of related variables above the variable of interest in the structure.

The cumulative distribution of local relevance numbers at each node can be computed and plotted if desired. This program also prints out at each node the local relevance numbers tagged with the source, together with the percentage of the distribution below each relevance number.

Data Reduction

Relevance methodology data reduction is accomplished through four subsystems:

1. Ballot generation.
2. Calculation and data editing.
3. Report generation.
4. Revision.

The subsystems are integrated through the structure or TDR (total direct relevance) tape. The present programs are written in COBOL. The subsystems in the computer program perform the following functions:

- *Ballot generation. subsystem:* Generates tree structure, criteria, and ballots for each structure level, and revises structure below Level 1 to enable study continuation in selected detailed areas.
- *Calculation and data-editing subsystem:* Accepts card ballot input data from matrix and questionnaire ballots and also checks the cards for structural consistency. The program then accomplishes the zeroing of selected criteria and the isolation of selected ballots for limited processing. The program next calculates the local relevance number for each node, the average relevance of ballots, and the standard deviations expressed as a percentage of the relevance figures. The total direct relevance and root sum square (RSS) of standard deviations, expressed as a percentage of the relevance figures, are then computed.

This subsystem also computes relevance number ratios, that is, R_B/R_U, etc., at the option of the analyst and may be modified to compute products of relevance numbers over identical trees. It has also been

TOTAL DIRECT RELEVANCE OF THE TASKS

RANKED BY RELEVANCE NUMBER (HIGH TO LOW)

RANK	ID	TITLE	RFLEVANCE	RSS
0001	910601	SENSING MEANS	INTEGRATED SYS INDIVIDUAL STRUCTURES BUILDING PROTECTION	0.0519857	31.0
0002	910605	RESPONSE	INTEGRATED SYS INDIVIDUAL STRUCTURES BUILDING PROTECTION	0.0374687	37.5
0003	910602	INFO TRANS	INTEGRATED SYS INDIVIDUAL STRUCTURES BUILDING PROTECTION	0.0358080	39.0
0004	910603	ANALYSIS	INTEGRATED SYS INDIVIDUAL STRUCTURES BUILDING PROTECTION	0.0326279	39.6
0005	410211	SENSING MEANS	INTRUDER D?R DEF?OFFICIAL	0.0242640	27.6
0006	910604	DISPLAY	INTEGRATED SYS INDIVIDUAL STRUCTURES BUILDING PROTECTION	0.0238263	29.7
0007	1101F1	SENSING MEANS	FIRE DET?REP%EDUC?OFFICE	0.0195285	37.0
0008	410212	INFO TRANS	INTRUDER D?R DEF?OFFICIAL	0.0164053	32.7
0009	210211	SENSING MEANS	INTRUDER D?R INSTITUTIONAL	0.0141252	32.9
0010	310211	SENSING MEANS	INTRUDER D?R INDUSTRIAL	0.0126400	36.6
0011	2201F1	SENSING MEANS	FIRE DET?REP%INSTITUTIONAL	0.0123154	30.1
0012	1101F5	RESPONSE	FIRE DET?REP%EDUC?OFFICE	0.0119136	50.4
0013	960201	SENSING MEANS	INTEGRATED SYS PROPRIETARY MULTIPLE BLDG	0.0118858	29.8
0014	1101F2	INFO TRANS	FIRE DET?REP%EDUC?OFFICE	0.0117477	40.0
0015	960101	SENSING MEANS	INTEGRATED SYS CENTRAL STATION BLDG PROTECTION	0.0115898	51.8
0016	4301F1	SENSING MEANS	FIRE DET?REP%UNATTENDED AREAS	0.0113220	33.5
0017	410213	ANALYSIS	INTRUDER D?R DEF?OFFICIAL	0.0111458	43.4
0018	410214	DISPLAY	INTRUDER D?R DEF?OFFICIAL	0.0107483	35.5
0019	410215	RESPONSE	INTRUDER D?R DEF?OFFICIAL	0.0105190	46.6
0020	1101F3	ANALYSIS	FIRE DET?REP%EDUC?OFFICE	0.0104594	45.6
0021	960401	SENSING MEANS	INTEGRATED SYS DIR CON%REMOTE MULTIPLE BLDG	0.0102917	21.5
0022	4301F2	INFO TRANS	FIRE DET?REP%UNATTENDED AREAS	0.0099071	25.3

ID	Code	Category	Description	Value	
0023	210212	INFO TRANS	INTRUDER D?R INSTITUTIONAL	0.0096644	26.-
0024	960202	INFO TRANS	INTEGRATED SYS PROPRIETARY MULTIPLE BLDG	0.0091680	?d.0
0025	310212	INFO TRANS	INTRUDER D?R INDUSTRIAL	0.0087772	29.1
0026	3301F1	SENSING MEANS	FIRE DET?REP%INDUSTRIAL	0.0083742	33.4
0027	210213	ANALYSIS	INTRUDER D?R INSTITUTIONAL	0.0083898	41.5
0028	110211	SENSING MEANS	INTRUDER D?R EDUCATIONAL	0.0083422	46.8
0029	960402	INFO TRANS	INTEGRATED SYS DIR CON/REMOTE MULTIPLE BLDG	0.0080242	39.0
0030	2201F5	RESPONSE	FIRE DET?REP%INSTITUTIONAL	0.0079889	53.7
0031	2201F2	INFO TRANS	FIRE DET?REP%INSTITUTIONAL	0.0078650	35.8
0032	960205	RESPONSE	INTEGRATED SYS PROPRIETARY MULTIPLE BLDG	0.0078587	27.3
0033	4301F5	RESPONSE	FIRE DET?REP%UNATTENDED AREAS	0.0077917	31.0
0034	1101F4	DISPLAY	FIRE DET?REP%EDUC?OFFICE	0.0075767	47.2
0035	510211	SENSING MEANS	INTRUDER D?R COMMERCIAL	0.0075033	26.5
0036	210215	RESPONSE	INTRUDER D?R INSTITUTIONAL	0.0075008	34.9
0037	210102	INFO TRANS	INTEGRATED SYS CENTRAL STATION BLDG PROTECTION	0.0073708	36.3
0038	960403	ANALYSIS	INTEGRATED SYS DIR CON/REMOTE MULTIPLE BLDG	0.0072408	53.9
0039	3301F2	INFO TRANS	FIRE DET?REP%INDUSTRIAL	0.0069854	25.9
0040	960405	RESPONSE	INTEGRATED SYS DIR CON/REMOTE MULTIPLE BLDG	0.0069212	21.3
0041	960203	ANALYSIS	INTEGRATED SYS PROPRIETARY MULTIPLE BLDG	0.0066352	24.6
0042	960105	RESPONSE	INTEGRATED SYS CENTRAL STATION BLDG PROTECTION	0.0066270	46.7
0043	4301F3	ANALYSIS	FIRE DET?REP%UNATTENDED AREAS	0.0065019	47.0
0044	960103	ANALYSIS	INTEGRATED SYS CENTRAL STATION BLDG PROTECTION	0.0062235	41.0
0045	2201F3	ANALYSIS	FIRE DET?REP%INSTITUTIONAL	0.0061857	44.0
0046	310215	RESPONSE	INTRUDER D?R INDUSTRIAL	0.0061485	36.4
0047	5101F1	SENSING MEANS	FIRE DET?REP%RETAIL	0.0059486	28.7
0048	960204	DISPLAY	INTEGRATED SYS PROPRIETARY MULTIPLE BLDG	0.0058634	36.2
0049	310213	ANALYSIS	INTRUDER D?R INDUSTRIAL	0.0057462	43.7
0050	2201F4	DISPLAY	FIRE DET?REP%INSTITUTIONAL	0.0056952	42.0

SAMPLE

Figure 4 Sample printout of relevance rankings.

expanded to enable computation of the cumulative distribution of local relevance numbers at each node.

- *Report generation subsystem:* Prints out balloted relevance numbers organized by relevance ranking and identification number in a standardized format (shown in Figure 4) for relevance number, ratio, and intersection data.
- *Revision subsystem:* Permits modification of the structure tree by combining or deleting nodes (horizontal summation), and enables changes in node names and expansion of the structure at lower levels for detailed studies.

In summary, this methodology permits a greater contribution of quantitative data to the technology-upgrading investment decision since:

- Large numbers of complex interrelated variables can be broken down into simple decision factors that can be expressed numerically and stored in a computer.
- These variables, when assigned quantitative weightings (or "relevance numbers") can be manipulated to present logical conclusions. This manipulation does not destroy the validity of the initial decision factors, nor does it introduce significant biases.
- Conclusions can be drawn and extrapolations of the analysis of these relevance numbers can be made from information that was inherent in their assignment but not yet explicit in the minds of the decision makers when the parameters were inserted.

PATTERN DATA USE

The rank-ordered printouts (by relevance number and/or R_B/R_U) constitute the computer-printed reports from the PATTERN methodology. These reports provide a partial basis for selection of technology areas for prosecution. In general, the top one-third of the rank-ordered items at any level constitute the group from which projects should be selected for pursuance. This group normally will comprise approximately 75% of the total upgrading required in the complete study area under consideration. Individual study items in this top one-third listing will amost invariably have a market and technology need which warrants significant investment.

In cases in which the tree structure departs significantly from symmetry and the input data from the balloters have a large dispersion (standard deviation percentages of 70–100), the decisions should be based on the R_B/R_U ranking rather than the total relevance ranking. This ratio represents the relationship between an equally expected relevance number and the balloted relevance number. A ratio greater than 1.0

indicates that the balloters believe the item to require more than an average amount of upgrading, whereas a ratio less than 1.0 indicates a less than average or normally expected amount of upgrading. A decision point based on a ratio greater than 1.2 will result in the selection of items for pursuance which have high validity. This breakpoint normally selects approximately the top one-third of the items in the structure.

Selection of items which appear within the acceptable group should be based on company capabilities and desires, together with further analysis of the source of highly ranked need for upgrading. These data may be derived in part from the criteria zeroing outputs of the PATTERN system, in which rank-ordered outputs of the needs for upgrading are based on the criteria which are active. For example, if all criteria except those pertaining to cost were set to zero, the resultant ranking would indicate the relative needs for upgrading of the items under consideration in terms of cost reduction. On the other hand, all criteria except performance-oriented criteria might be set to zero, and the resultant ranking would show the relative needs for upgrading based on performance only. The intersection of rankings based on performance and cost independently would indicate the items requiring upgrading in both cost and performance. Obviously other types of criteria could be considered here, and it might be desirable to make a selection based on the opinions of limited groups of balloters. In this case rank-ordered outputs would be printed out, based only on the ballot inputs selected through the input-editing programs.

The selected study structure (tree) may be functionally oriented in a fashion which is not directly related to hardware systems. If this is the case, the relevance numbers applicable to functions which may be met by selected hardware systems should be assembled by the horizontal summed programs on the bases of fitting the functions and the available hardware systems together. In this event, where different hardware systems supply different functional capabilities, the appropriate functional upgrading requirements should be summed for each hardware system and the relative needs for upgrading the hardware systems then compared on the basis of the summed relevance numbers. This approach can result in a comparison of the need for upgrading the systems presently available with the need for upgrading the functions of a hypothetical system, thus providing a comparative evaluation of the system- or hardware-upgrading needs.

PATTERN METHODOLOGY APPLIED TO BIOMEDICINE

The PATTERN relevance tree methodology, as stated earlier, can be applied to any problem area in which decisions must be made under conditions of uncertainty. Some time ago a study was performed within Honeywell to identify future needs in biomedicine. This study was given the acronym Project MEDICINE (MEDical Instrumentation and Control Identified and Numerically Evaluated), and used the tree structuring and relevance number assignment techniques developed in the original military version of PATTERN. The study was conducted by a group of medical doctors, including Honeywell personnel and external consultants.

The team defined the principal national objective in the biomedicine study as *the maximizing of the human lifespan with optimal health and activities in all environments.* The generalized tree structure shown in Figure 5 illustrates the thought processes used in going from the national objective down to the technology and tools required to perform the various functions. For example, at the TASK level of the tree, "diagnosis" would be one of the primary activities necessary to achieve the objective. The APPROACH level contains the procedures to be applied to scientific tasks, such as surgery under "treatment." At the SYSTEM level are the bodily activities carried out by several organs operating together under integrated control (i.e., reflexive control of locomotion, blood circulation, etc.). The SUBSYSTEM, or organ, level contains the

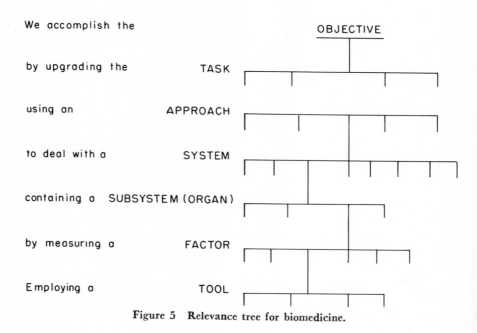

Figure 5   Relevance tree for biomedicine.

units, either natural or artificial, which perform a specialized activity. The FACTOR level lists the parameters which need to be measured, analyzed, and controlled to evaluate or cope with the normal or abnormal operation of an organ. Finally, the TOOL level contains the devices in the form of hardware or software used to acquire or process data, or to treat, cure, or prevent disease.

APPENDIX: METHODOLOGY

The example discussed in the section on "Relevance Number Determination" illustrates the calculation of partial relevances for Level 1 of the transportation structure as related to Criterion 1. The following examples illustrate the calculation of partial and total direct relevances over the balance of the structure.

The partial relevance numbers for functions listed under Criterion 2 (weighting 50) would, under the same approach, be:

Accommodate passengers	$0.25 \times 0.50 = 0.125$
Provide environment	$0.05 \times 0.50 = 0.025$
Provide performance monitoring capability	$0.10 \times 0.50 = 0.05$
Provide control capability	$0.60 \times 0.50 = 0.30$

The partial relevance numbers for functions listed under Criterion 3 (weighting 20) would, under the same approach, be:

Accommodate passengers	$0.40 \times 0.20 = 0.08$
Provide environment	$0.15 \times 0.20 = 0.03$
Provide performance monitoring capability	$0.40 \times 0.20 = 0.08$
Provide control capability	$0.05 \times 0.20 = 0.01$

The partial relevance numbers for functions listed under Criterion 4 (weighting 10) would, under the same approach, be:

Accommodate passengers	$0.35 \times 0.10 = 0.035$
Provide environment	$0.50 \times 0.10 = 0.05$
Provide performance monitoring capability	$0.05 \times 0.10 = 0.005$
Provide control capability	$0.10 \times 0.10 = 0.01$

As previously indicated, the local relevance for function is the sum of the partial relevance developed for the function by evaluation against the associated criteria. The local relevances for our example are accordingly:

For the first function, "Accommodate passengers," the local relevance is:

$$0.01 + 0.125 + 0.08 + 0.035 = 0.250$$

For "Provide environment" the local relevance is:

$$0.06 + 0.025 + 0.03 + 0.05 = 0.165$$

For "Provide performance-monitoring capability" the local relevance is:

$$0.12 + 0.05 + 0.08 + 0.005 = 0.255$$

For "Provide control capability" the local relevance is:

$$0.01 + 0.30 + 0.01 + 0.01 = 0.330$$

In accordance with the discussion of relevance number determination we will now calculate the total direct relevance (TDR) of the Level 2 functions. To illustrate, we will assume that local relevance numbers have been calculated for these functions:

Seat passengers	0.12
Protect passengers	0.23
Exclude external environment	0.08
Establish internal environment	0.15

(We are assuming here that the balance of the Level 2 local relevance total has been assigned to subfunctions of "Provide performance-monitoring capability" and "Provide control capability," which we are not considering in this illustration.)

The TDR for these functions is then determined as follows.

"Seat passengers" and "Protect passengers" are subfunctions of "Accommodate passengers," which has been assigned a total direct relevance of 0.250. Their total direct relevance is the product of their local relevance and the total direct relevance of their "parent function." Their respective TDR's are accordingly as follows:

Seat passengers	$0.12 \times 0.250 = 0.03$
Protect passengers	$0.23 \times 0.250 = 0.058$

Similarly, the TDR's for the other two subfunctions are:

Exclude external environment	$0.08 \times 0.165 = 0.0132$
Establish internal environment	$0.15 \times 0.165 = 0.0248$

(Note that in the calculation of TDR, total direct relevance and local relevance are identical for Level 1 functions. This follows from the formula for TDR calculation.)

XXIV. *A Research and Development Investment Model for Project Evaluation and Selection*[1]

MICHAEL L. COCHRAN AND A. DOUGLAS BENDER

The point of view of the directors of certain companies seems to be: what I do not understand, I do not ask about, and what I do not understand cannot possibly be worthwhile.
George Libik

INTRODUCTION

The successful commitment of an organization's resources is one of the most fundamental and crucial responsibilities facing a management team. Management literature abounds with suggested techniques to help the decision maker carry out his resource allocation responsibilities.

[1] We wish to acknowledge the technical contributions of Mr. Steven Dittmann of Com-Share, Inc. While at Smith Kline & French, he formulated the mathematical model and was responsible for the greater part of the coding for the Project Evaluation Program.

We also wish to express our appreciation to Mr. Harold A. Clymer and Dr. Leon C. Greene for their encouragement and to Mr. Edmund B. Pyle III for his valuable and outstanding technical contributions.

Three central themes in the literature become readily apparent:

- The investment must benefit the owner, that is, ensure continuity of the enterprise and maximize the probability that an adequate return will be achieved.
- All of the various investment opportunities available to the decision maker cannot be accepted because of the scarcity of both capital and physical resources.
- The information concerning the characteristics of a particular investment opportunity is, at best, incomplete, that is, uncertainties cloud each piece of data describing the investment.

Against this *background* the management team must decide to which investment opportunity it will commit the capital and the physical resources of the organization.

The pharmaceutical industry faces a relatively unique investment environment when committing its R&D resources. The average time from the conception of a research hypothesis to product introduction is extremely long (more than 10 years). In addition, the industry has an unusually high attrition rate for specific compounds (compared with durable consumer products), coupled with high R&D costs. This uniqueness of the pharmaceutical R&D commitment led us to the design of the Research and Development Investment Model used at Smith Kline & French. This model is designed to assist R&D management in its project *evaluation* and *selection* responsibilities.

In this chapter we describe the model and the way in which it has been incorporated as a tool to assist in the R&D decision-making process. Generally, descriptions of models in the literature are read with some skepticism, for, although of sound construction, these models are often ignored by management because either they are too complex or they do not truly reflect the environment in which they are designed to be used. Because of this situation we have stressed the management application of this model as each element of the system is described.

SUMMARY OF THE MODEL APPROACH

The R&D Investment Model is a return on investment evaluator, using the discontinued cash-flow technique. It is designed to evaluate the economic indices and to analyze the critical parameters of various potential projects with respect to their projected cash-flow characteristics. In addition, it is capable of selecting projects which will remain within the capital and physical resource limitations of alternative levels of budget considerations and will contribute the highest available return on investment within each level of resource limitation considered.

The approach used in the model can best be described in terms of four sequential elements.

1. *Determine the economic characteristics of each project.* The economic characteristics of a project can be shown by a cash-flow graph. The negative cash flow represents the dollar amount and the time that the management team must commit to each project. The positive cash flow represents the net income (return) to be generated by the project. The model assumes a 10-year product life which was defined by assumption.

2. *Consider the technological risks—expected net income.* The R&D management team's confidence in being able to produce a marketable product is expressed in terms of "probability of technical success." Because the Model is comparing the economic characteristics of one project with those of other projects which are competing for investment funds, the net income of a project with a *low* probability of success must be *penalized.* For example, if Project A has a total net income flow of $100.0 with a probability of success of 0.1, and Project B has a $20.0 flow with a 0.9 success factor, the management team may feel safer with the *expected* net income flow of $18.0 for Project B (20.0 × 0.9) than with Project A's *expected* net income of $10.0.

3. *Evaluate the adequacy of a project's economic characteristics.* The R&D Investment Model uses the expected net present value index (ENPV), which describes in one number the adequacy of the economic characteristics of a project under investment analysis. The net present value (NPV) of the cash-flow stream has been discounted by the cost of capital rate, and if the NPV is positive the economic characteristics are judged to be adequate. We selected the *expected* net present value index to define the overall value of a project because this one value considers:

- The dollar magnitude of the investment and resulting returns
- The timing of the cash flows
- The probability of technical success
- The cost of the capital invested in the project

A variation in any one of these considerations will change the ENPV characteristic.

4. *Select a combination of projects which yields the highest total ENPV for any R&D expenditure level.* After the R&D Investment Model

has computed one dollar figure (expected net present value) for each project under consideration, the model will then select a combination of projects that will meet the following objectives:

- Yield the highest combined ENPV
- Have total development costs which will not exceed the budget constraints determined by the R&D management team

On the basis of other considerations, management may decide to fund a project regardless of whether or not the optimization algorithm selects it. In this case, the budget figures are reduced by an amount equal to the development costs of the selected project, and the remaining development budget is allocated in accordance with the rules of the selection algorithm.

PROJECT EVALUATION MODULE

The Project Evaluation Module is a completely conversational, user-oriented tool for performing in-depth analyses concerning the economic characteristics of various potential projects under various management strategies and assumptions. Because of its time-sharing interactive nature, the mechanics of executing the program and selecting and using the various options available in the model are very quickly mastered. Even the user who has had no previous experience with computerized models finds himself working comfortably with it after one or two sessions. As a result, various managers are making direct use of it to evaluate and analyze their respective projects. This is particularly desirable, since many times the course of future analyses for a project depends on some intermediate results, and only the cognizant manager is in a position to evaluate these results and to determine the nature of follow-on analyses.

User Options and Output

The Project Evaluation Module consists of a main portion which allows record (project) creating, deleting, and updating on a random-access file; and a Return on Investment subroutine which calculates the ENPV, internal rate of return, and percentage of goals achieved, and also performs the input sensitivity analysis.

Upon execution of the main program the user is presented with the following options:

(U)PDATE, (R)OI, (S)EE FILE, (P)ROJECT LIST, (E)ND

He selects the desired option by merely typing the appropriate first letter.

The UPDATE option is utilized to create a new project record or to update an existing record. The steps involved in the use of this option to create a new record are shown in Figure 1. (*Note:* Underlined items indicate user answers to program queries.) Upon selecting the UPDATE option, the user is asked for a project name. If the six-character name supplied does not match any name already in the directory, the program assumes that a new project is to be added. The user is then queried:

(P)ERMANENT OR (T)EMPORARY?

If the PERMANENT option is chosen, all data items are written on a random-access disk file for future access and analysis. If the TEMPORARY option is selected, the data items are retained in core only and are lost after termination of the program. After this selection, the user is advised to change desired data items by codes and is offered an opportunity to view the list of codes and their respective meanings. When a project is being created, certain data items are considered to be vital: development start and end dates, development costs, net sales, marketing costs, cost of goods sold, other expenses, probability of success, and cost of capital. If any of these items are omitted, the program will prompt the user until they are properly entered. In addition, certain data items are considered optional: sales start and end dates, high probability estimate, low probability estimate, historical probability, present phase (of drug investigation), present-phase completion date, date of next decision point, and New Drug Application approval date. These data are for informational purposes only and do not affect the values of the economic indices. The program will continually request more changes until an N (No More Changes) is entered in response to the query, CODE? At this point, if all vital data have been entered, the program will execute the Return on Investment (ROI) subroutine, print out the ENPV and the internal rate of return, and query:

SEE SUMMARY DATA?

If the user responds N (No), the program presents him with the original five options for the next analysis. If the user selects Y (Yes), a complete investment report is printed (see Figure 2) containing all the economic information concerning the project. Then the program returns to the original five options.

If the UPDATE option is selected and the project name is found

```
(U)PDATE, (R)OI, (S)EE FILE, (P)ROJECT LIST, (E)ND
U
PROJECT NAME?
TEST
NOT ON FILE
ASSUME YOU WISH TO ADD
(P)ERMANENT OR (T)EMPORARY?
P
CHANGE ITEMS BY CODE
SEE CODES?
Y
         CODE    MEANING
••••••••••••••••••••••••••••••••••••••••••••••••••••••••••••••••••••
                                                        REQUIRED DATA
         DD      DEVELOPMENT START AND END DATES
         DC      DEVELOPMENT COSTS
         NS      NET SALES
         MC      MARKETING COSTS
         CG1     CGS %
         OE      OTHER EXPENSE %
         PS      PROBABILITY OF SUCCESS
         CC      COST OF CAPITAL %
         N       NO MORE CHANGES
                                                        REQUIRED DATA
••••••••••••••••••••••••••••••••••••••••••••••••••••••••••••••••••••
                                                        OPTIONAL DATA
         SD      SALES START AND END DATES
         HPR     HIGH PROBABILITY ESTIMATE
         LPR     LOW PROBABILITY ESTIMATE
         APR     AVERAGE PROBABILTY ESTIMATE
         HIS     HISTORICAL PROBABILITY
         PP      PRESENT PHASE
         PPC     PRESENT PHASE COMPLETION DATE
         DPT     DATE OF NEXT DECISION POINT
         NDA     NDA APPROVAL DATE
         NA      PROJECT NAME
                                                        OPTIONAL DATA
••••••••••••••••••••••••••••••••••••••••••••••••••••••••••••••••••••
CODE?
DD
  0, 0, 0, 0,
  1, 70, 1, 74
CODE?
DC
0.000,0.000,0.000,0.000,0.000,0.000,0.000,0.000,0.000,0.000,
% CHANGE?   (NO=0., YES=ACTUAL %--XX.)
0.
ENTER DATA
0.800, 1.300, 1.400, 0.600
CODE?
NS
  0.0, 0.0, 0.0, 0.0, 0.0, 0.0, 0.0, 0.0, 0.0, 0.0, 0.0,
% CHANGE?   (NO=0., YES=ACTUAL %--XX.)
0.
ENTER DATA
4.4, 5.6, 6.4, 7.9, 11.3, 15.7, 18.9, 19.9, 21.0, 23.4
CODE?
```

Figure 1 *(a)* **Update option for new project creation.**

in the directory, the user is queried:

(C)HANGE OR (D)ELETE?

If the CHANGE option is selected, the user is queried:

(P)ERMANENT OR (T)EMPORARY?

and the analysis proceeds exactly as described above. Figure 3 gives an example of an analysis performed utilizing the CHANGE option, and Figure 4 shows the resulting output if a complete report is desired.

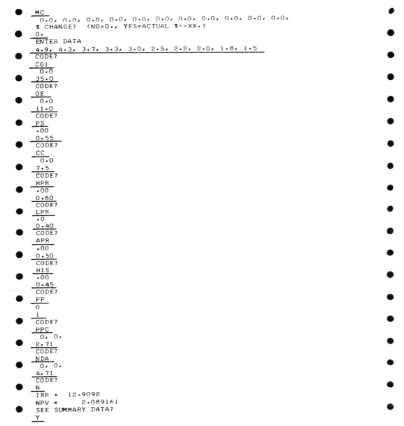

```
MC
  0.0,  0.0,  0.0,  0.0,  0.0,  0.0,  0.0,  0.0,  0.0,  0.0,  0.0,
% CHANGE?   (NO=0., YES=ACTUAL %--XX.)
0.
ENTER DATA
4.9,  4.3,  3.7,  3.3,  3.0,  2.5,  2.2,  2.0,  1.8,  1.5
CODE?
CG1
  0.0
35.0
CODE?
OE
  0.0
11.0
CODE?
PS
  .00
0.55
CODE?
CC
  0.0
7.5
CODE?
HPR
  .00
0.60
CODE?
LPR
  .0
0.40
CODE?
APR
  .00
0.50
CODE?
HIS
  .00
0.45
CODE?
PP
  0
1
CODE?
PPC
  0,  0,
2,71
CODE?
NDA
  0,  0,
4,71
CODE?
N
IRR  =   12.9092
NPV  =       2.089161
SEE SUMMARY DATA?
Y
```

Figure 1 (*b*)

In this case the net sales were increased by 20%, while the probability of success was decreased to 0.45. The effects on the economic indices may be seen by comparing the corresponding output reports. This option is very useful in performing the "what if" analysis discussed in the section "Management Use."

If the DELETE option is selected, the user is asked, SURE? If the answer is affirmative, the core is zeroed, the project data are erased from the random-access file, and the program returns to the original five options.

Selection of the ROI option causes the Return on Investment sub-

PROJECT TEST
R & D PLANNING AND FORECASTING INVESTMENT REPORT

DATE 5/20   UPDATED   5/20/70

COST OF GOODS SOLD % 35.0- 0.0   CHANGEOVER DATE 0/ 0

OTHER EXPENSES 11.0% OF SALES

	CURRENT	PREVIOUS		% 75-79 GOAL ABS	EXP
IRR	12.9	12.9	PRETAX	6.8	3.7
NPV	2.1	2.1	SALES	14.7	8.1

CURRENT COST OF CAPITAL 7.5%   CURRENT PROBABILITY OF SUCCESS 0.55
V

	START	FINISH
DEVELOPMENT DATES	1/70	1/74
SALES DATES	1/74	1/84

YEAR	70	71	72	73
DEVELOPMENT COSTS	0.800	1.300	1.400	0.600

YEAR	74	75	76	77	78	79	80	81	82	83

NET SALES

  MAN. COST
  MKTG. COST

PAP

  OTHER EXPS.

PRETAX PROFIT

NET PROFIT

EXP. NET PROFIT
E

	INPUT VARIABLE	
SENSITIVITY	PROBABILITY OF SUCCESS	0.29
ANALYSIS	DEVELOPMENT COSTS	68.48 %
(NPV = 0)	NET INCOME	-30.93 %
	NET SALES -21.08 %	
	MKTG.COST 43.79 %	
	MNFG.COST 46.38 %	
	OTH.EXPS. 22.38 %	

OTHER PROBABILITY ESTIMATES: AVERAGE BETWEEN DECISION POINTS 0.77

          HIGH 0.60 LOW 0.40 AVERAGE 0.50 HISTORICAL 0.45

PRESENT PHASE 1   NEXT DECISION POINT   2/71   NDA APPROVAL 4/71

Figure 2   Detailed investment report.

```
(U)PDATE, (R)OI, (S)EE FILE, (P)ROJECT LIST, (E)ND
U
PROJECT NAME?
TEST
ON PERMANENT FILE
(C)HANGE OR (D)ELETE?
C
(P)ERMANENT OR (T)EMPORARY?
T
CHANGE ITEMS BY CODE
SEE CODES?
N
CODE?
NS
 4.4, 5.6, 6.4, 7.9,11.3,15.7,18.9,19.9,21.0,23.4, 0.0,
% CHANGE?   (NO=0., YES=ACTUAL %--XX.)
20.0
CODE?
PS
.55
0.45
CODE?
N
IRR = 15.3258
NPV =     2.921590
SEE SUMMARY DATA?
Y
```

Figure 3   Update option for project record changes.

routine to be executed, utilizing the data existing in the file. Again, the user may obtain a complete investment report if desired.

The SEE FILE option allows the user to view the data on file for a specified project. If this option is chosen, the user is queried:

DATA TYPE? (A)LL, (E)CONOMIC (P)ARAMETRIC

ECONOMIC includes sales and cost data; PARAMETRIC, input sensitivity analysis data; and ALL, all data on file for the particular project. If the ALL option is chosen, the output is similar to the complete reports shown in Figures 2 and 4.

The PROJECT LIST option allows the user to view a list of all the project names for which data files exist.

The END option causes normal termination of the Project Evaluation Module and is used when all the analyses of the current session have been performed.

A macro flow chart for the Project Evaluation Module is shown in Figure 5.

R & D PLANNING AND FORECASTING INVESTMENT REPORT

DATE 5/20

UPDATED 5/20/70

COST OF GOODS SOLD % 35.0- 0.0

CHANGEOVER DATE 0/ 0

OTHER EXPENSES 11.0% OF SALES

	CURRENT	PREVIOUS			% 75-79 ABS	GOAL EXP
IRR	15.3	12.9		PRETAX	10.8	4.9
NPV	2.9	2.1		SALES	17.6	7.9

CURRENT COST OF CAPITAL 7.5%   CURRENT PROBABILITY OF SUCCESS 0.45

V

	START	FINISH
DEVELOPMENT DATES	1/70	1/74
SALES DATES	1/74	1/84

YEAR	70	71	72	73
DEVELOPMENT COSTS	0.800	1.300	1.400	0.600

YEAR	74	75	76	77	78	79	80	81	82	83
NET SALES										
MAN. COST										
MKTG. COST										
PAP										
OTHER EXPS.										
PRETAX PROFIT										
NET PROFIT										
EXP. NET PROFIT										

E

SENSITIVITY ANALYSIS (NPV = 0)	INPUT VARIABLE	
	PROBABILITY OF SUCCESS	0.20
	DEVELOPMENT COSTS	100.55 %
	NET INCOME	-43.43 %
	NET SALES	-30.03 %
	MKTG.COST	74.84 %
	MNFG.COST	51.22 %
	OTH.EXPS.	27.21 %

OTHER PROBABILITY ESTIMATES: AVERAGE BETWEEN DECISION POINTS 0.73

HIGH 0.60 LOW 0.40 AVERAGE 0.50 HISTORICAL 0.45

PRESENT PHASE 1   NEXT DECISION POINT 2/71   NDA APPROVAL 4/71

Figure 4 Detailed investment report reflecting results of changes.

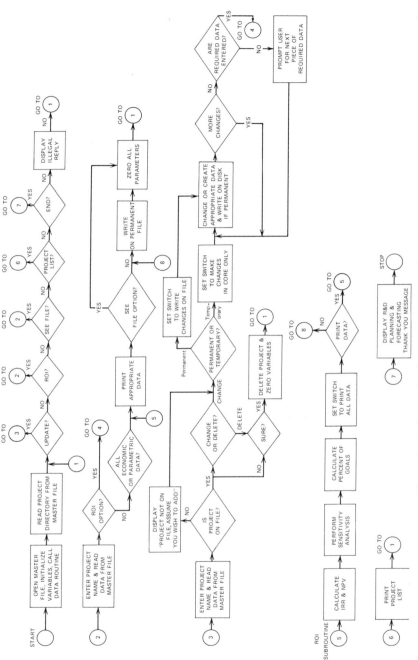

Figure 5 Project evaluation program: macro flow chart.

457

Management Use

When using the Project Evaluation Module of the R&D Investment Model, the manager can analyze the economic characteristics and adequacy of a specific project by temporarily changing the revenue stream, cost structure, cash-flow timing, project costs, success factor, and the cost of capital requirement. By using the "what if" analysis worksheet (see Figure 6) the manager can ask various questions concerning the input parameters in his office, and then go to the time-share terminal and immediately analyze the results and record the output in the "Results" section on the worksheet. The results are expressed in terms of three elements:

1. Economic indices—internal rate of return (IRR) and net present value (NPV).
2. Percentage of pretax and net sales goals during a specific time period produced by the project.
3. Sensitivity analysis of the three major inputs, that is, probability of technical success, project cost, and net income.

As the manager becomes familiar with the R&D Investment Model analysis, the sophistication of use and the subsequent analyses will increase. For example, if a project has a high NPV and IRR, which are indices of the *total* economic characteristics, but a low percentage of sales and pretax goal achievement, the short-term disadvantage (goal achievement) must be weighed against the long-term advantages (high NPV and IRR). No model can make this value judgment, and therefore the decision rests entirely on management.

The sensitivity analysis separates the "wheat from the chaff" as far as the inputs are concerned. If the probability of technical success for a specific project can go from, say 0.7 to 0.1 before the NPV becomes equal to zero, but net income can decrease by only 10% before the NPV becomes equal to zero, the projections of the revenue stream and the elements of the operating cost structure should be analyzed critically for reasonableness. The probability of success estimate is *relatively* insensitive to the adequacy of the economic characteristics of the project, and therefore needs minimum management attention to this point in time. The investment reports shown in Figures 2 and 4 extend the net income sensitivity analysis by showing the sensitivity of the elements generating net income, that is, net sales, manufacturing costs, marketing costs, and other expenses.

R&D INVESTMENT REPORT

"WHAT IF" ANALYSIS WORK SHEET

PROJECT _____ DATE _____

CURRENT STATUS		
ECONOMIC INDICES	% 19 ___ to 19 ___ **GOAL ACHIEVEMENT**	

			ABSOLUTE	EXPECTED
IRR %	[ ] %	PRETAX	%	%
NPV	$ [ ]	NET SALES	%	%

"WHAT IF CHANGES"	DATA									
1. TIMING: Development START and/or End Date (Code "DD")	New START Month _____ Year _____ New END Month _____ Year _____									
2. DEVELOPMENT COST: (Code "DC")	YR.	1	2	3	4	5	6	7		
a. DOLLAR CHANGE	AMT									
b. PERCENT CHANGE	[ ] %									
3. NET SALES: (Code "NS")	YR.	1	2	3	4	5	6	7	8	9	10
a. DOLLAR CHANGE	AMT									
b. PERCENT CHANGE	[ ] %									
4. COST OF GOODS SOLD: (Code "CGI") a. NEW PERCENT	[ ] %									
5. MARKETING COSTS: (Code "MC")	YR.	1	2	3	4	5	6	7	8	9	10
a. DOLLAR CHANGE	AMT									
b. PERCENT CHANGE	[ ] %									
6. OTHER EXPENSES: (Code "OE") a. NEW PERCENT	[ ] %									
7. PROBABILITY OF SUCCESS: (Code "PS")	[ ] %									
8. COST OF CAPITAL: (Code "CC")	[ ] %									

RESULTS		
ECONOMIC INDICES	% 19 ___ to 19 ___ GOAL ACHIEVEMENT	**SENSITIVITY ANALYSIS**

			ABSOLUTE	EXPECTED		(NPV = 0)	
IRR %	[ ] %	PRETAX	%	%	PROBABILITY OF SUCCESS	[ ] %
NPV	$ [ ]	NET SALES	%	%	DEV. COST	[ ] %
					NET INCOME	[ ] %

SEE REVERSE SIDE FOR TERMINAL OPERATING INSTRUCTIONS

Figure 6   "What if" analysis worksheet.

MATHEMATICAL COMPUTATIONS
FOR PROJECT EVALUATION

Expected Net Present Value

Once a project is selected for development, a commitment is made for expenditure at the present time and at various times in the future in the expectation of receiving benefits at various times even further in the future. The value of costs to be incurred or benefits to be received at different times cannot be compared directly. However, before development projects are selected, some comparison involving costs and benefits must be made among the projects being considered. Therefore, a method for putting the costs and benefits on a common basis is required. The concept commonly used is that of "present value," which states the value of future cost or benefit in terms of its equivalent value at some fixed point in time. The details of calculating a specific present value can be found in any elementary managerial textbook and hence are omitted here. The addition of the term net to "present value" merely implies that the present values for all of the years in a cash-flow stream are summed.

Since the present value of the net income sequence is not known with certainty (the project may succeed or fail), it would seem appropriate to use the expected values. These are arrived at by multiplying each present value in the net income sequence by the probability of technical success.

The same is also true of the cost sequence, but to a lesser extent. If a project is selected for development, the funding for the first year is committed, that is, the probability of spending the initial value in the cost sequence is unity. This is not true, however, for the remaining values in the cost sequence because there is a possibility that the project will be dropped at any time after the first year. Hence, for the remaining years of development, the probability that the cost will actually be incurred must lie somewhere between unity and the established value for the probability of technical success of the project.

Since historical information was not available concerning the exact variation of yearly probabilities during the development period, it was decided to use the numerical average between unity and the probability of technical success for the project. This was considered to be a reasonable approach, since all projects would be evaluated in the same manner.

Putting all this together, we obtain the equation for calculating the *expected net present value* (ENPV) for a project as:

$$\text{ENPV} = X_1 + \left(\frac{1 + P}{2}\right) \sum_{i=2}^{K} \frac{X_i}{(1 + R)^{i-1}} + (P) \sum_{i=K+1}^{N} \frac{X_i}{(1 + R)^{i-1}}$$

(1)

where X_i = cash flow for ith year (millions of dollars),

$(>0 \rightarrow$ net income)
$(<0 \rightarrow$ development cost),

P = probability of technical success,
R = cost of capital rate,
K = number of development years,
N = total number of years ($N = K + 10$, by assumption).

It should be noted that the ENPV is related to the end of the first consideration for development. This value is then used as the index year development cost is spent with certainty.

Equation 1 is used to compute the ENPV for every project under consideration for development. This value is then used as the index for obtaining the optimum subset of development projects, as explained in the next section.

Internal Rate of Return

The internal rate of return is, by definition, that value of R in Eq. 1 such that the expected net present value is equal to zero. It is found by setting the ENPV = 0 in Eq. 1 and solving for R. Since it is evident that R cannot be found explicitly, a trial-and-error iterative procedure is necessary. The method used is that of "false position." The details of this procedure can be found in most textbooks on computational methods and therefore are omitted here. The only restriction on the method is that there can be, at most, only one sign change in the cash-flow sequence. The method converges very rapidly and usually requires less than fifteen iterations.

Modified Sensitivity Analysis

The purpose of the sensitivity analysis is to identify the parameters most critical in the determination of the ENPV. The parameters which are investigated in this analysis are as follows:

- Probability of technical success
- Development costs
- Net income
    Net sales
    Marketing costs
    Manufacturing costs
    Other expenses

The analysis is conducted by holding two of the three primary parameters fixed and finding the value of the third parameter such that the ENPV becomes equal to zero in Eq. 1. Then the net income is investigated in detail to determine the sensitivity of the subparameters. The details peculiar to the analysis of each parameter are discussed separately in the following sections.

Probability of Technical Success. It can be seen that, if the ENPV is set equal to zero in Eq. 1, the necessary value of the probability of technical success (holding all other parameters constant) can be found explicitly as:

$$P_0 = -\frac{X_1 + \frac{1}{2}\sum_{i=2}^{K}[X_i/(1+R)^{i-1}]}{\frac{1}{2}\sum_{i=2}^{K}[X_i/(1+R)^{i-1}] + \sum_{i=K+1}^{N}[X_i/(1+R)^{i-1}]} \tag{2}$$

The subscript is used to differentiate this value from the actual probability of technical success associated with the project. If the value of P_0 should happen to lie outside the range $0 \to 1$ (i.e., $P_0 < 0$ or $P_0 > 1$), it would indicate that the probability of technical success could not be changed sufficiently to cause the ENPV to become zero. In this case it would be concluded that the ENPV was relatively insensitive to changes in the probability of technical success. If, on the other hand, the value of P_0 was very close to that of P, it would be concluded that the ENPV was extremely sensitive to changes in the probability of technical success.

Development Costs. It can be readily seen from Eq. 1 that, with the ENPV set equal to zero, it is not possible to solve explicitly for the required development costs $(X_i, i = 2, 3, \ldots, K)$. Therefore, an iterative procedure is required. Since there are theoretically an infinite number of combinations of absolute values for development costs that would make the ENPV equal to zero, it is necessary to choose a meaningful foundation upon which to base the analysis. A logical choice is the original development cost sequence. Hence, the percentage change in the original development cost sequence necessary to make the ENPV equal to zero is determined. Depending on whether the percentage is large or small, it can be concluded that the ENPV is either insensitive or sensitive, respectively, to changes in the development costs of the project.

Net Income. The effect of net income on the ENPV is determined in the same manner as is the effect of development cost. An iterative procedure is used to determine the percentage change in the net income sequence necessary to make the ENPV equal to zero. Then, depending on the magnitude of the percentage, conclusions concerning the sensitivity of the ENPV with respect to changes in the net income can be drawn.

Since four parameters contribute to the net income, each is investigated independently to determine its influence on the ENPV. The percentage change in the net sales and the marketing costs are determined in exactly the same manner as is the percentage change in the overall net income. The manufacturing costs and other expenses, however, are handled a little differently. Since they are expressed as a fixed percentage of the net sales, a new fixed percentage (rather than a percent change) is calculated which makes the ENPV become equal to zero in each case. Then, depending on how the new fixed percentage compares with the original value, conclusions may be drawn concerning the sensitivity of the ENPV with respect to manufacturing costs and other expenses.

It must be remembered that this is a modified sensitivity analysis in that the interdependence of parameters is not investigated; only the individual effects are obtained. However, this information is very useful in identifying the most sensitive parameters with regard to the weighting index, that is, the expected net present value.

PROJECT SELECTION MODULE

The second module in the R&D Investment Model system is the Project Selection Program. Its function is quite simple: given a set of projects, each with an established expected net present value and a sequence of yearly development costs, the program finds the subset of projects with the highest total ENPV for which the total development costs do not exceed fixed budgetary constraints.

Because this program is not run nearly as often as the Project Evaluation Program, it is not nearly as interactive in nature. The Project Selection Program is more of a planning tool and it is not economically feasible to run it in the same manner as the Project Evaluation Program.

User Input and Output

Upon execution of the program the user is supplied with a list of all the projects currently on file, including their respective expected net present values and development cost sequences. The user is then requested to supply the desired yearly budgetary constraints (at least one but not more than seven). After accepting these, the program eliminates all projects whose expected net present values are less than zero (these cannot possibly contribute toward maximizing the total ENPV) and checks to see that no more than sixteen projects remain in the set (this upper limit is due to computational inefficiencies and will be discussed in detail in the section entitled "Mathematical Considerations for Project Selection"). If more than sixteen projects remain, the user is requested to remove enough projects of his choosing so that this limit is not exceeded. Next, the program executes the selection logic (also discussed fully in the section on "Mathematical Considerations") and outputs the desired optimum subset of projects.

Figure 7 shows a sample execution of the Project Selection Program, utilizing a hypothetical set of projects with their corresponding expected net present values and development cost sequences.

Management Use

Research and development management is faced with the continuous problem of how much to invest in the development process before the added dollar of investment is not worth the additional dollar of return. The Project Selection Module of the R&D Investment Model is used to assist management in this type of marginal analysis.

The selection program can be run at a specified budget level to determine the total ENPV yielded by the projects (see Figure 7). The budget can then be parametrically increased, for example, in increments of $500,000, and the corresponding expected net present values observed and compared with those of previous runs. The additional ENPV yield, as the budget level is increased, can give management graphic insight into the value received from an additional commitment of funds.

```
CURRENT PROJECT LIST:
*******************************************************************************
                       DEV.COSTS(BY YEAR)
    PROJ        NPV        1       2       3

    TESTO1     1.291     0.23    0.35    0.76
    TESTO2     2.035     0.31    0.33    0.45
    TESTO3     0.497     0.15    0.30    0.40
    TESTO4     3.347     0.18    0.29    0.53
    TESTO5     9.136     0.31    0.39    0.56
    TESTO6     8.554     0.10    0.20    0.30
    TESTO7     6.976     0.14    0.33    0.71
    TESTO8     5.531     0.55    0.80    1.09
    TESTO9     4.971     0.44    0.73    0.94
    TEST10     2.224     0.12    0.28    0.44
    TEST11     3.004     0.23    0.29    0.35
    TEST12     5.097     0.35    0.39    0.51
    TEST13     6.014     0.31    0.46    0.63
    TEST14     0.976     0.11    0.16    0.21
*******************************************************************************
    TOTALS    59.653     3.53    5.30    7.88


HOW MANY BUDGET CONSTRAINTS? (MAX=7)
3

ENTER BUDGET FIGURES STARTING WITH THE FIRST
YEAR AND SEPARATING WITH COMMAS.
1.60, 2.10, 2.90


THE OPTIMUM SUBSET OF PROJECTS IS AS FOLLOWS:
*******************************************************************************
                       DEV.COSTS(BY YEAR)
    PROJ        NPV        1       2       3

    TESTO5     9.136     0.31    0.39    0.56
    TESTO6     8.554     0.10    0.20    0.30
    TESTO7     6.976     0.14    0.33    0.71
    TEST12     5.097     0.35    0.39    0.51
    TEST13     6.014     0.31    0.46    0.63
*******************************************************************************
    TOTALS    35.777     1.21    1.77    2.71

    CONSTRAINTS           1.60    2.10    2.90
```

Figure 7   Project selection program: sample run.

This type of budget level analysis requires a value judgment on the part of management, that is, *these executives* must decide at what point the additional value received is not sufficient in view of the additional amount expended. If the budget is determined and becomes the absolute constraint of allowable resources, management can analyze the effect of a new project coming into the existing project mix. When this project is added to the available list, the total ENPV may increase because an old project is dropped by the selection module and the new one is picked up in order to optimize the total economic characteristics of the project list.

MATHEMATICAL CONSIDERATIONS FOR PROJECT SELECTION

Formulation of the Optimization Problem

As mentioned previously, it is desired to determine which projects from a candidate list should be chosen for development, so that the best expected return on investment dollars is obtained while the total costs associated with the selected projects does not exceed a predetermined budget level. This problem may be formulated mathematically as follows.

Given a set of n candidate projects:

$$E = \{e_1, e_2, \ldots, e_n\} \tag{3}$$

and the associated set of weights:

$$W = \{W_1, W_2, \ldots, W_n\} \tag{4}$$

(*Note:* In our case the components of the weight vector are merely the expected net present values for the candidate projects.) and the associated set of costs:

$$C_j = \{C_{1j}, C_{2j}, \ldots, C_{nj}\} \quad (j = 1, 2, \ldots, K) \tag{5}$$

where C_{ij} = the development cost of the ith project in the jth year, and K = total number of development years.

The problem is to find the binary components of the decision vector:

$$\Delta = \{\delta_1, \delta_2, \ldots, \delta_n\} \tag{6}$$

where $\delta_i = \begin{cases} 0 \rightarrow \text{project } e_i \text{ is } not \text{ selected for development} \\ 1 \rightarrow \text{project } e_i \text{ is selected for development} \end{cases}$

such that

$$V = \max \left(\sum_{i=1}^{n} \delta_i W_i \right) \tag{7}$$

subject to the constraints:

$$\sum_{i=1}^{n} \delta_i C_{ij} \leq B_j \quad (j = 1, 2, \ldots, m) \tag{8}$$

where B_j = the budget level for the jth year of development, and m = number of years for which budget levels are specified.

Equation 7 is the objective function, and Eq. 8 specifies the constraints. If there were no monetary resource limitations, all the B_j's in Eq. 8 could be considered to be infinite. In this case, the solution would trivially be:

$$\Delta = \{1, 1, \ldots, 1\} \tag{9}$$

In other words, all projects would be selected for development. However, this is not the case, and the problems must be solved subject to finite budgetary constraints.

The Solution Algorithm

It is readily seen that, if we have n projects in the list, there are 2^n possible solutions for the components of the decision vector (including the trivial case of no projects selected). Therefore, if n is small, the problem is easily solved by looking at all possible solutions (total enumeration) and choosing the one with the largest total ENPV for which the total development costs remain within the budget limitations. For example, if only four projects were under consideration, we would have to look at 2^4 or 16 possible solutions; for five projects, 2^5 or 32 possible solutions; etc. Each time a project is added to the list, the number of possible solutions doubles over what it was before the addition of the project. At this rate it doesn't take very long before total enumeration becomes infeasible in terms of computation time. For example, for a list of twenty projects, we would have to examine 2^{20} or 1,048,576 possible solutions.

Fortunately, this problem can be solved through the use of integer programming techniques with 0–1 variables. The technique presently implemented for solving this problem is a computational procedure known as the Lawler-Bell algorithm. It is fully documented by the authors[2] and will be explained only briefly here.

Basically, the algorithm is a partial enumeration scheme (as opposed to the total enumeration scheme described earlier), in that it permits skipping certain solutions which *cannot* improve an existing optimum or *cannot* satisfy the budget constraints. Hence, only a fraction of the total possible solutions need be examined in order to obtain the desired optimum. The skipping rules are set up on the basis of the nature of

[2] E. L. Lawler and M. D. Bell, "A Method for Solving Discrete Optimization Problems," *Operations Research,* November–December 1966, pp. 1098–1112.

the functions involved and the fact that the various solution vectors are treated as binary numbers and are examined in binary numerical order.

The general form of the problem for which the Lawler-Bell algorithm is applicable is as follows.

Find:
$$V = \min [f(\Delta)] \tag{10}$$

subject to:

$$\sum_{i=1}^{K} [g_{i1}(\Delta) - g_{i2}(\Delta)] \geq 0 \tag{11}$$

where

$$\Delta = \{\delta, \delta_2, \ldots, \delta_n\}$$
$$\delta_i = 0 \text{ or } 1 \quad (i = 1, 2, \ldots, n)$$

and each of the functions $f(\Delta)$, $g_{11}(\Delta)$, $g_{12}(\Delta)$, $\ldots$, $g_{k1}(\Delta)$, $g_{k2}(\Delta)$ is monotonically nondecreasing in each of the variables $\delta_1, \delta_2, \ldots, \delta_n$. This problem can be alternatively stated as follows.

Find:
$$V = \max [f(\Delta)] \tag{12}$$

subject to:

$$\sum_{i=1}^{K} [g_{i1}(\Delta) - g_{i2}(\Delta)] \leq 0 \tag{13}$$

where Δ is as defined previously, and each of the functions $f(\Delta)$, $g_{11}(\Delta)$, $g_{12}(\Delta)$, $\ldots$, $g_{k1}(\Delta)$, $g_{k2}(\Delta)$ is monotonically nonincreasing in each of the variables $\delta_1, \delta_2, \ldots, \delta_n$.

A monotonically nonincreasing function is one that, given two decision vectors $\Delta^{(1)}$ and $\Delta^{(2)}$, such that $\Delta^{(1)} \leq \Delta^{(2)}$ (in the sense of partial vector ordering, i.e., $\delta_i^{(1)} \leq \delta_i^{(2)}$ for all i), then $f[\Delta^{(1)}] \leq f[\Delta^{(2)}]$.

Now, comparing Eqs. 7 and 8 with Eqs. 12 and 13, respectively, we can see that our problem apparently fits the general form of the Lawler-Bell problem. However, since W_i and C_{ij} are nonnegative, and since B_j is a constant, it can be seen that $\delta_i W_i$, $\delta_i C_{ij}$, and B_j are all monotonically nondecreasing in the δ_i. If our problem is to fit the Lawler-Bell problem, these functions must be made monotonically nonincreasing in the δ_i. This is accomplished by applying the transformation:

$$\delta_i = 1 - \delta_i' \tag{14}$$

Then our problem becomes as follows.

Find:
$$\Delta' = \{\delta_1', \delta_2', \ldots, \delta_n'\} \tag{15}$$

such that:

$$V = \max \left[\sum_{i=1}^{n} (1 - \delta_i') W_i \right] \qquad (16)$$

subject to:

$$\sum_{i=1}^{n} (1 - \delta_i') C_{ij} - B_j \leq 0 \quad (j = 1, 2, \ldots, m) \qquad (17)$$

It can be seen that now the objective and constraint functions are monotonically nonincreasing the δ_i'. It can also be seen that the net effect of the transformation given by Eq. 14 is to reverse the implied meaning of the decision variables, or:

$$\delta_i = \begin{cases} 0 \to \text{project } e_i \text{ is selected for development} \\ 1 \to \text{project } e_i \text{ is } not \text{ selected for development} \end{cases}$$

After being implemented on the time-sharing computer system, this algorithm was found to be computationally efficient, provided the number of projects does not exceed approximately sixteen. However, since the optimization procedure is performed only a few times a year, this program receives considerably less use then does the Project Evaluation Program, and therefore a certain level of computational inefficiency is acceptable. It should be noted that, if this program were to be implemented on a large-scale computer and run in a batch mode, many more than sixteen projects could be efficiently handled. This limit was arbitrarily fixed on the basis of what was considered to be the maximum desirable terminal waiting time (approximately 20 minutes).

Another optimization method being investigated for possible future implementation is a dynamic programming scheme which uses Lagrange multipliers to incorporate the budget constraints into the objective function. Preliminary investigation shows that the computation time will increase linearly with the number of projects rather than exponentially as is the case now.

FUTURE EXTENSIONS

Feasibility Test of the Economic Solution

The ultimate output from the R&D Investment Model is a list of projects which have the highest total expected net present value and whose total yearly development costs are within the imposed limitations. This is the optimum *economic* solution! The selection of projects on the basis of economic characteristics assumes the availability of all required manpower and facilities, that is, sufficient physical resources. This availability assumption must be tested.

It is planned to examine the optimum project list, using the McDonnell Management Scheduling and Control System (MSCS) software package in order to determine whether resource conflicts exist. In the event of conflicts, the project list will be altered slightly and tested again. This process will be continued until the best list of projects which satisfy both budgetary and resource limitations is found. The project management system used here at SK&F has been described in the literature.[3]

Alternative Development Strategies

A development project requires, on the average, 5.6 years from its establishment to submission of the New Drug Application. This time can be reduced by 1 year for selected projects by assuming risk in early starts for some of the activities in the development process. These decisions necessitate more rapid cost generation for the project, but should place the product on the market sooner, thereby changing the economic characteristics of the project, that is, the expected net present value.

The present capability of the R&D Investment Model considers only one revenue stream and, therefore, one development process strategy for each project. A project is selected either at the stated level of strategy or not at all. This approach has limitations in that it does not offer the capability to increase the overall contribution of product development to net income by selecting one of several alternative strategies for a project. For scientific or other noneconomic reasons, the alternative strategy concept may not be applicable to all projects. However, if used for suitable projects, alternative strategies may allow an increase in the contributions to profit. In addition, by considering alternative strategies, it may be possible to alter the optimum economic solution so that it fits within resource limitations.

Return on Investment Simulations

The Project Evaluation Module of the R&D Investment Model presently computes a single value index (the expected net present value), upon which the Project Selection Module bases its criterion for choice. The basis of the calculation is the cash-flow sequence, made up of the development cost and net sales estimates. Yearly variations in either

---

[3] R. M. Walsh, R. H. Ayres, R. L. Hayne, and R. G. Staples, "Pharmaceutical Project Management System," *Research Management*, in press.

of these parameters can alter the ENPV over a considerably wide range. It has been suggested[4] that, since the future is not known with certainty, an attempt should be made to set maximum and minimum levels on the yearly costs and sales, rather than to establish an absolute cash-flow stream. Then a Monte Carlo technique can be used to generate many cash flows and therefore many values for the ENPV of a particular project (i.e., expected net present value simulation). If enough values are generated (the number must be such that the mean value has stabilized), the distribution of the ENPV can be ascertained. As a result, the selection procedure may be based on both the mean and the variance of the distribution, rather than on the mean value alone. The variance provides a measure of the uncertainty involved in estimating costs and sales (i.e., the higher the variance, the more uncertain are the cost and net sales estimates and therefore the higher is the risk based on these parameters).

OBSERVATIONS AND CONCLUSIONS

The R&D Investment Model is now operational through a time-sharing computer service at Smith Kline & French Laboratories. It is not a decision maker, and its results become only other items of information to *assist* R&D management in carrying out its decision-making responsibilities. In its present form the model analyzes only the economic input to the total decision-making process. Management must consider many other intangible factors as well before making the final commitment of R&D resources to a project.

As mentioned earlier, the Project Evaluation Program is used more frequently than the Project Selection Program because it makes the economic considerations visible to management and allows for a "what if" analysis. Our job now is to develop techniques for input collection and subsequent data projections that will increase management's confidence in the information and analysis that the model provides.

[4] R. A. Elnicki, "ROI Simulations for Investment Decisions," *Management Accounting,* February 1970, pp. 37–41.

XXV. *One Way of Tying All the Pieces Together*[1]

MARVIN J. CETRON

Governmental reorganizations have aptly been compared to the mating of two elephants—it takes place at a very high level, requires about two years for anything meaningful to develop, and a lot of little people get stomped on in the process.
Patrick J. McGarvey

BACKGROUND

The United States seems to be beset with increasing numbers of problems crying for the attention of the country at large and the application of national resources. There is apparently no coordinated direction to our efforts, no national plan, no national assessment of goals and application of values to these goals. There is little persistent dedication of effort based commensurately on the value of national goals. Having very few specific goals, it is little wonder, then, that the nation seems to swing its attention fitfully from one problem to another with the consequence that none is pursued in any logical fashion. The nation

---

[1] This Chapter was adapted from a paper originally presented under the title GNP-T (Goals for National Planning in Technology) at the joint Institute of Management Sciences—World Future Society Symposium on Assessing the Future and Policy Planning, March 9, 1970, at Gaithersburg, Maryland. The views expressed are those of the author, and do not necessarily represent those of the United States Navy. It also appeared as an article *Technological Forecasting,* vol. 2, No. 1, 1970, under the title "A Method for Integrating Goals and Technological Forecasting into Planning."

gives the impression of having dawdled, be it in regard to the SST, the ghettos, social justice, transportation, or the maintenance of civil order, to name just a few issues. Almost the same situation is mirrored in the research and development world.

Here uncertainty, intangibility, uniqueness of accomplishments, and long-time delays in the feedback of results have discouraged and hindered attempts to develop a factual basis for the R&D field. These same phenomena, combined with the concentration of operations research analysts and management scientists on the more straightforward problems encountered in the production and distribution functions, have limited the quantitative developments applicable to R&D.

Despite the growth in importance of science and technology, R&D activities seem to remain among the most "undermanaged" of corporate and government functions./A number of factors contribute to this state of affairs but do not adequately explain it. The relative youth of organized R&D and its rapid growth have left it without firmly established managerial traditions and practices. Some mistaken ideas borrowed from the history of academic research even suggested that the least-managed R&D activity is the best-managed. This concept may hold true in the fundamental research but not in the applied research and development area, where relevance is important.

Until the past few years methods for planning, budgeting, and control of technical programs were simple in concept and implementation. A turning point, observable only after the fact, with regard to a more sophisticated and quantitatively based methodology for R&D management was the publication in 1963 of B. V. Dean's collection of a number of papers treating various areas of R&D.[2] This major work was accompanied concurrently by many books on the Program Evaluation and Review Technique (PERT), which under governmental pressure and mistakenly attributed acclaim rapidly became a widely used method for quantitative scheduling and control of R&D projects. In 1964, E. B. Roberts' *The Dynamics of Research and Development*[3] became the first published text that presented quantitative analyses of a large number of project management factors, based on a complex mathematical model and extensive computer simulation.

Rapidly increasing cost for R&D, scarce resources, and mounting competitive pressures have prompted many U.S. firms, particularly in the highly innovative industries, to take a close look at new methods which

[2] B. V. Dean, ed., *Operations Research in Research and Development* (New York: John Wiley & Sons, 1963).
[3] E. B. Roberts, *The Dynamics of Research and Development* (New York: Harper & Row, 1964).

might help them to prepare better plans for the direction of future work. In order to better anticipate the possibilities of new markets and to increase the effectiveness and return from research operations, management is striving to reduce, as much as possible, the "chance" element that characterizes much of its planning. Accordingly, there is growing interest in and acceptance of technological forecasting and long-range planning as aids in the resource allocation procedure.

Unfortunately, most early attempts to build better allocation systems, based on strictly economic theory, foundered on two basic questions: Which research areas are most likely to be the source of significant technical breakthroughs? Which breakthroughs are most likely to bring important new developments? The realization that technological forecasting methods could help to answer these questions was catching hold slowly when many R&D planners were rudely shaken by a new reality: a leveling-off or even a cutback in most government-sponsored research efforts. With NASA's post-Apollo projects whittled back, the Department of Defense research budgets cut extensively, and other usually expanding budgets on a shorter rein, the need to make hard choices in funding became more critical than ever.

Now many planners are turning to technological forecasting to help them make their difficult selections. The academic community, however, has been dragging its feet. The major books spawned by this technological forecasting activity, for example, those of Jantsch, Cetron, and Ayres, are of nonacademic origin. The volume edited by Professor Bright contains 28 papers; however none of these came from academicians, the total being split evenly among the military, industry, and nonprofit organizations.[4]

The truth is that this field is still in an evolutionary phase, and most work now being done in one organization cannot be modified enough for adoption in others. At best, what is being done can provide many helpful hints for planners grappling with their own problems of using technological forecasts to aid in allocation.[5,6]

It is vital to remember that a technological forecast is not a picture of what the future will bring. Instead, it is a prediction, with a level of confidence and, in a given time frame, of a technical achievement

[4] H. A. Linstone, "A University for the Postindustrial Society," *Technological Forecasting,* 1 (March 1970), p. 265.

[5] M. J. Cetron, J. Martino, and L. Roepke, "The Selection of R&D Program Content—Survey of Quantitative Methods, *IEEE Transactions on Engineering Management,* Vol. EM-14, No. 1 (March 1967), pp. 4–12.

[6] M. J. Cetron, R. Isenson, J. Johnson, A. B. Nutt, and H. Wells, *Technological Resource Management: Quantitative Methods* (Cambridge, Mass.: The M.I.T. Press, 1970).

that can be expected for a given level of budgetary and manpower support.

The foundation underlying technological forecasting is the tenet that individual R&D events are susceptible to influence. The times at which they occur—if they can occur at all—can be modified significantly by regulating the resources allocated to them. Another basic tenet of technological forecasting is the belief that many futures are possible and that the paths toward these futures can be *mapped*.[7]

In use, a technological forecast can provide two vantage points of outlook. One, in the present, gives the user a view of the path that technological progress will probably take if it is not consciously influenced. In addition, the user will see critical branch points in the road—the situation where alternative futures are possible. He will also gain a greater understanding of the price of admission to these branch paths.

The second vantage point is in the future. The user selects or postulates a technical situation he desires. Looking backward from this point, he can then discern the obstacles that must be overcome to achieve the result he wants. Once again, he is brought up against the hard realities of what he must do to achieve a desired result. As one user has said; "The process substitutes forecasting for forecrastination."

MAKING BASIC FORECASTS

At this point, it is worth reviewing some of the basic principles of making technological forecasts. Let me hasten to say that the idea is not new. Leonardo da Vinci is probably the prime example of the scientific and technical forecaster whose knowledge and imagination enabled him to foresee many developments far in the future. Science fiction writers from Jules Verne to Arthur Clarke have also peered into the future, often with great success.[8] As long as one remains within the general bounds of known natural laws, he is safe in forecasting almost any technical achievement, with the prospect of enjoying some success. But a highly developed imagination offers little help for the technological planner—the odds are not good enough.

To reduce the odds, most technological forecasts today fall into four

[7] M. J. Cetron and A. L. Weiser, "Technological Change, Technological Forecasting and Planning R&D—A View from the R&D Manager's Desk," *George Washington Law Review* (Technological Assessment and the Law), **35** (July 1968).
[8] *Ibid.*

categories: intuitive, trend extrapolating, trend correlating, and growth analogy.[9] These four techniques have one common aspect: they depend on historical data and projection. There is no provision in them for the systematic introduction of management plans and actions. To take these into account, the forecaster must still rely on intuitive judgment. Newer and more sophisticated attempts at forecasting, however, include a systems analysis and a mathematical modeling approach. Basic to these methods is the interaction of human awareness of economic, social, and geopolitical needs with the technical state of the art. The technical inputs are formulated by methods like those mentioned above, but they are then examined for nontechnical feasibility.

PUTTING FORECASTS TO WORK

In most cases, a manager does not have a total system to work with. Instead, he has the results of trend extrapolations or other regular technological forecasting projections. How does he use these data? There are many approaches; the following is one which the Navy Department is examining to determine which techniques can best help to choose the R&D projects to be funded.

We begin with a technical planning flow chart (Figure 1) that shows the "shredding out" of some of the bits and pieces that comprise the construction of a sea floor site. Assume that we have a technological forecast for each and every parameter of the shred-out. The forecasts, at each level of the breakdown, are the probable paths that various technologies will take. Armed with this type of data, the user and the producer can engage in meaningful discourse. To a given set of operational requirements and performance characteristics specified by the user, the technical planners can respond with data that tell the user by what alternative means his needs can be satisfied, and when he can expect these to be accomplished. Many of the tradeoffs—between metals, plastics, and glass, for example—become clear.

Construction officers, however, are not usually quite so acquiescent in accepting what a planner sees ahead. When faced with a military threat, or an anticipated threat, they want an effective answer to that threat by a specified date. The same holds true if they wish to create a new force of their own. In these situations, planners are taking a vantage point at some time in the future and are trying to discover whether they will have the technology needed at that time.

Quite probably an examination of the technology forecasts to the par-

[9] R. Lenz, *Technological Forecasting,* CSTI (AD 408 085), Springfield, Va., 1962.

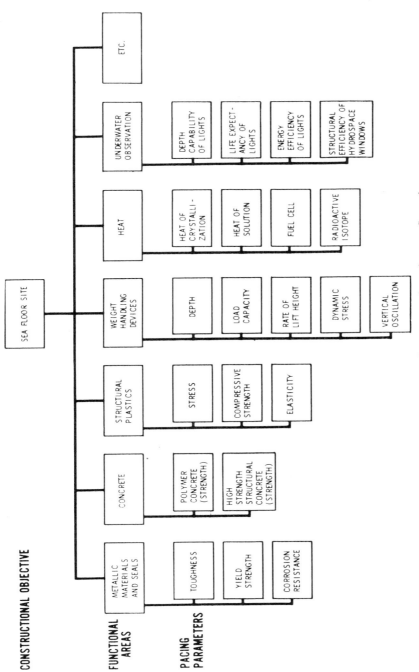

Figure 1 Technical planning flow chart for construction of a sea floor site.

ticular point in time will reveal that the users are not likely to get what they want. Now, this is useful information in itself, and represents an approach not yet widely used in industry.

However, this view of technological forecasting is not the only one. There is the question of which path we should take to achieve a desired result. By deciding on our needs in the future and looking at the forecasts, we can spot the principal obstacles standing in our way, and gain some idea of the magnitude of these obstacles. The inference is clear: if the given goal is to be achieved in a given time, our efforts must be applied in the areas containing the major obstacles. Alternatively, we can settle for something less with clear knowledge of what that something less will be. Often, this analysis will show that two or more paths may be taken to achieve the needed or acceptable capabilities. The point here is that an environment of flexible choice is engendered—choices of which the user was not previously aware.

A truly comprehensive technological forecast is backed up not only by the material and data used in generating the specific forecasts but also by supplementary analyses of various subfactors that could influence each technological forecast. Forecasts like these help to indicate the future posture of an enemy or a competitor. Although the user does not know what the opponent *will* do, he at least has a better idea of what the opponent *could* or *could not* do.

MECHANICS OF DECISION MAKING

Let's turn to an example and see how a specific decision can be analyzed, based on some technological forecasts generated by the Naval Civil Engineering Laboratory.[10] Forecasts for metallic materials and seals are given in terms of toughness, yield strength, and corrosion resistance. The next consideration might take us into the area of concrete and ultimate concrete strengths for, say, structural concrete versus polymer concrete, or possibly plastic composites. We also might want to consider forecasts of weight-handling devices, heating for sea floor sites, and underwater observations. Each of these functional considerations keys into the total sea floor site construction problem, in the same manner that each of the pacing parameters keys into each functional area. In this fashion we can work our way through the technical planning flow chart (Figure 1), eventually going into any degree of detail or considering as many functional areas as we wish.

[10] "Sea Floor Engineering" [excerpts] *Navy Technological Forecast,* October 1968 (prepared by Naval Civil Engineering Laboratory, Pt. Hueneme, Calif.).

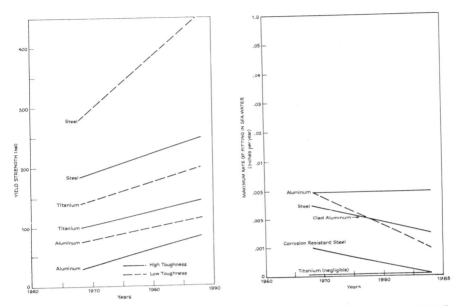

Figure 2 (*a*) **NASL forecast of strength of ship structural materials.** (*b*) **NASL forecast of corrosion resistance of ship stuctural materials.**

This information is used for very practical decisions. For instance, the pacing parameters of toughness, yield strength, and corrosion resistance forecast for the functional metallic materials and seals are shown in Figure 2. A technological forecast on metallic materials and seals and five other functional areas covered in Figure 1 is presented in *Technological Forecasting: A Practical Approach.*[11]

THE OVERALL PICTURE

Up to this point we have been discussing the technological forecasting needed for one problem in a laboratory. But any organization has many such problems.[12] Here the question becomes one of allocation of resources of men, money, and materials. The evaluation scene therefore shifts

[11] M. J. Cetron, *Technological Forecasting: A Practical Approach* (New York: Gordon & Breach, 1969), Appendix C.
[12] A. B. Nutt, "An Approach to Research and Development Effectiveness," *IEEE Transactions on Engineering Management,* September 1965, pp. 103–112.

from the technical specialist to the department manager, the head of research, and the overall planners. The forecast data must be fitted into their overall planning approach if it is to be really useful.

When management problems are simple, a decision maker can examine with relative ease the various factors he must consider. One man, such as the hermit in a cave, the individual homeowner, the small businessman, or the teacher in a one-room school, may be able to interrelate all of the necessary information and succeed in his endeavors.

As the management scope becomes larger and the complexity of problems increases, however, more and different factors must be considered to reach a decision. Soon staff and management procedures are needed to assist in all phases of management. Eventually, the point is reached where any one decision affects many facets of the operation; all efforts become interrelated to an alarming degree.

Increasing complexities are particularly characteristic of programs or projects which must operate within a fixed government or corporation resource ceiling. Choices must be made on alternative approaches; specifically, it must be decided which efforts should proceed and which should be dropped or delayed. Since numerous efforts are interrelated in time, resources required, purpose, and possible technical transfer one to another, choices must be made with consideration of the total effect. Every manager, whether he be a manufacturer, service industry director, government administrator, or university professor, seeks the greatest payoff for resource investments.

SOME FREQUENTLY USED METHODS
OF RESOURCE ALLOCATION

What alternatives does a manager have for developing resource allocation approaches? The resource allocation problem is usually too big to keep in one man's head, and often inputs come from levels completely outside his control. Hundreds of inputs can be involved when the alternatives are examined in depth.

A familiar resource allocation approach is termed the *squeaking wheel* process. A manager can cut resources from every area (he can be sophisticated and cut some areas more than others) and then wait to see which area complains the most. On the basis of the loudest and most insistent squeaking, the manager can then restore some of the resources previously withdrawn until he reaches his ceiling budget.

Another common approach develops the minimum noise level and results in fewer squeaks by allocating the current year's resources in just about the same manner as last year. The budget perturbations are mini-mized, and the status quo maintained. Unfortunately, if this *level funding* approach is continued very long within a rapidly changing techno-logical field, the company, group, or government agency will end up in serious trouble.

An effortless version of the preservation of management security ap-proach to resource allocation seeks to perpetuate the *glorious past*. Last year, or the year before, or perhaps several years ago, a division or organization had a very successful project; therefore why not fund the unit for the next 5 years on any projects that it advocates? The premise is "once successful, always successful." This method really means that no analysis should be made of the proposed project or its usefulness; instead, projects will be assigned resources solely on the basis of the past record of an individual or organization.

Still another way to allocate resources is called the *white charger* technique. Here the various departments come dashing in to top manage-ment with multicolor graphs, handouts, and well-rehearsed presentations. If they impress the decision-maker, they are rewarded with increased resources. Often the best speaker or the last man to brief the boss wins the jackpot.[13]

Finally, there is the *committee approach*, which frees the manager from resource allocation decisions. The committees tell the manager to increase, decrease, or leave all allocations as they are. A common danger is that the committee may not have enough actual experience in the organization or sufficient information on which to base its recom-mendations. If the committee is *ad hoc* or from outside the organization, the members can also avoid responsibility in not having to live through the risky process of implementing their recommendations.

Obviously, the allocation methods described are neither scientific nor objective, though they are utilized quite extensively. These naive ap-proaches point up the need of the manager and his staff for an aid to bring information into a form to which judgment may be applied. It is a common experience for an organization to have numerous reports on specific technical subjects which recommend increased resources for a particular area. But the direct use of these data only compounds the manager's problem when he tries to allocate resources among the many technical areas. If he is operating under a fixed budget ceiling, to increase funding for one area requires that one or more other technical areas must be correspondingly decreased.

[13] M. J. Cetron, P. H. Caulfield, and R. D. Freshman, "Facts and Folklore in R&D Management Revisited," Submitted to *Management Science* (TIMS), Winter, 1969.

TECHNOLOGICAL RESOURCE ALLOCATION SYSTEM

A more sophisticated alternative approach involves the use of staff or specialists in operations research. The information they assemble can be used to significantly assist managerial judgment. This is the point where quantitative evaluation techniques enter the picture. Each major aspect of a program can be examined, first by itself and then in interrelation to competing factors. Such items as timeliness, cost utility or payoff, confidence level or risk, personnel, and facilities can be evaluated by specialists in each field, and the total picture made available as a basis for decision. Greater payoff areas can be identified and problems highlighted. Inputs can be accurately recorded, made clearly visible, and analyzed for assisting in the final decision.

The use of quantitative techniques permits input factors and possible outcomes to be re-examined readily, and different managerial emphasis applied. The manager can still hedge his "allocation selections" by utilizing such criteria as increased resources to previously successful groups backing a high-risk effort, that is, a high-cost project with apparently slim chances of success, which might yield gigantic results. The decision maker can incorporate any desired additional criteria—such as the politics of selection, competitive factors, or technological barriers.

The question now becomes one of allocating the resources of men, money, and materials. Figure 3, the long-range planning program, which is really a broad allocation diagram, shows the interactions of numerous managers from the technical specialist to the agency head, the head of research, and the agency planners. The data must be fitted into an overall planning approach if they are to be really useful. National goals are the main topic and occupy the central position in the chart. In order to establish national goals, the preliminary steps of systems analysis, needs analysis, and deficiency analysis must be accomplished. After the goals and technical objectives are established, technology assessment and R&D programming take place to complete the R&D resources allocation process. Each of these steps will be explained in greater depth.

SYSTEMS ANALYSIS

National policy must be considered and involves philosophic and strategy questions, including these: Will our organization choose to be the world leader? Will it keep abreast of the world technically and see whether a major market develops? In the overall environment, other

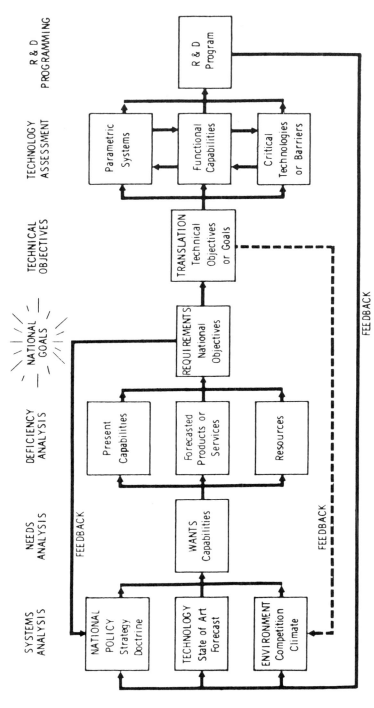

Figure 3 Long-range national R&D planning.

countries' actions must be followed closely, but there are other factors, such as GNP, balance of payments, interest rates, business expectation, and economic forecasts, to be identified.[14] Figure 3, viewed as the national planning chart, shows a recommended organization of considerations.

The technology forecasting element acts as a catalyst in setting and implementing overall national goals. At present only a handful of the largest countries are really utilizing their full technical potential. The next question is how to relate the technological forecasts with appraisal in this total picture. A discussion of the numerous appraisal methods would be a long story in itself. For example, all systems employed by the Department of Defense utilize three major factors in the appraisal or normative forecasting process: military utility, technical feasibility, and financial acceptability. Each of these factors is amenable to quantification and can be fitted into a model which compares the value of each component project or system. Because of the complexity of the analysis, it is necessary to program the job on a computer to obtain usable information quickly. It must be remembered, however, that these computer processes are simply a tool to aid the decision maker; the machine merely arranges the material in accordance with his instructions so that he can quickly focus his attention on the areas which require his special knowledge and judgment.

UNIVERSAL DECISION FACTORS

I have studied many decision models over a period of almost 20 years in government, industry, and the academic community. These models have embraced every segment of the R&D spectrum from the most fundamental research through operational development. To reiterate, in every instance the factors included as major elements have fallen into three general categories: *utility, feasibility,* and *cost.* Sometimes one of these categories has been omitted, and consequently the models have been considered deficient by other practitioners.

If these three factors could be expressed as single-valued quantities, the product desirability could be estimated easily. However, each is composed of a great many subfactors and also varies considerably over time (often in an unexpected manner) as forecasts are projected further and further into the future. The problem facing the planner at this

[14] H. A. Linstone, "Madness, Mediocrity, or Mastery—A Threat Analysis for a New Era," in *Quantitative Decision-Aiding Techniques for R&D Management,* ed. by M. Cetron, H. Davidson, and A. Rubenstein (New York: Gordon & Breach, 1971).

point, then, is how to consider explicitly all of the subfactors involved in a decision and how to express their relative importance.

The environment (competition, climate) also must be considered, and includes such questions as: Who are the competitors? What unique skills, products, or resources do these competitors possess? What is the international climate? Will the demand for consumer goods continue to expand rapidly, will there be a sudden drop in demand, or can a leveling of demand be expected? The factors considered under the systems analysis allow the needs (wants) as well as the unique or strong capabilities of the country to be identified. The "future environment" for the construction industry in this country is presented as Appendix D in *Technological Forecasting: A Practical Approach* (cited in footnote 11).

NEEDS ANALYSIS

Analysis of the wants or desirable areas of growth for the country is equally as important as defining the areas where no growth or decline is expected.

The national or international economy provides the broadest scope for analyzing the needs for this country's products or services. The stage of development in this country vis à vis the world, the international image, the availability and cost of capital, and international controls and treaties may all require attention in the process of determining what the United States "wants" to do.

The international share of the market for the country relates directly to its volume. That is, in a country of rapid growth an individual industry may grow while remaining constant relative to its competitors. Conversely, the share of the market may need to be greatly increased to remain at a level stage in a declining market.

Finally, the desires of the country and of the individual firms within the country can be assessed. However, these desires may not be attainable within the capability of the country. Thus, the national "wants" need to be balanced against the capabilities.

DEFICIENCY ANALYSIS

After the wants of the country have been established, the capabilities available must be delineated in order that areas of deficiency can be identified. Ordinarily, the present capabilities of a country will be known, but often effort is required by management to obtain a comprehensive statement of its technological capabilities in terms of men, money, and machines. Because we are dealing with futures, the products and services such as new manufacturing methods, new materials, and advanced skills that are forecasted to be available must also be carefully identified. Other resources available to the country will also be important information. Labor, natural resources, or facilities may exist that could be made available from outside the country when and if required.

By identifying and analyzing the present capabilities and the forecasted products and services, along with other resources available, the deficiencies and excesses will become evident. The analysis now permits the administration to focus on realistic national goals.

NATIONAL GOALS

The most important phase of the resource allocation system may now be brought into focus—the national goals (objectives). These goals may be viewed by the administration from the vantage point of the wants (desires or needs) of the country, which have been carefully considered for feasibility against the present or potential national capabilities. Several passes through the analysis described above usually are required before acceptable goals are achieved.

These national goals will be translated into guidance for performance of the country, to aid in its further planning.

TECHNICAL OBJECTIVES

The idea of applying quantitative approaches to resource allocation has too long been suspect by administrators. Currently, both industry and government are seeking tangible improvements in the results from use of available resources. Economy drives and/or cost/benefit analyses have resulted in paired budgets, with the need more critical than ever to make hard choices among alternative programs. The application of objective measurements to resource assignments has too long been classified as visionary and impractical.

For example, how does a corporation decide whether its current allocation for research and technology is adequate? And how does it determine the right balance between the R&D and the manufacturing project? How does a government do the same thing?

A prime example of lack of quantitative data exists in the area of assessing technological effort. Querying the scientist or engineer and requesting a justification of his selection of a program or a task (including the projected benefits to a mission- or product-oriented organization) has often been construed as an assault against the scientific professional's prestige and prerogatives. Today, scientists and engineers are beginning to realize, however, that they are accepted at the highest organization levels and that one sign of this ascendancy is their high visibility and responsibility to the interrogation of criteria and rational judgments. The technical manager's intuition can no longer be accepted as infallible and beyond managerial review.[15]

Several project evaluation and selection techniques have as their basis a belief in the efficacy and acceptance of Bayesian statistics and theories of probability.[16-18] Bayesians believe that it is correct to quantify feelings about uncertainty in terms of subjectively assessed numerical probabilities. Thus, assessments are made of probabilities for events that determine the profitability or utility of alternative actions open to the decision maker.

For example, there is a necessity to assess the criterion of whether a piece of research is technically feasible (technological forecasts) or what the probability is that it will be successfully accomplished (level of confidence criterion). Bayesian theory believes that it is possible for an "expert" in the field being assessed to assign a figure of merit or "subjective" probability number that the event will actually occur. This theory states that on this very subject matter an expert can assign a "subjective" probability number from a scale, for example, between 0 and 1. Men of considerable experience in a field usually have no difficulty in utilizing a Bayesian probability scale. In a like manner, other criteria, such as the utility of the research to the objectives of the organization, or the relevance of desired priority systems or corporation products, are assessed (criterion of utility).

The use of Bayesian subjective probabilities makes feasible the incorporation into the decision process, in a formal and visible way, many of the subjective and objective criteria and variables previously taken into account by the decision maker informally and without visibility. The probability assignment, a number between 0 and 1, or for that matter from 0 to 10, to each facet, factor, criterion, or parameter inherent to a rational decision, reflects the degree of belief held by the individual expert(s) that the objective will be met.

Thus the experience, knowledge of the subject, and judgment of the various experts are summarized by the subjective probabilities that they assign against the respective criteria. The final or top decision maker

---

[15] Cetron, Caulfield, and Freshman, *op. cit.*
[16] Cetron, Martino, and Roepke, *op. cit.*
[17] Cetron, Isenson, Johnson, Nutt, and Wells, *op. cit.*
[18] Nutt, *op. cit.*

then has a clear view of the alternatives and can use the results of the probability assignments of the different experts. A computer can be used to summarize the choices or probabilities of the experts, and also to determine "consequences" if the probability assignments are changed or if the final decision maker adds new information or weighting factors.

Advocates of allocation and selection procedures are accused of assuming that the myriad of quantitative estimates of scientific relevance, importance, feasibility, and the like should and can be collected and manipulated.[19] Apparently the academic community also makes this assumption. For example, in the field of education, the university admission policy is based on a "myriad of quantitative estimates." Mr. Robert Freshman, a U.S. Air Force Laboratory planner who was previously a professional educator, relates the following example.[20] High school students are admitted to universities on the basis of the quantitative judgments of teacher grades as the key criterion. These teachers grade about 5 subjects a year, for 4 years of high school—thus, 20 teacher judgments. Different teachers, different subjects, different tests, different subject matter taken in high schools throughout the nation, are fused into one. Teacher opinions on how to grade, teacher biases and prejudgments, evaluations of oral recitations, grades on nonstandardized, unstructured subject matter, and test results are all injected into the above conglomeration to form the individual teacher's final grade in one subject.

High school grades for the 4 years are averaged to come up with one number—the high school average—the *magic number* which has great influence in college admission. More miraculous is that there is a good, positive correlation between this magic number and success in college. It is recognized that this "quantitative estimate" of many judgments is the best single criterion or indicator of success in *college;* but again it is just an aid to the decision maker. The personal interview, college board scores, and extracurricular activities also affect his judgment before making a final decision.

Opinions and judgments can be and should be weighed by every decision maker in his final decision. Several quantitative techniques gather and summarize the opinions and judgments to enable the final decision maker (such as the university dean of admissions utilizing teacher judgments) to visualize and weigh, as one input to his decision, the judgments of numerous people on diverse factors.

[19] E. B. Roberts, "Facts and Folklore in R&D Management," *Industrial Management Review,* Spring 1967.
[20] Cetron, Caulfield, Freshman (cited in footnote 12).

Two main points on quantitative decision making should be emphasized:

1. The quantitative management techniques discussed *do not make decisions*, but rather provide a basis of information on which decisions can be made.

2. A validity check cannot be made, since once the resources are allocated, the plan becomes self-fulfilling.

SUBSYSTEM ANALYSIS OR TECHNOLOGY ASSESSMENT

Assessment of technology or subsystem analysis is employed to answer the question, Which, when, and how many resources should be allocated among the alternative projects? Since the topic is multifaceted, it is necessary to draw information from a variety of sources, including operations research, project selection techniques, and technological forecasting.

Until recently "technology assessment" was not official jargon. The expression "assessment of technology" is not found listed in the table of contents or indexes of texts on management. Nor is it identified and found in the general literature of management or in official planning, programming, and policy documents of the government agencies.

Assessment is commonly considered to mean "setting a value to." "Assessment of technology," then, means setting a value to technology. Technologies include areas of special knowledge such as gas turbines, diesels, thermionics, thermoelectrics, fuel cells, and energy conversion, as opposed to the areas of science, which include items such as alloy theory, surface physics, cryogenics, and magnetism. The kinds or measures of value attributed to technologies will be discussed later. Also it can be demonstrated that the nature of the assessment of technology depends on who assesses, why the assessment is performed, and the nature of the technology itself. For a more detailed discussion of technology assessment, one should read the two latest publications by the Academy of Science and Engineering[21,22] and the report by the Legislative Reference Service.[23]

[21] *Technology: Process of Assessment and Choice,* Report of the National Academy of Science Committee on Science and Astronautics, U.S. House of Representatives, July 1969.
[22] *The Study of Technology Assessment,* Report of the Committee on Public Engineering Policy, National Academy of Engineering, Committee on Science and Astronautics, U.S. House of Representatives, July 1969.
[23] Technology Assessment Hearings before the Subcommittee on Science, Research, and Development of the Committee on Science and Astronautics, U.S. House of Representatives, Nov. 18 and 24 and Dec. 2, 3, 4, 8, and 12, 1969.

WHO ASSESSES TECHNOLOGY AND WHY—
OR FOR WHAT PURPOSE?

Intuitively, nearly everyone assesses technology at some time, for some purpose, and to some degree of sophistication. The "man on the street," for example, may essentially assess the aggregates of the technologies of color versus black and white television. He may consider the collective value of parameters such as cost, picture quality, repair frequency, and pressure from his wife and children in order to choose which type, if either, to buy. That nearly everyone has different values was pointed out by William D. Guth and Renato Tagiuri[24] in an article which emphasizes the following points:

- The personal values that businessmen and others have can be classified usefully as theoretical, economic, esthetic, social, political, and religious.
- The values that are most important to an executive have profound influence on his strategic decisions.
- Managers and employees often are unaware of the values they possess and also tend to misjudge the values of others.
- The executive who will take steps to better understand his own values and those of other men can gain an important advantage in developing workable and well-supported policies.

One difficulty in assessing technology is the problem of obtaining and maintaining an alignment of relative importance factors between the users of technologies and those responsible for improving the capabilities of technologies. *Technological Forecasting: A Practical Approach* gives an example in which the R&D engineer may not have been aware of the degree of importance of a particular parameter to a specific user. In other words, an R&D engineer may not recognize the need for a particular technological improvement. The importance of such need recognition as it contributes to the successful development of weapon systems is well illustrated by the comprehensive technology source study, Project Hindsight, conducted by Col. Raymond Isenson and Dr. Chalmers Sherwin of the Department of Defense.[25]

In addition to Project Hindsight, which was viewed from an engineer-

---

[24] W. D. Guth and R. Tagiuri, "Personal Values and Corporate Strategy," *Harvard Business Review,* September-October 1965.

[25] R. S. Isenson and C. W. Sherwin, *Project Hindsight* (Interim Report), Office of the Director of Defense Research and Engineering, CSTI (AD 642 400), Springfield, Va., June 30, 1966 (revised, Oct. 13, 1966).

ing standpoint and covered only 20 years, there is a study called TRACES, which was prepared for the National Science Foundation. It spans a much longer time frame and is more "acceptable" to the scientific community.[26]

RESEARCH AND DEVELOPMENT PROGRAMMING

To reiterate, three factors used by the U.S. Department of Defense to evaluate systems programs are military utility, technical feasibility, and financial acceptability. If one substitutes national utility for military utility, these factors can also be important when planners evaluate research and development. However, it is necessary to quantize these factors so that they may be compared for different R&D programs.

One simpler technique could be used to investigate the problem of the national utility. National utility with respect to development atmosphere is a measure of R&D work in terms of its usefulness in meeting U.S. national objectives. To be useful, hardware or information must provide a new or improved capability in the shortest possible time after the need for it is recognized. Thus, national utility is made up of three independent criteria: value to the country, responsiveness, and timeliness. In this condensed version "value to the country" will be considered.

This criterion is concerned with the extent of the contribution of a specific technology or innovation in terms of its value to the national goals. The importance of a task is measured by its relative impact on any individual goals, as well as the number of goals receiving a contribution from the technology or innovation. This is done by multiplying the assigned value of the national goal by the impact value of the contribution to arrive at a value for each individual goal. The sum of these values will determine the value of the technology or innovations.

Figures 4 and 5 illustrate the calculation procedure. The actual total number of points assigned to these 16 national goals is equal to 100, and the points are assigned for test purposes on the basis of the importance of each goal in the 1975 and 1980 time frame, since this is when most of our current applied research work will find its way into industrial applications.[27] The test figures are based on the present world situation

[26] B. Bartocha, F. Narin, and C. Stone, "TRACES—Technology in Retrospect and Critical Events in Science," in *The Science of Managing Organized Technology,* ed. by M. J. Cetron and J. Goldhar (New York: Gordon & Breach, 1970).
[27] The figures of merit, or point values assigned to each "national goal" (column 1) are dummy figures; they were assigned for this example only (the national goals taken from the appendix to this chapter are also for illustrative purposes only.)

MATERIALS TECHNOLOGY

| COLUMN 1 | COLUMN 2 | | | | | | | | | | COLUMN 3 |
| NATIONAL GOALS * | IMPACT OF "TECHNOLOGY OR INNOVATION" CONTRIBUTION | | | | | | | | | | VALUE TO INDIVIDUAL GOAL |
	1.0	0.9	0.8	0.7	0.6	0.5	0.4	0.3	0.2	0.1	
[6] AGRICULTURE									●		1.2
[7] AREA REDEVELOPMENT				●							4.9
[5] CONSUMER EXPENDIT									●		1.0
[8] EDUCATION										●	0.8
[7] HEALTH										●	0.7
[6] HOUSING	●										6.0
[3] INTERNATIONAL AID											0
[6] MANPOWER RETRAIN											0
[14] NATIONAL DEFENSE			●								11.2
[2] NATURAL RESOURCES		●									1.8
[4] PRIVATE PLANT & EQUIP			●								3.2
[3] RESEARCH & DEVELOP	●										3.0
[12] SOCIAL WELFARE								●			3.6
[4] SPACE					●						2.4
[5] TRANSPORTATION		●									4.5
[8] URBAN DEVELOPMENT		●									7.2
							TOTAL VALUE TO THE COUNTRY				51.5

* The national goals listed in the first column came from *Manpower Requirements for National Objectives in the 1970s* by Leonard A. Lecht, Center for Priority Analysis, National Planning Association, 1968.

Scale of Definitions for "Impact of Technology or Innovation" (Column 2)

Points	Descriptors
1.0	Meets overriding critical need (or creation of new opportunity)
0.5	Helps moderately to meet a need
0.2	Increase in economy
0.1	Minor contribution to the goal

Figure 4   Materials technology. Appraisal Sheet No. 1: Value to the country.

and the estimate of the most probable future situations. In the real world, these would be filled in by the administration.

When the goals commission specialist fills in column 2 of Appraisal Sheet No. 1 (Fig. 4), the impact of the technology or innovation contributions, he would consider the descriptors at the bottom of the figure (Scale of Definitions). In some cases the four descriptors would not adequately describe the contribution; he would then interpolate between these numbers.

The credibility of the ratings of technical feasibility and the probability of success increases if they are rated by personnel who have the necessary technical expertise and competence, as they can best judge these factors on the basis of the ability and experience of the individuals and/or organizations carrying on the development efforts under consider-

PROBABILITY OF SUCCESS

CHANCE OF MEETING THE REQUIRED LEVEL OF TECHNOLOGY OR MEETING THE OBJECTIVE OF AN INNOVATION

☐ 80 - 100 %   ☒ 60 - 80 %   ☐ 30 - 60 %   ☐ 0 - 30 %

NUMBER OF DIFFERENT CONCURRENT APPROACHES

☐ 1   ☐ 2   ☐ 3   ☒ 4   ☐ 5   ☐ 6   ☐ 7   ☐ 8   ☐ 9   ☐ 10 OR MORE

SACRED COW ?   WHO SAYS ?

☐ PRESIDENT   ☐ SPECIFIC AGENCY OR FOUNDATION   ☐ CONGRESS
☐ PROFESSIONAL ASSOC   ☐ INDUSTRIAL ASSOC   ☐ OTHER
                                                              (specify)

APPRAISAL SUMMARY

NUMBER OF GOALS ___14___ EXPECTED VALUE (E_V) ___48.3___
VALUE TO THE COUNTRY (V) ___51.5___ OPTIMUM FUNDING $(\$)$ ___I Billion___
PROBABILITY OF SUCCESS (P_S) ___.9375___ DESIRABILITY INDEX (D_i) ___48.3___

Figure 5   Materials technology. Appraisal Sheet No. 2.

ation. The Academy of Science or Engineering and the National Science Foundation's Office of Science and Technology are examples of organizations which might be consulted.

The top half of Appraisal Sheet No. 2 (Fig. 5) solicits the opinion of the technical specialist regarding the probability of achieving the technological objectives or the innovation undertaken. It considers whether the innovation could be successfully accomplished from a scientific and technical feasibility point of view. Technical risk also takes into consideration the degree of confidence or prediction of attaining the innovation. The degree of confidence or prediction that can be attained usually assesses the factors involved in the present state of the art, either implicit or explicit. This technical appraisal is naturally based on technical forecasts and includes time factors and resource levels, as well as the competence of the investigating team.

Therefore, the technical specialist checks the box that best describes his opinion regarding the technology or innovation being evaluated, as well as the number of different concurrent approaches being taken, which are also a measure of probability of success.

The area called "Sacred cow?" and "Who says?" was also considered in what we call the "management environment." This section solicits opinions on the acceptability of the effort in the management structure. Here, the evaluator is asked to give what he believes to be "the Washington environment" considerations concerning this effort, and he checks the applicable box.

The bottom of Appraisal Sheet No. 2 is then analyzed. The total program is calculated by value, expected value, and desirability index for three funding levels, by the computer. The inputs for national utility come from Appraisal Sheet No. 1. For example, suppose that the proposed R&D effort is to determine the desirability of materials technology to the United States. We shall consider the criterion "value to the country." Of the 16 national goals shown in column 1 of Appraisal Sheet No. 1 (see the Appendix at the end of the chapter for a description of the goals), materials technology would be of value and would contribute significantly to 14 of the 16 goals.

With respect to agriculture, materials technology in this hypothetical example is considered an "increase in economy" and is accorded 0.2 point. At the same time, agriculture is said to contribute 6 of the 100 units assigned to all the national goals. Thus, the value of materials technology to the national goals with respect to agriculture is $0.2 \times 6 = 1.2$. Materials technology can similarly be evaluated for its contribution to the other individual goals, and the total value of materials technology is summed at 51.5, as shown on Appraisal Sheet No. 1.

For our calculation of the probability of success (P_s) in meeting the technology objective (TO) we use the probability chart shown in Table 1. In this chart, n is the number of concurrent approaches used to accomplish the TO, and C is a number arbitrarily assigned to the chances of succeeding in a given approach. We use:

$$80\text{--}100\% \text{ chance of success: } C = 0.8$$
$$60\text{--}80\% \quad \text{chance of success: } C = 0.5$$
$$30\text{--}60\% \quad \text{chance of success: } C = 0.3$$
$$0\text{--}30\% \quad \text{chance of success: } C = 0.2$$

We assume that all approaches n have the same chance of success, and therefore the same value of C. If each n were to have a different C, a more involved calculation would be necessary.

The number assigned to the probability of n approaches failing is then $(1 - C)^n$. Furthermore, if we assume that at least one of the approaches taken will succeed, the number assigned to the probability of success P_s is $1 - (1 - C)^n$. This figure for P_s is filled in on Appraisal Sheet No. 2 under the "Probability of Success" column.

For example, on an Appraisal Sheet No. 2, we might have had 4 approaches $(n = 4)$ with a 60–80% chance of meeting TO $(C = 0.5)$. Then the number corresponding to the probability of success is 0.93750 or 93.75%. From our previous example we calculated the total value of a given TO to be 51.5. Therefore, the expected value is $51.5 \times 0.9375 = 48.3$.

The preceding discussion has been concerned with concurrent approaches. If the task area were made up of phased or sequential operations, the probabilities would be handled in a different manner.

Table 1   Tabulation of P_s

	C			
n	0.8	0.5	0.3	0.2
1	0.80000	0.50000	0.30000	0.20000
2	0.96000	0.75000	0.51000	0.36000
3	0.99200	0.87500	0.65700	0.48800
4	0.99840	0.93750	0.75990	0.58040
5	0.99968	0.96875	0.83193	0.67230
6	0.99993	0.98438	0.88235	0.73786
7	0.99997	0.99219	0.91765	0.79029
8	0.99999	0.99609	0.94235	0.83223
9	0.99999	0.99805	0.95965	0.86578
10	0.99999	0.99902	0.97175	0.89363

Three funding levels are utilized in the "concurrent" approach: the actual/optimum, maximum, and minimum. The actual/optimum consists of the latest approved fiscal data. For each subsequent year, funds are entered on the basis of what is estimated as necessary to achieve the completion date if the task area is supported at an optimum rate, that is, one which permits aggressive prosecution using orderly developmental procedures—not a crash program.

The maximum consists of what could effectively be expended in advancing the task area completion date. Maximum funding is the upper limit in which unlimited resources are assigned in order to accelerate the accomplishment of a task area.

The minimum consists of what could be effectively utilized to maintain continuity of effort and some progress toward fulfilling the task area objective. Minimum funding is the threshold limit below which it would not be feasible to continue further efforts in the task area.

The simplified formula is:

$$\text{Value } (V) \times \text{Probability of success } (P_s) = \text{Expected value } (E_v)$$

$$\frac{\text{Expected value } (E_v)}{\text{Funding level (\$)}} = \text{Desirability index } (D_i)$$

To finish the analysis of the rating sheet, "goals" represent the number of national goals affected by the technology; P_s, as previously stated, is read from a probability chart; and the optimum funding level is determined according to the resources needed to complete the project in the time span of the study. The final desirability index numbers now provide a way to compare a great multitude of current and proposed R&D technologies. By carrying out similar evaluations on the basis of

Navmat Program Evaluation Report

(Ranking of 00240012 By Total Warfare Valle RR. CETRCA 69TRE)

Task Area Number	Title	SC	Exp. Valle	Funding Max	Cum	Opt	Cum	Min	Ranking* Cum	
WF11511751 WF0190101	(U) Space Systems Engineering		26.446875	300	300	300	300	300	300	27.3
XF0322001 XF01902011	(U) Communications Satellite Support		22.050000	2000	2300	1375	1675	1000	1300	25.2
WF03222751 WF0190101	(U) Satellite Communications		10.350000	350	2650	350	2025	0	1300	21.8
WF12552751 WF0190202	(U) Satellite Oceanographic Data Collection		9.375000	900	3550	700	2725	150	1450	12.5
WF12551752 WF0190202	(U) Solar Radiation Monitoring Satellite		8.000370	3000	6550	2800	5525	1200	2650	11.9
WF03230751 WF0190101	(U) Satellite Navigation			2250	8800	2250	7775	0	2650	10.2
WF12551751 WF0190202	(U) Meteorological Satellite Data Readout		8.750000	600	9400	200	7975	150	2800	10.0
WF02112751 WF0190102	(U) Advanced Techniques For Space Object Detection and Identification		2.800000	850	10250	850	8825	0	2800	5.6
WF02111752 WF0190202	(U) Ocean Surveillance Systems Analysis			5500	15750	5000	13825	4000	6800	4.8
WF05311751 WF0190102	(U) Satellite Interceptor Systems Analysis			500	16250	500	14325	200	7000	1.0
WF05372751 WF0190102	(U) Astro-Defense Threat Studies			300	16550	200	14525	100	7100	1.0

DUMMY DATA

Figure 6   NAVMAT Program evaluation report. Ranking by value.

responsiveness to expected needs, the timeliness of the project, and other criteria, it is possible to combine all the information about the project and arrive at its "total national value."

The end results of an R&D planning effort like this one are computer printouts (Figs. 6 and 7) which rank every project according to its

Navmat Program Evaluation Report

(Ranking by Opt Desirability)

Task Area Number	Title	SC	Max	Cum	Funding Opt	Cum	Min	Cum	Ranking*
SF08452002	(U) Acoustical Silencing (Internal Ships Systems)	S6	320	320	220	220	185	185	0.266477
SF08452004	(U) Acoustical Silencing Ship Isolation Devices	S6	535	855	435	655	333	518	0.181034
XF10532001	(U) Test Equipment	S3	2400	3255	1300	1955	770	1288	0.124614
SF08452005	(U) Acoustical Silencing, Hull Vibration and Radiation	S6	955	4210	680	2635	610	1898	0.093750
SF02132001	(U) Direct View Image Intensifier Techniques	S4	400	4610	300	2935	65	1963	0.080000
SF08452001	(U) Ship Silencing Measurements, Analysis and Problem Definition	S6	1360	5970	1095	4030	860	2823	0.072602
WF02132601	(U) Imaging Reconnaissance Sensor Development	S3	1000	6970	750	4780	200	3023	0.056666
RF08412002	(U) Deep Research Vehicle Program	S6	1700	8670	1510	6290	1180	4203	0.048344
SF01121003	(U) Domes and Self Noise	S6	600	9270	550	6840	540	4743	0.041236
XF10545001	(U) Advanced Active Devices and Techniques	S3	4000	13270	2600	9440	2000	6743	0.039711
PF11521004	(U) Improved Navy Criteria	S6	500	13770	500	9940	253	6996	0.38400
SF01121007	(U) System Analysis and Engineering	S6	1000	14770	850	10790	500	7496	0.037058
SF08452003	(U) Acoustical Silencing, External Ship System	S6	1920	16690	1735	12525	1412	8908	0.033789
TF10531001	(U) Cargo Movement and Distribution	S6	700	17390	550	13075	300	9208	0.018039
SF01121004	(U) Transducers and Acoustic Power Generators	S6	4500	21890	4009	17084	2700	11908	0.011785
SF01121002	(U) Sonar Signal Processing and Classification	S6	7000	28890	6520	23604	5800	17708	0.007246
SF01121001	(U) Underwater Sound Propagation	S6	6400	35290	6000	29604	4800	22508	0.005250
SF09443004	(U) Nuclear Propulsion Plant Materials Development	S4	1100	36390	1100	30704	0	22508	
SF09443001	(U) Nuclear Propulsion Plant Technology	S4	1000	37390	1000	31704	0	22508	
SF09442003	(U) Surface Ship Refueling Equipment and Procedures Development	S4	2200	39590	2200	33904	0	22508	

DUMMY DATA

Figure 7   NAVMAT Program evaluation report: Ranking by optimum desirability.

value in the overall program. In the U.S. Navy, where Figs. 6 and 7 were generated, the total comes to over **700** separate R&D projects. It would be a mistake, however, to think that the impressive-looking computer printouts are taking over the final decision-making job. Most of those who design and work with information systems like the one described realize fully that technological forecasts and quantitative estimates of project value are no more or less than planning tools and are among many that a manager must use in making final decisions.

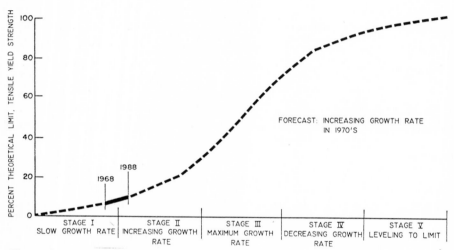

Figure 8 **Structural metals, homogeneous, thick sections, low toughness, projected growth, tensile yield strength, 1966–88 (shown in relationship to typical S-shaped growth curve). Source: Naval Applied Science Laboratory.**

Incidentally, one might be interested in knowing how the probability of success confidence levels are arrived at. Figures 8 and 9 are the types of technological forecasts that might be used in determining what growth potential still exists in a particular area. For instance, in regard to the tensile-yield strength of structural metals (Fig. 8), four structural metals in thick sections have the potential for over 100,000 pounds per square inch by 1988 (Fig. 9). These four metals—aluminum, molybdenum, steel, and titanium—would then seem to represent the four concurrent approaches to be taken in this area, depending on other properties required for a specific application.

Appraisal Sheets Nos. 1 and 2 were also completed for ocean tech-

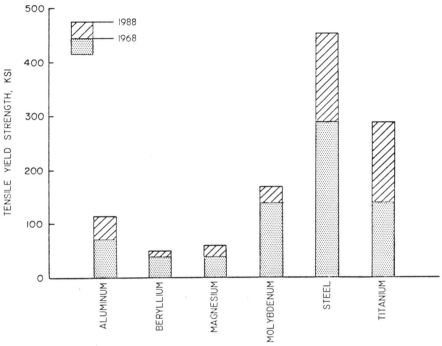

Figure 9 Structural metals, homogeneous, thick sections, low toughness, tensile yield strength, 1968–88. Values indicated are best properties of selected alloys of the element and are not necessarily representative of all alloys of the given element. Source: Naval Applied Science Laboratory.

nology (see Figs. 10 and 11), with a total value to the country of 25.2 and a probability of success of 0.75, thus yielding an expected value of 18.9 and a desirability index of 36.6. Two technological forecasts for the ocean technology could have been Figs. 12 and 13.

This technique, in addition to having been tested in the military, has been used quite extensively in private industry. These modified industrial applications have been referred to as BRAILLE and RALPH.[28,29]

[28] M. Cetron and B. Bartocha, "BRAILLE—A forecasting model to Aid Research and Development Planning," *Futures,* 1 (December 1969), pp. 479–487.
[29] C. A. Ralph, "RALPH I—Resource Allocation Logic for Planning Heuristically—Applied to the Electronics Industry," EIA International Meeting, California, October 1969.

OCEAN TECHNOLOGY

COLUMN 1 NATIONAL GOALS *	COLUMN 2 IMPACT OF "TECHNOLOGY OR INNOVATION" CONTRIBUTION										COLUMN 3 VALUE TO INDIVIDUAL GOAL
	1.0	0.9	0.8	0.7	0.6	0.5	0.4	0.3	0.2	0.1	
6 AGRICULTURE						●					2.4
7 AREA REDEVELOPMENT										●	0.7
5 CONSUMER EXPENDIT											
8 EDUCATION											
7 HEALTH											
6 HOUSING							●				1.8
3 INTERNATIONAL AID											
6 MANPOWER RETRAIN											
14 NATIONAL DEFENSE		●									12.6
2 NATURAL RESOURCES			●								1.6
4 PRIVATE PLANT & EQUIP											
3 RESEARCH & DEVELOP		●									2.7
12 SOCIAL WELFARE											
4 SPACE										●	0.4
5 TRANSPORTATION						●					3.0
8 URBAN DEVELOPMENT											

TOTAL VALUE TO THE COUNTRY   25.2

* The national goals listed in the first column came from *Manpower Requirements for National Objectives in the 1970s* by Leonard A. Lecht, Center for Priority Analysis, National Planning Association, 1968.

Scale of Definitions for "Impact of Technology or Innovation" (Column 2)

Points	Descriptors
1.0	Meets overriding critical need (or creation of new opportunity)
0.5	Helps moderately to meet a need
0.2	Increase in economy
0.1	Minor contribution to the goal

Figure 10   Ocean technology. Appraisal Sheet No. 1: Value to the country.

The technique just described related to technology and innovations. For *applied research* QUEST or a similar weighted-matrix technique is recommended.[30,31]

ON GOAL DETERMINATION

It should be reiterated at this point, that none of the decision-aiding models, including the one just illustrated, can be very effective unless it is based on goals.

[30] M. Cetron, "QUEST—Quantitative Utility Estimates for Science and Technology," *IEEE Transactions Engineering Management,* Vol. EM 14, No. 1, 1967.

[31] *Quantitative Techniques for Research Program Planning in Structural Mechanics,* a Report of the National Materials Advisory Board, National Research Council, Washington, D.C., September 1969.

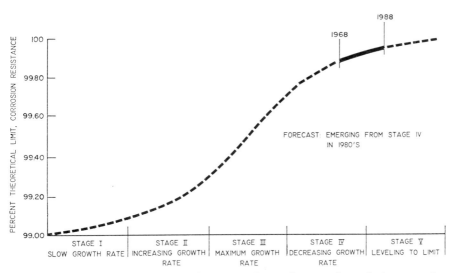

PROBABILITY OF SUCCESS

CHANCE OF MEETING THE REQUIRED LEVEL OF TECHNOLOGY OR MEETING THE OBJECTIVE OF AN INNOVATION

☐ 80 - 100 %   ☒ 60 - 80 %   ☐ 30 - 60 %   ☐ 0 - 30 %

NUMBER OF DIFFERENT CONCURRENT APPROACHES

☐ 1   ☒ 2   ☐ 3   ☐ 4   ☐ 5   ☐ 6   ☐ 7   ☐ 8   ☐ 9   ☐ 10 OR MORE

SACRED COW ? WHO SAYS ?

☐ PRESIDENT   ☐ SPECIFIC AGENCY OR FOUNDATION   ☐ CONGRESS
☐ PROFESSIONAL ASSOC   ☐ INDUSTRIAL ASSOC   ☐ OTHER
                                                                (specify)

APPRAISAL SUMMARY

NUMBER OF GOALS __8__   EXPECTED VALUE (E_V) __18.9__
VALUE TO THE COUNTRY (V) __25.2__   OPTIMUM FUNDING ($) __.516 Billion__
PROBABILITY OF SUCCESS (P_S) __.75__   DESIRABILITY INDEX (D_i) __36.6__

Figure 11   Ocean technology. Appraisal Sheet No. 2.

Figure 12   Environmental applications, corrosion resistance of metals in sea water, projected growth, 1968–88 (shown in relationship). Source: Naval Applied Science Laboratory.

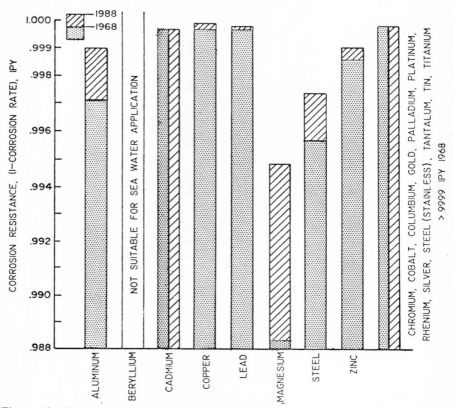

Figure 13   Environmental applications, corrosion resistance of metals in sea water, 1968–88. Values indicated are best properties of selected alloys of the element and are not necessarily representative of all alloys of the given element. Source: Naval Applied Science Laboratory.

On July 13, 1969 President Nixon established, within the White House, a National Goals Research Staff to assess the future of the United States for the purpose of offering alternative courses of action.[32] In his statement when creating the staff, he said:

We can no longer afford to approach the longer-range future haphazardly. As the pace of change accelerates, the process of change becomes more complex. Yet at the same time, an extraordinary array of tools and techniques has been developed by which it becomes increasingly possible to project future

[32] Cf. *Technological Forecasting,* **1** (Fall 1969), p. 217.

trends—and thus to make the kind of informed choices which are necessary if we are to establish mastery over the process of change. These tools and techniques are gaining widespread use in business, and in the social and physical sciences, but they have not been applied systematically and comprehensively to the science of government. The time is at hand when they must be used.

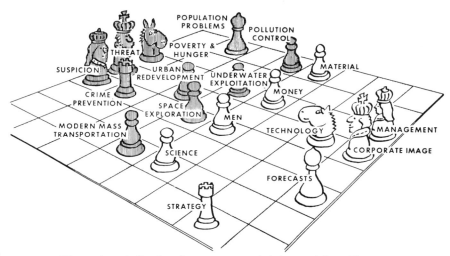

Figure 14   A "business" approach to fighting social problems.

Figure 14 tries to show how these business techniques are used against our national problems. The "problems" were gleaned from those given in Table 2. For one who would like to look deeper into our national problems, *Agenda for the Nation* is recommended.[33]

Since the United States has recently embarked on this first step of what could be called a "national plan," perhaps some benefit can be derived from an examination of the planning systems of other major powers and the effects on their industrial planning. A book and an article recently appeared, both of which could prove worthwhile in this context: *Industrial Planning in France*[34] and "Planning of Production and Consumption in the U.S.S.R."[35]

[33] K. Gordon, ed., *Agenda for the Nation* (Washington, D.C.: The Brookings Institution, 1968).

[34] J. H. MacArthur and B. R. Scott, *Industrial Planning in France* (Cambridge, Mass.: Harvard University Press, 1969).

[35] N. P. Fedorenko, "Planning of Production and Consumption in the U.S.S.R.," *Technological Forecasting,* 1 (June 1969), p. 87.

Table 2   Federal Government Spending for Social Need Projects during the Next 10 Years[a]

Project	Expenditure, billions of $
Agricultural research	$ 2.0
Highways	50.0
Mass transit	15.0
Transportation services	20.0
Education	300.0
Health	450.0
Welfare	700.0
Urban redevelopment	60.0
Water and power	50.0
Retraining	19.0
Total	more than $1.6 trillion

[a] "Source: Long-Range Planning Study," *Marketing Magazine*, July 15, 1967, p. 15, Douglas Aircraft Missiles and Space-Systems Division.

In the book, MacArthur and Scott point out that they were concerned only with the industrial sector of the French economy, specifically with five industries—energy, building materials, steel, chemicals, and "general manufacturing." When the authors completed their research, they were convinced that the national planning process had much less influence on company strategies than they had originally anticipated. This was true across the board in both light and heavy industry. Another key discovery was a decline in the influence of the national planning process on industry, which appeared to have taken place since the early 1950s. This decline, which occurred during the transition from wartime scarcity to postwar abundance, was evident both in France and in the U.S.S.R.

It should be noted that in France the industries most strongly influenced by the government were energy, computers, and steel. (Not too different, it will be seen, from those of the Soviet Union.) There was moderate state influence on chemicals and heavy industrial equipment, and either little or no state influence on the textile and food processing industries.

It seems to be much more than coincidence that these classifications tend to match those of what I choose to call "the degree of technological dynamism" of the industry. In other words, the industries in the United States that spend 10–20% of their profits on R&D (technologically dynamic) are the electronics, aerospace, pharmaceutical, and chemical industries. Those that spend an average 8% of their profits on R&D (technologically moderate) are the farm equipment, automotive, and petroleum industries. The industries spending less than 2–3% of their profits on R&D (technologically static) are food, lumber, cement, and construction. It is further worth noting that 83% of the funds spent in the technologically dynamic industries in the United States (with the exception of the chemical industry) were provided by the federal government.

The French planning process, then, was found to have its major positive effect when serving high political authorities as a staff activity assigned to analyze alternative policy choices at the overall economic (macro) level. At the industrial (micro) level, in contrast, the planning process was found to have little impact. It did not play a leading role in helping either business or the state to reach major policy decisions.

Fedorenko, director of the Central Economic-Mathematical Institute of the Soviet Academy of Sciences, says in his article, "Planning of Production and Consumption in the U.S.S.R.," that the early plans of economic development—the first 5-year plans—gave priority to industrial areas concerned with the main producers of goods and raw materials for the Soviet national economy. In Russia, the principal areas in which national plans were developed were metallurgy, power supply, and heavy industry. Not only was planning for these three industries essential, but also these plans (and their outputs) served as the inputs for the plans of the other industries. To use Fedorenko's words, "At that time this was the only way to safeguard the very existence of Soviet economy and pave the way for successful future development."

Perhaps the biggest difference between the U.S. National Goals Research Staff and the other national planning systems is that the U.S. group is not to be a planning agency, and will not in any way usurp or replace the political processes of decision making. Rather, it is intended to provide information about alternatives and options upon which decisions can be based. It is hoped that by stating goals, where they are required, these goals can be utilized as inputs in the strategic planning process.

Our national goals will also give some indication of priorities to the industrial manager so that he may use them as guides in developing his own corporate plans. There is nothing so futile as working without a plan, unless it is planning and then not using the plan in making decisions and allocating resources. In summary, it can be said that

- We need goals or objectives to plan, and
- the plans should be used as a guide in the allocation of resources.

The same idea can be expressed in another way: "If we lose sight of our objectives, we may have to redouble our effort."

CROSS IMPACT OF GOALS

One should also look at the impact of one goal on another. This function of "cross support" between goals really means that by working

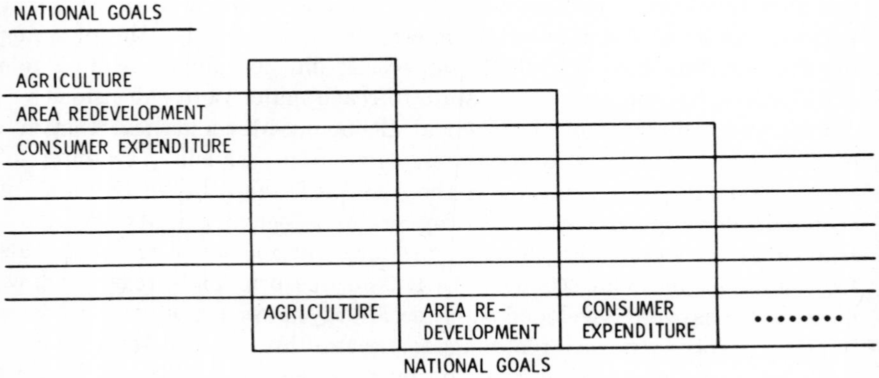

NATIONAL GOALS

Figure 15   Goal cross-support, cross-impact matrix.

on one goal a synergistic effect is created which helps other goals (see Fig. 15). Some work has already been undertaken in this area by T. Gordon[36] and by C. A. Ralph.[37]

CONCLUSIONS

I am well aware of many of the omissions and weaknesses of these quantitative selection or resource allocation techniques. It should be stressed again that they are intended, not to produce decisions, but rather to produce information which will facilitate decisions. Indeed, these techniques are merely thinking structures to force methodical, meticulous consideration of all the factors involved in resource allocation.

[36] T. Gordon, "Cross-Impact Matrices," *Futures,* 1 (December 1969), pp. 527–531.
[37] C. A. Ralph, "An Illustrative Example of DIANA—Applied to the Fishing Industry," a report of Synergistic Cybernetics, Inc., Alexandria, Va., February 1969; see also Chapter XVI of this book.

I am firmly convinced that, if I had to choose between any machine and the human brain, I would select the brain. The brain has a marvelous system that learns from experience, and an uncanny way of extracting the salient factors and rejecting useless information. It is wrong to say that one must select intuitive experience over analysis or minds over machines—really they are *not* alternatives; they complement each other. Used together, they yield results far better than if used individually.

A close look at a few "facts" concerning the quantitative resource allocation methods shows these approaches to be merely experimental management techniques. The fact that a computer or an adding machine can facilitate data handling should in no way detract from the basic fact that human subjective inputs are the foundation of these systems. Accurate human calculation, as opposed to use of a computer for the calculations of all the interrelationships considered would not alter the basic principles of these management tools in any respect. Nevertheless, I often hear the reactionary complaint that quantitative measurements cannot be applied to management processes because human judgment cannot be forsaken and machines cannot replace the seasoned-experience expertise of the manager.[38]

The real concern should be directed toward using the collective judgment of technical staffs (technological forecasts) and decision makers in such a manner that logically sound decisions are made, greater payoff is achieved for the resources committed, and less, not more, valuable scientific and engineering time is expended. To make an incorrect decision is understandable, but to make a decision and not really know the basis for the judgment is unforgivable. The area of good resource allocation certainly must have advanced beyond this point; otherwise, a pair of dice could replace the decision maker.

Most of the managers who design and work with information systems fully realize that technological forecasts such as quantitative estimates of project value and other aids to resource allocation are merely planning tools—and only a part of a brand-new kit of advanced decision-making devices.

Even this caveat, however, does not dissuade critics of the whole idea—and there are some very vocal ones around in government and business.[39,40] Some of the criticism is a reaction to the fear of "mecha-

[38] Roberts, *The Dynamics of Research and Development, op. cit.*

[39] R. A. Frosch, "A New Look at Systems Engineering," *IEEE Spectrum*, September 1969, pp. 24–28.

[40] E. B. Roberts, "Exploratory and Normative Technological Forecasting: A Critical Appraisal," in *Technological Forecasting: A Practical Approach,* ed. by M. J. Cetron (New York: Gordon & Breach, 1969), pp. 245–261.

nization" of a task felt to be rightfully in the province of human evaluation. Other critics claim that building up a logical system, computerizing the output, and quantifying what are essentially intuitive and judgment decisions may insulate some managers with a false sense of security. The validation of the process will not be continued, and management responsibility will be abandoned. Another criticism stems from the use of estimates as basic figures in the analysis. This kind of objection can also be applied, however, to decisions based on "experience" and made without a quantitative approach.

In a poem called "Bagpipe Music" by Louis MacNiece, the final couplet is:

> The glass is falling hour by hour
> the glass will fall forever.
> But if you break the bloody glass,
> you won't hold up the weather.

These lines express the fact that the barometer which is forecasting the weather does not control the weather. But it forgets to say that if one knows it *will* rain, he can prepare for it, or possibly in the future modify the weather enough to "hold it up."

Technological forecasting and systematic analysis tend to force managers to consider their resource allocation tasks more comprehensively and to highlight problem areas that might easily be overlooked by more traditional approaches. However, regardless of the high degree of sophistication being attributed to these planning devices, managers should use them with caution.

May 27, 1970

Appendix: Classification of Goals and the Abstract of Standards, National Goals Project

Source: *Manpower Requirements for National Objectives in the 1970's* by Leonard A. Lecht, Center for Priority Analysis, National Planning Association, 1968.

1. Agriculture	Includes cost of programs to raise income of commercial farm families to a close approximation to income of nonfarm families, plus the cost of programs to encourage

movement of 150,000 low-income members of the farm labor force into nonfarm employment each year.

2. Area Redevelopment

Includes cost of expanded redevelopment programs, following the objectives of the Area Redevelopment Act.

3. Consumer Expenditures

Sets living standards rise to limit fixed by savings rate of approximately 8% of disposable personal income. Includes additional increases in consumer expenditures from other goals, such as health, education, and transportation, plus family allowance system to increase family incomes below $3300 to this level.

4. Education

Assumes an increase in proportion of students from eligible age group receiving high school and higher education amounting to a 50% increase in proportion for college group. Allows for doubling of faculty salaries over decade, increased teacher-supporting staff, expansion of adult education and vocational training role of junior colleges, and increased plant and equipment at all levels of education.

5. Health

Stresses programs to enlarge access to modern health technologies by providing families with a level of health care equal to that enjoyed currently by families with most comprehensive health insurance plus expanded provisions for dental and psychiatric care. For persons over 65 years includes level of medical care costing 50% more than HEW estimate of cost of adequate medical care for the aged in early 1960s, with two-thirds of costs financed by public funds. Also includes increase in ratio of hospital beds to population following Hill-Burton Act standards, together with increase in health research expenditures sufficient to employ the 77,000 health research professionals NIH estimates will be needed in early 1970s.

6. Housing

Includes elimination of all remaining substandard housing between 1966 and 1975, plus increase in number of housing starts from 1.5 million in 1962 to 2.5 million by 1975 to provide for new family formation, adequate housing for nonwhites, higher income levels, greater emphasis on special housing for the aged, and vacation "second" housing. Also includes cost of R&D program to develop synthetic building materials, mass production of housing components, and building codes geared to potentialities of modern technology.

7. International Cooperation Act

Includes cost to United States of UN Decade of Development target that each industrialized nation contribute 1% of GNP from public and private sources to supply capital to developing nations. Also includes military support to developing nations at early 1960 levels, plus support for international nonfinancial organizations rising to $1.5 billion in 1975, primarily for WHO, UNESCO, FAO, and an expanded UN Peace Force.

8. Manpower Retraining

Includes cost of programs for retraining 1% of the labor force a year, following the outlines of the Manpower Development and Training Act passed in 1962, and providing basic literacy training as provided by 1963 amendments to the MDTA.

9. National Defense

Outlines expenditures for an adequate national defense, taking into account applications of technological advances such as antimissile missiles, nuclear aircraft carriers, and space vehicles, as well as requirements to maintain conventional armed forces.

10. Natural Resources

Includes cost of programs for increasing and economizing the supply of natural resources required in an urbanized and affluent society. Projects largest expansion in expenditures for water purification and storage with programs derived from studies of Senate Select Committee on Water Resources.

11. Private Plant and Equipment

Outlines expenditures for plant and equipment needed to sustain economic growth in the 1970s, plus the additional private plant and equipment expenditures projected for specific goals: utilities in urban development, transportation equipment in transportation, private and non-profit facilities for schools, hospitals, welfare, etc.

12. Research and Development

Stresses increases in "civilian economy" R&D with total R&D expenditures projected to increase from 3% of GNP in early 1960s to 4% of trillion-dollar GNP in mid-1970s. Includes substantial increases in expenditures for basic research, water desalination and oceanography, health and social science research, R&D information systems, and an R&D extension service for the private economy with objectives similar to those of the State Technical Services Act of 1965.

13. Social Welfare

Includes expenditures from public and private sources for providing typical pension covering cost of "modest but adequate" standard of living for an elderly retired couple in American cities in early 1960s, plus allowance for increases in earnings levels and standards of living. Also includes family allowance system to establish income maintenance floor for families with poverty incomes in the 1970s, and provisions for incorporating nationwide protection against income loss from illness as part of OASDI, expansion of unemployment compensation, and benefits similar to proposals of Johnson Administration.

14. Space

Includes expenditures for sustained space research and development program, involving further manned lunar landing followed by exploration of moon, earth-orbiting laboratories, and development of technology leading to human landing on Mars before year 2000. Also stresses expansion of research in basic space sciences and in applications of space technology in such areas as weather observation satellites and long-distance telecommunications.

15. Transportation

Outlines expenditures for transportation equipment and R&D, allowing for projected increase in automobile stock and for changes in transportation resource use following line of President Kennedy's 1962 Transportation Message to Congress. Also includes cost of R&D and advances such as supersonic planes, nuclear ships, hydrofoils, and gas-turbine engines.

16. Urban Development

Includes expenditures, generally derived from other goals, which are attributable to programs for providing adequate transportation, housing, cultural and recreation facilities, schools, hospitals, and industrial, commercial, and governmental buildings for the over three-fourths of the population who are expected to be living in urban areas in 1975. Also includes expenditures for new mass-transit technologies and for equipping automobiles with devices for controlling air pollution. Involves overall increase in spending for urban facilities, rising from 11% of GNP in 1962 to 13% in 1975.

Appendix: A More Detailed Analysis of the Sample and the Responses

THE SIZE AND MAKEUP OF SAMPLE

The initial list came from four sources:

1. Subscribers to *Innovation Magazine* (the majority of these are top-level R&D managers, e.g., vice presidents for research or directors of R&D).   4000
2. Individuals who attended lectures and seminars on technological forecasting for which Marvin Cetron served as an instructor (this group is composed primarily of R&D managers, R&D planners, and R&D project engineers).   1500
3. Individuals selected from a personally accumulated mailing list of those who requested reprints of articles published by Marvin Cetron (these are mostly planners, operations researchers, and systems analysts).   1000
4. Members of the R&D working group of the Military Operations Research Society (MORS); COLRAD (the College of Research and Development of The Institute of Management   1500

Science (TIMS); and the R&D marketing group of the Electronics Industry Association (EIA).

This list included 8000 names; but when they were typed and put in zip code order, duplications were found, and only 5980 questionnaires were mailed. Of that total, 1114 filled in the forms, and 325 others mailed in letters explaining why they could not answer the questionnaire. This means that approximately 24% answered the query. The 1114 responses were distributed as follows:

Industrial Classification	Responses[a]
Chemical and pharmaceuticals	128
Electronics	240
Plastics	42
Foods and feeds	30
Metallurgical and metals	87
Aerospace	128
R&D only firms	85
Government/military	119
Other	245

Occupation	Responses
Scientist	135
Engineer	188
Operations researcher	44
Planner or staff expert	173
Sales and other	41

Role in Organization in Relation to Forecasting and Planning	Responses
Personally responsible	252
General supervision	251
Staff capacity	251
Ad hoc basis or less	242

Age of Respondent (years)	Responses
Under 30	51
31–35	117
36–40	204
41–45	264
46–50	234
Over 50	236

Number of Technical and Professional Personnel in the Firm	Responses
1–25	347
26–100	248
101–400	223
401–750	71
Over 750	164

[a] Numbers do not add up to 1114 since not all respondents answered every question on the questionnaire.

THE RESPONSES

Tools of Analysis

One of four types of analyses was performed on the raw data: T tests, F tests, chi-square tests, and in one case a correlation analysis. The specific test selected depended on whether the data were along a continuum, whether one sample was being compared with one other sample, whether one sample was being compared with many other samples, or whether ordinal rankings were being compared.

The analysis of the significant data performed in each of the four tests is presented in the body of this chapter. The analysis of these data was based on a level of significance of 5% or better.

Level of Significance

In testing a given hypothesis, the maximum probability with which one would be willing to risk an error is called the level of significance of the test. This probability, often denoted by the subscript a, is generally specified before any samples are drawn, so that the results obtained will not influence our choice.

In practice a level of significance of 0.05 or 0.01 is customary, although other values are used. If, for example, a 0.05 or 5% level of significance is chosen in designing a test of hypothesis, there are about 5 chances in 100 that we would reject the hypothesis when it should be accepted, that is, we are about 95% confident that we have made the right decision. In such cases, we say that the hypothesis has been rejected at a 0.05 level of significance, which means that we could be wrong with probability 0.05.

t Tests

The t test (also called Student's distribution) is used to test the hypothesis that the difference between the mean $(\bar{X})$ scores of (1) two different sample populations from normal distributions responding to the same question, or (2) the same sample population responding to two different questions—with similar response categories—is statistically significant. The t test is used in cases where the two samples have approximately equal variations, and where the response categories fall along a continuum (ordinal scales).

The t test is used to test the hypothesis is that the two groups come from the same population $(\bar{X}_1 - \bar{X}_2)$. In cases where $t = 1.96$ (0.05 level of significance) or $t = 2.56$ (0.01 level of significance), statistically there is a significant difference between the mean scores. The formula is:

$$\bar{X}_1 - \bar{X}_2 / [(SD_1{}^2/N_2)(SD_2{}^2/N_2)]^{\frac{1}{2}}$$

where $\bar{X}$ = mean,
$\quad$ SD = standard deviation,
$\quad$ N = sample size.

Observations by Industry

1. The chemical and pharmaceutical industry is more knowledgeable about trend extrapolation than the electronics industry $(t = 2.07)$ and the aerospace industry $(t = 2.12)$.

2. The chemical and pharmaceutical industry is more knowledgeable about trend correlation than the electronics industry $(t = 2.18)$ and the aerospace industry $(t = 3.23)$.

3. The chemical and pharmaceutical industry is more knowledgeable about growth analogy than the electronics industry $(t = 2.13)$ and the aerospace industry $(t = 2.50)$.

4. The aerospace industry is more knowledgeable about the PAT-TERN relevance tree for allocation of resources technique than the chemical and pharmaceutical industry $(t = 2.11)$, the electronics industry $(t = 2.33)$, and the plastics industry $(t = 3.53)$.

5. The aerospace industry is more knowledgeable about the TORQUE military marginal utility technique than the chemical and pharmaceutical industry $(t = 3.48)$, the electronics industry $(t = 3.61)$, and the plastics industry $(t = 3.18)$.

6. The aerospace industry is more knowledgeable about the MACRO civilian marginal utility technique than the electronics industry $(t = 2.57)$.

7. The electronics industry is *less* knowledgeable about cash-flow allocation of resources techniques (such as the Disman technique) than

the chemical and pharmaceutical industry ($t = 3.96$) and the plastics industry ($t = 2.42$).

8. The aeronautical industry is *less* knowledgeable about cash-flow allocation of resources techniques (such as the Disman technique) than the plastics industry ($t = 3.22$).

9. The chemical and pharmaceutical industries use technological forecasts more as an aid in planning than as an aid in allocating resources, with positive scores of $t = 3.09$ and $t = 3.11$, respectively. There are no significant differences in the aerospace or plastics industries.

10. The electronics industry uses technological forecasts more than the chemical and pharmaceutical industries ($t = 2.26$).

11. The aeronautical industry considers probability of marketing success, as a criterion for project selection, to be *less* important than does the chemical and pharmaceutical industry ($t = 2.64$) and the electronics industry ($t = 2.51$).

12. The aeronautical industry considers market life of a product, as a criterion for project selection, to be *less* important than does the chemical and pharmaceutical industry ($t = 3.59$) and the electronics industry ($t = 4.69$).

13. The aeronautical industry considers revenue from sales, as a criterion for project selection, to be *less* important than does the chemical and pharmaceutical industry ($t = 3.52$), the electronics industry ($t = 3.12$), or the plastics industry ($t = 1.96$).

14. The aeronautical industry considers cost reduction as a criterion for project selection to be *less* important than does the chemical and pharmaceutical industry ($t = 3.81$) or the electronics industry ($t = 2.32$).

15. The chemical and pharmaceutical industry believes probability of technical success, as a criterion for project selection, can be determined *less* accurately than does the electronics industry ($t = 4.29$) or the plastics industry ($t = 2.33$).

16. The plastics industry believes manpower requirements, as a criterion for project selection, can be determined *more* accurately than does the electronics industry ($t = 2.54$), the aeronautical industry ($t = 2.41$), or the chemical and pharmaceutical industry ($t = 2.14$).

17. The aeronautical industry believes probability of marketing success, as a criterion for project selection, can be determined *less* accurately than does the electronics industry ($t = 3.26$) or the plastics industry ($t = 2.61$).

18. The chemical and pharmaceutical industry believes market life, as a criterion for project selection, can be determined *less* accurately than does the electronics industry ($t = 3.18$) or the plastics industry ($t = 2.13$).

Observations by Occupation

1. Staff members have greater familiarity with intuitive technological forecasting techniques than do managers ($t = 4.51$) or scientists ($t = 2.50$).

2. Scientists have greater familiarity with intuitive technological forecasting techniques than do managers ($t = 2.50$).

3. Scientists have greater familiarity with trend extrapolation as a technological forecasting technique than do engineers ($t = 3.89$) or managers ($t = 2.82$).

4. Engineers have *less* familiarity with trend extrapolation as a technological forecasting technique than do staff members ($t = 4.23$), scientists ($t = 3.89$), or managers ($t = 1.99$).

5. Staff members have greater familiarity with trend correlation as a technological forecasting technique than do managers ($t = 4.23$) or engineers ($t = 4.19$).

6. Scientists have greater familiarity with trend correlation as a technological forecasting technique than do engineers ($t = 3.10$) and managers ($t = 2.77$).

7. Scientists have greater familiarity with growth analogy as a technological forecasting technique than do managers ($t = 2.99$) or engineers ($t = 2.57$).

8. Staff members have greater familiarity with growth analogy as a technological forecasting technique than do managers ($t = 5.31$) or engineers ($t = 4.33$).

9. Engineers have *less* familiarity with normative technological forecasting techniques than do managers ($t = 4.65$), staff members ($t = 3.80$), or scientists ($t = 2.51$).

10. Engineers have *less* familiarity with discounted cash-flow techniques than do managers ($t = 3.67$) or staff members ($t = 3.62$).

11. Staff members are more familiar with linear programming techniques for allocation of resources than are engineers ($t = 4.85$), scientists ($t = 2.22$), or managers ($t = 2.16$).

12. Engineers are *less* familiar with double-matrix allocation of resource techniques than are scientists ($t = 2.42$) or staff members ($t = 2.38$).

F Ratios

The F ratio is also used to test the hypothesis that the difference between two population means is the same or that it is significantly different. This test, however, depends basically on a process which relies on a partitioning of the total variance among each of several sources.

This process has the advantage that it can be extended to test several means at the same time (a "multiple T test").

In the one-way analysis of variance we are testing the hypothesis that several subcategories are significant from one another. In cases with 3 degrees of freedom and an N of over 1000 (the role category), where $F = 2.60$ (0.05 level of significance) or $F = 3.78$ (0.01 level of significance), statistically there is a significant difference between the several subcategories. In cases with 4 degrees of freedom and an N of over 1000 (the size category), when $F = 2.37$ (0.05 level of significance) or $F = 3.32$ (0.01 level of significance), statistically there is a significant difference between the several subcategories. In cases with 6 degrees of freedom and an N of over 1000 (the age category), where $F = 2.10$ (0.05 level of significance) or $F = 2.82$ (0.01 level of significance), statistically there is a significant difference between the several subcategories.

Role

1. Individuals in no formal role, or in an *ad hoc* role, perceive their organization as having fewer written objectives (both corporate and R&D) than the more directly involved personnel ($F = 3.16$).

2. Individuals in no formal role, or in an *ad hoc* role, perceive their organization as having fewer forecasts, economic ($F = 6.64$) and marketing ($F = 3.39$), than those more directly involved.

3. The greater the direct involvement (i.e., personally responsible, staff capacity, general supervision, *ad hoc* basis or less), the more one believes that his organization uses technological forecasting as an aid in planning ($F = 8.76$) and in allocating resources ($F = 4.88$).

4. Staff and *ad hoc* personnel perceive their organization as using forecasts more to justify a previously made decision ($F = 6.49$) and to satisfy a fad ($F = 2.68$) than does the person responsible or the general supervisor.

5. The more responsible the individual's role is (i.e., personality responsible, general supervision, staff capacity), the more he believes that his organization formulates long-range plans ($F = 13.83$) and uses technological forecasting in preparing these long-range plans ($F = 4.14$).

6. The more responsible the individual's role is, the less familiar he is with intuitive ($F = 12.44$), trend extrapolation ($F = 5.13$), and trend correlation ($F = 4.77$) technological forecasting techniques.

7. Individuals in no formal role, or in an *ad hoc* role, are less familiar with all the normative forecasting techniques than individuals directly involved with the planning of technological forecasting areas, specifically: scoring techniques ($F = 2.76$), discount cash-flow model ($F =$

11.28), linear programming $(F = 7.31)$, cost-effective model based on technical feasibility $(F = 3.60)$, heuristic relevance tree technique (PROFILE) $(F = 2.63)$, double-matrix technique $(F = 4.08)$, and marginal utility technique, military $(F = 3.51)$ and civilian $(F = 4.78)$.

8. The more responsible an individual's role, the more he believes that long-range plans for the organization should be for a shorter period, both for applied research $(F = 8.70)$ and for development $(F = 6.39)$.

Age. The older an individual becomes, the more he believes his organization has:

1. more quantitative objectives, both corporate $(F = 4.86)$ and R&D $(F = 6.05)$;
2. a higher percentage of trend extrapolation $(F = 3.23)$ and normative (goal-oriented) forecasts $(F = 3.22)$;
3. a higher percentage of environmental forecasts $(F = 6.02)$;
4. a higher utilization of technological forecasting, both as an aid in planning $(F = 2.68)$ and in allocating resources $(F = 2.06)$;
5. been formulating specific long-range plans for its R&D efforts $(F = 3.52)$;
6. been using technological forecasting in preparing its long-range plans $(F = 4.05)$.

The younger an individual is, the more he is willing to try a new fad (such as technological forecasting) $(F = 2.69)$.

Size (based on the number of technical and professional personnel involved in the R&D effort)

1. The larger the organization, the more it uses economic $(F = 6.51)$, technological $(F = 11.01)$, and environmental $(F = 17.44)$ forecasts.
2. The larger the organization, the more it uses long-range planning in developing its R&D effort $(F = 12.38)$, and technological forecasts in preparing its long-range plans $(F = 4.49)$.
3. The larger the organization, the more it uses trend extrapolation $(F = 4.83)$, trend correlation $(F = .285)$, and growth analogy $(F = 2.90)$.
4. The larger the organization, the more it uses the following resource allocation methodologies:

    (a) Discount cash-flow optimization models, such as Disman $(F = 4.20)$.
    (b) Linear programming models, such as RDE $(F = 4.46)$.

(c) Cost-effective models based on technology, such as BRAILLE ($F = 3.11$).

(d) Heuristic relevance tree models, such as PATTERN ($F = 11.72$) and PROFILE ($F = 4.28$).

(e) Double-matrix techniques, such as QUEST ($F = 2.97$), and marginal utility models, such as TORQUE ($F = 5.25$).

Chi-Square Tests

The chi-square (χ^2) test is used to test the hypothesis that two classifications—either two different groups responding to the same question, or two different issues responded to by the same group—are statistically independent of each other.

The χ^2 test in this study is used on the basis of contingency analysis, whereby we are hypothesizing that the difference in the frequency of responses between the two classifications is not significantly different.

The χ^2 does not assume normal distributions, nor must the response categories be continuous. In cases where $\chi^2 = 5.99$ (0.05 level of significance) with 2 df (degrees of freedom), there is a significant difference between the mean scores; with 3 df, at the 0.05 level $\chi^2 = 7.81$ and at the 0.01 level $\chi^2 = 11.3$; with 4 df, at the 0.05 level $\chi^2 = 9.49$ and at the 0.01 level $\chi^2 = 13.3$.

The chi-square formula is as follows:

2 × 2 Table

$$\chi^2 = \frac{N(a_1 b_2 - a_2 b_1)^2}{(a_1 + b_1)(a_2 + b_2)(a_1 + a_2)(b_1 + b_2)}$$

		I	II	Total
A		a_1	a_2	N_A
B		b_1	b_2	N_B
	Totals	N_1	N_2	N

2 × 3 Table

$$\chi^2 = \frac{N}{N_A} \frac{a_1{}^2}{N_1} \frac{a_2{}^2}{N_2} \frac{a_3{}^2}{N_3} \frac{N}{N_B} \frac{b_1{}^2}{N_1} \frac{b_2{}^2}{N_2} \frac{b_3{}^2}{N_3} - N$$

		I	II	III	Total
A		a_1	a_2	a_3	N_A
B		b_1	b_2	b_3	N_B
	Totals	N_1	N_2	N_3	N

Objectives

Industry \ Criteria	Written Quantitative	Written Qualitative	Oral or None
Chemical and Pharmaceutical	65	41	17
Electronics	87	94	55

$\chi^2 = 9.41137$ on 2 degrees of freedom

Therefore, the chemical and pharmaceutical industry has more quantitative objectives than does the electronics industry.

Chemical Industry

Objectives \ Frequency of Review	More Often than Annual	Annual	1–3 Years	3 Years or More
Corporate	29	70	13	10
R&D	63	49	6	4

$\chi^2 = 21.4215$ on 3 degrees of freedom

Therefore, the R&D objectives for the chemical and pharmaceutical industry are reviewed and updated more frequently than the corporate objectives.

Electronics Industry

Objectives \ Frequency of Review	More Often than Annual	Annual	Less than Annual
Corporate	93	107	33
R&D	119	96	14

$\chi^2 = 11.4318$ on 2 degrees of freedom

Therefore, the R&D objectives for the electronic industry are reviewed and updated more frequently than the corporate objectives.

Aerospace Industry

Objectives / Frequency of Review	More Often than Annual	Annual	Less than Annual
Corporate	31	81	13
R&D	62	55	7

$\chi^2 = 17.1002$ on 2 degrees of freedom

Therefore, the R&D objectives for the aerospace industry are reviewed and updated more frequently than the corporate objectives.

Technological Forecasting Techniques

Trend Extrapolation

Occupation / Usage	1–10%	11–20%	21–30%	31–40%	41% or More
Scientists	26	19	19	16	46
Managers	108	88	98	93	108

$\chi^2 = 12.5378$ on 4 degrees of freedom

Therefore, scientists use the trend extrapolation technique of technological forecasting more than managers.

Intuitive

Occupation / Usage	1–10%	11–30%	31–40%	41% or More
Staff	55	37	17	53
Manager	176	152	54	108

$\chi^2 = 8.59375$ on 3 degrees of freedom

Therefore, staff members use the intuitive method of technological forecasting more than managers.

Growth Analogy

Usage Industry	1–10%	11–20%	21–30%	31–40%	41% or More
Chemical and pharmaceutical	47	15	13	22	23
Aerospace	59	19	12	8	8

$\chi^2 = 14.8502$ on 4 degrees of freedom

Therefore, the aerospace industry uses the growth analogy method of technological forecasting more than the chemical or pharmaceutical industry.

Rank Correlation Coefficients

When random samples are drawn from some population which is known to be bivariate but the distributions of whose variables are not known, or are known not to be normal, the traditional product-moment formulation cannot be used to measure the degree of association between the two variables. If, however, in such a situation the members of each sample can be ordinally ranked according to the variables of interest (such as this criterion), a non-parametric measure of correlation, devised by Spearman, may be computed and, within limits (in this case 5%), may be used to derive inferences about the degree of association of variables in the parent populations. In cases where $r = .43$ (0.05 level of significance) or $r = .61$ (0.01 level of significance), statistically there is significant "agreement" or "concordance" between the rankings.

The Spearman coefficient of rank correlation is given by the formula

$$ r = 1 - \frac{\Sigma_i d_i}{\frac{1}{6}(n^3 - n) + 1} $$

where d_i = the difference between the two rankings of the ith item,

$\quad n$ = the number of items ranked,

$\quad r$ = the Spearman rank correlation coefficient.

Project Selection. Spearman rank correlation analysis was performed on the importance and accuracy of the ranked criteria for project selection, for both initial and continued funding (See Chapter 12 Page 211–215). The results were as follows:

1. The rank correlation between the importance criterion and the accuracy criterion *is not* significant; *one cannot* accurately determine the ranking of the degree of accuracy needed for initial funding on the basis of the degree of importance for *initial* funding ($r = .356$).

2. The rank correlation between importance for initial funding and importance for continued funding is highly significant. At the 0.01 level of significance ($r = .919$), the ranking of the criteria for initial funding remains practically the same during continued funding.

3. Although the relationship between level of importance and degree of accuracy is not substantial during initial funding, the accuracy of the relationship between level of importance and degree of accuracy is significant for continued funding (0.05 level of significance) ($r = .500$).

Biographical Sketches of Contributors and Advisors

ROSS C. ALDERSON

Ross C. Alderson was a key participant in the initial development of the Honeywell PATTERN methodology for determining technical upgrading requirement in the aerospace industry. Subsequently, he participated actively in the Honeywell Medical Instrumentation Study and at present serves in a staff capacity to the manager of the Systems Analysis Department of the Honeywell Corporate Research Center. In this latter capacity he has directed requirements determination studies of the hydrocarbon processing industry, building protection, and the technological upgrading needs in the housing industry.

Before his participation in requirements determination and technological forecasting Mr. Alderson served as technical director of research projects in inertial navigation and guidance, aircraft flight-control systems and automatic landing systems, and miscellaneous long-range missile systems (ballistic and cruise) studies and developments. He has been with Honeywell from 1943 to the present, serving in various research, development, and design capacities.

ROBERT U. AYRES

Robert U. Ayres is vice president and director of the International Research and Technology Corporation in Washington, D.C. He received his B.S. degree from the University of Chicago, his M.S. degree from the University of Maryland, and his Ph.D. degree from the University of London.

From 1962 to 1966, Mr. Ayres served as a research staff member with the Hudson Institute, and from 1966 to 1967, as a senior research associate with the Hudson Laboratories of Columbia University. He was associated with Resources for the Future, Incorporated, from 1966 to 1968, as a nonresident staff member, and later as a visiting scholar. He subsequently joined the International Research and Technology Corporation in his present position, where he is responsible for the direction of projects on transportation, urban and program planning, and forecasting.

Dr. Ayres is the author of a number of articles, books, and papers, including *Hypercryogrnics, Technological Forecasting and Long-Range Planning,* and "Forecasting by the Envelope Curve Technique." He is a member of the Editorial Board of *European Business* and the Editorial Advisory Board of *Technological Forecasting.* He has served as a consultant for a number of other business organizations.

ROBERT H. BALDWIN

Robert H. Baldwin received his engineering degree from the University of Michigan. He is presently the director of the Technical Division of the Sherwin Williams Company. This positions entails administrative and technical services for four major laboratories and six plant sites.

Before joining the Sherwin Williams Company, Mr. Baldwin was employed as the director of research of the Maumee Chemical Company, which merged with Sherwin Williams in September 1969.

Among the various organizations of which Mr. Baldwin is a member are the American Chemical Society, American Institute of Engineers, New York Academy of Sciences, and American Society of Metals.

JOSEPH L. BARACH

Joseph L. Barach's scholastic background includes a B.A. in physics from Cornell University and an M.S. in physics from the University of Pennsylvania. He is presently manager of program evaluation and administration for the Technical Department of the Celanese Fibers Marketing Company.

During the last 17 years he has held a variety of positions, both in research for Celanese Corporation and in the Fibers Marketing Company. Before that, he was employed by the Alexander Smith Carpet Company (now Mohasco, Incorporated) and the Propeller Division of the Curtiss-Wright Corporation.

Mr. Barach holds a large number of patents issued in his name and has contributed many times to the scientific literature in the area of fiber science.

ROBERT BAWER

Robert Bawer is president of Radiation Systems, Incorporated, of McLean, Virginia. In addition to filling the presidential role, he also provides technical coordination in many areas of communication electronics.

Before this, Mr. Bawer held positions as assistant director for research for Aero Geo Astro Corporation, technical consultant to Emerson Research Laboratories, project engineer at Melpar Incorporated, and research assistant at Massachusetts Institute of Technology.

A. DOUGLAS BENDER

A. Douglas Bender received his bachelor's degree from Williams College, master's degree in physiology from the University of Iowa, and a Ph.D. degree in physiology from the Jefferson Medical College. He is director of the Science Information, Research and Development Division, Smith Kline & French Laboratories. In this post he is responsible for a variety of information and management services, including long-range planning and technological forecasting. He has been responsible for R&D planning activities for the past 3 years, and his group has performed a number of studies, including "A Delphic Study of the Future of Medicine."

Dr. Bender is a Fellow in the American College of Cardiology, the Gerontological Society, and the American Institute of Chemists, and a member of the American Physiological Society and the American Society for Information Science.

WILLIAM W. BEWLEY, JR.

William W. Bewley is the manager of the Economic Research Division of Hercules Incorporated. In this capacity, he is responsible for performing economic forecasts, economic and financial analyses, and capital expenditure analysis.

Mr. Bewley has been employed at Hercules since 1950 and has held such positions as controller-treasurer of the company's Mexican subsidiary, manager of the General Accounting Division, and senior financial analyst.

A. WADE BLACKMAN

A. Wade Blackman received his undergraduate degree in engineering from the University of Alabama and graduate degrees in engineering and in management from Massachusetts Institute of Technology. He is currently employed as manager of advanced systems research at United Aircraft Research Laboratories and is in charge of the areas of technological forecasting, economics, urban dynamics, and industrial dynamics.

His previous experience includes employment at MIT as a research assistant and at United Aircraft Research Laboratories as, successively, research engineer; group leader; supervisor, chemical kinetics; chief, rocket and air-breathing propulsion; and chief, propulsion. He was instrumental in the development of theory and design procedures for the elimination of combustion instabilities in turbojet afterburners and rockets and in establishing the feasibility of hydrogen-fueled rocket engines.

Mr. Blackman was appointed a Sloan Fellow at MIT during 1965–66. He returned to United Aircraft Research Laboratories as manager, hypersonic propulsion.

He served as an ensign in the U.S. Naval Reserve, received the American Institute of Aeronautics and Astronautics Goddard Award in 1966 for work on combustion instabilities, and is the author of 15 patients and numerous publications in the field. His memberships include Tau Beta Pi, Pi Tau Sigma, Theta Tau, Alpha Tau Omega, American Institute of Aeronautics and Astronautics (Associate Fellow), Combustion Institute, Connecticut Society of Professional Engineers, Society of Sloan Fellows, and University Club of Hartford. He is listed in *American Men of Science, Who's Who in the East,* and *Who's Who in Finance and Industry.*

RAUL DE BRIGARD

Raul de Brigard obtained B.A. and B.Arch. degrees from Harvard University and a M. Arch. degree (in urban design) at the University of California. He joined the staff of Institute for the Future soon after completing his studies.

In addition to studies, the two years from 1964 to 1966 included work in Canada (ARCOP, Place Bonaventure) and South America (Dicken Castro, Exposicion Panamericana del 64, Bogota, Pavilion Bavaria). Mr. de Brigard's 1966 thesis at Harvard was part of the proposal of the Harvard School of Education to the city of Pittsburgh. A year later he received one of the first scholarships awarded by the Department of Housing and Urban Development for urban studies.

During the summer of 1968 Mr. de Brigard worked at Charles Eames and Associates on display techniques to be used in urban simulation exhibits by IBM, and from 1966 to 1968 participated in a number of projects with Henry C. K. Liu, Warren Chalk, R. Hafner, and others. These projects included the development of possible futures for cities and proposals examining the impact of the Los Angeles Freeway on urban development, as well as assisting in instruction and setting up the framework for a study on urban design education sponsored by the Ford Foundation.

For the past year at the Institute, Mr. de Brigard has been engaged in a number of projects. These include an investigation of some possible issues and opportunities in the future of the state of Connecticut, a study of major future societal trends in the nation, and work specifically related to the future of housing. He is presently working on a project concerned with measures of social progress to be used by communities in Connecticut.

MARVIN J. CETRON

Marvin J. Cetron is president and chairman of the board of Forecasting International Limited in Fairfax, Virginia. Dr. Cetron gained his technical experience as head of the Planning Branch at the U.S. Naval Marine Engineering Laboratory, engineering assistant to the technical director of the Navy Applied Science Laboratory, and head of the Management Planning Review Branch of the Applied Science Laboratory. He was responsible for the Navy's technological forecast and appraisal efforts in the Advanced Concepts Branch at the Headquarters of the Naval Material Command in Washington, D.C.

Dr. Cetron has published extensively in the fields of planning, resource allocation, technological forecasting, and operations research. Some of his most recent publications are *Technological Forecasting: A Practical Approach* and *Technical Resource Management: Quantitative Methods*. Both books received the Armed Forces Management Literary Award for 1969 and 1970 respectively. His latest book, *The Science of Managing Organized Technology*, consists of 4 volumes.

Dr. Cetron is a member of the Military Operations Research Symposia, the American Institute of Industrial Engineers, the Interservice Technological Forecasting Methodology Group, the Interagency Group for Research on Research, and two *ad hoc* committee's of the National Materials Advisory Board of the National Academy of Science.

MICHAEL L. COCHRAN

Michael L. Cochran, currently vice president for finance, Smith Kline Instruments, Inc., Palo Alto, California, has spent a major portion of his career in the area of developing management information control systems, particularly for financial management. Upon completion of graduate school, he started his career as a systems analyst, changing over to financial reviews, with special emphasis on developing management accounting systems which allow planning and control reaction.

Mr. Cochran's previous experience was gained as systems analyst with Colgate-Palmolive, financial analyst with Burroughs Corporation, and assistant director for planning and forecasting with Smith Kline & French.

Mr. Cochran is a member of the National Association of Accountants and the World Future Society.

UGO A. COTY

Ugo A. Coty holds a B.S. degree in aeronautical engineering from Indiana Institute of Technology, and B.S. and M.S. degrees from the University of

Michigan. He is now manager of advanced programs analysis for the Lockheed-California Company, a post he has held since 1967.

Mr. Coty's varied experience includes positions as group test pilot and technical inspector, U.S. Air Force; group engineer for systems analysis of missile and aircraft weapon systems; assistant project engineer for X-17 re-entry test vehicle; manager of *Polaris* missile system project operations; division manager of *Polaris* design, Van Nuys; and senior research and development engineer for advanced concepts. Other posts have included manager or manufacturing and assistant works manager for design and production of aerospace systems, components, and propulsion systems.

MARCEL A. CORDOVI

Marcel A. Cordovi received a Bachelor of Mechanical Engineering degree in 1941 from the Polytechnic Institute of Brooklyn, where he also received a Master of Mechanical Engineering degree in 1942, and a Mechanical Engineer degree in 1947. Since 1950 he has been an adjunct professor in metallurgical engineering at the Institute.

Mr. Cordovi has been mechanical group leader in the Application Engineering Section of the Market Development Department since 1967. He joined the company in 1958 as a metallurgical engineer in the Development and Research Department, and later that year was appointed in charge of the Power Industry Section of the Market Development Department. In 1966 he was named senior application engineer.

Active in the American Society for Testing and Materials, Mr. Cordovi is also a member of the American Society of Mechanical Engineers, American Nuclear Society, American Society for Metals, American Welding Society, Metals Science Club of New York, National Association of Corrosion Engineers, Society of Naval Architects and Marine Engineers, New York Academy of Sciences, Sigma Xi, French Engineers in the United States, Inc., and Societe des Ingenieurs Civils de France (Paris).

The author of numerous papers on nuclear materials, welding, and steam generation materials, he was awarded the Industrial Achievement Award of the Society for Metals in 1967, the Award of Merit of the American Society for Testing and Materials in 1967, and a certificate by the Boiler and Pressure Vessel Code of American Society of Mechnical Engineers in 1968.

J. KENNETH CRAVER

J. Kenneth Craver obtained his B. Ed. degree at Southern Illinois University in 1936 and his M.S. degree at Syracuse University in 1938. He has held numerous positions in research and development with Monsanto Company, and now heads the Technological and Business Environmental Forecasting Department, Central Research Division.

Mr. Craver is a member of the American Chemical Society, American Association for the Advancement of Science, Commercial Chemical Development Association (past president), Chemists Club, Les Amis, and De Gustibus. He holds numerous patents and has written several scientific papers.

JAMES F. DALBY

James F. Dalby is currently advisory engineer, Components Division, IBM East Fishkill Facility, Hopewell Junction, New York.

His previous experience was as chief, Rendezvous Analysis Branch, MSC, Houston, Texas; chief, Mathematics Physics Branch, MSC, Houston, Texas; Executive engineer, Mission Planning and Analysis Division, MSC, Houston, Texas; manager of systems analysis, Manual Orbiting Laboratory Program, General Electric Company, Valley Forge, Pennsylvania.

DANIEL J. FINK

Daniel J. Fink is vice president and general manager of one of the nation's largest industrial space research and development complexes, General Electric's Space Division, with headquarters at Valley Forge, Pennsylvania. A major participant in U.S. manned and unmanned space programs, such as Apollo, Saturn V Test Range, Nimbus weather satellite, and the Orbiting Astronomical Observatory, the Space Division employs almost 9000 persons at eleven locations throughout the country.

Mr. Fink was named general manager of the Space Division in 1969, after serving as general manager of the GE Space Systems Organization at Valley Forge for almost 2 years. In his previous position, he was responsible for the research and development organization involved in the following major space programs: U.S. Air Force Manned Orbiting Laboratory, Nimbus, Orbiting Astronomical Observatory, SNAP-27 thermonuclear power source, Apollo color television transmission system, Applications Technology Satellites F/G, and Mariner/Mars '71 attitude and scan control subsystem.

As head of the Space Division for GE, Mr. Fink is responsible for the research, development, and testing of space vehicles, ground support equipment, and engineering services for NASA and the Department of Defense.

JOHN C. FISHER

John C. Fisher, consulting scientist at RESD and a member of the Division's Advanced Development Council, is the technical director of the Division's Independent Research and Development Council. His education includes an

A.B. degree in mathematics from Ohio State in 1941 and a Sc.D. degree from Massachusetts Institute of Technology in 1947. Dr. Fisher joined the staff of General Electric's Research Center upon receipt of his doctorate.

His background includes some 22 years' experience with the General Electric Company, including assignments as research and development manager for programs and systems at the company's Research and Development Center in Schenectady; and as manager of information disciplines at TEMPO, the General Electric Center for Advanced Studies, in Santa Barbara. Dr. Fisher has rejoined the company at RESD after a recent tour with the Air Force as chief scientist.

JOSEPH M. FOX

Joseph M. Fox has B.S. and M.S. degrees in chemical engineering from the University of Pennsylvania and is a licensed professional engineer. He joined Sharp & Dohme in 1946 and held various positions in engineering and production, including chief industrial engineer and manager of production control and warehousing. He initiated the application of quantitative techniques to the evaluation of effectiveness of advertising and promotion while manager of promotion research in the Merck Sharp & Dohme Division of Merck.

In 1965 he assumed his present position, where he is responsible for coordination of the company's strategic planning, monitoring of the environment affecting the company's operations, and recommending the company objectives. .

HERBERT I. FUSFELD

Herbert I. Fusfeld received his B.A. degree from Brooklyn College. Subsequently, he was awarded the M.A. and Ph.D. (physics) degrees, both from the University of Pennsylvania.

Dr. Fusfeld is currently director of research for the Kennecott Copper Corporation, New York City. Before joining Kennecott in 1963, he was director of research at the American Machine and Foundry Company, New York City. Earlier, he was head of the Physics and Foundry Company, New York City. Earlier, he was head of the Physics and Mathematics Division, Frankford Arsenal, Philadelphia, Pennsylvania.

He has also been a member of the faculties of the University of Pennsylvania and Temple University. He has published in many scientific journals and holds several patents in industrial testing and electronics.

Dr. Fusfeld is known for his contributions to metal physics and the plastic flow of metals. He is an authority on the organization of general physical research and industrial research management.

He has been a member of the Board of Governors, American Institute of Physics; a member of the Advisory Committee on Corporation Associates, American Chemical Society; a member of the Board of Directors, Industrial Research Institute, Inc.; and a member of the Scientific Research Society of

America, the Institute of Aeronautics and Astronautics, and the American Institute of Mining, Metallurgical, and Petroleum Engineers.

SAM GOODMAN

Sam Goodman received a B.B.A degree in accounting and economics from the City College of New York in 1951, and an M.B.A. degree in accounting and economics in 1957 from New York University. He received his Ph.D. degree in the areas of marketing, accounting, and corporate finance from New York University in 1968.

Dr. Goodman is controller and chief financial officer for The Nestle Company, Inc., in White Plains, New York. Prior to his current position, he had experience with the Crowell Collier Publishing Company and General Foods Corporation.

Dr. Goodman is an associate professor of marketing and finance at Pace College Graduate School of Business Administration. He specializes in teaching courses at the evening school in marketing and financial decision making.

He is a member of the Financial Executives Institute, the National Association of Accountants, the Planning Executives Institute, and the American Statistical Association.

Dr. Goodman has written several articles for such journals as *Financial Executive, Business Management,* and *Budgeting and Business Management,* as well as for the premier issue of *Innovation Magazine.* His book, *Techniques of Profitability Analysis,* was published by John Wiley & Sons in 1970.

GEORGE M. HAIR

George M. Hair is manager of technological forecasting and product planning for the Electronics Division of General Dynamics in Rochester, New York. He received his B.S. degree from the University of Rochester in 1953.

Mr. Hair joined the General Dynamics Corporation as business manager of the Radio Communications Laboratory in 1959, and became manager of advanced products in 1965. He became executive planning assistant in 1967 and assumed his present position in 1929. He is currently responsible for the development and implementation of the division's forecasting and planning procedures, and the generation of its strategic plan and technological forecast.

Mr. Hair is president of the Rochester planners.

OLAF HELMER

Olaf Helmer received Ph.D. degrees in mathematics and logic from the University of Berlin and London, respectively. He taught at the Universities of Chicago and Illinois, at New York City College, and at the New School for Social Research.

In 1946 he joined Project RAND, which in 1948 became The Rand Corporation; he was a senior staff member of the Mathematics Department there until 1968. During the academic year 1965–66 he also held a half-time appointment as research associate in the Institute of Government and Public Affairs at the University of California at Los Angeles.

In recent years his principal interest have been in gaming and other simulation studies, in long-range forecasting, and in scientific methodology. Among his publications are the book *Social Technology* (1966) and numerous articles, such as "On the Epistomology of the Inexact Sciences" (coauthor: N. Rescher), *Management Science*, Vol. 6 (1959); *Report on a Long-Range Forecasting Study* (coauthor: T. J. Gordon), first published as a Rand Paper, P-2982 (1964), and subsequently included as an appendix in *Social Technology* (see above) and also published in French, German, Italian, Japanese, and Russian; and "Planning Education for the Future" (coauthors: M. Adelson, M. Alkin, and C. Carey), *American Behavioral Scientist*, Vol. 10 (1967).

E. WEBER IVY

E. Weber Ivy is a 1949 graduate of the U.S. Military Academy and holds M.S. and Ph.D. degrees in electrical engineering from Texas A&M University. He is a member of the Institute of Electrical and Electronics Engineers, Eta Kappa Nu, Tau Beta Phi, and the General Dynamics Management Association, Orlando.

Dr. Ivy is currently the manager of advanced planning at Dynatronics, Orlando, Florida, an operation of the General Dynamics Electronics Division, Rochester, New York. In this capacity he is responsible for technological forecasting, new product planning, and market analysis associated with the Dynatronics product line of digital telemetry systems and data handling products. He has conducted recent studies concerning the application of advanced digital techniques to future requirements for data communications and environmental control systems.

Before joining Dynatronics, Dr. Ivy served 20 years with the Air Force, where he spent the last 12 years in DOD and NASA programs associated with planning, development, and evaluation of missile and space systems. He was DOD representative for network operations at the NASA Manned Spacecraft Center, Houston, and chief of the Strategic Analysis Division, Hq Air Force Systems Command, Washington D.C., before leaving the Air Force in 1969.

ERIC JOHNSON

Eric Johnson received a B.S. degree in metallurgy from Massachusetts Institute of Technology in 1967. He attended graduate school at Case Western Reserve University and will soon complete an M.S. in operations research.

Mr. Johnson is currently employed by the Metal Mining Division Engineering Department, Kennecott Copper Corporation, as associate planning engineer. Previously, he was employed at the Casting Laboratory, Chase Brass and Copper Company, from 1967 to June 1970, as manager of operations research.

Mr. Johnson is a member of The Institute of Management Science.

JACK KEVERIAN

Jack Keverian is general manager of Kennecott Refining Corporation, Anne Arundel County, Maryland, a subsidiary of Kennecott Copper Corporation. He received his bachelor's, master's, and doctor of science degrees in metallurgy from the Massachusetts Institute of Technology.

Previously, he was associated with Chase Brass and Copper Company at Cleveland, Ohio, also a Kennecott subsidiary. He organized and was director of the Casting Laboratory, a metallurgical research facility designed for the advancement of continuous casting technology and the refining of secondary coppers. Before joining Chase, he organized and served as manager of the Applied Research and Development Laboratory, Foundry Department, for General Electric Company at Schenectady, New York.

JAMES F. LANGSTON

James F. Langston was awarded the B.E.E degree from the University of Louisville (1945) and the M.S. degree from Iowa State University (1947). During the period 1948–53 he was with the Sperry Gyroscope Company, assigned to development of aircraft microwave landing and ECM systems. In 1953 he joined the Consolidated Vultee Aircraft Corporation, which subsequently became part of the General Dynamics Corporation; there he participated in the Atlas Weapon System development in the Convair and Astronautics Divisions.

In 1962 Mr. Langston became manager of field operations for electronic programs involved with missile tracking and satellite programs. During 1964 he became associated with SESTRO, a General Dynamics joint-venture French company, participating in a market survey and management planning.

He joined the Electronics Divisions' San Diego Operations in 1965, where he has held positions as program manager, manager of engineering services, and acting director of engineering, and is currently manager of long-range planning.

RALPH C. LENZ, JR.

Ralph C. Lenz, Jr., is currently assistant deputy for development planning with the Aeronautical Systems Division, Wright-Patterson AFB, Ohio. He has played a major role in the concept formulation for several large Air Force systems. He developed a provocative view of "Air Force Systems for the Next Thirty Years," which stimulated new industrial concepts and a favorable Command reaction. Before this, as technical director of the advanced system planning organization at ASD, he also had major responsibility for concept formulation for other aeronautical systems.

Mr. Lenz has published extensively in the field of technological forecasting, and is, at present, editor of the *Journal of Technological Forecasting*. Among his most recent publications are the Foreword to *Technological Forecasting: A Practical Approach*, by Marvin J. Cetron, Gordon & Breach, 1969; "Forecasts of Exploding Technologies by Trend Extrapolation," in *Technological Forecasting for Industry and Government*, by James R. Bright, Prentice-Hall, 1968; and "Practical Application of Technical Trend Forecasting," NATO Defense Research Group Seminar on "Technological Forecasting and its Application to Defense Research," United Kingdom, November 1968.

HAROLD A. LINSTONE

Harold A. Linstone received his B.S. degree in 1944 from the City College of New York (Phi Beta Kappa). He holds a master's degree from Columbia University and a Ph.D. in mathematics from the University of Southern California.

His industrial experience includes 11 years at Hughes Aircraft Company, where he was senior scientist, and 7 years at Lockheed Aircraft Corporation, where he is now associate director of corporate development planning—systems analysis.

He has also been a member of The Rand Corporation and a visiting member of the Institute for Defense Analyses. He is a consultant to the Stanford Research Institute and to Portland State University.

Dr. Linstone serves as adjunct professor of industrial and systems engineering at the University of Southern California. There he has introduced courses in "Technological Forecasting" and "Planning Alternative Futures."

He has given seminars on technological forecasting and planning in the United States, England, and France, as well as at the Weizmann Institute in Israel.

Since 1969, Dr. Linstone has been coeditor of the journal *Technological Forecasting and Social Change*.

WILLIAM GLEN MCLOUGHLIN

William Glen McLoughlin is general manager of the Industrial Management Center, Inc., and adjunct professor, Braniff Graduate School of Management, University of Dallas. He was formerly director of technical planning for Ling-Temco-Vought, Inc.

Mr. McLoughlin received his professional engineering degree from The Catholic University of America, his master's degree in business administration from the University of Dallas, and his training in economics at the Graduate School of Georgetown University.

He is the author of *Fundamentals of Research Management* (American Management Association, 1970), *The Case For Research Accountability* (1967), and an *Introduction to the Principles of Infrared Physics* (1956).

In addition to serving on the Board of Directors of Hydroponics in Texas, Inc., he is a member of the American Physical Society, American Institute of Aeronautics and Astronautics, and the American Ordinance Association.

JAY S. MENDELL

J. S. Mendell is currently at the University of Connecticut, Graduate School of Business Administration, M.B.A. Program, and is a lecturer in technological forecasting. Previously Dr. Mendell was at the University of Hartford, as an adjunct assistant professor of mathematics. Before obtaining a Ph.D., he was at Rensselaer Polytechnic Institute as a graduate assistant in electrical engineering and physics.

Some of his more recent articles are "Attempt to Generate Plasma Oscillations with a Relativistic Electron Beam," *Journal of Applied Physics;* Invited Commentary on "The Case of the Precarious Program," *Harvard Business Review;* "The Case of the Straying Scientist," *Harvard Business Review;* "Will the 21st Century Repeal the Laws of Nature?" *The Futurist: A Journal of Forecasts, Trends and Ideas about the Future;* and "Technological Forecasting: State of the Art."

Dr. Mendell is a member of The World Future Society, American Academy of Political and Social Science, The Health Physics Society, The Institute of Electrical and Electronics Engineers and the IEEE Group on Engineering Management, The Society for Long-Range Planning Ltd., and The National Society for Corporate Planning.

M. EUGENE MERCHANT

M. Eugene Merchant's undergraduate work, in mechanical engineering, was done at the University of Vermont, from which he graduated *magna cum laude* in 1936 with the degree of B.S. in mechanical engineering. His graduate work was done at the University of Cincinnati in the Graduate Department of Applied Science under a cooperative fellowship sponsored by The Cincinnati Milling Machine Co. Here he majored in physics and received the D.Sc. degree in 1941.

He has been employed since in the Research Division of The Cincinnati Milling Machine Co. (now named Cincinnati Milacron, Inc.), and is at present director of research planning. His research activities have included basic and applied research on manufacturing processes and equipment and the future of manufacturing technology. He has presented and published numerous papers on these subjects, both in the United States and abroad.

He is a Fellow of the American Society of Mechanical Engineers and of the Ohio Academy of Science, and a member of various other technical societies, including ASLE, American Society of Metals, Society of Mechanical Engineers, and the Engineering Society of Cincinnati. He is a member also of the International Institute for Production Engineering Research (CIRP).

EUGENE R. MONTANY

Since 1962, Eugene R. Montany has been assistant manager of advanced planning for Pratt & Whitney Division, United Aircraft Corporation. Before this, his work had been in the Research Department, Curtiss-Wright Corporation, Airplane Division, Columbus, Ohio; Aerophysics Department, North American Aviation, Downey, California; UAC Research Department, East Hartford, Connecticut; and P&WA Division-United Aircraft Corporation.

JACK A. MORTON

Jack A. Morton, vice president in charge of electronic materials and components development at Bell Telephone Laboratories, Inc., received the B.S. degree in electrical engineering from Wayne University in 1935 and the M.S. degree in engineering from the University of Michigan in 1936. He joined Bell Laboratories in 1936 and continued part-time postgraduate studies in physics at Columbia University until 1941.

During the early part of his career with Bell Laboratories, Mr. Morton did research on coaxial cable repeaters and microwave amplifiers. In 1948, he took charge of the first development work on semiconductor devices. In 1952, he became assistant director of electronic apparatus development, and a year later he was named director of transistor development. In 1955, he became director of device development.

Mr. Morton is the author of numerous articles. His book, *Organizing for Innovation,* will be published shortly.

Mr. Morton is actively serving on various committees, including those of the Institute of Electrical and Electronics Engineers, National Association of Engineers, National Association of Scientists, and the government.

WILLIAM S. MOUNCE

William S. Mounce is currently manager of the Market Development Department, The International Nickel Company, Inc., in New York. Previously, he was manager of the Application Engineering Section of the Market Development Department.

His earlier experience was in plant metallurgy with Hamilton Standard Division, United Aircraft Corporation, Hartford, Connecticut. He joined International Nickel in 1945 as an employee of the New England office. In 1955, he was transferred to the Alloy Constructural Steel Section of the Development and Research Department in the New York office. In 1958, Mr. Mounce was transferred to the newly established Application Engineering Section of the Development and Research Department, in charge of the construction and Machinery Group. He was assigned to the director of the European Information Bureau of International Nickel Limited, as a special assistant to introduce market development techniques in 1961. He returned to Inco Inc., in New York, in 1963, as manager of product development in the Development and Research Department.

PAUL POLISHUK

Paul Polishuk currently is senior staff physicist, Plans Office, Air Force Flight Dynamics Laboratory. From 1959 to June 1968, he was senior research physicist in the Air Force Flight Dynamics Laboratory. Mr. Polishuk was nuclear research officer, Flight Control Laboratory, Wright-Patterson AFB, Ohio, from 1956 to 1959, and was a staff physicist for the Lincoln Laboratory, Lincoln, Massachusetts, from June 1956 to October 1956.

Some of Mr. Polishuk's most recent papers are "Planning Method for the Air Force Flight Dynamics Laboratory," Internal Flight Dynamics Laboratory Report; "Management Study of the Air Force Nuclear Engineering Center," Air Force Flight Dynamics Laboratory Internal Management Report; and "Air Force Flight Dynamics Laboratory Long-Range Plan," written in January 1970.

ROBERT W. PREHODA

Robert W. Prehoda is the head of Technological Forecasting Associates, Inc., a California consulting organization specializing in technological forecasting and related studies for industry and government. His 1967 monograph, *Designing the Future: The Role of Technological Forecasting,* was one of the first popularized American books to cover in depth the importance of this vital new discipline

Mr. Prehoda has a broad scientific background and has been associated with the American space program since its inception. His varied aerospace experience has given him a thorough knowledge of the most intimate, often frustrating, details of American science. He has an extensive background in the biological sciences and has written books on cryobiology and cosmetic surgery. Mr. Prehoda has been particularly concerned with the prolongation of youthful vitality, and his book, *Extended Youth: The Promise of Gerontology,* is the most comprehensive current review of aging theories and therapies that promise to permit aging to be controlled—possibly reversed.

Mr. Prehoda has participated in original research in both the physical and biological sciences. His numerous technical articles and papers contain a number of original conceptual approaches that offer new options in our current ecology-pollution-population struggle.

ROBERT H. PRY

Robert H. Pry is manager of the Metallurgy and Ceramics Laboratory in the Research and Development Center of General Electric in Schenectady, New York. In this position, he directs the activities of a staff of over 100 persons, including 60 scientists and engineers engaged in research on metals, ceramics, and glass. He was appointed to his present position in January 1968.

He joined General Electric in 1951 after receiving his B.S. degree from Texas College of A & I, and both his M.A. and Ph.D. degrees in physics from Rice Institute.

He previously served as manager of liaison and transition at the GE Research and Development Center. In this capacity he directed the activities of a group of senior scientists responsible for maintaining a two-way flow of information between the Center and the more than 150 operating components of the company.

Dr. Pry is a member of the American Physical Society, the American Institute of Mining, Metallurgical, and Petroleum Engineers, The New York Academy of Sciences, and the American Society of Metals, and is a Fellow of the American Association for the Advancement of Science.

DONALD L. PYKE

Donald L. Pyke received his B.S. (1946) and M.S. (1953) degrees in engineering from Purdue University, where he served for 4 years as a teaching assistant and instructor, while an undergraduate and a graduate student. He has spent 9 years in the academic field as an educator and administrator. In addition to his experience at Purdue, he has held posts of assistant professor, assistant dean, and acting dean of engineering at Dartmouth College's Thayer School of Engineering.

Mr. Pyke's industrial experience includes 2 years as a college representative of John Wiley & Sons, publishers of scientific and engineering books; 1 year with Systems Development Corporation, where he served as technical assistant to the vice president for plans and operations; and 14 years with TRW, where he has held the posts of director of technical staff development; director of administration, Intellectronics Laboratories; assistant to the vice president for research and development; and manager of technical liaison and forecasting, the position he now occupies.

Mr. Pyke has continued to maintain his interest in academic affairs through active participation in the American Society for Engineering Education, the Southern California Industry Education Council, and the Visiting Committee to review the engineering curricula at the University of Southern California, and as a cofounder of PORTE, a nonprofit corporation formed to promote international education.

CHRISTINE A. RALPH

Christine A. Ralph is a staff member with the International Research and Technology Corporation in Washington, D.C. She attended London University and George Washington University.

From 1967 to 1969, she served as a systems analyst with the Advanced Systems Team at Plessey Radar, Limited. She joined the International Research and Technology Corporation in her present capacity in 1969.

She is the author of several articles, including "The Application of New Analysis Techniques to Automatic Radar Plot Extraction," "Aspects of Pattern Recognition and Real-Time Image Processing," "The Application of Decision Impact Analysis to the Solution of Multi-Variable Problems," "Ralph I—Applied to the Electronics Industry," and "Ralph II."

WILLIAM C. SPROULL

William C. Sproull's educational background includes a B.S. in aeronautical engineering, an M.B.A. from the University of Michigan, and is currently completing his doctoral work in business administration at American University. Mr. Sproull is currently manager of space and information systems planning for Honeywell's Aerospace and Defense Group.

Mr. Sproull assisted in the original development of the PATTERN concept within Honeywell. His participation in relevance tree analysis has continued through several studies, both within and external to the company's planning operations. Mr. Sproull served as study manager on three external space-related studies using the relevance tree approach.

Prior to his present position, Mr. Sproull held various posts with Honeywell's research and engineering groups in Minneapolis.

MURRAY TUROFF

Murray Turoff obtained B.S. degrees in mathematics and physics from the University of California at Berkeley and a Ph.D. in theoretical physics from Brandeis University. He began work in computer applications in 1959 as a research assistant at the MIT Computation Center and later was employed by IBM as a systems engineer.

Five years of experience with the Institute for Defense Analyses led him further into the areas of model building, information systems, and operations research in general. Since 1968, Dr. Turoff has been employed as an operations research analyst in the Office of Emergency Preparedness of the Executive Office of the President.

Dr. Turoff is the author of a number of papers in the areas of simulation, gaming, immediate-access systems, and information management systems, and recently has conducted a number of Delphi studies.

Bibliography (Books Only)*

Resource Allocation

Ackoff, Russell L., ed. *Progress in Operations Research*, Vol. 1. New York: John Wiley & Sons, 1961.

Ackoff, Russell L. *Scientific Method: Optimizing Applied Research Decisions.* New York: John Wiley & Sons, 1962.

Ackoff, Russell L., *A Concept of Corporate Planning*, New York: John Wiley & Sons, 1970.

Ackoff, Russell L., E. Leonard Arnoff, and C. West Churchman. *Introduction to Operations Research.* New York: John Wiley & Sons, 1957.

Ansoff, I. H. "Evaluation of Applied Research in a Business Firm." *Research, Development, and Technical Innovation: An Introduction,* edited by James R. Bright. Homewood, Ill.: Richard D. Irwin, 1964.

Anthony, Robert N. *Planning and Control Systems—A Framework for Analysis.* Boston: Harvard Business School, Division of Research, 1965.

Battersby, A. *Network Analysis for Planning and Scheduling.* New York: St Martin's Press, 1964.

Baumgartner, John S. *Project Management.* Homewood, Ill.: Richard D. Irwin, 1963.

Blood, Jerome W., ed. *The Management of Scientific Talent.* New York: The American Management Association 1963.

Bock, R. H., and W. K. Holstein. *Production Planning and Control.* Columbus, Ohio: Charles E. Merrill Books, 1963.

Bonini, Charles P., Robert K. Jaedicke, and Harvey M. Wagner. *Management Controls: New Directions in Basic Research.* New York: McGraw-Hill Book Company, 1964.

Boothe, Norton, et al. *From Concept to Commercialization, A Study of the*

---

* This bibliography is adapted from a more comprehensive one, including books, papers, articles and unpublished works which are published in Dr. Cetron's PhD thesis, entitled "Evaluation of an R & D Project Selection and Resource Allocation Model, Using Technological Forecasting for Technology Assessment," American University, June 1971.

R&D Budget Allocation Process. Stanford, Calif.: The Graduate School of Business, Stanford University, 1962.

Brabb, George J. *Introduction to Quantitative Management.* New York: Holt, Rinehart and Winston, 1968.

Brandenberg, R. G. "Project Selection in Industrial R&D: Problems and Decisions." *Research Program Effectiveness,* edited by M. C. Yovits et al. New York: Gordon & Breach, 1966.

Busaker, Robert F., and Thomas L. Saaty. *Finite Graphs and Networks: An Introduction with Applications.* New York: McGraw-Hill Book Company, 1965.

Bush, George P. *Bibliography on Research Administration, Annotated.* Washington, D.C.: The University Press, 1964.

Carroll, Phil. *Profit Control—How to Plug Profit Leaks.* New York: McGraw-Hill Book Company, 1962.

Cetron, Marvin J. *Technological Forecasting: A Practical Approach.* New York: Gordon & Breach, 1969.

Cetron, Marvin J., and Joel Goldhar (ed.). *The Science of Managing Organized Technology.* New York: Gordon & Breach, 1970.

Cetron, Marvin J., and T. I. Monahan. "An Evaluation and Appraisal of Various Approaches to Technological Forecasting." *Technological Forecasting for Industry and Government,* edited by James R. Bright. Englewood Cliffs, N.J.: Prentice-Hall, 1968.

Cetron, Marvin J., et al. *Technical Resource Management: Quantitative Methods.* Cambridge, Mass.: The M.I.T. Press, 1970.

Chou, Ya-Lun. *Statistical Analysis with Business and Economic Applications.* New York: Holt, Rinehart and Winston, 1969.

Churchman, C. West. *Prediction and Optimal Decision.* Englewood Cliffs, N.J.: Prentice-Hall, 1961.

Clark, Wallace, *The Gantt Chart.* London: Isaac Pitman and Sons, 1938.

Davis, Keith, and S. Sengupta. "On a Method for Determining Corporate Research Development Budgets." *Management Sciences, Models, and Techniques,* Vol. 11, edited by C. W. Churchman and M. Verhulst. New York: Pergamon Press, 1960.

Dean, Burton V., ed. *Operations Research in Research and Development.* New York: John Wiley & Sons, 1963.

Dean, Burton V., ed. *Operations Research in Research and Development.* Proceedings of a Conference at Case Institute of Technology. New York: John Wiley & Sons, 1963.

Dean, Burton V. *Evaluating, Selecting, and Controlling R&D Projects.* AMA Research Study Number 89. New York: American Management Association, 1968.

Dean, Joel. *Managerial Economics.* Englewood Cliffs, N.J.: Prentice-Hall, 1951.

Easton, David. *A Systems Analysis of Political Life*. New York: John Wiley & Sons, 1965.

Ewing, David W., ed. *Long-Range Planning of Management*. New York: Harper and Brother, 1958.

Fishborn, Peter C. *Utility Theory for Decision Making*. New York: John Wiley & Sons, 1970.

Flood, Merrill W. "Research Project Evaluation." *Coordination, Control, and Financing of Industrial Research*, edited by Albert R. Rubenstein. New York: Columbia University, King's Crown Press, 1955.

Ford, L. R., Jr., and D. R. Fulkerson. *Flows in Networks*. Princeton, N.J.: Princeton University Press, 1962.

Freund, John E. *Mathematical Statistics*. Englewood Cliffs, N.J.: Prentice-Hall, 1962.

Galbraith, John Kenneth. *The Affluent Society*. New York: Mentor Books, 1958.

Gass, Saul I. *Linear Programming: Methods and Applications*. New York: McGraw-Hill Book Company, 1964.

Guy, K. *Laboratory Organizations and Administration*. London: Macmillan & Company; also New York: St Martin's Press, 1962.

Hansen, B. J. *Practical PERT Including Critical Path Method*. Washington, D.C.: America House, 1964.

Harrel, C. G. "Selecting Projects for Research." *Research in Industry: Its Organization and Management*, edited by C. C. Furnas. New York: Van Nostrand, 1948.

Heckert, J. E., and J. B. Willson. *Business Budgeting and Control*. New York: The Ronald Press, 1955.

Henke, Russ. *Effective Research and Development for the Smaller Company*. Houston: Gulf Publishing Company, 1963.

Hertz, David B. *The Theory and Practice of Industrial Research*. New York: McGraw-Hill Book Company, 1950.

Hertz, David B., and Phillip G. Carlson. "Selection, Evaluation, and Control of Research and Development Projects." *Operations Research in Research and Development*, edited by Burton V. Dean. New York: John Wiley & Sons, 1963.

Hertz, David B., and A. H. Rubenstein. *Costs, Budgeting and Economics of Industrial Research*. Proceedings of the First Annual Conference of Industrial Research. New York: Columbia University Press, 1951.

Hertz, David B., and A. H. Rubinstein, eds. *Research Operations in Industry*, Proceedings of the Third Annual Conference on Industrial Research. New York: Columbia University Press, 1953.

Heyel, Carl, ed. *Handbook of Industrial Research Management*. New York: Reinhold Publishing Corporation, 1959.

Jantsch, Erich, ed. *Perspectives of Planning.* Paris: OECD, 1969.

Johnson, Richard A., Fremont E. Kast, and James E. Rosenzweig. *The Theory and Management of Systems.* New York: McGraw-Hill Book Company, 1963.

Karger, D. C., and R. G. Murkick. *Managing Engineering and Research.* New York: The Industrial Press, 1963.

Klein, B. "The Decision-Making Problem in Development." *The Rate of Direction of Inventive Activity.* Princeton, N.J.: Princeton University Press, 1962.

Koontz, Harold. *Toward A Unified Theory of Management.* New York: McGraw-Hill Book Company, 1963.

Leermakers, J. A. "The Selection and Screening of Projects." *Getting the Most from Product Research and Development.* New York: American Management Association, 1955.

Lipetz, Ben-Ami. *Measurement of Effectiveness of Science Research.* Carlisle, Mass.: Intermedia, Inc., 1965.

McMillan, Claude, and Richard F. Gonzales. *Systems Analysis: A Computer Approach to Decision Models.* Homewood, Ill.: Richard D. Irwin, 1965.

Mansfield, Edwin. *The Economics of Technological Change.* New York: W. W. Norton & Company, 1968.

Marschak, T. A. "Models, Rules of Thumb, and Development Decisions." *Operations Research in Research and Development,* edited by B. V. Dean. New York: John Wiley & Sons, 1963.

Marshall, A. W., and W. H. Mecklong. "Predictability of the Costs, Time and Success of Development." *The Rate and Direction of Inventive Activity.* Princeton, N.J.: Princeton University Press, 1962.

Mees, C. E. K., and J. A. Leermakers. *The Organization of Industrial Scientific Research,* 2nd ed. New York: McGraw-Hill Book Company, 1950.

Mellon, W. Giles. *An Approach to a General Theory of Priorities: An Outline of Problems and Methods.* Princeton University Econometric Research Program, Memorandum No. 42. Princeton, N.J.: Princeton University Press, 1962.

Miller, D. W., and M. K. Starr. *Executive Decisions and Operations Research.* Englewood Cliffs, N.J.: Prentice-Hall, 1960.

Miller, Robert W. *Schedule, Cost and Profit Control with PERT.* New York: McGraw-Hill Book Company, 1963.

Miller, T. T. "Projecting the Profitability of New Products." Special Report No. 20. New York: American Management Association, 1957.

Mills, Frederick C. *Statistical Methods.* New York: Holt and Company, 1955.

Morris, William T. *The Analysis of Management Decisions.* Homewood, Ill.: Richard D. Irwin, 1964.

Moshman, Jack, Jacob Johnson, and Madalyn Larson. "RAMPS—A Technique for Resource Allocation and Multi-Project Scheduling." *Proceedings of the Spring Joint Computer Conference, 1963*. Baltimore: Spartan Books, 1963.

Olsen, F. "The Control of Research Funds." *Coordination, Control and Financing of Industrial Research*, edited by A. H. Rubenstein. New York: Columbia University, King's Crown Press, 1955.

Pessemier, E. A. *New Product Decisions: An Analytical Approach*. New York: McGraw-Hill Book Company, 1966.

Peters, Charles C., and Walter R. Van Voorhis. *Statistical Procedures and Their Mathematical Bases*. New York: McGraw-Hill Book Company, 1940.

Quinn, James Brian. *Yardsticks for Industrial Research: The Evaluation of Research and Development Output*. New York: The Ronald Press, 1959.

Roberts, E. G. *The Dynamics of Research and Development*. New York: Harper & Row, 1964.

Rubenstein, Albert H., ed. *Coordination, Control, and Financing of Industrial Research*. New York: Columbia University, King's Crown Press, 1955.

Rubinstein, Albert H., "Studies of Project Selection Behavior in Industry." *Operations Research in Research and Development*, edited by B. V. Dean. New York: John Wiley & Sons, 1963.

Rubinstein, Albert H., and C. J. Haverstroh, eds. *Some Theories of Organization*. Homewood, Ill.: Richard D. Irwin, 1960.

Saaty, Thomas L. *Mathematical Methods of Operations Research*. New York: McGraw-Hill Book Company, 1959.

Sasiene, Maurice, Arthur Yaspin, and Lawrence Friedman. *Operations Research*. New York: John Wiley & Sons, 1959.

Savage, J. J. *The Foundations of Statistics*. New York; John Wiley & Sons, 1954.

Schlaifer, Robert. *Introduction to Statistics for Business Decisions*. New York: McGraw-Hill Book Company, 1961.

Seiler, Robert E. *Improving the Effectiveness of Research and Development*. New York: McGraw-Hill Book Company, 1963.

Shank, R. J. "Planning to Meet Goals." *Optimum Use of Engineering Talent*. AMA Report No. 68. Cambridge: Riverside Press, 1961.

Silk, Leonard S. *The Research Revolution*. New York: McGraw-Hill Book Company, 1960.

Silk, Leonard S. *The New Science of Management Decisions*. New York: Harper & Row, 1960.

Spencer, Milton H. *Managerial Economics*, 3rd ed. Homewood, Ill.: Richard D. Irwin, 1968.

Spencer, Milton H., and L. Siegelman. *Managerial Economics*. Homewood, Ill.: Richard D. Irwin, 1964.

Stanely, A. O., and K. K. White. *Organizing the R&D Function*. AMA Research Study No. 72. New York: American Management Association, 1965.

Steiner, George A. *Managerial Long-Range Planning*. New York: McGraw-Hill Book Company, 1963.

Stilian, C. N., et al. *PERT—A New Management Planning and Control Technique*. New York: American Management Association, 1962.

Walters, J. E. *Research Management: Principles and Practice*. Washington, D.C.: Spartan Books, 1965.

Wasson, Chester R. *The Economics of Managerial Decision*. New York: Appleton-Century-Crofts, 1965.

Watson, Donald Stevenson. *Price Theory and Its Uses*. Boston: Houghton Mifflin, 1963.

Wilson, E. Bright. *An Introduction to Scientific Research*. New York: McGraw-Hill Book Company, 1952.

Technological Forecasting

Allen, T. *Technology and Social Change*. New York: Appleton, 1957.

Ayres, Robert U. *Technological Forecasting and Long-Range Planning*. New York: McGraw-Hill Book Company, 1969.

Baade, Fritz. *The Race to the Year 2000*. New York: Doubleday & Company, 1962.

Bell, Arthur S. "Toward the Year 2000," *Daedalus*, Summer 1967.

Bell, Daniel. "Twelve Modes of Prediction." *Penguin Survey of the Social Sciences*, Edited by J. Gould. Baltimore: Penguin Books, 1965.

Bliven, Bruce. *Preview for Tomorrow: The Unfinished Business of Science*. New York: Alfred A. Knopf, 1953.

Bright, James R., ed. *Technological Planning on the Corporate Level*. Division of Research, Harvard Business School, Boston, Mass., 1961.

Bright, James R., ed. *Research, Development, and Technological Innovation*. Homewood, Ill.: Richard D. Irwin, 1964.

Bright, James R., ed. *Technological Forecasting for Industry and Government: Methods and Applications*. Englewood Cliffs, N.J.: Prentice-Hall, 1968.

Brown, Harrison. *The Challenge of Man's Future: An Inquiry Concerning the Condition of Man During the Years That Lie Ahead*. New York: The Viking Press, 1954.

Buchholz, A. *Die Grosse Transformation*. Stuttgart: Deutsche Verlagsanstalt, 1969.

Calder, Richie. *After the Seventh Day: The World Man Created*. New York: Simon and Schuster, 1961.

Calder, Richie, ed. *The World in 1984*. Baltimore: Penguin Books, 1965.

Cetron, Marvin J. *Technological Forecasting: A Practical Approach*. New York: Gordon & Breach, 1969.

Clarke, Arthur S. *Profiles of the Future*. London: Harper, 1962.

Conant, James B. *Science and Common Sense*. New Haven: Yale University Press, 1952; Yale Paperbound (tenth printing), July 1964.

Conklin, L., ed. *17X Infinity*. New York: Dell Publishing Company, 1963.

Darwin, Charles Galton. *The Next Million Years*. London: Rupert Hart-Davis, 1952.

De Jouvenel, B. *The Art of Conjecture*. Translated by Nikita Lang. New York: Basic Books, 1967.

De Solla Price, D. J. *Little Science, Big Science*. New York: Columbia University Press, 1963; Columbia Paperback Edition, 1965.

Docks, S., and P. Bernays, eds. *Information and Prediction in Science*. New York: Academic Press, 1965.

Dusenberry, J. R. et al., eds. *The Brookings Quarterly Econometric Model of the United States*. Chicago: Rand McNally, 1965.

Ellison, K., ed. *Dangerous Visions*. New York: Doubleday & Company, 1968.

Ellul, Jacques. *The Technological Society*. New York: Alfred A. Knopf, 1964.

Emme, Eugene M. *A History of Space Flight*. New York: Holt, Rinehart and Winston, 1965.

Falk C. and Mendlovitz A., eds. *The Strategy of World Order*. World Law Fund, 1968.

Foreign Policy Association. *Toward the Year 2018*. New York: Cowles, 1968.

Forrester, Jay. *Industrial Dynamics*. Cambridge, Mass.: The M.I.T. Press, 1961.

Fromm, G. and P. Taubman. *Policy Simulations with an Econometric Model*. Washington, D.C.: The Brookings Institution, 1968.

Furnas, C. C. *The Next Hundred Years—The Unfinished Business of Science*. Baltimore, Md.: Williams & Wilkins, 1936.

Gabor, Dennis. *Inventing the Future*. London: Secker & Warburg, 1963; Pelican Book A 663, Penguin Books, Harmondsworth, Middlesex, 1964.

Gilfillan, S. Colum. *The Sociology of Invention*. Chicago: Follett Publishing Company, 1935.

Gilman, William. *Science: U.S.A.*. New York: The Viking Press, 1965.

Greenberger, Martin, ed. *Computers and the World of the Future*. Cambridge, Mass.: The M.I.T. Press, 1962.

Hamilton, H. R., et al. *System Simulation for Regional Analysis*. Cambridge: The M.I.T. Press, 1968.

Heinlein, L. J. *The Past through Tomorrow*. New York: Doubleday & Company, 1968.

Hertz, D. B. *International Politics in the Atomic Age*. New York: Columbia University Press, 1962.

Hitch, Charles J. *Decision-Making for Defense*. Berkeley and Los Angeles: University of California Press, 1965.

Holton, Gerard, ed. *Science and Culture—A Study of Cohesive and Disjunctive Forces*, Vol. 4: The Daedalus Library. Boston: Houghton Mifflin, 1965.

Jantsch, Erich. *Technological Forecasting in Perspective*. Paris: OECD, 1967.

Jewkes, John, David Sawers, and Richard Stillerman. *The Sources of Invention*. London: The Macmillan Company, 1958.

Kahn H., and T. Weiner. *The Year 2000*. New York: The Macmillan Company, 1967.

Kaplan, N. *New Approaches to International Relations*. New York: St. Martin's Press, 1968.

Lanford, Horace W. *A Synthesis of Technological Forecasting Methodologies*. New York: American Management Association, 1971.

Lien, Arthur P., Paul Anton, and Joseph W. Duncan. *Technological Forecasting: Tools, Techniques, Applications*. New York: American Management Association, 1968.

Mansfield, Edwin. *Industrial Research and Technological Innovation*. New York: W. W. Norton & Company, 1968.

Mansfield, Edwin. *The Economics of Technological Change*. New York: W. W. Norton & Company, 1968.

Martino, Joseph P. *Technological Forecasting for Decision Making*. New York: American Elsevier Publishing Company, 1971.

McHale, John. *The Future of the Future*. New York: George Braziller, 1969.

McLuhan, Marshall. *Understanding Media: The Extensions of Man* (third printing). New York: McGraw-Hill Paperbacks, 1966.

Nord, O. C. *Growth of a New Product*. Cambridge, Mass.: The M.I.T. Press, 1963.

Page, Robert Morris. *The Origin of Radar. Science Study Series*. Garden City, N.Y.: Anchor Books, Doubleday & Company, 1962.

Parsons, S. A. J. *The Framework of Technical Innovation*. London: Macmillan & Company, 1969.

Prehoda, Robert W. *Designing the Future*. Philadelphia: Chilton Books, 1967.

Ridenour, Louis N. "Physical Science and the Future." *Facing the Future's Risks—Studies Toward Predicting the Unforeseen*, Edited by Lyman Bryson. New York: Harper and Brothers, 1953.

Roberts, E. B. "Questioning the Cost/Effectiveness of the R&D Procurement Process." *Research Program Effectiveness*. New York: Gordon & Breach, 1966.

Roberts, E. B. "Exploratory Normative Technological Forecasting: A Critical Appraisal." *Technological Forecasting: A Practical Approach*, Marvin J. Cetron, ed. New York: Gordon & Breach, 1969.

Rogers, Everett M. *Diffusion of Innovations*. New York: The Free Press, 1962.

Spanier, G. *World Politics in an Age of Revolution*. New York: Frederick A. Praeger, 1968.

Teilhard de Chardin, Pierre. *The Future of Man*. London: Collins, 1964.

Thirring, Hans. *Energy for Man: From Windmills to Nuclear Power*. New York: Harper & Row, 1958.

Thompson, Sir George. *The Foreseeable Future*. London: Cambridge University Press, 1955.

Toffler, Alvin. *Future Shock*. New York: Random House, 1970.

Ubbelohde, A. R. *Man and Energy*. New York: George Braziller, 1955.

U.S. National Bureau of Economic Research. *The Rate of Direction of Inventive Activity—Economic and Social Factors*. A Conference of Universities. Princeton, N.J.: Princeton University Press, 1962.

Vassilev, M., and S. Gouschev, eds. *Life in the Twenty-First Century*. Translated from the Russian. First published in Russia 1959; Penguin Special, Penguin Books, Harmondsworth, Middlesex, 1961.

Warner, Aron W., and Alfred S. Eichner, eds. *The Impact of Science on Technology*. New York: Columbia University Press, 1965.

Warner, Aron W., and Dean Morse, eds. *Technological Innovation and Society*. New York: Columbia University Press, 1966.

Weymar, F. H. *The Dynamics of the World Cocoa Market*. Cambridge, Mass.; The M.I.T. Press, 1968.

Wills, Gordon, David Ashton, and Bernard Taylor, eds. *Technological Forecasting and Corporate Strategy*. New York: American Elsevier Publishing Company, 1969.

Wolstenholme, Gordon, ed. *Man and His Future*. A Ciba Foundation Volume. Boston: Little Brown and Company, 1963.

Zwicky, Fritz, and A. G. Wilson. *New Methods of Thought and Procedure*. New York: Springer-Verlag New York, 1967.

R&D Management

Ackoff, R. L., and P. A. Rivett. *A Manager's Guide to Operations Research*. New York: John Wiley & Sons, 1963.

Alderson, W., V. Terpsta, and S. J. Shapiro. *Patents and Progress*. Homewood, Ill.: Richard D. Irwin, 1965.

Allison, David, ed. *The R&D Game: Technical Men, Technical Managers, and Research Productivity*. Cambridge, Mass.: The M.I.T. Press, 1969.

Anthony, R. N., and J. S. Day. *Management Controls in Industrial Research Organizations*. Cambridge, Mass.: Harvard University Printing Office, 1952.

Barber, R. J. *The Politics of Research*. Washington, D.C.: Public Affairs Press, 1966.

Barish, N. N., and M. Verhulst, eds. *Long Range Planning International Symposium*. New York: Gordon & Breach, 1967.

Battersby, Albert. *Network Analysis for Planning and Scheduling*, 2nd ed. London: The Macmillan Company, 1967.

Bauer, Raymond A., ed. *Social Indicators*. Cambridge, Mass.: The M.I.T. Press, 1966.

Baumgartner, J. S. *Project Management*. Homewood, Ill.: Richard D. Irwin, 1963.

Bennett, Rawson. "Obsolescence of Engineers and Scientists." *Improving Effectiveness in Research and Development*, Edited by Ralph I. Cole. Washington, D.C.: Thompson Book Company, 1967.

Berners-Lee, C. M., ed. *Models for Decision*. London: The English Universities Press, 1965.

Cetron, Marvin J., R. Isenson, J. J. Johnson, A. B. Nutt, and H. A. Wells. *Technical Resources Management: Quantitative Methods*. Cambridge, Mass.: The M.I.T. Press, 1970.

Cetron, Marvin J., and J. Goldhar, (eds.) *The Science of Managing Organized Technology*. New York: Gordon & Breach, 1970.

Dean, B. V. *Evaluating, Selecting and Controlling R&D Projects*. New York: American Management Association, 1968.

Derman, Cyrus, and Morton Klein. *Probability and Statistical Inference*. New York: Oxford University Press, 1959.

Dupre, J. S., and S. A. Lakoff. *Science and the Nation: Policy and Politics*. Englewood Cliffs, N.J.: Prentice-Hall, 1962.

Enke, S., ed. *Defense Management*. Englewood Cliffs, N.J.: Prentice-Hall, 1967.

Enrick, N. L. *Management Planning: A Systems Approach*. New York: McGraw-Hill Book Company, 1967.

Forrester, Jay W. *Industrial Dynamics*. Cambridge, Mass.: The M.I.T. Press, 1961.

Galbraith, John Kenneth. *The New Industrial State*. Boston: Houghton Mifflin, 1967.

Glatt, E., and M. W. Shelly, eds. *The Research Society*. New York: Gordon & Breach, 1968.

Gordon, Kermit, ed. *Agenda for the Nation*. Washington, D.C.: The Brookings Institution, 1968.

Greenberg, D. S. *The Politics of Pure Science*. New York: New American Library, 1967.

Gregory, Carl E. *The Management of Intelligence; Scientific Problem Solving and Creativity*. New York: McGraw-Hill Book Company, 1967.

Gruber, W. H., and D. G. Marquis, eds. *Factors in the Transfer of Technology*. Cambridge, Mass.: The M.I.T. Press, 1969.

Hetman, Francois. *The Language of Forecasting*. Paris: S.E.D.E.I.S., 1969.

Hertz, David B. *New Power for Management; Computer Systems and Management Science*. New York: McGraw-Hill Book Company, 1969.

Heyel, C., ed. *Handbook of Industrial Research Management*. New York: Reinhold Publishing Corporation, 1964.

Higbee, Edward. *A Question of Priorities; New Strategies for Our Urbanized World*. New York: William Morrow and Company, 1970.

Hitch, C. J., and Roland N. McKean. *The Economics of Defense in the Nuclear Age*. New York: Atheneum, 1965.

Jackson, Thomas W., and Jack M. Spurlock. *Research and Development Management*. Homewood, Ill.: Dow Jones-Irwin, 1966.

Jewkes, J., D. Sawers, and R. Stillerman. *The Sources of Invention*. New York: St Martin's Press, 1959.

Johnson, R. A., F. E. Kast, and J. E. Rosenzweig. *The Theory and Management of Systems*, 2nd ed. New York: McGraw-Hill Book Company, 1965.

Kahn, H., and A. J. Wiener. *The Year 2000*. New York: The Macmillan Company, 1967.

Kaplan, N., ed. *Science and Society*. Chicago: Rand McNally, 1965.

Karger, D. W., and R. G. Murdoch. *Managing Engineering and Research*. New York: Industrial Press, 1963.

Kart, F., and J. Rosenzweig. *Science, Technology and Management*. New York: McGraw-Hill Book Company, 1963.

Kaufmann, A., and G. Desbuzeille. *The Critical Path Method*. New York: Gordon & Breach, 1969.

Kipp, E. M. *People Aspects of Research and Development Management: Attracting and Retaining R&D Personnel*. New York: Gordon & Breach, 1967.

Komhauser, W. *Scientists in Industry*. Berkeley, Calif.: University of California Press, 1962.

Koontz, Harold, and Cyril O'Donnell. *Principles of Management*. New York: McGraw-Hill Book Company, 1955.

Kuhn, J. W. *Scientific and Managerial Manpower in Nuclear Industry*. New York: Columbia University Press, 1966.

Lawrence, Paul R., and Jay W. Lorsch. *Organization and Environment*. Homewood, Ill.: Richard D. Irwin, 1969.

Le Breton, Preston P. *Planning Theory*. Englewood Cliffs, N.J.: Prentice-Hall, 1961.

Mansfield, E. *The Economics of Technological Change*. New York: W. W. Norton & Company, 1968.

Mansfield, E. *Industrial Research and Technological Innovation*. New York: W. W. Norton & Company, 1968.

Mansfield, E., ed. *Defense, Science, and Public Policy*. New York: W. W. Norton & Company, 1968.

Marschak. T., T. Glennan, and R. Summers. *Strategy for R&D*. New York: Springer-Verlag New York, 1967.

MacArthur, John H., and Bruce R. Scott. *Industrial Planning in France*. Boston: Division of Research, Graduate School of Business Administration, Harvard University, 1969.

National Bureau of Economic Research. *The Rate and Direction of Inventive Activity*. Princeton, N.J.: Princeton University Press, 1962.

Nelson, R., M. Peck, and E. Kalachek. *Technology, Economic Growth and Public Policy*. Washington, D.C.: The Brookings Institution, 1967.

Newman, William H., Charles E. Summer, and E. Kirby Warren. *The Process of Management: Concepts, Behavior and Practice*, 2nd ed. Englewood Cliffs, N.J.: Prentice-Hall, 1967.

Okun, Arthur M. *The Political Economy of Prosperity*. Washington, D.C.: The Brookings Institution, 1970.

Orth, C., J. Bailey, and F. Wolek. *Administering Research and Development*. Homewood, Ill.: Richard D. Irwin, 1964.

Pelz, D. C., and F. N. Andrews. *Scientists in Organizations: Productive Climates for Research and Development*. New York: John Wiley & Sons, 1966.

Price, D. K. *The Scientific Estate*. Cambridge, Mass.: Harvard University Press, 1965.

Raudsepp, E. *Managing Creative Scientists and Engineers*. New York: The Macmillan Company, 1963.

Reeves, E. Duer. *Management of Industrial Research*. New York: Reinhold Publishing Corporation, 1967.

Roberts, E. B. *The Dynamics of Research and Development*. New York: Harper & Row, 1964.

Roman, D. D. *Research and Development Management: The Economics and Administration of Technology*. New York: Appleton-Century-Crofts, 1968.

Schmookler, J. *Invention and Economic Growth*. Cambridge, Mass.: Harvard University Press, 1966.

Scott, B. W. *Long-Range Planning in American Industry*. New York: American Management Association, 1965.

Seiler, R. E. *Improving the Effectiveness of Research and Development*. New York: McGraw-Hill Book Company, 1965.

Simon, Herbert A. "Some Strategic Considerations in the Construction of Social Science Models." *Mathematical Thinking in the Social Sciences*, Edited by P. L. Lazarsfield. Glencoe, Ill.: The Free Press, 1954.

Spencer, M. H. *Managerial Economics*, 3rd ed. Homewood, Ill.: Richard D. Irwin, 1968.

Suits, C. Guy. *Suits: Speaking of Research*. New York: John Wiley & Sons, 1965.

Taylor, C. W., and F. Barron, eds. *Scientific Creativity: Its Recognition and Development*. New York: John Wiley & Sons, 1962.

TyBout, R., ed. *The Economics of Research and Development*. Columbus, Ohio: Ohio State University Press, 1965.

Vollmer, H. M., et al. *Adaptations of Scientists in Five Organizations: A Comparative Analysis*. Menlo Park, Calif.: Stanford Research Institute, 1964.

Walton, Clarence C., ed. *Business and Social Progress*. New York: Frederick A. Praeger, 1970.

Warren, E. K. *Long-Range Planning: The Executive Viewpoint*. Englewood Cliffs, N.J.: Prentice-Hall, 1966.

Willings, D. *The Human Element in Management*. New York: Gordon & Breach, 1969.

Wills, Gordon, David Ashton, and Bernard Taylor, eds. *Technological Forecasting and Corporate Strategy*. New York: American Elsevier Publishing Company, 1969.

Withington, Frederic G. *The Real Computer: Its Influence, Uses and Effects*. Reading, Mass.: Addison-Wesley Publishing Company, 1969.

Work, Harold K. "Continuing Education." *Improving Effectiveness in Research and Development*, Edited by Ralph I. Cole. Washington, D.C.: Thompson Book Company, 1967.

Yovits, M. C., D. Gilford, R. Wilcox, and H. Lerner, eds. *Research Program Effectiveness*. New York: Gordon & Breach, 1966.

Index

518, 524
Guth, William D., 490

Hacke, James, E., Jr., 44
Hahn, Otto, 333
Hahn-Strassmann point, 333, 334
Hair, George M., 62, 535
Hall, Arthur D., 361
Harvard University, 244
Hayes, Robert H., 362
Hayne, R. L., 470
Hayward, H., 21, 97, 259, 260, 262
Helmer, Dr. Olaf, xvii, xix, 12, 14, 44, 164,
    200, 308, 362, 535
Historical analogy, 19
Honeywell, 429, 430
Hudson Institute, 244
Hunter, Maxwell, II, 362

ICE, 411
Illinois Institute of Technology, 304
INCO, see International Nickel Co.
Institute for the Future, 244, 312, 322
International Nickel Co., 193-197
Interservice Technological Forecasting Meth-
    odology Study Group, 12
Isenson, Raymond S., 7, 10, 474, 487, 490
Ivy, E. Weber, 536

Jantsch, Erich, 11, 18, 20, 23, 239, 259,
    360, 474, 536
Jay, Anthony, 513
Johns Hopkins University, 244
Johnson, Dr. H., 244
    J. N., 365, 474
    Samuel, 81
Jones, Prof. A., 244
JOSS, 255

Kahn, Herman, 353, 363
Kavesh, Robert A., 361
Kay, Dr. M., 244
Kelvin, Lord, 364
Keverian, Jack, 537
Kiefer, David M., 359
Killefer, David, 361
Kitson, Kenneth, 447
Kozmetsky, George, 356
Kuhn, Thomas, 361
Kuhns, J. P., 240

Langston, James F., 64, 537
Language and Systems Development, Inc., 255
Lawler-Bell algorithm, 467, 468
Lawler, E. L., 467
Lawrence, Paul R., 362
Lecht, Leonard A., 492, 500, 508
Lenz, Ralph C., Jr., v, xvi, xix, 14, 15, 17-
    20, 225, 240, 476, 537
Libik, George, 447
Lien, Arthur P., 5, 14
Linear programming, 32, 33
    model, 38
Ling-Temco-Vought, Inc., see LTV
Linstone, Harold A., 43, 128, 474, 484, 538
Little, A. D., Inc., 411
Lockheed Aircraft Corporation, 128, 244
Lockheed-California Co., 137
Longfellow, xi
Long-range planning, vii, 60, 109, 111, 121,
    127, 158, 185, 198, 202, 205-207,
    213, 392-417, 419-427, 482, (10, 68,
    83, 161)
LRP, see Long-range planning
LTV, 171, 172, 175-178, 182, 183
Lubbock, John, 290

MacArthur, Donald, 34
    J. H., 503, 504
McDonnell Management Scheduling and
    Control System, see MSCS
McGarvey, Patrick J., 472
McLaughlin, Laurence D., 362
McLoughlin, William G., 171, 178, 538
MacNiece, Louis, 508
MACRO, 413, 516
Madden, Carl, 347
Mahinske, Capt. Edmund B., xviii
Maines, N. Robert, 415
Mansfield, Edwin, 42
Martino, Joseph P., 5-7, 43, 244, 360, 365,
    474, 487
Maumee Chemical Co., 100
MEDical Instrumentation and Control Iden-
    tified and Numerically Evaluated, see
    MEDICINE
MEDICINE, 444
Mendell, Jay S., xvii, xix, 347, 361, 539
Merchant, M. Eugene, 539
Merck and Co., 121
MIRAGE, 130, 131, 136, 413